Valuation Methods and Shareholder Value Creation

Valuation Methods and Shareholder Value Creation

Pablo Fernández

PricewaterhouseCoopers Professor of Corporate Finance
IESE Business School
University of Navarra
Madrid, Spain

ACADEMIC PRESS

An imprint of Elsevier Science

Amsterdam   Boston   London   New York   Oxford   Paris
San Diego   San Francisco   Singapore   Sydney   Tokyo

Valuation Methods and Shareholder Value Creation was published in a different form as *Valoración de Empreses* in 1999 by Ediciones Gestión 2000.

Cover photo credit: Images Copyright © GettyImages 2002.

This book is printed on acid-free paper. ∞

Academic Press
An Elsevier Science Imprint
525 B Street, Suite 1900, San Diego, California 92101-4495, USA
http://www.academicpress.com

Academic Press
84 Theobalds Road, London WC1X 8RR, UK
http://www.academicpress.com

Library of Congress Catalog Card Number: 2002101284

International Standard Book Number: 0-12-253841-2

PRINTED IN THE UNITED STATES OF AMERICA
02   03   04   05   06   07   MM   9   8   7   6   5   4   3   2   1

Contents

Part I
Basics of Valuation Methods and Shareholder Value Creation

Chapter 1
Shareholder Value Creation, Basic Concepts

Chapter 2
Company Valuation Methods

Chapter 3

Price-Earnings Ratio, Profitability, Cost of Capital, and Growth

Chapter 4

Splitting the Price-Earnings Ratio: Franchise Factor, Growth Factor, Interest Factor, and Risk Factor

Chapter 5
Market Value and Book Value

Chapter 6
Dividends and Market Value

Chapter 9

Cash Flow and Net Income

Chapter 10

Inflation and Value

Chapter 12

Valuations of Internet Companies: The Case of Terra-Lycos

Part II

Shareholder Value Creation

Chapter 13

Proposed Measures of Shareholder Value Creation: EVA™, Economic Profit, MVA, CVA, CFROI, and TSR

Chapter 14

EVA, Economic Profit, and Cash Value Added do not Measure Shareholder Value Creation

Chapter 15
The RJR Nabisco Valuation

Chapter 16
Valuation and Value Creation in Internet-Related Companies

Part III

Rigorous Approaches to Discounted Cash Flow Valuation

Chapter 17
Discounted Cash Flow Valuation Methods: Perpetuities, Constant Growth, and General Case

Chapter 18

Optimal Capital Structure: Problems with the Harvard and Damodaran Approaches

Chapter 19

Financial Literature about Discounted
Cash Flow Valuation

Chapter 20

Application of the Different Theories to RJR Nabisco

Chapter 21

Eight Methods and Seven Theories for Valuing Companies by Cash Flow Discounting

Part IV

Real Options and Brands

Chapter 22

Real Options. Valuing Flexibility: Beyond Discounted Cash Flow Valuation

Chapter 23

Valuation of Brands and Intangibles

Appendix A

Capital Asset Pricing Model (CAPM)

Preface

Valuation Methods and Shareholder Value Creation is a complete book about business valuation and value creation. The book explains the nuances of different valuation methods and provides the reader with the tools for analyzing and valuing any business, no matter how complex. With 23 chapters divided into four parts, *Valuation Methods and Shareholder Value Creation* uses 140 diagrams, 211 tables, and more than 100 examples to help the reader absorb these concepts.

This book contains materials of the MBA and executive courses that I teach in IESE Business School. It also includes some material presented in courses and congresses in Spain, US, Austria, Mexico, Argentina, Peru, Colombia, United Kingdom, Italy, France, and Germany. The chapters have been modified many times as a consequence of the suggestions of my students since 1988, my work in class, and my work as a consultant specialized in valuation and acquisitions. I want to thank all my students for their comments on previous manuscripts and their questions. The book also includes results of the research conducted in the International Center for Financial Research at IESE.

PART I – BASICS OF VALUATION METHODS AND SHAREHOLDER VALUE CREATION

The book begins with the definition of Shareholder Value Creation and with a description of the most popular valuation methods, with particular emphasis on Price Earnings Ratio, the relationship between market value and book value, dividends, and the impact of interest rates on valuation. Later chapters take an in-depth look at valuing a company by discounting a stream of potential future income back to the present. It lays out the differences between using net income or cash flow as the relevant stream. It offers various examples of valuations and explains real-life valuations. Chapter 11 tackles the question of which discount rate to use in discounting income streams. It shows the problems that may arise in measuring company betas and the difficulty of obtaining the market risk premium starting from historical data.

PART II – SHAREHOLDER VALUE CREATION

Part II describes some of the tools used to measure value creation, e.g., economic value-added and economic benefit, analyzing their limitations and applicability in various situations. Chapter 15 contains several valuations of RJR Nabisco and the value creation of each strategy. Chapter 16 analyzes the evolution of a number of Internet-related companies (Terra, Amazon, America Online, Microsoft, B2B companies, online brokers, etc.), although the focus is the valuation of Amazon.

PART III – RIGOROUS APPROACHES TO DISCOUNTED CASH FLOW VALUATION

Part III examines in greater depth discounted cash flow valuation and starts with the analysis of the eight most commonly used methods for valuing companies by cash flow discounting:

1. Free cash flow discounted at the WACC.
2. Equity cash flows discounted at the required return to equity.
3. Capital cash flows discounted at the WACC before tax.
4. APV (Adjusted Present Value).
5. The business's risk-adjusted free cash flows discounted at the required return to assets.
6. The business's risk-adjusted equity cash flows discounted at the required return to assets.
7. Economic profit discounted at the required return to equity.
8. EVA discounted at the WACC.

It is shown how all eight methods always give the same value. This result is logical, since the methods analyze the same reality under the same hypotheses; they only differ in the cash flows taken as starting point for the valuation.

Chapter 18 is a revision of the financial literature about discounted cash flow valuation. We will analyze in greater detail the most important theories about value creation by leverage: Modigliani and Miller, Damo-daran, Practitioners method, Harris and Pringle, Ruback, Myers, and Miles and Ezzell. Chapter 20 is the application of the theories studied in previous chapters to RJR Nabisco. Chapter 21 is a summarized compendium of all the methods and theories on company valuation using cash flow discounting presented in the previous chapters.

PART IV – REAL OPTIONS AND BRANDS

The final portion of the book reviews the most important methods to value real options and shows the usefulness and limitations of option pricing theory for company valuation, clarifying the differences between financial options and real options. It also addresses the valuation of brands and intangible assets.

Some issues covered in *Valuation Methods and Shareholder Value Creation:*

- Definition of shareholder value creation.
- Shareholder value creation of 142 American companies in the period 1993–2000.
- Valuation and shareholder value creation of Internet-related companies.
- Differences of increase of equity market value, shareholder value added, and created shareholder value.
- Different flows used in valuation: free cash flow, flows available to shares, and capital cash flow.
- Different discount rates used: weighted average cost of capital (WACC), required return to shareholders, required return to assets, and WACC before taxes.
- Basic stages in the performance of a valuation.
- Critical aspects in performing a company valuation.
- Determination of the risk premium in international markets and in the U.S.
- How to value Amazon.
- The similarities and differences of the methods for valuing companies by discounted cash flows streams.
- The methods for valuing companies by discounted cash flows streams must provide the same result.
- Inconsistency of calculating the market risk premium from historic data.
- The break out of Price Earnings Ratio in Price Earnings Ratio without growth, and franchise value.
- Valuation of businesses and projects using option pricing theory.
- Differences between a financial option and a real option.

- Problems of using formulae of financial options to value real options.
- Multiples used in valuation.
- Inflation and value.
- ROE (Return on Equity) is not shareholder return.
- The market risk premium has decreased worldwide in the last decade.
- How do analysts reach their conclusions?
- Fewer companies are paying dividends and dividend yield has decreased worldwide.
- Duration of shares.
- Instability of volatilities and betas of companies.
- Different approaches to estimate a qualitative beta.
- Usefulness and limitations of the proposed measures of value creation for shareholders: Economic Value Added, economic profit and others.
- Speculative bubbles on the stock market.
- Value Creation due to debt.
- Value of the tax shield.
- Key factors that affect value and value creation: growth, profitability, risk and interest rates.
- Factors influencing the equity's value (value drivers).
- EVA is not a good measure of shareholder value creation.
- Accounting magnitudes can not measure the shareholder value creation.
- Optimal capital structure
- Main errors in valuations.

Most of the tables and spreadsheets included in the book and up-dated financial data may be found and downloaded on my website: http://web.iese.edu/pablofernandez/valuation.html.

Pablo Fernández
June, 2002

Acknowledgments

CIIF (the IESE Center for Finance Research) and PricewaterhouseCoopers have so kindly sponsored this book. I would like to publicly express my deepest gratitude to Rafael Termes and Natalia Centenera CIIF President and CEO respectively, for their on-going support and guidance throughout the project. The support provided by CIIF's own sponsoring companies and PricewaterhouseCoopers has also been greatly appreciated.

This book would never have been possible without the excellent work done by a group of students and research assistants, namely José Ramón Contreras, Teresa Modroño, Gabriel Rabasa, Laura Reinoso. It has been 5 years since we began and their contribution has been essential.

My secretary, Laura Parga, has been able to cope with making corrections, draft after draft.

The book has been revised by such IESE Finance Professors as José Manuel Campa, Javier Estrada and María Jesús Grandes, who have provided their own enhancements.

I want to thank my dissertation committee at Harvard University, Carliss Baldwin, Timothy Luehrman, Andreu Mas-Colell, and Scott Mason for improving my dissertation as well as my future work habits. Special thanks go to Richard Caves, chairman of the Ph.D. in Business Economics, for his time and guidance. Some other teachers and friends have also contributed to this work. Discussions with Franco Modigliani, John Cox, and Frank Fabozzi (from M.I.T.), and Juan Antonio Palacios (BBVA) were important for developing ideas which have found a significant place in this research.

Lastly, I would like to dedicate this book to my wife Lucia and my parents for their unfledging, on-going encouragement and invaluable advice.

PART I

Basics of Valuation Methods and Shareholder Value Creation

Chapter 1

Shareholder Value Creation, Basic Concepts

In this chapter, we will define and analyze shareholder value creation. To help us understand this concept better, we will use the example of a listed company, General Electric (GE), between 1991 and 2000.

On December 31, 1991, General Electric had 866.59 million shares outstanding and the price of each share on the stock market was $76.50. On December 31, 2000, General Electric had 9,932 million shares outstanding and the price of each share on the stock market was $47.9375. Consequently, General Electric's equity market value[1] increased from $66.3 billion in December 1991 to $476.1 billion in December 2000.[2] The increase of equity market value during this period was $409.8 billion. However, this is not General Electric's created shareholder value during those years.

To obtain the created shareholder value, we must first define the increase of equity market value, the shareholder value added, the shareholder return, and the required return to equity. It is important to not confuse the created shareholder value with any of the other concepts we have mentioned. All of these concepts will be explained in this chapter.

Figure 1.1 shows that between December 1991 and December 2000, General Electric's equity market value increased $409.8 billion, the shareholder value added was $452 billion, and the created shareholder value was $279.2 billion.

---

[1] The equity market value is the value of all of the company's shares.
[2] On December 31, 2000: 9.932 million shares × $47.9375/share = $476.1 billion.

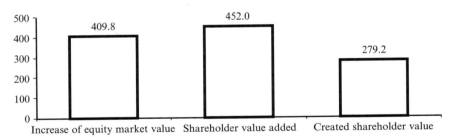

Figure 1.1   General Electric. December 1991–December 2000. Increase of equity market value, shareholder value added, and created shareholder value (billion dollars).

1.1. INCREASE OF EQUITY MARKET VALUE

The equity market value of a listed company is the company's market value, that is, each share's price multiplied by the number of shares. The increase of equity market value in one year is the equity market value at the end of that year less the equity market value at the end of the previous year. The equity market value is also called capitalization.

Table 1.1 shows the evolution of General Electric's equity market value and the increase of equity market value during each year.

It is important not to confuse the *increase of equity market value* with the *shareholder value added*, as they are two different concepts, as we shall see in the following section.

1.2. SHAREHOLDER VALUE ADDED

Shareholder value added is the term used for the difference between the wealth held by the shareholders at the end of a given year and the wealth they

Table 1.1

**General Electric. Equity Market Value and Increase of
Equity Market Value during Each Year (Billion dollars)**

	1991	1992	1993	1994	1995	1996	1997	1998	1999	2000
Equity market value	66.29	73.02	89.45	87.19	120.26	162.79	240.14	334.24	507.22	476.12
Increase of equity market value	15.95	6.73	16.43	−2.26	33.07	42.53	77.35	94.10	172.98	−31.10

held the previous year. The increase of equity market value is not the shareholder value added.

One talks of an increase in the equity market value, but not of a shareholder value added when:

1. Shareholders subscribe to new shares of the company paying money.
2. A conversion of convertible debentures takes place.

One talks of a decrease of the equity market value, but not of a decrease of shareholder value[3] when:

1. The company pays money to all of the shareholders: dividends.
2. The company buys shares on the market (share buy-backs or stock repurchases).

The shareholder value added is calculated as follows:

Shareholder value added =
Increase of equity market value
+ Dividends paid during the year
+ Other payments to shareholders
(discounts on par value, share buy-backs. . . .)
− Outlays for capital increases, exercise of options and warrants
− Conversion of convertible debentures

Table 1.2 shows the calculation of the shareholder value added for the period 1991–2000. The shareholder value added has exceeded the increase of

---

[3]When the company pays dividends or buys shares on the market to the shareholders, they receive money, but the company's equity market value also decreases by a similar amount.

Table 1.2

General Electric. Increase of Equity Market Value and Shareholder Value Added Each Year (Billion dollars)

	1992	1993	1994	1995	1996	1997	1998	1999	2000	Total
Increase of equity market value	6.73	16.43	−2.26	33.07	42.53	77.35	94.10	172.98	−31.10	409.82
+ Dividends	1.93	2.15	2.46	2.77	3.05	3.41	3.91	4.59	5.40	29.67
+ Other payments to shareholders	1.21	0.77	1.12	2.52	2.32	2.82	2.82	1.00	0.00	14.58
− Outlays by shareholders	0.43	0.41	0.77	0.00	0.00	0.00	0.00	0.00	0.47	2.07
− Convertible debentures converted	0.00	0.00	0.00	0.00	0.00	0.00	0.00	0.00	0.00	0.00
= **Shareholder value added**	9.43	18.95	0.56	38.36	47.90	83.57	100.83	178.57	−26.17	452.00

equity market value every year. This is because the dividends and other payments to shareholders exceeded the outlays the shareholders had to make.

However, the *shareholder value added* is not the *created shareholder value*. For value to be created during a period, the shareholder return must exceed the required return to equity.

1.3. SHAREHOLDER RETURN

The *shareholder return* is the shareholder value added in one year, divided by the equity market value at the beginning of the year.

Shareholder return = Shareholder value added / Equity market value

---

For example, as Table 1.3 shows, General Electric's shareholder return in 1998 was 42%: the shareholder value added in 1998 ($100,833 million) divided by the equity market value at the end of 1997 ($240,136 million).

Another way to calculate the shareholder return is increase in the share's price plus dividends, rights and other payments (discounts on par value, special payments, etc.) divided by the share's price at the start of the year.

Table 1.3

Shareholder Return of General Electric

	1992	1993	1994	1995	1996	1997	1998	1999	2000	average
Shareholder return	14%	26%	1%	44%	40%	51%	42%	53%	−5%	28%

1.4. REQUIRED RETURN TO EQUITY

The required return to equity (also called cost of equity) is the return that shareholders *expect* to obtain in order to feel sufficiently remunerated. The required return to equity depends on the interest rates of long-term Treasury bonds and the company's risk. Let us look at an example. On December 1997, the return provided by 10-year Treasury bonds was 5.74%. A shareholder would therefore demand a return on his investment that was higher than the 5.74% he could get risk-free. How much higher? That depends on the company's risk. Obviously, he would require a higher return on an investment in shares of a high-risk company than on an investment in shares of a lower risk company.

The required return is the sum of the interest rate of long-term Treasury bonds plus a quantity that is usually called the company's **risk premium** and which depends on its risk.

$$\begin{array}{ccc} \text{required return} & = & \text{return of long-term} + \text{risk} \\ \text{to equity} & & \text{treasury bonds} \quad \text{premium} \end{array}$$

Ke is the term used for the required return to equity (return on the investment required by the shareholder), also known as the equity cost.

If the one-year risk-free interest rate is 6%, this means that one million dollars to be paid in one year's time with the guarantee of the State (this is what we mean with the expression "risk-free") today has a value of $1,000,000/1.06 = \$946,396$. The value today of obtaining a million dollars in one year's time, as a result of an investment in a company's shares, will be less because that million has more risk (we have less certainty of obtaining it). For the value today of our investment in the company to be less than $946,396, we must divide the million we expect to obtain by a quantity greater than 1.06. If we give our investment in the company a value of $909,091 ($1,000,000/1.10 =

909,091), this means that we are restating at 10% the million we expect to obtain in one year's time.

Another way of saying this is that the return we require on an investment guaranteed by the State is 6% (the risk-free interest rate) and the required return on an investment in the company is 10%. The difference between 10 and 6% is due to the risk perceived in a company and is usually called the company's risk premium.

Stating this idea as an equation, we could say that the required return on the investment in the company's shares (Ke) is equal to the risk-free rate plus the company's risk premium. The company's risk premium is a function of the company's perceived risk[4]:

$$Ke = \text{return of Treasury bonds} + \text{company's risk premium}$$

Table 1.4 shows the evolution of 10-year Treasury bonds and the required return to equity of General Electric.

1.5. CREATED SHAREHOLDER VALUE

A company creates value for the shareholders when the shareholder return exceeds the cost of equity (the required return to equity). In other words, a company creates value in one year when it outperforms expectations.

The created shareholder value is quantified as follows:

Table 1.4

Yield on 10-Year Treasury Bonds and Required Return to Equity of General Electric (Data Corresponding to December)

	1991	1992	1993	1994	1995	1996	1997	1998	1999	2000	average
Yield on 10-year Treasury bonds	6.7%	6.7%	5.8%	7.8%	5.6%	6.4%	5.7%	4.6%	6.4%	5.1%	6.1%
Required return to equity (Ke)	11.5%	11.5%	10.0%	13.5%	9.6%	11.0%	9.9%	8.0%	11.1%	8.8%	10.5%

[4]If, instead of investing in a single company's shares, we were to invest in all companies' shares (in a diversified portfolio), we would then require a return which is the following: Ke = return of Treasury bonds + market risk premium.

Created shareholder value = Equity market value ×
(Shareholder return - Ke)

As we already saw that the shareholder return is equal to the shareholder value added divided by the equity market value. The created shareholder value can also be calculated as follows:

Created shareholder value =Shareholder value added −
(Equity market value × Ke)

Consequently, the value created is the shareholder value added above expectations, which are reflected in the required return to equity.

Table 1.5 shows the created shareholder value of General Electric. General Electric has created value for its shareholders every year except 1994 and 2000.

Table 1.6 shows in simplified form the relationship between three variables, which are sometimes confused: increase of equity market value, shareholder value added, and created shareholder value.

1.6. THE ROE IS NOT THE SHAREHOLDER RETURN

ROE means return on equity. However, it is not true that the ROE, which is calculated by dividing the net income by the shares' book value, is the

Table 1.5

General Electric. Evolution of the Increase of Equity Market Value, Shareholder Value Added, and Created Shareholder Value (Billion Dollars)

	1992	1993	1994	1995	1996	1997	1998	1999	2000	Total
Increase of equity market value	6.73	16.43	−2.26	33.07	42.53	77.35	94.10	172.98	−31.10	409.82
Shareholder value added	9.43	18.95	0.56	38.36	47.90	83.57	100.83	178.57	−26.17	452.00
Created shareholder value	1.79	10.55	−8.36	26.63	36.38	65.60	77.12	151.85	−82.37	279.20

In Chapter 11, we will discuss the market risk premium in detail. By way of reference, in 1999 and 2000, most market analysts used a market risk premium around 4%.

Table 1.6

**Increase of Equity Market Value, Shareholder Value Added,
and Created Shareholder Value**

Increase of equity market value	Equity market value$_t$ Equity market value$_{t-1}$
	$\downarrow$
Shareholder value added	Increase of equity market value − payments from shareholders + dividends + repurchases − conversions.
	$\downarrow$
Created shareholder value	Shareholder value added − (Equity market value × Ke)

shareholder return. In Section 1.3, we already defined the shareholder return as the shareholder value added divided by the equity market value and this is not the ROE.

Table 1.7, which shows General Electric's ROE and shareholder return prove this for each year. We can see that the ROE follows a different course from the shareholder return.

1.7. COMPARISON OF GENERAL ELECTRIC WITH OTHER COMPANIES

Table 1.8 shows the created shareholder value of selected American companies during the three-year period 1998–2000 and during the 8-year period 1993–2000. General Electric was the first company in created shareholder value in both periods, and in capitalization (equity market value) in 2000.

Table 1.9 shows the return of listed American companies in the 3-year period, 1998–2000 and in the 8-year period, 1993–2000. It can be seen that General Electric was the forty-eighth most profitable company during the period 1998–2000. Bea Systems and Network Appliance were the most profitable. General Electric was the 39th most profitable company during the period 1993–2000. America Online and EMC were the most profitable in that period.

Table 1.7

General Electric's ROE and Shareholder return

	1992	1993	1994	1995	1996	1997	1998	1999	2000	Average
Shareholder return	14%	26%	1%	44%	40%	51%	42%	53%	−5%	28%
ROE	21%	18%	18%	23%	24%	25%	25%	26%	27%	23%

Table 1.8

Created Shareholder Value and Market Capitalization of Selected American Companies (Billion Dollars)

	Company Name	Created shareholder value		Capitalization (year end)	
		1998–00	1993–00	2000	1992
1	General Electric	146.6	277.4	476.1	73.0
2	Oracle	120.0	126.8	162.7	4.0
3	Cisco Systems	101.0	129.4	268.7	4.8
4	EMC	99.4	106.8	145.0	0.9
5	American International G.	91.2	119.9	228.2	24.5
6	Wal-Mart Stores	88.5	66.7	237.3	73.6
7	Citigroup	70.6	102.7	229.4	5.3
8	Merck	54.3	97.3	215.9	49.8
9	Sun Microsystems	47.3	54.7	89.7	3.4
10	Pfizer	45.6	100.2	290.2	23.9
11	Amgen	41.5	39.3	65.7	9.6
12	Solectron	40.0	41.9	21.8	0.6
13	Morgan Stanley, Dean Witter,	38.7		89.7	
14	Texas Instruments	38.4	44.4	82.0	3.8
15	Enron	37.8	38.0	61.4	5.4
16	Tyco International	31.5	35.2	97.1	0.9
17	Home Depot	29.5	33.7	106.1	22.3
18	Exxon-Mobil	28.6	69.1	302.2	75.9
19	Medtronic	27.5	40.6	72.4	5.7
20	Corning	23.6	20.8	46.7	7.3
21	Johnson & Johnson	23.1	51.1	146.1	33.1
22	Bristol-Myers Squibb	22.6	67.5	144.6	35.0
23	Network Appliance	20.6		20.3	
24	Siebel Systems	19.2		29.1	
25	American Home Products	18.9	34.3	83.3	21.1
26	Schering-Plough	18.5	43.5	83.0	12.7
27	Walgreen	18.4	24.4	42.2	5.4
28	American Express	17.5	40.5	73.1	11.9
29	Anheuser-Busch	17.1	18.0	41.2	16.2
30	QUALCOMM	16.4	17.0	61.5	0.5
31	Merrill Lynch & Co., Inc.	16.2	31.3	54.9	6.1

(continues)

Table 1.8 (*continued*)

	Company Name	Created shareholder value		Capitalization (year end)	
		1998–00	1993–00	2000	1992
32	Bea Systems	14.5		25.6	
33	Immunex Corporation	13.7		21.8	
34	Ford Motor	13.7	30.3	42.8	20.9
35	Intel	13.7	79.2	202.3	18.1
36	Automatic Data Processing	13.3	18.1	40.0	7.5
37	Charles Schwab Corp.	13.3	20.9	39.3	1.0
38	BellSouth	12.1	32.4	76.4	25.4
39	Bank of New York	12.1	25.6	40.9	4.3
40	Kohl's	11.2	13.8	20.2	1.1
41	United Technologies	11.1	16.3	36.8	6.0
42	Comverse Technology	10.9	11.1	18.0	0.2
43	CIGNA Corporation	10.8	16.1	20.3	4.2
44	12 Technologies	10.8		22.0	
45	Comcast	10.5	12.2	36.4	1.6
46	Safeway	10.4	19.7	31.3	1.3
47	Qwest Communications	10.3		67.9	
48	Veritas Software	10.3		35.8	
49	Sysco	10.1	10.7	20.0	4.9
50	Abbott Laboratories	10.0	22.8	74.9	25.4
51	3M	9.4	12.9	47.5	22.1
52	IBM	9.3	64.2	149.1	28.8
53	MBNA Corporation	9.2	17.7	31.5	2.5
54	Wells Fargo & Company	9.0	22.6	95.2	6.0
55	Providian Financial Corp.	8.9	12.4	16.4	3.4
56	Cardinal Health	8.9	11.4	27.8	0.6
57	Analog Devices	8.8	10.5	18.3	0.8
58	Baxter International	8.2	9.7	25.8	9.0
59	Xilinx	8.0	8.5	15.2	0.6
60	State Street Corporation	7.4	11.1	20.0	3.3
61	Viacom	6.9	1.0	64.5	2.8
62	Cox Communications	6.9		26.6	
63	Alcoa	6.8	8.2	29.0	6.1
64	Linear Technology	6.5	8.0	14.7	0.9

(*continues*)

Table 1.8 (*continued*)

	Company Name	Created shareholder value		Capitalization (year end)	
		1998–00	1993–00	2000	1992
65	Colgate-Palmolive	6.1	12.7	37.1	8.9
66	Target	5.6	11.1	28.9	5.4
67	Mellon Bank Corporation	5.6	15.1	24.0	2.9
68	Applied Materials	5.4	10.3	31.0	1.3
69	Micron Technology	5.3	6.2	20.2	0.7
70	Eli Lilly	5.2	55.2	105.1	17.8
71	J.P. Morgan & Company	4.8	7.0	26.6	12.6
72	CVS Corp	4.5	3.9	23.4	5.6
73	Fifth Third Bancorp	4.3	10.8	27.8	3.2
74	Emerson Electric	4.2	9.2	33.8	12.3
75	First Data Corp	4.1	−1.4	20.8	3.8
76	Tellabs	4.0	10.4	23.2	0.3
77	Omnicom	3.4	7.1	14.7	1.2
78	Kimberly-Clark	3.2	3.1	38.0	9.5
79	American General Corp.	3.1	5.4	20.5	6.2
80	Kroger	3.1	7.9	22.2	1.3
81	Bestfoods	2.7	6.5	20.2	7.6
82	Boeing	2.3	7.4	58.6	13.6
83	HCA Healthcare	2.0	−4.8	23.4	0.6
84	U.S. Bancorp	1.7	12.2	21.9	2.4
85	McDonald's	1.5	3.4	44.6	17.7
86	PNC Bank Corp.	0.9	5.9	21.2	8.0
87	Texaco	0.8	8.4	34.3	15.5
88	TENET Healthcare	0.6	2.4	14.1	2.1
89	Alltel Corporation	0.5	1.6	19.5	4.2
90	Phillips Petroleum	0.3	3.4	14.5	6.5
91	PepsiCo	0.3	2.6	71.5	33.1
92	JDS Uniphase	0.1		40.1	
93	Household International	0.1	6.3	25.9	2.4
94	Electronic Data Systems	−0.3	−7.2	26.9	6.8
95	The Gap	−0.5	5.9	21.7	4.8
96	Time Warner	−1.1	5.1	63.4	10.9
97	Chubb Corporation	−1.6	−1.7	15.1	7.8

(*continues*)

Table 1.8 (*continued*)

	Company Name	Created shareholder value		Capitalization (year end)	
		1998–00	1993–00	2000	1992
98	Dow Chemical	−2.8	1.2	24.8	15.6
99	Chevron	−3.9	12.6	55.1	23.7
100	Nextel Communications	−4.1	−3.8	18.0	1.0
101	Gannett Co	−4.3	1.7	16.6	7.3
102	H.J. Heinz	−4.3	−0.9	16.5	11.2
103	Caterpillar	−4.7	3.0	16.3	5.4
104	Chase Manhattan Corp.	−5.4	6.5	59.2	9.5
105	Schlumberger	−5.6	11.2	45.5	13.8
106	General Motors	−5.8	−1.0	28.8	22.7
107	Illinois Tool Works	−6.2	0.1	18.0	3.7
108	ConAgra	−6.4	−2.9	13.9	8.1
109	America Online	−6.7	−1.0	80.9	0.2
110	International Paper	−7.1	−10.3	19.7	8.2
111	FleetBoston	−7.3	−1.6	33.9	4.0
112	SunTrust Banks, Inc.	−7.3	−0.2	18.7	5.5
113	Clear Channel Comm.	−7.4	−2.7	28.3	0.2
114	Verizon Communications	−7.4	1.6	135.3	22.2
115	Hewlett-Packard	−7.5	17.2	62.4	17.6
116	Honeywell	−7.7	−2.8	38.1	8.6
117	Halliburton	−8.5	−2.5	16.2	3.1
118	National City Corporation	−8.5	−3.7	17.5	3.9
119	Sara Lee	−9.6	−4.8	20.5	14.4
120	Lockheed Martin	−10.2		14.6	
121	Allstate Corporation	−10.3		31.9	
122	SBC Communications	−11.7	−4.0	161.6	22.2
123	Sprint	−14.0	−3.3	16.2	5.6
124	Campbell Soup	−14.2	−2.2	14.6	10.6
125	Waste Management	−14.6	1.0	17.3	0.2
126	Motorola	−17.2	−21.5	44.2	14.0
127	Philip Morris	−17.2	6.3	97.8	68.9
128	Dell Computer	−18.0	7.3	45.8	1.8
129	E.I. Du Pont De Nemours	−26.2	−0.2	50.4	31.8
130	Walt Disney	−26.6	−11.2	60.3	22.5

(*continues*)

Table 1.8 (*continued*)

	Company Name	Created shareholder value		Capitalization (year end)	
		1998–00	1993–00	2000	1992
131	Gillette	−31.6	−12.7	38.1	12.5
132	Banc One Corporation	−33.0	−35.0	42.3	12.3
133	Procter & Gamble	−33.3	12.8	102.3	36.5
134	First Union Corporation	−36.9	−27.4	27.3	5.8
135	Yahoo!	−41.0		16.5	
136	Compaq Computer	−43.1	−17.8	25.6	3.8
137	BankAmerica Corporation	−50.9	−42.6	75.4	12.5
138	Coca-Cola	−62.9	1.8	151.1	54.9
139	WorldCom	−96.1		40.5	
140	Microsoft	−96.8	−4.3	231.3	23.5
141	Lucent Technologies	−112.0		45.1	
142	AT&T	−122.2	−120.9	64.8	68.1

Source: Fernández (2001).

Table 1.9

Shareholder Return of Selected Companies (Average Annual Return)

	Company Name	Average shareholder return			Company Name	Average shareholder return	
		1998–00	1993–00			1998–00	1993–00
1	Bea Systems	149.6%		12	Solectron	92.5%	60.4%
2	Network Appliance	143.7%		13	America Online	83.2%	87.4%
3	QUALCOMM	139.0%	65.7%	14	Sun Microsystems	77.5%	50.7%
4	Siebel Systems	134.8%		15	Xilinx	73.9%	47.1%
5	Veritas Software	126.3%		16	Amgen	67.8%	28.1%
6	EMC	113.2%	75.4%	17	Corning	64.1%	24.5%
7	Immunex Corp.	108.2%		18	Texas Instruments	61.9%	42.8%
8	Comverse Tech.	102.9%	44.5%	19	Enron	60.9%	30.4%
9	12 Technologies	102.0%		20	Cisco Systems	60.3%	56.0%
10	JDS Uniphase	100.5%		21	Providian Financial	56.7%	35.8%
11	Oracle	98.4%	59.3%	22	Analog Devices	54.6%	44.4%

(*continues*)

Table 1.9 (*continued*)

Company Name	Average shareholder return		Company Name	Average shareholder return	
	1998–00	1993–00		1998–00	1993–00
23 Kohl's	53.0%	41.7%	54 Citigroup	25.1%	39.1%
24 Yahoo!	51.4%		55 Target	25.0%	24.5%
25 Linear Technology	48.0%	40.3%	56 Merrill Lynch & Co	24.7%	34.1%
26 Charles Schwab	45.3%	55.7%	57 Baxter International	24.5%	18.1%
27 Morgan Stanley, DW	40.4%		58 Nextel Comm.	23.9%	13.1%
28 Qwest Comm.	40.1%		59 CVS Corp	23.9%	15.0%
29 Micron Technology	39.9%	44.5%	60 Pfizer	23.8%	31.0%
30 Wal-Mart Stores	39.8%	16.9%	61 Schering-Plough	23.5%	30.3%
31 Sysco	39.8%	22.6%	62 American Express	23.5%	31.2%
32 Walgreen	39.4%	30.4%	63 Merck	22.8%	22.8%
33 Comcast	38.4%	27.7%	64 Colgate-Palmolive	22.1%	23.5%
34 American Int. G.	36.9%	30.2%	65 First Data Corp	21.9%	15.3%
35 Applied Materials	36.4%	43.6%	66 American Home Pr.	20.5%	21.6%
36 Tyco International	35.2%	38.9%	67 Mellon Bank	20.2%	28.0%
37 CIGNA Corporation	34.1%	30.6%	68 Intel	19.8%	35.4%
38 Home Depot	32.9%	19.6%	69 Fifth Third Bancorp	19.6%	26.2%
39 Medtronic	32.5%	34.4%	70 Time Warner	19.4%	18.0%
40 Cox Comm.	32.5%		71 Dell Computer	18.6%	48.3%
41 Viacom	31.2%	10.6%	72 Johnson & Johnson	18.3%	21.5%
42 United Technologies	31.0%	29.1%	73 IBM	18.2%	28.5%
43 Anheuser-Busch	29.7%	18.3%	74 The Gap	17.8%	23.9%
44 State Street Corp.	29.7%	25.7%	75 Bristol-Myers Squibb	17.6%	24.0%
45 Tellabs	28.8%	65.5%	76 Alltel Corporation	17.5%	16.1%
46 Automatic Data Proc.	28.2%	22.6%	77 American General	17.5%	17.8%
47 MBNA Corporation	28.0%	38.0%	78 J.P. Morgan	17.0%	16.2%
48 General Electric	26.7%	29.5%	79 3M	16.6%	15.2%
49 Omnicom	26.2%	31.9%	80 Abbott Laboratories	15.8%	17.9%
50 Bank of New York	26.1%	33.5%	81 BellSouth	15.4%	19.5%
51 Alcoa	26.0%	20.2%	82 Bestfoods	15.2%	17.6%
52 Cardinal Health	26.0%	32.4%	83 Wells Fargo	15.1%	25.9%
53 Safeway	25.5%	44.7%	84 Kimberly-Clark	15.0%	14.7%
			85 Exxon-Mobil	14.9%	17.8%

(*continues*)

Table 1.9 (*continued*)

Company Name	Average shareholder return 1998–00	1993–00	Company Name	Average shareholder return 1998–00	1993–00
86 HCA Healthcare	14.5%	15.5%	114 Motorola	2.7%	11.9%
87 Emerson Electric	14.2%	16.7%	115 Schlumberger	2.2%	16.1%
88 Ford Motor	13.8%	19.1%	116 Gannett Co	2.0%	14.2%
89 Kroger	13.8%	28.4%	117 Caterpillar	1.9%	19.4%
90 McDonald's	13.1%	14.4%	118 Procter & Gamble	0.9%	16.5%
91 PepsiCo	12.6%	14.4%	119 H.J. Heinz	0.8%	9.7%
92 PNC Bank Corp.	12.3%	17.1%	120 Illinois Tool Works	0.8%	19.0%
93 Boeing	11.9%	17.9%	121 Allstate Corporation	0.6%	
94 Eli Lilly	11.6%	28.6%	122 International Paper	0.4%	5.0%
95 SBC Comm.	11.5%	16.0%	123 National City	−0.7%	15.6%
96 Electronic Data Sys.	10.9%	8.7%	124 Coca-Cola	−1.9%	15.7%
97 Household Int.	10.6%	26.7%	125 SunTrust Banks	−2.0%	16.7%
98 TENET Healthcare	10.3%	17.9%	126 Sara Lee	−2.4%	8.8%
99 Microsoft	10.3%	29.9%	127 Walt Disney	−3.6%	9.9%
100 Chase Manhattan	10.1%	20.5%	128 E.I. Du Pont	−4.8%	12.4%
101 Hewlett-Packard	9.8%	22.3%	129 ConAgra	−4.9%	8.6%
102 U.S. Bancorp	8.9%	27.8%	130 BankAmerica	−6.0%	11.1%
103 Phillips Petroleum	8.5%	14.4%	131 Banc One	−6.1%	5.4%
104 Honeywell	8.4%	17.1%	132 Sprint	−6.7%	13.9%
105 Texaco	8.0%	14.0%	133 Gillette	−9.2%	13.8%
106 Clear Channel Comm.	6.8%	52.8%	134 Lockheed Martin	−9.8%	
			135 Halliburton	−10.1%	15.1%
107 Chubb Corporation	6.6%	11.0%	136 Lucent Technologies	−10.2%	
108 Dow Chemical	6.3%	12.7%	137 Waste Management	−10.9%	8.5%
109 Verizon Comm.	6.2%	13.2%	138 WorldCom	−11.3%	
110 Chevron	6.2%	15.7%	139 Campbell Soup	−12.9%	9.4%
111 Philip Morris	4.7%	12.4%	140 First Union	−14.6%	7.2%
112 General Motors	3.4%	12.1%	141 Compaq Computer	−18.7%	21.3%
113 FleetBoston	3.0%	14.8%	142 AT&T	−23.5%	−1.6%

Source: Fernández (2001).

Table 1.10 shows the top ten value creators and value destroyers in 2000, 1999, and 1998.

Table 1.10

Top Ten Value Creators and Value Destroyers in 2000, 1999, and 1998 (Billion Dollars)

	Top value shareholder creators. Shareholder value created in $billion					
		2000		1999		1998
1	Philip Morris	52.8	Microsoft	192.8	Microsoft	159.1
2	Merck	49.3	Cisco Systems	172.6	Wal-Mart Stores	85.2
3	American International Group	44.8	General Electric	151.8	Lucent Technologies	82.3
4	PMC-Sierra	42.8	Oracle	114.8	Cisco Systems	77.3
5	Pfizer	41.8	Wal-Mart Stores	106.4	General Electric	77.1
6	American Home Products	28.4	QUALCOMM	92.6	IBM	65.5
7	Solectron	25.8	Sun Microsystems	81.0	Intel	65.2
8	Enron	25.2	Citigroup	63.4	Dell Computer	64.0
9	Medtronic	24.5	EMC	61.5	Pfizer	56.1
10	Eli Lilly	23.9	Yahoo!	58.1	America Online	53.1

	Top value shareholder destroyers. Shareholder value created in $billion					
		2000		1999		1998
1	Microsoft	−448.6	Philip Morris	−84.1	Boeing	−22.1
2	Lucent Technologies	−224.5	Pfizer	−52.3	Schlumberger	−20.7
3	Cisco Systems	−148.9	Coca-Cola	−39.3	Coca-Cola	−17.0
4	WorldCom	−128.1	Compaq Computer	−33.7	Cendant	−15.2
5	AT&T	−123.8	Eli Lilly	−33.4	E.I. Du Pont	−13.4
6	America Online	−116.6	First Union Corp.	−33.4	Walt Disney	−12.9
7	Yahoo!	−116.0	Merck	−33.1	Citigroup	−12.8
8	Intel	−104.6	Banc One Corp.	−30.9	Allstate Corporation	−9.8
9	Dell Computer	−104.5	BankAmerica Corp.	−29.7	Computer Associates	−9.5
10	Wal-Mart Stores	−103.1	American Home	−29.3	Gillette	−8.9

Source: Fernández (2001).

1.8. VALUE CREATION AND VALUE DESTRUCTION OF THE S&P 500

Table 1.11 shows the value creation of the S&P 500 in years 1997, 1998, and 1999 and the destruction of value in 2000 and 2001 (until September). It is interesting to see that the value destruction in the last 2 years was higher than the value creation of the previous 3 years.

1.9. WHAT SHOULD THE SHAREHOLDER RETURN BE COMPARED WITH?

In Section 1.5, we saw that the company creates value if the shareholder return exceeds the required return (and it destroys value in the opposite case).

However, the shareholder return is often compared with other benchmarks.[5] The most common benchmarks are

1. *Zero.* If the shareholder return is positive (above zero), the shareholders have more money in nominal terms than at the beginning of the year.
2. *The return of Treasury bonds.* If the shareholder return exceeds that of investing in Treasury bonds, the shareholders have obtained an additional return for bearing more risk (the additional risk of investing in the company instead of investing in Treasury bonds).
3. *Required return to equity.* If the shareholder return exceeds the expected return, the company has created value: the shareholders have obtained a return that is greater than that required to compensate the additional risk of investing in the company instead of investing in Treasury bonds.

Table 1.11
Value Creation of the S&P 500 (Billion Dollars)

	1997	1998	1999	2000	Sep. 28, 2001
S&P 500 index level	970.4	1,229.2	1,469.3	1,320.3	1,035.2
Capitalization (year-end)	7,555	9,942	12,310	11,735	9,437
Shareholder return	33.4%	28.6%	21.0%	−9.1%	−20.9%
Shareholder value added	1,890	2,158	2,092	−1,120	−2,456
Created shareholder value	1,286	1,411	1,295	−2,487	−3,226

[5]Comparing different benchmarks enables different questions to be answered.

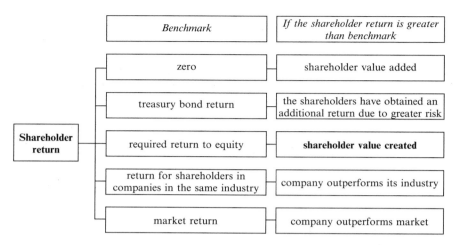

4. *Shareholder return of companies in the same industry.* If the shareholder return exceeds the shareholder return of companies in the same industry, the company has created more value than the other companies in its industry (for an equal investment and risk).

5. *Return of the stock market index.* If the shareholder return exceeds the return of the stock market index, the company has outperformed the market as a whole.

REFERENCE

Fernandez, P. (2001), "Shareholder value creators and shareholder value destroyers in USA. Year 2000," Social Science Research Network (SSRN), Working Paper No. 272252.

Chapter 2

Company Valuation Methods

For anyone involved in the field of corporate finance, understanding the mechanisms of company valuation is an indispensable requisite. This is not only because of the importance of valuation in acquisitions and mergers but also because the process of valuing the company and its business units helps identify sources of economic value creation and destruction within the company.

The methods for valuing companies can be classified in six groups:

Main Valuation Methods

Balance sheet	Income statement	Mixed (goodwill)	Cash flow discounting	Value creation	Options
Book value	Multiples	Classic	Free cash flow	EVA	Black and Scholes
Adjusted book value	PER	Union of European Accounting Experts	Equity cash flow	Economic profit	Investment option
	Sales		Dividends	Cash value added	Expand the project
Liquidation value	P/EBITDA	Abbreviated income	Capital cash flow		Delay the investment
Substantial value	Other multiples	Others	APV	CFROI	Alternative uses

In this chapter, we will briefly describe the four main groups comprising the most widely used company valuation methods. Each of these groups is discussed in a separate section: balance sheet-based methods (Section 2.2), income statement-based methods (Section 2.3), mixed methods (Section 2.4), and cash flow discounting-based methods (Section 2.5). The methods based on value creation measures are discussed in depth in Chapters 13 and 14, and company valuation using option theory is introduced in Chapter 22.

Section 2.7 uses a real-life example to illustrate the valuation of a company as the sum of the value of different businesses, which is usually called the *break-up value*. Section 2.8 shows the methods most widely used by analysts for different types of industry.

The methods that are becoming increasingly popular (and are conceptually "correct") are those based on cash flow discounting. These methods view the company as a cash flow generator and, therefore, assessable as a financial asset. We will briefly comment on other methods since—even though they are conceptually "incorrect"—they continue to be used frequently. The rest of the book will basically concentrate on valuation by cash flow discounting. There are also chapters on the price-earnings ratio (PER) (Chapters 3 and 4), and market value and book value (Chapter 5), but in all cases we will look at these methods through the looking glass of cash flow discounting. Chapter 8 addresses valuation by multiples.

2.1. VALUE AND PRICE: WHAT PURPOSE DOES A VALUATION SERVE?

Generally speaking, a company's value is different for different buyers and it may also be different for the buyer and the seller.

Value should not be confused with price, which is the quantity agreed between the seller and the buyer in the sale of a company. This difference in a specific company's value may be due to a multitude of reasons. For example, a large and technologically highly advanced foreign company wishes to buy a well-known national company in order to gain entry into the local market, using the reputation of the local brand. In this case, the foreign buyer will only value the brand but not the plant, machinery, etc., as it has more advanced assets of its own. However, the seller will give a very high value to its material resources, as they are able to continue producing. From the buyer's viewpoint, the basic aim is to determine the maximum value it should be prepared to pay for what the company it wishes to buy is able to contribute. From the seller's viewpoint, the aim is to ascertain what should be the minimum value at which it should accept the operation. These are the two figures that face each other across the table in a negotiation until a price is finally agreed on, which is usually somewhere between the two extremes.[1] A company may also have different values for different buyers due to economies of scale, economies of scope, or different perceptions about the industry and the company.

A valuation may be used for a wide range of purposes:

1. In company buying and selling operations:
   - For the buyer, the valuation will tell him the highest price he should pay.
   - For the seller, the valuation will tell him the lowest price at which he should be prepared to sell.
2. Valuations of listed companies:
   - The valuation is used to compare the value obtained with the share's price on the stock market and to decide whether to sell, buy or hold the shares.
   - The valuation of several companies is used to decide the securities that the portfolio should concentrate on: those that seem to it to be undervalued by the market.
   - The valuation of several companies is also used to make comparisons between companies. For example, if an investor thinks that the future course of GE's share price will be better than that of Amazon, he may buy GE shares and short-sell Amazon shares. With this position, he will gain provided that GE's share price does better (rises more or falls less) than that of Amazon.
3. Public offerings:
   - The valuation is used to justify the price at which the shares are offered to the public.
4. Inheritances and wills:
   - The valuation is used to compare the shares' value with that of the other assets.
5. Compensation schemes based on value creation:
   - The valuation of a company or business unit is fundamental for quantifying the value creation attributable to the executives being assessed.
6. Identification of value drivers:
   - The valuation of a company or business unit is fundamental for identifying and stratifying the main value drivers.
7. Strategic decisions on the company's continued existence:

---

[1]There is also the middle position that considers both the buyer's and seller's viewpoints and is represented by the figure of the neutral arbitrator. Arbitration is often necessary in litigation, for example, when dividing estates between heirs or deciding divorce settlements.

- The valuation of a company or business unit is a prior step in the decision to continue in the business, sell, merge, milk, grow, or buy other companies.
8. Strategic planning:
   - The valuation of the company and the different business units is fundamental for deciding what products/business lines/countries/customers . . . to maintain grow or abandon.
   - The valuation provides a means for measuring the impact of the company's possible policies and strategies on value creation and destruction.

2.2. BALANCE SHEET-BASED METHODS

These methods seek to determine the company's value by estimating the value of its assets. These are traditionally used methods that consider that a company's value lies basically in its balance sheet. They determine the value from a static viewpoint, which, therefore, does not take into account the company's possible future evolution, money's temporary value. These methods do not take into account other factors that also affect the value such as the industry's current situation, human resources or organizational problems, contracts, etc., that do not appear in the accounting statements.

Some of these methods are the following: book value, adjusted book value, liquidation value, and substantial value.

2.2.1. BOOK VALUE

A company's book value, or net worth, is the value of the shareholders' equity stated in the balance sheet (capital and reserves). This quantity is also the difference between total assets and liabilities, that is, the surplus of the company's total goods and rights over its total debts with third parties.

Let us take the case of a hypothetical company whose balance sheet is that shown in Table 2.1. The shares' book value (capital plus reserves) is $80 million. It can also be calculated as the difference between total assets (160) and liabilities (40 + 10 + 30), that is, $80 million.

This value suffers from the shortcoming of its own definition criterion: accounting criteria are subject to a certain degree of subjectivity and differ from "market" criteria, with the result that the book value almost never matches the "market" value. Chapter 5 discusses the relationship between market value and book value.

Table 2.1
Alfa Inc. Official Balance Sheet (Million Dollars)

Assets		Liabilities	
Cash	5	Accounts payable	40
Accounts receivable	10	Bank debt	10
Inventories	45	Long-term debt	30
Fixed assets	100	Shareholders' equity	80
Total assets	160	Total liabilities	160

2.2.2. ADJUSTED BOOK VALUE

This method seeks to overcome the shortcomings that appear when purely accounting criteria are applied in the valuation.

When the values of assets and liabilities match their market value, the adjusted net worth is obtained. Continuing with the example of Table 2.1, we will analyze a number of balance sheet items individually in order to adjust them to their approximate market value. For example, if we consider that:

1. Accounts receivable includes $2 million of bad debt, this item should have a value of $8 million.
2. Stock, after discounting obsolete, worthless items and revaluing the remaining items at their market value, has a value of $52 million.
3. Fixed assets (land, buildings, and machinery) have a value of $150 million, according to an expert.
4. The book value of accounts payable, bank debt, and long-term debt is equal to their market value.

The adjusted balance sheet would be that shown in Table 2.2.

The adjusted book value is $135 million: total assets (215) less liabilities (80). In this case, the adjusted book value exceeds the book value by $55 million.

2.2.3. LIQUIDATION VALUE

This is the company's value if it is liquidated, that is, its assets are sold and its debts are paid off. This value is calculated by deducting the business's liquidation expenses (redundancy payments to employees, tax expenses and other typical liquidation expenses) from the adjusted net worth.

Table 2.2
Alfa Inc. Adjusted Balance Sheet (Million Dollars)

Assets		Liabilities	
Cash	5	Accounts payable	40
Accounts receivable	8	Bank debt	10
Inventories	52	Long-term debt	30
Fixed assets	150	Capital and reserves	135
Total assets	215	Total liabilities	215

Taking the example given in Table 2.2, if the redundancy payments and other expenses associated with the liquidation of the company Alfa Inc. were to amount to $60 million, the shares' liquidation value would be $75 million $(135 - 60)$.

Obviously, this method's usefulness is limited to a highly specific situation, namely, when the company is bought with the purpose of liquidating it at a later date. However, it always represents the company's minimum value, as a company's value, assuming it continues to operate, is greater than its liquidation value.

2.2.4. SUBSTANTIAL VALUE

The substantial value represents the investment that must be made to form a company having identical conditions as those of the company being valued.

It can also be defined as the assets' replacement value, assuming the company continues to operate, as opposed to their liquidation value. Normally, the substantial value does not include those assets that are not used for the company's operations (unused land, holdings in other companies, etc.)

Three types of substantial value are usually defined:

1. Gross substantial value: this is the asset's value at market price (in the example of Table 2.2: 215).
2. Net substantial value or corrected net assets: this is the gross substantial value less liabilities. It is also known as adjusted net worth, which we have already seen in the previous section (in the example of Table 2.2: 135).
3. Reduced gross substantial value: this is the gross substantial value reduced only by the value of the cost-free debt (in the example of Table 2.2: $175 = 215 - 40$). The remaining $40 million correspond to accounts payable.

2.2.5. BOOK VALUE AND MARKET VALUE

In general, the equity's book value has little bearing with its market value. This can be seen in Table 2.3, which shows the price/book value (P/BV) ratio of several international stock markets in September 1992 and August 2000.

Figure 2.1 shows the evolution of the P/BV ratio of the British, German, and United States stock markets. It can be seen that the book value, in the 1990s, has lagged considerably below the shares' market price.

Chapter 5 deals with the relationship between market value (price) and book value in greater detail.

2.3. INCOME STATEMENT-BASED METHODS: RELATIVE VALUATION

Unlike the balance sheet-based methods, these methods are based on the company's income statement. They seek to determine the company's value through the size of its earnings, sales, or other indicators. Thus, for example,

Table 2.3

Market Value/Book Value (P/BV), PER, and Dividend Yield (Div/P) of Different National Stock Markets

| | September 1992 | | | August 2000 | | |
	P/BV	PER	Div/P (%)	P/BV	PER	Div/P (%)
Spain	0.89	7.5	6.3	3.38	22.7	1.5
Canada	1.35	57.1	3.2	3.29	31.7	0.9
France	1.40	14.0	3.7	4.60	37.9	1.7
Germany	1.57	13.9	4.1	3.57	28.0	2.0
Hong Kong	1.69	14.1	3.9	1.96	8.4	2.3
Ireland	1.13	10.0	3.2	2.55	15.2	2.1
Italy	0.78	16.2	4.1	3.84	23.8	2.0
Japan	1.82	36.2	1.0	2.22	87.6	0.6
Swizerland	1.52	15.0	2.2	4.40	22.1	1.4
UK	1.88	16.3	5.2	2.90	24.4	2.1
US	2.26	23.3	3.1	5.29	29.4	1.1

P/BV is the share's price (P) divided by its book value (BV). PER is the share's price divided by the earnings per share. Div/P is the dividend per share divided by the price.
Source: Morgan Stanley Capital International Perspective.

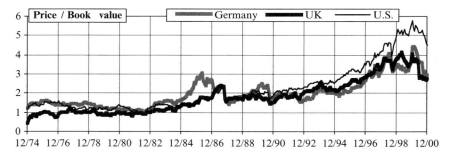

Figure 2.1 Evolution of the price/book value ratio on the British, German, and United States stock markets. (Source: Morgan Stanley.)

it is a common practice to perform quick valuations of cement companies by multiplying their annual production capacity (or sales) in metric tons by a ratio (multiple). It is also common to value car parking lots by multiplying the number of parking spaces by a multiple and to value insurance companies by multiplying annual premiums by a multiple. This category includes the methods based on the PER: according to this method, the share's price is a multiple of the earnings. The use of multiples is often called relative valuation because the multiples used are chosen among comparable companies.

The income statement for the company Alfa Inc. is shown in Table 2.4:

2.3.1. VALUE OF EARNINGS, PER[2]

According to this method, the equity's value is obtained by multiplying the annual net income by a ratio called PER, that is:

$$\text{Equity value} = \text{PER} \times \text{Net income}$$

Table 2.3 shows the mean PER of a number of different national stock markets in September 1992 and August 2000. Figure 2.2 shows

[2]The PER of a share indicates the multiple of the earnings per share that is paid on the stock market. Thus, if the earnings per share in the last year has been $3 and the share's price is $26, its PER will be 8.66 (26/3). On other occasions, the PER takes as its reference the forecast earnings per share for the next year, or the mean earnings per share for the last few years. The PER is the benchmark used predominantly by the stock markets. Note that the PER is a parameter that relates a market item (share price) with a purely accounting item (earnings).

Table 2.4

Alfa Inc. Income Statement (Million Dollars)

Sales	300
Cost of sales	136
General expenses	120
Interest expense	4
Profit before tax	40
Tax (35%)	14
Net income	26

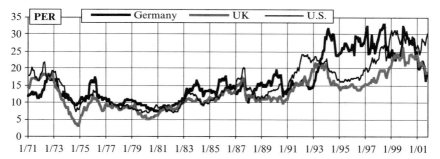

Figure 2.2   Evolution of the PER of the German, British, and United States stock markets. (Source: Morgan Stanley.)

the evolution of the PER for the German, British, and United States stock markets.

Sometimes, the **relative PER** is also used, which is simply the company's PER divided by the country's PER.

PER is studied in detail in Chapter 3 which shows the relationship existing between the PER (the most commonly used ratio in valuation, particularly for listed companies), the required return to equity, and the estimated mean growth of the cash flow generated by the company. This simple relationship often enables us to quickly find out whether a company is over- or under-valued. Chapter 4 shows how the PER breaks down into a number of different factors.

2.3.2. VALUE OF THE DIVIDENDS

Dividends are the part of the earnings effectively paid out to the shareholder and, in most cases, are the only regular flow received by shareholders.[3]

According to this method, a share's value is the net present value of the dividends that we expect to obtain from it.[4] In the perpetuity case, that is, a company from which we expect constant dividends every year, this value can be expressed as follows:

$$\text{Equity value} = \text{DPS}/\text{Ke}$$

where: DPS = dividend per share distributed by the company in the last year;
Ke = required return to equity

If, on the other hand, the dividend is expected to grow indefinitely at a constant annual rate g, the above formula becomes the following[5]:

$$\text{Equity value} = \text{DPS}_1/(\text{Ke} - \text{g})$$

Where DPS_1 is the dividends per share for the next year.

Empirical evidence[6] shows that the companies that pay more dividends (as a percentage of their earnings) do not obtain a growth in their share price as a result. This is because (as we shall see in Chapter 5) when a company distributes more dividends, normally it reduces its growth because it distributes the money to its shareholders instead of plowing it back into new investments.

Table 2.3 shows the dividend yield of several international stock markets in September 1992 and August 2000. Japan was the country with the lowest dividend yield (0.6%) and Spain had a dividend yield of 1.5%.

Figure 2.3 shows the evolution of the dividend yield of the German, Japanese, and United States stock markets.

---

[3]Other flows are share buy-backs and subscription rights. However, when capital increases take place that give rise to subscription rights, the shares' price falls by an amount approximately equal to the right's value.

[4]The dividend discounting-based method for valuing shares is discussed extensively in Chapter 6. Depending on the hypothesis made about the dividends' growth, a number of different formulas are obtained.

[5]This formula is called the formula of Gordon-Shapiro and is derived in Appendix 6.1.

[6]There is an enormous and highly varied literature about the impact of dividend policies on equity value. Some recommendable texts are to be found in Sorensen and Williamson (1985) and Miller (1986).

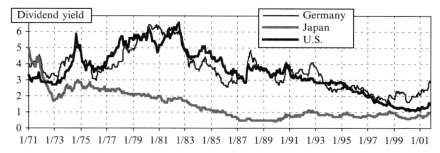

Figure 2.3 Evolution of the dividend yield of the German, Japanese, and United States stock markets.
(*Source*: Morgan Stanley.)

2.3.3. SALES MULTIPLES

This valuation method, which is used in some industries with a certain frequency, consists of calculating a company's value by multiplying its sales by a number. For example, a pharmacy is often valued by multiplying its annual sales (in dollars) by 2 or another number, depending on the market situation. It is also a common practice to value a soft drink bottling plant by multiplying its annual sales in liters by 500 or another number, depending on the market situation.

In order to analyze this method's consistency, Smith Barney analyzed the relationship between the price/sales ratio and the return on equity. The study was carried out in large corporations (capitalization in excess of $150 million) in 22 countries. He divided the companies into five groups depending on their price/sales ratio: group 1 consisted of the companies with the lowest ratio, and group 5 contained the companies with the highest price/sales ratio. The mean return of each group of companies is shown in Table 2.5.

It can be seen from this table that, during the period December 1984–December 1989, the equity of the companies with the lowest price/sales ratio in December 1984 on average provided a higher return than that of the

Table 2.5
Relationship between Return and the Price/Sales Ratio

	Group 1	Group 2	Group 3	Group 4	Group 5
December 1984–December 1989	38.2%	36.3%	33.8%	23.8%	12.3%
December 1989–September 1997	10.3%	12.4%	14.3%	12.2%	9.5%

Source: Smith Barney.

companies with a higher ratio. However, this ceased to apply during the period December 1989–September 1997: there was no relationship between the price/sales ratio in December 1989 and the return on equity during those years.

The price/sales ratio can be broken down into a further two ratios:

$$\text{Price/sales} = (\text{price/earnings}) \times (\text{earnings/sales})$$

The first ratio (price/earnings) is the PER and the second (earnings/sales) is normally known as return on sales.

2.3.4. OTHER MULTIPLES

In addition to the PER and the price/sales ratio, some of the frequently used multiples are

1. Value of the company/earnings before interest and taxes (EBIT)
2. Value of the company/earnings before interest, taxes, depreciation, and amortization (EBITDA)
3. Value of the company/operating cash flow
4. Value of the equity/book value[7]

Obviously, in order to value a company using multiples, multiples of comparable companies must be used.[8]

2.3.5. MULTIPLES USED TO VALUE INTERNET COMPANIES

In Chapter 8 we will see that the multiples most commonly used to value Internet companies are price/sales, price/subscriber, price/pages visited, and price/inhabitant.

For example, in March 2000, a French bank published its valuation of Terra based on the price/sales ratio of comparable companies:

	Freeserve	Tiscali	Freenet.de	Infosources	**Average**
Price/sales	110.4	55.6	109.1	21.0	**74.0**

[7]We could also list a number of other ratios which we could call "sui-generis." One example of such ratios is the value/owner. In the initial stages of a valuation I was commissioned by a family business to perform that was on sale, one of the brothers told me that he reckoned that the shares were worth about 30 million euros. When I asked him how he had arrived at that figure, he answered: "We are three shareholder siblings and I want each one of us to get 10 million."

[8]For a more detailed discussion of the multiples method, see Chapter 8.

Applying the mean ratio (74) to Terra's expected sales for 2001 ($310 million), they estimated the value of Terra's entire equity to be $19.105 billion ($68.2 per share).

2.4. GOODWILL-BASED METHODS[9]

Generally speaking, goodwill is the value that a company has above its book value or above the adjusted book value. Goodwill seeks to represent the value of the company's intangible assets, which often do not appear on the balance sheet but which, however, contribute an advantage with respect to other companies operating in the industry (quality of the customer portfolio, industry leadership, brands, strategic alliances, etc.). The problem arises when one tries to determine its value, as there is no consensus regarding the methodology used to calculate it. Some of the methods used to value the goodwill give rise to the various valuation procedures described in this section.

These methods apply a mixed approach: on the one hand, they perform a static valuation of the company's assets and, on the other hand, they try to quantify the value that the company will generate in the future. Basically, these methods seek to determine the company's value by estimating the combined value of its assets plus a capital gain resulting from the value of its future earnings: they start by valuing the company's assets and then add a quantity related with future earnings.

2.4.1. THE "CLASSIC" VALUATION METHOD

This method states that a company's value is equal to the value of its net assets (net substantial value) plus the value of its goodwill. In turn, the goodwill is valued as n times the company's net income, or as a certain percentage of the turnover. According to this method, the formula that expresses a company's value is:

$$V = A + (n \times B), \text{ or } V = A + (z \times F)$$

---

[9]The author feels duty bound to tell the reader that he does not like these methods at all but as they have been used a lot in the past, and they are still used from time to time, a brief description of some of them is included. However, we will not mention them again in the rest of the book. The reader can skip directly to Section 2.5. However, if he continues to read this section, he should not look for much "science" in the methods that follow because they are very arbitrary.

where: A = net asset value;
        n = coefficient between 1.5 and 3;
        B = net income;
        z = percentage of sales revenue;
        F = turnover

The first formula is mainly used for industrial companies, while the second is commonly used for the retail trade.

When the first method is applied to the hypothetical company Alfa Inc., assuming that the goodwill is estimated at three times the annual earnings, it would give a value for the company's equity amounting to $213 million ($135 + 3 \times 26$).

A variant of this method consists of using the cash flow instead of the net income.

2.4.2. THE SIMPLIFIED "ABBREVIATED GOODWILL INCOME" METHOD OR THE SIMPLIFIED UEC[10] METHOD

According to this method, a company's value is expressed by the following formula:

$$V = A + a_n(B - iA)$$

where: A = corrected net assets or net substantial value;
        a_n = present value, at a rate t, of n annuities, with n between 5 and 8 years
        B = net income for the previous year or that forecast for the coming year;
        i = interest rate obtained by an alternative placement, which could be debentures, the return on equities, or the return on real estate investments (after tax); $a_n(B - iA)$ = goodwill

This formula could be explained in the following manner: the company's value is the value of its adjusted net worth plus the value of the goodwill. The value of the goodwill is obtained by capitalizing, by application of a coefficient a_n, a "superprofit" that is equal to the difference between the net income and the investment of the net assets "A" at an interest rate "i" corresponding to the risk-free rate.

---

[10]UEC: This is the acronym for Union of European Accounting Experts.

In the case of the company Alfa Inc., $B = 26$; $A = 135$. Let us assume that 5 years and 15% are used in the calculation of a_n, which would give $a_n = 3.352$. Let us also assume that $i = 10\%$. With this hypothesis, the equity's value would be:

$$135 + 3.352(26 - 0.1 \times 135) = 135 + 41.9 = 176.9 \text{million}$$

2.4.3. UEC METHOD

The company's value according to this method is obtained from the following equation:

$$V = A + a_n(B - iV) \quad \text{giving}: \quad V = [A + (a_n \times B)]/(1 + ia_n)$$

For the UEC (Union of European accounting experts), a company's total value is equal to the substantial value (or revalued net assets) plus the goodwill. This is calculated by capitalizing at compound interest (using the factor a_n) a superprofit, which is the profit less the flow obtained by investing at a risk-free rate i a capital equal to the company's value V.

The difference between this method and the previous method lies in the value of the goodwill, which, in this case, is calculated from the value V we are looking for, while in the simplified method, it was calculated from the net assets A.

In the case of the company Alfa Inc., $B = 26$; $A = 135$, $a_n = 3.352$, $i = 10\%$. With these assumptions, the equity's value would be:

$$(135 + 3.352 \times 26)/(1 + 0.1 \times 3.352) = 222.1/1.3352 = 166.8 \text{million}$$

2.4.4. INDIRECT METHOD

The formula for finding a company's value according to this method is the following:

$$V = (A + B/i)/2, \quad \text{which can also be expressed as } V = A + (B - iA)/2i$$

The rate i used is normally the interest rate paid on long-term Treasury bonds. As can be seen in the first expression, this method gives equal weight to the value of the net assets (substantial value) and the value of the return. This method has a large number of variants that are obtained by giving different weights to the substantial value and the earnings' capitalization value.

In the case of the company Alfa Inc., $B = 26$; $A = 135$, $i = 10\%$. With these assumptions, the equity's value would be $197.5 million.

2.4.5. ANGLO-SAXON OR DIRECT METHOD

This method's formula is the following:

$$V = A + (B - iA)/t_m$$

In this case, the value of the goodwill is obtained by restating for an indefinite duration the value of the superprofit obtained by the company. This superprofit is the difference between the net income and what would be obtained from placing at the interest rate i, a capital equal to the value of the company's assets. The rate t_m is the interest rate earned on fixed-income securities multiplied by a coefficient between 1.25 and 1.5 to adjust for the risk.

In the case of the company Alfa Inc., B = 26; A = 135, i = 10%. Let us assume that t_m = 15%. With these assumptions, the equity's value would be $218.3 million.

2.4.6. ANNUAL PROFIT PURCHASE METHOD

With this method, the following valuation formula is used:

$$V = A + m(B - iA)$$

Here, the value of the goodwill is equal to a certain number of years of superprofits. The buyer is prepared to pay the seller the value of the net assets plus m years of superprofits. The number of years (m) normally used ranges between 3 and 5, and the interest rate (i) is the interest rate for long-term loans.

In the case of the company Alfa Inc., B = 26; A = 135, i = 10%. With these assumptions, and if m is 5 years, the equity's value would be $197.5 million.

2.4.7. RISK-BEARING AND RISK-FREE RATE METHOD

This method determines a company's value using the following expression:

$$V = A + (B - iV)/t \quad \text{giving} \quad V = (A + B/t)/(1 + i/t)$$

The rate i is the rate of an alternative, risk-free placement; the rate t is the risk-bearing rate used to restate the superprofit and is equal to the rate i increased by a risk ratio. According to this method, a company's value is equal to the net assets increased by the restated superprofit. As can be seen, the formula is a variant of the UEC's method when the number of years tends toward infinity.

In the case of the company Alfa Inc., $B = 26$; $A = 135$, $i = 10\%$. With these assumptions, if $t = 15\%$, the equity's value would be $185 million.

2.5. CASH FLOW DISCOUNTING-BASED METHODS

These methods seek to determine the company's value by estimating the cash flows it will generate in the future and then discounting them at a discount rate matched to the flows' risk.

The mixed methods described previously have been used extensively in the past. However, they are currently used increasingly less and it can be said that, nowadays, the cash flow discounting method is generally used because it is the only conceptually correct valuation method. In these methods, the company is viewed as a cash flow generator and the company's value is obtained by calculating these flows' present value using a suitable discount rate.

The second part of the book addresses the cash flow discounting valuation methods in greater detail. Chapter 9 discusses the difference between the different cash flows and net income.

Cash flow discounting methods are based on the detailed, careful forecast, for each period, of each of the financial items related with the generation of the cash flows corresponding to the company's operations, such as, collection of sales, personnel, raw materials, administrative, sales, expenses, loan repayments, etc. Consequently, the conceptual approach is similar to that of the cash budget.

In cash flow discounting-based valuations, a suitable discount rate is determined for each type of cash flow. Determining the discount rate is one of the most important tasks and takes into account the risk and historic volatilities. In practice, the minimum discount rate is often set by the interested parties (the buyers or sellers are not prepared to invest or sell for less than a certain return, etc.).

2.5.1. GENERAL METHOD FOR CASH FLOW DISCOUNTING

The different cash flow discounting-based methods start with the following expression:

$$V = \frac{CF_1}{1+k} + \frac{CF_2}{(1+k)^2} + \frac{CF_3}{(1+k)^3} + \cdots + \frac{CF_n + RV_n}{(1+k)^n}$$

where: CF_i = cash flow generated by the company in the period i;
        RV_n = residual value of the company in the year n;
        k   = appropriate discount rate for the cash flows' risk

Although at first sight it may appear that the above formula is considering a temporary duration of the flows, this is not necessarily so as the company's residual value in the year n (RV_n) can be calculated by discounting the future flows after that period. A simplified procedure for considering an indefinite duration of future flows after the year n is to assume a constant growth rate (g) of flows after that period. Then the residual value in year n is $RV_n = CF_n(1 + g)/(k - g)$.

Although the flows may have an indefinite duration, it may be acceptable to ignore their value after a certain period, as their present value decreases progressively with longer time horizons. Furthermore, the competitive advantage of many businesses tends to disappear after a few years.

Before looking in more detail at the different cash flow discounting-based valuation methods, we must first define the different types of cash flow that can be used in a valuation.

2.5.2. Deciding the Appropriate Cash Flow for Discounting and the Company's Economic Balance Sheet

In order to understand what the basic cash flows are that can be considered in a valuation, the following chart shows the different cash streams generated by a company and the appropriate discount rates for each flow.

Cash flows	Appropriate discount rate
Free cash flow (FCF)	Weighted average cost of capital (WACC)
Equity cash flow (ECF)	Required return to equity (Ke)
Debt cash flow (CFd)	Required return to debt (Kd)

There are three basic cash flows: the free cash flow, the equity cash flow, and the debt cash flow.

The easiest one to understand is the debt cash flow, which is the sum of the interest to be paid on the debt plus principal repayments. In order to determine the present market value of the existing debt, this flow must be discounted at the required rate of return to debt (cost of the debt). In many cases, the debt's market value shall be equivalent to its book value, which is why its book value is often taken as a sufficient approximation to the market value.[11]

The free cash flow (FCF) enables the company's total value[12] (debt and equity: D + E) to be obtained. The equity cash flow (ECF) enables the value of the equity to be obtained which, combined with the value of the debt, will also enable the company's total value to be determined. The discount rates that must be used for the FCF and the ECF are explained in the following sections.

Figure 2.4 shows in simplified form the difference between the company's full balance sheet and its economic balance sheet. When we refer to the company's (financial) assets, we are not talking about its entire assets but about total assets less spontaneous financing (suppliers, creditors, etc.). To put it another way, the company's (financial) assets consist of the net fixed assets plus the working capital requirements (WCR).[13] The company's (financial) liabilities consist of the shareholders' equity (the shares) and its debt (short and long-term financial debt).[14] In the rest of the book, when we talk

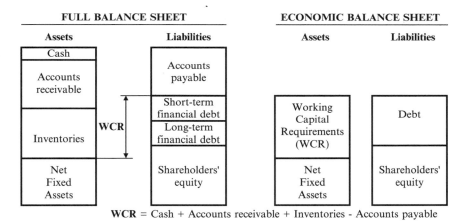

WCR = Cash + Accounts receivable + Inventories - Accounts payable

Figure 2.4   Full and economic balance sheet of a company.

[11]We shall see in subsequent chapters that this is only valid if the required return to debt is equal to the debt's cost.

[12]The "company's value" is usually considered to be the sum of the value of the equity plus the value of the financial debt.

[13]For an excellent discussion of WCR, see Faus (1996).

[14]The shareholders' equity or capital can include, among others, common stock, preferred stock, and convertible preferred stock; and the different types of debt can include, among others, senior debt, subordinated debt, convertible debt, fixed or variable interest debt, zero or regular coupon debt, short- or long-term debt, etc.

about the company's value, we will be referring to the value of the debt plus the value of the shareholders' equity (shares).

2.5.2.1. The Free Cash Flow

The FCF is the operating cash flow, that is, the cash flow generated by operations, without taking into account borrowing (financial debt), after tax. It is the money that would be available in the company after covering fixed asset investment and working capital requirements, assuming that there is no debt and, therefore, there are no financial expenses.

In order to calculate future FCF, we must forecast the cash we will receive and must pay in each period. This is basically the approach used to draw up a cash budget. However, in company valuation, this task requires forecasting cash flows further ahead in time than is normally done in any cash budget.

Accounting cannot give us this information directly as, on the one hand, it uses the accrual approach and, on the other hand, it allocates its revenues, costs, and expenses using basically arbitrary mechanisms. These two features of accounting distort our perception of the appropriate approach when calculating cash flows, which must be the "cash" approach, that is, cash actually received or paid (collections and payments). However, when the accounting is adjusted to this approach, we can calculate whatever cash flow we are interested in.

We will now try to identify the basic components of an FCF in the hypothetical example of the company XYZ. The information given in the accounting statements shown in Table 2.6 must be adjusted to give the cash flows for each period, that is, the sums of money actually received and paid in each period.

Table 2.6 gives the income statement for the company XYZ, SA. Using this data, we shall determine the company's FCF, which we know by definition must not include any payments to fund providers. Therefore, dividends and interest expenses must not be included in the free cash flow.

Table 2.7 shows how the FCF is obtained from earnings before interest and tax (EBIT). The tax payable on the EBIT must be calculated directly; this gives us the net income without subtracting interest payments, to which we must add the depreciation for the period because it is not a payment but merely an accounting entry. We must also consider the sums of money to be allocated to new investments in fixed assets and new WCR, as these sums must be deducted in order to calculate the FCF.

In order to calculate the FCF, we must ignore financing for the company's operations and concentrate on the financial return on the company's assets after tax, viewed from the perspective of a going concern, taking into account in each period the investments required for the business's continued existence.

Table 2.6

Income Statement for XYZ

	1999	2000	2001
Sales	1,000	1,100	1,210
− Cost of goods sold	− 650	− 715	− 786.5
− General expenses	− 189	− 207.9	− 228.7
− Depreciation	− 20	− 20	− 20
Earnings before interest and tax (EBIT)	141	157.1	174.8
− Interest expenses	− 10	− 10	− 10
Profit before tax (PBT)	131	147.1	164.8
− Tax	− 45.85	− 51.49	− 57.68
Net income or profit after tax (PAT)	85.15	95.62	107.1
− Dividends	− 34.06	− 38.25	− 42.85
Retained earnings	**51.09**	**57.37**	**64.28**

Table 2.7

Free Cash Flow of XYZ, SA

	1999	2000	2001
Earnings before interest and tax (EBIT)	141	157.1	174.8
− Tax paid on EBIT	− 49.4	− 55	− 61.2
Net income without debt	91.65	102.1	113.6
+ Depreciation	20	20	20
− Increase in fixed assets	− 61	− 67.1	− 73.8
− Increase in WCR	− 11	− 12.1	− 13.3
Free cash flow	**39.65**	**42.92**	**46.51**

Finally, if the company had no debt, the FCF would be identical to the equity cash flow, which is another cash flow variant used in valuations and which will be analyzed below.

2.5.2.2. The Equity Cash Flow

The equity cash flow (ECF) is calculated by subtracting from the FCF the interest and principal payments (after tax) made in each period to the debt holders and adding the new debt provided. In short, it is the cash flow remaining available in the company after covering fixed asset investments and working capital requirements and after paying the financial charges and repaying the corresponding part of the debt's principal (in the event that there exists debt). This can be represented in the following expression:

$$ECF = FCF - [\text{interest payments} \times (1 - T)]$$
$$- \text{principal repayments} + \text{new debt}$$

In Chapter 9, we will see that, when making projections, the dividends and other expected payments to shareholders must match the ECFs.

This cash flow assumes the existence of a certain financing structure in each period, by which the interest corresponding to the existing debts is paid, the installments of the principal are paid at the corresponding maturity dates and funds from new debt are received. After that there remains a certain sum which is the cash available to the shareholders, which will be allocated to paying dividends or buying back shares.

When we restate the ECF, we are valuing the company's equity (E), and, therefore, the appropriate discount rate will be the required return to equity (Ke). To find the company's total value (D + E), we must add the value of the existing debt (D) to the value of the equity (E).

2.5.2.3. Capital Cash Flow

Capital cash flow (CCF) is the term given to the sum of the debt cash flow plus the equity cash flow. The debt cash flow is composed of the sum of interest payments plus principal repayments. Therefore:

$$CCF = ECF + DCF = ECF + I - \Delta D \text{ separated } I = DKd$$

It is important to not confuse the capital cash flow with the free cash flow.

2.5.3. CALCULATING THE VALUE OF THE COMPANY USING THE FREE CASH FLOW

In order to calculate the value of the company using this method, the FCFs are discounted (restated) using the weighted average cost of debt and equity or weighted average cost of capital (WACC):

$$E + D = \text{present value [FCF; WACC] where WACC} = \frac{EKe + DKd(1 - T)}{E + D}$$

D = market value of the debt;
E = market value of the equity;
Kd = cost of the debt before tax = required return to debt;
T = tax rate;
Ke = required return to equity, which reflects the equity's risk

The WACC is calculated by weighting the cost of the debt (Kd) and the cost of the equity (Ke) with respect to the company's financial structure. This is the appropriate rate for this case, since we are valuing the company as a whole (debt plus equity), we must consider the required return to debt and the required return to equity in the proportion to which they finance the company.

2.5.4. CALCULATING THE VALUE OF THE COMPANY AS THE UNLEVERED VALUE PLUS THE DISCOUNTED VALUE OF THE TAX SHIELD

In this method, the company's value is calculated by adding two values: on the one hand, the value of the company assuming that the company has no debt and, on the other hand, the value of the tax shield obtained by the fact that the company is financed with debt. This method is called APV or adjusted present value. For a more detailed discussion, see Chapter 17.

The value of the company without debt is obtained by discounting the FCF, using the rate of required return to equity that would be applicable to the company if it were to be considered as having no debt. This rate (Ku) is known as the unlevered rate or required return to assets. The required return to assets is smaller than the required return to equity if the company has debt in its capital structure as, in this case, the shareholders would bear the financial risk implied by the existence of debt and would demand a higher equity risk premium. In those cases where there is no debt, the required return to equity (Ke = Ku) is equivalent to the WACC, as the only source of financing being used is capital.

The present value of the tax shield arises from the fact that the company is being financed with debt, and it is the specific consequence of the lower tax paid by the company as a consequence of the interest paid on the debt in each period. In order to find the present value of the tax shield, we would first have to calculate the saving obtained by this means for each of the years, multiplying the interest payable on the debt by the tax rate. Once we have obtained these flows, we will have to discount them at the rate considered appropriate. Although the discount rate to be used in this case is somewhat controversial, many authors suggest using the debt's market cost, which need not necessarily be the interest rate at which the company has contracted its debt.

Consequently, the APV condenses into the following formula:

$$D + E = NPV(FCF; Ku) + \text{value of the debt's tax shield}$$

2.5.5. CALCULATING THE VALUE OF THE COMPANY'S EQUITY BY DISCOUNTING THE EQUITY CASH FLOW

The market value of the company's equity is obtained by discounting the ECF at the rate of required return to equity for the company (Ke). When this value is added to the market value of the debt, it is possible to determine the company's total value.

The required return to equity can be estimated using any of the following methods:

1. Gordon and Shapiro's constant growth valuation model:

$$Ke = [Div_1/P_0] + g$$

   Div_1 = dividends to be received in the following period = $Div_0(1 + g)$;
   P_0 = share's current price;
   g = constant, sustainable dividend growth rate
   For example, if a share's price is \$200, it is expected to pay a dividend of \$10 and the dividend's expected annual growth rate is 11%:

$$Ke = (10/200) + 0.11 = 0.16 = 16\%$$

2. The capital asset pricing model (CAPM), which defines the required return to equity in the following terms:

$$Ke = R_F + \beta(R_M - R_F)$$

   R_F = rate of return for risk-free investments (Treasury bonds);
   β = share's beta;[15]
   R_M = expected market return;
   $R_M - R_F$ = market risk premium
   And thus, given certain values for the equity's beta, the risk-free rate, and the market risk premium; it is possible to calculate the required return to equity.[16] The CAPM and the market risk premium are discussed in Chapter 11, where the relationship between beta and volatility is shown.

---

[15]The beta measures the systematic or market risk of a share. It indicates the sensitivity of the return on a share held in the company to market movements. If the company has debt, the incremental risk arising from the leverage must be added to the intrinsic systematic risk of the company's business, thus obtaining the levered beta.

[16]The classic finance textbooks provide a full discussion of the concepts analyzed here. For example, Brealey and Myers (2000) and Copeland and Weston (1988).

2.5.6. CALCULATING THE COMPANY'S VALUE BY DISCOUNTING THE CAPITAL CASH FLOW

According to this model, the value of a company (market value of its equity plus market value of its debt) is equal to the present value of the capital cash flows (CCF) discounted at the weighted average cost of capital *before tax* ($WACC_{BT}$):

$$E + D = \text{present value } [CCF; WACC_{BT}]$$

$$WACC_{BT} = \frac{EKe + DKd}{E + D}$$

$$CCF = (ECF + DCF)$$

2.5.7. BASIC STAGES IN THE PERFORMANCE OF A VALUATION BY CASH FLOW DISCOUNTING

The basic stages in performing an accurate valuation by cash flow discounting are

1. Historic and Strategic Analysis of the Company and the Industry

A. Financial analysis	B. Strategic and competitive analysis
Evolution of income statements and balance sheets	Evolution of the industry
Evolution of cash flows generated by the company	Evolution of the company's competitive position
Evolution of the company's investments	Identification of the value chain
Evolution of the company's financing	Competitive position of the main competitors
Analysis of the financial health	Identification of the value drivers
Analysis of the business's risk	

2. Projections of Future Flows

A. Financial forecasts	B. Strategic and competitive forecasts	C. Consistency of the cash flow forecasts
Income statements and balance sheets	Forecast of the industry's evolution	Financial consistency between forecasts
Cash flows generated by the company	Forecast of the company's competitive position	Comparison of forecasts with historic figures

| Investments | Competitive position of the main competitors | Consistency of cash flows with the strategic analysis |

Financing

Terminal value

Forecast of various
    scenarios

3. Determination of the cost (required return) of capital

| For each business unit and for the company as a whole | Cost of the debt, required return to equity and weighted cost of capital |

4. Net present value of future flows

| Net present value of the flows at their corresponding rate. Present value of the terminal value | Value of the equity |

5. Interpretation of the results

| Benchmarking of the value obtained: comparison with similar companies | Identification of the value creation. Sustainability of the value creation (time horizon) |
| Analysis of the value's sensivity to changes in the fundamental parameters | Strategic and competitive justification of the value creation |

The critical aspects in performing a company valuation are

Critical Aspects of a Valuation

Dynamic. The valuation is a process. The process for estimating expected risks and calibrating the risk of the different businesses and business units is crucial.

Involvement of the company. The company's managers must be involved in the analysis of the company, of the industry and in the cash flow projections.

Multifunctional. The valuation is not a task to be performed solely by financial management. In order to obtain a good valuation, it is vital that managers from other departments take part in estimating future cash flows and their risk.

Strategic. The cash flow restatement technique is similar in all valuations, but estimating the cash flows and calibrating the risk must take into account each business unit's strategy.

Compensation. The valuation's quality is increased when it includes goals (sales, growth, market share, profits, investments, etc.) on which the managers' future compensation will depend.

Real options. If the company has real options, these must be valued appropriately. Real options require a totally different risk treatment from the cash flow restatements.

Historic analysis. Although the value depends on future expectations, a thorough historic analysis of the financial, strategic, and competitive evolution of the different business units helps assess the forecasts' consistency.

Technically correct. Technical correction refers basically to: (a) calculation of the cash flows; (b) adequate treatment of the risk, which translates into the discount rates; (c) consistency of the cash flows used with the rates applied; (d) treatment of the residual value; (e) treatment of inflation.

2.6. WHICH IS THE BEST METHOD TO USE?

Table 2.8 shows the value of the equity of the company Alfa Inc. obtained by different methods based on shareholders' equity, earnings, and goodwill. The fundamental problem with these methods is that some are based solely on the balance sheet, others are based on the income statement, but none of them consider anything but historic data. We could imagine two companies with identical balance sheets and income statements but different prospects: one with high sales, earnings, and margin potential, and the other in a stabilized situation with fierce competition. We would all concur in giving a higher value to the former company than to the latter, in spite of their historic balance sheets and income statements being equal.

The most suitable method for valuing a company is to discount the expected future cash flows, as the value of a company's equity—assuming it

Table 2.8

**Alfa Inc. Value of the Equity According to
Different Methods (Million Dollars)**

Book value	80
Adjusted book value	135
Liquidation value	75
PER	173
Classic valuation method	213
Simplified UEC method	177
UEC method	167
Indirect method	197
Direct or Anglo-Saxon method	218
Annual profit purchase method	197
Risk-bearing and risk-free rate method	185

continues to operate—arises from the company's capacity to generate cash (flows) for the equity's owners.

2.7. THE COMPANY AS THE SUM OF THE VALUES OF DIFFERENT DIVISIONS. BREAK-UP VALUE

On many occasions, the company's value is calculated as the sum of the values of its different divisions or business units.[17]

The best way to explain this method is with an example. Table 2.9 shows the valuation of a North American company performed in early 1980. The company in question had three separate divisions: household products, ship-building, and car accessories.

A financial group launched a takeover bid on this company at $38 per share and a well-known investment bank was commissioned to value the company. This valuation, which is included in Table 2.9, would serve as a basis for assessing the offer.

Table 2.9 shows that the investment bank valued the company's equity between $430 and $479 million (or, to put it another way, between $35 and $39 per share). But let us see how it arrived at that value. First of all, it projected each division's net income and then allocated a (maximum and minimum) PER to each one. Using a simple multiplication (earnings × PER), it calculated the value of each division. The company's value is simply the sum of the three divisions' values.

We can call this value (between $387 and $436 million) the value of the earnings generated by the company. We must now add to this figure the company's cash surplus, which the investment bank estimated at $77.5 million. However, the company's pension plan was not fully funded (it was short by $34.5 million), and consequently, this quantity had to be subtracted from the company's value.

After performing these operations, the conclusion reached is that each share is worth between $35 and $39, which is very close to the offer made of $38 per share.

2.8. VALUATION METHODS USED DEPENDING ON THE NATURE OF THE COMPANY

Holding companies are basically valued by their liquidation value, which is corrected to take into account taxes payable and managerial quality.

---

[17]For a more detailed discussion of this type of valuation, we recommend Chapter 14 of Copeland *et al.* (2000).

Table 2.9

Valuation of a Company as the Sum of the Value of its Divisions; Individual Valuation of Each Business using the PER Criterion

(Million dollars) Expected net income	Household products 28.6		Shipbuilding 14.4		Car accessories 5.8		Total company 48.8	
	Minimum	Maximum	Minimum	Maximum	Minimum	Maximum	Minimum	Maximum
PER for each business	9	10	5	6	10	11		
Value (million dollars)	257.4	286.0	72.0	86.4	58.0	63.8	387.4	436.2
Plus: estimated net cash surplus at year end[a]							77.5	77.5
Less: non-funded retirement pensions at year end							34.5	34.5
Value of equity (million dollars)							430.4	479.2
Value per share (based on 12,201,000 shares)							35.3	39.3

[a]Cash surplus: $103.1 million in cash, less $10 million for operations and less $15.6 million of financial debt.

The growth of utility companies is usually fairly stable. In developed countries, the rates charged for their services are usually indexed to the CPI, or they are calculated in accordance with a legal framework. Therefore, it is simpler to extrapolate their operating statement and then discount the cash flows. In these cases, particular attention must be paid to regulatory changes, which may introduce uncertainties.

In the case of banks, the focus of attention is the operating profit (financial margin less commissions less operating expenses), adjusting basically for bad debts. Their industry portfolio is also analyzed. Valuations such as the PER are used, or the net worth method (shareholders' equity adjusted for provision surpluses/deficits, and capital gains or losses on assets such as the industry portfolio).

In the case of industrial and commercial companies, the most commonly used valuations—apart from restated cash flows—are those based on financial ratios (PER, price/sales, price/cash flow).

These issues are discussed in greater detail in Chapter 8.

2.9. KEY FACTORS AFFECTING VALUE: GROWTH, RETURN, RISK, AND INTEREST RATES

The equity's value depends on expected future flows and the required return to equity. In turn, the growth of future flows depends on the return on investments and the company's growth. However, the required return to equity depends on a variable over which the company has no control, the risk-free interest rate, and on the equity's risk which, in turn, we can divide into operating risk and financial risk.

Table 2.10 shows that the equity's value depends on three primary factors (*value drivers*):

1. Expectations of future flows
2. Required return to equity
3. Communication with the market[18]

These factors can be subdivided in turn into return on the investment, company growth, risk-free interest rate, market risk premium, operating risk, and financial risk. However, these factors are still very general. It is

---

[18]The communication with the market factor not only refers to communication and transparency with the financial markets in the strict sense but also to communication with: analysts, rating companies, regulatory agencies, board of directors, employees, customers, distribution channels, partner companies, suppliers, financial institutions, and shareholders.

Table 2.10
Factors influencing the Equity's Value (Value Drivers)

VALUE OF EQUITY							
Expections of future cash flows		Required retured to equity					
Expected **return** on investment	*Expected* company **growth**	Risk-free interest rate	Market risk premium	Operating risk	Financial risk		
Competitive advantage period / Assets in place / Profit margin / Regulator environment / Taxes / Managers, People, Corporate culture	Actual business, Barriers to entry / Aquisitions / disposals / Industry, Competitive structure / New businesses / products / Technologe / Real options			Industry, countries, laws / Control of operations / Buyer / target / Risk perceived by the market	Financing / Liquidity / Size / Risk management		Market communication

very important that a company identify the fundamental parameters that have most influence on the value of its shares and on value creation. Obviously, each factor's importance will vary for the different business units.

The length of the competitive advantage period is critical and it weds strategy (competitive advantage) to valuation. A good article about competitive advantage period is Mauboussin and Johnson (1997).

2.10. SPECULATIVE BUBBLES ON THE STOCK MARKET

The advocates of fundamental analysis argue that share prices reflect future expectations updated by rational investors. Thus, a share's price is equal to the net present value of all the expected future dividends. This is the so-called fundamental value. In other words, the share price reflects current earnings generation plus growth expectations. The adjective fundamental refers to the parameters that influence the share price: interest rates, growth expectations, investment's risk, etc.

Another group of theories is based on psychological or sociological behaviors, such as Keynes' "animal spirits." According to these theories, share price formation does not follow any rational valuation rule but rather depends on the states of euphoria, pessimism, etc., predominating at any given time in the financial community and in society in general. It is these psychological phenomena that give hope to the chartists: if moods do not change too often and investors value equity taking into account the share prices' past evolution, one can expect that successive share prices will be correlated or will repeat in similar cycles.

The speculative bubble theory can be derived from fundamental analysis and occupies a middle ground between the above two theories, which seek to account for the behavior and evolution of share prices. MIT professor Olivier Blanchard developed the algebraic expression of the speculative bubble, and it can be obtained from the same equation that gives the formula normally used by the fundamentalists. It simply makes use of the fact that the equation has several solutions, one of which is the fundamental solution and another is the fundamental solution with a speculative bubble tacked onto it. By virtue of the latter solution, a share's price can be greater than its fundamental value (net present value of all future dividends) if a bubble develops simultaneously, which at any given time may: (1) continue to grow, or (2) burst and vanish. To avoid tiring ourselves with equations, we can imagine the bubble as an equity overvaluation: an investor will pay today for a share a quantity that is greater than its fundamental value if he hopes to sell it tomorrow for a higher price, that is, if he hopes that the bubble will continue growing. This process can continue so long as there are investors who trust that the speculative bubble will continue to grow, that is, investors who expect to find in the future other trusting investors to whom they can sell the bubble (share) for a price that is greater than the price they have paid. Bubbles tend to grow during periods of euphoria, when it seems that the market's only possible trend is upward. However, there comes a day when there are no more trusting investors left and the bubble bursts and vanishes: shares return to their fundamental value.

This theory is attractive because it enables fundamental theory to be synthesized with the existence of anomalous behaviors (for the fundamentalists) in the evolution of share prices. Many analysts have used this theory to account for the tremendous drop in share prices on the New York stock market and on the other world markets on October 19, 1987. According to this explanation, a bubble bursting that had been growing over the previous months caused the stock market crash. A recent study performed by Yale professor Shiller provides further evidence in support of this theory. Shiller interviewed 1000 institutional and private investors. The investors who sold before Black Monday said that they sold because they thought that the stocks were already overvalued. However, the most surprising finding is that more than 90% of the institutional investors who did not sell said that they too believed that the market was overvalued, but hoped that they would be able to sell before the inevitable downturn. In other words, it seems that more than 90% of the institutional investors were aware that a speculative bubble was being formed—the stock was being sold for more than its fundamental value—but trusted that they would be able to sell before the bubble burst. Among the private investors who did not sell before October 19, more than 60% stated that they also believed that the stocks were overvalued.

This bursting of a speculative bubble is not a new phenomenon in history. We can find recent examples in Spain in 1974 and in the U.S.: electronic and high-tech companies in 1962, "good concept" companies in 1970, and household name companies throughout the 1970s. In the electronic companies' bubble, many companies' shares in 1962 were worth less than 20% what they were worth in 1961. IBM's share price fell from $600+ in 1961 to $300 in 1962; and Texas Instruments' share price fell from $200+ to $50. Even larger was the bubble that grew in 1970 around the "good concept" companies: several of them lost 99% of their value in the space of just 1 year. Household name companies also suffered severe drops in their share prices during the 1970s: McDonald's PER fell from 83 to 9, Sony's from 92 to 17, and Polaroid's from 90 to 16, to give just a few examples. (See Figures 2.5 to 2.8.)

Speculative bubbles can also develop outside of the stock market. One often-quoted example is that of the Dutch tulips in the 17th century. An unusual strain of tulips began to become increasingly sought after and its price rose continuously, etc. In the end, the tulips' price returned to normal levels and many people were ruined. There have also been many speculative bubbles in the real estate business. The story is always the same: prices temporarily rocket upward and then return to "normal" levels. In the process, many investors who trust that the price will continue to rise lose a lot of

Figure 2.5 The 1929 American stock market crisis.

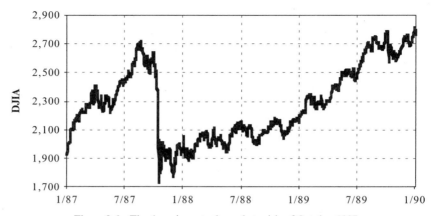

Figure 2.6   The American stock market crisis of October 1987.

Figure 2.7   The Internet speculative bubble of 1998 and 1999.

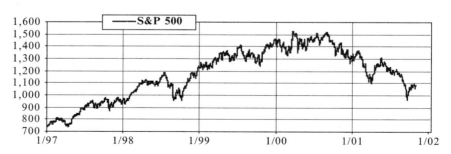

Figure 2.8   The American stock market crisis of 1998 and of September 11, 2001.

money. The problem with this theory, as with many of the economic interpretations, is that it provides an ingenious explanation to account for events *a posteriori* but it is not very useful for providing forecasts about the course that share prices will follow in the future. For this, we would need to know how to detect the bubble and predict its future course. This means to be able to separate the share price into two components (the fundamental value and the bubble) and know the number of investors who trust that the bubble will continue to grow (here many chartists can be included). What the theory does remind us is that the bubble can burst at any time. History shows that, so far, all the bubbles have eventually burst.

The only sure recipe to avoid being trapped in a speculative bubble is to not enter it: to never buy what seems to be expensive, even if advised to do so by certain "experts," who appeal to esoteric tendencies and the foolishness or rashness of other investors.

2.11. MOST COMMON ERRORS IN VALUATIONS

The following list contains the most common errors that the author has detected in the more than one thousand valuations he has had access to in his capacity as business consultant or teacher:

A. Procedural (method) errors
  1. Calculating the WACC using book values for E and D instead of market values.
  2. When calculating the FCF, using the taxes of the levered project.
  3. Using flows in constant currency and current rates or vice versa.
  4. Disparity between expected inflation and discount rates.
  5. Updating equity flows from years when no dividends were distributed.
  6. The equity flows do not match the dividends and payments expected by the shareholders.
  7. Confusing Ke with WACC.
  8. Valuing divisions using the company's WACC (+).
  9. Valuing all businesses at the same rate.
  10. Incorrect calculation of the FCF (equity flow if D = 0).
  11. Incorrect calculation of the ECF (equity flow with planned debt).
  12. Assuming that the debt's value matches the nominal value when this is not the case.
  13. Not using the correct formulas when the debt's value does not match its nominal value.
  14. Highly variable borrowing and constant WACC and Ke.

15. Calculating the market risk premium from historic data.
16. Calculating the beta from historic data.
17. Using averages of multiples with a high degree of scatter.

B. Data errors

18. In mature companies, disparity between historic and projected equity flows.
19. Hypotheses on sales, costs, prices, margins . . . are totally illogical.
20. Hypotheses on sales, costs, prices, margins . . . do not take into account the economic environment.
21. Hypotheses on sales, costs, prices, margins . . . do not take into account the industry's evolution.
22. Hypotheses on sales, costs, prices, margins . . . contradict the competitive analysis.
23. Incorrect calculation of the residual value.
24. Residual value calculated from the wrong flow.

REFERENCES

Brealey, R. A., and S. C. Myers (2000), *Principles of Corporate Finance*, Sixth edition. New York: McGraw-Hill.

Copeland, T. E., T. Koller, and J. Murrin (2000), *Valuation: Measuring and Managing the Value of Companies*. 3rd edition. New York: Wiley.

Copeland, T. E., and J. F. Weston (1988), *Financial Theory and Corporate Policy*, third edition. Reading, MA: Addison-Wesley.

Faus, Josep (1996), "Operational Finance: Analysis and Diagnosis," IESE Business School Technical Note No. 00803000.

Mauboussin, M., and P. Johnson (1997), Competitive Advantage period: The Neglected Value Driver, *Financial Management*, Vol. 26, No. 2, pp. 67–74.

Miller, M.H. (1986), "Behavioral Rationality in Finance: The Case of Dividends," *Journal of Business*, N. 59, pp. 451–468 (October).

Sorensen, E. H., and D.A. Williamson (1985), "Some evidence on the value of the dividend discount model," *Financial Analysts Journal*, 41, pp. 60–69.

Chapter 3

Price-Earnings Ratio, Profitability, Cost of Capital, and Growth

The PER is the most commonly used parameter in the stock market. The PER is the result of dividing the equity market value by the company's profit after tax.

PER = equity market value / profit after tax

The PER can also be calculated by dividing the price of each share by the earnings per share (profit after tax divided by the number of shares outstanding).

PER = price per share / earnings per share

Example. on October 6, 2000, General Electric had 9.901 billion shares outstanding. The price of one share was $59.4375. The price of all the shares (market capitalization) was therefore $588.52481 billion. The profit after tax in 1999 was $10.396679 billion and the earnings per share was $1.05. Therefore, General Electric's PER on October 6, 2000 was 56.607 (59.4375/

1.05 = 588.52481/10.396679). The earnings per share forecast for 2000 was $1.24. Therefore, General Electric's PER on October 6, 2000 on the basis of the expected earnings per share for 2000 was $47.93 (59.4375/1.24).

3.1. EVOLUTION OF THE PER ON THE INTERNATIONAL STOCK MARKETS

Figure 3.1 shows the evolution of the PER of two leading telecommunications companies in their respective countries: Telefónica in Spain and British Telecom in the United Kingdom. In the case of Telefónica, it can be seen that the PER peaked in February 1994 and then fell until October 1995, when it started to rise again. As we shall see in Figure 3.3, these variations were basically due to variations in the interest rates: when interest rates fall, the PER rises; and when interest rates rise, the PER falls.

Figure 3.1 also shows the "boom" experienced by the telecommunications companies during 1999, particularly at the end, and the beginning of 2000. In this period, all stocks related with the telecommunications world and the new Internet era were rewarded significantly on the stock market. The impressive rise in these companies' share price was due to the investors' expectations which, as can be seen, shifted down to more reasonable levels after February 2000.

Figure 3.2 shows the evolution of the PER of three of the largest North American companies. Particularly noteworthy is the case of Cisco Systems, whose PER is far above the rest. Thus, for example, in the last 5 years, Cisco has attained a maximum PER of 236.05, as opposed to the technology industry which attained a maximum PER of 67.32 and the "computer network" industry, whose maximum PER was 51.01. In addition, there is a marked difference when comparing with the maximum PER for the last 5 years of the

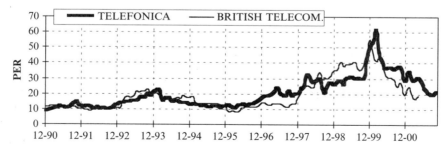

Figure 3.1   Evolution of the PER of Telefónica and British Telecom. (Source: Datastream.)

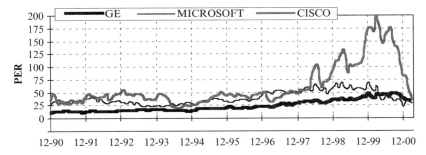

Figure 3.2 Evolution of the PER of GE, Microsoft, and Cisco. (Source: Datastream.)

S&P 500, which is 49.91. One can also see the fall in this Internet company's share price after February 2000.

Figure 3.3, which shows the evolution of the average PER of the Spanish stock market and the interest rate paid on 10-year public debt, confirms that when interest rates fall, the PER rises, and vice versa.

Figure 3.4 shows the evolution of the average PER of the Spanish, North American, and English stock markets. Note that the Spanish stock market's PER equaled that of the other two stock markets at the end of 1993, then fell behind and subsequently surpassed the English stock market at the end of 1996 and equaled the North American stock market in 1997 and 1998.

Figure 3.5 shows the ratio between the average PER of the United States stock market and the S&P 500. As PER = price/profit after tax, it is logical that the PER follows approximately the evolution of the S&P 500, which is an index that reflects the prices of the shares included in it. In this case, this ratio's denominator breaks this trend at certain times.

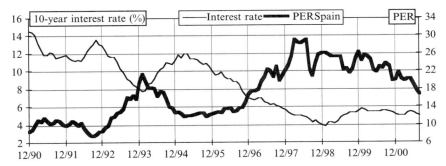

Figure 3.3 Evolution of interest rates and the average PER of the Spanish stock market. (*Source*: Morgan Stanley.)

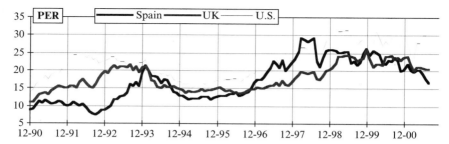

Figure 3.4 Evolution of the average PER of the Spanish, English, and United States stock markets.

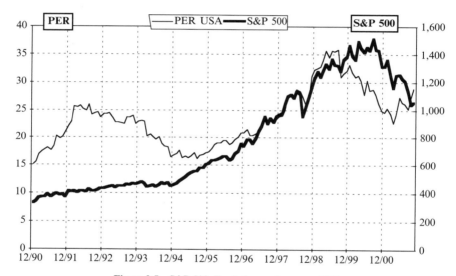

Figure 3.5 S&P 500. Evolution and average PER.

3.2. FACTORS AFFECTING THE PER

The best way to understand the influence of a company's growth and profitability on the PER is through simple examples. We use six different companies (see Table 3.1) growing at different rates. All six companies are financed solely by equity. The initial outlay in all cases is 100 million pesetas (Ebv_0). The required return to equity (Ke) in all the companies is 10%. The cost of capital is, therefore, 10%.

Table 3.1

PER of Six Companies. Influence of Growth and Return on Investments on the PER

	A	B	C	D	E	F
Required return to equity. Ke	10%	10%	10%	10%	10%	10%
Equity book value. Ebv_0	100	100	100	100	100	100
Return on equity. $ROE = PAT_1/Ebv_0$	10%	10%	**12%**	12%	12%	**13%**
Profit of the first year. PAT_1	10	10	12	12	12	13
Dividends in the first year. Div_1	4	**10**	12	**4**	**6**	6
Pay-out ratio. p = Dividends/PAT	40.00%	100.00%	100.00%	33.33%	50.00%	46.15%
Growth. g	6%	0%	0%	8%	6%	7%
Equity value. $E_0 = Div_1/(Ke - g)$	100	100	120	200	150	200
$PER = E_0/PAT_1$	**10.00**	**10.00**	**10.00**	**16.67**	**12.50**	**15.38**

3.2.1. COMPANIES A AND B

Companies A and B obtain a return on equity (ROE)[1] of 10%, which means that the first year's profit after tax will be $10 million in both cases.[2]

In the first year, company A distributes $4 million as dividends (and invests another $6 million at 10%). Consequently, year 2's profit after tax will be $10.6 million ($10 million from investments in year zero and $0.6 million from investments in year 1). Year 2's dividends will also be 40% of the profit after tax. Company A grows with the profit after tax that it does not distribute (which is withheld).

Company B distributes all the profit after tax ($10 million) as dividends. Consequently, profit after tax (and dividends) for all years will be $10 million (from the investments in year zero). Company B does not grow because it distributes 100% of the profit after tax as dividends.

It will be readily seen that the value of the equity (Eo) of companies A and B is equal to its book value ($100 million), because they invest in projects that have a return (10%) equal to the cost of capital. Consequently, the PER (price/profit after tax = 100/10) of both is 10. Even though company

---

[1]ROE is the company's profit after tax divided by the equity's book value.

[2]Appendix 3.3 shows that the relationship between the PER and growth (g), required return to equity (Ke), and return on equity (ROE) in a company with constant growth is PER = (ROE − g) /[ROE (Ke − g)].

A is growing at a rate of 6% (it withholds 60% of the profit after tax and invests it at 10%), its PER is equal to that of company B which does not grow: the growth of company A is not rewarded with a higher PER because it invests in investments having a return equal to its cost of capital (10%).

3.2.2. COMPANIES C AND D

Companies C and D obtain a return on equity (ROE) of 12%, which means that the first year's profit after tax will be $12 million in both cases.

Company C distributes all the profit after tax ($12 million) as dividends. Consequently, the profit after tax (and the dividends) for all years will be $12 million (from the investments in year zero). Company C does not grow because it distributes 100% of the profit after tax as dividends.

In the first year, company D distributes $4 million as dividends (and invests another $8 million at 12%). Consequently, year 2's profit after tax will be 12.96 million ($12 million from the investments in year zero and $0.96 million from the investments in year 1). Year 2's dividends will also be 33.33% of the profit after tax. Company D grows with the profit after tax that it does not distribute (which is withheld).

The value of company C's equity is $120 million, which is greater than its book value ($100 million), because it invests in projects having a return (12%) greater than the cost of capital (10%). The PER (price/profit after tax = 120/12) of company C is 10.

The value of company D's equity is $200 million. The PER (price/profit after tax = 200/12) of company D is 16.67. Company D grows at 8% (it withholds 66.66% of the profit after tax and invests it at 12%), and its PER is greater than that of company C, which does not grow: the growth of company D is rewarded with a higher PER because it invests in investments having a return (12%) greater than its cost of capital (10%).

3.2.3. COMPANY E

Company E obtains an ROE of 12%, which means that the first year's profit after tax will be 12 million. In the first year, company E distributes $6 million as dividends (and invests another $6 million at 12%). Consequently, year 2's profit after tax will be $12.72 million ($12 million from the investments in year zero and 0.72 from the investments in year 1). Year 2's dividends will also be 50% of the profit after tax. The value of company E's equity is $150 million and its PER (price/profit after tax = 150/12) is 12.5.

Company E grows at 6% (it withholds 50% of the profit after tax and invests it at 12%) while company D grows at 8%.

Considering companies C, D, and E, we see that the market rewards their growth with a higher PER: the company that grows most (company D) has a PER of 16.67, the company that does not grow (company C) has a PER of 10, the company with a middle-level growth (company E) has a PER of 12.5.

3.2.4. COMPANY F

Company F is identical to company E, but it is more profitable: it obtains an ROE of 13%, which means that the first year's profit after tax will be $13 million. It also distributes $6 million as dividends (and invests another $7 million at 13%). The value of company F's equity is $200 million and its PER (price/profit after tax = 200/13) is 15.38. Company E grows at 6% (it withholds 50% of the profit after tax and invests it at 12%) while company F grows at 7%.

Considering companies E and F, we see that the market rewards higher growth and return with a higher PER.

These examples enable us to conclude that the factors that affect the PER are

1. The company's return (ROE). $ROE = PAT_1/Ebv_0$
2. The company's expected growth (g), which is the growth of profit after tax and dividends. We have already seen that it is not enough to simply grow to have a high PER: the company must invest in projects having a return greater than the cost of capital.
3. The proportion of the profit after tax which is distributed as dividends. This parameter is related with growth. We have already seen that a company that distributes all the profit after tax as dividends does not grow (it does not hold capital for investing) and the more profit after tax it withholds, the more it grows. The ratio between the dividends paid by the company and the profit after tax it generates is called the pay-out ratio (p). $p = Div_1/PAT_1$
4. The required return to equity (Ke). The higher the required return to equity (also called cost of capital), the lower the PER.[3]

We can conclude that, in general, an improvement in the profit after tax (increase in the ROE) leads to an increase in the PER.[4] An increase in growth causes a decrease in the PER if ROE < Ke and an increase in the PER if

[3]Chapter 4 gives a breakdown of the PER into several factors: franchise, interest, growth, and risk.

[4]We are assuming that all the other factors (growth, etc.) remain constant.

ROE > Ke. It is also obvious that an increase in interest rates (increase in Ke) causes a decrease in the PER. An increase in the company's risk (increase in Ke) causes a decrease in the PER.

An increase in:	...makes...the PER
Profit (ROE)	Increase
Interest rates (Ke)	Decrease
Company's risk (Ke)	Decrease
Company's growth (g)	If ROE > Ke, increase
	If ROE = Ke, not change
	If ROE < Ke, decrease

The diagram below shows the factors that affect the value of the equity and, therefore, the PER:

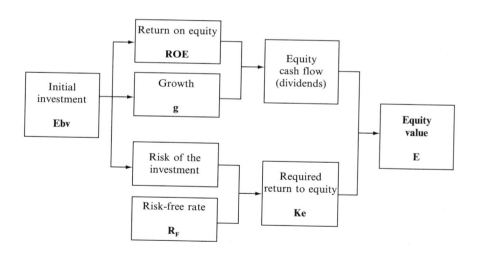

3.3. INFLUENCE OF GROWTH (g) ON THE PER

As we have seen in the previous examples, the company's expected growth has a considerable influence on the PER. Figure 3.6 shows how the PER increases with growth provided that the company's return (measured by the ROE) is greater than the required return to equity (Ke). It also shows

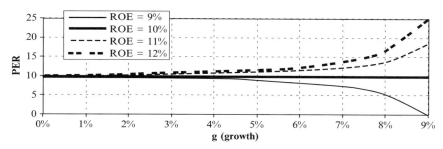

Figure 3.6   PER of a company depending on its growth (g). Ke = 10%.

that if the company's return is equal to the required return to equity (10%), growth does not affect the PER, which remains at 10. If the company's return is less than the cost of capital (ROE < Ke), the more the company grows, the lower its PER, because the more the company grows, the more value it destroys by investing in projects with a return less than the cost of capital.[5]

We have also seen that the growth of earnings per share depends on the dividends distributed by the company. If the return on investments remains constant, the company will grow more if it pays less dividends and reinvests more capital in new projects. A formula that relates the growth of the dividend per share (g) and the pay-out ratio (p) is: g = ROE (1−p). Figure 3.7 shows this formula in graph form.[6]

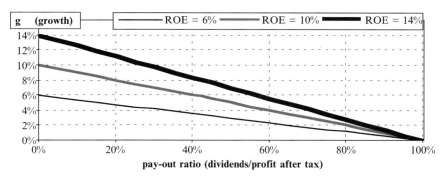

Figure 3.7   Relationship between the growth of the dividend per share (g) and the pay-out ratio (p).

---

[5]We will see further on that investing in projects with a return lower than the cost of capital destroys value.

[6]This is a formula for sustainable growth. It assumes that the company's growth is only dependent upon the resources it generates.

3.4. INFLUENCE OF THE ROE ON THE PER

Figure 3.8 shows the influence of the company's return (measured by the ROE) on the PER. If the company does not grow, its PER is always 10 (1/Ke). If the company grows, an increase in the return always increases the PER, and the PER increases more with higher growth.

3.5. INFLUENCE OF THE REQUIRED RETURN TO EQUITY ON THE PER

Figures 3.9 and 3.10 show the effect of the required return to equity on the PER. An increase in the required return to equity always decreases the PER, and decreases it more the more the company grows. Note how the PER falls

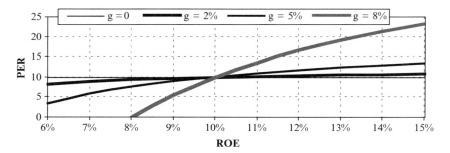

Figure 3.8   PER of a company depending on its ROE. Ke = 10%.

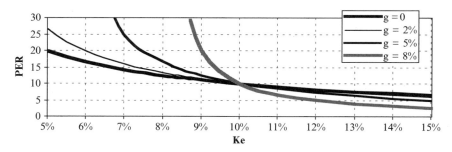

Figure 3.9   PER of a company depending on Ke. ROE = 10%.

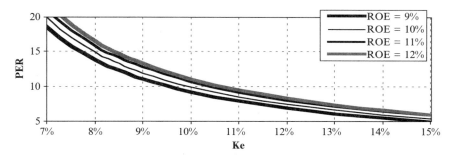

Figure 3.10   PER of a company depending on Ke. g = 4%.

much more when Ke is small. As we shall see in later chapters, the required return to equity increases when interest rates and the company's risk increase.

3.6. INFLUENCE OF INTEREST RATES ON THE PER

As we have already seen in Figure 3.3, when interest rates fall, the PER increases, and vice versa. This is because the required return to equity is related with interest rates: when interest rates increase, the required return to equity increases, and vice versa. In times of high interest rates, the PER is usually less than when interest rates are lower. For example, in December 1994, the long-term interest rate in Spain was 11.3% and the average PER of the Spanish stock market was 12.8. In January 1998, the long-term interest rate in Spain was 5.5%, and the average PER of the Spanish stock market was 23.4.

3.7. GROWTH VALUE AND PER DUE TO GROWTH

To quantify the influence of expected growth (g) on the share price and the PER, we can calculate the price that the share would have if the company did not grow, that is, if the previous year's profit after tax was constant and the company distributed it entirely as dividends. The share's price if the company did not grow is the earnings per share (EPS) divided by the required return to equity:

$$P \text{ no growth} = EPS/Ke$$

We can say that the share price is the price it would have if there was no growth (P no growth) plus the growth value:[7]

$$P = P \text{ no growth} + \text{growth value}$$

Example. GE's share price on 6 October 2000 was $59.4375. The earnings per share in 1999 was 1.05. If the required return to equity was 11%, the no growth price of GE's share would be $9.545 (1.05/0.11), and the growth value would be $49.89 (59.4375 − 9.545). Consequently, 16% (9.545/59.4375) of the value of GE's share was due to the profit after tax already attained by the company (P no growth) and 84% (49.89/59.4375) was due to the expected growth (growth value). By way of reference (see Appendix 3.2), on average, 47.5% of the value of the companies included in the Euro Stoxx 50 in May 2001 was due to the profit after tax already attained by the companies (P no growth) and 52.5% corresponded to the expected growth (growth value).

We can perform the same breakdown with the PER and consider it as the sum of the PER that the company would have if the incremental PER due to growth did not grow any further.

$$PER = PER \text{no growth} + PER \text{growth}$$

As the PER is the price per share divided by the earnings per share, this gives:

$$PER \text{no growth} = 1/Ke$$

$$PER \text{growth} = \text{growth value}/EPS$$

[7]The value of the growth is also called the present value of the growth opportunities.

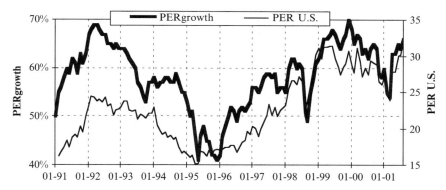

Figure 3.11.   U.S. Stock Market. PER due to growth as a percentage of PER and PER. (Sources: *PER USA MSDW* and PER due to growth: author's data.)

Figure 3.11 shows that in the nineties the PER due to growth was almost 70% of the PER in early 1992 and at the end of 1999.

Appendix 3.2 shows the breakdown of the price per share between the no growth price and the growth value and the breakdown of the PER of the companies included in the Euro Stoxx 50 on May 30, 2001. Appendix 3.3 shows the relationship between the PER and growth (g), required return to equity (Ke), and return on equity (ROE) in a company with constant growth.

SUMMARY

The PER is calculated by dividing the share price by the earnings per share. It is the main benchmark used in the stock markets.

The PER depends on a number of factors, some of which are out of the company's control, such as variations in interest rates, and others are intrinsic to the company, such as its risk, its growth, and the return on its investments.

The PER increases, *ceteris paribus*, if interest rates fall, if the company's risk decreases, and if the company's profit after tax increases.

The PER increases with growth if the return on the company's investments is greater than the cost of capital.

APPENDIX 3.1: PRICE PER SHARE, MARKET CAPITALIZATION, EARNINGS PER SHARE (EPS), DIVIDEND YIELD AND PER OF THE COMPANIES INCLUDED IN THE EURO STOXX 50 ON 30 MAY 2001

Company	Country	No. shares (million)	Price per share (euros)	Capitalization m. euros	%	EPS (euros) 2001	EPS (euros) 2002	Div. Yield (%)	PER 2001	PER 2002
ABN Amro	Holland	1,484	22.82	33,857	1.43	2.12	2.31	3.9	10.8	9.9
Aegon	Holland	1,344	31.25	41,994	1.77	1.76	1.98	2.4	17.7	15.8
Ahold	Holland	759	35.80	27,166	1.14	1.67	1.95	1.8	21.4	18.3
Air Liquide	France	91	162.20	14,786	0.62	8.02	9.08	2.1	20.2	17.9
Alcatel	France	1,141	29.26	33,373	1.41	1.37	1.79	1.9	21.3	16.3
Allianz	Germany	245	319.05	78,253	3.30	11.04	12.90	0.6	28.9	24.7
Aventis	France	780	85.70	66,831	2.82	2.05	2.64	0.7	41.8	32.5
Axa-uap	France	395	33.27	13,147	0.55	1.56	1.81	1.9	21.3	18.4
Basf	Germany	621	46.90	29,125	1.23	2.74	3.34	6.1	17.1	14.0
Bayer	Germany	730	46.27	33,793	1.42	2.64	3.16	4.0	17.5	14.7
BBVA	Spain	3,153	16.01	50,473	2.13	0.90	1.08	1.9	17.8	14.9
BNP	France	450	102.80	46,285	1.95	9.38	10.24	2.4	11.0	10.0
BSCH	Spain	4,515	10.98	49,580	2.09	0.65	0.78	2.5	16.8	14.1
Carrefour	France	698	65.40	45,633	1.92	1.82	2.22	0.9	35.9	29.4
DaimlerChrysler	Germany	1,014	53.65	54,387	2.29	1.23	3.42	6.3	43.6	15.7
Danone	France	149	150.00	22,322	0.94	5.38	6.29	1.6	27.9	23.8

(*continues*)

Appendix 3.1 (*continued*)

Company	Country	No. shares (million)	Price per share (euros)	Capitalization m. euros	Capitalization %	EPS (euros) 2001	EPS (euros) 2002	Div. Yield (%)	PER 2001	PER 2002
Deutsche Bank	Germany	614	90.42	55,549	2.34	5.81	6.83	2.1	15.6	13.2
Deutsche Telekom	Germany	3,030	23.81	72,135	3.04	0.62	0.57	3.4	38.3	41.6
Dresdner Bank	Germany	547	50.80	27,776	1.17	1.99	2.42	2.5	25.5	21.0
E.On	Germany	752	58.35	43,874	1.85	2.87	3.17	3.3	20.4	18.4
Endesa	Spain	1,059	19.20	20,328	0.86	1.59	1.80	3.2	12.1	10.7
Enel	Italy	12,113	3.72	45,061	1.90	0.16	0.15	3.2	24.0	24.1
ENI	Italy	8,004	7.70	61,632	2.60	0.70	0.65	2.4	11.0	11.8
Fortis	Belgium	734	29.87	21,932	0.92	2.41	2.71	2.5	12.4	11.0
France Telecom	France	1,154	65.80	75,921	3.20	1.16	1.81	2.1	56.6	36.5
Generali	Italy	1,253	33.78	42,326	1.78	1.11	1.28	0.8	30.4	26.3
Hypoverennsbank	Germany	395	55.60	21,936	0.92	3.57	4.26	2.2	15.6	13.1
ING	Holland	997	75.70	75,448	3.18	4.98	5.70	3.0	15.2	13.3
KPN	Holland	1,199	11.29	13,536	0.57	− 0.70	−0.57	3.0	−16.0	−19.8
L'Oreal	France	676	75.50	51,043	2.15	1.72	1.96	0.6	43.9	38.4
LVMH Moet Hennessy	France	490	67.30	32,967	1.39	1.44	1.69	1.4	46.6	39.9
Muenchener Re	Germany	180	314.94	56,664	2.39	9.55	11.39	0.4	33.0	27.6
Nokia	Finland	4,681	34.30	160,549	6.77	0.91	1.13	0.8	37.9	30.2
Philips	Holland	1,316	32.08	42,220	1.78	1.19	2.03	5.1	26.9	15.8
Pinault-Printemps	France	119	206.10	24,604	1.04	7.75	8.98	1.2	26.6	22.9

(*continues*)

Appendix 3.1 (*continued*)

Company	Country	No. shares (million)	Price per share (euros)	Capitalization (m. euros)	Capitalization %	EPS (euros) 2001	EPS (euros) 2002	Div. Yield (%)	PER 2001	PER 2002
Repsol–YPF	Spain	1,188	21.11	25,079	1.06	1.88	1.81	2.1	11.2	11.7
Royal Dutch	Holland	2,144	71.55	153,424	6.47	3.94	3.71	2.2	18.2	19.3
RWE	Germany	529	44.30	23,419	0.99	0.97	1.12	3.2	45.9	39.5
San Paolo–IMI	Italy	1,403	16.09	22,580	0.95	2.27	2.57	3.5	7.1	6.3
Sanofi–synthelabo	France	731	71.35	52,171	2.20	1.66	1.95	0.6	43.1	36.6
Siemens	Germany	595	85.40	50,799	2.14	3.26	4.01	2.7	26.2	21.3
Societe Generale	France	423	71.00	30,013	1.26	6.20	6.68	3.4	11.5	10.6
Suez Lyonnaise	France	199	35.75	7,120	0.30	1.78	1.97	2.1	20.0	18.2
Telecom Italia	Italy	5,260	11.18	58,802	2.48	0.33	0.38	2.8	33.8	29.7
Telefonica	Spain	4,218	17.32	73,057	3.08	0.62	0.71	0.0	27.8	24.3
Totalfina Elf	France	724	174.30	126,225	5.32	10.27	10.41	2.2	17.0	16.7
Unicredito Italiano	Italy	5,003	5.30	26,518	1.12	0.36	0.42	2.4	14.8	12.8
Unilever	Holland	572	64.65	36,952	1.56	2.71	3.29	2.2	23.9	19.6
Vivendi	France	1,080	75.90	81,974	3.45	1.57	2.17	1.5	48.3	35.0
Volkswagen	Germany	312	58.50	18,247	0.77	6.30	6.96	1.9	9.3	8.4
Euro Stoxx 50			**4,413.37**	**2,372,886**	**100.0**			**2.14**	**23.4**	**21.6**

APPENDIX 3.2:   BREAKDOWN OF THE PRICE PER SHARE BETWEEN NO-GROWTH PRICE AND GROWTH VALUE; AND BREAKDOWN OF THE PER (COMPANIES INCLUDED IN THE EURO STOXX 50 ON 30 MAY 2001)

Company	Country	Price per share (euros)	P no growth	P growth	PER	PER no growth	PER growth
ABN Amro	Holland	22.82	89.8%	10.2%	10.8	9.7	1.1
Aegon	Holland	31.25	51.6%	48.4%	17.7	9.1	8.6
Ahold	Holland	35.80	46.6%	53.4%	21.4	10.0	11.4
Air Liquide	France	162.20	44.1%	55.9%	20.2	8.9	11.3
Alcatel	France	29.26	43.4%	56.6%	21.3	9.2	12.1
Allianz	Germany	319.05	35.0%	65.0%	28.9	10.1	18.8
Aventis	France	85.70	23.8%	76.2%	41.8	10.0	31.8
Axa-Uap	France	33.27	46.9%	53.1%	21.3	10.0	11.3
Basf	Germany	46.90	59.5%	40.5%	17.1	10.2	6.9
Bayer	Germany	46.27	58.5%	41.5%	17.5	10.2	7.3
BBVA	Spain	16.01	55.3%	44.7%	17.8	9.8	8.0
BNP	France	102.80	88.1%	11.9%	11.0	9.7	1.3
BSCH	Spain	10.98	56.7%	43.3%	16.8	9.5	7.3
Carrefour	France	65.40	27.0%	73.0%	35.9	9.7	26.2
DaimlerChrysler	Germany	53.65	21.3%	78.7%	43.6	9.3	34.3
Danone	France	150.00	36.1%	63.9%	27.9	10.1	17.8
Deutsche Bank	Germany	90.42	63.6%	36.4%	15.6	9.9	5.7
Deutsche Telekom	Germany	23.81	22.5%	77.5%	38.3	8.6	29.7
Dresdner Bank	Germany	50.80	39.3%	60.7%	25.5	10.0	15.5
E.On	Germany	58.35	50.5%	49.5%	20.4	10.3	10.1
Endesa	Spain	19.20	92.6%	7.4%	12.1	11.2	0.9
Enel	Italy	3.72	41.4%	58.6%	24.0	9.9	14.1
ENI	Italy	7.70	89.7%	10.3%	11.0	9.9	1.1
Fortis	Belgium	29.87	73.4%	26.6%	12.4	9.1	3.3
France Telecom	France	65.80	17.1%	82.9%	56.6	9.7	46.9
Generali	Italy	33.78	31.2%	68.8%	30.4	9.5	20.9
Hypoverennsbank	Germany	55.60	56.6%	43.4%	15.6	8.8	6.8
ING	Holland	75.70	61.4%	38.6%	15.2	9.3	5.9

(continues)

Appendix 3.2 (*continued*)

Company	Country	(euros)	P no growth	P growth	PER	PER no growth	PER growth
			Price per share				
KPN	Holland	11.29	−60.3%	160.3%	−16.0	9.6	−25.6
L'Oreal	France	75.50	19.2%	80.8%	43.9	8.4	35.5
LVMH Moet Hennessy	France	67.30	18.7%	81.3%	46.6	8.7	37.9
Muenchener Re	Germany	314.94	30.6%	69.4%	33.0	10.1	22.9
Nokia	Finland	34.30	20.2%	79.8%	37.9	7.6	30.3
Philips	Holland	32.08	38.6%	61.4%	26.9	10.4	16.5
Pinault-Printemps	France	206.10	37.0%	63.0%	26.6	9.8	16.8
Repsol-YPF	Spain	21.11	85.7%	14.3%	11.2	9.6	1.6
Royal Dutch	Holland	71.55	54.2%	45.8%	18.2	9.9	8.3
RWE	Germany	44.30	24.8%	75.2%	45.9	11.4	34.5
San Paolo-IMI	Italy	16.09	133.7%	−33.7%	7.1	9.5	−2.4
Sanofi-synthelabo	France	71.35	22.3%	77.7%	43.1	9.6	33.5
Siemens	Germany	85.40	32.5%	67.5%	26.2	8.5	17.7
Societe Generale	France	71.00	84.7%	15.3%	11.5	9.7	1.8
Suez Lyonnaise	France	35.75	51.5%	48.5%	20.0	10.3	9.7
Telecom Italia	Italy	11.18	27.5%	72.5%	33.8	9.3	24.5
Telefonica	Spain	17.32	33.1%	66.9%	27.8	9.2	18.6
Totalfina Elf	France	174.30	60.3%	39.7%	17.0	10.3	6.7
Unicredito Italiano	Italy	5.30	66.3%	33.7%	14.8	9.8	5.0
Unilever	Holland	64.65	42.3%	57.7%	23.9	10.1	13.8
Vivendi	France	75.90	21.2%	78.8%	48.3	10.2	38.1
Volkswagen	Germany	58.50	100.8%	−0.8%	9.3	9.4	−0.1
Euro Stoxx 50		**4,413.37**	**47.5%**	**52.5%**	**23.4**	**11.1**	**12.3**

APPENDIX 3.3: RELATIONSHIP BETWEEN THE PER AND GROWTH (g), REQUIRED RETURN TO EQUITY (Ke) AND RETURN ON EQUITY (ROE) IN A COMPANY WITH CONSTANT GROWTH

This appendix shows that, for a company with constant annual growth, the relationship between the PER, growth (g), required return to equity (Ke), and return on equity (ROE) is

$$PER = \frac{ROE - g}{ROE\,(Ke - g)}$$

The PER is the price of all the shares (E) divided by the company's profit after tax:

$$PER = E_0/PAT_1 \qquad (3.1)$$

The shares' value is the present value of the dividends, which, in the case of a company with constant growth, is:

$$E_0 = Div_1/(Ke - g) \qquad (3.2)$$

The ratio between the dividends paid by the company and the profit after tax it generates is called the pay-out ratio (p)

$$p = Div_1/PAT_1 \qquad (3.3)$$

ROE (return on equity) is the company's profit after tax divided by the shares' book value:

$$ROE = PAT_1/Ebv_0 \qquad (3.4)$$

Substituting [3.2] and [3.3] in [3.1] gives:

$$PER = \frac{E_0}{PAT_1} = \frac{Div_1}{(Ke - g)PAT_1} = \frac{p}{Ke - g} \qquad (3.5)$$

For a company in which everything (balance sheet and income statement) grows at a constant rate g and with a constant return on its investments (ROE), the relationship between growth (g) and the pay-out ratio (p) is given by:

$$g = ROE(1 - p) \qquad (3.6)$$

Isolating p gives: $p = (ROE - g)/ROE \qquad (3.7)$

Substituting (3.7) in (3.5) gives:

$$PER = \frac{ROE - g}{ROE(Ke - g)}.$$

If we use the last profit after tax (PAT_0) to calculate the PER instead of the expected profit after tax for the coming year (PAT_1), the relationships change a little. One has simply to see that in a company in which everything grows at the rate g, $PAT_1 = PAT_0(1 + g)$. Consequently:

$$PER^* = E_0/PAT_0 = PER(1 + g)$$
$$ROE^* = PAT_0/Ebv_0 = ROE/(1 + g)$$

$$g = ROE(1 - p) = ROE^*(1 - p)(1 + g); \qquad p = \frac{ROE^*(1 + g) - g}{ROE^*(1 + g)}$$

Therefore, the relationship between PER*, growth (g), required return to equity (Ke), and return on equity (ROE*) is

$$PER^* = \frac{[ROE^*(1 + g) - g]}{ROE^*(Ke - g)}$$

Chapter 4

Splitting the Price-Earnings Ratio: Franchise Factor, Growth Factor, Interest Factor, and Risk Factor

In the previous chapter, we studied the PER, the most widely used indicator in the stock market, how it is defined, how it is calculated, the factors it depends on, etc. The PER is the multiple of the profits at which the market values a company's shares. This multiple basically depends on the market's expectations regarding the company's growth, profitability, and risk. Growth alone is not enough to give a high PER, the company must invest in projects having a return greater than the cost of capital. In order to study in greater depth the factors that affect the PER, we shall split[1] the PER into two addends: the first is the PER the company would have if it did not grow and the second is the contribution made by the company's growth to the PER, which in turn splits into a product of two factors: the *Franchise Factor*, which measures the growth's quality, and the *Growth Factor*. We shall see that for growth to contribute to the PER, the company must invest in projects having a return greater than the cost of capital.

Further on, the PER's first addend is split into another two factors: the *Interest Factor* and the *Risk Factor*. The Interest Factor is, approximately, the PER of a long-term Treasury bond. The Risk Factor depends on the company's risk, which is defined as the required return to equity.

---

[1]This splitting of the PER is discussed in the article of Leibowitz and Kogelman (1992).

4.1. PER, FRANCHISE FACTOR, AND GROWTH FACTOR

The PER can be split into two addends as follows (see the proof in Appendix 4.1):

$$PER = \frac{1}{Ke} + FF \times G \qquad FF = \frac{ROE - Ke}{ROE\ Ke} \qquad G = \frac{g}{Ke - g}$$

The first addend, $1/Ke$ (in the previous chapter $1/10\% = 10$), is the company's PER if it has no growth, regardless of the return on its investments.

The second addend ($FF \times G$) is the contribution made by growth to the PER. It consists of two factors:

1. The Growth Factor, G, which basically depends on the company's growth.
2. The Franchise Factor, FF, which mainly depends on the difference between the return on investment and the cost of capital employed. The Franchise Factor measures what we could call the growth's "quality," understanding this to be the return above the cost of the capital employed.

This formula tells us that a company's PER is the PER of the no-growth company plus an "extra PER" due to growth, which depends on the growth (G) and the "quality" of that growth (Franchise Factor).

We shall now apply this split to the six companies analyzed in Chapter 3.

Table 4.1 shows all six companies' Growth Factor G and Franchise Factor FF. Obviously, the companies that do not grow (company B and company C) have a Growth Factor of zero. The company that grows most (company D with 8%) has the highest Growth Factor: 4.

The companies investing in projects with a return equal to the cost of capital (company A and company B) have a Franchise Factor of zero. The companies investing in projects with a return of 12% (companies C, D, and E)

Table 4.1

PER, FF, and G of Six Companies

	A	B	C	D	E	F
PER	10.00	10.00	10.00	16.67	12.50	15.38
G	1.5	0	0	4	1.5	2.333
FF	0	0	1.667	1.667	1.667	2.308
G × FF	0	0	0	6.667	2.500	5.385

have a Franchise Factor of 1.667 and the company investing in projects with a return of 13% (company F) has a Franchise Factor of 2.308. The higher the return on investment, the higher the Franchise Factor.

We have seen with these simple examples that growth alone is not enough to have a high PER: growth is important, but only if the new investments have a return greater than the cost of capital (growth with "quality").

A word of caution: in the above examples, the PER has been calculated by dividing the shares' price today by next year's expected profit. Very often, the PER is calculated by dividing the shares' price today by last year's profit. In this case (as we shall see in the following section), the PER's breakdown is identical but the expression of the Franchise Factor changes a little: all we have to do is add 1 and calculate the return on investment (ROE) also with this year's profit, instead of with next year's profit.

4.2. PER*, FRANCHISE FACTOR*, AND GROWTH FACTOR

We use the asterisk (*) to identify the PER* calculated by dividing the shares' price today by this year's profit.

$$\text{If } PER^* = \frac{P_0}{EPS_0} = \frac{E_0}{PAT_0} \text{ and } PER = \frac{P_0}{EPS_1} = \frac{E_0}{PAT_1}$$

As $PAT_1 = PAT_0(1 + g)$, the relationship between PER and PER* is

$$PER^* = PER (1 + g)$$

We use the asterisk (*) to identify the ROE* calculated by dividing this year's profit by the equity's book value this year.

Performing similar operations, we obtain:

$$ROE^* = PAT_0/Ebv_0 = ROE/(1 + g)$$

In Appendix 4.1, we show that PER* is split as follows:

$$PER^* = \frac{1}{Ke} + FF^* \times G \qquad FF^* = \frac{ROE^* - Ke}{ROE^*Ke} + 1 \qquad G = \frac{g}{Ke - g}$$

In Appendix 4.1, we also show that the difference between FF and FF* is

$$FF^* - FF = 1 - \frac{g}{ROE} = 1 - \frac{g}{ROE^* (1 + g)}$$

Table 4.2 shows PER* and FF* for all six companies in the previous example.

4.3. PER, INTEREST FACTOR, AND RISK FACTOR

We have already said that $(1/Ke)$ is the PER the company would have if it did not grow. This term can be split into two terms:

$$\frac{1}{Ke} = \frac{1}{R_F} - \frac{Ke - R_F}{Ke\,R_F}$$

The first term $(1/R_F)$ is the PER the company would have if it did not grow and had no risk. It is, approximately, the PER of a long-term Treasury bond. This term is called Interest Factor. The second term depends primarily on the difference between the required return to equity (Ke) and the risk-free interest rate (R_F). The value of this term increases as the required return to equity increases (which depends on the risk perceived by the market). This is why it is called Risk Factor.

$$\text{Interest Factor} = \frac{1}{R_F} \qquad \text{Risk Factor} = \frac{Ke - R_F}{Ke\,R_F} = \frac{1}{R_F} - \frac{1}{Ke}$$

$$PER = \frac{1}{R_F} - \frac{Ke - R_F}{Ke\,R_F} + FF \times G$$

Table 4.2
PER* and FF* of Six Companies

	A	B	C	D	E	F
PATo	9.434	10	12	11.111	11.321	12.150
DIV$_0$ = ECF$_0$	3.774	10	12	3.704	5.660	5.607
PER*	**10.60**	**10.00**	**10.00**	**18.00**	**13.25**	**16.46**
ROE*	9.43%	10.00%	12.00%	11.11%	11.32%	12.15%
G	1.5	0	0	4	1.5	2.333
FF*	0.4	1	2.667	2	2.167	2.769
G × FF*	0.6	0	0	8.000	3.250	6.462

$$\text{PER} = \text{Interest Factor} - \text{Risk Factor} + \\ \text{Franchise Factor} \times \text{Growth Factor}$$

Likewise:

$$\text{PER*} = \frac{1}{R_F} - \frac{Ke - R_F}{Ke\ R_F} + FF^* \times G$$

$$\text{PER*} = \text{Interest Factor} - \text{Risk Factor} + \\ \text{Franchise Factor*} \times \text{Growth Factor}$$

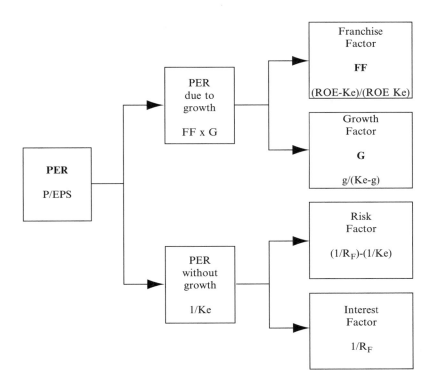

4.4. VALUE GENERATION OVER TIME IN COMPANIES WITH GROWTH

Figure 4.1 shows the evolution over time of the profits and dividends of companies A (annual growth = 6%) and B (without growth). Both companies have the same equity value (100 million). The expected dividends of company B are 10 million every year. The expected dividends of company A are 4 million in year 1, growing thereafter at an annual rate of 6% in the following years. The dividends of company A will not reach 10 million (the dividends of company B) until 16 years from now.

Figure 4.2 shows the evolution over time of the profits and dividends of companies A (annual growth = 6%) and C (without growth). The equity value of company A is 100 million and the equity value of company C is 120 million. The expected dividends of company C are 12 million every year. The dividends of company A will not reach 12 million (the dividends of company C) until 19 years from now.

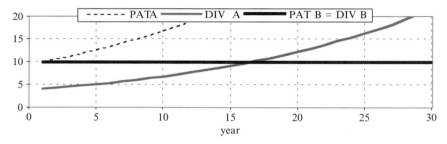

Figure 4.1   Evolution of the profits and dividends of companies A and B.

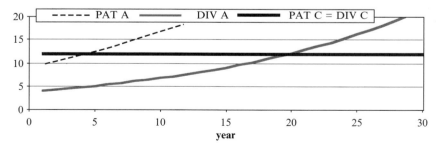

Figure 4.2   Evolution of the profits and dividends of companies A and C.

Figure 4.3 shows the evolution over time of the profits and dividends of companies D (annual growth = 8%) and F (annual growth = 7%). Both companies have the same equity value (200 million). The expected dividends of company D are 4 million in year 1, growing thereafter at an annual rate of 8%. The expected dividends of company F are 6 million in year 1, growing thereafter at an annual rate of 7%. Although it seems in Figure 4.3 that the dividends of company D are always less than those of company F, they will in fact catch up with the dividends of company F in 45 years' time.

Figure 4.4 and Table 4.3 show the equity value generation over time: the present value of the dividends until a certain year. Thus, the present value of the dividends for the first 20 years is 52 million for company A, 85 million for company B, 61 million for company D, and 85 million for company F. The present value of companies B and F match in year 20 and that of companies B and D in year 36.

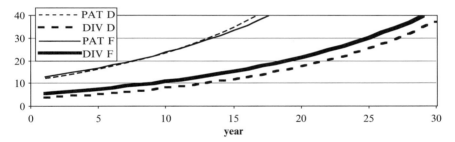

Figure 4.3   Evolution of the profits and dividends of companies D and F.

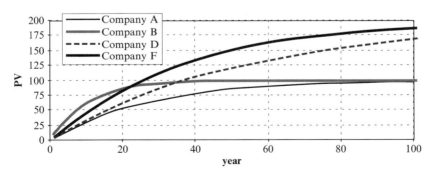

Figure 4.4   Equity value generation over time. Present value of the dividends until the year indicated.

Table 4.3

Equity Value Generation Over Time

Present Value of the Dividends until the Year Indicated

Year	Company A	Company B	Company C	Company D	Company E	Company F
5	17	38	45	18	25	26
10	31	61	74	34	46	48
15	43	76	91	48	64	68
20	52	85	102	61	78	85
30	67	94	113	85	101	113
40	77	98	117	104	116	134
50	84	99	119	120	126	150
75	94	100	120	149	141	175
100	98	100	120	168	146	187
125	99	100	120	180	149	194
150	100	100	120	187	149	197
175	100	100	120	192	150	198
200	100	100	120	195	150	199

Figure 4.5 shows the equity value generation over time: the present value of the dividends until a certain year as a percentage of the equity's value today. Thus, the present value of the first 20 years' dividends is 52% of its value (100 million) for company A, 85% of its value (100 million) for company B, 31% of its value (200 million) for company D, and 42% of its value (200 million) for company F.

4.5 INFLUENCE OF GROWTH ON THE FRANCHISE FACTOR AND ON THE GROWTH FACTOR

Figure 4.6 shows the relationship between the Franchise Factor multiplied by the Growth Factor and the growth rate for four companies with different ROEs. Note that in the company with ROE = 9%, that is, less than the required return to equity, which is 10%, the higher the growth rate, the lower the product FF × G, which becomes negative. In the case of the company with ROE = 10% (equal to the required return to equity), the product FF × G is always 0. For companies with a ROE greater than the required return to equity, the higher the growth rate, the higher the product FF × G.

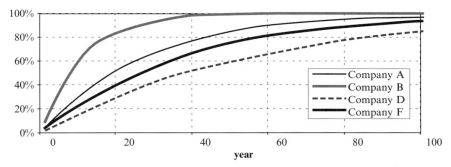

Figure 4.5   Equity value generation over time. Present value of the dividends until the year indicated as a percentage of the equity value.

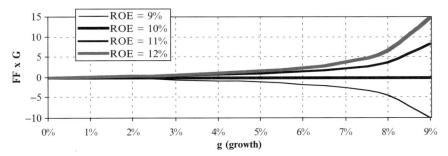

Figure 4.6   FF × G of a company with different growth rates (g). Ke = 10%.

4.6 INFLUENCE OF THE ROE ON THE FRANCHISE FACTOR

Figure 4.7 shows the Franchise Factor at different ROEs. Companies with different growth rates have an identical Franchise Factor, as the Franchise Factor does not depend on growth. Figure 4.7 also shows that if the ROE is equal to the required return to equity, i.e., 10%, the Franchise Factor is 0. For companies with a ROE less than 10%, the Franchise Factor is negative and, for companies with a ROE greater than 10%, the Franchise Factor is positive.

Figure 4.8 shows the product of the Franchise Factor by the Growth Factor at different ROEs, for companies with different growth rates. Again it is showed that for a ROE of 10%, the Franchise Factor multiplied by the

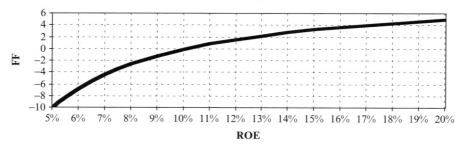

Figure 4.7   FF of a company with different values for ROE. Ke = 10%.

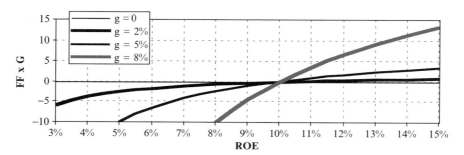

Figure 4.8   FF × G of a company with different values for ROE. Ke = 10%.

Growth Factor is 0, irrespective of the company's growth rate. Companies with high growth have a product FF × G greater than 0 if the ROE is greater than 10%, and less than 0 if the ROE is less than 10%.

4.7. INFLUENCE OF THE REQUIRED RETURN TO EQUITY ON THE FRANCHISE FACTOR AND ON THE PER

Figure 4.9 shows the relationship between the Franchise Factor multiplied by the Growth Factor and the required return to equity. As was to be expected, when the required return to equity increases, the product FF × G decreases. In the case of companies whose ROE is greater than the required

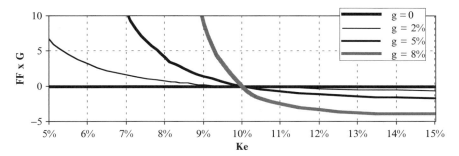

Figure 4.9   FF × G of a company with different values for Ke. ROE = 10%.

return to equity, the product FF × G increases rapidly when the required return to equity decreases.

Figure 4.10 shows the relationship between the Franchise Factor multiplied by the Growth Factor and Ke but this time we can see how this relationship changes when the ROE changes: the higher a company's ROE, the higher the product FF × G.

Figure 4.11 shows how the Franchise Factor changes depending on the required return to equity. As is logical, the Franchise Factor decreases as the required return to equity increases.

Figure 4.12 shows the evolution of the U.S. stock market's Franchise Factor and the its average PER. The Franchise Factor increased from 1994–1998, but was negative in 1992.

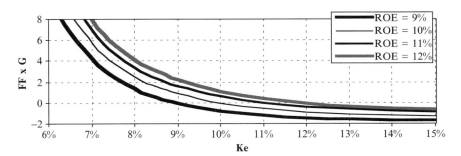

Figure 4.10   FF × G of a company with different values for Ke. g = 4%.

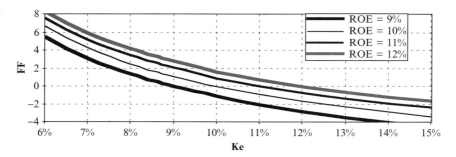

Figure 4.11 FF of a company with different values for Ke. g = 4%.

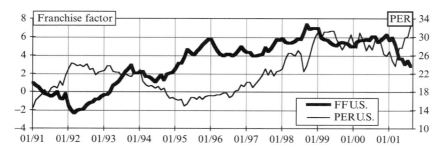

Figure 4.12 FF and PER of the U.S. stock market.

APPENDIX 4.1: SPLITTING THE PER

In Appendix 3.3 in Chapter 3, the following equation was proven:

$$\text{PER} = \frac{p}{\text{Ke} - g} = \frac{\text{ROE} - g}{\text{ROE (Ke} - g)} \qquad (4.1)$$

In a company with constant growth and performing algebraic operations, it is readily deduced that[2]:

$$\frac{E_0}{\text{Ebv}_0} = \frac{\text{ROE} - g}{\text{Ke} - g}$$

[2]Comparing ROE (which is an accounting number) with Ke (which is the required return) is always dangerous. As a general rule, it is not true (except for perpetuities, which is the case we are considering here) that the condition for a company to "create value" is that ROE be greater than Ke. We will develop on this in Chapter 13.

Substituting this expression into the previous one, we obtain:

$$PER = \frac{p}{Ke - g} = \frac{ROE - g}{ROE\ (Ke - g)} = \frac{1}{ROE}\frac{E_0}{Ebv_0}$$

As $g = ROE\ (1 - p)$, substituting and performing algebraic operations, we obtain:

$$PER = \frac{p}{Ke - g} = \frac{1}{Ke}\frac{Ke\ p}{Ke - g} = \frac{1}{Ke}\frac{Ke\ (ROE - g)}{ROE\ (Ke - g)}$$

$$= \frac{1}{Ke}\left[1 + \frac{Ke\ (ROE - g) - ROE\ (Ke - g)}{ROE\ (Ke - g)}\right]$$

$$= \frac{1}{Ke} + \frac{(ROE - Ke)\ g}{ROE\ Ke\ (Ke - g)} = \frac{1}{Ke} + FF \times G$$

$$PER = \frac{1}{Ke} + FF \times G$$

Where:

$$FF = \frac{ROE - Ke}{ROE\ Ke} \qquad G = \frac{g}{Ke - g}$$

Furthermore, performing algebraic operations, the first addend can be expressed as:

$$\frac{1}{Ke} = \frac{1}{R_F} - \frac{Ke - R_F}{Ke\ R_F}$$

We call the first term Interest Factor and the second term Risk Factor:

$$\text{Interest Factor} = \frac{1}{R_F} \qquad \text{Risk Factor} = \frac{Ke - R_F}{Ke\ R_F}$$

$$PER = \frac{1}{R_F} - \frac{Ke - R_F}{Ke\ R_F} + FF \times G$$

$$PER = \frac{1}{R_F} - \frac{Ke - R_F}{Ke\ R_F} + \frac{ROE - Ke}{ROE\ Ke} \times \frac{g}{Ke - g}$$

$$
\boxed{
\begin{array}{c}
PER = \text{Interest Factor} - \text{Risk Factor} + \\
\text{Franchise Factor} \times \text{Growth Factor}
\end{array}
}
$$

If

$$PER^* = \frac{P_0}{EPS_0} = \frac{E_0}{PAT_0}$$

As $PAT_1 = PAT_0 (1 + g)$, the relationship between PER and PER* is

$$PER^* = PER (1 + g)$$

$$ROE^* = PAT_0/Ebv_0 = ROE/(1 + g)$$
$$g = ROE (1 - p) = ROE^* (1 - p)(1 + g)$$

$$p = \frac{ROE^* (1 + g) - g}{ROE^* (1 + g)}$$

$$PER^* = \frac{p (1 + g)}{Ke - g} = \frac{1}{Ke} \frac{Ke\, p (1 + g)}{Ke - g} = \frac{1}{Ke} \frac{Ke\, [ROE^* (1 + g) - g]}{ROE^*(Ke - g)} =$$
$$= \frac{1}{Ke}\left[1 + \frac{Ke\, [ROE^* (1 + g) - g] - ROE^* (Ke - g)}{ROE^* (Ke - g)}\right] =$$
$$= \frac{1}{Ke} + \frac{(ROE^* - Ke + Ke\, ROE^*)g}{ROE^*Ke\, (Ke - g)} = \frac{1}{Ke} + FF^* \times G$$

$$FF^* = \frac{ROE^* - Ke}{ROE^*\, Ke} + 1 \qquad G = \frac{g}{Ke - g}$$

$$PER^* = \frac{1}{Ke} + FF^* \times G \qquad PER^* = \frac{1}{R_F} - \frac{Ke - R_F}{Ke\, R_F} + FF^* \times G$$

$$FF^* - FF = 1 - g/ROE = 1 - g/[ROE^* (1 + g)]$$

REFERENCE

Leibowitz, M. L., and S. Kogelman (1992), "Franchise Value and the Growth Process," *Financial Analysts Journal*, 48, pp. 53–62.

Chapter 5

Market Value and Book Value

The relationship between share prices (their market value for listed companies) and their book value is the subject of considerable study by financial analysts. In this chapter, we will analyze the relationship between the two parameters in several companies and different countries. We will also analyze the influence of the PER and the ROE on this relationship.

5.1. MARKET VALUE AND BOOK VALUE ON THE NORTH AMERICAN STOCK MARKET

Figure 5.1 shows the evolution of the market-to-book ratio of the U.S. stock market and the S&P 500 in recent years. Obviously, both lines move in parallel: when stock prices rise, the shares' market-to-book ratio also rises and viceversa. However, it is important to remember that the equity book value increases when there are capital increases, when companies retain earnings and also when assets appreciate.

Figure 5.2 shows the evolution of the market-to-book ratio (E/Ebv) of Coca Cola and Pepsico. It is interesting to see that although Coca Cola's ratio has been markedly higher during the period 1991–2001, the two companies' ratios have been converging since mid-1998 and had almost met by 2001.

Figure 5.3 shows the evolution of the ratio of three of the world's largest companies: General Electric, Microsoft, and Cisco. Note the enormous market-to-book ratio of Cisco in the second half of 1999 and 2000, coinciding with the Internet Speculative Bubble. In the first months of 2000, the market-to-book ratio (E/Ebv) for Cisco was higher than 40.

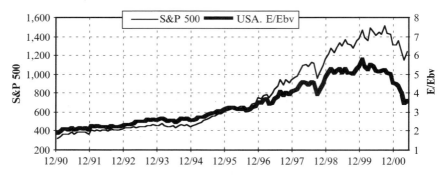

Figure 5.1   Evolution of the average market-to-book ratio of the U.S. stock market and evolution of the S&P 500. (Sources: Morgan Stanley and Datastream.)

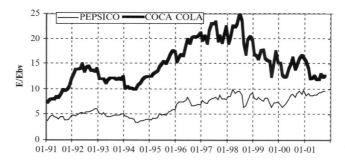

Figure 5.2   Evolution of the market-to-book ratio of Coca Cola and Pepsico. (Source: Datastream.)

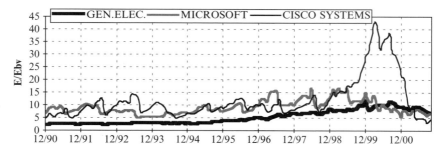

Figure 5.3   Market-to-book ratio of General Electric, Microsoft, and Cisco. (Source: Datastream.)

5.2. MARKET-TO-BOOK RATIO ON THE INTERNATIONAL STOCK MARKETS

Figure 5.4 shows the evolution of the market-to-book ratio (E/Ebv) in the United States and compares it with the evolution of the same ratio in the United Kingdom and Spain. As can be seen, during the period between 1991 and 1999, the North American market had the highest ratio and Spain the lowest ratio, although it was above the British ratio in 2000 and 2001. The market-to-book ratio grew enormously in all three countries until December 1999, and then fell in 2000 and 2001, following the general trend of the world stock markets.

5.3. MARKET-TO-BOOK RATIO AND INTEREST RATES ON THE NORTH AMERICAN STOCK MARKET

Share prices and interest rate variations are closely linked, as we will see in greater depth in Chapter 7. Consequently, it is to be assumed that shares' market-to-book ratio will also be related with interest rates. Figure 5.5 enables this ratio's evolution to be compared with the evolution of the interest rates. It can be seen that, historically, when interest rates have risen, the market-to-book ratio has fallen, and when interest rates have fallen, as happened after 1995, the market-to-book ratio has increased.

5.4. RELATIONSHIP BETWEEN THE MARKET-TO-BOOK RATIO AND THE PER AND THE ROE

The market-to-book ratio (E/Ebv) is closely related with the price-to-earnings ratio (PER) and the return on equity (ROE).

It can be readily verified by means of a simple algebraic operation that the E/Ebv ratio is equal to the PER multiplied by the ROE:

$$\frac{E}{Ebv} = \frac{\text{Market value}}{\text{Book Value}} = \frac{\text{Market value}}{\text{Net income}} \times \frac{\text{Net income}}{\text{Book Value}} = PER \times ROE \quad (5.1)$$

Table 5.1 shows the values of these three ratios for British Telecom, General Electric, Microsoft, and Cisco in recent years. The reader can see that the previous equation: E/Ebv = PER × ROE, is met in all cases.

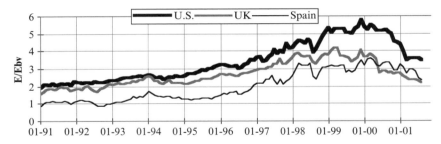

Figure 5.4   Evolution of the average market-to-book ratio of the U.S., U.K., and Spanish stock markets. (Source: Morgan Stanley.)

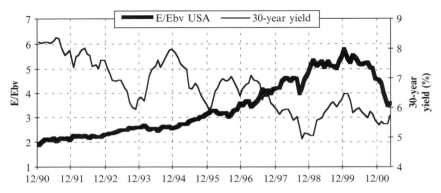

Figure 5.5   Evolution of the average market-to-book ratio of the U.S. stock market and the long-term interest rates. (Source: Morgan Stanley.)

Figure 5.6 shows the evolution of the average ROE of the U.S., U.K., and Spanish stock markets. Note that the average ROE of the Spanish stock market has been less than the ROE of the American and British stock markets until 2000. However, in 2001 it was the highest of the three.

Figure 5.7 shows the evolution of the ROE of Coca Cola and Pepsico. As can be seen, Coca Cola's ROE has been markedly higher than Pepsico's until the end of 1999. The fall in Coca Cola's ROE in 1998, 1999, and 2000 is surprising.

Figure 5.8 shows the evolution of the ROE of three of the world's largest companies. Cisco's ROE was negative after the first quarter of 2001 as a consequence of the losses reported by the company. It is also interesting to see the cyclical evolution of Microsoft's ROE and the growth of General Electric's ROE.

Table 5.1

Evolution of the E/Ebv, PER, and ROE of British Telecom, General Electric, Microsoft, and Cisco

		1991	1992	1993	1994	1995	1996	1997	1998	1999	2000
British Telecom	ROE	19.7%	17.4%	10.0%	13.6%	14.4%	15.7%	18.7%	15.8%	21.0%	20.5%
	PER	8.7	11.7	22.5	14.4	12.2	14.4	15.2	26.1	46.8	18.1
	E/Ebv	1.7	2.0	2.3	2.0	1.8	2.3	2.8	4.1	9.8	3.7
General Electric	ROE	20.5%	20.1%	17.1%	17.9%	22.2%	23.4%	23.8%	23.9%	25.2%	25.2%
	PER	14.9	15.5	20.3	18.4	18.2	22.3	29.2	35.9	47.4	37.4
	E/Ebv	3.05	3.12	3.47	3.3	4.05	5.22	6.96	8.58	11.94	9.43
Microsoft	ROE	34.3%	32.3%	29.4%	25.8%	27.3%	31.8%	35.1%	28.5%	28.3%	22.7%
	PER	26.9	23.0	17.9	26.2	27.8	31.9	28.3	45.2	52.8	24.4
	E/Ebv	9.2	7.43	5.26	6.74	7.58	10.15	9.95	12.9	14.91	5.54
Cisco Systems	ROE	33.9%	34.4%	36.2%	37.1%	30.5%	32.4%	24.5%	19.0%	18.0%	10.1%
	PER	23.9	29.8	27.1	18.7	28.1	30.7	33.4	68.4	167.2	212.8
	E/Ebv	8.11	10.24	9.82	6.94	8.59	9.95	8.17	13	30.01	21.43

Source: Datastream and own data.

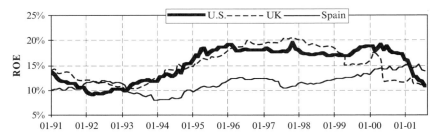

Figure 5.6 Evolution of the average ROE of the U.S., U.K., and Spanish stock markets. (Source: Morgan Stanley.)

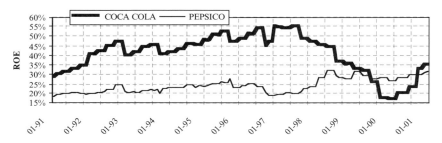

Figure 5.7 Evolution of the ROE of Coca Cola and Pepsico. (Source. Datastream.)

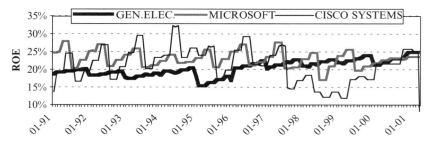

Figure 5.8 Return on equity (ROE) of General Electric, Microsoft, and Cisco. (Source. Datastream.)

The relationship between the equity market value (E) and book value (Ebv) depends on only three factors: ROE, required return to equity (Ke), and expected growth of dividends (g). To prove this statement, we will use another mathematical equation. From the expression obtained for the PER in Appendix 3.3, we can conclude that:

$$\frac{E}{Ebv} = \frac{ROE - g}{Ke - g} \tag{5.2}$$

Figure 5.9 seems to indicate a significant parallelism between the market-to-book ratio and ROE/risk-free rate (R_F). When ROE/risk-free rate has grown, the market-to-book ratio has usually increased. As R_F, we have chosen the yield on 30–year Treasury Bonds. The correlation coefficient (using monthly data) between the market-to-book ratio and ROE/R_F was 85%. But the correlation coefficient (using monthly data) between the increase of the market-to-look ratio and the increase of ROE/R_F was only 19.4%.

The highest values for ROE/R_F were attained in December 1995 and August 1998.

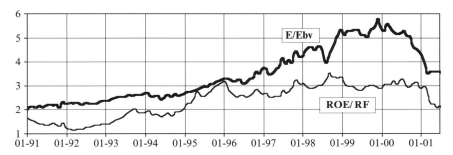

Figure 5.9   Relationship between E/Ebv and ROE/R_F.

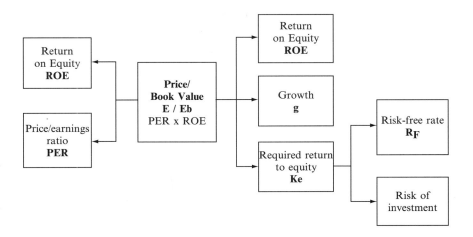

5.5. VALUE CREATION AND THE DIFFERENCE BETWEEN MARKET VALUE AND BOOK VALUE

The difference between the equity market value and its book value is called Market Value Added (MVA), and it is often related with companies' *value creation*. However, in actual fact, it is only true for a company that has just been created and is completely false if we are talking about an active company that has been created some time previously: in this case, value creation has nothing to do with the difference between market value and book value. This is a very important and also very controversial issue, which we will analyze in more detail in Chapters 13 and 14.

This reasoning is based on the view that the book value represents the investment that the equity's holders have made in the company. However, as we have said in the previous paragraph, this only happens when the company is created. At any later time, the book value is not equal to the shareholder's investment but is the sum of the initial capital outlay and other items. Thus, a company's book value is usually the partners' initial investment plus the earnings obtained in each period plus the capital increases less share repurchases plus capital increase due to asset value increases. To associate the equity book value with the quantity invested by the shareholders is, as a general rule, a mistake.

As the market-to-book ratio depends on the PER and the ROE, Figures 5.10 and 5.11 show the relationship existing between the market-to-book ratio and the PER, and the relationship existing between the market-to-book ratio and the ROE of the 30 companies comprising the Dow Jones Industrial Average Index in July 2000. In both figures, we see that none of the relationships is very clear: there are companies with a high PER and a low market-to-

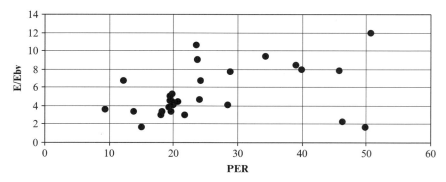

Figure 5.10 Relationship between the PER and the market-to-book ratio of the Dow Jones Industrial Average, July 2001.

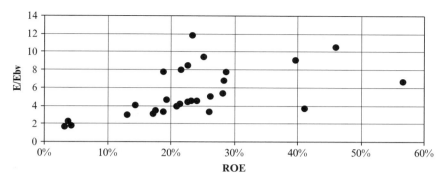

Figure 5.11   Relationship between the ROE and the market-to-book ratio of the Dow Jones Industrial Average, July 2001.

book ratio, and others in which the opposite case is true. Neither does a higher ROE imply a higher market-to-book ratio. In July 2001, the correlation coefficient was 36.6% between the market-to-book ratio and the PER, and 55% between the market-to-book ratio and the ROE.

According to Morgan Stanley, in July 2001, the U.S. market had a PER of 32.6, a market-to-book ratio of 3.5, and an average ROE of 10.7%.

Fama and French (1992) show that, on average, the companies with lower PER and E/Ebv have higher shareholder returns than the companies with higher PER and E/Ebv.[1] In the period 1963–1990, there was quite a strong relationship between the shareholder return and the market-to-book ratio. The authors divided the shares into portfolios and the portfolios with lower market-to-book ratios had higher shareholder returns. Table 5.2 shows this effect.

5.6. EQUITY BOOK VALUE MAY BE NEGATIVE: THE CASE OF SEALED AIR

Sealed Air Co. paid its shareholders a special dividend of $40 per share in May 1989. In the month prior to the special dividend, its share price had ranged between $44 and $46. The company had 8,245,000 shares outstanding. The special dividend meant paying $329.8 million (87% of the shares' market value). As the company only had $54 million in cash, it borrowed most of the funds required to pay the dividend. After paying the dividend, the company had a *negative equity book value of $160 million.*

[1]This paper is discussed in more detail in Section 11.4 in Chapter 11.

Table 5.2

Relationship between Market-to-Book Ratio and Shareholder Return

Market-to-book ratio	Annual average shareholder return
Portfolio 1 (high)	5.9%
Portfolio 2	10.4%
Portfolio 3	11.6%
Portfolio 4	12.5%
Portfolio 5	14.0%
Portfolio 6	15.6%
Portfolio 7	17.3%
Portfolio 8	18.0%
Portfolio 9	19.1%
Portfolio 10 (low)	22.6%

Source: Fama and French (1992).

On the day after announcing the extraordinary dividend, there was a rush to buy the company's shares.[2] The opening price was $53 per share, and it closed at $50.5 dollars, $4.38 above the previous day. Subsequently, the new shares increased value and ended 1989 at $20.4. Figure 5.12 shows how the share's price dropped after paying the dividend and its subsequent rise.

The company's tremendous leverage was accompanied by a substantial increase in its efficiency ratios. Sealed Air gave its shareholders a 290% return from April 1989 to December 1992, while the stock market rose 36% during the same period. Before the special dividend, from December 1986 to April 1989, the shareholder return was 6%, while the market return was 48%.

Table 5.3 shows that the shareholder's equity was negative in 1989 due to the dividend payment. It can also be seen the debt increased during that year to cover the dividend payment. The shareholder's equity became positive again in 1994. Sales, operating profit, and net income also grew during this period.

Founded in 1960, Sealed Air manufactured and sold a broad range of packaging products. One of its most famous products was the plastic wrapping with air bubbles. Other products were self-sealing envelopes, paper for

[2]In the press release, the company's president said: "The special dividend will enable the company's shareholders to realize in cash a very significant portion of the company's value, while at the same time maintaining their holding in it. Our strategy has always been to be market leader in packaging products. With the present investments, we believe that the company has sufficient production capacity to satisfy the growing demand for its products for several years without any significant additional investments. We also believe that it is unlikely, in the present market circumstances that we will find opportunities for major acquisition at an acceptable price that are consistent with our strategy. The special dividend is not a response to any takeover offer."

Table 5.3

Sealed Air, 1987–1997

($ million)	1987	1988	1989	1990	1991	1992	1993	1994	1995	1996	1997
Sales	302.7	345.6	385.0	413.3	435.1	446.1	451.7	519.2	723.1	789.6	842.8
Operating profit	38.2	43.6	53.7	67.4	69.5	72.2	74.1	83.9	108.9	130.1	138.1
Net income	20.5	25.3	7.2	11.4	16.2	20.8	27.4	31.6	52.7	69.3	80.0
Current assets	80.7	96.0	86.7	22.3	18.5	29.4	33.8	15.8	41.9	58.9	87.2
Inventories	32.0	36.2	25.9	25.6	28.3	28.3	32.0	38.3	43.3	42.3	48.3
Shareholder's equity	141.1	162.3	−160.5	−131.6	−94.6	−66.3	−29.4	11.0	106.3	186.6	257.3
Long-term debt	34.4	33.5	311.1	259.0	253.7	225.3	190.1	155.3	149.8	99.9	48.5
Investments	13.1	13.9	13.8	12.1	15.9	11.2	22.4	29.9	21.0	17.0	24.3

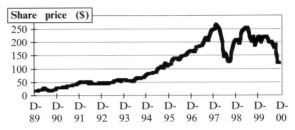

Figure 5.12　Share price of Sealed Air from 1987 to 1989, and from 1989 to 2000.

absorbing meat fluids for supermarkets, and plastic materials for packaging fragile goods.

When it announced the special dividend to the banks, the company found that many banks did not want to lend money to a company with negative shareholder's equity.

In spite of these problems, Sealed Air obtained a loan from Bankers Trust for $136.7 million (with the possibility of increasing it to $210 million) at an interest rate of 11.5%.[3] It also issued $170 million in 10-year subordinated bonds paying an interest rate of 12.625%. To finance the remaining $23.1 million, the company realized short-term investments. The agreement with the banks also required that any proceeds from the sale of assets should be used to pay back loans. In addition, Sealed Air would not be able to take out any additional loans.

Commissions and other expenses associated with the special dividend amounted to $20.9 million.

After the special dividend, the company's management shifted the emphasis in its policies to new priorities: (1) putting the customer first; (2)

---

[3]The Bankers Trust prime rate plus 1.5%.

cash flow; (3) working capital focus; (4) innovation; and (5) earnings per share.

The company implemented a new incentive plan for its managers. Before the recapitalization,[4] the incentives were based on the earnings per share, then on the EBITDA (earnings before interest, tax, depreciation and amortization), inventory level, level of accounts receivable, and working capital. The aim of the new incentive plan was to focus the managers' attention on the importance of generating cash flow. The president explained this change in incentives as follows: "In our company, our managers never had to worry about the balance sheet and the company accepted the investments recommended by managers without demur. By changing from earnings per share to EBITDA, we have focused our managers more on the cash flow." The company also implemented a plan to enable employees to hold more shares in the company. In April 1989, the employees had 7.9% of the company's shares; by March 1992, their holding had increased to 24.6%.

Figure 5.13 shows that the company's operating profit/sales ratios were higher than that of the industry. It also shows the reduction in net working capital and the inventories/sales ratio after paying the dividend.[5]

On 31 March 1998, the company merged with Cryovac, W.R. Grace & Co.'s packaging products division. The merged company continues to be called Sealed Air.

Not all leveraged recapitalizations have been as profitable for shareholders as Sealed Air's. Table 5.4 shows the shareholder return of 33 leveraged recapitalizations.

SUMMARY

The E/Ebv ratio depends on the ROE, Ke, and the dividends' expected growth. When interest rates rise, *ceteris paribus*, the ratio decreases, and vice versa, as happens with share prices.

The equity book value increases when there are capital increases, the company's retained earnings increase, and when the value of its assets increases.

---

[4]Recapitalization is the name given to the increase in the company's indebtedness as a result of the payment of the special dividend.

[5]Those readers interested in finding out more about the company can see the Harvard Business School cases 9-294-122/3 "Sealed Air Corporation's Leveraged Recapitalization," written by Karen Wruck.

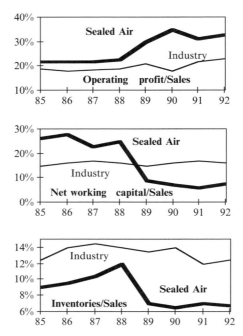

Figure 5.13 Behavior of Sealed Air compared with the industry. (Source: Wruck (1998).)

To associate the difference market value − book value (E − Ebv) with the companies' value creation, as a general rule, is a mistake. It is only true in the case of companies that have just been created, as only then will the book value match the amount invested by shareholders.

REFERENCES

Fama, E.F., and K.R. French (1992), "The Cross-Section of Expected Stock Returns," *Journal of Finance*, 47, pp. 427–466.
Wruck, K. (1994), "Sealed Air Corporation's Leveraged Recapitalization," Harvard Business School cases Number 9–294–122 and 9–294–123.
Wruck, K. (1998), "Financial Policy, Internal Control, and Performance: Sealed Air Corporation's Leveraged Special Dividend," Working Paper, Harvard Business School.

Table 5.4

Leveraged Recapitalizations, Shareholder Return in the Year after the Leveraged Recap

Company	Annual return		Difference	Company	Annual return		Difference
	Company	S&P 500			Company	S&P 500	
Sealed Air Corp	62.8%	10.8%	52.1%	*Whittaker*	-1.8%	*10.6%*	-12.3%
Holiday Corp	59.8%	5.5%	54.3%	Phillips-Van Heusen	-1.8%	5.2%	-7.0%
Holly Corp	40.8%	12.0%	28.8%	*Triad Systems*	-3.7%	0.3%	-3.9%
Shoney's	40.6%	11.8%	28.8%	Service Merchandise	-5.6%	8.4%	-14.0%
CUC International	39.5%	7.6%	31.9%	Swank Inc	-11.5%	6.1%	-17.6%
Barry Wright	31.8%	22.5%	9.4%	*GenCorp*	-19.5%	6.9%	-26.4%
Kroger	25.8%	13.0%	12.8%	WNS Inc	-28.0%	11.6%	-39.5%
Colt Industries	24.1%	8.5%	15.6%	Butler Manufacturing	-30.0%	-0.1%	-29.9%
Cleveland-Cliffs	22.8%	13.8%	9.0%	*USG Corp*	-35.3%	12.8%	-48.1%
Di Giorgio	18.8%	11.6%	7.2%	*Interlake Corp*	-36.2%	7.5%	-43.7%
FMC Corp	17.6%	9.4%	8.2%	Quantum Chemical	-38.5%	13.5%	-52.0%
Owens Corning	12.6%	10.5%	2.1%	*Standard Brands Paint*	-39.0%	13.2%	-52.1%
Vista Chemical	12.0%	10.5%	1.6%	*Carter Hawley Hale*	-44.0%	5.8%	-49.8%
Union Carbide	10.0%	12.1%	-2.0%	*HBJ*	-49.2%	6.4%	-55.6%
Optical Coating Lab	8.5%	5.7%	2.8%	*Interco*	-63.1%	13.9%	-77.0%
Goodyear	5.8%	8.4%	-2.6%	*Bank Bldg Equip*	-79.7%	3.7%	-83.5%
General Signal	5.3%	13.6%	-8.4%	Average	-1.5%	9.5%	-10.9%

The operations carried out as a defense measure against takeovers are in Italics.
Source: Wruck (1998).

APPENDIX 5.1: MARKET VALUE (E) AND BOOK VALUE (Ebv) OF SELECTED U.S. COMPANIES IN DECEMBER 1995 AND JULY 2001 ($ MILLION)

($ million)	Equity Book Value (Ebv)		Capitalization (E)		E/Ebv		Annualized return
	Dec-1995	Jul-2001	Dec-1995	Jul-2001	1995	2001	Dec.95-Jul.01
GENERAL ELECTRIC	29,609	50,492	120,260	432,166	4.1	8.6	27.8%
MICROSOFT	5,333	53,210	51,975	356,241	9.7	6.7	33.4%
EXXON MOBIL	40,436	70,757	99,962	288,134	2.5	4.1	16.5%
CITIGROUP	35,994	66,206	19,811	252,744	0.6	3.8	31.9%
WAL MART	12,726	31,343	51,081	249,926	4.0	8.0	28.0%
INTEL	12,140	37,322	46,603	200,562	3.8	5.4	25.6%
IBM	22,423	20,624	51,016	182,714	2.3	8.9	28.9%
JOHNSON & JOHNSON	9,045	23,369	55,372	168,783	6.1	7.2	18.3%
MERCK	11,736	14,832	80,805	155,636	6.9	10.5	16.0%
SBC COMMUNICATIONS	6,256	31,608	34,914	151,387	5.6	4.8	10.2%
CISCO	1,379	26,497	20,420	140,670	14.8	5.3	31.6%
HOME DEPOT	3,442	15,004	22,768	117,545	6.6	7.8	31.2%
COCA COLA	5,392	9,316	93,136	110,947	17.3	11.9	5.5%
PHILIP MORRIS	13,985	15,005	75,335	99,406	5.4	6.6	14.2%
AT & T	17,274	107,908	103,073	71,401	6.0	0.7	-0.8%
PEPSICO	7,313	7,249	44,025	68,508	6.0	9.45	12.8%
DISNEY	6,651	24,100	30,778	55,070	4.6	2.3	4.9%

(continues)

Appendix 5.1 (*continued*)

($ million)	Equity Book Value (Ebv)		Capitalization (E)		E/Ebv		Annualized return
	Dec-1995	Jul-2001	Dec-1995	Jul-2001	1995	2001	Dec.95-Jul.01
AMER.EXPRESS	8,220	12,184	20,042	53,380	2.4	4.4	19.1%
HEWLETT-PACKARD	11,839	14,209	42,863	47,928	3.6	3.4	7.4%
BOEING	9,898	11,020	26,894	47,181	2.7	4.3	7.4%
DU PONT	8,436	13,299	38,803	44,519	4.6	3.3	6.3%
MCDONALDS	8,262	9,204	31,420	37,508	3.8	4.1	5.8%
GENERAL MOTORS	23,345	30,314	39,624	34,982	1.7	1.2	9.8%
UNITED TECHNOLOGIES	4,419	8,094	11,576	34,567	2.6	4.3	22.3%
ENRON	3,542	12,374	9,593	34,006	2.7	2.7	13.3%
ALCOA	4,445	11,422	9,370	33,897	2.1	3.0	20.2%
HONEYWELL INTL.	3,592	9,707	13,436	29,924	3.7	3.1	9.8%
DUKE ENERGY	5,469	11,709	9,705	29,921	1.8	2.6	14.5%
INTL PAPER	8,247	13,839	9,642	19,688	1.2	1.4	3.2%
CATERPILLAR	3,388	5,600	11,604	18,920	3.4	3.4	11.6%
UNION PACIFIC	6,364	10,162	13,568	13,334	2.1	1.3	4.6%
EASTMAN KODAK	5,121	3,428	22,921	12,593	4.5	3.7	-4.6%
FEDEX	2,246	5,900	4,174	12,308	1.9	2.1	15.2%
AMERICAN AIRLINES	3,720	7,176	5,669	5,402	1.5	0.8	7.3%
EDISON INTL	7,069	3,930	7,848	4,574	1.1	1.2	1.6%
NORTHWEST AIRLINES	745	1,021	4,053	2,203	5.4	2.2	-14.1%
UAL	-179	5,860	2,261	1,848	-12.6	0.3	-7.3%
Sum \ Average	369,321	805,295	1,336,402	3,620,525	3.6	4.5	13.2%

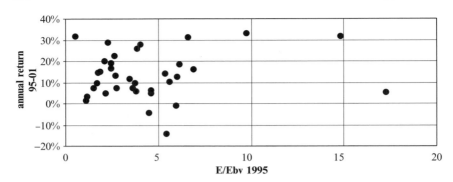

Chapter 6

Dividends and Market Value

6.1. EVOLUTION OF DIVIDENDS ON THE U.S. STOCK MARKET

Figure 6.1 shows the evolution of the dividend yield[1] of three of the largest North American companies: GE, Boeing, and Coca-Cola.

Figure 6.2 shows the evolution of the yield on 30-year Government bonds and the dividend yield in the United States. Both yields have fallen in the last 20 years. Although Figure 6.2 seems to show that the yield on Government bonds has always been greater than the stock market's dividend yield, Fisher and Statman (2000) show that the dividend yield was greater than the yield on Government bonds in every year from 1879 to 1958. The average difference during those years between the dividend yield and the yield on Government bonds was 1.87%.

6.2. INCREASINGLY FEWER COMPANIES DISTRIBUTE DIVIDENDS AND MORE BUY BACK SHARES

There are increasingly fewer companies that distribute dividends. In 1998, only 20.7% of the 5,655 companies listed on the main U.S. stock markets (NYSE, AMEX, and NASDAQ) paid dividends. As Table 6.1 shows, of the 4,484 companies that did not pay dividends in 1998, 3,981 companies had

[1]The dividend yield is the dividend per share (DPS) divided by the share price (P).

109

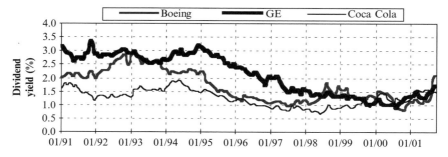

Figure 6.1   Evolution of the dividend yield of GE, Boeing, and Coca-Cola.

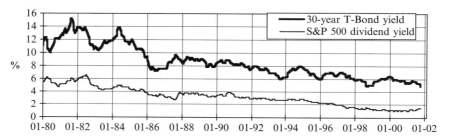

Figure 6.2   Dividend yield and yield on 30-year Government bonds in the United States.

Table 6.1

**Dividend Distribution by Companies Listed on the Main
U.S. Stock Markets (NYSE, AMEX, and NASDAQ)**

	1926–62	1963–77	1978–82	1983–87	1988–92	1993–97	1998
Number of companies	787	2,531	3,742	4,391	4,326	5,202	5,655
Paid dividend	**74.7%**	**65.5%**	**58.3%**	**36.3%**	**29.5%**	**24.5%**	**20.7%**
Did not pay dividend	25.3%	34.5%	41.7%	63.7%	70.5%	75.5%	79.3%
Did pay	*118*	*233*	*378*	*540*	*523*	*531*	*503*
Never paid	*81*	*640*	*1,182*	*2,257*	*2,526*	*3,397*	*3,981*

Source: Fama and French (1999).

never paid dividends since they were incorporated, and 503 companies had
paid dividends in previous years.

Itemizing by markets, in 1998, 52% of the companies listed on the NYSE,
19% of the companies listed on the AMEX, and the 9% of the companies
listed on the NASDAQ paid dividends.

Table 6.2 shows the reduction of the dividend yield. This reduction is not only because less companies pay dividends. The dividend yield of the companies that do distribute dividends has also fallen from 4.7% in the 1980s to 2.2% in the 1990s. It also shows that stock repurchases are increasing. The reason is that it is fiscally more efficient for shareholders to distribute money in the form of stock repurchases than by paying dividends. Stock repurchases as a percentage of profits increased from 3.5% in the mid-1970s to 27.1% in the 1990s.

Between 1995 and 1999, North American companies announced stock repurchase programs with a total value of 750 billion dollars. In 1998, for the first time in history, North American companies distributed more money to shareholders through stock repurchases than through dividends,[2] as can be seen in Figure 6.3.

The large increase in stock repurchases is related with the increase in employee options. Kahle (1991) finds that firms announce repurchases when executives have large numbers of options outstanding and when employees have large numbers of options exercisable. She also finds that the shareholder return due to the announcement of a stock repurchase is significantly lower for firms with large amounts of employee stock options.

Table 6.2

Selected Financial Data on the Companies Listed on the Main U.S. Stock Markets (NYSE, AMEX, and NASDAQ)

	1973–77	1978–82	1983–87	1988–92	1993–97
Dividend/Market capitalization					
Total companies	3.1%	4.4%	3.1%	2.6%	1.7%
Dividend payers	3.2%	4.7%	3.5%	3.0%	2.2%
Share repurchases/net income	3.5%	4.9%	24.7%	27.1%	27.1%
Dividend/net income	33.9%	35.2%	40.7%	55.8%	40.3%
(Repurchase + dividend)/net income	37.4%	40.1%	65.4%	82.8%	67.3%
Share issues/net income	8.7%	11.4%	23.0%	32.2%	34.0%
ROE. Dividend payers	12.8%	14.5%	12.0%	10.7%	13.3%
ROE. Nondividend payers	7.6%	8.4%	4.4%	3.4%	3.9%
Share of total market capitalization					
Dividend payers	96.3%	94.1%	88.4%	86.8%	77.5%
Nondividend payers	3.7%	5.9%	11.6%	13.2%	22.5%

Source: Fama and French (1999).

[2] See Grullón and Ikenberry (2000).

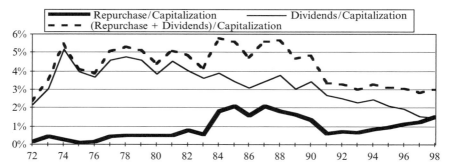

Figure 6.3 Cash payments to shareholders: dividends and stock repurchases. (North American companies included in COMPUSTAT.)

6.3. EVOLUTION OF DIVIDENDS ON THE INTERNATIONAL MARKETS

Table 6.3 shows the evolution of dividends, profits, GDP, and CPI in several European countries during the period 1976–1996.

Figure 6.4 shows the evolution of the dividend yield in United States, England, and Germany. The dividend yield has fallen in all markets in the last 10 years.

6.4. THE SHARE VALUE IS THE PRESENT VALUE OF THE EXPECTED DIVIDENDS

A share's value is the current value of the expected dividends.[3] Further on, we shall see several methods for valuing companies by discounting expected dividends. The methods vary depending on how dividends are expected to grow.

The investor who buys a share today normally expects to receive dividends in the future[4] and resell the share in the future at a higher price. It may also be the case that he buys the share with the intention of holding it indefinitely.

---

[3]When we talk about dividends, we are referring to payments to shareholders. We have already seen that this remuneration can take the form of dividends, share repurchases, reduction of nominal value, expected bid-offer, etc.

[4]He will also charge subscription rights. However, what he receives in subscription rights, he loses in decreased share value due to the dilution produced by the capital increase.

Table 6.3
Growth of the Nominal and Real Dividends per Share in Several European Stock Markets (1976–1996)

	Germany	France	Italy	Holland	Spain	Sweden	Switzerland	U.K.
Nominal dividends	3.4%	9.1%	11.2%	6.0%	9.6%	9.5%	4.7%	11.7%
Real dividends	0.4%	3.4%	2.0%	3.1%	1.7%	4.4%	1.7%	5.0%
Net income	4.7%	8.1%	10.3%	6.6%	8.3%	13.2%	5.6%	10.9%
Real GDP	2.6%	2.1%	2.1%	2.2%	2.2%	1.4%	1.4%	2.1%
Nominal GDP	5.8%	7.7%	12.1%	4.6%	11.9%	8.1%	8.1%	9.1%
CPI	3.0%	5.7%	9.2%	3.0%	9.4%	5.5%	5.5%	6.7%

Source: Hoare Bovett

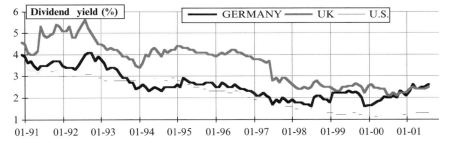

Figure 6.4   Evolution of the dividend yield on the German, English, and North American stock markets. (*Source*: Morgan Stanley Dean Witter.)

Let us imagine that the investor who intends to hold the share indefinitely buys it today. A company that distributes dividends each year has issued the share. If the return that our investor requires from the investment is Ke, the maximum price that he must pay for this share (P_0) is the present value of the dividends (DPS) that he expects[5] to obtain from the share:

$$P_0 = \frac{DPS_1}{1 + Ke} + \frac{DPS_2}{(1 + Ke)^2} + \frac{DPS_3}{(1 + Ke)^3} + \frac{DPS_4}{(1 + Ke)^4} + \ldots \qquad (6.1)$$

Another investor expects to receive dividends for the next two years (DPS_1 and DPS_2) and then sell the share at a price P_2. If the return that our investor

[5]DPS is the abbreviation for dividend per share. Although we only use DPS, we are always referring to the *expected* dividend per share.

requires from the investment is Ke, the maximum price that he must pay for this share (P_0) is

$$P_0 = \frac{DPS_1}{1 + Ke} + \frac{DPS_2 + P_2}{(1 + Ke)^2}$$

However, the investor who buys the share in 2 years' time will make a calculation similar to his. Assuming that he too wishes to hold it for 2 years, the calculation he will perform to obtain the share's price in 2 years' time (P_2) will be

$$P_2 = \frac{DPS_3}{1 + Ke} + \frac{DPS_4 + P_4}{(1 + Ke)^2}$$

However, the price in year 4 will also depend on the following years' dividends. Repeating this reasoning, we obtain:

$$P_0 = \frac{DPS_1}{1 + Ke} + \frac{DPS_2}{(1 + Ke)^2} + \frac{DPS_3}{(1 + Ke)^3} + \frac{DPS_4}{(1 + Ke)^4} + \cdots$$

Consequently, the share's value is the present value of the dividends that the share is expected to generate, even if the investor is thinking of selling it soon.

Example. Calculate the value of a share that distributes an annual dividend of \$100 and which is expected to remain constant over time. The yield on long-term Government bonds is 6% and the required return from this company is 10%.

The share's value is \$1,000 dollars because

$$P_0 = 1,000 = \frac{100}{1.1} + \frac{100}{(1.1)^2} + \frac{100}{(1.1)^3} + \frac{100}{(1.1)^4} + \cdots$$

Note that if instead of expecting those \$100 from the investment in the share, they were expected from a perpetual Government bond, its value would be \$1,667 (higher because it has no risk):

$$1,667 = \frac{100}{1.06} + \frac{100}{(1.06)^2} + \frac{100}{(1.06)^3} + \frac{100}{(1.06)^4} + \cdots$$

6.5. SHARE VALUE WHEN DIVIDENDS HAVE CONSTANT GROWTH, GORDON AND SHAPIRO FORMULA

We now address the valuation of a share whose dividends are expected to grow each year at a rate g.

$$DPS_1 = DPS_0(1 + g)$$

$$DPS_2 = DPS_0(1 + g)^2 = DPS_1(1 + g)$$

$$DPS_n = DPS_0(1 + g)^n = DPS_1(1 + g)^{n-1}$$

The share's price will be

$$P_0 = \frac{DPS_1}{1 + Ke} + \frac{DPS_1(1 + g)}{(1 + Ke)^2} + \frac{DPS_1(1 + g)^2}{(1 + Ke)^3} + \frac{DPS_1(1 + g)^3}{(1 + Ke)^4} + \cdots$$

Appendix 6.1 shows that the share's price can be expressed in the form of the Gordon and Shapiro formula (1956):

$$P_0 = \frac{DPS_1}{Ke - g} \qquad (6.2)$$

Example. Calculate the value of a share whose annual dividend was \$100 and which is expected to grow at a rate of 4% over time. The required return from this company is 10%.

The dividend expected next year is \$104. Consequently, the share's value is \$1733 because, applying the expression (6.2): $1733 = 104/(0.1 - 0.04)$.

Note that if we did not expect any growth in the dividend ($g = 0$), the share's value would be \$1,000: $1,000 = 100/(0.1 - 0)$

Example. The price of the Coca-Cola share on December 31, 2000 was \$60.94. The dividend per share in 2000 was \$0.68. If the required return to Coca-Cola's equity was 9.044%, the reader can see that the average expected growth of the dividends was 7.84%:

$$\$60.94 = \frac{\$0.68 \times 1.0784}{0.09044 - 0.0784}$$

Figure 6.5 shows the expected dividend growth implicit in the year-end share price and the actual dividend growth of Coca-Cola. The expected growth of the dividend per share is calculated by repeating the above calculation at the end of each year. Figure 6.6 compares the expected dividend growth of Coca-Cola and PepsiCo.

Figures 6.7 and 6.8 compare the evolution of the dividends per share of Coca-Cola and PepsiCo with the earnings per share, both expressed in nominal dollars. It is seen, particularly in the case of Coca-Cola, that the DPS growth is smoother than the EPS growth. Figure 6.9 shows both companies' market capitalization.

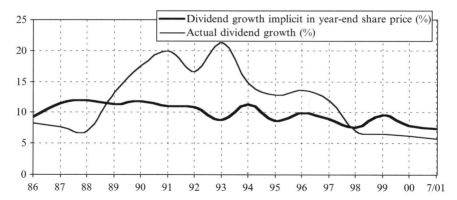

Figure 6.5   Coca-Cola—expected dividend growth implicit in the year-end share price and actual dividend growth.

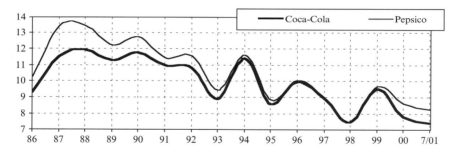

Figure 6.6   Coca-Cola and PepsiCo—expected dividend growth implicit in the year-end share price.

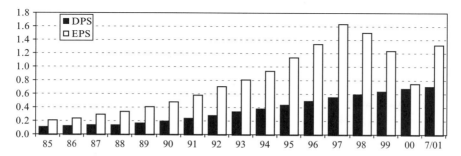

Figure 6.7   Evolution of the dividend and earnings per share of Coca Cola ($ per share).

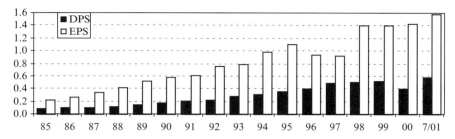

Figure 6.8   Evolution of the dividend and earnings per share of PepsiCo ($ per share).

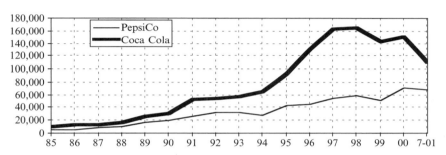

Figure 6.9   Market value (capitalization) of Coca Cola and PepsiCo ($ million).

6.6. SHARE VALUE WHEN DIVIDENDS GROW AT A FIXED QUANTITY EACH YEAR

We will now address the valuation of a share whose dividends are expected to grow each year at a fixed quantity Δ.

$$DPS_1 = DPS_0 + \Delta. \qquad\qquad DPS_n = DPS_0 + n\Delta.$$

The share's price will be

$$P_0 = \frac{DPS_0 + \Delta}{1 + Ke} + \frac{DPS_0 + 2\Delta}{(1 + Ke)^2} + \frac{DPS_0 + 3\Delta}{(1 + Ke)^3} + \frac{DPS_0 + 4\Delta}{(1 + Ke)^4} + \cdots$$

In Appendix 6.2, it is shown that the share's value reduces to:

$$P_0 = \frac{DPS_1}{Ke} + \frac{\Delta}{Ke^2}$$

The first addend is the dividends' value if they were constant (equal to next year's dividend) and the second addend is the value of the dividends' growth.

6.7. BINOMIAL VALUATION MODEL OF DISCOUNTED DIVIDENDS

In this section, we will value shares when we do not have a clear idea as to whether the dividends will grow. We only assign a probability to the dividends growing.[6]

6.7.1. ADDITIVE BINOMIAL MODEL

We value a share when we do not have a clear idea as to whether the dividends will grow: we assign a probability (p_u) to the dividends growing at a quantity Δ and another probability ($p_c = 1 - p_u$) to them remaining constant.

$$DPS_{t+1} = \begin{cases} DPS_t + \Delta & \text{probability } p_u \\ DPS_t & \text{probability } p_c = 1 - p_u \end{cases}$$

Appendix 6.3 shows that the share's value is

$$P_0 = \frac{DPS_0}{Ke} + \left[\frac{1}{Ke} + \frac{1}{Ke^2} \right] p_u \, \Delta$$

6.7.2. ADDITIVE BINOMIAL MODEL WITH PROBABILITY OF BANKRUPTCY

This model completes the previous model by assigning a probability to the company going bankrupt and ceasing to pay dividends:

$$DPS_{t+1} = \begin{cases} DPS_t + \Delta & \text{probability } p_u \\ DPS_t & \text{probability } p_c = 1 - p_u - p_q \\ 0 = P_{t+1} & \text{probability } p_q \end{cases}$$

In this case, the share's value is

$$P_0 = \frac{DPS_0(1 - p_q)}{Ke + p_q} + \left[\frac{1}{Ke + p_q} + \frac{1}{(Ke + p_q)^2} \right] p_u \, \Delta$$

---

[6]See Hurley and Johnson (1994).

Note that when $p_q = 0$, this formula matches the additive binomial model without probability of bankruptcy.

6.7.3. GEOMETRIC BINOMIAL MODEL

We value a share when we do not have a clear idea as to how the dividends will evolve: we assign a probability (p_u) to the dividends growing at a percentage g and another probability ($p_c = 1 - p_u$) to them remaining constant.

$$DPS_{t+1} = \begin{cases} DPS_t\ (1+g) & \text{probability } p_u \\ DPS_t & \text{probability } p_c = 1 - p_u \end{cases}$$

Appendix 6.4 shows that the share's value is

$$P_0 = \frac{1 + p_u g}{Ke - p_u g} DPS_0$$

If $p_u = 1(p_c = 0)$, we have the Gordon and Shapiro formula:

$$P_0 = DPS_0(1 + g)/(Ke - g)$$

6.7.4. GEOMETRIC BINOMIAL MODEL WITH PROBABILITY OF BANKRUPTCY

This model completes the previous model by assigning a probability to the company going bankrupt and ceasing to pay dividends:

$$DPS_{t+1} = \begin{cases} DPS_t\ (1+g) & \text{probability } p_u \\ DPS_t & \text{probability } p_c = 1 - p_u - p_q \\ 0 = P_{t+1} & \text{probability } p_q \end{cases}$$

In this case, the share's value is

$$P_0 = \frac{1 + p_u g - p_q}{Ke - p_u g + p_q} DPS_0$$

When $p_q = 0$, this formula matches the geometric binomial model without probability of bankruptcy.

6.8. TRINOMIAL VALUATION MODEL OF DISCOUNTED DIVIDENDS

In this section, we will value shares when we do not have a clear idea as to whether the dividends will grow, decrease, or remain constant. To value the share, we must assign probabilities to all three options.[7]

6.8.1. ADDITIVE TRINOMIAL MODEL

We value a share when we do not have a clear idea as to how the dividends will evolve: we assign a probability (p_u) to the dividends growing at a quantity Δ, another probability (p_d) to them decreasing in the same[8] quantity Δ, and another probability ($p_c = 1 - p_u - p_d$) to them remaining constant.

$$DPS_{t+1}=\begin{cases} DPS_t + \Delta & \text{probability } p_u \\ DPS_t & \text{probability } p_c = 1 - p_u - p_d \\ DPS_t - \Delta & \text{probability } p_d \end{cases}$$

The share's value is

$$P_0 = \frac{DPS_0}{Ke} + \left[\frac{1}{Ke} + \frac{1}{Ke^2} \right] (p_u - p_d)\, \Delta$$

6.8.2. ADDITIVE TRINOMIAL MODEL WITH PROBABILITY OF BANKRUPTCY

This model completes the previous model by assigning a probability to the company going bankrupt and ceasing to pay dividends:

$$DPS_{t+1}=\begin{cases} DPS_t + \Delta & \text{probability } p_u \\ DPS_t & \text{probability } p_c = 1 - p_u - p_d - p_q \\ DPS_t - \Delta & \text{probability } p_d \\ 0 = P_{t+1} & \text{probability } p_q \end{cases}$$

---

[7]See Yao (1997).

[8]The model can also be extended to the case when the quantity by which the dividends may decrease is different from the quantity by which they may increase.

In this case, the share's value is

$$P_0 = \frac{DPS_0(1 - p_q)}{Ke + p_q} + \left[\frac{1}{Ke + p_q} + \frac{1 - p_q}{(Ke + p_q)^2} \right] (p_u - p_d)\,\Delta$$

When $p_q = 0$, this formula matches the additive trinomial formula without probability of bankruptcy.

6.8.3. GEOMETRIC TRINOMIAL MODEL

We value a share when we do not have a clear idea as to how the dividends will evolve: we assign a probability (p_u) to the dividends growing at a percentage g, another probability (p_d) to them decreasing in the same[9] percentage g, and another probability ($p_c = 1 - p_u - p_d$) to them remaining constant:

$$DPS_{t+1} = \begin{cases} DPS_t\,(1+g) & \text{probability } p_u \\ DPS_t & \text{probability } p_c = 1 - p_u - p_d \\ DPS_t\,(1-g) & \text{probability } p_d \end{cases}$$

Appendix 6.5 shows that the share's value is

$$P_0 = \frac{1 + (p_u - p_d)g}{Ke - (p_u - p_d)g} DPS_0$$

If $p_u = 1(p_d = p_c = 0)$, we have the Gordon and Shapiro formula.

6.8.4. GEOMETRIC TRINOMIAL MODEL WITH PROBABILITY OF BANKRUPTCY

This model completes the previous model by assigning a probability to the company going bankrupt and ceasing to pay dividends:

$$DPS_{t+1} = \begin{cases} DPS_t\,(1+g) & \text{probability } p_u \\ DPS_t & \text{probability } p_c = 1 - p_u - p_d - p_q \\ DPS_t\,(1-g) & \text{probability } p_d \\ 0 = P_{t+1} & \text{probability } p_q \end{cases}$$

[9]The model can also be extended to the case when the quantity by which the dividends may decrease is different from the quantity by which they may increase.

In this case, the share's value is

$$P_0 = \frac{1 - p_q + (p_u - p_d)g}{Ke + p_q - (p_u - p_d)g} DPS_0$$

When $p_q = 0$, this formula matches the geometric trinomial model without probability of bankruptcy.

6.9. THE SHARE'S VALUE WHEN THE DIVIDENDS HAVE TWO GROWTH RATES: THE TWO-STAGE GROWTH MODEL

It is assumed that the DPS and the earnings per share (EPS) grow at the rate g until year n and that after year $n + 1$, they grow at the rate g_n. Therefore, the dividend per share for year n is $DPS_n = DPS_1(1 + g)^{n-1}$, and the dividend per share for year $n + 1$ is $DPS_{n+1} = DPS_1(1 + g)^{n-1}(1 + g_n)$

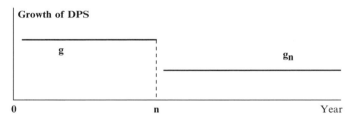

The share's price today is

$$P_0 = \frac{DPS_1}{Ke - g}\left[1 - \left(\frac{1+g}{1+Ke}\right)^n\right] + \frac{DPS_1(1 + g)^{n-1}(1 + g_n)}{(Ke - g_n)(1 + Ke)^n}$$

This expression reduces to:

$$P_0 = \frac{DPS_1}{Ke - g}\left[1 - \left(\frac{1+g}{1+Ke}\right)^{n-1}\left(\frac{g - g_n}{Ke - g_n}\right)\right]$$

One problem with this model is that the growth jump, which immediately goes from g to g_n, rarely happens.

A good approximation to this expression is obtained with the following formula:

$$P_0 = \frac{DPS_0}{Ke - g_n}[(1 + g_n) + n(g - g_n)]$$

Appendix 6.6 shows the error made with this approximation.

6.10. STOCK VALUATION WHEN DIVIDENDS HAVE TWO GROWTH RATES: MODEL H[10]

It is assumed that the DPS grows at the initial rate g_i in the first year. During 2H years, the growth rate gradually falls until it reaches the rate g_n. From then onward, it grows every year at the rate g_n.

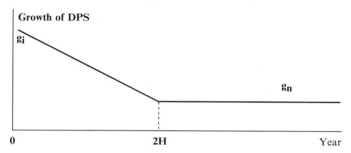

The share's value today can be approximated by:

$$P_0 = \frac{DPS_0(1 + g_n)}{Ke - g_n} + \frac{DPS_0\, H(g_i - g_n)}{Ke - g_n}$$

Appendix 6.7 shows the error made with this approximation.

6.11. STOCK VALUATION WITH THREE PERIODS OF DIVIDEND GROWTH

It is assumed that the DPS grows at the initial rate g_i for N1 years. From N1 to the year N2, the growth rate gradually falls until it reaches the rate g_n. From then onward, it grows every year at the rate g_n.

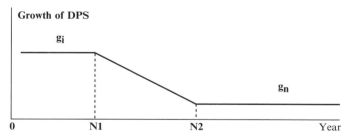

[10]See Fuller and Hsia (1984).

The share's value today is

$$P_0 = \sum_{t=1}^{N1} \frac{DPS_0(1 + g_i)^t}{(1 + Ke)^t} + \sum_{t=N1+1}^{N2} \frac{DPS_t}{(1 + Ke)^t} + \frac{DPS_{N2}(1 + g_n)}{(Ke - g_n)(1 + Ke)^{N2}}$$

The first addend is the dividends' value during the initial growth stage at the rate g_i (the first N1 years). The second addend is the dividends' value during the transitional growth stage (years N1 + 1 to N2). The third addend is the dividends' value during the final growth stage at the rate g_n (years N2 + 1 and following).

For a comprehensive compilation of the many papers published on dividends and shareholder remuneration, see the book published by Kalay et al. (1999).

APPENDIX 6.1: DERIVATION OF THE GORDON AND SHAPIRO FORMULA

We wish to prove the following equality: $P_0 = DPS_1/(Ke - g)$
We start with the Equation [6.1]:

$$P_0 = \frac{DPS_1}{1 + Ke} + \frac{DPS_2}{(1 + Ke)^2} + \frac{DPS_3}{(1 + Ke)^3} + \ldots \qquad (6.1)$$

If the dividends grow at an annual rate g, it is met that:

$$DPS_2 = DPS_1(1 + g); \quad DPS_n = DPS_1(1 + g)^{n-1}$$

Substituting in (6.1):

$$P_0 = \frac{DPS_1}{1 + Ke} + \frac{DPS_1(1 + g)}{(1 + Ke)^2} + \frac{DPS_1(1 + g)^2}{(1 + Ke)^3} + \ldots$$

Multiplying both sides of the equality by $(1 + g)/(1 + Ke)$:

$$P_0 \frac{1 + g}{(1 + Ke)} = \frac{DPS_1(1 + g)}{(1 + Ke)^2} + \frac{DPS_1(1 + g)^2}{(1 + Ke)^3} + \frac{DPS_1(1 + g)^3}{(1 + Ke)^4} + \ldots$$

Subtracting the last two expressions gives:

$$P_0 - P_0(1 + g)/(1 + Ke) = DPS_1/(1 + Ke)$$

Consequently:

$$P_0 = DPS_1/(Ke - g) \qquad (6.2)$$

This formula can also be expressed as:

$$P_0 = [DPS_1/Ke] + gDPS_1/[Ke(Ke - g)]$$

The first addend is the dividends' value if they did not grow (if they were always equal to next year's dividends) and the second term is the value of the dividends' growth.

APPENDIX 6.2: DERIVATION OF THE SHARE VALUE FORMULA WHEN THE DIVIDEND GROWS AT A FIXED QUANTITY EVERY YEAR

The share's price is the present value of the dividends discounted at the required return to equity (Ke). As the dividends grow at a quantity Δ every year:

$$P_0 = \frac{DPS_1}{1 + Ke} + \frac{DPS_2}{(1 + Ke)^2} + \frac{DPS_3}{(1 + Ke)^3} + \ldots$$
$$= \frac{DPS_0 + \Delta}{1 + Ke} + \frac{DPS_0 + 2\Delta}{(1 + Ke)^2} + \frac{DPS_0 + 3\Delta}{(1 + Ke)^3} + \ldots$$

Upon regrouping terms:

$$P_0 = \frac{DPS_0}{1 + Ke} + \frac{DPS_0}{(1 + Ke)^2} + \frac{DPS_0}{(1 + Ke)^3} + \ldots$$
$$+ \frac{\Delta}{1 + Ke} + \frac{2\Delta}{(1 + Ke)^2} + \frac{3\Delta}{(1 + Ke)^3} + \ldots = S_1 + S_2$$

We separate the expression into two addends. The first addend is

$$S_1 = \frac{DPS_0}{1 + Ke} + \frac{DPS_0}{(1 + Ke)^2} + \frac{DPS_0}{(1 + Ke)^3} + \ldots = \frac{DPS_0}{Ke}$$

The value of the second addend is

$$S_2 = \frac{\Delta}{1 + Ke} + \frac{2\Delta}{(1 + Ke)^2} + \frac{3\Delta}{(1 + Ke)^3} + \ldots =$$
$$= \left[\frac{\Delta}{1 + Ke} + \frac{\Delta}{(1 + Ke)^2} + \frac{\Delta}{(1 + Ke)^3} + \ldots\right]$$
$$+ \left[\frac{\Delta}{(1 + Ke)^2} + \frac{\Delta}{(1 + Ke)^3} + \ldots\right] + \left[\frac{\Delta}{(1 + Ke)^3} + \ldots\right] + \ldots =$$
$$= \frac{\Delta}{Ke} + \frac{\Delta}{Ke(1 + Ke)} + \frac{\Delta}{Ke(1 + Ke)^2} + \ldots$$

$$= \frac{\Delta}{Ke} \left[1 + \frac{1}{1+Ke} + \frac{1}{(1+Ke)^2} + \frac{1}{(1+Ke)^3} + \ldots \right] =$$

$$= \frac{\Delta}{Ke} \left[1 + \frac{1}{Ke} \right] = \left[\frac{1}{Ke} + \frac{1}{Ke^2} \right] \Delta$$

Thus:

$$P_0 = \frac{DPS_0}{Ke} + \left[\frac{1}{Ke} + \frac{1}{Ke^2} \right] \Delta = \frac{DPS_1}{Ke} + \frac{\Delta}{Ke^2}$$

APPENDIX 6.3: DERIVATION OF THE SHARE VALUE FORMULA IN THE ADDITIVE BINOMIAL MODEL

Each year's dividend is

$$DPS_{t+1} = DPS_t + \Delta \quad \text{with a probability } p_u$$
$$DPS_t \qquad\qquad \text{with a probability } p_c = 1 - p_u$$

The share's price at zero time (now) is

$$P_0(DPS_0) = p_u \frac{DPS_0 + \Delta + P_1(DPS_0 + \Delta)}{1 + Ke} + ((1 - p_u) \frac{DPS_0 + P_1(DPS_0)}{1 + Ke}$$

As $P_0(DPS_0) = P_1(DPS_0)$, and $P_0(DPS_0 + \Delta) = P_1(DPS_0 + \Delta)$, this gives:

$$P_0(DPS_0) = a \, DPS_0 + b\Delta + b \, P_0(DPS_0 + \Delta),$$

where:

$$a = 1/(Ke + p_u) \qquad\qquad b = p_u/(Ke + p_u)$$

Likewise,

$$P_0(DPS_0 + \Delta) = a(DPS_0 + \Delta) + b\Delta + b \, P_0(DPS_0 + 2\Delta),$$
$$P_0(DPS_0 + 2\Delta) = a(DPS_0 + 2\Delta) + b \, \Delta + b \, P_0(DPS_0 + 3\Delta)$$

Substituting in the previous equation, the following is obtained:

$$P_0(DPS_0) = [a \, DPS_0 + b\Delta] (1 + b + b^2 + \ldots + b^{n-1}) +$$
$$+ a\Delta(b + 2b^2 + 3b^3 + \ldots + (n - 1)b^{n-1}) + b^n \, P_0(DPS_0 + n\Delta).$$

When n tends to infinity, $b^n \, P_0(DPS_0 + n\Delta)$ tends to zero because b is less than 1.

When n tends to infinity, $(1 + b + b^2 + \ldots + b^{n-1}) = 1/(1 - b)$ because b is less than 1.

When n tends to infinity, $(b + 2b^2 + 3b^3 + \ldots + (n-1)b^{n-1}) = 1/(1-b)^2$ because b is less than 1.

Consequently:

$$P_0(DPS_0) = \frac{b\Delta + aDPS_0}{1-b} + \frac{a\ b\Delta}{(1-b)^2} = \frac{DPS_0}{Ke} + \left[\frac{1}{Ke} + \frac{1}{Ke^2}\right]p_u\ \Delta$$

APPENDIX 6.4: DERIVATION OF THE SHARE VALUE FORMULA IN THE GEOMETRIC BINOMIAL MODEL

Each year's dividend is

$$DPS_{t+1} = DPS_t(1+g) \quad \text{with a probability } p_u$$
$$DPS_t \qquad\qquad \text{with a probability } p_c = 1 - p_u$$

The share's price at zero time (now) is

$$P_0(DPS_0) = p_u\frac{DPS_0(1+g) + P_1(DPS_0(1+g))}{1+Ke} +$$
$$(1 - p_u)\frac{DPS_0 + P_1(DPS_0)}{1+Ke}$$

As $P_0(DPS_0) = P_1(DPS_0)$, and $P_0(DPS_0(1+g)) = P_1(DPS_0(1+g)) = (1+g)P_0(DPS_0)$, this gives:

$$P_0(DPS_0) = p_u\frac{DPS_0(1+g) + (1+g)P_0(DPS_0)}{1+Ke} +$$
$$(1 - p_u)\frac{DPS_0 + P_0(DPS_0)}{1+Ke}$$

Consequently:

$$P_0 = \frac{1 + p_u\ g}{Ke - p_u\ g}DPS_0$$

APPENDIX 6.5: DERIVATION OF THE SHARE VALUE FORMULA IN THE GEOMETRIC TRINOMIAL MODEL

Each year's dividend is

$$DPS_{t+1} = DPS_t(1+g) \quad \text{with a probability } p_u$$
$$DPS_t(1-g) \quad \text{with a probability } p_d$$
$$DPS_t \qquad\quad \text{with a probability } p_c = 1 - p_u - p_d$$

The share's price at zero time (now) is

$$P_0(DPS_0) = p_u \frac{DPS_0(1+g) + P_1(DPS_0(1+g))}{1+Ke} +$$

$$p_d \frac{DPS_0(1-g) + P_1(DPS_0(1-g))}{1+Ke} +$$

$$+ (1 - p_u - p_d)\frac{DPS_0 + P_1(DPS_0)}{1+Ke}$$

Taking into account that $P_0(DPS_0) = P_1(DPS_0),$

$P_0(DPS_0(1+g)) = P_1(DPS_0(1+g)) = (1+g)P_0(DPS_0),$ and

$P_0(DPS_0(1-g)) = P_1(DPS_0(1-g)) = (1-g)P_0(DPS_0),$ this gives:

$$P_0(DPS_0) = p_u\frac{DPS_0(1+g) + (1+g)P_0(DPS_0)}{1+Ke} +$$

$$p_d\frac{DPS_0(1-g) + (1-g)P_0(DPS_0)}{1+Ke} +$$

$$+(1 - p_u - p_d)\frac{DPS_0 + P_0(DPS_0)}{1+Ke}$$

Consequently:

$$P_0 = \frac{1 + (p_u - p_d)g}{Ke - (p_u - p_d)g}\,DPS_0$$

APPENDIX 6.6: ERROR MADE WITH THE SHARE PRICE APPROXIMATION WHEN THE SHARE'S DIVIDENDS GROW AT TWO DIFFERENT RATES

Error made when using the approximation:

$$P_0 = \frac{DPS_0}{Ke - g_n}[(1 + g_n) + n(g - g_n)]$$

instead of the exact formula:

$$P_0 = \frac{DPS_1}{Ke - g}\left[1 - \left(\frac{1+g}{1+Ke}\right)^{n-1}\left(\frac{g - g_n}{Ke - g_n}\right)\right]$$

Error = (Approximate Value − Exact Value) / Exact Value. (Ke = 12%)

g	g_n	n = 2	n = 3	n = 4	n = 5	n = 6	n = 7	n = 8	n = 9	n = 10
11%	5%	0.0%	0.1%	0.2%	0.4%	0.6%	0.8%	1.0%	1.2%	1.4%
10%	5%	0.1%	0.2%	0.4%	0.7%	1.0%	1.3%	1.7%	2.1%	2.5%
9%	5%	0.1%	0.3%	0.5%	0.8%	1.2%	1.6%	2.1%	2.6%	3.2%
8%	5%	0.1%	0.3%	0.5%	0.9%	1.3%	1.7%	2.2%	2.8%	3.4%
7%	5%	0.1%	0.2%	0.5%	0.7%	1.1%	1.5%	1.9%	2.4%	2.9%
6%	5%	0.1%	0.1%	0.3%	0.5%	0.7%	0.9%	1.2%	1.5%	1.9%
5%	5%	0.0%	0.0%	0.0%	0.0%	0.0%	0.0%	0.0%	0.0%	0.0%
4%	5%	−0.1%	−0.2%	−0.4%	−0.7%	−1.0%	−1.3%	−1.8%	−2.2%	−2.7%
3%	5%	−0.2%	−0.5%	−0.9%	−1.5%	−2.3%	−3.1%	−4.1%	−5.3%	−6.5%
2%	5%	−0.3%	−0.8%	−1.6%	−2.6%	−3.9%	−5.5%	−7.2%	−9.2%	−11.3%
1%	5%	−0.4%	−1.2%	−2.4%	−4.0%	−6.0%	−8.4%	−11.1%	−14.1%	−17.5%
0%	5%	−0.6%	−1.7%	−3.4%	−5.7%	−8.5%	−11.9%	−15.8%	−20.2%	−25.0%
8%	1%	0.2%	0.6%	1.1%	1.8%	2.6%	3.4%	4.3%	5.3%	6.4%
8%	2%	0.2%	0.5%	1.0%	1.6%	2.3%	3.0%	3.9%	4.8%	5.7%
8%	3%	0.2%	0.5%	0.9%	1.4%	2.0%	2.6%	3.4%	4.2%	5.0%
8%	4%	0.1%	0.4%	0.7%	1.1%	1.6%	2.2%	2.8%	3.5%	4.2%
8%	5%	0.1%	0.3%	0.5%	0.9%	1.3%	1.7%	2.2%	2.8%	3.4%
8%	6%	0.1%	0.2%	0.4%	0.6%	0.9%	1.2%	1.6%	1.9%	2.4%
8%	7%	0.0%	0.1%	0.2%	0.3%	0.5%	0.6%	0.8%	1.0%	1.3%
8%	8%	0.0%	0.0%	0.0%	0.0%	0.0%	0.0%	0.0%	0.0%	0.0%
8%	9%	0.0%	−0.1%	−0.2%	−0.3%	−0.5%	−0.7%	−0.9%	−1.2%	−1.5%
8%	10%	−0.1%	−0.2%	−0.4%	−0.7%	−1.0%	−1.5%	−1.9%	−2.5%	−3.1%
8%	11%	−0.1%	−0.3%	−0.6%	−1.1%	−1.6%	−2.3%	−3.1%	−4.1%	−5.1%

APPENDIX 6.7: ERROR MADE WITH THE SHARE PRICE APPROXIMATION USING THE MODEL H

Error made when using the approximation:

$$P_0 = \frac{DPS_0(1 + g_n)}{Ke - g_n} + \frac{DPS_0 \, H(g_i - g_n)}{Ke - g_n}$$

instead of the exact formula:

$$P_0 = \sum_{t=1}^{2H} \frac{DPS_{t-1}(1 + g_i - [(t - 1)(g_i - g_n)/(2H - 1)])}{(1 + Ke)^t} + \frac{DPS_{2H}(1 + g_n)}{(Ke - g_n)(1 + Ke)^{2H}}$$

Error = (Approximate Value − Exact Value) / Exact Value. (Ke = 12%)

g_i	g_n	H = 1	H = 2	H = 3	H = 4	H = 5	H = 6	H = 7
15%	4%	0.0%	−0.2%	−0.4%	−0.5%	−0.7%	−0.9%	−1.0%
14%	4%	0.0%	−0.1%	−0.1%	−0.1%	0.0%	0.0%	0.1%
12%	4%	0.0%	0.1%	0.3%	0.6%	1.0%	1.5%	2.0%
10%	4%	0.0%	0.2%	0.5%	1.0%	1.6%	2.3%	3.1%
8%	4%	0.0%	0.2%	0.6%	1.1%	1.7%	2.5%	3.3%
6%	4%	0.0%	0.1%	0.4%	0.8%	1.2%	1.8%	2.4%
4%	4%	0.0%	0.0%	0.0%	0.0%	0.0%	0.0%	0.0%
2%	4%	0.0%	−0.2%	−0.7%	−1.3%	−2.1%	−3.0%	−4.1%
1%	4%	0.0%	−0.4%	−1.1%	−2.1%	−3.5%	−5.1%	−6.9%
0%	4%	0.0%	−0.6%	−1.6%	−3.2%	−5.1%	−7.5%	−10.3%
−2%	4%	0.0%	−1.0%	−2.9%	−5.7%	−9.3%	−13.8%	−18.9%
−4%	4%	0.0%	−1.6%	−4.6%	−9.1%	−14.9%	−22.1%	−30.5%
−5%	4%	0.0%	−1.9%	−5.6%	−11.1%	−18.3%	−27.1%	−37.5%
4%	11%	0.0%	−0.6%	−1.8%	−3.7%	−6.2%	−9.6%	−13.8%
4%	10%	0.0%	−0.5%	−1.6%	−3.1%	−5.3%	−8.0%	−11.4%
4%	8%	0.0%	−0.4%	−1.0%	−2.1%	−3.4%	−5.1%	−7.1%
4%	6%	0.0%	−0.2%	−0.5%	−1.0%	−1.7%	−2.4%	−3.3%
4%	4%	0.0%	0.0%	0.0%	0.0%	0.0%	0.0%	0.0%
4%	2%	0.0%	0.2%	0.5%	1.0%	1.6%	2.3%	3.1%
4%	0%	0.0%	0.4%	1.0%	2.0%	3.1%	4.4%	5.9%
4%	−2%	0.0%	0.5%	1.6%	2.9%	4.6%	6.5%	8.6%
4%	−4%	0.0%	0.7%	2.1%	3.9%	6.1%	8.5%	11.1%
4%	−6%	0.0%	0.9%	2.6%	4.8%	7.5%	10.4%	13.5%
4%	−8%	0.0%	1.1%	3.1%	5.8%	8.8%	12.2%	15.8%

REFERENCES

Fama, E.F., and K.R. French (1999), "Disappearing Dividends: Changing Firm Characteristics or Lower Propensity to Pay?" Center for Research in Security Prices, Working Paper No. 509.

Fisher, K., and M. Statman (2000), "Cognitive Biases in Market Forecasts," *Journal of Portfolio Management*, Fall, pp. 72–81.

Fuller, R.J., and C. Hsia (1984), "A Simplified Common Stock Valuation Model," *Financial Analysts Journal*, No. 40, pp. 49–56.

Gordon, M., and E. Shapiro (1956), "Capital Equipment Analysis: The Required Rate of Profit," *Management Science*, 3, October, pp. 102–110.

Grullón, G., and D. Ikenberry (2000), "What do we know about Stock Repurchases?" *Journal of Applied Corporate Finance*, Volume 13, Number 1, pp. 31–51.

Guay, W., and J. Harford (2000), "The Cash-Flow Permanence and Information Content of Dividend Increases Versus Repurchases," *Journal of Financial Economics*, Vol. 57, Issue 3, September.

Hurley, W.J., and L.D. Johnson (1994), "A Realistic Dividend Valuation Model," *Financial Analysts Journal*, July/August, pp. 50–54.

Ikenberry, D, J. Lakonishok, and T. Vermaelen (1994), "Market Underreaction to Open Market Share Repurchases," National Bureau of Economic Research Working Paper No. W4965.

Kahle, K. M. (2001), "When a Buyback isn't a Buyback: Open Market Repurchases and Employee Options," Social Science Research Network (SSRN) Working Paper No. 273041, *Journal of Financial Economics*, forthcoming.

Kalay et al. (1999), *Dividend Policy: Its Impact on Firm Value*, Harvard Business School Press.

Yao, Yulin (1997), "A Trinomial Dividend Valuation Model," *The Journal of Portfolio Management*, Vol. 23, No. 4, Summer, pp. 99–103.

Chapter 7

Interest Rates: Their Importance in the Valuation

Interest rates have a considerable bearing on share prices. Any investor's experience shows that, in general, when interest rates fall, share prices rise, and vice versa.

In this chapter, we will begin by observing the evolution of interest rates in recent years in the United States and other countries, followed by the evolution of interest rates with different maturities. We will then show the relationship between the evolution of interest rates and the S&P 500 and the relationship between interest rates and the PER. We will also show the relationship between interest rates and the dividend yield.

7.1. EVOLUTION OF INTEREST RATES

Figure 7.1 shows the evolution of the interest rates on 10-year Government bonds in the United States, Japan, Spain, and Germany. It can be seen that interest rates in the United States have fallen from 9% in early 1989 to 5% in mid-1993. Subsequently, interest rates rose to 8% by the end of 1995, from that point, interest rates have varied within a two-point band until they reached 5.5% in June 2001. The evolution of interest rates has been similar in the United States and Germany. Interest rates in Spain were substantially higher than those of the other countries until 1997.

In June 2001, the 10-year risk-free interest rates in the United States and the European countries were around 5.5%. Another interesting point is the convergence of interest rates in Spain and Germany, both member countries of the European Monetary Union (EMU).

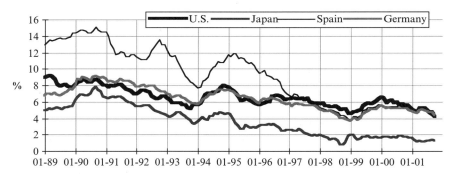

Figure 7.1 Evolution of the yields on 10-year government bonds in the United States, Japan, Spain, and Germany. (Yield on 10-year government bonds.) (*Source*: Datastream.)

Figure 7.2 compares the evolution of interest rates in the United States with the evolution of interest rates in three European countries: Italy, France, and the United Kingdom. It is seen that interest rates in the United States have been below those of the United Kingdom and France until mid-1996, and a long way from the Italian interest rates, with spreads of up to 9%. It can also be seen that, after the early months of 1995, interest rates have fallen both in Italy and in France, while they have held relatively constant in the United Kingdom. This figure also shows the convergence of interest rates in the EMU member countries.

7.2. INTEREST RATES WITH DIFFERENT MATURITIES (YIELD CURVE)

In this section, we will talk about the interest rate curve, which is simply the representation of the interest rates available for different maturities. Figure 7.3 shows the evolution of interest rates in the United States for three different maturities: a very short-term interest rate (the 3-month T-Bills), a medium-term interest rate (the 3-year Government bonds), and a long-term interest rate (the 30-year Government bonds). This figure also shows that all of these interest rates move uniformly, while maintaining differences between each other. For example, in 1991, medium- and short-term interest rates fell sharply—as did long-term interest rates, although less so—and recovered in 1994.

Figure 7.4 shows the evolution of what is usually called the yield curve in the United States. This figure describes the changes that have taken place in the yield curve in the United States from December 1990–June 2001. It also

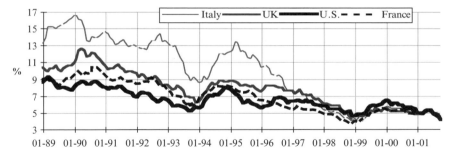

Figure 7.2   Evolution of 10-year interest rates in the United States, Italy, France, and the United Kingdom. (Yield on 10-year government bonds.) (*Source*: Datastream.)

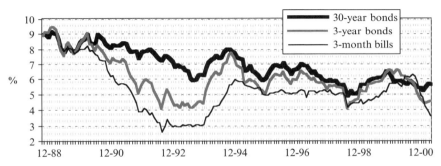

Figure 7.3   Evolution of the yields on U.S. Treasuries: 3 months, 3 years, and 30 years. (*Source*: Datastream.)

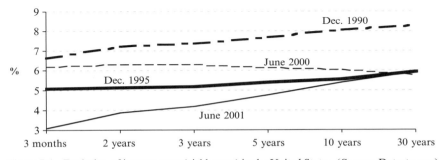

Figure 7.4   Evolution of interest rates (yield curve) in the United States. (*Source*: Datastream.)

shows that, in general, the longer term interest rates have been higher than the shorter term interest rates, although this was not the case in June 2000. From December 1995 until June 2001 there was a significant fall in short-term interest rates, although without any significant differences in the long-term interest rates (10–30 years).

7.3. RELATIONSHIP BETWEEN INTEREST RATES AND SHARE PRICES

Figure 7.5 shows the relationship between share prices (as represented by the S&P 500) and the 30-year interest rates in the United States. Normally, there is a negative correlation between interest rates and share prices, which means that when interest rates fall, share prices rise, and vice versa. This correlation is very clear during the period June 1997–October 1998, when interest rates fell from 7–5% and the S&P 500 rose from 800 to 1,000 points. Note the positive correlation in 1994, 1996, and 1997 and after January 1999: the two curves' movements are parallel.

7.4. RELATIONSHIP BETWEEN INTEREST RATES AND THE PER

We already saw in Figure 3.3 that when interest rates fall, the PER normally increases, and vice versa.

Figure 7.6 shows the relationship between the reciprocal of the S&P 500 PER and the yield on 30-year T-bonds in the United States. Again a strong parallelism is seen between the reciprocal of the PER and the interest rates.

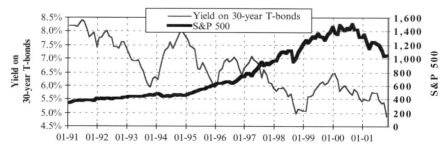

Figure 7.5 Evolution of the 30-year interest rates in the United States and the S&P 500. (*Source*: Datastream.)

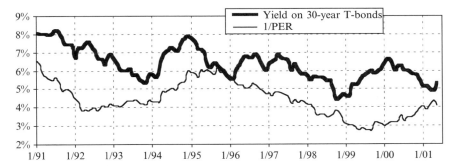

Figure 7.6   Evolution of interest rates and reciprocal of the S&P 500 PER. (*Source*: Datastream.)

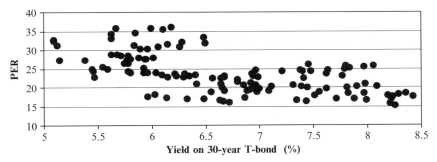

Figure 7.7   Relationship between interest rates and the PER of the U.S. stock market (1991–2000). (*Source*: Datastream.)

This relationship is to be expected as the PER is the share price divided by the earnings per share, and the reciprocal of the PER is the earnings per share divided by the share price.

Figure 7.7 shows the relationship between the 30-year interest rates and the PER of the U.S. stock market. Note that there is an inverse relationship: generally speaking, the higher the interest rates, the lower the PER and vice versa, although this relationship is not exact. This means that the PER and share prices are not only affected by interest rates, but there are also other factors that also influence the PER and the share price.

7.5. RELATIONSHIP BETWEEN INTEREST RATES AND DIVIDEND YIELD IN THE UNITED STATES

Figure 7.8 shows the relationship between the S&P 500 dividend yield and 30-year interest rates. Again, a strong parallelism is observed; also, the dividend yield has always been less than the yield on 30-year Government bonds. The correlation between the yield on 30-year Government bonds and the dividend yield during the period 1991–2001 was 85%; however, the correlation between the increase in the yield on 30-year Government bonds and the increase in the dividend yield was 21% in the same period.

Figure 7.8 shows that, in general, it is never worthwhile to buy shares purely for the dividends, as the dividend yield is less than the yield on 30-year Government bonds. An investor who buys shares must necessarily hope for their price to increase as dividends alone give a yield below the yield he would obtain if he were to invest in government debt.

7.6. EQUITY DURATION

The duration of a share is a parameter that measures the price's sensitivity to changes in the interest rate. Thus, a duration of 8 years means that if interest rates increase 1% (for example, from 6–7%) the share price falls 8%. Likewise, if interest rates fall 1% (for example, from 6–5%) the share's price increases 8%.

Figure 7.9 shows the duration of the S&P 500 in recent years[1]. It is a parameter that varies considerably over time and depends on the interest rate

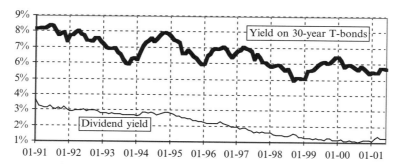

Figure 7.8   Evolution of the yield on 30-year Government bonds and the dividend yield in the United States.

[1]The simplest way of calculating the duration is by performing a regression between the index's yield and the variation in interest rates: $\Delta P/P = a + \text{duration} \, \Delta R/(1 + R)$, where P is the price, ΔP is the variation in the price, and R is the interest rate. a and duration are the parameters obtained in the regression.

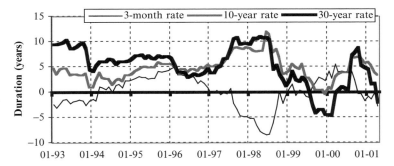

Figure 7.9 Duration of the S&P 500. Calculated using monthly data from the last two years. (*Source*: Datastream.)

used to measure it. In Figure 7.9, the duration has been calculated using the interest rates of two years. The duration calculated with all the data (1991–2001) was 0.3 (3-month), 4.7 (10-year), and 5.1 (30-year).

Using the Gordon and Shapiro formula, some authors conclude that a share's modified duration must be[2] $1/(Ke - g)$. However, the future growth of dividends is also affected by variations in interest rates. And if interest rates increase 1%, Ke normally increases more than 1%.

Leibowitz and Kogelman (1993) provide a solution to the paradox: while, according to many authors, the equity duration should range between 7 and 20 years, the durations calculated empirically are between 2 and 6 years. Any reader interested in equity duration is recommended to read this article, as it provides considerable help in understanding this concept.

7.7. RELATIONSHIP BETWEEN THE YIELD OF THE S&P 500 AND THE VARIATION IN INTEREST RATES

The correlation should be negative as when interest rates rise, the S&P 500 return is usually negative, and when interest rates fall, the S&P 500 return is usually positive.

The correlation is a very interesting parameter because it enables us to know what percentage of the S&P 500 return is due to changes in the interest rates. Thus, for example, a correlation of -20% (R = 0.2) implies that its square (R^2) is 0.04. This indicates that the variations in the interest rates account for the 4% yield of the S&P 500. Likewise, a correlation of -40%

---

[2]This is based on assuming $\partial P / \partial Ke = -DPA/(Ke - g)^2$

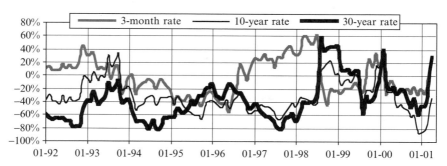

Figure 7.10   Correlation (monthly data from the previous year) between the S&P 500 return and the increase of risk-free interest rates. (*Source*: Datastream.)

means that the variations in the interest rate account for 16% of the S&P 500 return. During 1995, the correlation using monthly data was about −90%. This means that using monthly data, the variations in the interest rates accounted for approximately 81% of the S&P 500 return.

Figure 7.10 shows the correlation between the S&P 500 return and the variation in interest rates with different maturities using monthly data from the previous year. A first point to make is that, during several periods (1992, 1993, June 1996–June 1998, July–December 1999, and 2001), the correlation with short-term interest rates was positive, which means that, on average, when interest rates rise, the share price also rises, and vice versa. With long-term interest rates, more logical correlations, i.e., negative correlations, are more frequently obtained. The figure also shows how the correlation between the S&P 500 return and the variations in the interest rates is much higher with long-term interest rates (10 and 30 years) than with short-term interest rates (3 months).

The correlation calculated with all the data (1991–2001) was −1.7% (3-month), −25.1% (10-year), and − 25.2% (30-year).

7.8. RISK AND REQUIRED RETURN TO DIFFERENT DEBT ISSUES

Table 7.1 contains the definitions of the ratings used by the two leading credit rating agencies: Moody's and Standard and Poor's.

Throughout the chapter, we have only used risk-free interest rates, that is, interest rates for different maturities in bonds issued by governments. Figure 7.11 shows the costs of corporate debt depending on its maturity and quality.

Table 7.1

Rating Definitions

Moody's		Standard and Poor's	
Aaa	Exceptional financial security.	AAA	Extremely strong capacity to meet its financial commitments.
Aa	Excellent financial security. Together with the Aaa group, they constitute what are generally known as high-grade entities. Rated lower than Aaa-rated entities because long-term risks appear somewhat larger.	AA	Very strong capacity to meet its financial commitments. It differs from the highest rated obligors only in a small degree.
A	Good financial security. However elements may be present which suggest a susceptibility to impairment sometime in the future.	A	Strong capacity to meet its financial commitments but is somewhat more susceptible to the adverse effects of changes in circumstances and economic conditions than obligors in higher-rated categories.
Baa	Adequate financial security. However, certain protective elements may be lacking or may be unreliable over any great period of time.	BBB	Adequate capacity to meet its financial commitments. However, adverse economic conditions or changing circumstances are more likely to lead to a weakened capacity of the obligor to meet its financial commitments.
Ba	Questionable financial security. Often the ability of these entities to meet obligations may be moderate and not well safeguarded in the future.	BB	Less vulnerable in the near term than other lower rated obligors. However, it faces major ongoing uncertainties and its exposure to adverse business, financial, or economic conditions, which could lead to the obligor's inadequate capacity to meet its financial commitments.
B	Poor financial security. Assurance of payment of obligations over any long period of time is small.	B	More vulnerable to nonpayment than obligations rated "BB", but the obligor currently has the capacity to meet its financial commitment on the obligation. Adverse business, financial, or economic conditions will likely impair the obligor's capacity or will to meet its financial commitments.
Caa	Very poor financial security. They may be in default on their obligations or there may be present elements of danger with respect to punctual payment of obligations.	CCC	Currently vulnerable, and is dependent upon favorable business, financial, and economic conditions to meet its financial commitments.

(*continues*)

Table 7.1 (*continued*)

Moody's		Standard and Poor's	
Ca	Extremely poor financial security. Such entities are often in default on their obligations or have other marked shortcomings.	CC	Currently highly vulnerable.
C	Lowest-rated class of entity, are usually in default on their obligations, and potential recovery values are low.	C	Currently highly vulnerable to nonpayment. The "C" rating may be used to cover a situation where a bankruptcy petition has been filed or similar action taken, but payments on this obligation are being continued.
		R	Under regulatory supervision owing to its financial condition.
		D	Has failed to pay one or more of its financial obligations (rated or unrated) when it came due.
	Moody's applies numerical modifiers 1, 2, and 3 in each generic rating category from Aa to Caa. The modifier 1 indicates that the issuer is in the higher end of its letter-rating category.		Plus (+) or minus (−) The ratings from "AA" to "CCC" may be modified by the addition of a plus or minus sign to show relative standing within the major rating categories.
			Obligors rated "BB", "B", "CCC", and "CC" are regarded as having significant speculative characteristics. "BB" indicates the least degree of speculation and "CC" the highest.

Sources: moodys.com and standardandpoors.com.

The bottom line shows the yield of U.S. Government bonds for different maturities, and the other lines show the cost of corporate debt depending on the respective companies' credit rating. Companies with an AAA rating have debt with minimum risk. Consequently, their required return (cost) is only slightly above that of Government debt. Of the debt shown in Figure 7.11, the lowest quality is rated B and, logically, demands a higher return.

Table 7.2 contains the bond default spread according to rating and maturity in September 2001. The default spread is the difference between the interest rate on a corporate bond and the interest on a Treasury bond having the same maturity.

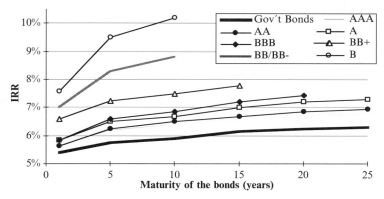

Figure 7.11   Yield curve of the debt of U.S. industrial corporations with different ratings and maturities, 13 November 1997. (*Source*: Standard & Poor's Fixed-Income research.)

Table 7.2

Bond Default Spread According to Rating and Maturity

Rating	1 year	2 year	3 year	5 year	7 year	10 year	30 year
Aaa/AAA	0.44%	0.57%	0.64%	0.80%	1.01%	1.18%	1.38%
Aa1/AA+	0.55%	0.69%	0.75%	0.99%	1.12%	1.25%	1.45%
Aa2/AA	0.57%	0.74%	0.78%	1.03%	1.17%	1.31%	1.51%
Aa3/AA−	0.59%	0.77%	0.81%	1.06%	1.22%	1.37%	1.57%
A1/A+	0.71%	0.82%	0.87%	1.13%	1.31%	1.49%	1.69%
A2/A	0.74%	0.84%	0.89%	1.15%	1.33%	1.51%	1.72%
A3/A−	0.77%	0.86%	0.91%	1.18%	1.36%	1.54%	1.75%
Baa1/BBB+	1.02%	1.20%	1.27%	1.55%	1.88%	2.20%	2.41%
Baa2/BBB	1.09%	1.28%	1.35%	1.60%	1.91%	2.25%	2.46%
Baa3/BBB−	1.14%	1.33%	1.40%	1.65%	1.96%	2.30%	2.51%
Ba1/BB+	3.00%	3.10%	3.20%	3.30%	3.50%	3.70%	3.90%
Ba2/BB	3.10%	3.20%	3.30%	3.40%	3.60%	3.80%	4.00%
Ba3/BB−	3.20%	3.30%	3.40%	3.50%	3.70%	3.90%	4.10%
B1/B+	5.80%	5.90%	6.00%	6.30%	6.70%	7.10%	7.60%
B2/B	5.90%	6.00%	6.10%	6.40%	6.80%	7.20%	7.70%
B3/B−	6.00%	6.10%	6.20%	6.50%	6.90%	7.30%	7.80%
Caa/CCC	8.05%	8.15%	8.25%	8.50%	8.90%	9.40%	9.90%

The default spread is the difference between the interest rate on a corporate bond and the interest on a Treasury bond having the same maturity.
Source: www.bondsonline.com, 15 September 2001.

7.9. RATES OF THE FEDERAL RESERVE (UNITED STATES) AND THE EUROPEAN CENTRAL BANK (GERMANY BEFORE 1998)

Figure 7.12 shows the evolution of the year-end leading rates of the Federal Reserve (United States) and the European Central Bank (Germany before 1998) during the period 1990–2001.

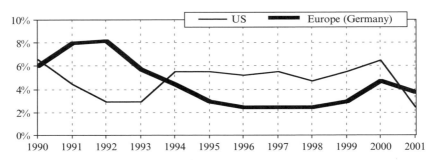

Figure 7.12 Year-end interest rates of the Federal Reserve (United States) and the European Central Bank (Germany before 1998).

REFERENCE

Leibowitz, M. L., and S. Kogelman (1993), "Resolving the Equity Duration Paradox," *Financial Analysts Journal*, January–February.

Chapter 8

Valuation Using Multiples. How Do Analysts Reach their Conclusions?

This chapter focuses on equity valuation using multiples. The basic conclusion is that multiples almost always have a broad dispersion, which is why valuations performed using multiples are almost always highly debatable. We agree with Damodaran (2001, page 253) who says "a biased analyst who is allowed to choose the multiple on which the valuation is based and to pick the comparable firms can essentially ensure that almost any value can be justified."

However, multiples are useful in a second stage of the valuation: after performing the valuation using another method, a comparison with the multiples of comparable firms enables us to gauge the valuation performed and identify differences between the firm valued and the firms it is compared with.

8.1. VALUATION METHODS USED BY THE ANALYSTS

Figure 8.1 shows the valuation methods[1] most widely used by Morgan Stanley Dean Witter's analysts for valuing European companies. Surprisingly, the discounted cash flow (DCF) is in fifth place, behind multiples such as the PER, the EV/EBITDA, and the EV/EG.

Defond and Hung (2001) report that only 7% of the 34,787 earnings forecasts done by analysts about U.S. companies from 1993 through 1999 included cash flow forecasts. But the proportion of earnings forecasts that also included a cash flow forecast increased from 1% in 1993 to 15% in 1999.

---

[1]Weighted by the market capitalization of the industry in which it is applied.

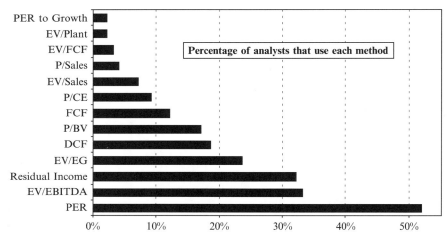

Figure 8.1 Most widely used valuation methods. (*Source*: Morgan Stanley Dean Witter Research.)

8.2. MOST COMMONLY USED MULTIPLES

Although, as Figure 8.1 shows, the PER and the EV/EBITDA seem to be the most popular multiples for valuing firms (the most used and misused), it is also true that, depending on the industry being analyzed, certain multiples are more appropriate than others.

Table 8.1 Shows the Most commonly used multiples.

Table 8.1
Most Commonly Used Multiples

P/E, PER	Price earnings ratio	P/output	Price to output
P/CE	Price to cash earnings	EV/EBITDA	Enterprise value to EBITDA
P/S	Price to sales	EV/S	Enterprise value to sales
P/LFCF	Price to levered free cash flow	EV/FCF	Enterprise value to unlevered free cash flow
P/BV	Price to book value	EV/BV	Enterprise value to book value
P/AV	Price to asset value	PEG	Price earnings (PER) to growth
P/Customer	Price to customer	EV/EG	Enterprise value to EBITDA growth
P/units	Price to units		

The multiples can be divided into three groups[2]:

1. Multiples based on the company's capitalization (equity value: E).
2. Multiples based on the company's value (equity value and debt value: E + D).[3]
3. Growth-referenced multiples.

8.2.1. MULTIPLES BASED ON CAPITALIZATION

The price- or capitalization-based multiples have the advantage of being very easy to understand and calculate.

8.2.1.a. Price-Earnings Ratio (PER)

PER = market capitalization/total net income =
share price/earnings per share

Sometimes, the mean of last or next few years' earnings is used.

8.2.1.b. Price to Cash Earnings (P/CE)

P/CE = market capitalization/
(net income before depreciation and amortization)

8.2.1.c. Price to Sales (P/S)

P/S = market capitalization/sales = Share price/sales per share

[2]Morgan Stanley Dean Witters Report, *How We Value Stocks*, 15 September 1999.
[3]The value of the firm (E + D) is often called enterprise value (EV). However, the initials are also used sometimes to indicate the value of the shares (equity value).

This multiple compares sales with capitalization (the shares' value) only. However, sales are attributable to all the company's stakeholders: shareholders, creditors, pensioners, Inland Revenue, etc. As we will see in the next chapter, this multiple is often used to value Internet companies, etc., and also telecommunications infrastructure companies, bus companies, and pharmacies.

8.2.1.d. Price to Levered Free Cash Flow (P/LFCF)

P/LFCF = Market capitalization/(operating income after interest and tax + depreciation + amortization − increased working capital requirements − investments in existing businesses[4]).

One variant of this multiple is the P/FAD (funds available for distribution).

8.2.1.e. Price to Book Value (P/BV)

P/BV = market capitalization/
book value of shareholder's equity

We saw in Chapter 4 that in a firm with constant growth g, the relationship between market value and book value is

$$P/BV = (ROE - g)/(Ke - g)$$

This multiple is often used to value banks. Other industries that use P/BV or its derivatives are the paper and pulp industry, real estate and insurance. One variant of this multiple for the insurance industry is the capitalization/ *embedded value* (shareholder's equity + present value of the future cash flows on signed insurance contracts).

---

[4]"Investments in existing businesses" are those in businesses that the company already has. They do not include growth-oriented investments, either for new businesses or to increase capacity.

8.2.1.f. Price to Customer

P/Customer = market capitalization/number of customers

This multiple is very commonly used to value cellular phone and Internet companies.

8.2.1.g. Price to Units

This multiple is often used to value soft drinks and consumer product companies.

8.2.1.h. Price to Output

This multiple is used to value cement and commodities companies.

8.2.1.i. Price to Potential Customer

As we will see in the next chapter, some analysts use this multiple to value Internet companies.

8.2.2. MULTIPLES BASED ON THE COMPANY'S VALUE

These multiples are similar to those in the previous section, but instead of dividing the market capitalization by another parameter, they use the sum of the firm's market capitalization and financial debt. This sum is usually called the enterprise value (EV).[5]

1. *Enterprise value to EBITDA (EV/EBITDA)*

EV/EBITDA = enterprise value/earnings before interest,
tax, depreciation, and amortization

---

[5]If there are preferred shares and minority interests, the enterprise value is market capitalization + preferred shares + minority interests + net debt.

This is one of the most widely used multiples by analysts. However, the EBITDA (earnings before interest, tax, depreciation, and amortization) has a number of limitations, including[6]:

1. It does not include the changes in the working capital requirements (WCR).
2. It does not consider capital investments.

2. *Enterprise value to sales (EV/sales)*

$$EV/Sales = \text{Enterprise value/Sales}$$

3. *Enterprise value to unlevered free cash flow (EV/FCF)*

$$EV/FCF = \text{enterprise value/(earnings before interest and after}$$
$$\text{tax} + \text{depreciation} + \text{amortization} - \text{increased working capital}$$
$$\text{requirements} - \text{capital investments}[7]).$$

8.2.3. GROWTH-REFERENCED MULTIPLES

1. *PEG—PER to EPS growth.*

$$PEG = PER/g = PER/\text{growth of earnings}$$
$$\text{per share in the next few years}$$

This multiple is mainly used in growth industries, such as luxury goods, health and technology.

[6]For a good report on the limitations of the EBITDA, see *Putting EBITDA in Perspective*, Moody's Investors Service, June 2000.

[7]Sometimes recurrent *free cash flow* is used as well. In this case, investments in existing businesses are considered.

2. *EV/EG—Enterprise value to EBITDA growth.*

EV/ EG = EV/EBITDA (historic)/growth of
EBITDA in the next few years

As with the previous multiple, it is mainly used in growth industries, particularly health, technology and telecommunications.

8.3. RELATIVE MULTIPLES

All of these multiples by themselves can tell us very little. They need to be placed in a context. There are basically three relative valuations:

1. With respect to the firm's own history
2. With respect to the market
3. With respect to the industry

   1. *With respect to the firm's history.*

History-referenced multiple = multiple/
mean of recent years' multiple

One problem with historic multiples is that they depend on exogenous factors, such as interest rates and stock market situation. In addition, the composition and nature of many firms' businesses changes substantially over time, so it does not make much sense to compare them with previous years.

   2. *With respect to the market.*

Market-referenced multiple = firm multiple/
market multiple

3. *With respect to the industry.*

> Industry-referenced multiple = firm multiple/
> industry multiple

This comparison with the industry is more appropriate than the two previous comparisons. However, one problem is that when the industry is overvalued, all of the companies in it are overvalued: clear examples of this situation were the Internet companies up to 2000. We shall also see in Section 8.4 that the multiples of companies operating in the same industry normally have a very wide dispersion.

Table 8.2 is a summary of the most commonly used multiples for valuing different industries.

Table 8.3 shows the average multiple of different industries in the U.S. stock market in September 2000. The total number of companies analyzed was 5,903.

Liu, Nissim, and Thomas (2001) find that multiples derived from forward earnings perform the best and that multiples derived from sales perform the worst.

8.4. THE PROBLEM WITH MULTIPLES: THEIR DISPERSION

8.4.1. DISPERSION OF THE UTILITIES' MULTIPLES

Table 8.4 shows multiples used to value European utilities. Table 8.5 concentrates solely on English utilities. Note the multiples' wide dispersion in all cases.

8.4.2. DISPERSION OF THE MULTIPLES OF CONSTRUCTION AND HOTEL COMPANIES

Table 8.6 shows different multiples for construction and building materials companies in Europe, America, Asia, and Spain. Table 8.7 contains multiples for hotel companies

Table 8.2

Most Commonly Used Multiples in Different Industries

Industry	Subsector	Most commonly used multiples
Automobiles	Manufactures	P/S
	Components	P/CE relative and P/S
Banks		P/BV
Base materials	Paper	P/BV
	Chemicals	EV/EBITDA, EV/S, and P/CE
	Metals and mining	P/LFCF and EV/EBITDA
Building and construction		P/LFCF, EV/FCF, PER, and EV/EBITDA
Business services		EV/EBITDA, ROCE, P/LFCF, PER, and PER to growth
Capital goods	Engineering	PER, EV/EBITDA, and EV/S
	Defense	PER, EV/EBITDA, and EV/S
Food, drink, and tobacco	Food Producers	EV/EBITDA and EV/CE
	Brewers and pubs	ROCE, PER to growth, and PER relative
	Alcoholic beverages	EV/EBITDA
	Tobacco	ROCE
Healthcare		PER, PER relative to S&P, and EV/EBITDA
Insurance		P/AV
Leisure		EV/EBITDA
Media		PER relative and EV/EBITDA
Oil and Gas	Integrated	PER and EV/CE
Real estate		P/FAD, EV/EBITDA, and P/NAV
Retail and consumer goods	Clothing	PER relative to market and sector, EV/EBITDA
	Food	PER relative
	Luxury goods	PER, PER to growth, EV/S, and EV/E to EBITDA growth
Technology	Software, equipment, and semiconductors	PER and PER relative
Telecom		EV/E to EBITDA growth, EV/S, and P/customer
Transport	Air	EV/EBITDA
	Travelers through road	P/S
Utilities		PER and P/CE

Table 8.3

Mean Multiples of different American industries, September 2000

Industry	PER	P/S	EV/S	P/BV	EV/BV	EV/EBITDA	PEG	ROE	ROC	Payout	Beta	Dividend yield	Volatility	Capitalization (nm)
Air transport	12.0	0.4	0.7	1.8	1.6	3.8	1.0	13.9%	15.3%	10.7%	1.1	0.98%	53.1%	64
Auto & truck	14.7	0.7	1.4	2.1	1.5	4.9	1.0	12.6%	12.5%	28.7%	0.9	1.15%	45.8%	378
Bank	12.2	NA	NA	2.2	2.1	4.0	1.1	18.9%	28.1%	38.1%	0.8	3.28%	32.5%	524
Beverage (soft drink)	39.8	3.5	3.9	9.4	5.4	13.4	2.6	22.1%	19.6%	46.5%	0.8	0.68%	38.3%	236
Chemical (diversified)	24.0	2.0	2.4	4.0	2.7	7.4	1.6	15.7%	16.7%	44.2%	0.8	1.51%	39.7%	183
Computer & peripherals	75.8	3.9	3.9	12.5	12.9	25.2	2.7	18.3%	24.5%	9.2%	1.1	0.06%	88.8%	1,418
Computer software & svcs	73.1	7.3	7.1	12.6	17.5	25.3	2.3	19.2%	33.4%	4.3%	1.0	0.09%	91.1%	1,223
Drug	59.0	9.2	9.3	14.3	13.6	27.2	2.1	23.9%	28.3%	48.2%	0.9	0.08%	95.6%	1,490
Electric utility (east)	13.2	1.0	1.9	1.7	1.3	5.3	1.6	13.5%	11.7%	70.6%	0.5	4.83%	30.1%	137
Electrical equipment	43.8	4.3	4.4	9.5	8.2	23.9	2.2	22.9%	17.9%	40.9%	0.9	0.68%	76.5%	650
Electronics	110.8	2.8	2.9	8.2	7.3	27.8	4.5	10.9%	12.4%	9.2%	0.9	0.19%	75.4%	260
Entertainment	125.8	2.8	3.3	2.8	2.2	11.1	5.7	2.5%	7.9%	17.9%	0.9	0.16%	70.0%	306
Financial services	21.3	5.7	7.6	3.6	2.4	8.0	1.3	17.7%	17.4%	18.9%	0.9	1.36%	48.8%	784
Food processing	14.0	0.8	0.9	2.3	2.4	5.3	1.1	15.0%	19.9%	42.0%	0.7	1.61%	41.8%	247
Foreign electron/entertn	342.6	2.6	2.7	3.2	3.3	8.9	20.2	2.8%	11.8%	122.6%	0.9	1.50%	42.6%	437
Foreign telecom.	82.3	9.9	10.6	10.8	6.8	17.3	5.2	10.3%	19.1%	49.8%	1.1	1.23%	45.7%	1,765
Household products	20.8	1.8	2.0	7.1	4.0	8.2	1.4	35.0%	24.4%	39.2%	0.8	1.23%	43.4%	172
Insurance (life)	14.9	NA	NA	2.2	2.1	4.2	1.4	15.0%	31.6%	23.6%	0.9	1.43%	42.4%	125
Internet	NA	26.7	26.1	16.2	26.4	NA	NA	-18.3%	-13.0%	0.0%	2.0	0.00%	134.0%	672

(continues)

Table 8.3 (*continued*)

Industry	PER	P/S	EV/S	P/BV	EV/BV	EV/ EBITDA	PEG	ROE	ROC	Payout	Beta	Dividend yield	Volatility	Capitalization (mm)
Medical services	21.8	0.7	0.8	2.3	2.1	6.5	1.0	10.0%	14.1%	8.2%	0.9	0.18%	76.1%	136
Medical supplies	34.9	2.2	2.3	7.3	5.8	14.8	1.6	21.7%	20.9%	27.8%	0.8	0.16%	73.2%	442
Natural gas (diversified)	36.4	1.2	1.6	3.6	2.1	9.1	2.0	12.1%	10.4%	46.0%	0.7	2.73%	44.8%	142
Newspaper	37.9	2.8	3.3	4.4	3.2	11.1	3.2	12.6%	13.6%	33.6%	0.8	1.40%	38.8%	142
Petroleum (integrated)	23.6	1.2	1.3	3.0	2.6	6.4	1.6	12.3%	17.4%	68.6%	0.8	2.43%	40.3%	973
Retail building supply	41.6	2.0	2.0	7.1	6.3	18.8	2.8	18.0%	17.9%	9.6%	0.9	0.43%	42.9%	136
Retail store	26.9	0.8	1.0	4.5	2.9	10.2	1.8	16.8%	13.8%	18.7%	1.1	1.06%	45.0%	373
Securities brokerage	18.9	1.7	3.0	4.4	2.0	5.4	1.1	27.4%	19.8%	11.6%	1.2	1.20%	62.5%	271
Semiconductor	80.9	8.6	8.5	11.3	13.6	25.7	2.7	18.8%	26.5%	6.8%	1.3	0.01%	90.7%	978
Semiconductor cap equip	86.8	9.2	8.9	13.6	25.4	40.6	3.2	26.2%	33.6%	0.0%	1.8	0.00%	72.0%	108
Telecom. equipment	122.0	6.1	6.2	11.0	9.5	30.3	3.8	9.9%	15.1%	7.5%	1.1	0.02%	98.7%	489
Telecom. services	111.3	4.2	4.8	4.6	3.2	11.2	3.7	2.8%	11.4%	87.2%	1.2	0.24%	83.9%	1,120
Tobacco	8.6	0.7	0.8	3.8	2.8	4.5	1.1	43.6%	31.1%	55.2%	0.6	5.61%	48.8%	89
Total market	34.6	2.2	2.6	4.6	3.1	9.6	1.7	14.4%	15.9%	35.0%	0.9	**1.14%**	**60.5%**	20,057

Source: Damodaran (2001).

Table 8.4

Multiples of European Utilities (Excluding the English Utilities), September 2000

	PER		P/CE		Dividend yield (%)		EV/EBITDA		P/BV
	1999	2000E	1999	2000E	1999	2000E	1999	2000E	1999
EVN	−5.9	14.4	3.8	5.3	2.2	2.4	6.4	7.7	1.4
Verbund	32.6		8.9		1.2		11.8		3.7
Electrabel	15.0	15.1	7.4	7.7	5.6	5.8	8.5	8.2	2.8
Fortum	4.3	10.0	6.1	3.7	4.7	4.5	6.1	6.3	0.6
Vivendi	32.2		9.7		1.9		13.7		4.7
Suez LdE	27.2	24.5	6.8	7.0	2.7	2.9	9.7	8.3	2.4
RWE	19.4	18.4	4.9	4.7	3.6	3.9	4.7	4.5	3.4
E.ON	14.0	10.6	5.8	8.0	3.1	3.4	7.7	7.9	1.8
Edison	32.5	31.6	13.4	13.3	1.3	1.4	11.8	10.4	3.6
ENEL	22.8	25.6	7.7	8.9	2.7	3.0	7.3	8.6	7.9
EDP	21.0	19.2	8.4	8.2	3.9	4.2	9.3	9.3	1.8
Agbar	18.6	16.2	9.5	8.2	1.8	2.0	10.9	8.9	2.1
Endesa	18.1		5.7		2.7		10.6		2.5
Iberdrola	17.6		7.1		3.6		8.6		1.6
Unión Fenosa	10.6	23.4	11.0	10.5	1.7	2.1	7.5	6.9	2.3
Hidrocantábrico	21.2	18.6	9.3	8.5	2.6	2.8	9.6	8.5	2.2
REE	19.6	18.4	8.8	8.4	3.4	3.7	6.7	6.5	2.1
Sydkraft A	14.8	13.3	7.6	7.0	3.3	3.4	6.2	5.9	1.4
Average	18.6	18.5	7.9	7.8	2.9	3.3	8.7	7.7	2.7
Maximum	*32.6*	*31.6*	*13.4*	*13.3*	*5.6*	*5.8*	*13.7*	*10.4*	*7.9*
Minimum	*−5.9*	*10.0*	*3.8*	*3.7*	*1.2*	*1.4*	*4.7*	*4.5*	*0.6*

Source: Morgan Stanley Dean Witter Research.

8.4.3. DISPERSION OF THE MULTIPLES
OF TELECOMMUNICATIONS

Table 8.8 shows the leading telecommunications operators divided by geographical area. In the case of North America, Europe, and Latin America, it can be seen that the PER is the multiple with the most dispersion, particularly for the year 2000E, ranging between 13.5–73, 12.2–63.6, and 14.9–45.1,

Table 8.5

Multiples of English Utilities, September 2000

	PER		P/CE		Dividend yield (%)		EV/EBITDA		P/BV
	2000	2001E	2000	2001E	2000	2001E	2000	2001E	2000
British Energy	7.4	−26.1	1.8	2.4	4.6	4.6	4.4	5.7	0.8
National Grid	25.0	29.8	17.2	14.7	2.3	2.5	11.6	11.4	4.5
National Power	12.8	14.7	7.6	8.9	3.2	3.4	8.1	10.0	3.3
PowerGen	8.9	7.4	5.7	5.1	6.2	6.8	6.9	6.3	1.9
Scottish Power	7.3	18.2	7.8	8.7	4.7	5.0	9.1	7.6	1.5
Scottish & Southern	12.3	12.4	9.0	8.9	4.9	5.1	7.5	7.6	2.9
Anglian Water	9.6	12.0	5.5	5.8	7.4	7.6	6.9	7.1	1.0
Hyder	5.2	5.0	2.1	2.2	5.6	5.9	5.9	5.2	0.6
Kelda	6.8	10.6	4.0	4.8	6.5	6.9	6.7	7.1	0.8
Pennon	7.7	11.9	5.3	6.3	7.2	5.4	6.9	7.9	1.0
Severn Trent	9.9	10.9	4.4	4.9	6.2	6.5	6.9	6.3	1.0
Thames	12.5	27.7	7.8	11.7	3.9	4.1	7.8	8.6	1.9
United Utilities	8.4	12.1	5.0	6.0	6.5	6.7	6.8	7.3	1.5
Average	10.3	11.3	6.4	7.0	5.3	5.4	7.3	7.5	1.7
Maximum	*25.0*	*29.8*	*17.2*	*14.7*	*7.4*	*7.6*	*11.6*	*11.4*	*4.5*
Minimum	*5.2*	*−26.1*	*1.8*	*2.2*	*2.3*	*2.5*	*4.4*	*5.2*	*0.6*

Source: Morgan Stanley Dean Witter Research.

respectively. In the case of Asia, the differences are substantial in all multiples, particularly the EV/EBITDA, which ranges between 3.4 and 136.7 (for 2000E) and 3.1 and 117.1 (for 2001E), and the P/CE, with data between 3.2–196.9 and 2.9–171.4 for 2000E and 2001E, respectively.

Table 8.9 shows multiples for cellular phone companies. Note, again, the multiples' wide dispersion.

8.4.4. DISPERSION OF THE MULTIPLES OF BANKS

Table 8.10 shows multiples for Spanish and Portuguese banks in November 2000. The PER in 2000 ranges between 10.4 and 30.9, the price to book value multiple ranges between 1.5 and 4.7, and the ROE ranges between 12.9

Table 8.6

Multiples of Construction Companies, August 2000

	PER				EV/EBITDA				P/CE			
	1999	2000E	2001E	2002E	1999	2000E	2001E	2002E	1999	2000E	2001E	2002E
CRH	17.5	14.4	13.0	12.4	10.1	7.6	7.3	7.0	10.7	8.8	8.4	8.0
Holderbank	19.5	17.1	13.7	12.2	8.7	7.6	7.0	6.5	8.9	8.2	7.1	6.6
Lafarge	15.2	12.2	11.8	10.2	7.2	5.9	5.8	5.5	6.8	6.1	6.0	5.7
Saint Gobain	18.0	11.5	9.8	8.4	5.4	4.6	4.1	3.7	8.0	5.9	5.2	4.7
Cemex	5.5	6.6	6.1	5.7	5.1	5.7	5.1	4.9	4.1	5.0	4.7	4.5
Lafarge Corporation	6.5	6.0	5.8		5.3	4.8	4.7					
Martin Marietta	15.8	15.0	13.0		6.7	6.2	5.6		7.9	7.2	6.6	
Vulcan Materials	19.2	17.0	13.5		9.8	8.9	7.5		2.4	2.7	3.5	
Siam Cement	9.6	6.6	5.6		8.5	5.7	5.1	4.9	4.1	3.2	2.6	2.3
Acciona	26.5	22.3	18.5	16.1	12.5	9.1	7.8	7.0	15.4	11.5	9.9	9.0
ACS	18.8	15.3	13.7	12.1	10.6	7.8	7.1	6.4	12.4	10.6	9.7	8.8
Dragados	14.1	13.6	10.4	9.1	7.2	6.5	5.9	5.0	9.6	9.6	8.0	7.6
FCC	11.4	11.3	11.1	10.6	5.8	5.6	5.3	5.0	6.1	5.7	5.3	5.1
Ferrovial	16.9	13.0	10.5	9.2	21.2	16.2	14.2	12.3	10.1	8.3	7.2	6.3
Average	15.3	13.0	11.2	10.6	8.9	7.3	6.6	6.2	8.2	7.1	6.5	6.2
Maximum	*26.5*	*22.3*	*18.5*	*16.1*	*21.2*	*16.2*	*14.2*	*12.3*	*15.4*	*11.5*	*9.9*	*9.0*
Minimum	*5.5*	*6.0*	*5.6*	*5.7*	*5.1*	*4.6*	*4.1*	*3.7*	*2.4*	*2.7*	*2.6*	*2.3*

Source: Morgan Stanley Dean Witter Research.

and 28.2%. The multiples are much more homogenous in the case of the Portuguese banks.

8.4.5. DISPERSION OF THE MULTIPLES OF INTERNET COMPANIES

Table 8.11 contains the price/sales multiple of Internet companies. Note the wide dispersion and the multiple's decrease in 2000.

8.5. VOLATILITY OF THE MOST WIDELY USED PARAMETERS FOR MULTIPLES

Table 8.12 shows the average volatility of several of the most commonly used parameters for multiples and of some of the multiples for the 26 largest

Table 8.7

Multiples of Hotel Companies, November 2000

	EV/EBITDA		PER	
	2000E	2001E	2000E	2001E
Accor	10.0	9.0	23.1	20.0
Bass	5.8	6.3	11.8	10.7
Club Med	10.5	8.2	26.2	18.4
Hilton Group	10.0	8.8	13.2	11.4
Hilton Hotels Corp.	7.6	7.3	13.5	12.8
Marriott Int'l	10.6	9.4	20.5	18.4
Millennium & Copthorne	8.7	8.0	11.2	9.8
NH Hoteles	12.8	9.9	21.4	18.1
Scandic Hotels	7.7	6.5	15.2	14.5
Sol Meliá	10.0	8.7	17.6	14.4
Starwood	7.4	7.1	16.0	14.2
Thistle Hotels	8.1	7.8	9.2	9.2
Average	**9.1**	**8.1**	**16.6**	**14.3**
Maximum	*12.8*	*9.9*	*26.2*	*20.0*
Minimum	*5.8*	*6.3*	*9.2*	*9.2*

Spanish companies during the period 1991–1999. PER, EBITDA, and profit after tax were more volatile than equity value.

8.6. ANALYSTS' RECOMMENDATIONS: HARDLY EVER SELL

Table 8.13 shows the recommendations of 226 brokers during the period 1989–1994. Note that the recommendations range mostly between hold and buy. Less than 10% of the recommendations are to sell.

Table 8.14 shows the analysts' recommendations for Spanish companies in the IBEX 35 index. Note that the recommendations mostly range between holding and buying. Less than 15% of the recommendations are to sell. On February 14, 2000, the IBEX stood at 12,458 points; by 23 October it had fallen to 10,329 points.

Table 8.8

Valuation by Multiples of Telecommunications Companies

		P/E		EV/EBITDA		P/CE		EV/Sale	
		2000E	2001E	2000E	2001E	2000E	2001E	2000E	2001E
North America	AT&T	18.6	18.9	7.6	6.7	13.6	13.1	2.7	2.5
	Verizon	13.5	11.9	5.9	5.3			2.6	2.4
	BellSouth	16.7	14.7	6.8	6.1	15.7	13.9	3.1	2.9
	Broadwing			15.5	11.5			3.8	3.0
	CenturyTel	17.3	13.8	6.3	5.0	14.1	11.7	3.1	2.5
	Commonwealth Telephone Ent.	73.0	53.9	11.5	9.5			3.8	3.4
	WorldCom	15.7	12.3	8.2	6.6	12.7	10.3	2.8	2.4
	SBC Communications	19.6	17.0	8.1	7.2	18.6	16.1	3.3	3.0
	Sprint FON Group	14.3	12.0	5.7	5.1	13.9	11.8	1.7	1.5
	TELUS Corp.	15.4	17.2	4.7	4.8	5.5	5.5	1.9	1.9
	Qwest	62.2	71.9	13.7	11.6	16.8	14.1	5.2	4.6
Europe	British Telecom	53.6		11.6	12.4	13.8	16.0	3.4	2.9
	Cable & Wireless	63.6	44.2	17.7	15.5	24.0	18.1	4.4	4.3
	Deutsche Telekom	17.5	18.5	9.6	9.7	9.7	13.3	5.4	5.0
	KPN	20.4		13.2	11.4	7.3	11.5	4.2	3.6
	OTE	16.4	15.2	7.8	7.3	10.0	8.9	3.4	3.3
	Portugal Telecom	25.9	26.8	9.0	8.5	11.3	11.4	4.3	4.0
	Swisscom	12.2	34.3	10.1	9.8	6.9	10.9	3.0	2.8
	Telefónica	47.6	39.5	12.9	12.2	18.6	17.9	5.2	4.8
	Telia		57.0	17.2	13.5	18.6	15.4	3.8	3.4
Latin America	CANTV		38.1	3.2	3.3	3.4	3.4	1.4	1.4
	CTC	45.1	24.2	8.3	7.7	7.6	6.5	3.7	3.5
	Embratel	21.5	15.1	7.3	5.5	8.2	6.6	2.1	1.7
	Brasil Telecom	24.6	18.4	3.7	3.0	4.9	4.2	1.8	1.5
	Telemar	42.8	19.5	3.8	3.0	4.0	3.3	1.8	1.4
	Telecom Argentina	14.9	14.1	4.8	4.4	3.9	3.6	2.2	2.1
	TelMex	16.6	15.7	7.2	6.4	9.1	8.5	3.8	3.3
	Korea Telecom	19.7	13.3	6.6	5.3	5.3	4.6	2.5	2.3
	MTNL	4.4	4.2	3.4	3.1	3.2	2.9	1.7	1.6
	PLDT			7.2	5.6	7.4	7.3	3.5	3.1
	Indosat	5.5	5.4	3.8	3.7	5.0	4.8	2.2	2.1

(continues)

Table 8.8 (*continued*)

		P/E		EV/EBITDA		P/CE		EV/Sales	
		2000E	2001E	2000E	2001E	2000E	2001E	2000E	2001E
Asia	PT TELKOM	10.1	7.7	5.4	4.7	5.2	4.5	3.7	3.3
	Singapore Telecom	20.1	19.6	13.2	13.1	15.8	15.1	7.0	6.9
	Telecom New Zealand	14.3	13.2	7.7	6.8	7.9	7.3	3.5	3.0
	VSNL (GDR)			136.7	117.1	196.9	171.4	45.3	43.2
	Japan Telecom	59.8	59.4	6.6	5.3	9.6	7.4	1.6	1.4
	NTT		59.3	6.2	5.8	6.4	5.9	2.2	2.0
	Average	19.1	22.8	19.7	17.1	26.3	23.1	7.3	6.9

Source: Morgan Stanley Dean Witter Research, 15 September 2000.

Womack (1996) also found that the ratio of new buy to new sell recommendations issued by the 14 major U.S. brokerage firms was 7:1 in the 1989–1991 period. He also found that after buy recommendations the abnormal return was 2.4% and short-lived, whereas for sell recommendations the abnormal return was −9% and extended for 6 months.

On the other hand, Hilary and Menzly (2001) found that analysts who predict earnings more accurately than the average analysts tend to be relatively inaccurate and more out of consensus in their subsequent earnings predictions.

Bolliger (2001) found that the analysts forecast accuracy is positively associated with analysts firm specific experience and the number of companies covered by the analysts, but negatively associated with analysts's job experience, the number of countries for which they provide forecasts, and the size of their brokerage house.

Groysberg, Nanda, and Prats (2001) report that focusing on the 2,602 analysts in the United States that belonged to the top 24 firms in the period 1988–1996, they identified 1,777 moves. Of the analysts that moved, 1,065 moved to competitors and 712 exited the industry. Among those that exited the industry, 45 started their own company.

8.7. STRANGE MULTIPLES

An alumnus wrote to me: I have just received a valuation from an investment bank that values my company as a combination of multiples:

$$\text{Value} = (1 \times \text{Sales} + 8 \times \text{EBITDA})/2.$$

Do you think that it makes any sense?

Table 8.9

Multiples of Cellular Phone Companies, September 2000

	PER		EV/EBITDA		P/CE		EV/Sales	
	2000E	2001E	2000E	2001E	2000E	2001E	2000E	2001E
Europolitan	42.0	39.4	22.1	20.0	28.0	25.0	8.4	7.9
Libertel	55.3	38.2	17.9	12.3	22.0	15.2	4.6	3.9
Mobistar			30.0	17.8	63.7	28.8	5.0	3.9
Panafon	34.0	31.6	16.3	14.2	23.9	21.7	6.8	5.8
Sonera		65.3	46.0	37.1	45.2	35.8	13.4	11.3
STET Hellas	52.7	35.6	11.0	8.8	15.2	11.1	3.0	2.6
Telecel	34.8	28.8	13.2	11.2	16.8	14.2	4.5	4.3
Turkcell	36.7	22.3	16.5	10.8	18.6	11.9	6.1	4.2
Vodafone Group	72.7	52.7	25.7	21.1	37.8	29.6	8.8	7.6
Average, Europe	*46.9*	*39.2*	*22.1*	*17.0*	*30.1*	*21.5*	*6.7*	*5.7*
Iusacell			13.1	10.9	14.1	10.2	4.5	3.9
Tele Celular Sul	46.9	30.4	9.2	7.0	11.2	8.8	2.9	2.5
Tele Centro Oeste	30.9	26.2	8.1	7.2	11.1	9.0	3.2	2.5
Tele Leste Celular		23.1	10.6	5.5	13.1	6.2	2.3	1.9
Tele Nordeste Celular	34.7	23.3	6.9	5.4	9.8	7.6	2.2	1.9
Tele Norte Celular	60.4	27.8	6.4	4.6	6.4	5.0	1.5	1.3
Telemig Celular Part.	72.7	54.1	8.2	6.5	8.5	7.1	2.8	2.3
Telesp Celular Part.	61.6	46.5	12.8	11.3	13.3	11.6	5.4	4.5
Average, Latin America	*51.2*	*33.1*	*9.4*	*7.3*	*10.9*	*8.2*	*3.1*	*2.6*
Adv. Info. Service (AIS)	24.1	23.8	9.1	8.5	11.8	10.8	3.2	2.9
China Mobile (HK)	42.3	38.6	18.8	15.5	24.7	20.4	10.6	8.7
SK Telecom	23.0	23.0	8.0	7.8	11.4	11.8	3.6	3.6
SmarTone	44.8	37.3	13.9	10.4	58.8	12.0	2.0	1.9
Total Access Com.	21.0	19.9	12.6	12.0	15.0	12.9	4.6	4.2
DDI		50.9	8.2	6.2	6.7	4.9	1.8	1.4
NTT DoCoMo			24.5	20.0	32.4	26.5	7.4	6.3
Average Asia	*31.0*	*32.3*	*13.6*	*11.5*	*23.0*	*14.2*	*4.7*	*4.1*

Table 8.10

Multiples of Spanish and Portuguese banks, November 2000

	PER			P/BV		P/NAV	Dividend yield		ROE		ROE/P/BV	
	2000	2001	2002	2000	2001	2000	2000	2001	2000	2001	2000	2001
BBVA	21.5	17.3	13.9	3.9	3.5	3.4	2.2%	2.6%	20.2%	21.4%	5.2	6.1
BSCH	19.6	15.8	12.9	3.2	2.9	4.2	2.6%	3.4%	19.6%	19.2%	6.2	6.6
Banco Popular	16.5	14.2	12.5	4.7	4.1	4.1	3.3%	3.9%	28.2%	30.7%	6.0	7.5
Bankinter	30.9	29.9	27.0	4.0	3.8	3.2	2.2%	2.3%	12.9%	12.8%	3.2	3.3
Banco Pastor	10.4	9.5	9.2	1.5	1.4	1.5	2.8%	3.1%	14.7%	14.2%	9.5	10.3
Banco Zaragozano	17.8	16.6	16.6	1.7	1.6	n.a.	2.4%	2.9%	15.0%	16.0%	8.8	10.0
Banco Valencia	13.7	12.4	11.5	2.2	2.0	2.2	3.5%	5.7%	16.4%	17.0%	7.4	8.5
Spain	*18.6*	*16.5*	*14.8*	*3.0*	*2.9*	*3.1*	*2.7%*	*3.4%*	*18.1%*	*18.8%*	*6.3*	*6.8*
BCP	17.7	16.2	14.4	3.0	2.8	3	2.4%	2.6%	18.6%	19.8%	6.3	7.0
BES	13.7	12.2	11.6	2.6	2.4	2.6	3.5%	4.0%	18.6%	14.4%	7.3	6.0
BPI	14.0	12.8	11.4	2.6	2.4	2.6	2.9%	3.1%	18.6%	21.4%	7.0	8.9
Portugal	*15.1*	*13.7*	*12.5*	*2.7*	*2.5*	*2.7*	*2.9%*	*3.3%*	*18.6%*	*18.5%*	*6.9*	*7.3*

Table 8.11

Multiples of Internet Companies in 1999 and 2000

e.service companies	Price / Sales				
Company	Dec-99	Mar-00	Jun-00	Sep-00	Dec-00
Agency.Com	20.7	8.1	4.3	3.0	0.7
Answerthink	5.8	3.8	2.4	2.3	0.5
Braun Consulting	30.4	11.7	6.7	5.4	0.9
Cambridge Technology	2.6	1.4	0.9	0.5	0.3
C-bridge Internet Solutions	44.8	36.8	7.8	6.0	0.9
CMGI	312.0	88.9	24.2	9.4	1.3
Diamond Tech. Partners	18.2	11.8	13.3	9.5	3.4
Digitas Inc.		6.7	4.0	3.9	1.0
Inforte Corp.		16.2	9.5	7.8	2.6
iXL Enterprises, Inc.	19.2	7.4	3.0	0.9	0.2
iGate Capital Corporation	3.6	6.1	1.7	0.7	0.4
Internet Capital Group	2881	1658.8	733.0	208.6	9.2
Lante Corporation		26.5	13.1	2.7	0.8
Luminant Worldwide	23.7	5.5	2.1	0.6	0.2
MarchFIRST	16.8	8.9	3.2	2.1	0.2
Modem Media, Inc	23.3	8.8	2.9	0.9	0.6
Organic, Inc		19.6	7.3	3.0	0.5

(continues)

Table 8.11 (*continued*)

| e.service companies | Price / Sales | | | | |
Company	Dec-99	Mar-00	Jun-00	Sep-00	Dec-00
Proxicom	84.8	23.2	19.0	6.2	1.1
Razorfish	53.1	13.0	6.4	3.3	0.5
Sapient	60.4	31.2	33.3	10.8	2.8
Scient Corporation	63.7	42.6	14.0	5.1	0.6
Viant Corporation	77.5	19.1	12.7	2.2	1.5
Xpedior	10.8	7.2	3.7	0.8	0.1
Average	**197.5**	**89.7**	**40.4**	**12.8**	**1.3**

| Dot coms | Price / Sales | | | | |
Company	Dec-99	Mar-00	Jun-00	Sep-00	Dec-00
About.com	60.3	39.5	10.0	7.7	5.0
Amazon.com	16.5	12.4	5.9	5.6	2.2
El sitio	221.2	72.4	15.3	6.2	0.9
Excite@Home	51.2	29.5	15.8	9.9	3.6
Gemstar	140.1	145.8	96.8	128.6	66.8
Homestore.com	97.3	41.8	17.8	21.5	7.2
iGo	9.0	6.0	2.7	1.8	1.0
InfoSpace.com	1351.4	669.8	189.0	75.9	10.9
iTurf	10.6	6.6	1.6	0.7	
Liberate	1260.1	268.6	107.6	92.6	39.2
Promotion.com	27.0	8.0	3.2	0.9	0.2
Quepasa.com	426.7	89.4	11.7	4.9	
Salon.com	11.1	7.6	2.0	2.4	0.8
Sportsline	22.0	10.8	5.4	3.9	1.4
StarMedia	131.2	69.3	32.3	9.9	2.0
Student Adverage	29.0	10.7	6.5	6.0	3.1
Switchboard		77.2	17.8	9.3	3.5
Terra	559.0	462.6	149.1	113.9	34.3
TheKnot Inc.	24.0	12.2	3.7	2.4	0.6
TicketMaster CitySearch	32.3	16.3	8.2	7.4	3.4
Tickets.com	18.4	10.5	3.6	1.1	0.3
Travelocity.com		18.0	7.1	4.7	3.2
Women.com Networks	22.2	9.4	2.0	2.6	0.2
Yahoo	403.8	132.0	79.6	50.2	14.8
Average	**223.8**	**92.8**	**33.1**	**23.7**	**9.3**

Table 8.12

Average Volatility of Several Parameters Used for Multiples—26 Spanish companies, 1991–1999

	Equity value	Profit after tax	EBITDA	Dividends	Book value	ROE	ROA	PER
Average volatility	41%	49%	59%	20%	18%	4%	2%	76%

Table 8.13

North American Analysts' Recommendations, 1989–1994

From ↓ to →	Strong buy	Buy	Hold	Sell	Strong sell	Sum	%
Strong buy	8,190	2,234	4,012	92	154	14,682	27.5%
Buy	2,323	4,539	3,918	262	60	11,102	20.8%
Hold	3,622	3,510	13,043	1,816	749	22,740	42.5%
Sell	115	279	1,826	772	375	3,367	6.3%
Strong Sell	115	39	678	345	407	1,584	3.0%
Sum	14,365	10,601	23,477	3,287	1,745	53,475	
%	26.9%	19.8%	43.9%	6.1%	3.3%		

Source: Welch (2000).

Table 8.14

Analysts' Recommendations on Spanish Stocks

	February 14, 2000			October 23, 2000		
	Buy	Hold	Sell	Buy	Hold	Sell
ACS	90.0%	0.0%	10.0%	81.8%	18.2%	0.0%
Acciona	37.5%	25.0%	37.5%	88.9%	0.0%	11.1%
Aceralia	82.4%	5.9%	11.8%	79.0%	21.1%	0.0%
Acerinox	68.8%	18.8%	12.5%	70.6%	17.7%	11.8%
Acesa	54.6%	36.4%	9.1%	72.7%	27.3%	0.0%
Aguas Bna.	69.2%	15.4%	15.4%	50.0%	36.7%	13.1%
Alba	80.0%	0.0%	20.0%	62.5%	25.0%	12.5%
Altadis	72.7%	18.2%	9.1%	76.9%	15.4%	7.7%
Amadeus	75.0%	0.0%	25.0%	58.6%	34.3%	7.1%
Bankinter	31.6%	47.4%	21.1%	33.3%	38.9%	27.8%
BBVA	57.7%	34.6%	7.7%	54.7%	33.5%	11.8%
BSCH	63.0%	37.0%	0.0%	51.8%	48.2%	0.0%

(continues)

Table 8.14 (*continued*)

	February 14, 2000			October 23, 2000		
	Buy	Hold	Sell	Buy	Hold	Sell
Cantábrico	42.9%	42.9%	14.3%	27.8%	44.4%	27.8%
Continente	71.4%	14.3%	14.3%	53.3%	40.0%	6.7%
Dragados	50.0%	41.7%	8.3%	66.7%	33.3%	0.0%
Endesa	67.9%	28.6%	3.6%	52.9%	44.4%	2.8%
FCC	70.0%	30.0%	0.0%	51.3%	48.7%	0.0%
Ferrovial	50.0%	30.0%	20.0%	70.0%	30.0%	0.0%
Gas natural	18.8%	43.8%	37.5%	22.2%	50.0%	27.8%
Iberdrola	57.9%	36.8%	5.3%	50.0%	38.0%	12.0%
Indra	55.6%	33.3%	11.1%	76.9%	23.1%	0.0%
NH Hoteles	85.0%	15.0%	0.0%	81.3%	18.8%	0.0%
Popular	54.6%	36.4%	9.1%	70.0%	30.0%	0.0%
Repsol	75.8%	18.2%	6.1%	48.6%	45.9%	5.6%
Sogecable	87.5%	0.0%	12.5%	62.4%	25.9%	11.8%
Sol Melia	60.0%	26.7%	13.3%	76.5%	17.7%	5.9%
Terra	87.5%	0.0%	12.5%	59.1%	31.8%	9.1%
Tele pizza	50.0%	37.5%	14.3%	41.5%	35.4%	23.1%
Telefónica	94.7%	5.3%	0.0%	86.3%	11.8%	2.0%
TPI	50.0%	37.5%	18.5%	38.5%	30.8%	30.8%
Unión Fenosa	88.2%	11.8%	0.0%	85.7%	14.3%	0.0%
Vallehermoso	50.0%	10.0%	40.0%	76.9%	23.1%	0.0%
Average	**64.1%**	**23.1%**	**13.1%**	**61.8%**	**29.8%**	**8.4%**

Source: Actualidad Económica.

REFERENCES

Bolliger, G. (2001), "The Characteristics of Individual Analysts' Forecasts in Europe," Social Science Research Network, Working Paper No. 264764.

Damodaran, A. (2001), *The Dark Side of Valuation*, New York: Prentice Hall.

Defond, M., and M. Hung (2001), "An Empirical Analysis of Analysts' Cash Flow Forecasts," Social Science Research Network, Working Paper No. 265773.

Groysberg, B., A. Nanda, and M.J. Prats (2001), "Entrepreneurship among Knowledge Workers: Evidence from Equity Analyst Market," Harvard Business School Working Paper No. 02011.

Hilary, G., and L. Menzly (2001), "Do Past Success Lead Analysts to Become Overconfident?" Social Science Research Network, Working Paper No. 261476.

Liu, J., D. Nissim, and J. Thomas (2001), "Equity Valuation Using Multiples," *Journal of Accounting Research*, forthcoming.

Welch, I. (2000b), "Herding among Security Analysts," *Journal of Financial Economics*, 58, pp. 369–396.
Womack, K. L. (1996), "Do Brokerage Analysts' Recommendations Have Investment Value?" *Journal of Finance*, Vol. LI, No. 1, pp. 137–167.

Chapter 9

Cash Flow and Net Income

There is a financial and accounting maxim which, although it is not absolutely true, comes very close to and is a good idea to remember: "Net income is just an opinion, but cash flow is a fact."

9.1. NET INCOME IS JUST AN OPINION, BUT CASH FLOW IS A FACT

Still today, many analysts view net income as the key and only truly valid parameter for describing how a company is doing. According to this simple approach, if the net income increases, the company is doing better; if the net income falls, the company is doing worse. It is commonly said that a company that showed a higher net income last year "generated more wealth" for its shareholders than another company with a lower net income. Also, following the same logic, a company that has a positive net income "creates value" and a company that has losses "destroys value." Well, all these statements can be wrong.

Other analysts "refine" net income and calculate the so-called *accounting cash flow*, adding depreciation to the net income.[1] They then make the same remarks as in the previous paragraph but referring to "cash flow" instead of net income. Of course, these statements too may be wrong.

---

[1]The sum of net income plus depreciation is often called "cash generated by operations" or "cash flow earnings" (see Anthony and Reece (1983), page 343). Net income is also called profit after tax (PAT).

The classic definition of net income (revenues for a period less the expenses that enabled these revenues to be obtained during that period), in spite of its conceptual simplicity, is based on a series of premises that seek to identify which expenses were necessary to obtain these revenues. This is not always a simple task and often implies accepting a number of assumptions. Issues such as the scheduling of expense accruals, the treatment of depreciation, calculating the product's cost, allowances for bad debts, etc., seek to identify in the best possible manner the quantity of resources that it was necessary to sacrifice in order to obtain the revenues. Although this "indicator," once we have accepted the premises used, can give us adequate information about how a company is doing, the figure obtained for the net income is often used without full knowledge of these hypotheses, which often leads to confusion.

Another possibility is to use an *objective measure*, which is not subject to any individual criterion. This is the difference between cash inflows and cash outflows, called cash flow in the strict sense: the money that has come into the company less the money that has gone out of it. Two definitions of cash flow in the strict sense are used: *equity cash flow* and *free cash flow*. Also, the so-called *capital cash flow* is used. Generally speaking, it can be said that a company is doing better and "generates wealth" for its shareholders when the cash flows improve. In the following section, we will take a closer look at the definitions of these cash flows.

9.2. ACCOUNTING CASH FLOW, EQUITY CASH FLOW, FREE CASH FLOW, AND CAPITAL CASH FLOW

Although the financial press often gives the following definition for accounting cash flow:

accounting cash flow = Profit after Tax (PAT) + depreciation

we will use three different definitions of cash flow: equity cash flow (ECF), free cash flow (FCF), and capital cash flow (CCF).

ECF is the money that remains available in the company after tax, after having covered capital investment requirements and the increase in working capital requirements (WCR), after having paid financial expenses, after having repaid the debt's principal, and after having received new debt.

The ECF represents the cash available in the company for its shareholders, which shall be used for dividends or share repurchases. The equity cash flow in a period is simply the difference between cash inflows[2] and cash outflows[3] in that period.

> equity cash flow = cash inflows − cash outflows in a period

---

When making forecasts, the forecast equity cash flow[4] in a period must be equal to forecast dividends plus share repurchases in that period.

Free cash flow is the cash flow generated by operations after tax, without taking into account the company's debt level, that is, without subtracting the company's interest expenses. It is, therefore, the cash that remains available in the company after having covered capital investment requirement,[5] and working capital requirements[5], assuming that there is no debt.[6] The FCF is the company's ECF assuming that it has no debt.

> Free cash flow = equity cash flow if the company has no debt

---

It is often said that the FCF represents the cash generated by the company for the providers of funds, that is, shareholders and debtholders.[7] This is not true, the parameter that represents the cash generated by the company for its shareholders and debtholders is the capital cash flow.

Capital cash flow is the cash flow available for debtholders plus the equity cash flow. The cash flow for debtholders consists of the sum of

---

[2]Cash inflows normally consist of sums collected from customers and the increases in financial debt.

[3]Cash outflows normally consist of payments to employees, suppliers, creditors, taxes, etc., and interest payments and repayment of financial debt.

[4]Equity cash flow is also called equity free cash flow, equity cash flow, and levered cash flow.

[5]Some authors call it noncash working capital investments. See, for example, Damodaran (2001, page 133).

[6]Free cash flow is also called cash flow to the firm, free cash flow to the firm, and unlevered cash flow.

[7]See, for example, Damodaran (1994, page 144) and Copeland, Koller, and Murrin (2000, page 132).

the interest payments plus repayment of the principal (or less the increase in the principal).

Capital cash flow = equity cash flow + debt cash flow

9.3. CALCULATING THE CASH FLOWS

Equity cash flow corresponds to the concept of cash flow. The ECF in a period is the difference between all cash inflows and all cash outflows in that period. Consequently, the ECF is calculated as follows:

Profit after tax (PAT)
+Depreciation and amortization
−Increase in WCR (working capital requirements)
−Principal payments of financial debt
+Increase in financial debt
−Increase in other assets
−Gross investment in fixed assets
+Book value of disposals and sold fixed assets
_____
ECF

The ECF in a period is the increase in cash (above the minimum cash, whose increase is included in the increase in WCR) during that period, before dividend payments, share repurchases, and capital increases.

The free cash flow is equal to the hypothetical equity cash flow that the company would have had if it had no debt on the liabilities side of its balance sheet. Consequently, in order to calculate the FCF from the net income, the following operations must be performed:

Profit after tax (PAT)
+Depreciation and amortization
−Increase in WCR (working capital requirements)
−Increase in other assets
−Gross investment in fixed assets
+Interest $(1 - T)$
+Book value of disposals and sold fixed assets
_____
FCF

Taking into account the above two calculations, it can be seen that, in the case of perpetuity, the relationship between ECF and FCF is the following:

$$FCF = ECF + I(1 - T) - \Delta D$$

If the company has no debt in its liabilities, ECF and FCF are the same.

The capital cash flow is the cash flow available for all debt and equity holders. It is the ECF plus the cash flow corresponding to the debtholders (CFd), which is equal to the interest received by the debt (I) less the increase in the debt's principal (Δ D).

$$CCF = ECF + CFd = ECF + I - \Delta D \quad \text{where } I = DKd$$

The diagram below summarizes the company valuation approaches using discounted cash flows.[8]

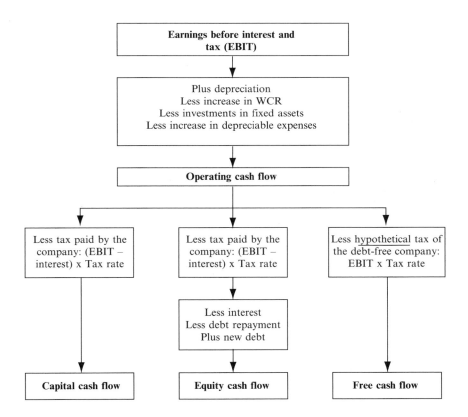

[8]For a company without extraordinary net income or asset disposals.

Another diagram that enables us to see the difference between the different cash flows is the following:

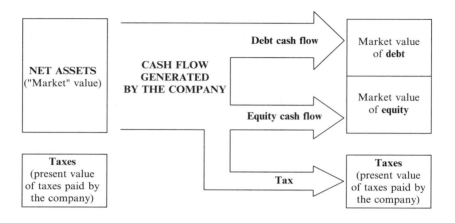

May a company have positive net income and negative cash flows? Of course: one has only to think of the many companies that file for voluntary reorganization after having a positive net income. This is precisely what happens to the company we show in the following example.

9.4. A COMPANY WITH POSITIVE NET INCOME AND NEGATIVE CASH FLOWS

To give a better idea, we give an example in the four tables below. Table 9.1 shows the income statements for a company with strong growth in sales and also in net income. Table 9.2 shows the company's balance sheets. We assume that the minimum cash is zero. Table 9.3 shows that, even though the company generates a growing net income, the free cash flow is negative, and becomes increasingly negative with each year that passes. The equity cash flow is also negative. Table 9.4 is another way of explaining why the free cash flow is negative: because the cash inflows from operations were less than the cash outflows. Finally, Table 9.5 provides a few ratios and some additional information.

Table 9.1
FausCommerce—Income Statements

Income statements (million euros)	1996	1997	1998	1999	2000
Sales	2,237	2,694	3,562	4,630	6,019
Cost of sales	1,578	1,861	2,490	3,236	4,207
Personnel expenses	424	511	679	882	1,146
Depreciation	25	28	39	34	37
Other expenses	132	161	220	285	370
Interest	62	73	81	96	117
Extraordinary profit (disposal of fixed assets)		−15	32		
Taxes (30%)	4	13	25	29	42
Profit after tax	**12**	**32**	**60**	**68**	**100**

1997: Assets with a book value of 15 were written off (gross fixed assets = 25; accumulated depreciation = 10). 1998: At the end of the year, assets with a book value of 28 (gross fixed assets = 40; accumulated depreciation = 12) were sold for 60.

Table 9.2
FausCommerce—Balance Sheets

Balance sheets (million euros)	1996	1997	1998	1999	2000
Cash and temporary investments	32	28	26	25	25
Accounts receivable	281	329	439	570	742
Inventories	371	429	583	744	968
Gross fixed assets (original cost)	307	335	342	375	410
Accumulated depreciation	50	68	95	129	166
Net fixed assets	257	267	247	246	244
Total assets	**941**	**1,053**	**1,295**	**1,585**	**1,979**
Banks. Short-term debt	402	462	547	697	867
Taxes payable	2	6	12	14	21
Other expenses payable	22	26	36	47	61
Accounts payable	190	212	303	372	485
Long-term debt	95	85	75	65	55
Shareholders' equity	230	262	322	390	490
Total liabilities and shareholders' equity	**941**	**1,053**	**1,295**	**1,585**	**1,979**

Table 9.3

**FausCommerce—Free Cash Flow, Equity Cash Flow,
Debt Cash Flow and Capital Cash Flow**

Cash flow (million euros)	1997	1998	1999	2000
Profit after tax	**32**	**60**	**68**	**100**
+ Depreciation	28	39	34	37
− Purchase of fixed assets	53	47	33	35
+ Book value of sold assets	15	28		
− Increase of WCR	76	157	210	262
+ Interest × (1 − 30%)	51	57	67	82
Free cash flow	**−3**	**−20**	**−74**	**−78**
− Interest × (1 − 30%)	51	57	67	82
+ Increase of short-term financial debt	60	85	150	170
− Principal payments of long-term financial debt	10	10	10	10
Equity cash flow	**−4**	**−2**	**−1**	**0**
Interest	73	81	96	117
+ Principal payments of long-term financial debt	10	10	10	10
− Increase of short-term financial debt	60	85	150	170
Debt cash flow	**23**	**6**	**−44**	**−43**
Capital cash flow	**19**	**4**	**−45**	**−43**

Table 9.4

FausCommerce—Cash Inflows and Cash Outflows; New Funding (million euros)

Cash inflows and cash out flows	1997	1998	1999	2000
Cash inflows: collections from clients	**2,646**	**3,452**	**4,499**	**5,847**
Cash outflows:				
Payments to suppliers	1,897	2,553	3,328	4,318
Labor	511	679	882	1,146
Other expenses	157	210	274	356
Interest payments	73	81	96	117
Tax	9	19	27	35
Capital expenditures	53	47	33	35

(continues)

Table 9.4 (*continued*)

Cash inflows and cash out flows	1997	1998	1999	2000
Total cash outflows	**2,700**	**3,589**	**4,640**	**6,007**
Cash inflows − cash outflows	**−54**	**−137**	**−141**	**−160**
Financing				
Increase of short-term debt	60	85	150	170
Reduction of cash	4	2	1	0
Sale of fixed assets	0	60		
Payments of long-term debt	−10	−10	−10	−10
Source of funds	**54**	**137**	**141**	**160**

Table 9.5
FausCommerce—Ratios

RATIOS	1996	1997	1998	1999	2000
Net income/sales	0.5%	1.2%	1.7%	1.5%	1.7%
Net income/net worth (mean)	5.4%	13.0%	20.5%	19.1%	22.7%
Debt ratio	68.4%	67.9%	66.3%	66.6%	65.8%
Days of debtors (collection period)	45.8	44.6	45.0	45.0	45.0
Days of suppliers (payment period)	40.3	40.3	41.8	40.0	40.0
Days of stock	85.8	84.1	85.5	84.0	84.0
Cash ratio	5.2%	4.0%	2.9%	2.2%	1.7%
Sales growth	27.9%	20.4%	32.2%	30%	30%

9.5. WHEN IS PROFIT AFTER TAX A CASH FLOW?

Using the formula that relates profit after tax (PAT) with the equity cash flow, we can deduce that the PAT is the same as the equity cash flow when the addends of the following equality, which have different signs, cancel out.

Equity cash flow =
profit after tax (PAT)
+ depreciation
− gross investment in fixed assets
− increase in WCR (Working Capital Requirements)
− decrease in financial debt
+ increase in financial debt
− increase in other assets
+ book value of fixed assets sold

A particularly interesting case in which this happens is when the company is not growing (and therefore its customer, stock, and supplier accounts remain constant), buys fixed assets for an amount identical to depreciation, keeps debt constant, and only writes off or sells fully depreciated assets. Another case is that of a company which collects from its customers in cash, pays in cash to its suppliers, holds no stocks (these three conditions can be summarized as this company's working capital requirements being zero), and buys fixed assets for an amount identical to depreciation.

9.6. WHEN IS THE ACCOUNTING CASH FLOW A CASH FLOW?

Following the reasoning of the previous section, the accounting cash flow is equal to the equity cash flow in the case of a company that is not growing (and keeps its customer, stock, and supplier accounts constant), keeps debt constant, only writes off or sells fully depreciated assets, and does *not* buy fixed assets. Also in the case of a company that collects from its customers in cash, pays in cash to its suppliers, holds no stock (this company's working capital requirements are zero), and does *not* buy fixed assets.

Is cash flow more useful than net income? This question cannot be answered if we have not defined beforehand who is the recipient of this information and what it is sought to find out by analyzing the information. Also, both parameters come from the same accounting statements. But, as a general rule, yes: the reported net income is one among several that can be given (one opinion among many), while the equity cash flow or free cash flow is a fact—a single figure.

9.7. EQUITY CASH FLOW AND DIVIDENDS

We have already said that when making projections, the equity cash flow must be equal to the forecast dividends.[9] When making projections, the forecast dividends must be exactly equal to the equity cash flow. Otherwise, we will be making hypotheses about what use is given to the part of the equity cash flow that is not to be used for dividends (cash, investments, repaying debt, etc.) and it will be necessary to subtract it beforehand from the equity cash flow.

Distributing dividends in the form of shares is not stated as a cash flow because it isn't: the shareholder who receives shares now has more shares with a lower value but the same total value.

Let us see an example. Tables 9.6 and 9.7 contain the forecast income statements and balance sheets for the company Santoma & Co., which plans to start operating at the end of 2001. The initial investment is 64 million euros, which is funded in equal proportions with long-term debt and equity. The company does not plan to distribute dividends in 2002 so as to reduce its medium-term funding requirements for funding its working capital requirements.

Table 9.8 shows the company's different cash flows. It can be seen that the equity cash flow is equal to the forecast dividends.

It also enables another statement made in Section 9.5 to be verified. As in the year 2004, the company:

Table 9.6
Forecast Income Statements for Santoma & Co. (Thousand euros)

Year	2002	2003	2004	2005
Sales	110,275	170,367	170,367	192,288
Cost of sales	75,417	116,456	116,456	137,810
Personnel expenses	10,735	10,950	10,950	11,169
Depreciation	4,141	4,381	4,381	4,478
Other expenses	9,532	6,872	6,872	6,885
Interest	1,920	2,356	2,356	2,356
Profit before tax (PBT)	8,530	29,352	29,352	29,590
Tax	2,730	9,686	9,686	10,356
Profit after tax (PAT)	**5,801**	**19,666**	**19,666**	**19,233**
Dividends	**0**	**18,388**	**19,666**	**8,817**
To reserves	5,801	1,278	0	10,417

[9]When we say dividends, we are referring to payments to shareholders, which may be dividends, share repurchases, par value repayments, etc.

Table 9.7

Forecast Balance Sheets for Santoma & Co. (Thousand euros)

Assets	2001	2002	2003	2004	2005
Cash and temporary investments	1,000	1,103	1,704	1,704	1,923
Accounts receivable		18,788	21,471	21,471	24,234
Inventories	6,300	14,729	14,729	14,729	16,335
Gross fixed assets	56,700	56,700	62,700	67,081	72,081
Accumulated depreciation	0	4,141	8,522	12,903	17,381
Net fixed assets	56,700	52,559	54,178	54,178	54,700
Total assets	**64,000**	**87,179**	**92,082**	**92,082**	**97,191**

Liabilities	2001	2002	2003	2004	2005
Accounts payable		9,195	10,502	10,502	12,244
Taxes payable		910	3,229	3,229	3,452
Medium-term financial debt	0	7,273	7,273	7,273	0
Long-term financial debt	32,000	32,000	32,000	32,000	32,000
Shareholders' equity	32,000	37,801	39,078	39,078	49,495
Total liabilities	**64,000**	**87,179**	**92,082**	**92,082**	**97,191**

1. Does not grow (the income statement is identical to 2003)
2. Keeps its working capital requirements constant
3. Keeps its financial debt constant
4. Buys fixed assets for an amount identical to depreciation, the net income forecast for 2004 is identical to the forecast equity cash flow (and the forecast dividends)

9.8. RECURRENT CASH FLOWS

Sometimes, people talk about recurrent equity cash flow and recurrent free cash flow. These cash flows are calculated in the same manner as the cash flows explained in the chapter with just one difference: only the businesses in which the company was already present at the beginning of the year are considered. Therefore, net income, increases in WCR, increases in depreciable expenses or gross investment in fixed assets arising from acquisitions of companies, new business lines, and, in general, investments in businesses that are still incipient, are not included.

Table 9.8

Forecast Cash Flows for Santoma & Co. (Thousand euros)

Year	2001	2002	2003	2004	2005
Net income (PAT)	0	5,801	19,666	19,666	19,233
+ Depreciation	0	4,141	4,381	4,381	4,478
− Increase in WCR	7,300	17,214	−341	0	2,622
− Increase in fixed assets	56,700	0	6,000	4,381	5,000
+ Increase in short-term financial debt	0	7,273	0	0	−7,273
+ Increase in long-term financial debt	32,000	0	0	0	0
Equity cash flow	**−32,000**	**0**	**18,388**	**19,666**	**8,817**
− Increase in short-term financial debt	0	7,273	0	0	−7,273
− Increase in long-term financial debt	32,000	0	0	0	0
+ Interest (1–T)	0	1,248	1,532	1,532	1,532
Free cash flow	**−64,000**	**−6,025**	**19,920**	**21,197**	**17,621**
Accounting cash flow	0	9,942	24,047	24,047	23,711
Debt cash flow	**−32,000**	**−5,353**	**2,356**	**2,356**	**9,629**
Capital cash flow	**−64,000**	**−5,353**	**20,744**	**22,022**	**18,446**
Dividends		**0**	**18,388**	**19,666**	**8,817**

SUMMARY

A company's PAT (or net income) is a quite arbitrary figure obtained after assuming certain accounting hypotheses regarding expenses and revenues. On the other hand, the cash flow is an objective measure, a single figure that is not subject to any personal criterion.

In general, to study a company's situation, it is more useful to operate with the cash flow (ECF, FCF, or CCF) as it is a single figure, while the net income is one of several that can be obtained, depending on the criteria applied.

PAT is equal to the equity cash flow when the company is not growing (and keeps its customer, inventory, and supplier accounts constant), buys fixed assets for an amount identical to depreciation, keeps debt constant, and only writes off or sells fully depreciated assets.

PAT is also equal to the equity cash flow when the company collects in cash, pays in cash, holds no stock (this company's working capital requirements are zero), and buys fixed assets for an amount identical to depreciation.

The accounting cash flow is equal to the equity cash flow in the case of a company that is not growing (and keeps its customer, inventory, and supplier accounts constant), keeps debt constant, only writes off or sells fully depreciated assets and does *not* buy fixed assets.

When making projections, dividends and other payments to shareholders forecasted must be exactly equal to expected equity cash flows.

APPENDIX 9.1: ATTENTION TO THE ACCOUNTING AND THE MANAGING OF NET INCOME

When analyzing accounting statements, which are used by most listed companies, it is important to consider the accounting standards and techniques used by the firm. The most importants ones are

- *Recognition of revenues.* Some firms recognize revenues too early and others too late: companies have some degrees of freedom to recognize revenues.[10]
- *Capitalizing expenses.* Companies may make payments that do not appear in the income statement but are entered directly as an increase in assets (capitalized). For example, oil companies capitalize exploration costs,[11] electric utilities capitalize interest expense, etc.
- *Use of accrual and reserves.* Firms may build up accruals and reserves for court settlements, consumer's demands, bad debts, and other potential losses and expected payments. However, many firms build up excess accruals and reserves in good years to use this excess in bad years. By doing that, companies smooth out net income.
- *Extraordinary profits from investments.* Many firms hold in their balance sheets marketable securities valued below their market values and sell these investments in bad years to smoothout net income.
- *In many countries outside the* U.S. *it is quite easy for some companies to charge some payments against retained earnings, without going through the profit and loss statements.* This is the case of the staff reduction costs due to early retirement incurred by the Spanish banks. The table below shows the charges to retained earnings for early retirement costs incurred by the main Spanish banks:

Million euros	1996	1997	1998	1999	2000e	Total
BBVA	0	225	395	384	666	1,670
BSCH	250	56	210	802	480	1,798
Popular	60	72	102	106	0	340

[10]See, for example, the HBS case—The O. M. Scott & Sons Company.
[11]See, for example, the HBS case Gulf Oil Corp.—Takeover.

When analyzing international consolidated accounting statements, which are used by most listed companies, it is important to take into account the consolidation method used. Readers interested in a more detailed discussion of this subject are recommended to read Chapter 25 of the book *Contabilidad para dirección* written by my colleagues at IESE's control department, headed by Professor Pereira. There are three ways of consolidating the purchase of another company's shares:

1. *Passive consolidation.* The shares purchased are entered in the assets at purchase cost, the dividends received are entered as financial income, and the proceeds of the sale of the shares are entered as extraordinary income. In addition, a provision must be made for future losses, including potential losses. In order to calculate the provisions, the reference taken must be the share's price on the stock market.
2. *Equity method.* Recommended for holdings between 20 and 50% in unlisted companies and 3 and 5% in listed companies. The shares purchased are entered in the assets at purchase cost (distributed between the shares' book value and goodwill); the corresponding percentage of the net income appears in the income statement (the balancing entry in the investment); the dividends received are entered as a decrease in the investment; and the proceeds of the sale of the shares are entered as extraordinary income. The goodwill generated in the purchase (difference between the shares' purchase value and book value) is depreciated over 20 years.
3. *Overall consolidation.* In this case, the income statements and the balance sheets are added together, eliminating the accounting operations that start and end within the group. If the company is not fully owned, the percentage of the net income corresponding to outside partners is deducted in the income statement. On the liabilities side, the quantity of shareholders' equity corresponding to outside partners, also called minority holdings, is also indicated.

It is important to adequately analyze consolidation in order to correctly calculate the cash flows generated by the company. To calculate the cash flows in the case of overall consolidation, each company must be analyzed separately.

An excellent book on the analysis of financial statements is *Financial Statement Analysis and Security Valuation*, McGraw-Hill. Chapters 7–12 provide a very useful guide for interpreting balance sheets and income statements.

REFERENCES

Anthony, R. N., and J. S. Reece (1983), *Accounting: Text and Cases*, New York: Irwin.

Copeland, T. E., T. Koller, and J. Murrin (2000), *Valuation: Measuring and Managing the Value of Companies*, third edition. New York: Wiley.

Damodaran, A. (1994), *Damodaran on Valuation*, New York: John Wiley and Sons.

Damodaran, A. (2001), *The Dark Side of Valuation*, New York: Prentice Hall.

Pereira, F., E. Ballarín, M. J. Grandes, J. M. Rosanas, and J. C. Vazquez-Dodero (2000), *Contabilidad para dirección*, 17th edition. Pamplona, Spain: Eunsa.

Penman, S. H. (2001), *Financial Statement Analysis and Security Valuation*, New York: McGraw-Hill.

Unknown Author, "Gulf Oil Corp.-Takeover," Harvard Business School Case No. 9–285–053.

Unknown Author, "The O. M. Scott & Sons Company," Harvard Business School Case No. 9–209–102.

Chapter 10

Inflation and Value

As we shall see in this chapter, the return on investments depends on the effects of inflation. To analyze the effect of inflation, we shall use the case study Campa Spain and Campa Argentina. This case study concerns two companies engaging in the same business and in identical market conditions but with very different inflation rates. The problem of inflation and its consequences is expressed very clearly. And its solution is very simple.

10.1. CAMPA SPAIN AND CAMPA ARGENTINA

Victor Campa wondered where part of the money from his businesses in Argentina went. His brother Alberto was engaging in a business that was identical to his business in Spain but his profits were much higher.

Alberto Campa sold undecipherable wave radio transmitters through Campa Spain. The Campa brothers had developed a device (with the appearance of a black box) in which they placed a normal radio transmitter. Over a 1-year period, the transmitter acquired certain special magnetic properties so that the waves it emitted were impossible to decipher. They kept the black box at home and the patent gave them worldwide protection.

Complete manufacture of the black box—Campa Spain's only fixed asset—cost 20 million euros. The box operated for 5 years, at the end of which it could no longer be used and it had no residual value. The business was very simple. On December 31, 2000, they bought a normal transmitter for 80 million euros in cash, put it in the black box and sold it to the government (converted into an undecipherable wave transmitter) on December 31, 2001, also in cash, for 104 million euros. On that same day, they bought another normal transmitter, put it into the black box and sold it on December 31, 2002. This process was continued until December 31, 2005 when the last transmitter would be sold and the black box would be unusable. The tax authorities allowed the black box to be depreciated over a 5-year period at a rate of 4 million euros per year.

Alberto Campa founded Campa Spain on December 31, 2000, with a share capital of 100 million euros, which he used to pay for the black box (20 million) and buy the first transmitter (80 million). During those years, there was no inflation in Spain so Campa Spain obtained the same profit during each of the 5 years the black box lasted: 14 million euros (sales 104, cost of sales 80, depreciation 4, tax on earnings 6, net income 14). The tax rate was 30% and tax was paid on December 31, of the year in which it was generated. Alberto Campa received 14 million euros each year as dividends and another 4 million euros as an advance on account.

A well-known consultant calculated the cash flow generated by Campa Spain for its owner: investment of 100 million euros in 2000, payback of 18 million euros in 2001, 2002, 2003, and 2004, and 98 million euros in 2005. He also estimated the investment's net present value (NPV) at 0% (there was no inflation in Spain) at 70 million euros and the internal rate of return (IRR) at 15.04%.

Victor Campa started operating in Argentina at the same time as his brother Alberto in Spain. On December 31, 2000, the euro-peso exchange rate was 1 euro = 1 peso. Victor formed Campa Argentina with an upfront investment of 100 million pesos. With this money, he paid for the black box (20 million) and bought the first transmitter (80 million). Annual inflation in Argentina was 25%. The transmitter selling and buying prices adjusted exactly to inflation. Victor had sold his transmitters for 130 million pesos in 2001, 162.5 million pesos in 2002, and so on. The transmitters had cost 80 million pesos in 2000; 100 million pesos in 2001; 125 million pesos in 2002, etc. Tax, whose rate in Argentina was 30%, as in Spain, was also paid on December 31, of the year on which it was generated and the black box was depreciated over 5 years at a rate of 4 million pesos a year. All conditions—except for inflation—were identical to those existing in Spain.

Everything seemed to indicate that Campa Argentina should have the same return (after adjusting for inflation) as Campa Spain. However, the net income for 2001 was 32.2 million pesos (equivalent to 25.76 million euros), which was more than that obtained by Campa Spain. In spite of this, at the end of 2001, Victor only received 16.2 million pesos (equivalent to 12.96 million euros) in dividends, which is less than the amount received by Alberto. He could not receive more dividends because there was no more cash available. During the following years, Campa Argentina's net income was greater than that of Campa Spain, but Victor received a lower remuneration than his brother Alberto. Earnings for 2001 amounted to 32.2 million pesos (sales 130, cost of sales 80, depreciation 4, tax 13.8, and net income 32.2), but the cash flow was 16.2 million. The euro-peso exchange rate adjusted to the inflation differential (1 euro = 1 peso at the value in 2000; 1.25 pesos at the value in 2001; 3.0518 pesos at the value in 2005).

Alarmed, Victor asked his brother's consultant for help. The consultant calculated Campa Argentina's cash flow: investment of 100 million pesos in 2000 and paybacks of 16.2, 19.95, 24.64, 30.50, and 281.96 in 2001, 2002, 2003, 2004, and 2005, respectively. The NPV of the investment at 25% was 43.23 million pesos at the value in 2000 (equivalent to 43.23 million euros) and the IRR was 36.69%, but falling to 9.35% after adjusting for inflation (25%).[1]

Victor reasoned as follows: "the net present value of the cash flow generated by my company is worth 43.23 million pesos at the value in 2000 (equivalent to 43.23 million euros). The net present value of the cash flow generated by Alberto's company is worth 70 million euros. We both do the same and generate the same wealth. Or my calculations are wrong or someone else is pocketing the 26.77 million euros difference (70 − 43.23)."

The reader is asked to help Victor Campa find out the reason for this difference of 26.77 million euros between the two companies' cash flows.

10.2. ANALYSIS OF THE DIFFERENCES BETWEEN CAMPA SPAIN AND CAMPA ARGENTINA

We shall create two tables that shall give a clearer view of the two companies' situation. Table 10.1 shows the income statements and balance sheets for Campa Spain after the year 2000. It will be seen that Alberto Campa's remuneration, which is the equity cash flow, is equal to the free cash flow because the company has no debt. The investment's IRR is 15.04%.

The balance sheets, income statements, and cash flows of Campa Argentina are shown in Table 10.2. It is seen again that Victor Campa's remuneration (the equity cash flow) is identical to the free cash flow because this company has no debt either. The investment's IRR is 36.69%. To compare it with the IRR obtained by his brother in Spain (where zero inflation is assumed), we perform the following operation:

$$[(1 + 0.3669)/1.25] - 1 = 9.35\%$$

---

[1]To adjust for inflation, the following expression is used:

$$1 + \text{nominal IRR} = (1 + \text{adjusted IRR})(1 + \text{inflation rate})$$

Table 10.1

Campa Spain (Million euros)

	2000	2001	2002	2003	2004	2005	Sum
Income statement							
Sales		104	104	104	104	104	520
Cost of sales		80	80	80	80	80	400
Depreciation		4	4	4	4	4	20
EBT		20	20	20	20	20	100
Tax (30%)		6	6	6	6	6	30
Net income		14	14	14	14	14	70
Remuneration of Alberto Campa (equity cash flow)							
Dividends		14	14	14	14	14	70
Advance on account		4	4	4	4	−16	0
Investment in the company	−100	0	0	0	0	0	−100
Liquidation of the company		0	0	0	0	100	100
Total	**−100**	**18**	**18**	**18**	**18**	**98**	**70**
Balance sheet							
Cash	0	0	0	0	0	0	
Advance on account		4	8	12	16	0	
Stocks	80	80	80	80	80	0	
Net fixed assets	20	16	12	8	4	0	
Assets	**100**	**100**	**100**	**100**	**100**	**0**	
Capital	100	100	100	100	100	100	
Reserves		0	0	0	0	−100	
Liabilities	**100**	**100**	**100**	**100**	**100**	**0**	
Free cash flow							
Net income	0	14	14	14	14	14	70
+ Depreciation		4	4	4	4	4	20
− Investments in working capital requirements	−80	0	0	0	0	80	0
− Investments in fixed assets	−20	0	0	0	0	0	−20
Total	**−100**	**18**	**18**	**18**	**18**	**98**	**70**

IRR of the free cash flow = 15.04%

Table 10.2
Campa Argentina (Million pesos)

	2000	2001	2002	2003	2004	2005	Sum	NPV 25%	Campa Spain sum
Income statement									
Sales		130	162.5	203.13	253.91	317.38	1066.91	520.00	520
Cost of sales		80	100	125	156.25	195.31	656.56	320.00	400
Depreciation		4	4	4	4	4	20	10.76	20
EBT		46	58.5	74.13	93.66	118.07	390.35	189.24	100
Tax (30%)		13.8	17.55	22.24	28.10	35.42	117.11	56.77	30
Net income		**32.2**	**40.95**	**51.89**	**65.56**	**82.65**	**273.25**	**132.47**	**70**
Remuneration of Victor Campa (equity cash flow)									
Dividends		16.2	19.95	24.64	30.5	181.96	273.25	110.46	70
Investment	−100	0	0	0	0	0	0	−100.00	−100
Liquidation of the company		0	0	0	0	100	100	32.77	100
Total	**−100**	**16.2**	**19.95**	**24.64**	**30.5**	**281.96**	**373.3**	**43.23**	**70**
Balance sheet									
Cash	0	0	0	0	0	0			
Stocks	80	100	125	156.25	195.31	0			
Net fixed assets	20	16	12	8	4	0			

(*continues*)

Table 10.2 (*continued*)

	2000	2001	2002	2003	2004	2005	Sum	NPV 25%	Campa Spain sum
Assets	**100**	**116**	**137**	**164.25**	**199.31**	**0**			
Capital	100	100	100	100	100	100			
Reserves		16	37	64.25	99.31	−100			
Liabilities	**100**	**116**	**137**	**164.25**	**199.31**	**0**			
Free cash flow									
Net income	0	32.2	40.95	51.89	65.56	82.65	273.25	132.47	70
+ Depreciation		4	4	4	4	4	20	10.76	20
−Δ Working capital requirements	−80	−20	−25	−31.25	−39.0625	195.313	80	0.00	0
−Δ Fixed assets	−20						0	0.00	−20
Total	**−100**	16.2	19.95	24.64	30.4975	281.963	373.25	143.23	70

IRR = 36.69%; IRR adjusted for inflation = 9.35% [(1.3669/1.25) − 1 = 9.35%]

Table 10.3

Cash Flows and IRR of Campa Spain and Campa Argentina

	2000	2001	2002	2003	2004	2005	IRR
Campa Spain (million euros)	−100	18	18	18	18	98	**15.04%**
Campa Argentina (million pesos)							
Current pesos	−100	16.2	19.95	24.64	30.5	281.96	**36.69%**
Constant pesos	−100	12.96	12.77	12.61	12.49	92.39	**9.35%**

The inflation adjustment operation we have just performed is equivalent to calculating Campa Argentina's IRR considering real (or constant) pesos, that is, pesos discounted for the effect of inflation and not current pesos. Table 10.3 shows the cash flows and IRRs of Campa Spain and Campa Argentina (in current pesos and constant pesos). This table shows that, in real terms (after discounting the effect of inflation), Campa Spain has a return of 15.04%, while Campa Argentina has a lower return of only 9.35%.

What happens to the cash flows? Upon calculating the cash flows' NPV at the inflation rate, in Spain this gives 70 and only 43.23 in Argentina. Where has the 26.77 million pesos difference gone? If we take a close look at Table 10.2 and analyze the different accounts included in the cash flow, we can see the difference between the NPVs of the tax paid by the two companies during the last 5 years. Thus, in Spain at 0%, we obtain 30 million, while in Campa Argentina the NPV of the tax payment at 25% is 56.77 million.

$$56.77 - 30 = 26.77 \text{ million}$$

We have found the difference: Campa Argentina has paid 26.77 million more in tax than Campa Spain, while both companies perform the same activity and in identical conditions, except for the inflation rate. Hence our result $56.77 - 30 = 26.77$. The project in Argentina is less profitable than in Spain because, as a result of inflation, a large part of the company's business is eaten up by tax.

The project in Argentina is less profitable than in Spain because, as a result of inflation, earnings before tax (EBT), which is the basis on which the tax is calculated, is artificially increased. This means that the amount of tax that must be paid is greater, taking away large part of the company's revenues.

Table 10.4 shows the valuation of Campa Spain and Campa Argentina with different rates. If the required return to equity in Spain were to be

Table 10.4

Differences in the Valuation of Campa Spain and Campa Argentina with Different Discount Rates[a]

		Shareholder + Taxes		Shareholder		
Ke$_{SPAIN}$	Ke$_{ARGENTINA}$	NPV$_{SPAIN}$ (million euros)	NPV$_{ARGENTINA}$ (million pesos)	NPV$_{SPAIN}$ (million euros)	NPV$_{ARGENTINA}$ (million pesos)	Difference
0.0%	25.0%	100.0	100.0	70.0	43.2	26.8
1.0%	26.3%	92.6	92.6	63.5	37.5	26.0
2.0%	27.5%	85.6	85.6	57.3	32.1	25.2
3.0%	28.8%	78.9	78.9	51.4	27.0	24.5
4.0%	30.0%	72.6	72.6	45.9	22.1	23.8
5.0%	31.3%	66.6	66.6	40.6	17.5	23.1
10.0%	37.5%	40.7	40.7	17.9	−2.3	20.2
15.0%	43.8%	20.2	20.2	0.1	−17.7	17.8
16.0%	45.0%	16.7	16.7	−3.0	−20.4	17.4
20.0%	50.0%	3.9	3.9	−14.0	−29.9	15.9

[a]Ke$_{ARGENTINA}$ = (1 + Ke$_{SPAIN}$) × 1.25 − 1.

10%, the required return to equity in Argentina[2] should be 37.5% ($0.375 = 1.1 \times 1.25 - 1$). Thus, the present value of the sum of equity cash flow and tax is identical: 40.7 million (euros and pesos). In this situation, the value of Campa Spain's shares would be 17.9 million euros and the value of Campa Argentina's shares would be −2.3 million pesos.

Figure 10.1 shows the present value of the equity cash flows for different discount rates.

10.3. ADJUSTMENTS TO CORRECT FOR THE EFFECTS OF INFLATION

Table 10.5 shows how the disadvantage of Campa Argentina with respect to Campa Spain disappears after reappraisal (adjustment for inflation) of fixed assets and stocks.

Table 10.6 summarizes the cash flows of Campa Spain and Campa Argentina, in all the cases seen in this chapter.

Looking at Tables 10.5 and 10.6, we can see that once the assets have been restated and the necessary adjustments for inflation have been made, earnings (which were artificially increased by inflation) decrease but the cash flow increases because tax is reduced. Thus, the NPV of each company's cash flows, discounted at the corresponding inflation rate, is the same and, likewise, the internal rates of return of the project in Spain and in Argentina is equal: the two investments' return is the same.

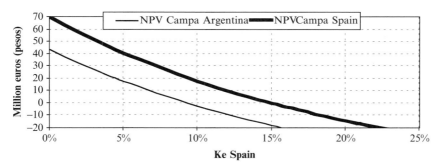

Figure 10.1   Net present value (NPV) of the cash flows of Campa Spain and Campa Argentina.

---

[2]Assuming that the only risk difference affecting business in both countries is caused by inflation.

Table 10.5

Campa Argentina with Restatement (million pesos)

	2000	2001	2002	2003	2004	2005	Sum	NPV 25%	Campa Spain Sum
Income statement									
Sales		130	162.5	203.13	253.91	317.38	1066.91	520	520
Cost of sales		80	100	125	156.25	195.31	656.56	320	400
Reappraisal of stocks (1)		20	25	31.25	39.06	48.83	164.14	80	0
Depreciation		4	4	4	4	4	20	10.76	20
Depreciation due to reappraisal of fixed assets (2)		1	2.25	3.81	5.77	8.21	21.04	9.24	
EBT		25	31.25	39.06	48.83	61.04	205.18	100	100
Tax (30%)		7.5	9.37	11.72	14.65	18.31	61.55	30	30
Net income		17.5	21.88	27.34	34.18	42.72	143.62	70	70
Remuneration of Victor Campa									
Dividends		17.5	21.88	27.34	34.18	42.72	143.62	70	70
Advance on account		5	6.25	7.81	9.77	−28.83	0	6.55	0
Investment	−100	0	0	0	0	0	−100	−100	−100
Liquidation of the company		0	0	0	0	285.18	285.18	93.45	100
Total	−100	22.5	28.13	35.15	43.95	299.07	328.8	70	70

(*continues*)

Table 10.5 (*continued*)

	2000	2001	2002	2003	2004	2005	Sum	NPV 25%	Campa Spain Sum
Balance sheet									
Cash	0	0	0	0	0	0			
Advance on account. Victor Campa		5	11.25	19.06	28.83	0			
Stocks	80	100	125	156.25	195.31	0			
Gross fixed assets	20	20	20	20	20	20			
Reappraisal gross fixed assets		1	3.25	7.06	12.83	21.04			
Accum. dep initial assets		4	8	12	16	20			
Accum. dep reappraised assets		1	3.25	7.06	12.83	21.04			
Net fixed assets	20	16	12	8	4	0			
Total assets	**100**	**121**	**148.25**	**183.31**	**228.14**	**0**			
Capital	100	100	100	100	100	100			
Reserves (retained earnings)		0	0	0	0	–100			
Reserves (reappraisal stocks)		20	45	76.25	115.31	0			
Reserves (reappraisal fixed assets)		1	3.25	7.06	12.83	0			
Total liabilities	**100**	**121**	**148.25**	**183.31**	**228.14**	**0**			

(*continues*)

Table 10.5 (*continued*)

	2000	2001	2002	2003	2004	2005	Sum	NPV 25%	Campa Spain Sum
Free cash flow									
Net income	0	17.5	21.88	27.34	34.18	42.72	143.62	70	70
+ Depreciation		5	6.25	7.81	9.77	12.21	41.04	20	20
− Δ WCR	−80	−20	−25	−31.25	−39.06	195.31	0	−80	0
+ Reappraisal stocks		20	25	31.25	39.06	48.83	164.14	80	
− Investments in fixed assets	−20						−20	−20	−20
Total	**−100**	**22.5**	**28.13**	**35.16**	**43.95**	**299.07**	**328.80**	**70**	**70**

[1] Reappraisal of stocks in year n = 80 $(1.25^n - 1.25^{n-1})$.
[2] Depreciation due to reappraisal of fixed assets in year n = 4 $(1.25^n - 1)$.

Table 10.6

**Cash Flows and IRR of Campa Spain and Campa Argentina
(in Current Pesos and Constant Pesos) Without and With Restatement**

	2000	2001	2002	2003	2004	2005	IRR
1 Campa Spain (million euros)	−100	18	18	18	18	98	15.04%
Campa Argentina without restatement (without adjustments) (million pesos)							
2 current pesos	−100	16.20	19.95	24.64	30.50	281.96	36.69%
3 constant pesos	−100	12.96	12.77	12.61	12.49	92.39	9.35%
Campa Argentina with restatement (with adjustments) (million pesos)							
4 current pesos	−100	22.50	28.13	35.16	43.95	299.07	43.79%
5 constant pesos	−100	18.00	18.00	18.00	18.00	98.00	15.04%

If the country's current legislation does not allow assets to be restated, tax will take away a significant part of the company's value, and this part will be higher at higher inflation rates.

Table 10.7 shows the evolution of inflation in Spain, Argentina, Peru, Chile, and Mexico from 1970 to 2000. Note that Argentina had 2 years of 4-digit inflation, 12 years of 3-digit inflation, 9 years of 2-digit inflation, and only 8 years of 1-digit inflation. Spain had 19 years of 1-digit inflation and 12 years of 2-digit inflation.

Table 10.8 shows the credit rating histories of Argentina and Spain.

SUMMARY

When inflation is high, company earnings are artificially high (i.e., not caused by an improvement in the company's situation), which means that the tax paid is higher than if there was no inflation. Consequently, investments' real return is less.

When the tax authorities allow reappraisal or restatement of assets, the company's return is not decreased as a result of inflation.

Table 10.7

Annual inflation in Spain, Argentina, Peru, Chile and Mexico

	70	71	72	73	74	75	76	77	78	79	80	81	82	83	84	85	86	87	88	89	90	91	92	93	94	95	96	97	98	99	00
Spain	5.7	8.2	8.3	11	16	17	18	25	20	16	16	15	14	12	11	8.8	8.8	5.3	4.8	6.8	6.7	5.9	5.9	4.6	4.7	4.7	3.6	2.0	1.8	2.3	3.4
Argentina	22	39	64	44	40	335	348	160	170	140	88	131	210	434	688	385	82	175	388	4924	1344	84	18	7.4	3.9	1.6	0.1	0.3	0.7	-2	-1
Peru	5.1	6.8	7.2	10	17	24	33	38	58	-76	59	75	64	11	11	16	NA	NA	70	NA	3000	40	74	49	24	11	12	8.5	7.2	3.5	3.8
Chile	35	22	163	508	376	341	174	63	30	39	31	10	21	23	23	26	17	21	13	21	27	19	13	12	9	8.2	6.6	6.0	4.7	2.3	4.5
Mexico	5.0	5.5	4.9	12	24	15	16	29	17	18	26	28	59	102	65	58	86	132	114	20	27	23	16	10	7.0	35	34	21	16	17	9.5

Source: Datastream, IN Argentina, IN Chile.

Table 10.8

Credit Rating Histories of Argentina and Spain Rated by Standard & Poor's as of August 3, 2001, Long-Term/Outlook/Short Term

	Date	Local currency rating	Foreign currency rating
Argentina	July 12, 2001	B–/Negative/C	B–/Negative/C
	June 6, 2001	B/Negative/C	B/Negative/C
	May 8, 2001	B/CW Neg./C	B/CW Neg./C
	March 26, 2001	B+/CW Neg./B	B+/CW Neg./B
	March 19, 2001	BB/CW Neg./B	BB–/CW Neg./B
	Nov. 14, 2000	BB/Stable/B	BB–/Stable/B
	Oct. 31, 2000	BBB–/CW-Neg./A–3	BB/CW–Neg./B
	Feb. 10, 2000	BBB–/Stable/A–3	BB/Stable/B
	July 22, 1999	BBB–/Negative/A–3	BB/Negative/B
	April 2, 1997	BBB–/Stable/A–3	BB/Stable/B
	March 8, 1995	BBB–/Stable/A–3	BB– /Stable/B
	Sept. 1, 1994	BBB–/Positive/A–3	BB– /Postive/B
	Aug. 22, 1994	—/Positive/A–3	BB–/Positive/B
	Feb. 4, 1994		BB–/Positive/—
	Aug. 25, 1993		BB–/Stable/—
Spain	March 31, 1999	AA+/Stable/A–1+	AA+/Stable/A–1+
	May. 6, 1998	AA/Positive/A–1+	AA/Positive/A–1+
	Feb. 6, 1996	AAA/Stable/A–1+	AA/Stable/A–1+
	Dec. 11, 1992	AAA/Stable/A–1+	AA/Positive/A–1+
	June 26, 1989		AA/Positive/A–1+
	Aug. 1, 1988		AA/—/A–1+
	May 25, 1987		Strong/A–1+
	Jan. 3, 1984		—/—/A–1+

Source: www.standard and poors.com/Ratings Actions/Ratings Lists/Sovereigns/index.html.

The reader interested in a deeper analysis of the effect of inflation on investment can see Baldwin and Ruback (1986).

REFERENCE

Baldwin, C. Y., and R. S. Ruback (1986), "Inflation, Uncertainty and Investment," *Journal of Finance*, Vol. XLI, No. 3 (July), pp. 657–669.

Chapter 11

Cost of Equity: Beta and Risk Premium

The market risk premium is one of the most important but elusive parameters in finance. It is also called equity premium, market premium, and risk premium. The market risk premium is the expected rate of return on the aggregate stock market in excess of the risk-free interest rate.

The market value of the company's equity is obtained by discounting the equity cash flow at the required return to equity for the company (Ke).

The capital asset pricing model (CAPM)[1] defines the required return to equity in the following terms:

$$Ke = R_F + \beta[E(R_M) - R_F]$$

R_F = rate of return for risk-free investments (Treasury bonds);
β = share's beta;
$E[R_M]$ = expected market return;
$[E(R_M) - R_F]$ = market risk premium

Therefore, given certain values for the equity's beta, the risk-free rate and the market risk premium, it is possible to calculate the required return to equity[2]. The CAPM and the market risk premium are discussed in this chapter, where the relationship between beta and volatility is shown.

In addition to the beta, in order to calculate the required return to equity (as postulated by the CAPM), we need to know the value of the market risk premium. The market risk premium is the difference between the *expected*

---

[1]See Appendix A for a derivation of the CAPM.
[2]The classic finance textbooks provide a full discussion of the concepts analyzed here. For example, Brealey and Myers (2000) and Copeland and Weston (1988).

return on the market portfolio and the risk-free rate, that is, the incremental return demanded by investors on stocks, above that of risk-free investments.

We will see that the market risk premium is an expectation and not the market's historical return above the risk-free rate, as is often stated, and we will study the different methods proposed for calculating the market risk premium.

In this chapter, we will see that the betas and volatilities are very unstable parameters over time. They are also parameters whose value depends to a great extent on the data used (daily, weekly, and monthly) to calculate it.

One practical consequence of this analysis of the *betas* is that using a share's historical beta in a valuation, without analyzing this beta and the company's future prospects, is a very risky and imprecise practice as historical betas are *unstable* and *depend on the data used* (daily, weekly, monthly . . .), in almost all companies. As a result, it is very risky to handle a single beta or historical volatility for a share without analyzing it and the company's future prospects.

11.1. BETAS AND VOLATILITIES

When talking about volatility and beta, we must have a clear idea of the risk associated with these concepts. Any holder of a stock portfolio faces a risk, which means that there is a likelihood that circumstances may occur in the future that are different from those expected for his portfolio. Volatility and beta are two parameters that measure the risk.

We can distinguish between two different types of risk:

1. *Diversifiable risk*.[3] This is the risk that can be eliminated by diversifying the portfolio.
2. *Market risk*.[4] This is the market's intrinsic risk, and cannot be eliminated by diversifying the portfolio.

Diversifying consists of forming a portfolio with shares from different companies. This has the effect of reducing the degree of variation in the portfolio's total value, as movements in different directions in different companies' share prices will tend to offset each other. However, there is one risk that cannot be eliminated no matter how much you diversify: this is the market risk, which arises from the circumstances of the economy as a whole, which affects all businesses.

The volatility measures the portfolio's total risk, that is, both the market risk and the diversifiable risk, while the beta only measures the portfolio's market risk.

---

[3]Diversifiable risk may be called specific risk, unsystematic risk, residual risk, or unique risk.
[4]Market risk may be called systematic risk or undiversifiable risk.

Any holder of a stock portfolio faces a risk, that is, the possibility that situations other than those expected for his portfolio may arise.

When an investor has an adequately diversified portfolio, the relevant risk here is the market risk, which is measured by the beta. On the other hand, the volatility is a correct measure of the risk for a holder of a non-diversified stock portfolio and is indispensable for valuing other financial assets, such as options, convertible debentures, etc.

11.2. VOLATILITY (σ) AND DIVERSIFICATION

A share's volatility measures that share's *total risk*, that is, both the market risk and the diversifiable risk.

Volatility is the correct measure of risk for the holder of a non-diversified portfolio and is also indispensable for calculating the value of options, warrants, stock market bonds, convertible debentures, and financial instruments packaged with options.

In mathematical terms, volatility is the annualized standard deviation of the shareholder returns. Standard deviation (σ) and variance (σ^2) are two statistical measures of the variability (risk) of a parameter which, in the case concerning us, is a company's equity return.[5]

Therefore, volatility provides a measure of the scatter of a share's return. Share volatility normally ranges between 25 and 45% in 75% of the cases.

If a share's volatility is high, it means that the return obtained from the share in the future may vary within a relatively broad range. A low volatility implies that the share's future return will differ little from its expected value.

The effect of portfolio diversification on volatility can be seen in Figure 11.1. This figure shows that when a portfolio is diversified from holding the shares of a single company to holding the shares of 19 companies, the portfolio's annual volatility falls from 71.3–22.6%.

11.3. BETA (β)

A share's beta measures the *incremental risk* added by a share to a given portfolio. This risk, called *market risk*, is the risk that cannot be eliminated by creating a diversified portfolio.

---

[5]Mathematically speaking, the variance in a share's return is the expected value of the square of the deviation from the expected return. The standard deviation is the square root of the variance. Variance $(R_i) = \sigma^2 =$ expected value of $[R_i - E(R_i)]^2$

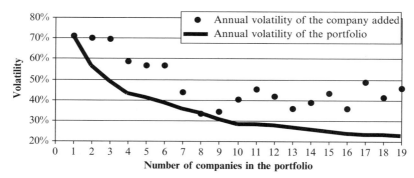

Figure 11.1 Effect of diversification on the volatility of equal-weighted portfolios. Annual volatility calculated with daily data during the period January 1998–June 2001.

Number corresponding to the company added to the portfolio, according to the numbering given in the following table. For example, company no. 3 = Xerox.

Number of companies in the portfolio	Company added	Annual volatility of the company	Annual volatility of the portfolio
1	CHARLES SCHWAB	71.3%	71.3%
2	APPLE	70.3%	56.1%
3	XEROX	69.6%	48.7%
4	BARNES & NOBLE	58.6%	42.6%
5	INTEL	56.5%	40.8%
6	GAP	56.9%	38.2%
7	AT & T	44.0%	35.4%
8	GENERAL ELECTRIC	33.4%	33.3%
9	COCA COLA	34.3%	30.3%
10	PHILIP MORRIS	40.2%	28.0%
11	MICROSOFT	45.4%	27.9%
12	IBM	41.8%	27.6%
13	ESTEE LAUDER	36.0%	26.2%
14	FORD	38.8%	25.6%
15	HERTZ	43.2%	24.7%
16	KELLOGG	35.9%	23.7%
17	NIKE	48.9%	23.2%
18	DISNEY	41.2%	22.9%
19	TOYS R US	45.9%	22.6%

The market risk exists because in the economy as a whole, in addition to the specific risk of a company or business, there are other factors that threaten all businesses (such as expectations concerning interest rates and inflation rates, political events, etc.). This is why investors are exposed to market uncertainties, regardless of the shares that they hold.

In the case of a reasonably well-diversified portfolio, the only major risk is the market risk of the securities included in the portfolio. Therefore, the main source of uncertainty for an investor who diversifies is whether the market rises or falls: this movement will drive the investor's portfolio.

Trying to measure the market risk is like measuring a share's sensitivity to market movements. This sensitivity is precisely what is known as the share's beta.

A share's beta is calculated as the covariance between the stock and market returns, divided by the variance of the market return. It is also the correlation coefficient between the two returns (ρ_{im}) multiplied by the share's volatility and divided by the market volatility. In other words:

$$\beta_i = \mathrm{Cov}(R_i, \ R_M)/\sigma_M^2 = \rho_{im} \ \sigma_i/\sigma_M$$

The value of the beta indicates the sensitivity of the share's return with respect to the market return. The average beta of all securities is 1. If a beta is greater than 1, it means that the share is very sensitive to market movements, while a beta less than 1 indicates a low level of sensitivity of the share to market variations.

It is important to also consider that the beta may have negative values. The beta's sign indicates the direction of the movement of the share's return with respect to the market return. Thus, a negative beta indicates that when the market return increases, that of the share decreases, and vice versa, while a positive beta would indicate that both returns rise or fall simultaneously. To calculate a portfolio's beta, the beta of each share (β_i) is weighted by the share's price (P_i) with respect to the portfolio's total value (P_{total}), i.e.:

$$\beta \text{ of a portfolio} = (\textstyle\sum P_i\beta_i)/P_{total}$$

The betas usually have values between 0.7 and 1.3 in 80% of the cases.

11.4. DRAWBACKS OF BETAS AND VOLATILITIES: INSTABILITY AND PERIOD DEPENDENCE

Figures 11.2–11.7 show the betas of IBM, Microsoft, and Coca-Cola. All of the figures show the betas' instability and the differences in the values calculated depending on whether daily, weekly, or monthly data are used (period dependence).

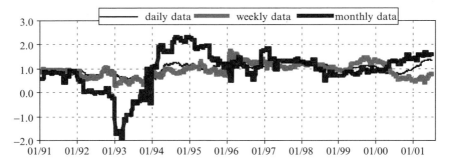

Figure 11.2   Beta of IBM (calculated with data from the last year).

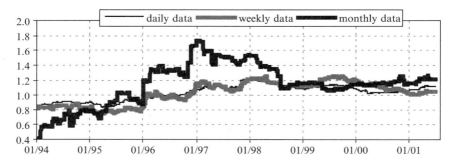

Figure 11.3   Beta of IBM (calculated with data from the last 5 years).

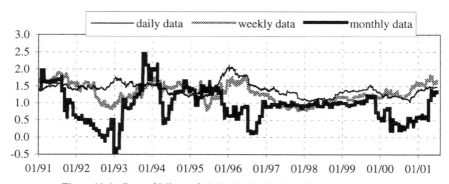

Figure 11.4   Beta of Microsoft (calculated with data from the last year).

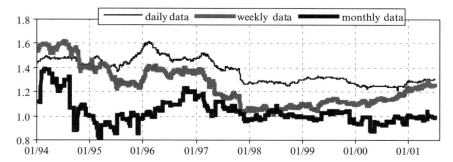

Figure 11.5   Beta of Microsoft (calculated with data from the last 5 years).

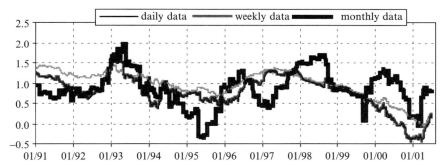

Figure 11.6   Beta of Coca-Cola (calculated with data from the last year).

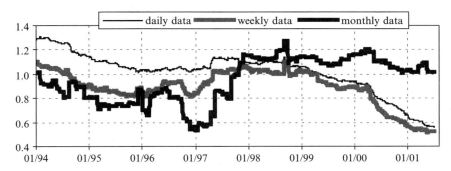

Figure 11.7   Beta of Coca-Cola (calculated with data from the last 5 years).

The beta's instability is particularly important when determining a share's expected return, as this may vary depending on the data used to calculate the beta.

To conclude this analysis of *betas*, we can say that using a share's historical beta, without any analysis of this beta and the company's future prospects, is highly risky, as historical betas are unstable and depend on the data used (daily, weekly, monthly, etc.), in almost all companies.[6]

Damodaran (2001, page 72) also calculates different betas for Cisco versus the S&P 500:

Beta Estimates for Cisco versus the S&P 500

	Daily	Weekly	Monthly	Quarterly
2 years	1.72	1.74	1.82	2.7
5 years	1.63	1.7	1.45	1.78

Source: Damodaran (2001), page 72.

Figures 11.8 to 11.12 show the annual volatilities of the S&P 500 and of IBM, Microsoft, and Coca-Cola. These figures also clearly show the instability of some companies' volatilities over these years.

The figures mentioned in the previous section show that the parameter being calculated (betas or volatilities) depends substantially on the data used, i.e., whether these are daily, weekly, or monthly.

The article that dealt the hardest blow to the CAPM was that published by Fama and French (1992). This article showed that in the period 1963–1990, the correlation between the stocks' returns and their betas was very small, while the correlation with the companies' size and their price/book value ratio was greater. The authors divided the shares into portfolios. Table 11.1 shows the article's main findings.

---

[6]Damodaran (1994) also makes this point by calculating the beta of Disney. With daily data, he gets 1.33; 1.38 with weekly data; 1.13 with monthly data; 0.44 with quarterly data; and 0.77 with annual data. With a 3-year period, he gets 1.04; 1.13 with 5 years; and 1.18 with 10 years. Also, the beta depends on the index taken as the benchmark; thus, the beta with respect to the Dow 30 is 0.99; with respect to the S&P 500, it is 1.13, and with respect to the Wilshire 500, it is 1.05. Another interesting study is Bartholdy and Peare (2001).

Table 11.1

Main Findings of Fama and French's article (1992)

Size of the companies	Average beta	Annual average return	Beta of the companies	Average beta	Annual average return	Price / book value	Average beta	Annual average return
1 (biggest)	0.93	10.7%	1 (high)	1.68	15.1%	1 (high)	1.35	5.9%
2	1.02	11.4%	2	1.52	16.0%	2	1.32	10.4%
3	1.08	13.2%	3	1.41	14.8%	3	1.30	11.6%
4	1.16	12.8%	4	1.32	14.8%	4	1.28	12.5%
5	1.22	14.0%	5	1.26	15.6%	5	1.27	14.0%
6	1.24	15.5%	6	1.19	15.6%	6	1.27	15.6%
7	1.33	15.0%	7	1.13	15.7%	7	1.27	17.3%
8	1.34	14.9%	8	1.04	15.1%	8	1.27	18.0%
9	1.39	15.5%	9	0.92	15.8%	9	1.29	19.1%
10 (smallest)	1.44	18.2%	10 (low)	0.80	14.4%	10 (low)	1.34	22.6%

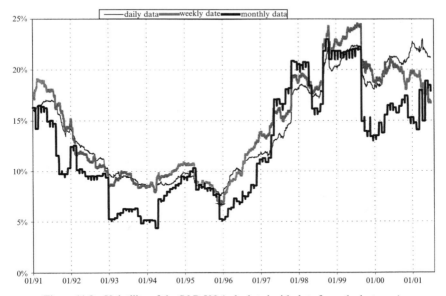

Figure 11.8   Volatility of the S&P 500 (calculated with data from the last year).

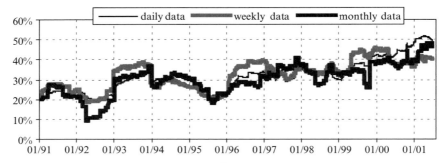

Figure 11.9   Volatility of IBM (calculated with data from the last year).

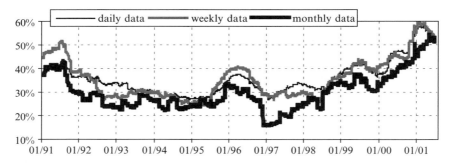

Figure 11.10   Volatility of Microsoft (calculated with data from the last year).

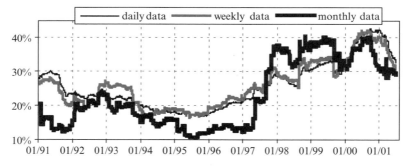

Figure 11.11   Volatility of Coca-Cola (calculated with data from the last year).

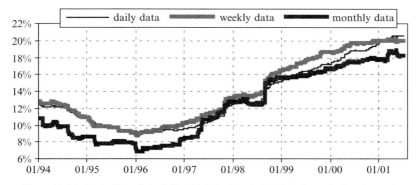

Figure 11.12   Volatility of the S&P 500 (calculated with data from the last 5 years).

11.5. QUALITATIVE CALCULATION OF THE BETA

Given the betas' instability and the low significance of the historical betas, there are increasingly more companies who calculate the qualitative beta of companies or investment projects.

Example. A company uses the MASCOFLAPEC method (initials of the parameters considered to assess each project's risk) to estimate the beta, see Table 11.2. The parameters are obtained from the historical analysis (learning from past misjudgments about the estimation of the risk of projects and acquisitions) of several of the company's projects to identify the variables that most affected their risk, both *a priori* and *a posteriori*. Each parameter is scored from 1–5 depending on its contribution to the risk. It is also necessary to define each factor's weight. In the example below, the sum of each parameter's scores, taking into account their weight, was 3.5. When this quantity was multiplied by 0.5, the beta of 1.75 was obtained. Using the parameter 0.5, the beta may range between 0.5 and 2.5, which was the range of variance that seemed most suitable to the company. With a parameter of 0.8 (instead of 0.5), the beta could range between 0.8 and 4.0.

Other alternatives to the MASCOFLAPEC method are the MARTILLO method and the BAMCELLEX method.

Of course, the risk of a project must be calculated on a stand-alone basis.

Table 11.2

Qualitative Beta. MASCOFLAPEC Method

			Risk					
			Low	Average	Substantial	High	Very high	*Weighted*
Weight			1	2	3	4	5	*risk*
10%	**M**	Management	1					*0.10*
25%	**A**	Assets: business / industry / products					5	*1.25*
3%	**S**	Strategy				4		*0.12*
15%	**C**	Country risk				4		*0.60*
10%	**O**	Operational leverage				4		*0.40*
15%	**F**	Financial leverage		2				*0.30*
5%	**L**	Liquidity of investment					5	*0.25*
5%	**A**	Access to sources of funds			3			*0.15*
2%	**P**	Partners				4		*0.08*
5%	**E**	Exposure to other risks (currency...)		2				*0.10*
5%	**C**	Cash flow stability			3			*0.15*
100%								*3.50*

Beta of equity = 3.5 × 0.5 = 1.75

11.6. MARKET RISK PREMIUM

We will now discuss the determination of the market risk premium. We will also analyze two of the main explanations for the growth in sale prices in recent years: a fall in the market risk premium and overvaluation (speculative bubble). One of the conclusions is that whether the stock markets are overvalued or the market risk premium has fallen, the consequence is the same: with regard to the yield of fixed-income securities, equity investors will gain less in coming years than they gained in the past.

The market risk premium is also the answer to a question to which we all want to know the answer: What return can I expect from the stock market above the risk-free rate over the next few years? This is also crucial for any company because the answer to this question is fundamental for determining the cost of the money invested in the company by its shareholders (Ke).

The market risk premium is the incremental return demanded by investors from equity above the risk-free rate. If R_F is the risk-free rate and $E(R_M)$ is the *expected* market return:

$$\text{Market risk premium} = [E(R_M) - R_F]$$

As we will see below, the main problem in determining the market risk premium is that it is an expectation. We will see that the market risk premium is not, contrary to what is often said, the stock market's historical return above the bond market. Indeed, Byron Wien, from Morgan Stanley, recently wrote an article entitled "Risk premium—R.I.P." We will also see that while it does not make much sense to talk of market risk premium, it does make sense to talk of *each investor's* market risk premium.

The market risk premium and the expected market return are the most important parameters in finance, but they are expectations and, therefore, non-observable parameters. An anecdote from the Nobel prizewinner Merton Miller:

> "I still remember the teasing we financial economists, Harry Markowitz, William Sharpe, and I, had to put up with from the physicists and chemists in Stockholm when we conceded that the basic unit of our research, the expected rate of return, was not actually observable. I tried to tease back by reminding them of their neutrino—a particle with no mass whose presence was inferred only as a missing residual from the interactions of other particles. But that was eight years ago. In the meantime, the neutrino has been detected."[7]

However, Booth (1999) suggests a forecasting method to estimate the expected market return by adding a current inflation expectation to 9% (the historical average real equity return from 1871–1999). We do not agree with this, as we will comment later.

In one highly controversial article, Porter (1992) said that the United States economy grew less than that of Japan and Germany during the 1980s because the cost of capital and the market risk premium was higher in the United States. The evolution of the United States economy during the 1990s leads one to doubt the present relevance of this argument.

[7]See Miller (2000), page 3.

11.7. METHODS PROPOSED FOR CALCULATING THE MARKET RISK PREMIUM

11.7.1. Historical Differential Return of the Market Portfolio and the Risk-Free Rate

It is very common to use historical data to compare the return of an investment in shares with the return of the risk-free rate. Some conclude that the difference between the historical return of the stock market (of a stock market index) and the historical return of the risk-free rate[8] is a good indicator of the market premium.[9] In support of this statement, it is often argued that, on average, the market is right. Thus, although the equity gain above bonds in a particular year is not considered to be the market risk premium, the incremental return of stocks over bonds over a number of years is considered to be a good estimator of the market risk premium. Another of the contradictions of this approach is that after a very good year for the stock market, the market risk premium will have risen and, after a bad year, the market risk premium will have fallen, even if there is no reason for this. This means that, given equal expectations, the market will value a share higher after a bad year than after a good year (after a good year, the risk premium would be greater).

This method, sometimes called Ibbotson's method, assumes that the required return to equity in the past was equal to the return actually received, and that the market is all investors' efficient portfolio. As we will see further on, this method provides inconsistent results and, at present, exaggerates the market risk premium.

However, many textbooks suggest using this method to calculate the market risk premium. Brealey and Myers suggested 8.2–8.5% in the fifth edition of their book in 1996; on page 160 of their sixth edition (2000), they say "Brealey and Myers have no official position on the exact market risk premium, but we believe a range of 6–8.5 percent is reasonable for the United States. We are most comfortable with figures toward the upper end of the range." Further on, on page 195, they say: "How about the *market risk premium*? From past evidence it appears to be 8 to 9 percent, although many economists and financial managers would forecast a lower figure." Copeland,

---

[8]As we will see further on, the difference can be calculated as an arithmetic average or geometric average. For the historical return of the risk-free rate, the long- or short-term bonds can be used. Furthermore, there are authors who use the return of the risk-free rate (the return gained from buying bonds today and selling them in the next period), and others use the IRR of the risk-free rate at the beginning of the period. In the following sections, we will analyze which of these alternatives is the most suitable.

[9]This is an error for the reasons given above and for others that we will see further on.

Koller, and Murrin (2000) recommend 4.5–5% (in the second edition of 1995, they recommended 5–6%); Ross, Westerfield, and Jaffe (1993) recommend 8.5%; Van Horne (1992) recommends 3–7%; Weston, Chung, and Siu (1997) recommend 7.5%; and Damodaran (1994, pages 22–24) recommends 5.5%.[10] In the examples given in their book, Bodie and Merton (2000) use 8% for the U.S. Damodaran (2001, page 63) says

> "6.05%, which is the geometric average premium for stocks over Treasury bonds from 1928 to 1999 if you use historical premiums. In using this premium, however, you are assuming that there are no trends in the risk premium and that investors today demand premiums similar to those they used to demand two, four, or six decades ago. Given the changes that have occurred in the markets and in the investor base over the last century, you should have serious concerns about using this premium, especially in the context of valuation."

I completely agree with Damodaran on this point.

One parameter is the market risk premium (an expectation) and another is the historical differential return of stocks over treasury bonds. It is a common mistake to think that they are equal.

11.7.2. USING THE GORDON AND SHAPIRO FORMULA

Other authors propose calculating the market risk premium from the Gordon and Shapiro equation. This enables one to determine the share price by discounting the dividends when the latter grow at an annual rate g each year: $P_0 = EPS_1/(Ke - g)$.

Isolating Ke in the formula, we get: $Ke = (EPS_1/P_0) + g$.

The argument given by the advocates of this method is the following: Ke is the return required from the market (from a diversified portfolio), and must match the return expected by "the market": $Ke = E(R_M) = R_F + P_M$.

Consequently, $P_M = (EPS_1/P_0) + g - R_F$.

Applying the latter expression to the market as a whole, (EPS_1/P_0) is the average dividend-based market return, g is the growth of the dividends expected by "the market," and R_F is the risk-free rate. It would be sufficient to estimate the growth of the dividends expected by "the market" to calculate the market risk premium.

---

[10]5.5% was the geometric average differential return of the S&P 500 versus 30-year T-Bonds.

The problem with this method is, once again, that investors' expectations are not homogenous. If they were, it would make sense to talk in terms of market risk premium, as all investors would have the market portfolio and the same expectations regarding the portfolio.[11] However, as expectations are not homogenous, it is obvious that the investors who expect a higher growth will have a higher market risk premium. On the other hand, not all investors expect dividends to grow geometrically at a constant rate.

11.7.3. SURVEY OF ANALYSTS AND INVESTORS

Perhaps the most direct way for trying to calculate the market risk premium is to carry out a survey of analysts or investors.

One example of this method is Welch's study (2000). Welch performed two surveys, in 1998 and 1999, with several finance professors, asking them what they thought the market risk premium was. He obtained 226 replies and the average put the market risk premium (measured as the arithmetic average) about 7% above long- term Treasury bonds (5.2% when measured as a geometric average). Surprisingly, this figure is very high. The interest rate paid by long-term Treasury bonds in April 1998 was approximately 6%. The inflation rate expected by most banks and companies specializing in making forecasts was less than 2.5%. Consequently, the actual expected return of long-term Treasury bonds was 3.5%. A market risk premium of 6% implies an actual expected stock return of 9.5%. At that time, the forecasts of the real growth of the gross national product were running at about 2.5%. As the dividends paid by American companies were less than 3% of the shares' price, the forecast annual increase in the companies' equity market value would be 1.095 divided by $1.03 - 1 = 6.3\%$. This means that companies' real equity market value will grow much more than the gross national product. According to these forecasts, in 2048, the stock return would be equal or greater than the U.S. gross national product. This extrapolation is impossible; it is unfeasible to think that the annual stock return is greater than the U.S. gross national product.

The magazine *Pensions and Investments* (12/1/1998) carried out a survey among professionals working for institutional investors and the mean market risk premium obtained was 3%. In another survey of pension fund professionals (1997, Greenwich Associates Survey), the mean market risk premium obtained was 5%.

---

[11]Even this method requires knowing the expected growth of dividends. A higher growth estimate implies a higher premium.

11.7.4. FROM THE IRR OF THE SHARE PRICE AND THE EXPECTED DIVIDENDS

This method is similar to that obtained from the Gordon and Shapiro equation. According to this method, the market risk premium can be calculated as the difference between the IRR (internal rate of return) of the share price—expected dividends and the risk-free rate. The main problem is calculating the expected dividends, and that the premium calculated using this method depends on the estimate of the expected dividends and their future growth.

11.7.5. FROM THE INVERSE OF THE PER

The proponents of this method start with the formula (5.2): $E/Ebv = (ROE - g)/(Ke - g)$. If it is assumed that $g = 0$, then $Ke = ROE \times Ebv/E = PAT/E = 1/PER$. If we believe this (the hypothesis of $g = 0$, generally speaking, is not particularly credible), then: risk premium $= (1/PER) - R_F$.

Applying this to the U.S. market in July 2001, when the PER of the S&P 500 was 26.2 and R_F was 5.04%, this gives a negative market risk premium (-1.2%), which is absurd.

11.7.6. AS THE DIFFERENCE BETWEEN STOCK AND LONG-TERM BOND VOLATILITIES

This method also often gives absurd results. Reilly, Wright, and Chan (2000) show that, in the period 1950–1999, the annualized average bond volatility was 4.9% and the annualized average stock volatility was 14.1%. The difference is 9.2%, which is too high for the equity risk premium in the U.S.

11.7.7. MORE RECENT STUDIES

Pastor and Stambaugh (2001) find that

> "the estimated equity premium since 1834 fluctuates between 4 and 6 percent. It rises through much of the 1800s, reaches its peak in the 1930s, and declines fairly steadily thereafter, except for a brief upward spike in the early 1970s. The sharpest

decline in the premium occurs in the 1990s. The later inference is influenced by the prior belief that the premium and the price tend to change in opposite directions. When that aspect of the model is omitted, the estimated premium instead increases during the last decade."

Fama and French (2000) estimate the market risk premium for the period 1950–1999 as being between 3.4 and 4.83%. They say that these figures are far below the stock return over risk-free rate (8.28%) because the reduction in the market risk premium has caused an unexpected increase in share prices.

Li and Xu (1999) prove that the "survivorship bias"[12] does not account for the higher differential return of the market over equity in the American stock market.

11.7.8. Differences between the Arithmetic Average and the Geometric Average

There are four properties that differentiate the arithmetic averages from the geometric averages.

1. The geometric average is always equal or less than the arithmetic average.
2. The more variable (volatile) the returns, the greater will be the difference between the arithmetic average and the geometric average.
3. The geometric average only depends on the price level at the beginning and end of the period studied. However, the arithmetic average tends to rise as the period used shortens. For example, the arithmetic average calculated using monthly returns is usually greater than the arithmetic average obtained using annual returns.
4. The difference between the geometric averages of two series is not equal to the geometric average of the difference. However, the arithmetic average of the difference between two series is equal to the difference in the arithmetic average of each of the series.

---

[12]The *survivorship bias* in this context refers to the fact that, during the period 1926–2000, the U.S. stock market gave the highest returns in the world. Jorion and Goetzmann (1999) show that of the 39 stock markets existing in 1921, none obtained the returns of the American market and most of them had some critical period, mostly wars. According to them, the real mean return of the U.S. market was 4.3% and that of the other markets was 0.8%. For a discussion of what the *survivorship bias* is, see Brown, Goetzmann, and Ross (1995).

11.8. HISTORICAL DIFFERENTIAL RETURN OF THE MARKET PORTFOLIO AND THE RISK-FREE RATE IN THE U.S.

In this section, we will analyze the behavior of the equity and bond markets in the U.S.

Figure 11.13 shows the evolution of the equity market and inflation in the U.S. An investment of $100 in December 1925 in shares became (excluding tax) $258,000 in the year 2000. An investment of $100 in December 1925 in Government bonds became (excluding tax) $3,600 in the year 2000. An investment of $100 in December 1925 in 3-month T-bills became (excluding tax) $1,700 in the year 2000. In the meantime, goods that could be purchased for $100 in 1925 cost $971 in December 2000.

11.8.1. RETURN

Figure 11.14 shows the annual returns of the stock market (shares), the 3-month risk-free rate (T-bills) and the 30-year risk-free rate (T-bonds) after 1926.

11.8.2. VOLATILITY

Figure 11.15 shows the annual volatility, calculated using data from the last 10 years, of stocks, inflation, long-term bonds, and short-term Treasury

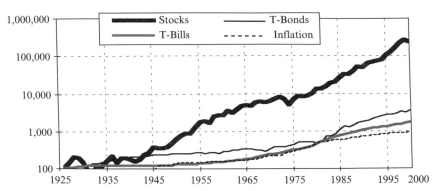

Figure 11.13   Evolution of an investment of $100 in December 1925 in the S&P 500 (stocks), 3-month T-bills and T- bonds, assuming reinvestment of dividends and interest. Goods that could be purchased for $100 in 1925 cost $971 in December 2000 (inflation).

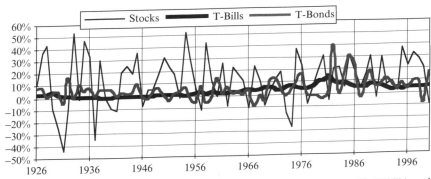

Figure 11.14   Annual return of the S&P 500 (stocks), 3-month U.S. Treasury bills (T-bills), and 30-year U.S. Treasury bonds (T-bonds).

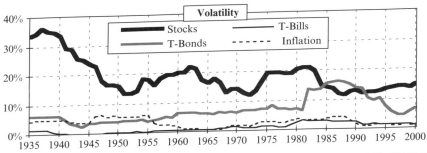

Figure 11.15   Annual volatility of the S&P 500 (Stocks), 3-month U.S. Treasury bills (T-bills), 30-year U.S. Treasury bonds (T-bonds), and inflation. Volatility calculated using yearly data for the past 10 years.

bills. The first conclusion that can be drawn from this figure is that, on average, stock volatility in recent years has been less than stock volatility in the previous periods: during the periods 1935–1945, 1955–1965 and 1972–1983, volatility was greater than in the 1990s. The volatility of long-term bonds (T-bonds) has been significant, particularly at the end of the 1980s, when the volatility of long-term bonds was greater than that of stocks. The volatility of short-term bonds (T-bills) has been markedly less and remained almost always below the volatility of inflation.

Figure 11.16 shows the monthly shareholder return of the S&P 500 from 1926 to early 2001, and Figure 11.17 shows the volatility of the S&P 500 Index using monthly data. We can see here too that the volatility of the S&P 500 in the 1990s has not been greater, on average, than the volatility of previous periods.

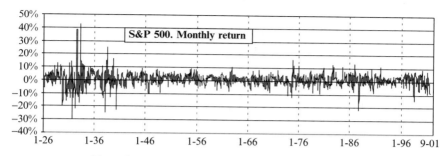

Figure 11.16   Monthly shareholder return of the S&P 500.

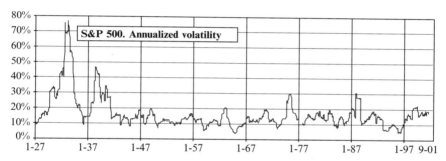

Figure 11.17   Annual volatility of the U.S. stock market (S&P 500 stocks). Volatility calculated using monthly data corresponding to one year.

Figures 11.15–11.17 show that the volatility of the U.S. stock market is not greater than the volatility in previous periods, as some proclaim, but that it is in fact less. Data from previous years and centuries can be found in Ineiche (2000).

11.9. RETURN OF STOCKS OVER BONDS IN U.S.

11.9.1. THE PERIOD 1926–1999

Figure 11.18 shows the geometric average of the last 20 years of the annual difference between the annual return of the market and the return of the 3-month risk-free rate (difference T-bills) and the 30-year risk-free rate (difference T-bonds) between 1946 and 1999.

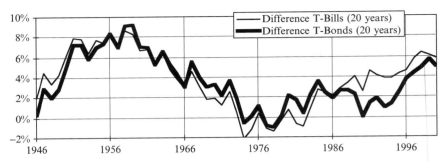

Figure 11.18   Historical differential return (geometric average) between the market and T-bills and T-bonds, over the last 20-year period.

Figure 11.19 shows the arithmetic average for the last 10 years of the annual difference between the annual return of the market and the return of the 3-month risk-free rate (premium bills) between 1936 and 1999 and compares it with the short-term interest rates in each year. Note that the premium has been greater in the years with low interest rates. It is also seen that when rates rise, the premium falls, and vice versa. This is logical: we have already seen that the market normally rises when interest rates fall.

Table 11.3 shows the market return, the return of the short-term risk-free rate, and the return of the long-term risk-free rate in different periods. The arithmetic average and geometric average have been calculated for all parameters.

Table 11.4 shows the average differential return between the market and the short-term risk-free rate (T-bills) and the average differential return between the market and the long-term risk-free rate (T-bonds) in different time periods. The arithmetic average and geometric average have been calculated for all parameters. Damodaran (1994) calculates the geometric average

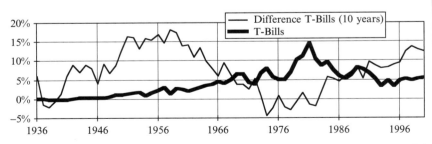

Figure 11.19   Average during the last 10 years of the *premium bills*, and annual return of the 3-month risk-free rate (T-bills).

Table 11.3

**U.S. Stock Market, Average (Arithmetic Average and Geometric Average)
in Different Periods of the Annual Return of the Market,
the 3-Month Risk-Free Rate (T-bills) and the 30-year Risk-Free Rate (T-bonds)**

	Return on Stocks		Return on T- Bills		Return on T-Bonds	
	Arithmetic	Geometric	Arithmetic	Geometric	Arithmetic	Geometric
1926–2000	13.0%	11.2%	3.9%	3.9%	5.2%	5.0%
1951–2000	14.0%	12.8%	5.3%	5.3%	5.7%	5.3%
1961–2000	13.1%	12.0%	6.2%	6.1%	6.8%	6.4%
1971–2000	14.5%	13.2%	6.8%	6.8%	8.6%	8.1%
1981–2000	16.5%	15.7%	6.8%	6.8%	10.8%	10.3%
1991–2000	18.5%	17.6%	5.1%	5.1%	7.2%	7.0%

Table 11.4

**U.S. Stock Market, Average (Arithmetic Average and Geometric Average)
in Different Periods of the Market Premium over the 3-Month Risk-Free Rate
(premium bills) and the 30-Year Risk-Free Rate (premium bonds)**

	Average differential return between the market and:			
	T-Bills		T-Bonds	
	Arithmetic	Geometric	Arithmetic	Geometric
1926–2000	9.1%	7.3%	7.8%	**6.2%**
1951–2000	8.7%	7.5%	8.3%	**7.4%**
1961–2000	6.9%	5.8%	6.3%	**5.6%**
1971–2000	7.7%	6.5%	5.9%	**5.1%**
1981–2000	9.7%	8.9%	5.7%	**5.4%**
1991–2000	13.4%	12.5%	11.3%	**10.6%**

differential return (T-bonds) for the period 1926–1990 and finds 5.5%: this is
the U.S. market risk premium that he uses all through his book.

Copeland, Koller, and Murrin (2000, page 221) recommend using a *risk
premium* between 4.5 and 5%. The argument used by Copeland, Koller, and
Murrin on page 221 is surprising:

> "It is unlikely that the U.S. Market index will do as well over the next century as
> it has in the past, so we adjust downward the historical arithmetic average market
> risk premium. If we substract a 1.5 percent to 2 percent survivorship bias from the

long-term arithmetic average of 6.5 percent,[13] we conclude that the market risk premium should be in the 4.5 percent to 5 percent range."

Further on, they acknowledge that, at the beginning of the year 2000, most investment banks used a risk premium between 3.5 and 5%. However, in 1995, in the second edition, they said (see page 268):

> "We recommend using a 5 to 6 percent market risk premium for U.S. companies. This is based on the long-run geometric average risk premium for the return of the S&P 500 versus the return on long-term government bonds from 1926 to 1992... we use a geometric average of rates of return because arithmetic averages are biased by the measurement period."

In the first edition (1990), they said (see page 196): "Our opinion is that the best *forecast* of the risk premium is its long-run geometric average." Obviously, in the third edition, they have changed their criterion. The advisability of adjusting for *survivorship bias* is not clear. We agree with Siegel (1999, pg. 13).

> "Although stock returns may be lower in foreign countries than in the U.S., the real returns on foreign bonds are substantially lower. Almost all disrupted markets experienced severe inflation, in some instances wiping out the value of fixed-income assets. (One could say that the equity premium in Germany covering any period including the 1922–1923 hyperinflation is over 100%, since the real value of fixed-income assets fell to zero while equities did not.)"

Mayfield (1999) performs an analytically more complex estimate of the risk premium and concludes that the risk premium over short-term bonds is 2.4% less than the difference between the market return and the risk-free rate. Claus and Thomas (1999) also argue that the risk premium is 3% less than the difference between the market return and the risk-free rate.

Figure 11.20 shows the geometric average of the annual difference between the annual market return and the 3-month risk-free rate (T-bills), and of the annual difference between the annual market return and the long-term risk-free rate (T-bonds) for all years between 1926 and 2000.

11.9.2. THE PERIOD 1802–1925

Schwert (1990) and Siegel (1998) studied the relationship between U.S. equity and bonds before 1926. The data on which they base their studies are less reliable than recent data, but, nevertheless, it is interesting. Table 11.5 shows their conclusions. It can be seen that the *risk premium* in the period 1802–1925 was substantially less than the risk premium in subsequent years. Likewise, it can be seen that inflation was substantially less before 1926.

---

[13]This is the arithmetic mean of 2-year returns from 1926–1998. The arithmetic mean of 1-year returns is 7.5%.

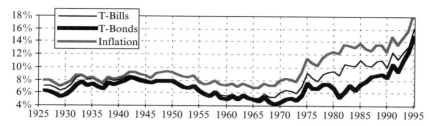

Figure 11.20   U.S. stock market. Annual average differential return in 2000 of the S&P 500 versus 3-month T-Bills (T-Bills), versus 30-year T-Bonds (T-Bonds) and versus inflation. (Annual average differential return from the year chosen until 2000.)

Table 11.5

U.S. stock market, Average (Arithmetic Average) in Different Periods of the Equity Premium above 3-Month Bills (Premium Bills) and 30-Year Bonds (Premium Bonds)

	Arithmetic average return				Arithmetic difference	
	Stocks	T-Bills	T-Bonds	Inflation	T-Bills	T- Bonds
1802–1870	**8.1%**	**5.1%**	**4.9%**	**0.1%**	**3.0%**	**3.2%**
1871–1925	**8.4%**	**3.2%**	**4.4%**	**0.6%**	**5.2%**	**4.0%**
1926–2000	13.0%	3.9%	5.2%	3.2%	9.1%	7.8%
1802–2000	10.0%	4.1%	4.9%	1.4%	5.9%	5.2%

However, the real return of bonds was significantly higher in the years before 1926.

One conclusion that can be drawn after studying all these periods is that the risk premium has varied so much in the past that it is almost impossible to say what its average has been and, of course, much more complicated to predict the future from historical data.

A more detailed look at the data given here raises the following doubts:

1. The equity return varies so much that it is not possible to accurately measure the risk premium even when data spanning a period of more than 70 years is used.

2. There is evidence—as we will show further on—that the risk premium has varied so much over time that it does not make much sense to calculate the average of years whose risk premiums have been radically different.

3. The use of long time periods seeks to eliminate the deviations caused as a result of business cycles, technological progress, political changes, wars,

etc. However, if we want to take the results obtained in one country and apply them in another country with different circumstances, or make comparisons between the two, our perceptions could be erroneous. Thus, in the period 1926–1998, the North American financial markets suffered from financial crises, but the North American economy was not exposed to another type of vicissitude that took place in other countries, such as a war fought on its own territory.

4. Inflation changed considerably in the years that followed the gold standard. With the abandonment of the gold standard, unexpected inflation became a much more important risk.

11.10. *PREMIUM* OVER THE RISK-FREE RATE IN DIFFERENT COUNTRIES AND COUNTRY RISK PREMIUM

Table 11.6 shows the difference between the geometric average of the return of stocks and the geometric average of the return of long-term bonds[14] in different countries. Note that in Germany and Italy, the difference was negative during that period, which is further proof that it is meaningless to call risk premium the difference between the historical market return and the risk-free rate.

It is also seen that the "difference" is greater in countries where the performance of the equity market was better during the period.

Table 11.6 serves a purely informative purpose: it cannot be used to determine each market's risk premium. It makes no sense to say that the risk premium (understood as the incremental return above the risk-free rate required to equity) in Spain during the period 1970–1996 was 0.31%, while in Holland it was 4.65% and 3.72% in the U.S.

To evaluate the country risk premium, one possibility is to multiply the default spread for the country (the country rating measures the default risk perceived in the country's bonds) by the volatility of the stocks and divide it by the volatility of the bonds:

Country risk premium =

Default spread for the Country $\times$ $[\sigma_{stocks}/\sigma_{Government\ bonds}]$

This figure should be added to the home (U.S.) country risk premium.

---

[14]Very often, this difference is called risk premium, although we have already said that the market risk premium has nothing to do with the historical differential return.

Table 11.6

Annual Geometric Average Differential Return in the Year 2000 of the Stock Market versus Long-Term Government Bonds in Several Countries

Country	Period	Average annual return		Difference
		Stocks	Government bonds	
Australia	1970–1996	8.47%	6.99%	**1.48%**
Canada	1970–1996	8.98%	8.30%	**0.68%**
France	1970–1996	11.51%	9.17%	**2.34%**
Germany	1970–1996	11.30%	12.10%	**−0.80%**
Hong Kong	1970–1996	20.39%	12.66%	**7.73%**
Italy	1970–1996	5.49%	7.84%	**−2.35%**
Japan	1970–1996	15.73%	12.69%	**3.04%**
Holland	1970–1996	15.48%	10.83%	**4.65%**
Switzerland	1970–1996	13.49%	10.11%	**3.38%**
UK	1970–1996	12.42%	7.81%	**4.61%**
US	1970–1996	12.34%	8.62%	**3.72%**
Spain	1970–1996	8.22%	7.91%	**0.31%**

Source: Ibbotson.http://www.ibbotson.com.

11.11. PREMIUM OF THE NORTH AMERICAN STOCK MARKET FROM THE GORDON AND SHAPIRO EQUATION

One can also attempt to calculate the implicit market premium from the Gordon and Shapiro equation. The Gordon and Shapiro equation simply says that the price of shares is the current value of the expected dividends discounted at the required return to equity (Ke):

$$P = \text{present value [Dividends;Ke]}$$

However, in turn, Ke is equal to the risk-free rate plus the market risk premium.

$$Ke = R_F + \text{Market risk premium}$$

To calculate the market risk premium, when the stock prices are known, all that we need to know are the expected dividends. Damodaran (2001) performs this exercise using the expected dividends obtained from analysts' forecasts. For the next 5 years after the year in which the calculation is performed, he uses analysts' estimates. There are data obtained from

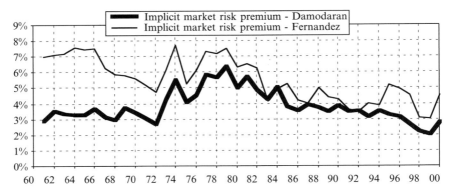

Figure 11.21   Implied market risk premium of the S&P 500 using the two-stage growth model.

analysts' estimates only after 1985. Before that date, he takes the dividends that were actually paid. After year 6, he assumes that dividends will grow at the same rate as long-term Treasury bonds.

Damodaran uses analyst-forecast growth for the first five years and then a stable growth rate equal to the T-bond rate. Fernandez uses an expected growth based on forecast inflation, past growth and the T-bond rate. (Sources: Damodaran (2001, page 65) and own data.)

Looking at Figure 11.21, Damodaran (2001, page 67) concludes,

> "The average implied equity-risk premium between 1970 and 2000 is approximately 4%. By using this premium, you are assuming that while markets might have been overvalued in some of these years and undervalued in others, it has been, on average, correct over this period."

Throughout his book, Damodaran (2001) uses a market risk premium of 4% for the U.S.

Figure 11.21 shows a growth in the market risk premium during the 1972 oil shock and a subsequent fall in the rate until it reached about 1.5% in 1998. The important point about this figure is not so much the specific parameter as that the market risk premium decreases from the 1980s onward.[15]

---

[15]A number of factors suggested as *possible* causes of the reduction of the market risk premium are computer and Internet access to the stock market, decrease in transaction costs, more favorable tax treatment, financial deregulation, the development of mutual and pension funds, the entry of the baby boom generation into the saving phase, and the observation by investors that, in the long run, stocks have almost always given a higher return than bonds.

11.12. RECENT COMPARISON OF THE STOCK MARKET EVOLUTION IN SPAIN, GERMANY, JAPAN, AND THE U.S.

Figure 11.22 shows the comparison of long-term interest rates (interest rate paid on 10–year bonds) in Spain, Germany, Japan, and the U.S. It can be seen that, until 1996, the interest rate paid on bonds in Spain was substantially higher than in the other countries. However, after that date, the long-term interest rates in Spain, U.S., and Germany converge until they reach the present level of about 5.5%. Although Japan has followed the same trend as the other countries (interest rates fell from December 1991 onward), it has always had lower interest rates than Spain, Germany, and the U.S.

Figure 11.23 shows the evolution of four countries' stock market indexes. The starting point for all indexes is 100 points in December 1991. It can be

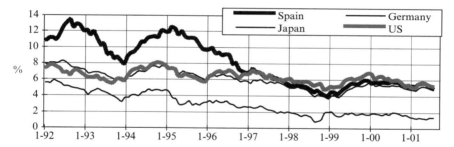

Figure 11.22   Long-term interest rates in Spain, Germany, Japan, and the U.S.

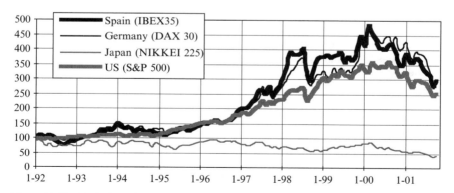

Figure 11.23   Evolution of the stock market indexes of Spain, Germany, Japan, and the U.S. December 1991 = 100 points.

seen that the IBEX 35, the S&P 500, and the DAX 30 have followed parallel paths: all of them have increased significantly. The behavior of the Japanese index Nikkei 225 has been completely different: not only has it not increased but its value in 2001 was less than its value in December 1991.

Table 11.7 shows the correlation matrix between the increase in interest rates between the different countries and the indexes' returns. The correlations between the North American, German, and Spanish stock market indexes have been greater than the correlations between these indexes and the Japanese market. Also, the correlation between the indexes' returns and the increase in interest rates has been greater (in absolute terms) in Spain (-45.3%) than in the other countries (-24.8, -12.3, and 23.5%). Regarding the correlation between interest rate increases, this has logically been greater between Spain and Germany than between Spain and the United States. There has also been a strong correlation between the interest rate increases in Germany and the United States. The correlation between the interest rate increases in Spain and Japan was virtually zero.

11.13. HAS THE MARKET RISK PREMIUM DECREASED OR IS THE MARKET OVERVALUED?

Both Figure 11.23 and many of the previous figures show that that market prices, with the exception of the Japanese market, have risen markedly during the 1990s. Two explanations are usually given to account for this phenomenon: one, that the market risk premium has fallen, and two, that the stock market is overvalued. When talking of market overvaluation, people often talk about the existence of a *speculative bubble*, which means that when this bubble bursts, the stock market will fall to correct price levels (according to those who believe that the market is overvalued).

Example. Greenspan, president of the U.S. Federal Reserve, said on December 5, 1996 (when the Dow Jones was at 6,437 points) that the stock market was showing "irrational exuberance." In August 1999, when the Dow Jones was at 11,090 points, he said that, in his opinion, the stock market was under the effects of a speculative bubble.

However, the data given in many graphs also support the belief of many that the market risk premium has fallen in recent years. Although this has no scientific value, we can take a look at the market risk premium used by American and European MBA students in their finance classes: most professors were using figures between 5 and 7% in 1999, although, admittedly, this was to try to resolve cases taken from the previous 20 years. However, when the professors were asked what was the market risk premium according to them, answers ranging between 2 and 5% were obtained in late 1999.

Table 11.7

Correlation Matrix, Monthly Data, December 1991–August 2001

	Market return of the index:				Increase of yields on Gov. bonds in:			
	S&P 500	DAX	NIKKEI	IBEX	U.S.	Germany	Japan	Spain
Return S&P 500	100.0%	60.4%	38.3%	54.1%				
Return DAX	60.4%	100.0%	30.7%	68.6%				
Return NIKKEI	38.3%	30.7%	100.0%	34.9%				
Return IBEX	54.1%	68.6%	34.9%	100.0%				
Δ Yield U.S.	−24.8%	1.1%	1.0%	1.5%	100.0%	55.1%	20.7%	28.6%
Δ Yield Germany	−10.2%	−12.3%	4.0%	−7.1%	55.1%	100.0%	24.3%	55.6%
Δ Yield Japan	5.8%	6.2%	23.5%	19.0%	20.7%	24.3%	100.0%	2.3%
Δ Yield Spain	−20.3%	−31.3%	−4.4%	−45.3%	28.6%	55.6%	2.3%	100.0%

Glassman and Hassett (2000), authors of the book *Dow 36,000*, calculated that the American market risk premium in 1999 was 3%.[16] Claus and Thomas, from Columbia, reached the same conclusion. Jeremy Siegel, Wharton professor and author of the book *Stocks for the Long Run*, says: "Although it may seem that stocks have more risk than long-term Treasury bonds, this is not true. The safest long-term investment (from the viewpoint of preserving the investor's purchasing power) has been stocks, not Treasury bonds." This fact has been the basic factor in inducing analysts and investors to use market premiums below the historical market return over the risk-free rent.

Whether stock markets are overvalued or the market risk premium has fallen, the consequence for equity investors is the same: equity investors will gain less in coming years than they did in the past (with respect to bonds).

The market risk premium says how much an investor can expect to earn, on average, above what he would earn by investing in long-term Treasury bonds. A fall in the market premium would also explain, at least in part, why the stock markets have been such a profitable investment in the 1990s. Indeed, taking an extreme position, Arnott and Ryan (2001) argue that the risk premium is gone in a paper entitled "The Death of the Risk Premium."

11.14. DOES THE MARKET RISK PREMIUM EXIST?

One of the hypotheses on which the CAPM—and most financial models— is based is that of homogenous expectations: all investors have the same return and risk expectations[17] for all assets. In such a case, all investors would have portfolios composed of risk-free debt and an equity portfolio with the same percentage composition as the market (the stock market). However, it is obvious that not all investors have the same expectations, that not all investors have equity portfolios having an identical composition, and that not all investors have a portfolio composed of all the stocks traded on the market.[18]

We can find out an investor's market risk premium by asking him, although, for many investors, the market risk premium is often not an explicit parameter but rather an implicit one, that manifests in the price that they are

---

[16]As there is always someone willing to go one stage better, Kadlec and Acampora (1999) titled their book *Dow 100,000: Fact or Fiction?*

[17]Identical risk expectations is when all investors agree on their expectations regarding the future volatility of each share's return and the correlation between the shares' returns.

[18]For a good article on the non-existence of homogenous expectations, see Levy and Levy (1996).

prepared to pay for the shares.[19] However, it is impossible to determine the premium for the market as a whole, because it does not exist. Even if we knew the market premiums of the different investors who operated on the market, it would be meaningless to talk of a premium for the market as a whole.

The rationale for this is to be found in the aggregation theorems of microeconomics, which in actual fact are non-aggregation theorems. One model that works well individually for a number of people may not work for all of the people together. For the CAPM, this means that although the CAPM may be a valid model for each investor, it is not valid for the market as a whole, because investors do not have the same return and risk expectations for all shares. The prices are a statement of expected cash flows discounted at a rate that includes the risk premium. Different investors have different cash flow expectations and different future risk expectations. One could only talk of a market risk premium if all investors had the same cash flow expectations.

Figure 11.24 is proof that investors do not have the same expectations: it shows the result of a survey performed among IESE MBAs in January 1998 regarding their return and risk (volatility) forecasts for the Spanish stock market in 1998. It is clearly seen that individual expectations vary

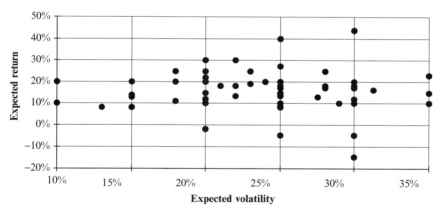

Figure 11.24 Return and risk (volatility) expectations for the Spanish stock market in 1998. Survey performed among IESE MBAs in January 1998.

---

[19]An example shows an investor is prepared to pay today $100 for a perpetual annual cash flow of $6 guaranteed by the state (risk-free fixed-income securities). This implies that the risk-free rate is 6%. However, for another perpetual annual cash flow of $6 in year 1 and growing at an annual rate of 3%, which he expects to obtain from a diversified equity portfolio, he is only prepared to pay $80. This means that the required market return is 10.5% ([6/80] + 0.03). Consequently, this investor's market premium is 4.5%.

enormously. The return of the IBEX 35 in 1998 was 36% and the volatility was 38%.

Table 11.8 shows the forecasts made at the end of 1997 by a number of North American analysts[20] about the level of the Dow Jones at the end of 1998. It also shows their recommendations for the composition of a portfolio: %S is the proportion of stocks that they recommended (the difference in fixed-income). Note the scatter of the forecasts (between 6,100 and 10,250), and the scatter of the proportion of stocks in the portfolio. One would expect that those who forecast a larger rise in the Dow Jones Index would recommend a higher proportion of stocks, but, as can be seen, this is not always so. The Dow Jones stood at 7,908 points on December 31, 1997 and 9,181 points on December 30, 1998.

> One thing is the market risk premium and another is the historical return of stocks over the risk-free rate. It is a common error to confuse them.

The problem with the market risk premium is that investors do not have homogeneous expectations. If they did, it *would* make sense to talk of a market risk premium because all investors would have the market portfolio. However, expectations are not homogeneous.

On top of that we have to take into consideration the inefficencies of the financial markets. For example, Abascal and Pregel (1994) find several inefficiencies exist in the U.S. stock market, the strongest one being the lead-lag effect that exists between large and small firms.

11.12. THE HMDYWD METHOD

My friend Guillermo Fraile, IAE professor at Buenos Aires, jokes in his classes by explaining a new method for calculating the risk premium for family business: the HMDYWD (How much do you want, Dad?) method. After what we have seen in this chapter, the HMDYWD is no joke: it does not make much sense to talk about market risk premium as a magnitude shared by all investors; but it does make sense to talk about *each investor's* market risk premium, including Dad's.

---

[20]Source: *Business Week*, 29 December 1997, page 65.

Table 11.8

Forecast Made at the End of 1997 by Analysts about the Level of the Dow Jones at the End of 1998

Analyst/company	Dow Jones 1998	%S
BIRINY JR. Birinyi Assoc.	10,250	75
J.FROEHLICH Zurich Kemper Invest.	10,000	75
E. PERONI JR. Janney Montgomery Scott	9,850	100
F. DWYER Ladenburg Thalmann & Co.	9,800	65
S. ROBBINS Robinson-Humphrey	9,455	60
J. APPLEGATE Lehman Brothers	9,200	75
J. CANELO Morgan Stanley, Dean Witter	9,000	70
J. DOMBICIK McDonald & Co.	9,000	75
G. RILEY JR BankBoston	8,950	60
S. RONESS JW Charles	8,900	85
T. McMANUS NatWest Markets	8,850	64
D. CLIGGOTT J.P. Morgan	8,800	60
A. GOLDMAN A.G. Edwards & Sons	8,800	70
M. SIMPSON Kirkpatrick Pettis	8,800	70
W. ZEMPEL Robert W. Baird & Co.	8,740	70
J. COHEN Goldman Sach	8,700	65
K. LYNCH Interstate Johnson Lane	8,700	60
R. DAVID JR. Rauscher Pierce Refsnes	8,666	65
E. CRIPPS Legg Mason Wood Walker	8,600	80
J. PRADILLA Cowen & Co.	8,600	45
F. SKRAINKA Edward Jones	8,600	70
T. MADDEN Federated Investors	8,500	55
A. SMITH Prudential Securities	8,500	85
J. MACKAY Bear Stearns	8,350	50
P. ANDERSON American Express Fin.Adv.	8,100	70
M. ACUFF Salomon Smith Barney	8,000	55
G. CRANE Key Asset Management	7,800	75
G. JACOBSEN Trevor Stewart Burton&J.	7,750	60
C. MOORE Principal Financial Securities	7,675	60
E. MILLER Donaldson, Lufkin&Jenrette	7,300	50
R. BROWN Feris, Baker Watts	7,061	40
H. BARTHEL Fahnestock	7,000	60
M. DION Ziegler Asset Management	7,000	95
M. METZ Cibc-Oppenheimer	7,000	25
R. HAYS Wheat First Butcher Singer	6,300	72
F. DICKEY Dain Bosworth	6,100	60

KEY CONCEPTS

- Methods proposed for calculating the market risk premium
- The market risk premium is not the difference between the historical market return and the risk-free rate
- Evolution of the stock market and inflation in Spain
- Evolution of the stock market and inflation in the U.S.
- Comparison of the Spanish and North American stock markets
- Has the market risk premium fallen or is the stock market overvalued?
- Does the market risk premium exist?
- The HMDYWD method

REFERENCES

Abascal, E. M., and G. Pregel (1994), "Weak Form Efficiency: A Comparison Between the Spanish and the U.S. Capital Stock Markets," IESE Business School Working Paper D/273.

Arnott, R. D., and R. J. Ryan (2001), "The Death of the Risk Premium," *Journal of Portfolio Management*, Spring, pp. 61–74.

Bartholdy, J., and P. Peare (2001), "The Relative Efficiency of Beta Estimates," Aarhus School of Business, Working Paper.

Bodie, Z., and R. Merton (2000), *Finance*, New Jersey: Prentice Hall.

Booth, L. (1999), "Estimating the Equity Risk Premium and Equity Costs: New Ways of Looking at Old Data," *Journal of Applied Corporate Finance*, Vol. 12, No. 1, pp. 100–112.

Brealey, R.A., and S.C. Myers (2000), *Principles of Corporate Finance*, 6th edition, New York: McGraw-Hill.

Brown, S. J., W. N. Goetzmann, and S. A. Ross (1995). "Survival," *The Journal of Finance*, July, pp. 853–873.

Claus, J. J., and J. K. Thomas, (1999), "The Equity Risk Premium Is Much Lower Than You Think It Is: Empirical Estimates From A New Approach," Research paper, Columbia Business School.

Copeland, T. E., T. Koller, and J. Murrin (2000), *Valuation: Measuring and Managing the Value of Companies*, 3rd, edition, New York: Wiley.

Copeland, T. E., and J. I. Weston (1988), *Financial Theory and Corporate Policy*, 3rd edition, Reading, MA: Addison-Wesley.

Damodaran, A. (1994), *Damodaran on Valuation*, New York: John Wiley and Sons.

Damodaran, A. (2001), *The Dark Side of Valuation*, New York: Prentice Hall.

Fama, E.F., and K.R. French (1992), "The Cross-Section of Expected Stock Returns." *Journal of Finance*, 47, pp. 427–466.

Fama, E.F., and K.R. French (2000), "The Equity Premium," Center for Research in Security Prices, Working Paper No. 522.

Glassman, J. K., and K. A. Hassett (2000). *Dow 36.000: The New Strategy for Profiting from the Coming Rise in the Stock Market*. New York: Three Rivers.

Ineiche, A. (2000), "Twentieth Century Volatility," *Journal of Portfolio Management*, Fall, pp. 93–102.

Jorion, P., and W. N. Goetzmann (1999), "Global Stock Markets in the Twentieth Century," *Journal of Finance*, 54 (June), pp. 953–80.

Kadlec, C., and R. Acampora (1999), *Dow 100.000: Fact or Fiction?*, New York: Prentice Hall.

Levy, M., and H. Levy, (1996), "The danger of assuming homogeneous expectations," *Financial Analysts Journal*, May/June, pp. 65–70.

Li, H., and Yuewu X. (1999), "Can Survival Bias Explain the 'Equity Premium Puzzle'?," Working Paper SSRN.

Mas-Colell, A, M. D. Whinston, and J. R. Green (1995), *Microeconomic Theory*, London: Oxford University Press.

Mayfield, E. S. (1999), "Estimating the Market Risk Premium," Research Paper, Graduate School of Business Administration, Harvard University.

Miller, M.H. (2000), "The History of Finance: An Eyewitness Account," *Journal of Applied Corporate Finance*, Vol. 13 No. 2, pp. 8–14.

Pastor, L., and R. F. Stambaugh (2001), "The Equity Premium and Structural Breaks," *Journal of Finance*, 56, No. 4, pp. 1207–1239.

Porter, M. (1992), "Capital Disadvantage: America's Failing Capital Investment System," *Harvard Business Review*, September–October.

Reilly, F. K., D. J. Wright, and K.C. Chan (2000), "Bond Market Volatility Compared to Stock Market Volatility," *Journal of Portfolio Management*, (Fall), pp. 82–92.

Ross, S. A., R. W. Westerfield, and J. F. Jaffe (1993), *Corporate Finance*, third edition, Homewood, IL.: Irwin/McGraw-Hill.

Schwert, G. W. (1990), "Indexes in the United States Stock Prices from 1802 to 1987," *Journal of Business*, Volume 63, July.

Siegel, J. (1998), *Stocks for the Long Run*, (2nd edition), New York: Irwin.

Siegel, J. (1999), "The Shrinking Equity Premium," *Journal of Portfolio Management*, Fall, pp. 10–17.

Termes, R. (1998), *Inversión y Coste de Capital*, Madrid: McGraw-Hill.

Van Horne, J. C. (1992), *Financial Management and Policy*, 9th edition Englewood Cliff, NJ: PrenticeHall.

Welch, I. (2000), "Views of Financial Economists on the Equity Premium and on Professional Controversies," *Journal of Business*, Volume 73, Number 4, pp. 501–537.

Weston, J. F., S. Chung, and J. A. Siu, (1997), *Takeovers, Restructuring and Corporate Governance*, 2nd edition, New York: Prentice Hall.

Chapter 12

Valuations of Internet Companies: The Case of Terra-Lycos

Terra started trading on the stock market in November 1999. The placement price was 13 euros per share (11.81 for retailers). In February 2000, its price stood at 139.75 euros. Between November 1999 and February 2000, Terra provided a return of 975% for its shareholders. However, by December 2000, the share price had plummeted to 11.6 euros, 8.3% of its February high. The average annual volatility of the Terra share was almost 100%.

In this chapter,[1] we review twelve valuations of Terra performed by Spanish and non-Spanish bank analysts and brokers.[2] We will look at several of them and we will also develop on the valuation by multiples we saw in the previous chapter.

We will start with the opinion of one Internet business analyst.

**Opinion of a Spanish Bank Analyst Regarding the
Valuation of Internet Companies**

There are obstacles that hinder the valuation of Internet companies. These obstacles include: difficulty in finding fully comparable

(continues)

---

[1] I would like to thank Natalia Centenera, Josep Faus, and Rafael Termes for their comments.
[2] Most of them can be described—depending on what the reader prefers—as highly questionable, esoteric, cabalistic, out of this world, or useless.

(continued)

companies; the limited track record of these companies and the industry, which makes analysis by cash flow discounting more complicated (as an example, we can mention Terra, which was formed in November 1998); the industry's significant degree of volatility; and the considerable divergence of multiples.

To calculate the value of an Internet company, we should consider the following methodologies:

a) Valuation by sum of the parts, applying the relevant multiples to each business line

b) The application of the Price/sales multiple of listed Internet companies

c) The book value, interpreted as the "absolute minimum valuation"

d) A maximum valuation, calculated from the multiples of industry leaders (AOL, Yahoo, etc.)

We consider that cash flow discounting is not the right tool for valuing a company like Terra. First, given the changes that the industry is experiencing (the Internet revolution) and the changes that the company could experience (new acquisitions), cash flow discounting would provide an incorrect valuation. In addition, almost all the value depends on the residual value. One could also discuss which is the right WACC and the appropriate perpetual growth. The right multiples are price/subscriber and price/sales. As all the Internet companies are still a long way from breaking even, in our opinion, price/sales is the most reasonable multiple for making comparisons.

As the above lines show, there are analysts and managers who maintain that the Internet companies cannot be valued using the traditional method of discounting expected cash flows.[3] This is not correct, it is a conceptual error, and it is the best recipe for creating speculative bubbles.

An investor is prepared to pay a price for a share (which is a piece of paper) if by having this piece of paper, he expects to receive money (flows) in the future. Therefore, the share's value is the current discounted value of the expected cash flows.[4] Otherwise, shares would be like sardine cans during the black market days in the 1940s. There is a joke[5] that says that one black

---

[3]There were many more in the first quarter of 2000.

[4]Plus the value of the real options, which are simply the expected flows contingent upon some future uncertainty. For more about real options, see Chapter 22.

[5]The author was told this joke by Rafael Termes.

marketeer sold a sardine can to another for one peseta. This black marketeer sold it to another for two pesetas and the third black marketeer sold it to another for three pesetas. The can continued to change hands and increase in price until a black marketeer bought it for 25 pesetas (an enormous sum at that time) and decided to open it. To his enormous surprise, he saw that the can was empty. He ran back to the black marketeer who had sold it to him to get his 25 pesetas back. However, this black marketeer simply told him, "How could you be so stupid as to open the can? This can is for selling, not for eating."

This joke also illustrates perfectly the distinction (with no basis) that some people make between shares for investing in (to hold them for a long time, so they say) and shares to speculate in (to sell quickly, so they say).

Expected cash flow discounting is the right method for valuing any company's shares. However, we should add that cash flow discounting should be complemented in certain cases with the valuation of the real options, but not all Internet companies have valuable real options. A real option only contributes value to a company when this company has some kind of exclusive right for exercising the option in the future. Furthermore, the real options to be found in Internet companies cannot be described as readily as the real options offered by the operation of a mine or the operation of an oil field. A good valuation of an Internet company should consider the reasonableness of the business plan (paying particular attention to the analysis of the expected growth of sales and margin), and it must recognize and quantify the value (if any) of the real options existing in the company.

12.1. TWELVE VALUATIONS OF TERRA: DIFFERENT EXPECTATIONS

Table 12.1 shows the projected sales and earnings provided by the twelve valuations of Terra. The table's second column shows the date on which the projections were made. Valuations [9], [11] and [12] give much higher sales figures than the others because their projections include Terra's merger with Lycos. It is interesting to observe that although there are differences in expected sales, the largest differences are to be found in the estimate of future earnings. For example, if we observe expected earnings for the year 2000, it seems that expected losses increased as time went by.

Of the twelve valuations, only one ([4]) used cash flow discounting. Another valuation ([6]) was based on multiples, but also used cash flow discounting to perform a reverse valuation.[6] Valuation [11] says that "we will perform

---

[6]Reverse valuation consists of calculating the hypotheses that are necessary to attain the share's price in order to then assess these hypotheses.

Table 12.1
Twelve Projections of Sales, Net Income, and EBITDA made by Different Companies (Million euros)

	Sales	1999	2000	2001	2002	2003	2004	2005
[1] Sept–99	American bank 1	76	149	269	456	748		
[2] Sept–99	Spanish bank 1	67	146	279	499	798		
[3] Sept–99	Spanish bank 2	74	153	265	409	604		
[4] Sept–99	American bank 2	72	138	220	375	610	919	1,311
[5] Sept–99	American bank 3	70	171	331	553	847		
[6] March–00	French bank	79	188	311	463	652	828	
[7] April–00	Euroamerican bank	79	178	323	539	860	1,238	1,617
[8] May–00	Spanish bank 2	79	182	340	548	753		
[9] June–00	American bank 4	79	576	905	1,166	1,465		
[10] July–00	German bank	79	196	414	773			
[11] Oct–00	American bank 5	79	572	988	1,374	1,735		
[12] Oct–00	Spanish bank 2	79	591	1,019	1,473	1,962		

	Net income	1999	2000	2001	2002	2003	2004	2005
[1] Sept–99	American bank 1	–152	–154	–138	–120	–51		
[2] Sept–99	Spanish bank 1	–154	–243	–221	–99	40		
[3] Sept–99	Spanish bank 2	–179	–185	–175	–136	–7		
[4] Sept–99	American bank 2	–146	–174	–135	–51	67	246	529
[5] Sept–99	American bank 3	–154	–206	–196	–95	51		

(continues)

Table 12.1 (*continued*)

Sales		1999	2000	2001	2002	2003	2004	2005
[6] March–00	French bank	−174	−269	−280	−208	−80	54	106
[7] April–00	Euroamerican bank	−174	−341	−337	−267	−112	173	368
[8] May–00	Spanish bank 2	−173	−532	−472	−317	−124		
[9] June–00	American bank 4	−174	−601	−400	−54	173		
[10] July–00	German bank	−173	−558	−641	−650			
[11] Oct–00	American bank 5	−173	−1,067	−2,750	−2,550	−2,442		
[12] Oct–00	Spanish bank 2	−173	−365	−595	−286	38		

EBITDA		1999	2000	2001	2002	2003	2004	2005
[1] Sept–99	American bank 1	−59	−51	−12	28	137		
[2] Sept–99	Spanish bank 1	−38	−149	−123	15	160		
[3] Sept–99	Spanish bank 2	−74	−68	−42	13	153		
[4] Sept–99	American bank 2	−132	−152	−107	−17	106	290	578
[5] Sept–99	American bank 3	−49	−103	−83	28	102		
[6] March–00	French bank	−86	−173	−145	−64	57	182	330
[7] April–00	Euroamerican bank	−86	−329	−307	−195	49	352	656
[8] May–00	Spanish bank 2	−86	−418	−336	−164	39		
[9] June–00	American bank 4	−86	−84	8	245	413		
[10] July–00	German bank	−86	−371	−380	−320			
[11] Oct–00	American bank 5	−86	−379	−245	−11	121		
[12] Oct–00	Spanish bank 2	−86	−258	−165	130	476		

the valuation by cash flow discounting when the company Terra-Lycos offers joint accounting statements."

Valuation [4] was performed by an American bank immediately before the subscription offer, based on its cash flow forecasts. They assumed that Terra's beta was 2.5 and the market premium was 3.5%.[7] As the yield on long-term Treasury stock was 5.15%, they estimated the required return to equity at 13.9%. This gave them a value per share of 16.3 euros. On the basis of this valuation, they recommended accepting the subscription offer (11.81 euros per share).

The only valuation report in which the recommendation was to sell was [6], made in March 2000, when Terra's share price was 117.15 euros. The French bank valued the share at 86 euros. The valuation was based on the [market value/sales] multiple of comparable companies: Freeserve, Tiscali, Freenet.de, and Infosources. The French bank also provided a reverse valuation by cash flow discounting. The bank argued that in order to obtain the market price of 117.15 euros per share, it was necessary to expect a growth in cash flows[8] of 14% after 2010. As this 14% growth seemed excessive to it, the French bank concluded that, at 117.15 euros, Terra was overvalued.

Figure 12.1 shows the evolution of Terra's share price in euros per share.

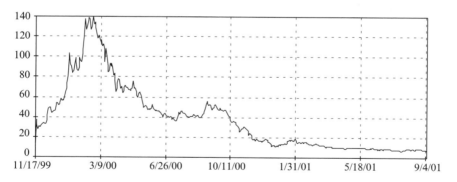

Figure 12.1   Terra's share price in euros per share.

[7]They justified Terra's beta on the betas of AOL, Amazon, and Yahoo, which were 2.3, 2.5 and 2.7.

[8]Assuming a beta of 2.5, a market premium of 3.5%, and a risk-free rate of 6%. These parameters gave a required return to equity of 14.75% and a weighted average cost of capital of 14.6%.

12.2. SOME COMPARISONS BETWEEN THE PROJECTIONS AND THE VALUATIONS

In this section, we will compare some of the projections. Thus, for example, Table 12.2 compares the earnings projections made by an American bank in September 1999 with those made by a French bank in March 2000. The difference shows that the American bank projected lower losses and higher earnings than the French bank. However, the American bank valued the Terra share at 16.3 euros per share, and the French bank (which expected much higher losses and much lower earnings) valued the Terra share at 86 euros per share.

Similarly, Table 12.3 compares the projections made by a Euroamerican bank in April 2000 with those of an American bank in June 2000. It is clear that the Euroamerican bank projected lower losses in 2000 and 2001 but higher losses in 2002 and 2003. However, the Euroamerican bank valued the Terra share at 104 euros per share while the American bank valued it at 53 euros per share.

The reader can make other inconsistent comparisons considering that the value per share in euros given by the valuations was:

Valuation	[1]	[2]	[3]	[4]	[5]	[6]	[7]	[8]	[9]	[10]	[11]	[12]
Date	Sept–99	Sept–99	Sept–99	Sept–99	Sept–99	March–00	April–00	May–00	June–00	July–00	Oct–00	Oct–00
Value (euros/share)	> 13	19.8	> 13	16.3	> 13	86	104	84.4	53	40	46	40
Share price (euros)	11.81	11.81	11.81	11.81	11.81	117.5	73.8	68	45	40	45.1	25.7

12.3. VALUATION PERFORMED BY A EUROAMERICAN BANK IN APRIL 2000: 104 EUROS

This section summarizes the valuation of Terra's shares performed by a Euroamerican bank in April 2000, when Terra's share price was 73.8 euros. As the valuation given by Table 12.4 is 104 euros per share, the bank advised its customers to buy Terra shares.

The valuation given in Table 12.4 is based on the 15 largest Internet companies in the U.S. The first column gives the price per share, the second column the number of shares outstanding, and the third column the companies' capitalization in million dollars. When the net debt is added to the capitalization, what the bank calls enterprise value (EV) is obtained, that is, the company's value. Thus, the sum of the EVs of the 15 largest Internet companies in the U.S. was $278.145 billion. The Euroamerican bank's analyst then divided this quantity by the number of inhabitants in the U.S., which he estimated to be 273 million, obtaining the EV per capita in the U.S.: $1,019.

Table 12.2

Projections of Terra's Earnings (Million Euros), Difference between Projections [4] and [6]

		Net income	1999	2000	2001	2002	2003	2004	2005
[4]	Sept–99	American bank 2	–146	–174	–135	–51	67	246	529
[6]	March–00	French bank	–174	–269	–280	–208	–80	54	106
[4] – [6]		**Difference**	**28**	**95**	**145**	**157**	**147**	**192**	**423**

Table 12.3

**Projections of Terra's Earnings (Million Euros),
Difference between Projections [7] and [9]**

		Net income	1999	2000	2001	2002	2003
[7]	April–00	Euroamerican bank	−174	−341	−337	−267	−112
[9]	June–00	American bank 4	−174	−601	−400	−54	173
[7] − [9]		**Difference**	**0**	**260**	**63**	**−213**	**−284**

At the bottom of Table 12.4, the analyst divided Terra's market into three geographical areas: Spain, *Hispanic* America,[9] and Latin America. Column 1 shows the gross national product per capita in each of the three geographical areas, and column 2 shows the percentage they represent with respect to the gross national product per capita in the U.S. ($32,328). Column 3 is the result obtained by multiplying the EV per capita in the U.S. ($1019) by the ratio between the gross national product per capita in each of the three geographical areas and the North American gross national product per capita (column 2). He then multiplied column 3 by the number of inhabitants in each geographical area (column 4) and by Terra's estimated market share in each of these markets (column 5), and obtained Terra's value in each of these geographical areas (column 6). Adding the three amounts in column 6, he arrived at the value for Terra: $27.117 billion. After subtracting the net debt from this amount, he obtained Terra's implicit capitalization: $27.642 billion. By dividing this quantity by the number of Terra shares (280 million) and by the euro's exchange rate, the analyst obtained the value of the Terra share: 104 euros per share.

Doesn't this valuation seem surprising to the reader? We can propose three more ways of getting the figure of $104 per share:

1. The value of the Terra share is twice the age of Manolo Gómez's mother-in-law, who is 52. We chose Manolo because he lives near Terra's corporate headquarters.
2. The value of the Terra share is eight times the price of the initial public offering (13 euros).
3. The speed of light in thousand of kilometers per second raised to the power of 0.3682.

Of course, these three valuations are absurd, but they have the same rigor as that given in Table 12.4. As the Spanish saying goes, "the blind man dreamt he saw and he dreamt what he wanted to see."

[9]American citizens who are Spanish speakers.

Table 12.4
Valuation of Terra Performed by a Euroamerican Bank on April 7, 2000

	Price per share ($)	Million shares	Capitalization ($ million)	Net debt	EV (enterprise value)
AOL	65.0	2,282	148,315	−1,472	146,843
Yahoo!	158.0	526	83,184	−1,208	81,976
Lycos	61,5	110	6,760	−618	6,142
Excite@Home	30,0	352	10,559	302	10,861
Go Networks	19.0	165	3,133	349	3,482
NBC Interactive	38.5	32	1,223	259	1,482
About.com	65.0	17	1,075	−176	899
The Go2Net	71.4	31	2,182	214	2,396
Ask Jeeves	59.0	35	2,062	−166	1,896
LookSmart	38.0	88	3,340	−97	3,243
Juno	13.8	39	531	−89	442
Infospace	65.5	217	14,186	−89	14,097
GoTo.com	43.0	49	2,107	−104	2,003
Earthink	18.0	138	2,489	−206	2,283
TheGlobe.com	5.0	30	152	−52	100
Sum of the 15 largest information hubs in the U.S.			281,298	−3,153	278,145

(continues)

Table 12.4 (*continued*)

No. inhabitants (million)	273
EV per capita (US$)	1,019
GNP per capita in the US (US$)	32,328

	GNP Per capita (US$) [1]	GNP per capita vs. USA (%) [2]	Adjusted EV per capita (U.S.$) [3]	Million inhabitants [4]	Terra market share (%) [5]	Value [6]
Spain	17,207	53%	542	39	30%	6,345
Hispanic America	16,164	50%	509	30	5%	764
Latin America	7,513	23%	237	338	25%	20,008
Average	*9,080*	*28%*	*286*	*407*	*23%*	
Value of Terra ($ million)						**27,117**
Net debt ($ million)						−525
Implicit capitalization ($ million)						**27,642**
Million shares: 280			Dollar/euro exchange rate: 0.94875		**Price per share**	**104**

12.4. VALUATION PERFORMED BY A SPANISH BANK IN MAY 2000: 84.4 EUROS

In this section, we transcribe the valuation of Terra performed by a Spanish bank in May 2000, when Terra's share price stood at 68 euros. As the valuation concluded that the value of the Terra share was 84.4 euros, the Spanish bank also advised in favor of buying.

Table 12.5 shows the valuation of Terra performed by the sum of the parts. The top of the table shows the result of the valuation performed by the analyst using a number of multiples. He used the capitalization/subscriber multiple for the years 1999, 2000, and 2001, and also the capitalization over sales multiple for the same years. He also performed an additional valuation assuming a time lag in the multiples. The valuation by the sum of the parts consists of adding the Internet access business (ISP), the valuation of the portal, the valuation of the B2B services, and Terra's holdings in other companies. To obtain a valuation for the ISP businesses, he used the multiples of the companies that seemed to have similar features (Earthlink, Prodigy, PSInet), and he calculated the average of these data and applied it to Terra. Thus, the ISP business according to the capitalization/subscriber multiple has a value which ranges between 1.89 and 4.49 billion euros. Using the capitalization over sales multiple, the value of the ISP would only be between 199 and 339 million euros. Using the multiples with a lag to take into account the companies' varying states of maturity, the valuation ranges between 9.39 billion and 846 million euros. To obtain the valuation of the portal, the analyst performed a similar analysis taking as his reference companies whose main business is the portal. Using the capitalization over sales multiple, he obtained values ranging between 1.92 and 11.01 billion euros.

To value the B2B services business, the analyst used Reuters as a guideline, using only the capitalization over sales multiple. In this case, the analyst arrived at figures with a much lower scatter: the value of this business of Terra's ranges between 107 and 112 million euros.

The top of Table 12.5 summarizes the valuation by the sum of the parts: the valuation of Terra ranges between 4.69 and 22.87 billion euros.

There is an enormous scatter in the multiples used of comparable companies. For example, in the valuation of the portal, depending on the year being considered, the multiples range between 11.1 and 111; between 6.3 and 60.7; and between 4.4 and 34.6. With such scatter, using the average of such different data has very little solid basis.

Table 12.6 shows the valuation of Terra performed by the analyst considering it as a complete company. To do this, he compared Terra with companies offering similar services. The multiples used are the same as in

Table 12.5
Valuation of Terra by the Sum of the Parts Performed by a Spanish Bank on May 10, 2000

Sum of the parts (million euros)

	Capitalization/subscriber			Capitalization/sales			With lag	
	1999	2000	2001	1999	2000	2001	Cap./Subscriber	Cap./Sales
ISP business	1,892	3,754	4,485	199	303	339	9,385	846
Portal business	8,201	1,915	3,378	8,201	1,915	3,378	11,012	11,012
Corporate services	107	108	112	107	108	112	107	107
Other shareholdings	2,364	2,364	2,364	2,364	2,364	2,364	2,364	2,364
Terra valuation (million euros)	12,564	8,141	10,339	10,871	4,690	6,193	22,869	14,329

Valuation of the "ISP" business

	Capitalization (million euros)	Capitalization/subscriber			Capitalization/sales			With lag		
		1999	2000E	2001F	1999	2000E	2001F	Lag	Cap/subs	Cap/sales
Earthlink	2,215	715	527	403	3.0	2.0	1.3	−2	715	3.0
Prodigy	834	556	261	194	4.0	2.8	2.0	−2	556	4.0
PSInet	3,074	2,196	1,464	1,025	5.0	2.8	1.8	−2	2,196	5.0
Average		1,437	961	687	4.1	2.5	1.7		1,681	2.5
Implied Terra valuation		1,892	3,754	4,485	199	303	339		9,385	846

(continues)

Table 12.5 (continued)

Valuation of the portal business

	Capitalization (million euros)	Capitalization/Sales			With lag	
		1999	2000E	2001F	Lag	Cap/sales
Yahoo	72,752	111.0	60.7	34.6	–2	111.0
Lycos	6,106	27.4	17.1	12.2	–2	27.4
Go2Net	1,684	72.0	21.6	12.6	–2	72.0
AskJeeves	1,014	41.4	13.0	6.1	–2	41.4
Go.com	2,466	11.1	6.3	4.4	–2	11.1
About	837	27.9	10.7	5.0	–2	27.9
Goto.com	1,450	100.3	20.1	10.4	–2	100.3
LookSmart	2,148	42.9	21.4	11.7	–2	42.9
NetZero	1,071	41.9	13.8	6.4	–2	41.9
Average		97.6	52.3	29.9		97.6
Implied Terra valuation (million euros)		8,201	1,915	3,378		11,012

Valuation of the "corporate services" business

	Capitalization/Sales		
	1999	2000	2001
Reuters	4.9	4.7	4.6
Terra implied valuation (million euros)	107	108	112

Table 12.6
Valuation of Terra Performed by a Spanish Bank on May 10, 2000

Valuation of the entire company

	Capitalization (million euros)	Capitalization/subscriber			Capitalization/sales			Lag	With lag	
		1999	2000E	2001F	1999	2000E	2001F		Cap/subs	Cap/sales
Terra	19,040	14,457	4,875	2,914	242.4	104.9	56.1	−2	2,914	56.1
Tiscali	10,461	11,955	3,487	2,092	330	65.4	34.9	−2	2,092	34.9
Freeserve	6,974	4,359	3,170	2,325	275.4	91.2	45.6	0	4,359	275.4
Freenet	3,360	4,098	2,100	1,344	960	187.7	84	−1	2,750	187.7
World On Line	3,300	2,750	1,100	550	51.6	16.5	8.2	−1	3,869	16.5
Liberty Surf	3,676	11,055	3,869	2,162	602.5	147	61.3	−1	12,106	147
T On Line	50,844	12,106	6,356	5,084	118.8	56.5	36.3	−1	6,007	56.5
AOL	142,975	6,007	5,199	4,399	22.6	17.1	14.3	0	5,988	22.6
Excite@Home	6,887	5,988	3,443	1,722	14.7	8.3	5.6	0	5,988	14.7
El Sitio	376	4,580	3,414	2,504	19.1	11.3	5.6	−2	2,504	5.6
Stamedia	1,408	NA	NA	NA	68.8	30.1	14.1	−2	NA	14.1
Average (ex-Terra)		7,004	4,740	3,843	82.1	32	20.7		6,552	31.0
Implied valuation (million euros)		9,225	18,511	25,107	6,447	5,802	7,035		42,805	11,866
Euros per share		35.5	71.2	96.6	24.8	22.3	27.1		164.6	45.6

the valuation by parts: capitalization by subscriber, capitalization by sales, and an adjustment for lag. This valuation gives values ranging between 5.802 and 42.805 billion euros. Observe here too the enormous scatter in the multiples used in Table 12.6: the multiples in the fifth column range between 14.7 and 960; those of the last column between 5.6 and 275.4.

Table 12.7 is the end of this analyst's valuation. It is a summary of the data obtained in Tables 12.5 and 12.6. The analyst used the maximum, minimum, and average values obtained in the valuation of the entire company (data from Table 12.6) and in the valuation by the sum of the parts (data from Table 12.5). Line (a) is the average of the data obtained for the valuation of the entire company and the valuation of the company as a sum of the parts. The analyst then calculated the average of all these numbers, which gave 17.232 billion euros.

Line (b) provides a data calculated by the analyst in which he adjusted the value of 17.232 billion euros for Terra's target population compared with the target population of other comparable companies and for the gross national product. He arrived at a valuation of 36.606 billion euros. The following line is the total valuation of Terra's shares: according to the analyst, 67% of line (a) plus 33% of line (b), which gives 23.623 billion euros. Dividing this value by the number of Terra shares (280 million), the analyst concluded that the value of each Terra share is 84.4 euros per share.

Another valuation with a rigor similar to that given above (i.e., none at all) would be to say that the value of Terra's shares is the average capitalization of the companies listed in Table 12.6, which gives 23.026 billion euros, a figure which is very close to that obtained in the valuation of Table 12.7 (23.626 billion euros).

12.5. VALUATION PERFORMED BY AN AMERICAN BROKER IN JUNE 2000: 53 EUROS

In this section, we summarize the valuation performed by an American broker in June 2000, when Terra's share price was 45 euros per share. As his valuation gave 53 euros per share, the broker recommended buying Terra shares.

Table 12.8 shows a summary of the valuation performed by the broker by geographical areas. First, he valued Terra's business in North America using the value per page viewed multiple. For Europe, he added together two values: on the one hand, the value of Lycos Europe at market price, and, on the other hand, the value of Terra's business in Spain using the value per subscriber multiple for comparable European companies. To value Latin America, he used the value per subscriber multiple. To value the business in

Table 12.7

Summary of the valuation of Terra performed by a Spanish bank on May 10, 2000

	Without adjustments			"Click Lag" adjustment			Average
	Maximum	Average	Minimum	Maximum	Average	Minimum	
Entire company	25,107	12,021	5,802	42,805	27,335	11,866	
Sum of the parts	12,564	8,800	4,690	22,869	18,599	14,329	
(a) Average	18,836	10,411	5,246	32,837	22,967	13,098	**17,232**
(b) Valuation with adjustments for population and gross national product per capita							36,606
Value of Terra shares = Weighted average [67% (a) + 33% (b)] (million euros)							23,626
Number of Terra shares (million)							280
Target price per share (euros)							**84.4**

Table 12.8

Valuation of Terra Performed by an American broker on June 20, 2000

	Methodology	Comparables	U.S.$ (million)
USA and Canada	EV/Pageview	Yahoo! (without Japan less 30%)	9,664
Total North America			**9,664**
Lycos Europe	Market price		1,264
Spain	EV/Sub	Comparable European companies	6,301
Total Europe			**7,565**
Brazil	EV/Sub	Comparable European companies	3,818
Mexico	EV/Sub	Comparable European companies	1,145
Other			,400
Total Latin America			**5,350**
Japan (50/50 JV)	EV/Pageview	Yahoo! (Japan) less 30%	2,353
Rest of Far East	Guesstimate	(n.b. All 50/50 JV's)	1,000
Total Far East			**3,353**
Total EV			25,932
Plus Cash			3,042
Total			**28,974**
No. shares (Post Issue) (million)			,591
		Euros per share: 53	U.S.$ per share: 49

Japan and other Asian countries, he used the value per page viewed multiple and a discretionary adjustment of 1.000 billion. This gave him a total value for Terra's and Lycos' shares of $28.974 billion. After dividing this quantity by the expected number of shares after the Terra/Lycos merger and adjusting for the exchange rate, he obtained a value of 53 euros per share.

Table 12.9 contains a verification of the value obtained by comparing Terra Lycos with Yahoo and America Online. The valuation of 53 euros per share gives a capitalization over sales ratio of 42.5. This ratio was 63.6 for Yahoo and 19.1 for American Online; the average of the two was 41.3. As 42.5 is close to 41.3, the valuation's author concluded that the valuation was correct. He also compared the capitalization over gross profit and capitalization over pages viewed ratios. Applying the same ratios to his valuation of Terra, he obtained 57.9 and 135.7. As both figures are close to the average multiples for Yahoo and American Online (56.8 and 117.7), he concluded that the valuation was correct.

Table 12.9

**Verification of the Valuation of Terra Performed by an
American Broker on June 20, 2000**

	Capitalization/ sales	Capitalization/ gross profit	Capitalization/ pageview
Yahoo! (without Japan)	63.6	74.3	117.7
AOL (without Time Warner)	19.1	39.3	
Average	*41.3*	*56.8*	.
Terra Lycos	**42.5**	**57.9**	**135.7**

12.6. VALUATION PERFORMED BY A SPANISH BANK
IN SEPTEMBER 1999: 19.8 EUROS

This valuation was performed before the initial public offering. The Spanish bank valued the shares at 19.8 euros. As this value was higher than the opening price, the bank advised its customers to buy.

Table 12.10 shows the companies that are comparable to Terra according to the Spanish bank and Table 12.11 shows the valuation. The multiples used by the Spanish bank for Terra are markedly below the average of the companies it calls comparable. It then applied these multiples to forecasts for 2002 and 2004.

Note the contradiction: it is argued that cash flow discounting is not used because it is very difficult to project Terra's future. However, multiples are applied to two- and four-year projections.

Table 12.10

Companies Comparable to Terra According to a Spanish Bank in September 1999

Access (ISP)	Capitalization/ sales		Portals	Capitalization/ sales		Services	Capitalization/ sales	
	1999E	2000E		1999E	2000E		1999E	2000E
America Online	20	16	Infoseek	13	9	Media Metrix	60	33
Earthlink	4	3	Lycos	22	14	Exodus	29	13
Excite@home	30	17	Yahoo	90	63	CMGI	34	22
mindspring	6	4						
Prodigy	7	5						
Weighted average	*20*	*15*		*78*	*55*		*32*	*19*

Table 12.11

Valuation of Terra Performed by a Spanish Bank in September 1999

	Capitalization/ sales	Sales growth	Remark	Value (million euros)
Access (ISP)				
Market	15	51%		
Terra	**8**	66%	8 × sales in 2002	**1,784**
Portal				
Market	55	51%		
Terra	**10**	57%	10 × sales in 2004	**2,367**
Corporate services in Brazil and Mexico				
Market	19	83%		
Terra	**4**	26%		**81**
E-commerce			Does not contribute to sales	**0**
Value of Terra shares (million euros)				**4,232**
Value of each share (euros)				**19.8**

12.7. HOW SHOULD TERRA BE VALUED?

What most analysts say about it being very difficult to make cash flow projections for Terra is true (although they do make projections for sales, earnings, and EBITDA, which we have seen in Table 12.1).

We do not know what Terra's growth will be like or what real options it may have. However, one analysis that we can carry out is to assume a future year in which Terra is a consolidated company, that is, a year after which Terra has moderate growth. If this year is 2010, Terra's capitalization at that time should be today's capitalization (2000) appreciated at the required return. This calculation is shown in Table 12.12.[10] If the required return is 13%, a price per share today of 50 euros (capitalization 31.063 billion euros) assumes a capitalization of 105.446 billion by 2010, provided that no dividends are paid or capital increases are made until then. This capitalization is greater than that of Telefónica in 2000 and is approximately the sum of the capitalizations of BSCH and BBVA. If it seems reasonable to the reader that Terra should have such a high capitalization in 10 years' time, then the price of 50 euros per share is also reasonable. However, if it seems too high to him, then he will value the share at less than 50 euros. Using the same reasoning

---

[10]This methodology is an alternative to that proposed by Copeland et al. (2000) in Chapter 15 (Valuing Dot.coms) of their book. This valuation is summarized in Section 19.3.3.

Table 12.12

Terra. Implicit Capitalization in November 2010 (Assuming a Required Return of 13%) and Equity Cash Flow in 2010 Required to Justify this Capitalization (Assuming a Required Return of 10%)

Price per share (euros) Nov–2000	Capitalization (million euros) Nov–2000	Capitalization (million euros) Nov–2010	Equity cash flow 2010 (million euros)			
			$g = 3\%$	$g = 4\%$	$g = 5\%$	$g = 6\%$
10	6,213	21,089	1,433	1,217	1,004	796
20	12,425	42,179	2,867	2,433	2,009	1,592
30	18,638	63,268	4,300	3,650	3,013	2,387
40	24,851	84,357	5,733	4,867	4,017	3,183
50	31,063	105,446	7,166	6,083	5,021	3,979
60	37,276	126,536	8,600	7,300	6,026	4,775
70	43,489	147,625	10,033	8,517	7,030	5,571
80	49,701	168,714	11,466	9,734	8,034	6,367
90	55,914	189,803	12,899	10,950	9,038	7,162
100	62,127	210,893	14,333	12,167	10,043	7,958
110	68,339	231,982	15,766	13,384	11,047	8,754
120	74,552	253,071	17,199	14,600	12,051	9,550
130	80,764	274,160	18,632	15,817	13,055	10,346
140	86,977	295,250	20,066	17,034	14,060	11,141

with 10 euros per share, Terra's capitalization in 2010 should be equal to that of Endesa today, or three times that of Unión Fenosa, Gas Natural, or Banco Popular.

Another way would be to compare the cash flows required to justify the capitalization in 2010. A price per share in 2000 of 50 euros assumes an equity cash flow in 2010 (if the required return then is 10%) of 6.083 billion euros, growing at an annual rate of 4%. In 1999, Telefónica's earnings were 1.805 billion euros, those of Endesa 1.278 billion, and those of Repsol 1.011 billion. General Electric's earnings were $12 billion and $5 billion were paid in dividends.

With these comparisons, unless one has exceptional expectations for Terra, it is difficult to justify a price per share greater than 10 euros.

Table 12.13 contains data on the world's largest companies to compare with Table 12.12.

To conclude, two morals.

Table 12.13

The World's 20 Largest Companies in Terms of Market Capitalization in November 2000 (Billion Dollars)

	Capitalization	Net income	PER	Dividend
General Electric	560.5	12.2	45.8	5.5
Cisco Systems	360.5	2.7	135.1	0.0
Exxon Mobil	326.6	11.8	27.7	6.1
Microsoft	298.6	9.4	31.7	0.0
Pfizer	278.6	4.0	69.9	2.3
Intel	237.5	9.4	25.3	0.5
Citigroup	222.6	11.7	19.1	2.5
American Int'l. Group	217.8	5.3	40.9	0.7
Wal-Mart	202.4	6.1	33.0	1.1
IBM	197.2	7.3	27.0	0.9
EMC	194.3	1.3	153.9	0.0
Merck	176.0	6.3	27.8	3.1
Oracle	175.6	6.6	26.8	0.0
SBC Comm.	166.5	7.9	21.0	3.4
Sun Microsystems	164.0	1.9	88.4	0.0
Coca-Cola	145.1	1.9	90.2	1.7
Johnson & Johnson	133.5	4.5	29.6	1.8
America Online	126.7	1.2	101.5	0.0
Verizon	126.2	7.5	16.8	4.2
Bristol-Myers Squibb	114.7	4.5	25.7	1.9

1. If you can't find a rational explanation for a share to continue rising, you can be sure that it will fall.
2. To become a millionaire, you must sell your shares at the right time.

12.8. AN ANECDOTE ON THE "NEW ECONOMY"

Letter received from a reader of an article on the valuation of Internet companies (July 2000):

Dear Mr. Fernández:
After reading your article published today, I felt compelled to convey to you my personal experience in this area.

In the last twelve months, I been involved as potential investor in two different Internet portal projects, one of them promoted by former senior consultants [of a consulting firm of acknowledged repute]. In neither case was any serious attempt made to quantify the potential market or establish any hypothesis regarding the expected market share. There was not even a single consideration about possible competitors, although knowing in both cases that they existed. If the market that each portal was targeting was infinite and, on top of this, each portal was definitely going to capture this infinite market, one can readily imagine the size of the results that they were expected to achieve: INFINITE.

To tell the truth, what saddened me most was to hear the former consultant of the consulting firm of acknowledged repute say that the traditional methods of company valuation were not applicable to this industry (I was clearly out of date with such infiniteness) and that—this he said "iocandi causa"—the greater the losses, the more potential the company had for increasing its value, clearly referring to Terra. And I say it saddened me for the following reason. I am an MBA and I specialized in *Financial Corporate Management* at an American university. How was it possible that after studying Bodie, Kane, Marcus, Brealey, Myers, Copeland, and I'll stop the list here . . . . I could be listening to such nonsense? And how was it possible that this nonsense was being said by someone who, until very recently, was advising top-notch companies and earning a fortune for doing so? And what was worse yet, how could the audience (consisting of 12 top-level executives) not raise any objection, any quibble, to what was clearly at odds with the most elemental common sense? Deep down, I believe that the other potential investors saw the same weaknesses as I did but their expectations were not centered on the growth of the business itself but on the capital gains they could realize within a year by selling.

In short, it was obvious that greed was silencing the warning voice of common sense, like a kind of Californian gold rush, and the profits were perceived to be substantial, quick, and sure, at the cost of passing on the future risks to secondary investors, who are always willing to invest their savings in unique opportunities, following the recommendations of "their advisors": the branch manager of the bank underwriting the issue, the dealer at the brokerage firm who receives a commission for placing the shares. . . . . And this brings me back to the initial question: Are family savings infinitely available? Of course, for the purpose in hand, this is not really the important point. Because what really matters is not the savings' infiniteness but their availability during the required time horizon, after which it doesn't matter if the sky comes crashing down on our heads!

PS. In the end, I decided not to invest in either of the two portals. Six months later, one of them continues to be inactive and the other one only offers the possibility of searching for domains.

REFERENCE

Copeland, T. E., T. Koller, and J. Murrin (2000), *Valuation: Measuring and Managing the Value of Companies*, third edition, New York: Wiley.

PART II

Shareholder Value Creation

Proposed Measures of Shareholder Value Creation: EVA™, Economic Profit, MVA, CVA, CFROI, and TSR[1]

This chapter describes and analyzes a series of parameters that have been proposed for measuring a firm's "value creation" for its shareholders. The parameters[2] analyzed are

1. EVA™ (economic value added), which is[3] earnings before interest less the firm's book value multiplied by the average cost of capital
2. EP (economic profit),[4] which is the book profit less the equity's book value multiplied by the required return to equity
3. MVA (market value added) seeks to measure a firm's value creation, which is understood as the difference between the market value of the firm's equity and the equity's book value (or initial investment)
4. CVA (cash value added), which is[5] earnings before interest plus amortization less economic depreciation less the cost of capital employed

---

[1] I must thank my IESE colleagues Josep Faus, Mª Jesús Grandes, and Toni Dávila for their perceptive comments, which have helped me improve this chapter.

[2] EVA is a registered trademark of Stern Stewart & Co. Some consultants use the Economic Profit as a synonym of the EVA, but we shall see further on that the two parameters are different. CVA, CFROI, TSR, and TBR are measures proposed by the Boston Consulting Group. See *Shareholder Value Metrics* (1996).

[3] According to Stern Stewart & Co's definition. See page 192 of their book *The Quest for Value. The EVA Management Guide*. Harper Business. 1991.

[4] Also called *residual income*. See McTaggart, Kontes, and Mankins (1994, page 317), a book published by the Marakon Associates.

[5] According to Boston Consulting Group's definition. See *Shareholder Value Metrics* (1996), Booklet 2, Page 16.

5. CFROI (cash flow return on investment) is the internal return on the investment unadjusted for inflation
6. TSR (total shareholder return) is the shareholder return, which is composed of the dividends paid and the equity's appreciation; TBR (total business return) is also the (hypothetical) shareholder return in unlisted companies and in corporate divisions

Many firms (Coca-Cola, Bank of America, Monsanto, among others) use EVA™, EP or CVA, instead of the book profit, to assess the performance of managers or business units and as a reference parameter for executive compensation. According to *CFO Magazine* (October 1996), 25 companies used EVA™ in 1993 and 250 in 1996. The advantage of EVA™, EP, and CVA over earnings is that they take into account the capital used to obtain the earnings and its risk. *Forbes* (20 May 1996) published that the average compensation of the CEOs of the 800 largest companies in the U.S. had the following breakdown: 41% fixed salary, 29% earnings-linked bonus, and 30% options and other long-term incentives.

In this chapter and in Chapter 14, we show that to claim that EP, EVA™, or CVA measures the firm's "value creation" in each period[6] is a tremendous error. These parameters may be useful for measuring the performance of managers or business units, but it does not make any sense at all to use EP, EVA™, or CVA to measure value creation in each period.

It is also shown that the present value of EP, EVA™, and CVA is the same as the MVA. Therefore, it is also possible to value firms by discounting EVA™, EP, or CVA, although these parameters are not cash flows and their financial meaning is much less clear than that of cash flows.

The problems with EVA™, EP, or CVA start when it is wished to give these parameters a meaning (that of value creation) that they do not have: value *always* depends on expectations.

13.1. BOOK PROFIT (EP) AND MVA

The MVA seeks to measure a firm's value creation, and is the difference between the market value of the firm's equity (or market value of the new investment) and the equity's book value (or initial investment).[7]

---

[6]For example, one can read in Stern Stewart & Co's advertising: "Forget about the EPS (earnings per share), ROE, and ROI. The true measure of your company's performance is EVA." "EVA™ is also the performance measure most directly linked to the creation of shareholder wealth over time."

[7]Although, as we will see in the course of the chapter, the difference between equity market value and book value corresponds to value creation when the firm is created.

Ebv$_0$ is the term used for the equity's book value and E$_0$ for its market value at t = 0 (now). Therefore:

$$MVA_0 = E_0 - Ebv_0 \qquad (13.1)$$

MVA (*market value added*) = Equity market value (price) − Equity book value

Economic profit (EP) is profit after tax (PAT) less equity book value (Ebv$_{t-1}$) multiplied[8] by required return to equity (Ke).

EP (economic profit) = Profit after tax − Equity book value × Cost of equity

$$EP_t = PAT_t - Ke \; Ebv_{t-1} \qquad (13.2)$$

Note that *the economic profit[9] mixes accounting parameters* (profit and the equity's book value) *with a market parameter* (Ke, the required return to equity).

The relationship between MVA and EP is shown in Appendix 13.1: the present value of the EP discounted at the rate Ke is the MVA.

$$MVA_0 = MVA_0 = E_0 - Ebv_0 = NPV(Ke;EP) \qquad (13.3)$$

As ROE = PAT$_t$/Ebv$_{t-1}$ we can also express the economic profit using (13.2), namely:

$$EP_t = (ROE - Ke) \; Ebv_{t-1} \qquad (13.4)$$

It is obvious that for the equity's market value to be higher than its book value (if ROE and Ke are constant),[10] ROE must be greater than Ke.

---

[8]Note that equity book value at the beginning of the period is used, that is, at the end of the previous period.

[9]The concept of economic profit is not new. Alfred Marshall was already using the term in 1890 in his book *Principles of Economics*.

[10]Some authors call this "creating value." Further on, we will explain why, as a general rule, we do not agree with this statement. The so-called "Value Creation Ratio" is also used, which is E$_0$/Ebv$_0$. In the case of perpetuities growing at a constant rate g, [E$_0$/Ebv$_0$] = (ROE − g) /(Ke − g).

13.2. EVA™ AND MVA

The difference ($[E_0 + D_0] - [Ebv_0 + D_0]$) is also called MVA and is identical (if the debt's market value is equal to its book value) to the difference ($E_0 - Ebv_0$).

EVA™[11] is the term used to define:

$$EVA_t = NOPAT_t - (D_{t-1} + Ebv_{t-1})WACC \qquad (13.5)$$

EVA is simply the NOPAT less the firm's book value ($D_{t-1} + Ebv_{t-1}$) multiplied by the average cost of capital (WACC). NOPAT (net operating profit after taxes) is the profit of the unlevered (debt-free) firm. Sometimes, it is also called EBIAT (earnings before interest and after tax).[12]

Note that *EVA mixes accounting parameters* (profit, and equity and debt book value) *with a market parameter* (WACC).

The relationship between MVA and EVA is shown in Appendix 13.2: the present value of the EVA discounted at the WACC is the MVA.

$$MVA_0 = [E_0 + D_0] - [Ebv_0 + D_0] = NPV(WACC; EVA) \qquad (13.6)$$

As[13] ROA = $NOPAT_t/(D_{t-1} + Ebv_{t-1})$, we can also express EVA as follows:

$$EVA_t = (D_{t-1} + Ebv_{t-1})(ROA - WACC) \qquad (13.7)$$

Thus, the EVA is simply the difference between the ROA and the WACC multiplied by the book value of the firm's capital (debt plus equity).[14] It is obvious that for EVA to be positive, the ROA must be greater than the WACC.[15]

---

[11]According to Stern Stewart & Co's definition. See page 192 of their book *The Quest for Value. The EVA Management Guide.*

[12]NOPAT is also called NOPLAT (net operating profit less adjusted taxes). See, for example, Copeland, Koller and Murrin (2000).

[13]ROA (return on assets) is also called ROI (return on investments), ROCE (return on capital employed), ROC (return on capital), and RONA (return on net assets). ROA = ROI = ROCE = *ROC = RONA.*

[14]The difference between ROA and WACC is usually called EVA spread.

[15]The creation of MVA is not a new concept. In 1924, Donaldson Brown, General Motors' CFO, said, "Managers' goal is not to maximize investment return but to achieve incremental earnings that are greater than the cost of capital employed."

> EVA = Capital book value × (Return on assets −
> Average cost of liabilities)

Copeland, Koller, and Murrin (2000, page 55) say that economic profit is a synonym of EVA. This is, obviously, not true.

13.3. CVA AND MVA

The Boston Consulting Group proposes cash value added[16] (CVA) as an alternative to the EVA. CVA is NOPAT plus book depreciation (DEP) less economic depreciation (ED) less cost of capital employed (initial investment multiplied by the weighted average cost of capital).

The definition of CVA is

$$CVA_t = NOPAT_t + DEP_t - ED - (D_0 + Ebv_0)WACC \qquad (13.8)$$

ED is the annuity that, when capitalized at the cost of capital (WACC), the assets' value will accrue at the end of their service life. The economic depreciation of certain gross fixed assets (GFA) depreciated over T years is

$$ED = GFA\ WACC/[(1 + WACC)^T - 1] \qquad (13.9)$$

Appendix 13.3 shows that the present value of the CVA discounted at the WACC is the same as the present value of the EVA discounted at the WACC (MVA) in firms that have fixed assets and constant working capital requirements.[17]

$$MVA_0 = [E_0 + D_0] - [Ebv_0 + D_0] = NPV(WACC;\ CVA) \qquad (13.10)$$

13.4. FIRST EXAMPLE: INVESTMENT WITHOUT VALUE CREATION

A firm funded entirely by equity is created to undertake a project that requires an initial investment of $12 billion (10 billion in fixed assets and 2 billion in working capital requirements).

---

[16]See *Shareholder Value Metrics*, Boston Consulting Group, 1996. Booklet 2, page 16.

[17]This may be a reasonable hypothesis in some projects. Also, it is necessary to not adjust for inflation.

The fixed assets are depreciated uniformly over the 5 years that the project lasts. The corporate income tax rate is 34% and the book profit is 837.976 million (constant over the 5 years).

Consequently, the project's (firm's) free cash flows (FCF) are -12 billion in year zero, 2.837976 billion in years 1–4, and 4.837976 billion in year 5. Therefore, this project's (firm's) IRR is 10%.

The risk-free rate is 6%, the market premium is 4%, and the project's beta is 1.0. Therefore, the required return to equity is 10%.

As the required return to equity is the project's IRR, the shares' price at $t = 0$ must be equal to their book value and there will be no value creation: the shares' value ($E_0 = 12$ billion) is equal to their baseline book value ($Ebv_0 = 12$ billion).

Table 13.1 gives the firm's accounting statements, valuation, and economic profit, EVA, and MVA. Lines 1–7 show the balance sheet and lines 8–14 the income statement. Line 17 contains the equity cash flow (in this case, equal to the FCF, as there is no debt).

Line 18 shows the ROE (in this case, equal to the ROA as there is no debt) and enables us to question its meaning: the ROE increases from 6.98–20.95%, which makes no economic or financial sense. The ROGI[18] (line 19) is 6.98% and does not make any economic or financial sense either.

The required return to equity (Ke) is equal to the WACC (line 20) and is 10%.

The equity's baseline value (line 21) is 12 billion, which is equal to the book value. Consequently, the baseline value creation (line 22) is nil. However, there "seems" to exist value creation at the end of successive years because the equity's market value is greater than its book value. This is obviously a mistake because the return on the investment is equal to the required return to equity. This "apparent" value creation in years 1–4 is because we are comparing a market value (present value of future cash flows) with a book value. *The difference between market value and book value makes sense in year zero* (because then the book value is a flow, which is the initial investment), *but not in the following years.*

As there is no debt, EP (line 23) is identical to EVA and WACC is the same as Ke. The present value of the EP discounted at Ke (line 24) is identical to the present value of the EVA discounted at the WACC and both agree with MVA $= E - Ebv$ (line 22).

Table 13.2 gives the CVA of the firm in Table 13.1.

Economic depreciation is the annuity that, when capitalized at the cost of capital (WACC), the fixed assets' value will accrue at the end of their service life. In our example, 1.638 billion per year capitalized at 10% provide, at the end of year 5, the 10 billion that was the initial investment in year zero.

---

[18]ROGI (return on gross investment) is NOPAT divided by the initial investment.

Table 13.1

EVA, EP, and MVA of a Company without Debt, ($ Million) IRR of Investment = Required Return to Equity (Ke) = 10%

Balance Sheet	0	1	2	3	4	5
1 WCR (Working Capital Requirements)	2,000	2,000	2,000	2,000	2,000	0
2 Gross Fixed Assets	10,000	10,000	10,000	10,000	10,000	10,000
3 – cumulative depreciation	0	2,000	4,000	6,000	8,000	10,000
4 NET ASSETS	**12,000**	**10,000**	**8,000**	**6,000**	**4,000**	**0**
5 Debt	0	0	0	0	0	0
6 Equity (book value)	12,000	10,000	8,000	6,000	4,000	0
7 NET WORTH & LIABILITIES	**12,000**	**10,000**	**8,000**	**6,000**	**4,000**	**0**
Income Statement						
8 Sales		10,000	10,000	10,000	10,000	10,000
9 Cost of sales		4,000	4,000	4,000	4,000	4,000
10 General & administrative expenses		2,730	2,730	2,730	2,730	2,730
11 Depreciation		2,000	2,000	2,000	2,000	2,000
12 Interest		0	0	0	0	0
13 Taxes		432	432	432	432	432
14 PAT		**838**	**838**	**838**	**838**	**8385**
15 + Depreciation		2,000	2,000	2,000	2,000	2,000
16 – Δ WCR		0	0	0	0	2,000
17 ECF = Dividends = FCF		**2,838**	**2,838**	**2,838**	**2,838**	**4,838**

(continues)

Table 13.1 (*continued*)

Balance Sheet	0	1	2	3	4	5
18 **ROE = ROA**		6.98%	8.38%	10.47%	13.97%	20.95%
19 **ROGI**		6.98%	6.98%	6.98%	6.98%	6.98%
20 **Ke = WACC**	10.00%	10.00%	10.00%	10.00%	10.00%	10.00%
21 **E = PV(Ke; ECF)**	12,000	10,362	8,560	6,578	4,398	0
22 **MVA = E − Ebv**	0.00	362.03	560.26	578.31	398.16	0.00
23 **EP = EVA**	0.0	−362.0	−162.0	38.0	238.0	438.0
24 **MVA = PV(Ke; EP) = PV (WACC; EVA)**	0.0	362.0	560.3	578.3	398.2	0.0

Table 13.2

CVA of a Company without Debt, IRR of the Investment = Required Return to Equity = 10%

Cash value added	1	2	3	4	5
NOPAT	838	838	838	838	838
+ Depreciation	2,000	2,000	2,000	2,000	2,000
− Economic depreciation	1,638	1,638	1,638	1,638	1,638
− Cost of capital employed	1,200	1,200	1,200	1,200	1,200
CVA	0	0	0	0	0

The cost of capital employed is the initial investment (12 billion) multiplied by the weighted cost of capital (in this case, 10% = WACC).

This firm's CVA (whose IRR is equal to the required return to equity) is zero in every year. The present value of the CVA is also equal to the MVA, which is zero.

One "apparent" advantage of the CVA over the EVA is that, while the EVA was negative for the first two years and positive for the following years, the CVA is zero for all the years, which, in this firm, makes more sense.

13.5. INCORRECT INTERPRETATION OF EVA, EP AND CVA

As the present value of the EVA[19] corresponds to the MVA, it is common for *the EVA to be interpreted incorrectly, saying that the EVA is each period's MVA.*[20]

It is sufficient to see the example of Table 13.1 to see this error: *this firm's EVA (line 23) is negative during the first two years and positive during the following years, which makes no economic or financial sense.* It makes no sense to say that this firm does worse in year 1 (EVA = −362) than in year 5 (EVA = 438). In this example, in which earnings and Ke are constant in

---

[19]A similar argument can be made for EP and CVA.

[20]However, one can read in Stern Stewart & Co's brochure: "EVA is the only measure that gives the right answer. All the others—including operating income, earnings growth, ROE and ROA—may be erroneous." In 2001, the message has been toned down and now says: "Economic value added is the financial performance measure that comes closer than any other to capturing the true economic profit of an enterprise." In a communiqué issued in February 1998 by Monsanto's management to its employees, one can read: "The larger the EVA, the more wealth we have created for our shareholders."

every year, EVA grows (from negative to positive) because the shares' book value decreases as the fixed assets are depreciated.

More recently, in a 1997 circular, Stern Stewart & Co. says: "what matters is the growth of EVA ... it is always good to increase the EVA." In our example, the EVA increases each year, but this does not mean that the company is doing better.

The Boston Consulting Group does recognize the limitations of these parameters. One can read in its advertising that "a major failure of EVA and CVA is that they ignore the cash flows produced by the business."

13.6. USEFULNESS OF EVA, EP, AND CVA

We have seen that, although the present value of EVA, EP, and CVA corresponds to MVA, it makes no sense to give EVA, EP, or CVA the meaning of value creation in each period.

However, *for many companies, EVA, EP, or CVA are more appropriate than the book profit for assessing the performance of executives or business units.*

It is obvious that the advantage of EVA, EP, and CVA over earnings is that they take into account the capital employed to obtain these earnings and also this capital's risk (which determines its required return).

Thus, many companies consider that EVA, EP, or CVA are better indicators of a manager's performance than earnings because they "refine" earnings with the quantity and risk of the capital required to obtain them.[21] For example, in AT&T's 1992 annual report, the CFO says that "our executives' remuneration in 1993 will be linked to the attainment of EVA goals." Likewise, Coca-Cola's president, Roberto Goizueta, referred to EVA to say that: "It is the way to control the company. It's a mystery to me why everyone doesn't use it."[22]

This is the usefulness of EVA, EP, and CVA. The problems with EVA, EP, or CVA start when one tries to give these numbers a meaning they do not have.

A policy of maximizing the EVA each year may be negative for the company. Let us imagine that the CEO of the company in Table 13.1 is assessed and remunerated on the basis of the EVA. One obvious way of improving the EVA during the first four years is to depreciate less during

---

[21]Many companies use different costs of capital for different activities within the company, logically applying a higher cost to activities with a higher risk. The RORAC (return on risk adjusted capital) seeks to do just this: determine each business unit's return while taking into account its risk.

[22]"The Real Key to Creating Wealth," *Fortune*, 20 September 1993.

the first years. Let us assume that it depreciates 1,000 during the first four years and 6,000 in year 5. Thus, the first 4 year's EVA would improve (it would be 298, 398, 498, and 598 million) and fifth year's EVA would be worse, -2.602 billion. With these depreciations, the shares' value would be 11.767 billion, instead of 12 billion if constant-rate depreciation were to be used.

It is obvious[23] that a period's EVA increases: (1) with increased NOPAT; (2) with reduced cost of capital; and (3) with reduced assets employed. But there are ways of increasing NOPAT, such as depreciating less, that decrease the company's cash flow and value. There are also many ways of reducing the cost of capital (for example, if interest rates fall) that have nothing to do with executive performance. There are also ways of decreasing assets employed (for example, deferring investment in new projects) that decrease or defer the cash flow and decrease the company's value.

On the other hand, it may happen that a particular year's EVA and economic profit have been very positive and even better than expected, but that the company's or business unit's value has decreased because the business's prospects have deteriorated due to poor management. To get partly round this problem, many consulting firms recommend (for those executives whose compensation is tied to the EVA or economic profit) to not pay the entire bonus immediately but to hold it as a provision that will be paid if the coming years' goals are also met.

Stern Stewart & Co proposes a series of adjustments to the NOPAT and the book value (see Appendix 13.4) with the intention of "giving more economic meaning" to EVA and the book value,[24] however, these adjustments[25] do not solve the EVA's problems, but rather tend to worsen them. In addition, when any of these adjustments is made, the EVA's present value is no longer the same as the MVA, unless another adjustment is made to the book value that is equal to the present value of the adjustments to the income statement.

13.7. CFROI, TSR, AND TBR

The CFROI (cash flow return on investment) tries to measure the "true return generated by a company's investments."[26] The CFROI is simply the

---

[23]See Formula (13.5).

[24]One can read in a Stern Stewart & Co brochure: "EVA also undoes accounting fictions and provides a much more accurate measure of operating income."

[25]Weaver (2001) reports that from a menu of up to 164 adjustments, the average EVA user makes 19 adjustments with a range between 7 and 34 adjustments.

[26]According to the Boston Consulting Group. See *Shareholder Value Metrics*, 1996. Booklet 2, pages 33 and 45.

IRR of the inflation-adjusted cash flows associated with the investment. In order to calculate it, we must first calculate the cash flows: the investment in year zero and the inflation-adjusted FCF generated by the project. In our example, the initial investment is 12 billion (year zero) and the cash flows are 2.838 billion in years 1–4 and 4.838 billion in year 5. One will see immediately that this project's (company's) CFROI is 10%.

In the case of a going concern, the BCG proposes calculating the initial investment as: book value + cumulative depreciation + adjustment for inflation + capitalization of current financial leases − spontaneous financing − goodwill. To determine the FCF, it proposes: profit + depreciation + interest after tax + payments of current financial leases + inflation adjustments of the WCR.

It should be stressed that the CFROI proposed by the BCG does not include inflation and, therefore, is a real, not nominal return.

Consequently, the CFROI measures better (although without taking inflation into account) what the ROA measures poorly. The CFROI should be compared with the WACC without inflation.[27] According to the Boston Consulting Group, "the CFROI represents the mean return of all of a firm's existing projects at a given time," and, consequently, a firm creates value for its shareholders if the CFROI is greater than the WACC without inflation[28] because the firm's projects have a higher return than the cost of capital.

TSR (total shareholder return) is the return for the shareholders, which is composed of the dividends and payments received and the shares' appreciation.

In the example of Table 13.1, the shareholder return in year 1 will be[29] 10%: 2.838 billion (dividends) less 1.638 billion (fall in the share price from 12–10.362 billion) divided by 12 billion (initial investment in year zero). The TSR in year 2 will also be 10%: 2.838 billion (dividends) less 1.802 billion (fall in the share price from 10.362–8.56 billion) divided by 10.362 billion (shares' value in year 1).

Consequently, the TSR measures well what the ROE measures poorly. The TSR should be compared with the required return to equity (Ke). A firm creates value for its shareholders if the TSR is greater than Ke.

TBR (total business return) is also the (hypothetical) shareholder return in unlisted companies and in corporate divisions. In our example, actually we have calculated the TBR because the firm in Table 13.1 is unlisted and the share prices we have calculated are hypothetical.

[27]WACC without inflation = $(1 + WACC)/(1 + inflation) - 1$

[28]See Chapter 11: influence of inflation on the value of firms, for the problems that may arise when analyzing companies or investment projects without inflation.

[29]If expectations are fully met.

In the example of Table 13.1, sales, WCR, etc., are constant every year. If we had included inflation, the effect on the investment's IRR and on the share value (keeping Ke at 10%) would be:

Inflation	IRR	Eo
0%	10.00%	12,000
1%	10.65%	12,219
2%	11.31%	12,444
3%	11.97%	12,674
4%	12.63%	12,910
5%	13.29%	13,152

During the period 1973–1992, the percentage of American companies that gave their shareholders a TSR greater than the S&P 500 stock market index was: 52% during one year, 29% during 2 years running, 17% during 3 years running, and 6% during 5 years running.

The correlation of the shareholder return of American companies during the period 1973–1992 (with respect to the S&P 500 stock market index) with EVA, growth of earnings per share, and growth of cash flow was:[30]

Correlation of TSR (with Respect to S&P 500) with:		
	1-year periods	3-year periods
EVA	13%	20%
Growth of EPS	25%	26%
Growth of cash flow	25%	45%

All of the correlations are relatively small, but the correlation with the EVA is the smallest of them all.

[30]Source: Boston Consulting Group. *Shareholder Value Metrics*, 1996. Booklet 1, page 2.

13.8. SECOND EXAMPLE: INVESTMENT WITH VALUE CREATION

Here, we come back to the firm of Table 13.1, but this time partly financed with 4 billions of debt at 8%.[31] The firm's FCFs are −12 billion in year zero, 2.837976 billion in years 1–4, and 4.837976 billion in year 5. Therefore, this firm's IRR is 10%.

Table 13.3 shows the firm's accounting statements, valuation, and economic profit, EVA, and MVA.

Line 21 shows the ROE (in this case, greater than the ROA, as there is debt with a cost after tax less than the ROA). Again, the ROE is economically and financially meaningless: it increases from 7.83–31.34%, and is infinite in the fifth year. The ROGI (line 23) is meaningless too: it is 6.98%. The project's internal rate of return (which ROA and ROGI try to give) is 10%. The internal rate of return on the investment in equity (which the ROE tries to give) is 13.879%. In this case, the debt ratio increases over time and, therefore, Ke (required return to equity) grows from 10.62–20.12% (line 24). As the debt ratio increases, the WACC decreases from 8.91–6.99% (line 26).

The shares' baseline value (lines 25 and 27) is 8.516 billion, which is 516 million more than the book value. Consequently, the baseline value creation (line 28) is 516 million.

As there is debt, the EP (line 29) is greater than the EVA (line 31). The EP's present value discounted at Ke (line 30) is identical to the EVA's present value discounted at the WACC (line 32) and both agree with MVA = E − Ebv (line 28). This does not mean that EP or EVA indicates "value creation" in each period: the value (516 million) "is created" at the beginning when an investment with an expected return (10%) greater than the cost of capital employed (WACC) is begun.

Looking at the course followed by the EVA, it is meaningless to say that this firm is doing worse in year 1 (EVA = −232) than in year 5(EVA = 558). Looking at the economic profit, it is also meaningless to say that this firm is doing worse in year 1(EP = −223) than in year 5 (EP = 627).

Table 13.4 shows the CVA of the firm in Table 13.3.

In this case, the CVA is not constant in all years because the WACC decreases each year as the leverage is increased. This firm's CVA (IRR > WACC) is positive every year and growing. The CVA's present value discounted at the WACC is equal to the MVA, which is 516 million. This does not mean that the CVA indicates value creation in each period: the value (516 million) "is created" at the beginning when an investment with an expected return (10%) greater than the cost of capital employed (WACC) is begun.

---

[31]Consequently, the beta associated with this debt cost is 0.5.

Table 13.3

EVA, EP, and MVA ($ Million) Company with Constant Debt Level ($4,000 Million), IRR of Investment = 10%

Balance Sheet	0	1	2	3	4	5
1 WCR (Working capital requirements)	2,000	2,000	2,000	2,000	2,000	0
2 Gross fixed assets	10,000	10,000	10,000	10,000	10,000	10,000
3 − cumulative depreciation	0	2,000	4,000	6,000	8,000	10,000
4 **NET ASSETS**	**12,000**	**10,000**	**8,000**	**6,000**	**4,000**	**0**
5 Debt	4,000	4,000	4,000	4,000	4,000	0
6 Equity (book value)	8,000	6,000	4,000	2,000	0	0
7 **NET WORTH & LIABILITIES**	**12,000**	**10,000**	**8,000**	**6,000**	**4,000**	**0**

Income Statement						
8 Sales		10,000	10,000	10,000	10,000	10,000
9 Cost of sales		4,000	4,000	4,000	4,000	4,000
10 General and administrative expenses		2,730	2,730	2,730	2,730	2,730
11 Depreciation		2,000	2,000	2,000	2,000	2,000
12 Interest		320	320	320	320	320
13 Taxes		323	323	323	323	323
14 **PAT**		**627**	**627**	**627**	**627**	**627**
15 + Depreciation		2,000	2,000	2,000	2,000	2,000
16 +Δ Debt		0	0	0	0	−4,000
17 −Δ WCR		0	0	0	0	2,000

(continues)

Table 13.3 (*continued*)

Balance Sheet	0	1	2	3	4	5
18 – Investment in fixed assets		0	0	0	0	0
19 ECF = Dividends		2,627	2,627	2,627	2,627	627
20 FCF		2,838	2,838	2,838	2,838	4,838
21 ROE		7.83%	10.45%	15.67%	31.34%	∞
22 ROA		6.98%	8.38%	10.47%	13.97%	20.95%
23 ROGI		6.98%	6.98%	6.98%	6.98%	6.98%
24 Ke	10.62%	10.78%	11.08%	11.88%	20.12%	10.00%
25 E = PV(Ke; ECF)	8,516	6,793	4,898	2,814	522	0
26 WACC	8.91%	8.74%	8.47%	8.00%	6.99%	10.00%
27 E = PV(WACC; FCF) – D	8,516	6,793	4,898	2,814	522	0
28 MVA = E – Ebv	516	793	898	814	522	0
29 EP = PAT – Ke × Ebv		–223	–20	184	389	627
30 MVA = PV(Ke; EP)	516	793	898	814	522	0
31 EVA		–232	–36	160	358	558
32 MVA = PV(WACC; EVA)	516	793	898	814	522	0
33 EP – EVA		9	16	23	32	68

Table 13.4

**CVA Firm with Constant Debt (4 Billion),
IRR of the Investment = 10%**

Cash value added	0	1	2	3	4	5
NOPAT		838	838	838	838	838
+ Depreciation		2,000	2,000	2,000	2,000	2,000
− Economic depreciation		1,712	1,712	1,712	1,712	1,712
− Cost of capital employed		1,070	1,049	1,017	961	839
CVA		57	77	110	166	287
PV(WACC; CVA)	516					

Looking at the course followed by the CVA, it is meaningless to say that this firm is doing worse in year 1 (CVA = 57) than in year 5 (CVA = 287).

The return for the shareholder who bought the shares in year zero for 8.516 billion (at "market value") will be 10.62% in year 1 (equal to Ke): 2.627 billion (dividends) less 1.723 billion (fall in the share price from 8.516–6.793 billion) divided by 8.516 billion (purchase of the shares in year zero). The TSR in year 2 will be 10.78% (Ke): 2.627 billion (dividends) less 1.895 billion (fall in the share price from 6.793–4.898 billion) divided by 6.793 billion (shares' value in year 1). Note that the value creation due to the investment (investment of 8 billion in shares that are worth 8.516 billion) is done in year zero.

The return of a founder shareholder who invested 8 billion in shares in year zero and sells them in year 1 will be 17.75%: he will receive the dividends corresponding to year 1 (2.627 million) and will then sell the shares at the expected price of 6.793 billion.

13.9. CONCLUSIONS

In the light of the foregoing sections, the following conclusions can be drawn.

- The information required to value a firm using the EP, EVA, and CVA is exactly the same as that required for valuing by cash flow discounting.
- The MVA, the difference between the market value and the book value, makes economic sense in year zero (because at that time the book value is a cash flow, which is the initial investment), but not in the following years.
- The present value of the EP, EVA, and CVA is equal to the MVA. Valuing the firm using the EP, EVA, and CVA gives the same result as valuing by cash flow discounting.

- Maximizing the present value of the EP, EVA, or CVA is equivalent to maximizing the value of the firm's shares.
- Maximizing a particular year's EP, EVA, or CVA is meaningless: it may be the opposite to maximizing the value of the firm's shares.
- The claim that the EP, EVA, or CVA measures the firm's value creation in each period is a tremendous error: it makes no sense to give the EP, EVA, or
- CVA the meaning of value creation in each period.
- The EVA, EP, and CVA do not measure value creation during each period.
- It is not possible to quantify value creation during a period on the basis of accounting data. Value always depends on expectations.
- An advantage of the EVA, EP, and CVA over earnings is that it takes into account the capital employed to obtain the earnings and also that capital's risk (which determines its required return). Therefore, many companies use the EVA, EP, or CVA as management performance indicators because they "refine" earnings with the quantity and risk of the capital employed to obtain them.
- It may happen that the EVA and the economic profit in one year have been positive, and even higher than expected, but that the value of the firm or business unit has fallen because the business's expectations have deteriorated due to poor management.
- The CFROI measures better (although without taking inflation into account) what the ROA measures poorly. The CFROI should be compared with the WACC without inflation. Undertaking a project creates value for shareholders if its CFROI is greater than the WACC without inflation.
- The TSR is the return for the shareholder and measures well what the ROE measures poorly. The TSR should be compared with the required return to equity (Ke). A firm creates value for its shareholders if the TSR is greater than Ke.
- The problems with EVA, EP, or CVA start when it is wished to give these parameters a meaning they do not have: value and shareholder value creation *always* depends on *expectations*.

APPENDIX 13.1: VERIFICATION THAT THE EP (ECONOMIC PROFIT) DISCOUNTED AT THE RATE KE IS THE MVA (MARKET VALUE – BOOK VALUE)

The value of equity is the present value of the equity's expected cash flows (ECF) discounted at the required return to equity (Ke):

$$E_0 = NPV(Ke; ECF) \tag{13.11}$$

The ECF is equal to the distributable dividends.[32] The part of the earnings that is not distributed will increase the equity's book value (Ebv). Consequently:[33]

$$ECF_t = DIV_t = PAT_t - \Delta Ebv_t = PAT_t - (Ebv_t - Ebv_{t-1}) \tag{13.12}$$

Replacing (13.12) in (13.11) gives:

$$
\begin{aligned}
E_0 = {} & \frac{PAT_1 - Ebv_1 + Ebv_0}{1 + Ke} \\
& + \frac{PAT_2 - Ebv_2 + Ebv_1}{(1 + Ke)^2} \\
& + \frac{PAT_3 - Ebv_3 + Ebv_2}{(1 + Ke)^3} + \dots
\end{aligned}
\tag{13.13}
$$

Taking into account the identity $Ebv_0/(1 + Ke) = Ebv_0 - Ke\ Ebv_0/(1 + Ke)$, equation (13.13) becomes:

$$
\begin{aligned}
E_0 = {} & \frac{PAT_1}{1 + Ke} + \frac{PAT_2}{(1 + Ke)^2} + \frac{PAT_3}{(1 + Ke)^3} + \dots \\
& + Ebv_0 - \frac{KeEbv_0}{1 + Ke} - \frac{KeEbv_1}{(1 + Ke)^2} - \frac{KeEbv_2}{(1 + Ke)^3} - \dots
\end{aligned}
\tag{13.14}
$$

$$
\begin{aligned}
E_0 = {} & Ebv_0 + \frac{PAT_1 - KeEbv_0}{1 + Ke} + \frac{PAT_2 - KeEbv_1}{(1 + Ke)^2} \\
& + \frac{PAT_3 - KeEbv_2}{(1 + Ke)^3} + \dots
\end{aligned}
\tag{13.15}
$$

$$E_0 - Ebv_0 = NPV(Ke; PAT_t - KeEbv_{t-1}) \tag{13.16}$$

The difference $(E_0 - Ebv_0)$ is called MVA. The economic profit is the numerator of Equation (13.16):

$$EP_t = PAT_t - KeEbv_{t-1} \tag{13.2}$$

---

[32]In actual fact, we are referring to expectations: Formula (13.11) indicates that the shares' value is the NPV of the expected value of the equity cash flows. We do not introduce the operator "expected value" in the formula in order to not complicate the expressions further. The expected value of the equity cash flow is, by definition, identical to the expected distributable dividend.

[33]We are assuming that $DIV_t = PAT_t - \Delta Ebv_t$. If this equality should not be met in a firm, for example, because it allocates a quantity Π directly to reserves, then the earnings should be adjusted as follows:

$$PAT_t = PATbv_t - \Pi,$$

where $PATbv_t$ is the profit shown by accounting methods.

Consequently, Equation (13.16) can be expressed as:

$$MVA_0 = E_0 - Ebv_0 = NPV(Ke; EP_t) \qquad (13.3)$$

As $PAT_t = ROE\ Ebv_{t-1}$, the economic profit can also be expressed as:

$$EP_t = (ROE - Ke)Ebv_{t-1} \qquad (13.4)$$

The relationship between profit and NOPAT is the following:

$$PAT_t = NOPAT_t - D_{t-1}Kd(1 - T) \qquad (13.17)$$

Therefore, the EP can also be expressed as:

$$EP_t = NOPAT_t - D_{t-1}Kd(1 - T) - KeEbv_{t-1} \qquad (13.18)$$

The WACC calculated using the equity and debt book values is

$$WACC_{bv} = \frac{D_{t-1}Kd(1 - T) + Ebv_{t-1}Ke}{D_{t-1} + Ebv_{t-1}} \qquad (13.19)$$

Consequently:

$$D_{t-1}Kd(1 - T) + KeEbv_{t-1} = WACC_{bv}(D_{t-1} + Ebv_{t-1}) \qquad (13.20)$$

The relationship between NOPAT and ROA is[34]

$$NOPAT_t = ROA(D_{t-1} + Ebv_{t-1}) \qquad (13.21)$$

Replacing (13.20) and (13.21) in (13.18) gives:

$$EP_t = (D_{t-1} + Ebv_{t-1})(ROA - WACC_{bv}) \qquad (13.22)$$

Consequently, another way of expressing the MVA is

$$MVA_0 = E_0 - Ebv_0 = NPV[Ke; (D_{t-1} + Ebv_{t-1})(ROA - WACC_{bv})] \qquad (13.23)$$

It is important to take into account that[35]

$$(D_{t-1} + Ebv_{t-1}) = NFA_{t-1} + WCR_{t-1} \qquad (13.24)$$

The relationships obtained are valid even if Ke is not constant over time. Equation (13.16) becomes:

$$E_0 - Ebv_0 = \sum_{t=1}^{\infty} \frac{PAT_t - Ke_tEbv_{t-1}}{\prod_{i=1}^{t}(1 + Ke_i)} \qquad (13.25)$$

[34]ROA (return on assets) is also called ROI (return on investments), ROCE (return on capital employed), ROC (return on capital) and RONA (return on net assets). ROA = ROI = ROCE = ROC = RONA. ROA = ROE if D = 0.

[35]NFA are net fixed assets. WCR are working capital requirements. The sum NFA + WCR is often called NAE (net assets employed).

APPENDIX 13.2: OBTAINMENT OF THE FORMULAS FOR EVA AND MVA FROM THE FCF AND WACC

In this Appendix, we perform a process that is fully analogous to that of Appendix 13.1, but using Formula (13.26), which postulates that the value of the debt plus the market value of the equity (also called the company's market value) is the present value of the expected FCF discounted at the WACC.[36]

$$E_0 + D_0 = \text{NPV}(\text{WACC}; \text{FCF}) \qquad (13.26)$$

The relationship between the FCF and profit (PAT) is[37]

$$\text{FCF}_t = \text{PAT}_t - \Delta \text{Ebv}_t + D_{t-1}\text{Kd}(1 - T) - \Delta D_t \qquad (13.27)$$

We know that $\text{PAT}_t = \text{NOPAT}_t - D_{t-1}\text{Kd}(1 - T)$. So

$$\text{FCF}_t = \text{NOPAT}_t - (\Delta \text{Ebv}_t + \Delta D_t) \qquad (13.28)$$

Replacing (13.28) in (13.26):

$$
\begin{aligned}
E_0 + D_0 &= \frac{\text{NOPAT}_1 - (\Delta \text{Ebv}_1 + \Delta D_1)}{1 + \text{WACC}} \\
&\quad + \frac{\text{NOPAT}_2 - (\Delta \text{Ebv}_2 + \Delta D_2)}{(1 + \text{WACC})^2} + \ldots = \qquad (13.29) \\
&= \frac{\text{NOPAT}_1}{1 + \text{WACC}} + \frac{\text{NOPAT}_2}{(1 + \text{WACC})^2} + \ldots - \frac{(\text{Ebv}_1 + D_1) - (\text{Ebv}_0 + D_0)}{1 + \text{WACC}} \\
&\quad - \frac{(\text{Ebv}_2 + D_2) - (\text{Ebv}_1 + D_1)}{(1 + \text{WACC})^2} - \ldots = \\
&= \frac{\text{NOPAT}_1}{1 + \text{WACC}} + \frac{\text{NOPAT}_2}{(1 + \text{WACC})^2} + \ldots + (\text{Ebv}_0 + D_0) \\
&\quad - \frac{\text{WACC}(\text{Ebv}_0 + D_0)}{1 + \text{WACC}} - \frac{\text{WACC}(\text{Ebv}_1 + D_1)}{(1 + \text{WACC})^2} + \ldots \\
&\quad \text{because } \frac{D_0 + \text{Ebv}_0}{1 + \text{WACC}} = D_0 + \text{Ebv}_0 - \frac{(D_0 + \text{Ebv}_0)\text{WACC}}{1 + \text{WACC}}
\end{aligned}
$$

---

[36]In actual fact, we are referring to expectations: Formula (13.11) indicates that the shares' value is the NPV of the expected value of the equity cash flows. We not introduce the operator "expected value" in the formula in order not to complicate the expressions further.

[37]We are assuming that $\text{DIV}_t = \text{PAT}_t - \Delta \text{Ebv}_t$. If this equality should not be met in a firm, for example, because it allocates a quantity Π directly to reserves, then the earnings should be adjusted as follows:

$\text{PAT}_t = \text{PATbv}_t - \Pi$, where PATbv_t is the profit shown by accounting methods.

Consequently:

$$[E_0 + D_0] - [Ebv_0 + D_0] = NPV[WACC; NOPAT_t -$$
$$(Ebv_{t-1} + D_{t-1})WACC] \tag{13.30}$$

Stern Stewart & Co. calls EVA the numerator of Expression (13.30)

$$EVA_t = NOPAT_t - (D_{t-1} + Ebv_{t-1})WACC \tag{13.5}$$

Consequently, the relationship between MVA and EVA is given by Equation (13.6).

$$MVA_0 = [E_0 + D_0] - [Ebv_0 + D_0] = NPV[WACC; EVA_t] \tag{13.6}$$

We know that $NOPAT_t = ROA(D_{t-1} + Ebv_{t-1})$. So:

$$EVA_t = (D_{t-1} + Ebv_{t-1})(ROA - WACC) \tag{13.7}$$

Replacing (13.7) in (13.6) gives:

$$MVA_0 = [E_0 + D_0] - [Ebv_0 + D_0] =$$
$$NPV[WACC; (D_{t-1} + Ebv_{t-1})(ROA - WACC)] \tag{13.31}$$

Comparing (13.7) with (13.22) gives:

$$EP_t - EVA_t = (D_{t-1} + Ebv_{t-1})(ROA - WACC_{bv})$$
$$- (D_{t-1} + Ebv_{t-1})(ROA - WACC) =$$

$$= (D_{t-1} + Ebv_{t-1})(WACC - WACC_{bv}) =$$

$$= (D_{t-1} + Ebv_{t-1})[\frac{D_{t-1}Kd(1-T) + E_{t-1}Ke}{D_{t-1} + E_{t-1}} - \frac{D_{t-1}Kd(1-T) + Ebv_{t-1}Ke}{D_{t-1} + Evc_{t-1}}]$$

$$= \frac{D_{t-1}[Kd(1-T)(Ebv_{t-1} - E_{t-1}) + Ke(E_{t-1} - Ebv_{t-1})]}{D_{t-1} + E_{t-1}} =$$
$$\frac{D_{t-1}(E_{t-1} - Ebv_{t-1})[Ke - Kd(1-T)]}{D_{t-1} + E_{t-1}}$$

$$EP_t - EVA_t = \frac{D_{t-1}(E_{t-1} - Ebv_{t-1})[Ke - Kd(1-T)]}{D_{t-1} + E_{t-1}}$$
$$= (D_{t-1} + Ebv_{t-1})(WACC - WACC_{bv}) \tag{13.32}$$

As $Ebv_{t-1} ROE = ROA(D_{t-1} + Ebv_{t-1}) - D_{t-1}Kd(1 - T)$, we can also express (13.5) as:

$$EVA_t = Ebv_{t-1} ROE + D_{t-1}Kd(1 - T) - (D_{t-1} + Ebv_{t-1})WACC \tag{13.5'}$$

The relationships obtained are valid even if the WACC is not constant over time. (13.30) becomes:

$$D_0 + E_0 - (D_0 + Ebv_0) = \sum_{t=1}^{\infty} \frac{NOPAT_t - WACC_t(D_{t-1} + Ebv_{t-1})}{\prod_{i=1}^{t}(1 + WACC_i)} \quad (13.33)$$

APPENDIX 13.3:   VERIFICATION THAT THE CVA DISCOUNTED AT THE WACC IS THE MVA

We wish to verify that:

$$MVA_0 = [E_0 + D_0] - [Ebv_0 + D_0] = NPV[WACC; CVA_t] \quad (13.10)$$

The definition of CVA is

$$CVA_t = NOPAT_t + DEP_t - ED - (D_0 + Ebv_0)WACC \quad (13.8)$$

where DEP_t is the book depreciation and ED is the economic depreciation.

The economic depreciation (ED) is the annuity that, when capitalized at the cost of capital (WACC), the fixed assets' (GFA) value will accrue at'the end of their service life. It will be immediately seen that the economic depreciation of certain gross fixed assets (GFA) depreciated over T years is:

$$ED = GFA \, WACC/[(1 + WACC)^T - 1] \quad (13.9)$$

The equality (13.10) for a firm with certain fixed assets (FA) that are depreciated over T years is

$$[E_0 + D_0] - [D_0 + Ebv_0] = \sum_{t=1}^{T} \frac{NOPAT_t + DEP_t - [D_0 + Ebv_0]WACC - ED}{(1 + WACC)^t}$$

$$(13.34)$$

Taking into account that:

$$\sum_{t=1}^{T} \frac{[D_0 + Ebv_0]WACC - ED}{(1 + WACC)^t}$$

$$= [D_0 + Ebv_0] - \frac{[D_0 + Ebv_0] - GFA}{(1 + WACC)^T} \quad (13.35)$$

$$= [D_0 + Ebv_0] - \frac{WCR_0}{(1 + WACC)^T}$$

Replacing (13.35) in (13.34) gives:

$$[E_0 + D_0] = \sum_{t=1}^{T} \frac{NOPAT_t + DEP_t}{(1 + WACC)^t} + \frac{WCR_0}{(1 + WACC)^T} \tag{13.36}$$

thus verifying and confirming its validity: (13.36) is valid for firms (projects) with constant gross fixed assets and constant WCR. These hypotheses can be valid for investment projects without inflation, without fixed assets purchases during the project's life, with constant income statement (after discounting inflation).

The relationships obtained are valid even if WACC is not constant over time. (13.10) becomes:

$$D_0 + E_0 - (D_0 + Ebv_0)$$

$$= \sum_{t=1}^{T} \frac{NOPAT_t + DEP_t - WACC_t(D_0 + Ebv_0) - ED}{\prod_{i=1}^{t} (1 + WACC_i)} \tag{13.37}$$

APPENDIX 13.4:   ADJUSTMENTS SUGGESTED BY STERN STEWART & CO. FOR CALCULATING THE EVA

Stern Stewart & Co. proposes (see page 112 of its book *The Quest for Value*) the following operations and adjustments for converting from book value to what it calls "economic book value." They recommend performing similar adjustments in the book NOPAT.

Operations for calculating the 'economic book value'	Operations for calculating the 'economic NOPAT'
Equity book value	Earnings available for common stock
+ Debt book value	+ Interest (1 − tax rate)
+ Preferred stock	+ Preferred dividends
+ Minority interest (equity)	+ Minority interest (earnings)

(continues)

(*continued*)

BOOK VALUE	NOPAT
Adjustments	**Adjustments**
+ Deferred taxes	+ Increase in deferred taxes
+ LIFO reserve	+ Increase in LIFO reserve
+ Cumulative depreciation of goodwill	+ Depreciation of goodwill
+ Uncapitalized goodwill	
+ Allowance for bad debts	+ Increase in allowance for bad debts
+ Allowance for stock obsolescence	+ Increase in allowance for stock obsolescence
+ Accrued R&D expenses	+ R&D expenses
− Cumulative depreciation of R&D	− Depreciation of R&D
+ Capitalization of non-cancelable contracts	+ Implicit interest on non-cancelable contracts
+ Accrued losses from sale of assets	+ Losses from sale of assets

REFERENCES

Boston Consulting Group (1996), *Shareholder Value Metrics.*
Copeland, T. E., T. Koller, and J. Murrin (2000), *Valuation: Measuring and Managing the Value of Companies*, third edition, New York: Wiley.
Fortune, (1993), "The Real Key to Creating Wealth," September 20.
McTaggart, J.M., P.W. Kontes, and M.C. Mankins (1994), *The Value Imperative*, Free Press.
Stewart, G. B. (1991), *The Quest for Value. The EVA Management Guide*, Harper Business.
Stern Stewart, www.eva.com.
Weaver, S. C. (2001), "Measuring Economic Value Added: A Survey of the Practices of EVA Proponents," *Journal of Applied Finance*, Fall/Winter, pp. 7–17.

Chapter 14

EVA, Economic Profit, and Cash Value Added do not Measure Shareholder Value Creation[1]

14.1. ACCOUNTING-BASED MEASURES CANNOT MEASURE VALUE CREATION

In the previous chapter, we saw that both a firm's value and the increase in the firm's value over a certain period are basically determined by the changes in expectations regarding the growth of the firm's cash flows and also by the changes in the firm's risk, which lead to changes in the discount rate. However, accounting only reflects the firm's history. Both the items of the income statement, which explain what has happened during a certain year, and those of the balance sheet, which reflect the state of a firm's assets and liabilities at a certain point in time, are historic data. Consequently, it is impossible for accounting-based measures, such as those we have seen (EVA, economic profit, cash value added), to measure value creation.

It is simple to verify this statement in quantitative terms: one has only to analyze the relationship between the shareholder value creation, or the shareholder value added, and the EVA, economic profit, and cash value added. This is what we will do in the following sections.

Market value added (MVA) does not help either. Yook and McCabe (2001) find a strong negative relationship between MVA and average returns.

[1] I would like to thank my colleagues, professors Josep Faus, Mª Jesús Grandes, and Toni Dávila, for their keen comments which have helped me improve this chapter.

14.2. EVA DOES NOT MEASURE THE SHAREHOLDER VALUE CREATION BY AMERICAN COMPANIES

Stern Stewart & Co.'s advertising contains such eye-catching statements as the following:

- "The EVA is the measure that correctly takes into account value creation or destruction in a company."
- "There is evidence that increasing the EVA is the key for increasing the company's value creation."
- "Forget about EPS (earnings per share), ROE, and ROI. The true measure of your company's performance is the EVA."
- "The EVA is the only measure that gives the right answer. All the others, including operating income, earnings growth, ROE, and ROA, may be erroneous."
- "The EVA is the parameter that is most directly linked to the creation of shareholder wealth over time."[2]

A communiqué issued in February 1998 by Monsanto's management to its employees says: "The larger the EVA, the more wealth we have created for our shareholders."

Roberto Goizueta, Coca-Cola's CEO said, referring to EVA, that "It is the way to control the company. It's a mystery to me why everyone doesn't use it."[3]

So much for the testimonials praising the EVA. We will now present evidence that enables these testimonials to be questioned. All of the data used here are taken from data calculated and published by Stern Stewart.[4] Stern Stewart makes adjustments both to the NOPAT and to the book value to calculate the EVA. These adjustments are summarized in Appendix 13.4.

Figure 14.1 shows the evolution of Coca-Cola's EVA and market value. In the case of Coca-Cola, it *is* possible to detect a correlation between the EVA and equity value. PriceWaterhouseCoopers[5] interprets this figure by saying that "Coca-Cola created enormous wealth for the shareholder through the appropriate implementation of EVA in 1987."

However, in Figure 14.2 (which shows the evolution of PepsiCo's EVA and market value), the correlation between EVA and equity value is much less clear.

---

[2]See www.eva.com.
[3]"The Real Key to Creating Wealth," *Fortune*, 20 September 1993.
[4]Stern Stewart calculates and sells the EVA, market value, MVA, and annual NOPAT of 1000 U.S. companies since 1978. These are the data that appear in the graphs in this section.
[5]See Corporate Valuation Guide, page 324.

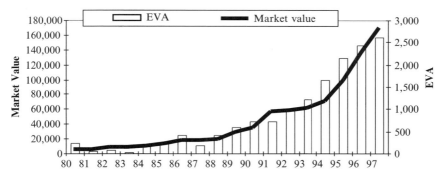

Figure 14.1   Evolution of Coca-Cola's EVA and market value (million dollars). (*Source*: Stern Stewart.)

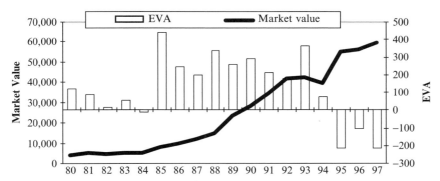

Figure 14.2   Evolution of PepsiCo's EVA and market value (million dollars). (*Source*: Stern Stewart.)

The correlation between EVA and equity value is not clear in Figures 14.3, 14.4, and 14.5 either, which show the evolution of the EVA and market value of Walt Disney, Boeing, and General Electric.

Of the 1000 American companies for which Stern Stewart provides data, 582 with data from at least 1987–1997 have been selected. For each of the 582 companies, we have calculated the correlation between the increase in the MVA each year and each year's EVA, NOPAT, and WACC. One surprising piece of information emerged: for 296 (of the 582) companies, the correlation between the increase in the MVA each year and the NOPAT was greater than the correlation between the increase in the MVA each year and the EVA. The NOPAT is a purely accounting parameter, while the EVA seeks to be a more precise indicator of the increase in the MVA.

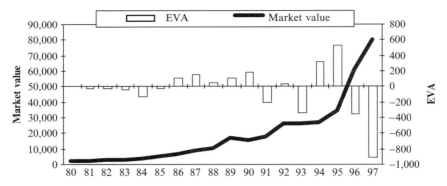

Figure 14.3   Evolution of Walt Disney's EVA and market value (million dollars). (*Source*: Stern Stewart.)

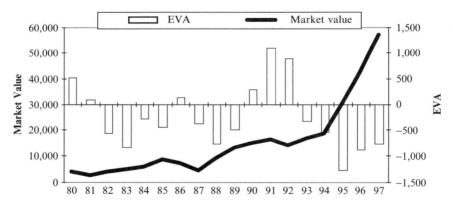

Figure 14.4   Evolution of Boeing's EVA and market value (million dollars). (*Source*: Stern Stewart.)

The correlations are summarized in Table 14.1. There are only 28 companies for which the correlation with the EVA has been significant (between 80 and 100%). There are 210 companies for which the correlation with the EVA has been negative.

Table 14.1 also shows how the correlation between the increase in the MVA and the NOPAT has been greater for more companies than the correlation between the increase in the MVA and the EVA. The third column of Table 14.1 shows the correlation between the increase in the MVA and the WACC. Although it is a rather meaningless correlation, both variables show a not insignificant correlation.

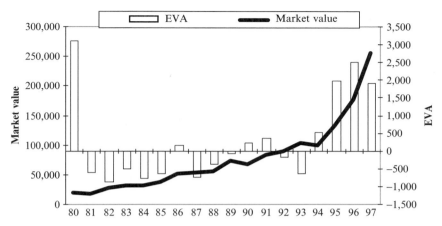

Figure 14.5   Evolution of General Electric's EVA and market value (million dollars). (*Source*: Stern Stewart.)

Table 14.1

**Summary of the Correlations between the Increase
in the MVA Each Year and Each Year's EVA, NOPAT,
and WACC for 582 American Companies**

Correlation of ΔMVA with:	Number of companies					
	EVA	NOPAT	WACC	Δ EVA	Δ NOPAT	ΔWACC
between 80 and 100%	28	53	0	22	39	2
between 60 and 80%	68	81	13	72	72	18
between 40 and 60%	94	98	20	94	89	51
between 20 and 40%	96	72	44	101	105	68
between 0 and 20%	86	80	79	108	114	124
between −20 and 0%	83	73	94	74	79	126
between −40 and −20%	59	70	144	60	50	94
between −60 and −40%	44	42	111	36	24	71
between −80 and −60%	22	12	67	13	9	24
between −100 and −80%	2	1	10	2	1	4
Total	*582*	*582*	*582*	*582*	*582*	*582*
Average	*16.0%*	*21.0%*	*−21.4%*	*18.0%*	*22.5%*	*−4.1%*
Standard deviation	*41.7%*	*43.6%*	*35.0%*	*39.3%*	*38.4%*	*35.1%*

Source: Stern Stewart.

Table 14.2 shows the results obtained for a number of companies. Microsoft was the company with the highest correlation (90.7%). Coca-Cola also had a very high correlation (78.2%), as we saw in Figure 14.1. Table 14.2 also shows that the correlation between the increase in the MVA and the EVA is not necessarily greater than the correlation between the MVA and the NOPAT.

Another item of evidence. Two studies performed by Richard Bernstein, from Merrill Lynch (19/12/97 and 2/3/98), showed that:

1. The portfolio composed of the 50 American companies with the highest EVA gained 0.2% less than the S&P 500
2. The portfolio composed of the 50 American companies with the largest increase in the EVA gained 0.3% less than the S&P 500

Fernandez (2001) compares EVA calculated by Stern Stewart and Co.[6] with created shareholder value. Figure 14.6 shows EVA and created shareholder value for 269 companies in 1999. The correlation of EVA with created shareholder value was only 17.66%. Sixty companies had negative EVA and positive created shareholder value. Sixty-four companies had positive EVA and negative created shareholder value. The difference of shareholder value creation minus EVA was, on average, -434% of EVA. The absolute value of the difference of shareholder value creation minus EVA was 8972% of EVA.

With this evidence, we conclude that EVA does not properly measure shareholder value creation.

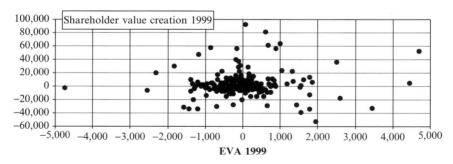

Figure 14.6 EVA (according to Stern Stewart and Co.) and created shareholder value for 269 companies in 1999 (million dollars).

---

[6]See *Fortune* (December 18, 2000), "America's Best and Worst Wealth Creators." This article contains EVA, calculated by Stern Stewart and Co., of several American companies for 1999.

Table 14.2

Correlations between the Increase in the MVA Each Year and Each Year's EVA, NOPAT, and WACC for the Largest American Companies (Million Dollars)

Company	Market value 1997	MVA 1997	Shareholders return		Correlation (1988–1997) of Δ MVA with					
			5 years	10 years	EVA	NOPAT	WACC	Δ EVA	Δ NOPAT	Δ WACC
General Electric	255,081	195,830	30.8%	24.0%	73.2%	80.3%	-10.1%	-24.2%	-6.4%	31.5%
Exxon	173,680	85,557	19.2%	17.1%	29.4%	40.8%	-18.2%	-33.7%	-32.0%	-12.2%
Coca-Cola	169,204	158,247	27.6%	32.1%	78.2%	76.6%	-71.9%	4.4%	29.5%	-19.9%
Microsoft	152,416	143,740	43.4%	45.6%	90.7%	90.5%	-48.9%	83.9%	84.4%	36.8%
Merck	130,530	107,418	22.3%	22.3%	29.4%	44.4%	27.4%	52.1%	35.8%	-10.3%
Philip Morris	125,557	82,412	16.8%	24.8%	22.8%	28.5%	58.1%	29.8%	50.6%	16.2%
IBM	115,521	49,101	34.8%	9.8%	13.3%	20.1%	19.0%	1.6%	18.4%	78.7%
Procter & Gamble	113,125	88,706	26.4%	24.7%	44.2%	68.3%	28.6%	-4.1%	-4.2%	26.9%
Intel	111,446	90,010	45.6%	35.9%	54.2%	53.6%	-69.2%	61.0%	63.3%	-40.2%
AT&T	105,621	35,214	6.3%	11.8%	37.0%	2.9%	-29.0%	55.9%	29.3%	-63.8%
Wal-Mart Stores	103,568	69,678	5.1%	20.5%	69.8%	7.6%	0.8%	71.1%	51.7%	46.4%
Bell Atlantic	99,757	48,414	17.1%	15.8%	89.3%	93.8%	-14.4%	87.8%	96.0%	9.5%
Bristol-Myers Squibb	95,939	81,312	27.5%	20.6%	49.9%	47.4%	0.6%	60.0%	53.6%	-14.4%
Johnson & Johnson	91,236	71,433	23.2%	23.7%	60.1%	61.6%	-20.7%	18.0%	56.4%	-10.6%
SBC Communications	86,395	45,136	18.3%	20.1%	77.7%	82.5%	-38.6%	88.5%	94.4%	1.6%
Walt Disney	79,576	46,869	18.8%	21.5%	-57.8%	75.2%	-62.4%	-34.8%	42.3%	-38.1%

(continues)

Table 14.2 (*continued*)

Company	Market value 1997	MVA 1997	Shareholders return		Correlation (1988–1997) of Δ MVA with					
			5 years	10 years	EVA	NOPAT	WACC	Δ EVA	Δ NOPAT	Δ WACC
Ford Motor	62,696	3,183	22.0%	15.5%	8.0%	7.6%	−55.8%	43.3%	33.3%	−31.3%
General Motors	61,478	−13,876	16.1%	11.7%	−2.4%	−10.3%	−31.5%	33.9%	21.8%	−64.9%
PepsiCo	59,251	40,743	13.5%	22.5%	−54.9%	14.3%	77.5%	−41.2%	−16.7%	43.7%
Boeing	56,887	28,725	21.4%	21.8%	−82.0%	−64.7%	−66.4%	−3.3%	−11.9%	−4.0%
Time Warner	53,032	20,020	17.2%	12.7%	−50.8%	2.5%	−52.0%	−9.1%	−19.3%	14.0%
McDonald's	41,763	22,817	15.2%	16.8%	2.2%	10.8%	−20.3%	37.7%	18.8%	−58.2%
3M	36,838	25,162	13.4%	13.2%	−42.2%	29.1%	−7.1%	−55.9%	−27.3%	36.5%
WorldCom	35,062	11,823	31.2%	64.2%	−78.1%	59.8%	5.2%	−28.5%	32.1%	−47.8%
CBS	27,626	10,103	18.8%	4.9%	−36.2%	−29.0%	8.4%	−34.8%	−33.2%	−8.6%
Chrysler	27,096	2,570	20.8%	17.0%	−28.5%	−32.6%	−45.7%	21.3%	6.8%	−77.9%
Coca-Cola Enterprises	23,075	5,896	54.6%	22.7%	−71.6%	89.1%	2.2%	−69.8%	54.5%	63.8%
Apple Computer	2,734	−1,594	−25.4%	−10.1%	−7.3%	−5.6%	19.7%	4.3%	8.3%	27.4%

Source: Stern Stewart.

14.3. THE CVA DOES NOT MEASURE THE SHAREHOLDER VALUE CREATION OF THE WORLD'S 100 MOST PROFITABLE COMPANIES[7]

Table 14.3 shows the equity value, shareholder return, and increase in the CVA (according to the Boston Consulting Group) of the world's 100 most profitable companies for their shareholders[7] during the period 1994–1998.

The correlation between the shareholder return in 1994–1998 and the increase in the CVA is 1.7%. The low correlation between the shareholder return and the increase in the CVA is striking. Table 14.3 is interesting for

Table 14.3

The World's 100 Most Profitable Companies for their Shareholders during the Period 1994–1998

Company	Country	Equity market value (million euros) 31/12/98	Shareholder return 1994–98	Δ CVA = CVA$_{98}$ − CVA$_{94}$ (million euros)
1 Dell Computer	USA	78,936	152.9%	1,088
2 America Online	USA	60,249	143.1%	149
3 Sap	D	17,991	90.6%	445
4 Nokia	FIN	48,687	78.8%	1,778
5 H&M	S	14,386	69.2%	147
6 Microsoft	USA	293,173	68.9%	2,178
7 Cisco Systems	USA	124,241	66.8%	604
8 Aegon	NL	61,004	66.2%	521
9 Charles Schwab	USA	19,097	64.7%	134
10 Compuware	USA	12,170	64.4%	226
11 Clear Channel Com.	USA	12,172	63.9%	75
12 Sun Microsystems	USA	27,626	63.7%	464
13 Tellabs	USA	11,293	63.3%	225
14 Safeway	USA	25,117	62.9%	517
15 Emc Corp.	USA	36,162	59.4%	370
16 Firstar*	USA	17,156	55.3%	−102
17 Staples	USA	11,381	54.0%	127

(continues)

[7]The 100 companies were chosen from a sample consisting of the 5316 largest listed companies in the world. The median return for all 5316 companies was 13%.

Table 14.3 (*continued*)

Company	Country	Equity market value (million euros) 31/12/98	Shareholder return 1994–98	$\Delta CVA = CVA_{98} - CVA_{94}$ (million euros)
18 Compaq	USA	60,529	53.6%	−1,356
19 Tyco	USA	41,397	52.3%	402
20 Pfizer	USA	137,525	51.2%	795
21 Intel	USA	167,551	50.6%	2,586
22 Gas Natural	Spain	13,860	49.8%	−25
23 Warner Lambert	USA	52,357	49.5%	601
24 Medtronic	USA	30,816	49.5%	256
25 BBV	Spain	27,316	48.7%	645
26 Schering-Plough	USA	68,834	48.3%	712
27 Rite Aid	USA	10,901	47.5%	11
28 IBM	USA	144,245	47.1%	7,672
29 Eli Lilly	USA	82,855	46.7%	919
30 Gap	USA	27,163	46.3%	475
31 Bank of New York	USA	25,955	45.7%	497
32 Pinault Printemps	F	19,121	45.6%	319
33 Mbna Corp.	USA	15,813	44.2%	389
34 Walgreen	USA	24,759	43.5%	209
35 MCI Worldcom	USA	111,519	43.2%	−4,428
36 Kroger	USA	13,141	43.2%	232
37 Banca Intesa	I	11,401	43.1%	270
38 Texas Instruments	USA	28,303	41.4%	113
39 Freddie Mac	USA	37,009	40.9%	424
40 Micron Technology	US	10,567	40.6%	−448
41 Rolo Banca 1473	I	10,060	40.5%	393
42 Bristol Myers Squibb	USA	112,710	40.3%	1,208
43 British Aerospace	UK	12,603	40.2%	783
44 Vodafone	UK	42,361	40.0%	234
45 Dayton-Hudson	USA	20,274	39.7%	506
46 Unicredito Italiano	I	23,569	39.2%	296
47 Swiss Re	CH	32,426	39.1%	1,203
48 Lloyds Tsb	UK	65,193	38.8%	1,112
49 Fifth Third Bancorp.	USA	16,127	38.4%	125

(*continues*)

Table 14.3 (*continued*)

Company	Country	Equity market value (million euros) 31/12/98	Shareholder return 1994–98	Δ CVA = $CVA_{98} - CVA_{94}$ (million euros)
50 Oracle	USA	35,086	38.3%	398
51 Ericsson	S	36,231	37.9%	940
52 Clorox	USA	10,252	37.4%	139
53 Smithkline Beecham	UK	65,746	37.1%	717
54 Merck	USA	148,933	36.9%	1,980
55 Ahold	NL	19,720	36.9%	354
56 Mannesmann	D	38,019	36.8%	1,264
57 Legal & General	UK	13,982	36.8%	65
58 Home Depot	USA	81,081	36.5%	831
59 Fortis	B	24,547	36.2%	431
60 Mellon Bank	USA	15,220	36.2%	371
61 Cardinal Healt	USA	12,912	35.3%	135
62 Sanofi	F	15,171	35.2%	197
63 Xerox	USA	32,803	34.6%	471
64 Applied Mats.	USA	13,301	34.5%	115
65 Williams Companies	USA	11,310	34.4%	−149
66 General Electric	USA	283,348	34.1%	3,965
67 Carnival	USA	24,229	33.9%	332
68 Progressive Corp.	USA	10,409	33.7%	75
69 Heineken	NL	16,080	33.7%	116
70 Cigna	USA	13,533	33.6%	865
71 Monsanto	USA	24,324	33.6%	253
72 Fannie Mae	USA	64,239	33.5%	940
73 Amgen	USA	22,561	33.4%	337
74 American Express	USA	39,284	33.1%	601
75 Takeda*	JP	28,909	32.9%	109
76 Bellsouth	USA	82,685	32.8%	815
77 Chase Manhattan	USA	50,908	32.8%	1,290
78 Waste Management Int.	USA	22,703	32.6%	768
79 Citigroup*	USA	95,700	32.5%	−411
80 American Home Prds.	USA	62,990	32.4%	918
81 Johnson & Johnson	USA	95,612	32.4%	1,433

(*continues*)

Table 14.3 (*continued*)

Company	Country	Equity market value (million euros) 31/12/98	Shareholder return 1994–98	Δ CVA = $CVA_{98} - CVA_{94}$ (million euros)
82 Household Int.	USA	16,218	32.3%	−29
83 Rentokil Initial	UK	18,201	32.3%	352
84 Sprint	USA	24,568	32.2%	134
85 Ameritech	USA	59,273	31.8%	476
86 Telefonica	Spain	39,645	31.7%	1,563
87 US Bancorp*	USA	21,840	31.6%	374
88 Northern Telecom	CN	28,091	31.4%	311
89 United Technologies	USA	20,819	31.3%	820
90 Promodes	F	11,684	31.3%	6
91 Telecom Italia	I	38,268	30.8%	3,051
92 3Com	USA	13,624	30.7%	19
93 American Inter. Group	USA	86,006	30.5%	979
94 KBC	B	19,984	30.5%	69
95 Suntrust Banks	USA	13,591	30.4%	178
96 Costco Companies	USA	13,360	30.3%	146
97 Banco Santander	Spain	19,837	30.2%	199
98 Wells Fargo*	USA	54,752	30.2%	58
99 Bank of Scotland	UK	12,442	29.8%	481
100 Abbott Laboratories	USA	63,041	29.7%	681

Source: Boston Consulting Group, The value Creators.

making comparisons between companies. Another interesting finding is the large number of American companies who are in the top 100 during the period 1994–1998.

14.4. THE ECONOMIC PROFIT DOES NOT MEASURE THE SHAREHOLDER VALUE CREATION

The relationship between shareholder value creation and various other parameters, including EP and EVA, during the period 1992–1998, has been analyzed. In this case, the sample consisted of the 28 largest Spanish companies. The relationship between economic profit and shareholder value added and shareholder value creation is rather tenuous.

Table 14.4 shows that the EVA had the highest correlation with shareholder return in only 2 companies, while in 16 companies the highest correlation was found for the variation in interest rates. The EVA had the highest correlation with shareholder value added or shareholder value creation in only 2 companies, while the variation in the interest rates had the highest correlation in 8 companies and the level of interest rates in 10 companies. The last column shows the correlation between value creation not due to interest rates (thereby eliminating the influence of interest rates) and the variables. Once again, the EVA had the highest correlation in only 2 companies, while the adjusted ROE had the highest correlation in 7 companies. Table 14.4 also shows that the economic profit obtained the highest correlation in more companies than the EVA did.

Table 14.5 shows the mean correlation between the parameters indicated for the 28 companies. It can be seen that, on average, the economic profit and the EVA had the best correlation with shareholder value added and shareholder value created than the other two parameters, but a lower mean correlation than the correlation with interest rates.

The basic conclusion to be drawn from this analysis is that the EVA is not the parameter that had the highest correlation with shareholder value creation. The EP and several other parameters had a higher correlation than the EVA did, although the EP was not the most highly correlated parameter either. The interest rates and the changes in interest rates were the variables showing the highest correlation.

Table 14.4

Number of Companies that Obtained the Highest Correlation between the Parameters Indicated, 28 Spanish Companies. 1992–1998

	Shareholder return	Shareholder value added	Shareholder value created	Shareholder value created without interest rate effect
Economic profit	3	4	5	9
EVA	2	2	2	2
Profit after taxes	0	0	0	0
ROE	0	1	1	3
Equity cash flow	2	1	1	2
Interest rate	1	10	10	5
Adjusted ROE	4	2	1	7
Δ Interest rate	16	8	8	0
Number of companies	28	28	28	28

Table 14.5

Mean Correlation between the Parameters Indicated, 28 Spanish Companies 1992–98

	Shareholder return	Shareholder value added	Shareholder value created	Shareholder value created without interest rate effect
Economic profit	26%	50%	45%	14%
EVA	28%	56%	50%	20%
Profit after taxes	19%	44%	38%	7%
ROE	11%	19%	16%	14%
Equity cash flow	16%	39%	33%	0%
Interest rate	5%	−64%	−59%	−14%
Adjusted ROE	27%	5%	8%	22%
Δ Interest rate	−57%	−48%	−48%	−13%

Given what we have seen in this chapter, it is difficult to argue that the EVA, the CVA, or the economic profit measure each year's value creation.

14.5. USEFULNESS OF EVA, EP, AND CVA

In spite of this, companies are increasingly using the EVA, EP, and CVA. In 1993, only 25 companies used the EVA; by 1996, they had increased to 250.

14.5.1. THE EVA, THE EP, AND THE CVA CAN BE USED TO VALUE COMPANIES

The present value of the future EPs, EVAs, and CVAs matches the MVA. Consequently, it is also possible to value companies by updating the EVA, EP, or CVA.[8]

This fact that the present value of the EVA, discounted at the WACC, matches the MVA leads some to say that each period's EVA can be interpreted as the increase in the MVA or the shareholder value creation during each period. However, this is a tremendous mistake: it is one thing to say that the present value of the future EVAs matches the MVA (equity's market

---

[8]In the previous chapter it was shown that:

MVA = E − Ebv = Net Present Value [WACC; future EVAs];

MVA = E − Ebv = Net Present Value [WACC; future CVAs]; and

MVA = E − Ebv = Net Present Value [Ke; future economic profit].

value – equity's book value) and another very different thing to say that each period's EVA is the value created during that period.

14.5.2. EVA, EP, AND CVA AS MANAGEMENT PERFORMANCE INDICATORS

Many firms use EVA, EP, and CVA as better management performance indicators than earnings because they "refine" earnings with the quantity and risk of the resources used to obtain such earnings.

The main advantage that these parameters have over book profit is that they take into account both the resources used to obtain the profit and these resources' risk (which determines their cost or required return).

We have already seen that the fact that a firm's EVA, EP, or CVA increase does not mean that the firm is creating value.

	Usefulness of EVA, EP, and CVA as Management Performance Indicators
Advantages	They take into account not only the earnings but also the cost of the resources used to generate those earnings
Usefulness	They may be better management performance indicators than book profit and they may be useful as benchmarks for their remuneration
Caution	Do not pay immediately the entire bonus to the manager but rather keep it as a provision which shall be paid if the following years' goals are also met

This is the usefulness of EVA, EP, and CVA: their use in valuing companies and as a performance indicator. The problems with these parameters start when it is wished to give these numbers a meaning they do not have: that of value creation.

14.6. CONSEQUENCES OF THE USE OF EVA, EP, OR CVA FOR EXECUTIVE REMUNERATION

A policy of maximizing the EVA each year may not be positive for the company, as the EVA may increase for several reasons:

1. Increase in the NOPAT. There may be increases in the NOPAT that decrease the cash flow and the company's value. For example, when depreciation is less.
2. Decrease in the cost of capital. This may decrease, for example, due to a drop in interest rates or in the market premium, which have nothing to do with management performance.
3. Decrease in the assets employed or a deferral of profitable investments.

Biddle, Bowen, and Wallace (1999)[9] conducted a study on 40 companies that used EVA, EP, or CVA as parameters for their executives' remuneration, that is, as the basis for calculating their variable compensation. They compared these 40 companies' progress with another 40 companies in which these parameters were not used for calculating remuneration and found the following differences shown in Table 14.6.

Table 14.6 shows that the companies that used EVA, EP, or CVA as parameters for their executives' remuneration

- Sold (or withdrew) 100% more assets (in order to decrease the book value of the assets employed) than those which did not use these parameters.
- Bought 21% less assets (in order to increase less the book value of the assets employed) than those which did not use these parameters.
- Bought 112% more shares on the market (in order to decrease the equity's book value) than those which did not use these parameters.

The effect on dividends is not significant.

Kleiman (1999)[10] compared the performance of 71 companies that adopted the EVA between 1987 and 1996 with that of its most direct competitors that did not adopt the EVA. The following table is a summary of his conclusions.

Year After (Before) the Introduction of EVA

	−3	−2	−1	0	1	2	3
Diferential shareholder return	0.9%	−0.4%	1.5%	2.6%	5.7%	−1.0%	11.1%
Debt / (Debt + Equity book value)	34.5%	35.8%	32.3%	31.9%	34.3%	36.6%	35.4%
Sales of assets/initial assets	17.2%	1.0%	1.0%	25.0%	14.8%	30.3%	19.4%
Investments/initial assets	6.1%	5.9%	6.3%	6.4%	6.2%	6.7%	6.2%
Increase of headcount	0.2%	−1.6%	−1.4%	−1.0%	1.1%	0.0%	1.7%

The first line shows that the companies that introduced EVA had, on average, a higher shareholder return than their immediate competitors:

[9]Biddle, Bowen, and Wallace (1999), "Evidence on EVA."

[10]Kleiman (1999), "Some New Evidence on EVA Companies," *Journal of Applied Corporate Finance*, Summer, pp. 80–91.

Table 14.6

Difference between 40 companies that used EVA, economic Profit, or CVA as Executive Remuneration Parameters and those that did not

Sales of assets	100%
Investments	-21%
Share repurchases	112%
Dividends per share	1%

2.6% in the year of introduction, and 5.7, −1, and 11.1% during the following years. It is also seen that debt ratio increases slightly. Sale of assets increases significantly after introduction of the EVA.

Now an anecdote to close this section. M. Volkema, CEO of Herman Miller, says that: "the analysis of the EVA showed that debt was cheaper than equity," and "the analysis of the EVA enabled us to identify where we were overinvesting. We cut down inventory by 24% and accounts receivable by 22%."[11]

14.7. MEASURES PROPOSED FOR MEASURING SHAREHOLDER RETURN

The measures proposed for measuring the shareholder return or return on investment by the consulting firms that use the EVA, EP, or CVA are

- ROA (return on assets)
- ROE (return on equity)
- CFROI (cash flow return on investment)

	EVA	EP	CVA
Measure of shareholder value creation	EVA = (D+Ebv) (ROA – WACC)	EP = Ebv (ROE – Ke)	CVA = (Do+Ebvo) (CFROI – WACC)
Measure of shareholder return	Return on Investment ROA = NOPAT / (D + Ebv)	Shareholder return ROE = PAT / Ebv	Return on Investment CFROI = (NOPAT + DEP − EDEP) / (Do+Ebvo)
Assets in place	(D + Ebv) = adjusted book value of debt and equity	Ebv = adjusted book value of equity	(Do + Ebvo) = working capital requirements + fixed assets + cum. depreciation + inflation adjustment

[11]See www.eva.com.

We already saw in Chapter 1 the low correlation between ROE and shareholder return. However, it can also be said that the correlation between ROA and CFROI, on the one hand, and return on the investment during the project's life, on the other hand, is equally low. The return on the investment and the shareholder return in any given year depend basically on the changes that have taken place in expectations during the year, and the ROA, ROE, and CFROI are calculated using accounting parameters that are completely unrelated with the changes in these expectations.

14.8. WHAT IS SHAREHOLDER VALUE CREATION?

When managers try to increase the EVA, EP, and CVA, are they really creating value for the shareholders?

A company creates value for the shareholders when the shareholder return exceeds the equity's cost (the required return to equity). A company destroys value when the opposite occurs.

We calculate shareholder value creation in the following manner:

Shareholder value creation $=$
Equity market value $\times$ (Shareholder return $-$ Ke)

Note the significant difference between the above formula and economic profit. Economic profit uses the equity book value instead of the equity market value, and the ROE instead of the shareholder return. It is not surprising that economic profit is very different from shareholder value creation.

Similarly, the EVA uses the book value of the company's debt and equity instead of the equity market value, and the ROA instead of the shareholder return. Therefore, it can come as no surprise that shareholder value creation has very little to do with the EVA, irrespective of whatever adjustments may be made to the accounting data used.

	EVA	EP	CVA	Created shareholder value (CSV)
Measure of shareholder value creation	EVA = NOPAT − (D + Ebv) WACC	EP = BFO − Ebv × Ke	CVA = NOPAT + DEP − EDEP − (Do + Ebvo) WACC	CSV = shareholder value added − E Ke
	EVA = (D + Ebv) (ROA − WACC)	EP = Ebv (ROE − Ke)	CVA = (Do + Ebvo) (CFROI − WACC)	CV = E (shareholder return − Ke)
Measure of shareholder return	ROA = NOPAT / (D + Ebv)	ROE = BFO / Ebv	CFROI = (NOPAT + DEP − EDEP)/ (Do+Ebvo)	Shareholder return = shareholder value added / E
Assets in place	(D + Ebv) = adjusted book value of debt and equity	Ebv = adjusted book value of equity	(Do + Ebvo) = working capital requirements + fixed assets + Cum. depreciation + inflation adjustment	E = equity market value

14.9. AN ANECDOTE ABOUT THE EVA

In October 1998, I published a summary of the previous version of this chapter in the Madrid Stock Market's journal (No. 70, pages 20–23) under the title "EVA, Economic Profit, and Value Creation." In reply to the article, the following e-mail was received by the journal, written by an analyst at Stern Stewart & Co.:

> Dear Sir,
>
> I am writing to you in my capacity as representative of the American firm Stern Stewart, creator of the "*economic value added*" concept or EVA, with reference to the article published in your journal last October under the title "EVA, Economic Profit, and Value Creation" and in response to the article's critical tone, as indicated by statements such as the following:
>
> "EVA is relegated to secondary positions with respect to other explanatory variable." "Some consulting firms say that EP and EVA measure the company's value creation in each period, and this is a tremendous error, as the study performed shows." "EVA was not the parameter that had the highest correlation with shareholder value creation. Economic profit and other parameters had a higher correlation with shareholder value creation than EVA." "One conclusion that can be drawn from this study is that EVA does not measure shareholder value creation in a period. But not only that: there are quite a few parameters that have had a much higher correlation with shareholder value creation than EVA."
>
> Statements such as these are a clear sign of a lack of understanding of the subject and contradict numerous studies and articles published by such renowned professors as Miller, Modigliani, Jensen, Drucker . . .
>
> Your measure may be interesting from an academic viewpoint but, in addition to being useless for measuring value creation at operational level, that is, as a management tool targeting value creation, the definition of EVA used in the article is incorrect.

Finally, I would point out that by questioning EVA as a valuation tool, you are questioning in turn the method for updating cash flows (equivalent to EVA), which was the work of the Economics Nobel Prize winner Merton Miller.

Thank you for your attention to this communication. I am at your disposal if you should wish to explore the issue in greater depth or would consider the possibility of publishing a different point of view.

Yours truly, AA, Financial Analyst, Stern Stewart & Co.

To conclude with this anecdote, the author sent the following e-mail in reply:

Dear D (Madrid Stock Market) and AA:
I have the following comments to make about the e-mail from AA, which I have just received.

1. AA says: "Statements such as these are a clear sign of a lack of understanding of the subject and contradict numerous studies and articles published by such renowned professors as Miller, Modigliani, Jensen, Drucker ..."

   Reply: It just so happens that Modigliani and Jensen were tutors of mine when I was studying for my doctorate at Harvard. I still keep in touch with them. I shall be seeing them in Boston next July. I would like to be shown any study or article by these professors that says anything that disagrees with my statements, as AA suggests.

2. AA says: "Your measure may be interesting from an academic viewpoint but, in addition to being useless for measuring value creation at operational level, that is, as a management tool targeting value creation, the definition of EVA used in the article is incorrect."

   Reply: The definition of EVA used in the article is that given on page 192 of the book *The Quest for Value. The EVA Management Guide* (1991), by Stern Stewart & Co., published by Harper Business. The article does not propose any measure as an alternative to EVA; it simply shows that EVA is not the parameter that had the highest correlation with shareholder value creation. This contradicts certain statements by Stern Stewart & Co., such as, for example, "Forget about EPS (earnings per share), ROE and ROI. The *true* measure of your company's performance is EVA" and "EVA is the only measure that gives the right answer. All the others— including operating income, earnings growth, ROE and ROA—may be erroneous."

3. AA says: "Finally, I would point out that by questioning EVA as a valuation tool, you are questioning in turn the method for updating cash flows (equivalent to EVA), which was the work of the Economics Nobel Prize winner Merton Miller."

   Reply: My article makes it quite clear that I do not question the usefulness of EVA as a valuation tool. Rather, I question the usefulness of EVA as a measure of value creation during a period. Discussing the usefulness of EVA as a value creation measure in a period has nothing to do with updating cash flows. Therefore, AA's statement is incorrect.

   Dear AA: Never in my experience as a consultant and professor have I received a letter anything like yours. If you should ever come to Madrid, I shall be delighted to chat with you and show you the IESE campus.

   Kindest regards, Pablo Fernández

REFERENCES

Biddle G., R. Bowen, and J. Wallace (1999), "Evidence on EVA," *Journal of Applied Corporate Finance*, Volume 12, No. 2, pp. 69–79.

Boston Consulting Group (1996), *Shareholder Value Metrics*.

Fernandez, P. (2001), "Shareholder Value Creators and Shareholder Value Destroyers in U.S.A. Year 2000," Social Science Research Network (SSRN), Working Paper No. 272252.

Fortune (1993), "The Real Key to Creating Wealth," September 20.

Fortune (2000), "America's Best and Worst Wealth Creators," December 18, pp. 207–216.

Kleiman, R. (1999), "Some New Evidence on EVA Companies," *Journal of Applied Corporate Finance*, Volume 12, No. 2, pp. 80–91.

Stewart, G. B. (1991), *The Quest for Value. The EVA Management Guide*, Harper Business.

Stern Stewart and Co., www.eva.com.

Yook, K. C., and G. M. McCabe (2001), "MVA and the Cross-Section of Expected Stock Returns," *Journal of Portfolio Management*, Spring, pp. 75–87.

Chapter 15

The RJR Nabisco Valuation

In this chapter, we shall analyze a real-life example of a valuation: the acquisition of RJR Nabisco in 1988. The main purpose of this chapter is to understand why the company's shares were bought at $108/share when their market price was $55.875/share. The example will also enable us to explore in greater depth the different valuations included in the chapter. Finally, we will see that the EVA (economic value added, a concept we studied in Chapter 14) offers little help in understanding this acquisition.

On 18 November 1988, there were two bids for buying RJR Nabisco's 229 million shares. F. Ross Johnson, RJR Nabisco's CEO, from a group, which we shall call "Management Group," headed one bid. The other bid was from the firm Kohlberg, Kravis, Roberts & Co. (KKR).[1] RJR Nabisco's share price immediately before the offers was $55.875/share.

---

[1] Three former executives of Bear Stearns & Co. founded KKR in 1976: Jerome Kohlberg, Henry Kravis, and George Roberts. Since then, KKR had bought more than 35 companies, paying more than 38,000 million dollars in total. For example, in 1986, KKR bought Beatrice Foods for 6,200 million dollars, the largest purchase made until then. KKR signed a confidentiality agreement with RJR Nabisco. This agreement enabled KKR to gain access to information about the company that was not available to the public. It also gave KKR the opportunity to hold regular meetings with RJR Nabisco's management. This was particularly important for KKR, because its rival—The Management Group—had access to this information thanks to its position in the company. KKR undertook to not buy RJR Nabisco stock, to not take part in shareholder maneuvers, and to not advise or influence any other participant in the acquisition for a two-year period, without the approval of RJR Nabisco's Board of Directors.

15.1. BACKGROUND OF THE COMPANY

RJR Nabisco started business in 1875 as a tobacco company. In 1967, it entered the food business. Table 15.1 shows the company's income statements for the previous six years. Table 15.2 shows the recent balance sheets.

The tobacco business included brands such as Winston, Salem, Camel, and Vantage. In 1987, the tobacco business generated sales amounting to 6330 million dollars, with an operating income of 1,800 million dollars.

The food businesses initially included drinks, oriental foods, desserts, flour, juices, and precooked meals. The Del Monte brand, which was acquired in 1979, added canned foods, fresh bananas, and pineapples. In 1985, the company purchased Nabisco Brands and added, among others, the Ritz and Quakers brands. In 1987, the food businesses generated sales amounting to $9,436 million and an operating income of $915 million.[2]

RJR Nabisco had tried to diversify into other businesses, although it subsequently withdrew from them. In 1969 it bought a containers company (Sea-Land), which it sold in 1984. In 1982 it bought Heublein, an alcoholic beverages company owned by Kentucky Fried Chicken. Kentucky Fried Chicken was sold in 1986, and Heublein was sold in 1987. In 1970 and 1976, it bought two oil companies (Independent Oil Company and Burmah Oil Company) and sold them in 1984.

Table 15.1

Income Statements and Stock Market Data for RJR Nabisco for the Years Prior to the Acquisition

(Million dollars)	1982	1983	1984	1985	1986	1987
Sales	7,323	7,565	8,200	11,622	15,102	15,766
Operating profit	1,142	1,205	1,412	1,949	2,340	2,304
Net income	834	819	1,154	910	962	1,179
Earnings per share ($)	2.96	2.89	4.47	3.63	3.84	4.77
Dividends per share ($)	1.14	1.22	1.30	1.41	1.51	1.76
Million shares*	281.5	283.2	258.4	250.6	250.4	247.4
Stock price*	20.4	24.3	28.8	31.4	49.2	45.0
Beta of the shares**	0.80	0.70	0.74	1.21	1.24	0.67

*   At year-end.
** Calculated using daily data for one year.

[2]The company's total operating income in 1987 (see Table 15.1) was $2,304 million. This figure is the sum of the operating income from tobacco ($1,800 million) and food ($915 million), plus the corporate headquarters' operating income (loss of $182 million), less reorganization expenses ($229 million).

Table 15.2

Balance Sheets of RJR Nabisco for the Years Prior to the Acquisition

	1986	1987		1986	1987
WCR	737	1,297	Debt	6,731	6,280
Fixed assets	11,306	11,021	Stockholder's Equity	5,312	6,038
Net Assets	12,043	12,318	Total	12,043	12,318

15.2. PRE-BID STRATEGY

Table 15.3 shows the projections made for RJR Nabisco assuming that it continued its pre-bid strategy. The largest investment in the tobacco business was related with the development of Premier, a smoke-free cigarette: the level of investment in this project already stood at $300 million.

Table 15.4 shows a valuation of the pre-bid strategy. The valuation has been carried out using the following assumptions:

- Risk-free interest rate = 8.5%
- Market risk premium = 8%
- Asset's beta, or unlevered beta = $0.65 = \beta_u$
- Growth of cash flows after 1998 = 2%

Line 1 of Table 15.4 shows the required return to equity. This parameter is calculated from the CAPM: $Ke = 8.5\% + \beta_L \times 8\%$. β_L is obtained from the equity value $(E)^3$ using the equation $\beta_L = \beta U(D + E)/E$.

Line 2 shows the equity value (E), which is $19,368 million ($84.6/share).[4] This figure is important for understanding the purchase of the company: the market rated the company ($55.875/share) considerably below its book value ($84.6/share).[5]

Line 3 shows the expected value of the debt in each year and line 4 contains the sum of debt plus equity.

---

[3]To calculate E and β_L in Table 15.4, it is necessary to iterate, because to calculate β_L we must know E and to calculate E we must know β_L.

[4]This value is obtained by discounting the equity cash flow given in Table 15.3 at the rate Ke. We compute the present value by using the compounded required return to equity over time. For example, the compounded discount rate for the equity cash flow of 1991 is (1.151)(1.152)(1.151). In 1988, there were 229 million shares outstanding.

[5]This may be because the market did not believe the projections of Table 15.3, or because it assigned much more risk to the business. In fact, at that time, the company's management came in for some heavy criticism. There were also several analysts who considered it unadvisable that the company should have two such different businesses as food and tobacco.

Table 15.3
Pre–Bid Strategy, Balance Sheets, Income Statements, and Cash Flows

(Million dollars)	1988	1989	1990	1991	1992	1993	1994	1995	1996	1997	1998
WCR	1,191	1,271	1,382	1,480	1,585	1,698	1,819	1,949	2,089	2,240	2,402
Net fixed assets	11,223	12,124	12,795	13,321	13,402	13,274	13,142	13,010	12,878	12,746	12,620
NET ASSETS	12,414	13,395	14,177	14,801	14,987	14,972	14,961	14,959	14,967	14,986	15,022
Debt	5,204	6,018	6,300	6,273	5,982	5,400	4,164	3,727	2,355	0	0
Equity	7,210	7,377	7,877	8,528	9,005	9,572	10,797	11,232	12,612	14,986	15,022
TOTAL	12,414	13,395	14,177	14,801	14,987	14,972	14,961	14,959	14,967	14,986	15,022
Sales	16,950	18,088	19,676	21,075	22,578	24,191	25,925	27,788	29,790	31,942	34,256
Operating income	2,653	2,898	3,336	3,838	4,216	4,634	5,093	5,596	6,149	6,756	7,424
Interest	551	582	662	693	690	658	594	458	410	259	0
Net income	**1,360**	**1,498**	**1,730**	**2,023**	**2,259**	**2,536**	**2,858**	**3,251**	**3,625**	**4,094**	**4,625**
Depreciation and deferred tax	730	807	791	819	849	866	867	867	867	867	861
Capital expenditures	1,142	1,708	1,462	1,345	930	738	735	735	735	735	735
Increase of WCR		80	111	98	105	113	121	130	140	151	162
Increase of debt		814	282	−27	−291	−582	−1,236	−436	−1,373	−2,355	0
Equity cash flow		**1,331**	**1,230**	**1,372**	**1,782**	**1,969**	**1,633**	**2,817**	**2,244**	**1,720**	**4,589**
− Increase of debt		−814	−282	27	291	582	1,236	436	1,373	2,355	0
Interest (1−0.34)		384	437	457	455	434	392	302	271	171	0
Free cash flow		**901**	**1,385**	**1,856**	**2,528**	**2,985**	**3,261**	**3,555**	**3,888**	**4,246**	**4,589**

Table 15.4
Pre-Bid Strategy, Valuation

($ Million)	1988	1989	1990	1991	1992	1993	1994	1995	1996	1997	1998
1 Ke		15.1%	15.2%	15.1%	15.0%	14.9%	14.7%	14.4%	14.3%	14.0%	13.7%
2 E = PV(ECF; Ke)	19,368	20,961	22,916	25,011	26,982	29,020	31,644	33,379	35,902	39,222	40,007
3 D	5,204	6,018	6,300	6,273	5,982	5,400	4,164	3,727	2,355	0	0
4 D + E	24,572	26,979	29,216	31,284	32,964	34,420	35,808	37,106	38,256	39,222	40,007
5 Kd		11%	11%	11%	11%	11%	11%	11%	11%	11%	0%
6 WACC		13.5%	13.4%	13.4%	13.5%	13.5%	13.5%	13.6%	13.6%	13.6%	13.7%
7 D + E = PV (FCF; WACC)	24,572	26,979	29,216	31,284	32,964	34,420	35,808	37,106	38,256	39,222	40,007
8 CCF		1,099	1,610	2,092	2,763	3,209	3,463	3,711	4,027	4,334	4,589
9 $WACC_{BT}$		14.3%	14.3%	14.2%	14.2%	14.2%	14.1%	14.0%	14.0%	13.9%	13.7%
10 D + E = PV (CCF; $WACC_{BT}$)	24,572	26,979	29,216	31,284	32,964	34,420	35,808	37,106	38,256	39,222	40,007

Value per share = 19,368/229 = $84.6/share.

Line 5 shows the cost of debt[6] (Kd) and line 6 the weighted average cost of capital (WACC) calculated using the following expression:

$$WACC = \frac{E\ Ke + D\ Kd\ (1 - T)}{E + D}$$

Line 7 is the present value of the expected free cash flow (FCF) discounted at the WACC, that is, debt plus equity (D + E). Obviously, this line is the same as line 4.

Line 8 shows the capital cash flow (CCF) and line 9 the weighted average cost of capital before taxes ($WACC_{BT}$) calculated using the following expression:

$$WACC_{BT} = \frac{E\ Ke + D\ Kd}{E + D}$$

Line 10 is the present value of the expected CCF discounted at the $WACC_{BT}$, that is, debt plus equity (D + E). Obviously, this line is the same as lines 4 and 7.

15.3. THE MANAGEMENT GROUP'S BID

The Management Group bid $99.3/share: $89.50 in cash, $6 of pay-in-kind preferred stock[7] and $3.80 of pay-in-kind convertible preferred stock. This convertible preferred stock could be converted into approximately 15% of the capital, which would remain in the company, but it could be redeemed at any time for its face value plus accrued dividends.

$2,500 million in shares and $18,000 million in debt would finance the cash portion.[8] The Management Group would also assume the $5,204 million of existing debt. Table 15.5 shows the balance sheet forecast by the Management Group.

The Management Group's strategy was to sell off all the food businesses and keep the tobacco business.[9] Table 15.6 shows the income statements and

---

[6]The cost of the debt is equal to the interest paid divided by the debt's nominal value at the start of the year. This chapter assumes that the value of the debt is equal to its nominal value.

[7]The term pay-in-kind is used for financial instruments that pay interest or dividends using new financial instruments of the same type, instead of paying in cash.

[8]$20,500 million divided among 229 million shares gives $89.5/share.

[9]This strategy was based on the idea that the market underrated the tobacco business's strong cash flows and did not fully value the food business due to its association with tobacco. If the assets of RJR Nabisco's food business were sold, leaving just the tobacco business, it was expected that the undervaluation would disappear and significant gains would be generated. F. Ross Johnson had experience in the sale of food businesses. He was Standard Brands' CEO when it was purchased by Nabisco to form part of Nabisco Brands in 1981. He was also Nabisco Brands' CEO when it was purchased by RJ Reynolds in 1985 to form RJR Nabisco.

Table 15.5
The Management Group's strategy, Balance Sheet

($ Million)	1988	1989	1990	1991	1992	1993	1994	1995	1996	1997	1998	1999	2000	2001
WCR	1,191	642	687	735	787	844	905	972	1,044	1,122	1,207	1,299	1,399	1,507
Net fixed assets	26,758	14,323	13,979	13,633	13,287	12,934	12,582	12,236	11,895	11,558	11,226	10,932	10,680	10,473
Net assets	27,949	14,965	14,666	14,368	14,074	13,778	13,487	13,208	12,939	12,680	12,433	12,231	12,079	11,980
Assumed debt	5,204	4,894	4,519	3,798	2,982	2,582	1,857	0	0	0	0	0	0	0
New debt	18,000	6,292	6,075	5,878	5,413	4,221	3,000	2,515	0	0	0	0	0	0
Preferred stock	1,374	1,632	1,939	2,304	2,737	3,251	3,863	4,589	5,170	2,811	0	0	0	0
Convertible preferred	871	1,035	1,229	1,460	1,735	2,061	2,449	2,909	3,456	4,106	4,552	1,548	0	0
Equity	2,500	1,112	904	928	1,207	1,663	2,319	3,195	4,313	5,763	7,881	10,683	12,079	11,980
Total	27,949	14,965	14,666	14,368	14,074	13,778	13,487	13,208	12,939	12,680	12,433	12,231	12,079	11,980

Table 15.6
The Management Group's Strategy, Income Statements and Cash Flows

($ million)	1988	1989	1990	1991	1992	1993	1994	1995	1996	1997	1998	1999	2000	2001
1 **Sales**	16,950	7,650	8,293	8,983	9,731	10,540	11,418	12,368	13,397	14,514	15,723	17,028	18,441	19,972
2 Operating income	2,653	1,917	2,385	2,814	3,266	3,589	3,945	4,337	4,768	5,243	5,766	6,130	6,639	7,190
3 Interest	551	2,792	1,353	1,286	1,183	1,037	850	624	351	0	0	0	0	0
4 Taxes (34%)	715	−298	351	520	708	868	1,052	1,262	1,502	1,783	1,960	2,084	2,257	2,445
5 Amortization		388	388	388	388	388	388	388	388	388	388	388	388	388
6 **Net income**	**1,360**	**−966**	**293**	**620**	**987**	**1,296**	**1,655**	**2,063**	**2,527**	**3,072**	**3,418**	**3,658**	**3,994**	**4,357**
7 −Preferred dividends		422	501	596	708	841	999	1,187	1,410	1,622	1,300	856	291	0
8 +Extraordinary profit														
9 **Net income-common stock**		**−1,388**	**−208**	**25**	**279**	**456**	**656**	**876**	**1,118**	**1,451**	**2,117**	**2,802**	**3,703**	**4,357**
10 Depreciation and deferred taxes	730	777	725	726	735	749	754	758	763	769	774	774	774	774
11 −Increase of fixed assets	1,142	432	381	380	389	396	402	412	422	432	442	480	522	567
12 −Increase of WCR		41	45	48	52	57	61	67	72	78	85	92	100	108
13 +Book value of disposals		12,680												
14 +Increase of debt		−12,018	−592	−918	−1,281	−1,592	−1,946	−2,342	−2,515	0	0	0	0	0
15 +Preferred dividends		422	501	596	708	841	999	1,187	1,410	1,622	1,300	856	291	0
16 −Reduction preferred									−282	−3,331	−3,339			
17 −Reduction convertible preferred										0	−325	−3,860	−1,839	
18 **ECF**	**0**	**0**	**0**	**0**	**0**	**0**	**0**	**0**	**0**	**0**	**0**	**0**	**2,307**	**4,456**
19 +(1 − 0.34) Interest paid		1,843	893	849	781	684	561	412	232	0	0	0	0	0
20 +Decrease of debt		12,018	592	918	1,281	1,592	1,946	2,342	2,515	0				
21 +Reduction preferred									282	3,331	3,339			
22 +Reduction convertible preferred											325	3,860	1,839	
23 **FCF**		**13,861**	**1,485**	**1,767**	**2,062**	**2,277**	**2,507**	**2,753**	**3,028**	**3,331**	**3,665**	**3,860**	**4,146**	**4,456**

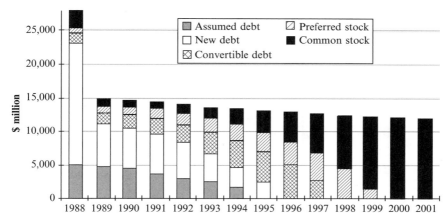

Figure 15.1   Liabilities structure according to The Management Group's strategy.

cash flows forecast by the Management Group. The net income does not include the sale of assets. They intended to sell all of the food assets for their book value of $12,680 million. Line 5 shows the amortization of the goodwill, which is not taxdeductible. The goodwill is calculated as the difference between the new company's total liabilities ($27,949) and the present company's total liabilities ($12,414). The goodwill is amortized in 40 years.[10]

Figure 15.1 shows the evolution of the liabilities structure (at book value) according to The Management Group's strategy.

15.4. VALUATION OF THE MANAGEMENT GROUP'S STRATEGY

Table 15.7 shows a valuation of The Management Group's strategy. The equity (E), the preferred stock (Pr), and the convertible preferred stock (PrCo) are valued separately. The valuation has been carried out with the following assumptions:

- Risk-free interest rate $= 8.5\%$
- Market risk premium $= 8\%$
- Asset's beta, or unlevered beta $= 0.65 = \beta_U$
- Growth of cash flows after 2001 $= 2\%$

---

[10]The annual amortization of the goodwill is $(27,949 - 12,414)/40 = 388$.

Table 15.7

Valuation of The Management Group's Strategy

($ million)	1988	1989	1990	1991	1992	1993	1994	1995	1996	1997	1998	1999	2000	2001
1 Ke		43.6%	25.4%	23.1%	21.2%	19.7%	18.5%	17.4%	16.6%	15.8%	15.1%	14.5%	13.9%	13.7%
2 E = PV(ECF; Ke)	4,453	6,393	8,016	9,865	11,959	14,315	16,960	19,918	23,219	26,890	30,962	35,454	38,088	38,850
3 CF prefer			0	0	0	0	0	0	282	3,331	3,339			
4 Kpref		31.4%	19.8%	18.3%	17.2%	16.2%	15.4%	14.7%	14.2%	13.7%	13.7%			
5 Pr = PV(CFpr; Kpr)	1,512	1,986	2,378	2,815	3,298	3,833	4,424	5,076	5,513	2,937	0			
6 CF prefer conv			0	0	0	0	0	0	0	0	325	3,860	1,839	
7 Kpref con		37.8%	22.7%	20.8%	19.3%	18.0%	17.0%	16.1%	15.4%	14.8%	14.2%	13.7%	13.7%	
8 PrCo = PV(CFprco; Kprco)	870	1,200	1,472	1,778	2,121	2,503	2,929	3,401	3,925	4,504	4,817	1,617		
9 D	23,204	11,186	10,594	9,676	8,395	6,803	4,857	2,515	0	0	0	0	0	0
10 D + E + Pr + PrCo	30,038	20,764	22,460	24,134	25,773	27,454	29,169	30,910	32,656	34,331	35,779	37,071	38,088	38,850

Line 1 of Table 15.7 shows the required return to equity. This parameter is calculated from the CAPM: $Ke = 8.5\% + \beta_E \times 8\%$. β_E is calculated using the equation

$$\beta_E = \beta_U \left(\frac{E + D + Pr + PrCo}{E} \right)$$

Line 2 shows the equity value (E), which is \$4,453 million. This value must be compared with the shareholders' contribution, which is \$2,500 million.

Line 3 shows the forecast cash flow for the preferred stock. Line 4 shows the required return to the preferred stock calculated from the CAPM: $Kpr = 8.5\% + \beta_{pr} \times 8\%$.

Where

$$\beta_{pr} = \beta_U \left(\frac{E + D + Pr + PrCo}{E + Pr + PrCo} \right).$$

Line 5 shows the value of the preferred stock, which is the present value of the expected cash flows (line 3) discounted at the required return (line 4).

Line 6 shows the forecast cash flow for the convertible preferred stock. Line 7 shows the required return to the convertible preferred stock, calculated from the CAPM: $K_{prco} = 8.5\% + \beta_{prco} \times 8\%$. β_{prco} is calculated using the equation .

$$\beta_{prco} = \beta_U \left(\frac{E + D + Pr + PrCo}{E + PrCo} \right).$$

Line 8 shows the value of the convertible preferred stock, which is the present value of the expected cash flows (line 6) discounted at the required return (line 7).

Line 9 shows the value forecast for the debt in each year and line 10 contains the sum of the debt, preferred stock, convertible preferred stock and equity.

Table 15.8 shows the valuation of The Management Group's strategy from the WACC. Line 1 shows the cost of debt (Kd) and line 2 the weighted average cost of capital (WACC) calculated using the following expression:

$$WACC = \left(\frac{E\ Ke + D\ Kd(1 - T) + PrKpr + PrCo\ Kprco}{E + D + Pr + PrCo} \right)$$

Line 3 is the present value of the forecast FCF discounted at the WACC, which is the sum of the debt, preferred stock, convertible preferred stock, and equity $(E + D + Pr + PrCo)$. Obviously, this line is the same as line 10 of Table 15.7.

Table 15.8

Valuation of The Management Group's Strategy with WACC and $WACC_{BT}$
$D + E + Pr + PrCo = PV(FCF;WACC) = PV(CCF;WACC_{BT})$

($ million)	1988	1989	1990	1991	1992	1993	1994	1995	1996	1997	1998	1999	2000	2001
1 Kd		12.0%	12.1%	12.1%	12.2%	12.4%	12.5%	12.8%	14.0%	0.0%	0.0%	0.0%	0.0%	0.0%
2 WACC		15.3%	15.3%	15.3%	15.3%	15.4%	15.4%	15.4%	15.4%	15.3%	14.9%	14.4%	13.9%	13.7%
3 PV(FCF; WACC)	30,038	20,764	22,460	24,134	25,773	27,454	29,169	30,910	32,656	34,331	35,779	37,071	38,088	38,850
4 CCF		14,810	1,945	2,204	2,464	2,629	2,796	2,966	3,147	3,331	3,665	3,860	4,146	4,456
5 $WACC_{BT}$		18.4%	17.5%	17.3%	17.0%	16.7%	16.4%	16.1%	15.8%	15.3%	14.9%	14.4%	13.9%	13.7%
6 PV(CCF; $WACC_{BT}$)	30,038	20,764	22,460	24,134	25,773	27,454	29,169	30,910	32,656	34,331	35,779	37,071	38,088	38,850

Line 4 shows each year's capital cash flow (CCF) and line 5 the weighted average cost of capital before tax (WACC$_{BT}$) calculated using the following expression:

$$\text{WACC}_{BT} = \left(\frac{\text{E Ke} + \text{D Kd} + \text{Pr Kpr} + \text{PrCo Kprco}}{\text{E} + \text{D} + \text{Pr} + \text{PrCo}} \right)$$

Line 6 is the present value of the forecast CCF discounted at the WACC$_{BT}$, which is the sum of the debt, preferred stock, convertible preferred stock, and equity (E + D + Pr + PrCo). Obviously, this line is the same as line 3 and line 10 of Table 15.7.

15.5. KKR'S BID

KKR's bid was $94 per share: $75 in cash, $11 of pay-in-kind preferred stock, and $6 of pay-in-kind convertible debt, which KKR valued at $8. The convertible debt would convert to shares at the end of 1993, unless the holder should decide to continue holding the debentures. If all the debt were to be converted, it would represent 25% of RJR Nabisco's capital. $1,500 million in shares and $15,880 million of debt would finance the cash portion of the bid. KKR also planned to assume the $5,204 million of existing debt. Table 15.9 shows the balance sheet forecast by KKR. It assumes that the convertible debt is converted in 1993.

KKR's strategy for managing RJR Nabisco was different from that of The Management Group: they intended to only sell a small part of the food businesses. According to KKR: "We do not plan to break up the company's operations. Our intention is to keep all the tobacco business. We also plan to keep a major part of the food operations." Table 15.10 contains the income statements and cash flows forecast for RJR Nabisco with KKR's strategy. Figure 15.2 shows the evolution of the liabilities structure (at book value) according to KKR's strategy.

15.6. VALUATION OF KKR'S STRATEGY

Table 15.11 shows a valuation of KKR's strategy. It assumes that the convertible debt is converted in 1993 and values jointly the common stock and the convertible debt (E + Co). The preferred stock (Pr) is valued separately. The valuation has been carried out with the following assumptions:

- Risk-free interest rate = 8.5%
- Market risk premium = 8%

Table 15.9
KKR's Strategy, Balance Sheet

($ million)	1988	1989	1990	1991	1992	1993	1994	1995	1996	1997	1998	1999	2000	2001
WCR	1,191	1,085	1,029	1,115	1,210	1,312	1,423	1,542	1,671	1,811	1,962	2,126	2,306	2,501
Net fixed assets	25,284	21,963	19,260	18,916	18,581	18,247	17,921	17,611	17,316	17,041	16,774	16,567	16,426	16,357
Net assets	26,475	23,048	20,289	20,031	19,791	19,559	19,344	19,153	18,987	18,852	18,736	18,694	18,732	18,858
Assumed debt	5,204	4,894	4,519	3,798	2,982	2,582	2,182	0	0	0	0	0	0	0
New debt	15,880	12,459	9,313	8,619	7,695	6,112	4,129	3,479	149	0	0	0	0	0
Convertible debt	1,373	1,579	1,816	2,128	2,494									
Preferred stock	2,518	2,896	3,330	3,956	4,700	5,583	6,633	7,880	9,362	7,320	4,377	549	0	0
Common stock	1,500	1,220	1,311	1,530	1,920	5,282	6,400	7,794	9,477	11,532	14,359	18,145	18,732	18,858
Total	26,475	23,048	20,289	20,031	19,791	19,559	19,344	19,153	18,987	18,852	18,736	18,694	18,732	18,858

	1989	1990
Sales of assets	3,694	2,850
Book value of assets	3,121	2,408
Taxes	194	150
Sales – taxes	3,500	2,700
Extraordinary profit	379	292

Table 15.10

KKR's Strategy, Income Statements and Cash Flows

($ million)	1988	1989	1990	1991	1992	1993	1994	1995	1996	1997	1998	1999	2000	2001
1 Sales	16,950	16,190	15,223	16,468	17,815	19,270	20,846	22,551	24,394	26,391	28,550	31,091	33,858	36,871
2 Operating income	2,653	2,862	3,228	3,811	4,140	4,508	4,906	5,341	5,815	6,335	6,902	7,516	8,185	8,914
3 Interest expense	551	2,754	2,341	1,997	1,888	1,321	1,088	806	487	21	0	0	0	0
4 Taxes (34%)	715	37	302	617	766	1,084	1,298	1,542	1,812	2,147	2,347	2,556	2,783	3,031
5 Amortization of goodwill		352	352	352	352	352	352	352	352	352	352	352	352	352
6 Net income	1,360	−281	233	845	1,134	1,751	2,168	2,641	3,164	3,815	4,203	4,609	5,050	5,531
7 −Preferred dividends		378	434	626	744	884	1,050	1,247	1,481	1,760	1,376	823	103	0
8 +Extraordinary profit		379	292	9										
9 Net income-common stock		−280	91	219	391	868	1,118	1,394	1,683	2,055	2,827	3,786	4,947	5,531
10 Depreciation and deferred taxes	730	1,159	991	899	907	920	924	928	933	939	945	945	945	945
11 −Increase of fixed assets	1,142	774	556	555	572	586	598	618	638	664	678	738	804	876
12 −Increase of WCR		79	84	86	95	102	111	119	129	140	151	164	179	195
13 +Book value of disposals		3,121	2,408											
14 +Increase of debt		206	237	312	366									
15 +Preferred dividends		−3,731	−3,521	−1,415	−1,740	−1,983	−2,383	−2,832	−3,330	−149				
16 −Reduction preferred		378	434	626	744	884	1,050	1,247	1,481	1,760	1,376	823	103	
17 −Reduction convertible preferred										−3,802	−4,319	−4,651		
18 ECF		0	0	0	0	0	0	0	0	0	0	0	4,360	5,405
19 +(1 − 0.34)Interest paid		1,682	1,389	1,112	1,005	872	718	532	321	14	0	0	0	0
20 −0.34× deferred interest		70	81	106	124	0	0	0	0	0	0	0	0	0
21 +Decrease of debt		3,731	3,521	1,415	1,740	1,983	2,383	2,832	3,330	149				
22 +Reduction preferred stock										3,802	4,319	4,651	652	
23 FCF		5,343	4,829	2,421	2,620	2,855	3,101	3,364	3,652	3,964	4,319	4,651	5,012	5,405

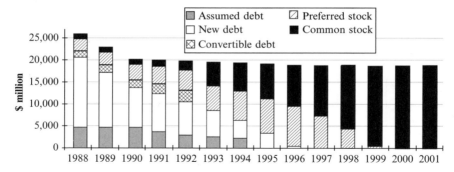

Figure 15.2   Liabilities structure according to KKR's strategy.

- Asset's beta, or unlevered beta $= 0.65 = \beta_U$
- Growth of cash flows after 2001 $= 2\%$

Line 1 of Table 15.11 shows the cash flows forecast for the stock and convertibles. Line 2 shows the required return to equity (and convertibles) calculated from the CAPM: $Ke = 8.5\% + \beta_E \times 8\%$. β_E is calculated using the equation

$$\beta_E = \beta_U \left(\frac{E + Co + D + Pr}{E + Co} \right)$$

Line 3 shows the equity value and the convertibles $(E + Co)$, which gives $6,030 million. This value must be compared with the shareholders' contribution, which is $1,500 million and the nominal value of the convertibles, which is $1,373 million. As the convertibles can be converted into 25% of the equity, their value is $1,507 million and that of the equity is $4,523 million.

Line 4 shows the cash flow forecast for the preferred stock. Line 5 shows the required return to the preferred stock calculated from the CAPM: $Kpr = 8.5\% + \beta_{pr} \times 8\%$. β_{pr} which is calculated using the equation

$$\beta_{pr} = \beta_U \left(\frac{E + Co + D + Pr}{E + Co + Pr} \right).$$

Line 6 shows the value of the preferred stock, which is the present value of the expected cash flows (line 4) discounted at the required return (line 5).

Line 7 shows the value forecast for the debt in each year and line 8 contains the sum of the debt, preferred stock, convertibles, and equity.

Table 15.12 shows the valuation of KKR's strategy from the WACC. Line 1 shows the cost of debt (Kd) and line 2 the weighted average cost of capital (WACC) calculated using the following expression:

Table 15.11
Valuation of KKR's Strategy

($ million)	1988	1989	1990	1991	1992	1993	1994	1995	1996	1997	1998	1999	2000	2001
1 ECF + CFcon		0	0	0	0	0	0	0	0	0	0	0	4,360	5,405
2 Ke		34.2%	27.1%	22.8%	20.9%	19.3%	18.1%	17.1%	16.3%	15.5%	14.9%	14.3%	13.8%	13.7%
3 E + Co = PV(ECF + CFcon; Ke)	6,030	8,093	10,283	12,627	15,260	18,207	21,505	25,185	29,282	33,834	38,877	44,442	46,200	47,124
4 CF preferred	0	0	0	0	0	0	0	0	0	3,802	4,319	4,651	652	
5 Ke preferred		26.2%	21.5%	18.7%	17.4%	16.3%	15.5%	14.8%	14.2%	13.7%	13.7%	13.7%	13.7%	
6 Pref = PV(CFpre; Kep)	2,718	3,431	4,170	4,949	5,808	6,757	7,805	8,962	10,237	7,840	4,595	574	0	
7 D	21,084	17,353	13,832	12,417	10,677	8,694	6,311	3,479	149	0	0	0	0	0
8 D + E + Pref + Co	29,832	28,877	28,284	29,993	31,745	33,658	35,621	37,626	39,668	41,674	43,472	45,015	46,200	47,124

Table 15.12
Valuation of KKR's Strategy with WACC and WACC$_{BT}$

($ million)	1988	1989	1990	1991	1992	1993	1994	1995	1996	1997	1998	1999	2000	2001
1 Kd		12.1%	12.1%	12.2%	12.3%	12.4%	12.5%	12.8%	14.0%	14.1%	0.0%	0.0%	0.0%	0.0%
2 WACC		14.7%	14.7%	14.6%	14.6%	15.0%	15.0%	15.1%	15.1%	15.1%	14.7%	14.2%	13.8%	13.7%
3 D + E + Pr + Co = PV (FCF; WACC)	29,832	28,877	28,284	29,993	31,745	33,658	35,621	37,626	39,668	41,674	43,472	45,015	46,200	47,124
4 CCF		6,279	5,625	3,100	3,262	3,304	3,471	3,638	3,817	3,971	4,319	4,651	5,012	5,405
5 WACC$_{BT}$		17.8%	17.4%	17.0%	16.7%	16.4%	16.1%	15.8%	15.6%	15.1%	14.7%	14.2%	13.8%	13.7%
6 D + E + Pr + Co = PV (CCF; WACC$_{BT}$)	29,832	28,877	28,284	29,993	31,745	33,658	35,621	37,626	39,668	41,674	43,472	45,015	46,200	47,124

$$\text{WACC} = \left(\frac{(E + Co)\ Ke + D\ Kd(1 - T) + Pr\ Kpr - Inp\ T}{E + Co + D + Pr} \right)$$

where Inp = not-paid interest,[11] but which is deductible from tax. This is the interest payable on the convertible debt. Note that the expression of the WACC changes due to the existence of not-paid interest that enables less tax to be paid.

Line 3 is the present value of the forecast FCF discounted at the WACC, which is the sum of the debt, preferred stock, convertible debt, and equity (E + D + Pr + Co). Obviously, this line is the same as line 8 of Table 15.11.

Line 4 shows the CCF of each period and line 5 the weighted average cost of capital before tax (WACC$_{BT}$) calculated using the following expression:

$$\text{WACC}_{BT} = \left(\frac{(E + Co)\ Ke + D\ Kd + Pr\ Kpr}{E + Co + D + Pr} \right)$$

Line 6 is the present value of the forecast CCF discounted at the WACC$_{BT}$, which is the sum of the debt, preferred stock, convertible debt, and equity (E + D + Pr + Co). Obviously, this line is the same as line 3 and line 8 of Table 15.11.

15.7. COMPARISON OF THE THREE ALTERNATIVES' FCF AND CCF

Table 15.13 shows the FCFs expected by KKR, The Management Group, and by the company before the bids. The next three lines are the differential FCFs between strategies. It also contains the IRR of the differential cash flow between KKR's and The Management Group's strategies based on different cash flow growth rates after 2001.

Table 15.14 shows the CCFs expected by KKR, The Management Group, and by the company before the bids. The next three lines are the differential CCFs between strategies. It also contains the IRR of the differential cash flow between KKR's and The Management Group's strategies based on different cash flow growth rates after 2001.

---

[11]Pay-in-kind interest.

Table 15.13

Comparison of the Two Bids' FCF with the Pre-Bid FCF

Free cash flows ($ million)	1989	1990	1991	1992	1993	1994	1995	1996	1997	1998	1999	2000	2001
KKR	5,343	4,829	2,421	2,620	2,855	3,101	3,364	3,652	3,964	4,319	4,651	5,012	5,405
The Management Group	13,861	1,485	1,767	2,062	2,277	2,507	2,753	3,028	3,331	3,665	3,860	4,146	4,456
Pre-bid strategy	901	1,385	1,856	2,528	2,985	3,261	3,555	3,888	4,246	4,589	0	0	0
KKR – Pre-bid	4,442	3,445	565	92	−130	−160	−191	−236	−282	−270	4,651	5,012	5,405
The Management Group – Pre-bid	12,960	100	−89	−467	−709	−754	−802	−860	−915	−924	3,860	4,146	4,456
KKR – The Management Group	−8,518	3,344	654	559	579	594	611	624	633	655	791	866	949

KKR – The Management Group	g = 0	g = 1%	g = 2%	g = 3%	g = 4%
IRR with different growth rates after 2001:	11.9%	12.3%	12.6%	13.0%	13.3%

Table 15.14

Comparison of the Two Bid's CCF with the Pre-Bid FCF

Capital cash flows ($ million)	1989	1990	1991	1992	1993	1994	1995	1996	1997	1998	1999	2000	2001
KKR	6,279	5,625	3,100	3,262	3,304	3,471	3,638	3,817	3,971	4,319	4,651	5,012	5,405
The Management Group	14,810	1,945	2,204	2,464	2,629	2,796	2,966	3,147	3,331	3,665	3,860	4,146	4,456
Pre-bid strategy	1,099	1,610	2,092	2,763	3,209	3,463	3,711	4,027	4,334	4,589	0	0	0
KKR – Pre-bid	5,180	4,015	1,008	499	95	8	–73	–210	–363	–270	4,651	5,012	5,405
The Management Group – Pre-bid	13,711	335	112	–299	–580	–667	–745	–880	–1,003	–924	3,860	4,146	4,456
KKR – The Management Group	–8,531	3,680	896	799	675	675	673	670	640	655	791	866	949

KKR – The Management Group	g = 0	g = 1%	g = 2%	g = 3%	g = 4%
IRR with different growth rates after 2001:	13.4%	13.6%	13.9%	14.2%	14.6%

15.8. EVA AND THE TWO ALTERNATIVES' VALUE CREATION

Table 15.15 shows the summary of the valuations. According to the valuations given, the value of all the company's liabilities with The Management Group's strategy is $30,038 million and, according to KKR's strategy, $29,832 million. The value of all the liabilities according to the pre-bid strategy is $24,572 million and the market valuation was only $17,999 million.[12] These calculations enable us to conclude that, according to the strategies shown, The Management Group could offer a maximum of $108.20 per share[13] and KKR a maximum of $107.50 per share.[14]

However, the most important issue is to answer the question of why a company valued by the market at $17,999 million can be worth $30,000 million for KKR and The Management Group. Table 15.15 helps us clarify this issue. The step-up from $17,999 to $24,572 million is due to the market undervaluation. As has already been suggested, this undervaluation could be because the market did not agree with the company's management (ostentatious management style, entering and exiting several businesses in recent years, uncertain, multimillion investments planned, etc.). The stepup from

Table 15.15

Summary of the Valuations

($ million)	The Management Group	KKR	Pre-bid strategy	Market value
Enterprise value (debt + equity)	**30,038**	**29,832**	**24,572**	**17,999**
Increase of value vs. pre-bid strategy	**5,466**	**5,260**		
Interest tax shield	1,202	1,950		
Cost of leverage	−3,816	−4,236		
Lower investment in fixed assets	4,400	2,675		
Lower depreciation of fixed assets	−1,100	−669		
Lower increase of WCR	488	88		
Lower operating income due to businesses sold	−7,456	−229		
Reduction in general expenses	952	516		
Sale of assets	11,005	5,104		
Other	−209	61		

[12]17,999 million is the sum of the debt, which is 5,204 million, and the equity, which is $12,795 million ($55.875/share × 229 million shares).

[13]$(30,038 − 5204)/229 = 108.20$, where 5,204 is the value of the assumed debt.

[14]$(29,832 − 5,204)/229 = 107.5$, where 5,204 is the value of the assumed debt.

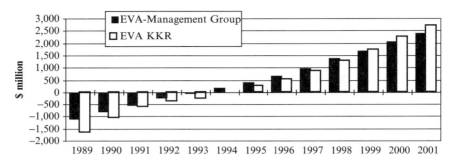

Figure 15.3   EVA of KKR's and The Management Group's strategies.

$24,572 million (the company's value according to the company's present strategy) to $30,000 million (the company's approximate value according to The Management Group's and KKR's strategy) is due to:

1. Greater leverage, which means a lower tax shield and higher leverage costs
2. Less investments planned, which also means lower depreciation
3. Sale of businesses, which also implies less operating income and a lower growth of working capital requirements

Figure 15.3 shows each year's EVA for The Management Group's and KKR's strategies. A literal interpretation of each year's EVA would indicate that both strategies destroy value during the first few years (those with a negative EVA) and create it after 1995. Obviously, this interpretation does not make sense.[15]

Figure 15.4 shows the sensitivity of the company's value (equity, debt, and convertibles, etc.) to the assets' beta.

15.9. FINAL BIDS AND OUTCOME

After a number of subsequent bids, on 30 November 1988 The Management Group and KKR tendered their final bids, which are shown in Table 15.17. The bids were identical in the total per share. The company was sold to KKR.

[15]Ross Johnson, RJR Nabisco's former Chairman and CEO, used to say "an accountant is someone with his head in the past and his butt in the future."

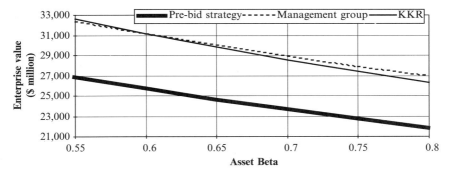

Figure 15.4   Value of the company at different values for the assets' beta (βu).

Table 15.16
Consultant Teams for KKR, The Management Group, and the Special Committee

KKR	The Management group
Investment Banks:	**Investment Banks:**
• Drexel Burnham Lambert	• Shearson Lehman Hutton
• Wasserstein Perella	• Salomon Brothers
• Merrill Lynch Capital Markets	**Comanaging Bank Agents**
• Morgan Stanley	• Citibank
Comanaging Bank Agents	• Bankers Trust
• Manufacturers Hanover Trust	**Legal Advisors:**
• Bankers Trust	• Davis Polk & Wardwell
• Citibank	
• Chase Manhattan	**Special Committee**
Other Investors	**Advisors:**
• Pension Funds	• Dillon Read
• University Endowments	• Lazard Freres
• Foreign Corporations	**Legal Advisors:**
Legal Advisors:	• Skadden, Arps, Slate,
• Simpson Thatcher & Bartlett	Meagher & Flom

Table 15.17

Final Bids Tendered by KKR and The Management Group

Management Group	$/share	KKR	$/share
Cash	84	Cash	81
Preferred stock	22	Preferred stock	17
Convertible preferred stock	2	Convertible debt	10
Total	**108**	**Total**	**108**

These bids are based on a somewhat different balance sheet structure to those given in this chapter. Specifically, KKR's bid was based on a higher cash outlay, thanks to new additional debt amounting to $1,220 million. Also, the previous shareholders were given more preferred stock and more convertible debt than in Table 15.9.

Can one talk of value creation in this operation? The reader has been able to see for himself that both KKR and The Management Group expected to pay less tax, invest less, spend less in operating costs, and sell business units for a profit. This is this operation's value creation. From the previous shareholders' viewpoint, they sold for $108 shares that 2 months previously were worth $55.875. However, whatever the reader's opinion may be about what name should be given to this, one very important point to consider is that the "value creation" occurred at the time of selling the 229 million old shares. Whatever happened after that was KKR's problem.

15.10. VALUATIONS GROUPING ALL THE FINANCIAL INSTRUMENTS AS DEBT OR EQUITY

This section shows that the valuations discussed earlier in this chapter for The Management Group and KKR penalize the company's valuation by valuing each financial instrument separately. If all the financial instruments are grouped in two groups, as debt or equity, the valuation is higher. This section shows the valuations obtained when the financial instruments are grouped (Table 15.8 and 15.9). It can be seen that:

- The company's value for The Management Group increases from $30,038 to $32,626 million
- The company's value for KKR increases from $29,832 to $32,342 million
- The WACC increases when the leverage decreases, which is the opposite of what happened before.

Table 15.18
Valuation of The Management Group's Strategy Grouping the Financial Instruments as Debt or Equity

($ million)	1988	1989	1990	1991	1992	1993	1994	1995	1996	1997	1998	1999	2000	2001
1 ECF + CFpref + CFconverpref		0	0	0	0	0	0	0	281	3,331	3,665	3,860	4,146	4,456
2 Ke, pref, and convert.pref.		26.5%	18.6%	17.6%	16.7%	15.9%	15.3%	14.7%	14.1%	13.7%	13.7%	13.7%	13.7%	13.7%
3 E + Pr + PrCo = PV (ECF+; Ke+)	9,422	11,920	14,135	16,621	19,402	22,496	25,932	29,738	33,661	34,942	36,064	37,145	38,088	38,850
4 D	23,204	11,186	10,594	9,676	8,395	6,803	4,857	2,515	0	0	0	0	0	0
5 D + E + Pr + PrCo	32,626	23,106	24,729	26,297	27,797	29,299	30,789	32,253	33,661	34,942	36,064	37,145	38,088	38,850
6 Kd		12.0%	12.1%	12.1%	12.2%	12.4%	12.5%	12.8%	14.0%	14.0%	0.0%	0.0%	0.0%	0.0%
7 WACC		13.3%	13.4%	13.5%	13.5%	13.6%	13.6%	13.7%	13.8%	13.7%	13.7%	13.7%	13.7%	13.7%
8 D + E + Pr + PrCo = PV (FCF; WACC)	32,626	23,106	24,729	26,297	27,797	29,299	30,789	32,253	33,661	34,942	36,064	37,145	38,088	38,850

Table 15.19

Valuation of KKR's Strategy Grouping the Financial Instruments as Debt or Equity

($ million)	1988	1989	1990	1991	1992	1993	1994	1995	1996	1997	1998	1999	2000	2001
1 ECF + CFconver + CFpref		0	0	0	0	0	0	0	0	3,801	4,319	4,651	5,012	5,405
2 Ke,con, and pref		23.4%	20.2%	18.0%	17.0%	16.1%	15.4%	14.8%	14.2%	13.7%	13.7%	13.7%	13.7%	13.7%
3 E + Co + Pr = PV (ECF +; Ke +)	11,258	13,897	16,702	19,710	23,055	26,769	30,888	35,448	40,485	42,238	43,705	45,042	46,200	47,124
4 D	21,084	17,353	13,832	12,417	10,677	8,694	6,311	3,479	149	0	0	0	0	0
5 D + E + Co + Pr	32,342	31,250	30,534	32,127	33,732	35,463	37,199	38,927	40,634	42,238	43,705	45,042	46,200	47,124
6 Kd		12.1%	12.1%	12.2%	12.3%	12.4%	12.5%	12.8%	14.0%	14.1%	0.0%	0.0%	0.0%	0.0%
7 WACC		13.1%	13.2%	13.1%	13.2%	13.6%	13.6%	13.7%	13.8%	13.7%	13.7%	13.7%	13.7%	13.7%
8 D + E + Co + Pr = PV (FCF; WACC)	32,342	31,250	30,534	32,127	33,732	35,463	37,199	38,927	40,634	42,238	43,705	45,042	46,200	47,124

What can be said about the diversification of RJR Nabisco? Campa and Kedia (2000) deal with the observed fact that diversified firms trade at a discount relative to similar single-segment firms. They argue in that this observed discount is not per se evidence that diversification destroys value. Firm characteristics, which make firms diversify, might also cause them to be discounted. Not taking into account these firm characteristics might wrongly attribute the observed discount to diversification. They find that the diversification discount always drops, and sometimes turns into a premium, when they take into consideration the endogeneity of the diversification decision.

15.11. VALUE CREATION IN ACQUISITIONS AND MERGERS

Bruner (2001) summarizes the evidence from 128 studies about mergers and acquisitions from 1974–2001. This mass of research suggests that target shareholders (sellers) earn sizable positive returns in the 20–30% range. However, the returns for buyer firms' shareholders are essentially zero. Almost all of the studies report positive combined returns (buyer firms' shareholders plus seller firms' shareholders). Based on the mass of research, Bruner's conclusions for managers are to be coldly realistic about the benefits of any acquisition, to structure the deals very carefully, to avoid overpaying, and to work very hard to achieve the expected economic gains.

REFERENCES

Bruner, R. F. (2001), "Does M&A Pay? A Survey of Evidence for the Decision-Maker," Darden Business School Working Paper No. 01–23.
Campa, J. M., and S. Kedia (2000), "Explaining the Diversification Discount," Social Science Research Network, Working Paper No. 264763.

Chapter 16

Valuation and Value Creation in Internet-Related Companies

The impressive escalation of the share prices of Internet-related companies during the late 1990s and their abrupt fall in 2000 render necessary a discussion of their value creation. Furthermore, most of these companies reported losses in 1999 and 2000, so most of their capitalization was due to investor expectations. At the beginning of 2000, the question was: Are they companies that create a lot of value or are they just a bubble?[1] The question at the beginning of 2001 is: Has the bubble disappeared, is there still some of it left, or is it that the market is unable to appreciate these companies' potential?

We start with three events that prove the bubble's existence:

1. Cooper, Dimitrov, and Rau (2000)[2] show that the 147 companies that *internetized* their name (they took on a name ending in .com or .net) between June 1998 and July 1999 gave a mean return, during the period between 15 days before changing their name to 15 days after changing their name, that was 142% above that of similar companies. This return was 122% for Internet companies and 203% for companies whose business had no relation with Internet.

---

[1]When, in January 2000, I wrote that "The analysis of what has happened with the railway business may give us some clues as to what may happen with the Internet companies. Several analyses and valuations of Internet companies are very similar to those that were made at the time of companies such as Boston Chicken (in voluntary reorganization), Levitz (bankrupt), and Home Shopping Network," a number of people—executives and professors—called me reactionary, antiquated, and retrograde.

[2]Cooper, Dimitrov and Rau (2000), "A rose.com by any other name," Working Paper, Purdue University.

2. In April 1999, the company dELIA*s floated 25.2% of its subsidiary iTurf (specializing in electronic commerce). From its flotation to February 2000, the capitalization of the parent company (dELIA*s) was less than the market value of the shares it held in iTurf (according to their market price). During the first month after the subsidiary went public, the market value of the iTurf equity held by the parent company (dELIA*s) was 54% higher than the market value of dELIA*s' entire equity. Isn't that surprising?

3. Another similar case occurred when Creative Computers floated 19.9% of its subsidiary uBid (specializing in electronic commerce) in February 1998. During the first month after the subsidiary went public, the market value of the uBid equity held by the parent company (Creative Computers) was 66% higher than the market value of Creative Computers' entire equity.[3]

Speculative bubbles are not a new phenomenon. We discuss a few of them in Section 2.10. To take a similar case, when the railways started building their lines, investors had tremendous expectations about these companies' future growth, which led to a dramatic increase in their share prices. However, what happened afterward with the railway business showed that the shares' price had been overvalued: the companies' return was much lower than expected. In the 1920s, the radio caused a stock market revolution. Companies such as RCA increased their value fivefold in 1928. Between 1929 and 1932, the share price of Radio Corporation of America fell 98%, even though the company was profitable for many years after that.

On the other hand, it is fairly obvious that Internet will reduce (it is already reducing them) the margins of banks as a whole. Some banks may succeed in benefiting partially from the Internet if it manages to increase its customers by taking them from other banks. However, for the industry as a whole, the Internet will bring about a decrease in their margins that will not be matched by a parallel decrease in their costs.

This chapter will analyze the evolution of a number of companies (Terra, Amazon, America Online, Microsoft, B2B companies, on-line brokers, etc.), although our focus will be the valuation of Amazon.

16.1. SOME EXAMPLES OF VALUE CREATION AND DESTRUCTION

Amazon.com started to sell books on the Internet in July 1995. Its shares were first traded on the stock market in May 1997. Between May 1997 and

---

[3]The reader interested in these anomalies can see Schill and Zhou (1999).

December 1999, the value created by Amazon for its shareholders amounted to $34.546 billion (a return of 7,013%). During the same period, the stock market yield (S&P 500) was 61% (see Table 16.1). However, its share price fell from $106.70 on December 10, 1999 to $15.56 on December 31, 2000.

America Online was incorporated in 1985. In the year 2000, it was the world leader in interactive services, Web brands, Internet technologies, and electronic commerce. The shareholders that bought America Online shares when it first went public obtained a return of 7,150% from December 1993–December 2000. During the same period, the stock market yield (S&P 500) was 223%. However, the equity did not rise continuously during this period: the return to equity was −67% between May and October 1996; −51% between March and September 1999; and −64% between December 1999 and December 2000.

In February 2000, Microsoft was the world's largest company in terms of stock market capitalization ($521.7 billion). The company was incorporated in 1975 and went public in March 1986. Between March 1986 and December 1999, the value created by Microsoft for its shareholders amounted to $479.418 billion (a return of 55,000%). During the same period, the stock market yield (S&P 500) was 712%. However, the share price fell from $119.9 in December 1999 to $43.38 on December 31, 2000 and the return to equity was −64%.

Terra went public in November 1999. The placement price was 13 euros per share. On 25 February 2000, it traded at 139.75 euros, but by December 2000 its share price had fallen to 11.6 euros. For a time, Terra was the second largest Spanish company, in capitalization terms (behind Telefónica). Between November 17, 1999 and February 25, 2000, the value created by Terra for its shareholders amounted to 34.798 billion euros (a return of 975%). During the same period, the stock market yield (IBEX 35) was 20%. However, during the period February 25 to December 31 2000, the value destroyed was 39.509 billion euros (a negative return of −92%), while the stock market fell 27%.

Table 16.2 shows the evolution of 13 B2B companies. Their total value in December 2000 was 8.9% what it had been in March.

16.2. AMAZON

16.2.1. Spectacular Growth in Sales and Losses

On November 24, 1999, Amazon's capitalization was $36.4 billion. On the Spanish market, only Telefónica and BSCH had a higher capitalization. This was surprising for many, because Amazon was still losing money, and losing it in increasing quantities. However, by December 2000, its capitalization stood at $8.1 billion. The company's accrued losses stood at $1.748 billion by September 2000.

Table 16.1
Periods of Value Creation and Destruction for a Number of Companies

		Period		Increase of value (million dollars)	Value creation (million dollars)	Shareholders return		Stock market return	
		From	To			(annualized)	(total)	(annualized)	(total)
Amazon		05–97	12–99	34,738	34,546	412%	7013%	20%	61%
		12–99	12–00	−31,442	−36,311	−85%	−85%	−10%	−10%
	Total	05–97	12–00	3,296	−1,765	91%	938%	11%	45%
America Online		12–93	05–96	8,307	6,933	152%	838%	22%	62%
		05–96	10–96	−5,667	−6,114	−93%	−67%	18%	7%
		10–96	03–99	152,077	151,105	425%	5,367%	31%	92%
		03–99	09–99	−79,345	−89,189	−76%	−51%	0%	0%
		09–99	12–99	105,434	102,861	2325%	140%	32%	8%
		12–99	12–00	−140,811	−171,406	−62%	−64%	−10%	−10%
	Total	12–93	12–00	39,994	−5,811	83%	7,150%	18%	223%
Microsoft		03–86	12–99	611,722	479,418	58%	55,000%	16%	712%
		12–99	12–00	−396,688	−480,275	−63%	−64%	−10%	−10%
	Total	03–86	12–00	215,035	−858	43%	19816%	14%	630%
Terra		11–99	02–00	34,920	34,798	581,522%	975%	92%	20%
		02–00	12–00	−35,305	−39,509	−95%	−92%	−31%	−27%
	Total	11–99	12–00	−386	−4,711	−10%	−11%	−11%	−13%

Table 16.2
B2B Companies, Evolution during 2000

| Company | Capitalization 2000 ($ million) | | | Public offering | Share price in 2000 | | | | Dec/March | low/high |
	24/March	03/Aug	31/Dec		low	high	31/Dec			
VerticalNet	6,547	3,676	492	11/Feb/99	4.1	148.4	5.6		7.5%	2.7%
FreeMarkets	6,529	1,872	665	10/Dec/99	16.9	370.0	17.5		10.2%	4.6%
Ventro	4,859	630	44	27/July/99	0.6	243.0	1.0		0.9%	0.2%
PurchasePro.com	3,740	1,328	962	14/Sept/99	9.2	87.5	14.5		25.7%	10.5%
Onvia.com	2,459	614	79	01/March/99	0.8	78.0	0.9		3.2%	1.0%
Neoforma	1,698	250	137	24/Jan/00	0.9	78.8	0.9		8.1%	1.1%
eMerge	1,248	877	135	04/Feb/00	3.6	70.5	3.9		10.8%	5.1%
FairMarket	1,036	134	48	14/March/00	1.1	53.5	1.7		4.6%	2.1%
SciQuest.com	966	273	39	19/Nov/99	1.3	91.0	1.3		4.0%	1.4%
iPrint	497	124	23	08/March/00	0.5	28.5	0.8		4.5%	1.8%
RoweCom	214	40	8	09/March/99	0.4	53.0	0.7		3.8%	0.8%
Partsbase.com	197	74	29	22/March/00	1.7	15.0	2.0		14.5%	11.3%
b2bstores.com	92	16	14	15/Feb/00	1.1	19.5	1.7		15.5%	5.8%
TOTAL	**30,082**	**9,908**	**2,674**						8.9%	3.7%

Amazon.com started to sell books on the Internet in July 1995 with a single purpose: to use the Internet to make book- buying the fastest, easiest, and most fun buying experience possible.

Jeffrey P. Bezos founded Amazon in 1994. Since its foundation, Bezos has been the company's president. He has also been its COO since May 1996, and was CFO from May 1996 to March 1997. In December 1998, Bezos and his family held 42% of Amazon's equity. (See Table 16.3.)

16.2.2. STOCK MARKET EVOLUTION

Amazon.com went public on 15 May 1997. At the time, the price was $1.50/share.[4] On 10 December 1999, Amazon's equity traded at $106.70/share. However, just one year later you could buy an Amazon share for $16. Figure 16.1 shows the evolution of the share price and the earnings per share.

Table 16.3
Amazon, Income Statements and Balance Sheets (Million Dollars)

($ million)	1995	1996	1997	1998	1999	2000
Sales	0.5	15.7	147.8	610.0	1,639.8	2,762.0
Cost of sales	0.4	12.3	119.0	476.2	1,349.2	2,106.2
Marketing and sales	0.2	6.1	40.5	133.0	413.2	594.5
Other expenses	0.2	3.8	20.9	67.3	268.6	623.1
Depreciation of intangibles				42.6	214.7	301.8
Losses on investments				2.9	76.8	304.6
Net interest	0.0	−0.2	−1.6	12.6	37.4	242.8
Net income	**−0.3**	**−6.2**	**−31.0**	**−124.5**	**−720.0**	**−1,411.0**
Cost of sales/sales	*80.0%*	*78.0%*	*80.5%*	*78.1%*	*82.3%*	*76.3%*
Marketing and sales/sales	*39.1%*	*38.7%*	*27.4%*	*21.8%*	*25.2%*	*21.5%*
Other expenses/sales	*40.1%*	*24.1%*	*14.2%*	*11.0%*	*16.4%*	*22.6%*
Cash	0.8	0.8	1.9	25.5	133.0	822.4
Temporary investments	0.2	5.4	123.5	347.9	573.0	278.0
Current assets, net	−0.9	−1.7	−93.2	−262.7	−299.0	−350.5
Total assets	1.1	8.4	149.8	648.5	2,472.0	2,135.1
Long-term debt	0.0	0.0	76.7	348.1	1,466.0	2,127.5
Shareholders' equity	1.0	2.9	28.6	138.8	266.0	−967.2
Million shares			144.9	159.3	345.2	357.1

[4]The price is adjusted for the splits: 2 × 1 on 1/September/99, 3 × 1 on 4/January/99, and 2 × 1 on 1/June/98. In actual fact, Amazon issued 3 million shares at $18/share.

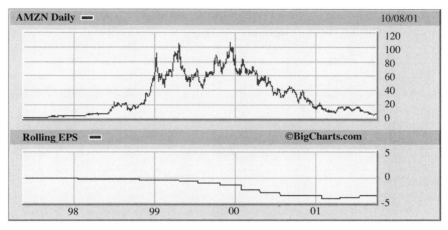

Figure 16.1   Amazon. Evolution of the share price and EPS.

Since it started business in 1995, this virtual bookstore was the example of electronic commerce that everyone wanted to imitate. By December 2000, it had 20 million customers in 160 countries.

Amazon	Dec. 98	March 99	June 99	Sept. 99	Dec. 00
Customers (million)	6.2	8.4	10.7	13.1	20

In December 2000 (as in the previous year), the analysts' recommendations were optimistic, even though the earnings per share forecast for 2000 and 2001 were −$1.20 and −$0.68, respectively.

		Number of analysts				
Date	Share price	Strong Buy	Buy	Hold	Sell	Strong sell
Dec. 1999	98	9	8	8	0	0
Dec. 2000	25.875	4	15	10	0	1

By the end of 1999, some analysts were already commenting that "Amazon's potential may not be as large as we think."

Amazon, like many other companies, implemented a compensation system for executives and employees using stock options. Table 16.4 shows that in December 1999, the company's personnel had 80.34 million options with an average exercise price of $27.755. In December 1999, the options were worth

Table 16.4

Options Held by Employees and Managers, 31 December 1999

Range of strike prices ($)	Million options	Average life (years)	Average strike price ($)
0.014–0.083	9.965	5.0	0.049
0.111–1.000	11.655	7.2	0.554
1.167–5.372	9.44	7.9	3.823
6.135–12.83	9.242	8.3	7.644
12.87–21.30	8.207	8.7	18.426
21.33–57.95	12.388	12.5	50.778
58.09–64.88	9.294	12.4	62.425
64.94–87.75	8.67	9.4	72.564
87.78–104.1	1.338	9.5	91.654
104.2–105.0	0.143	9.0	104.969
Total	80.342	9.0	27.755

	Million options	Strike price
January 1, 1996	21.23	0.012
Options granted	31.20	0.051
Canceled	−6.34	0.023
Exercised	−6.05	0.033
January 1, 1997	40.03	0.038
Options granted	36.12	1.148
Canceled	−5.10	0.297
Exercised	−16.39	0.032
January 1, 1998	54.66	0.751
Options granted	39.55	12.734
Canceled	−7.54	4.049
Exercised	−10.67	0.554
December 31, 1998	76.01	6.688
Options granted	31.74	63.602
Canceled	−11.28	3.860
Exercised	−16.13	19.703
December 31, 1999	80.34	27.755

approximately $8 billion, but by December 2000, their value had dropped to just above $1 billion.

16.2.3. ON-LINE LEADERSHIP: BARNES & NOBLE VERSUS AMAZON

Barnes & Noble was the world's largest bookstore chain, reporting sales amounting to $3.486 billion in 1999. It sold books only in the United States and had at least one store in every major city. In 1999, the company had 520 Barnes & Noble bookstores and 470 bookstores that operated under the name of B. Dalton. Barnes & Noble had developed other businesses: it offered books from small independent publishers and university papers. It also published books under the Barnes & Noble brand which were sold exclusively in its stores and through mail order catalogs. Barnes & Noble's greatest asset was its name, which had special connotations for its customers: a broad selection of titles, daily discounts, and a welcoming atmosphere to buy in.

In January 1997, Barnes & Noble announced plans to be the only bookseller for the largest Internet access provider (America Online) and its intention to launch its own web site that same spring. Barnesandnoble.com started operating in March 1997 and become one of the world's most visited sites and the fourth largest on-line retailer. It offered a broad range of products and services: books, music, software, posters, and related products, similar to those that could be found at amazon.com. Barnes & Noble staked their hopes on the company's name: its brand recognition would be the vehicle that would enable it to move from a small market (its bookstores) to a mass market (Internet). Referring to Barnes & Noble, Jeff Bezos said, "Quite frankly, I'm more worried about two guys in a garage."[5]

In December 2000, the company's market capitalization stood at $1.678 billion, three times less than that of Amazon. But one year before, Barnes & Noble's market capitalization was 23 times less than Amazon's. During that period, Barnes & Noble's return was 15%, while Amazon's was −75%. Figure 16.2 shows the evolution of Barnes & Noble's share price.

The main items of Barnes & Noble's financial statements were:

($ million)	1996	1997	1998	1999	2000
Sales	2,448	2,797	3,006	3,486	4,375
Net income	**51.2**	**64.7**	**92.4**	**124.5**	**−52.0**
Shareholders' equity	456.0	531.8	678.8	846.4	777.6
Number of stores	1,008	1,011	1,009	1,468	1,886

[5]*Fortune*, 9 December 1996.

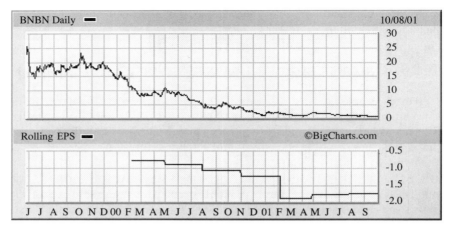

Figure 16.2 Evolution of Barnesandnoble.com's share price since its flotation.

Barnesandnoble.com went public on May 28, 1999. Barnes & Noble held 40% of this company's equity. Bertelsmann held another 40%. The company's market capitalization in December 2000 stood at $215 million, with expected sales during 2000 of about $300 million. Figure 16.2 shows a very different story from Amazon. However, in September 2000, the company's shareholders' equity stood at $100 million, which included accrued losses of $42.8 million.

16.3. VALUATIONS OF AMAZON

16.3.1. Valuation Made by an Analyst Using Cash Flow Discounting: $87.3/Share

On December 10, 1999, when the price had risen to $106.70/share, the forecasts given in Table 16.5 enabled one analyst, by discounting the cash flows at 12%, to reach a price per share for Amazon of $87.30/share, that is, a market capitalization of $30 billion.

Another way of justifying Amazon's share price was to view the share as a call option.[6] A call option on Amazon's future: an uncertain future in that the company could have many on-line businesses other than book selling.[7]

---

[6]In Chapter 22 we will deal with real options.

[7]There were some that were saying in early 2000 that "Amazon will be the Wal-Mart of the future." Copeland (2000, page 318) defines a possible scenario saying "suppose that Amazon is the next Wal-Mart."

Table 16.5

Forecasts Made by an Analyst for Amazon in December 1999 (Million Dollars)

($ million)	1995	1996	1997	1998	1999	2000	2001	2002	2003	2004	2005	2006	2007	2008	2009	2010
Sales	0.5	15.7	148	610	1,542	3,250	6,500	11,375	17,063	22,181	27,771	33,436	38,652	42,827	45,396	48,120
Net income	−0.3	−6.2	−31	−125	−425	−399	−322	169	540	649	918	1,335	1,533	1,962	2,321	2,799
Net income/sales	−60%	−39%	−21%	−20%	−28%	−12%	−5.0%	1.5%	3.2%	2.9%	3.3%	4.0%	4.0%	4.6%	5.1%	5.8%

With just book selling alone, it was virtually impossible to justify Amazon's share price of $106.70/share in December 1999.[8]

16.3.2. Damodaran's Valuation by Cash Flow Discounting: $35/Share

Damodaran (2000) published a valuation of Amazon in March 2000 and valued its equity at 11.955 billion dollars,[9] that is, $35/share. Table 16.6 gives Damodaran's forecasts. The valuation is a simple discount of the FCF at the WACC. From this quantity, we must deduct the debt and the value of the options held by the employees to obtain the equity's value.[10]

One error of Table 16.6 is that it considers that the company starts to pay taxes in 2003, even though the company has accrued losses of $1.748 billion in 2000. The depreciation is also very low, considering the historic depreciation and the level of investment. On the other hand, Damodaran considers a debt of only $349 million and a borrowing rate of 1.2% during the first 5 years, rising to 15% in years 9 and 10. Initial borrowing, according to the equity value obtained by Damodaran and considering the net debt in December 1999, is 5%. When these adjustments are entered into the valuation, the value of the equity would be about $1 billion higher.

16.3.3. Copeland's Valuation by Scenarios and Cash Flow Discounting: $66/Share

In the third edition of his book,[11] Copeland includes a valuation of Amazon. Copeland recommends drawing up different scenarios for 10 years' time. For the specific case of Amazon, he gives four scenarios for 10 years' time, ordered from most optimistic to least optimistic. Scenario A (see Table 16.7) corresponds to "suppose that Amazon is the next Wal-Mart":

[8]The company's comments on its performance in June 1999 included the following paragraphs: "Risk of new businesses. We want to expand our company by selling new or complementary products, introducing new services and new ways of selling. This will require additional expenditure and investment. We do not expect to benefit from the advantage of being the first mover, as in on-line book selling. Any unsuccessful business may damage the reputation of the Amazon brand."

[9]Value of shareholders' equity (14.847 billion) less value of the options held by employees (2.892 billion).

[10]Estrada (2001) suggests a new method to estimate the cost of equity of Internet companies. According to him, the required return to equity was 19.3% higher than the required return to equity estimated according to the capital asset pricing model.

[11]See Chapter 15 of Copeland, Koller, and Murrin (2000), *Valuation: Measuring and Managing the Value of Companies*.

Table 16.6

Forecasts of Damodaran for Amazon (Million Dollars)

	2000	2001	2002	2003	2004	2005	2006	2007	2008	2.009
Sales	2,793	5,586	9,776	14,663	19,062	23,866	28,735	33,217	36,805	39,013
EBIT	−373	−94	407	1,038	1,628	2,212	2,768	3,261	3,646	3,883
Taxes	0	0	0	167	570	774	969	1,141	1,276	1359
Depreciation	46	60	75	90	104	115	122	130	138	146
Capital expenditure	554	907	1,345	1,572	1,438	1,572	1,599	1,489	1,226	815
WCR expenditure	50	84	126	147	132	144	146	134	108	66
FCF	−931	−1,024	−989	−758	−408	−163	177	625	1,174	1,788
Ke	12.9%	12.9%	12.9%	12.9%	12.9%	12.42%	11.94%	11.46%	10.98%	10.50%
Kd	8.0%	8.0%	8.0%	8.0%	8.0%	7.8%	7.8%	7.7%	7.5%	7.0%

Table 16.7

Copeland's Forecasts and Valuation for Amazon (Billion Dollars)

| | Sales in 2010 | | | | | Equity value in each | Likelihood | Equity |
	Books	Music	Other	Total	EBITDA/sales	scenario (2000)	of scenario	value
Scenario A	24	13	48	85	14%	79	5%	3.9
Scenario B	20	9	31	60	11%	37	35%	13.0
Scenario C	16	6	19	41	8%	15	35%	5.3
Scenario D	7	5	5	17	7%	3	25%	0.8
								23.0

15% of book sales on the American market, 18% of music sales on the American market, success in the sale of new products and a good margin. Scenarios B and C are midway between A and the most pessimistic (D), which is defined as much lower shares of the book and music markets, little success with other products and a smaller margin. The value of Amazon's equity in 2000 is $79 billion according to scenario A and $3 according to scenario D. These valuations are obtained by cash flow discounting. The next step is to allocate a probability to each scenario: Copeland allocates 5% to the most optimistic, 25% to the most pessimistic, and 35% to the midway scenarios. With these assumptions, he obtains an equity value of $23 billion, that is, $66 per share. Note that Copeland does not allocate any probability to a voluntary reorganization or bankruptcy for the company.

16.3.4. OUR VALUATION BY SIMULATION AND CASH FLOW DISCOUNTING: $21/SHARE

In this section, we give our valuation of Amazon. The basic scenario is that given in Table 16.8.

The hypotheses given in Table 16.8 can be summarized as follows:

$$(\text{Cost of sales} + \text{ marketing } + \text{ other expenses})/\text{sales}^{12} = 95\%$$

Growth of sales $= 100\%$ in 2001, 80% in 2002, ..., 8% in 2008.

Both hypotheses are optimistic if we consider the historic evolution of the (Cost of sales + marketing + other expenses)/sales ratio and growth of sales shown in Figure 16.3.

With this data (without any type of future flexibility in costs or sales), the equity's value is calculated to be $2.721 billion (present value of the equity cash flows discounted at 12%).

Table 16.8

Basic Scenario for the Valuation of Amazon (Million Dollars)

	1999	2000	2001	2002	2003	2004	2005	2006	2007	2008	2009
Sales	1,640	2,650	5,300	9,540	15,264	22,133	29,105	35,522	40,222	43,415	45,482
Cost of sales, marketing and other expenses	2,030	2,518	5,035	9,063	14,501	21,026	27,649	33,746	38,211	41,244	43,208
FCF		33	65	117	187	271	357	436	493	532	558
Equity cash flow		−134	−10	34	97	173	250	321	279	318	420

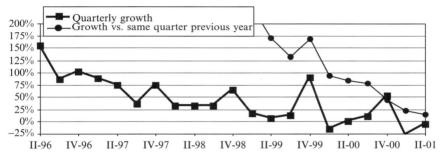

Figure 16.3   Historic growth of Amazon's sales.

In a company such as Amazon, it is necessary to introduce uncertainties in the expectations. We introduce uncertainty (volatility) in the hypotheses in the following manner:

$$(\text{Cost of sales} + \text{marketing} + \text{other expenses})/\text{sales}^{12} =$$
$$95\% \text{ with a volatility of } 5\% \text{ Sales growth in } 2001 =$$
$$100\% \text{ with a volatility of } 25\%$$

In order to take into account future flexibility in costs and sales, we carried out 10,000 simulations. The equity value obtained is $7.368 billion.[13] The distribution of the value of the 10,000 simulations is shown in Figure 16.4. Observe that 4343 of the 10,000 simulations give an equity value of zero. If we consider a liquidation value (or a value for the option of pulling out of the business), the equity's value would increase. For example, if we consider that the worst scenario is that proposed by Copeland (an equity value of $3 billion), the equity's value would increase to $8.671 billion.

[12]During the period 1995–1999, this ratio has been 159, 141, 122, 111, and 123%.
[13]7.368 billion dollars is the mean of the 10,000 valuations performed, one in each simulation.

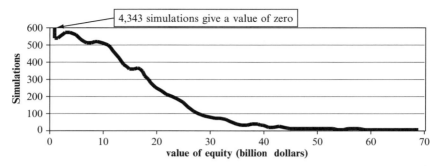

Figure 16.4 Distribution of the value of Amazon's equity in the year 2000—10,000 simulations.

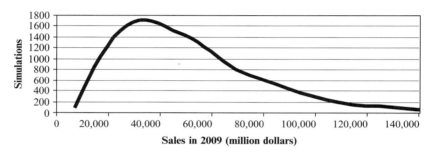

Figure 16.5 Distribution of Amazon's sales in the year 2009.

However, the reader should remember that this valuation considers that the likelihood of bankruptcy or voluntary reorganization is 43.43%.

The distribution of sales in 2009, according to the simulation, is shown in Figure 16.5.

Table 16.9 shows a sensitivity analysis for the valuation.

Schwartz and Moon (2000) also give a valuation of Amazon by simulation. They value the equity at \$4.210 billion, that is, \$12.42/share. In their simulation, Amazon applied for voluntary reorganization 27.9% of the times.

16.3.5. DIFFERENCES BETWEEN OUR VALUATION AND THOSE OF COPELAND AND DAMODARAN

Table 16.10 shows the differences between our valuation and Copeland's. In order to compare the two valuations, we have converted the 10,000 simulations of our valuation into 5 scenarios: for example, scenario A is the mean of the 49 simulations that gave the highest value to the shares.

Table 16.9

Value of Amazon's Equity (Million Dollars), Sensitivity Analysis

Cost of sales, marketing, and other expenses / sales	70%	80%	88%	90%	92%	94%	95%	96%	97%
Value of equity	35,426	26,816	18,399	15,523	12,311	9,099	7,386	5,944	4,741

Correlation between sales and costs' volatilities	−100%	−70%	−50%	−30%	0%	50%	100%
Value of equity	12,195	10,670	9,865	8,817	7,368	5,313	3,595

Cost volatility	2%	3%	4%	5%
Value of equity	5,021	6,030	6,824	7,368

Sales growth volatility	0%	10%	20%	25%	30%
Value of equity	6,518	6,693	7,049	7,368	7,691

Table 16.10

Difference between this Valuation and Copeland's (Billion Dollars)

	Equity value in each scenario (2000)	Likelihood of scenario		Equity value	
		Copeland	This valuation	Copeland	This valuation
Scenario A	79	5%	0.49%	3.9	0.39
Scenario B	37	35%	3.42%	13.0	1.27
Scenario C	15	35%	34.15%	5.3	5.16
Scenario D	3	25%	18.51%	0.8	0.56
Scenario E	0	0%	43.43%		0.00
				23.0	**7.4**

The main two differences are that Copeland allocates higher probabilities to the more optimistic scenarios and no probability to voluntary reorganization.

Table 16.11 shows the differences between our projections and Damodaran's. Our projections are more optimistic than Damodaran's regarding sales and the first years' FCFs. However, Damodaran expects much higher FCFs than we do after 2007. This is important because of the residual value: Damodaran's present value is $12.168 billion higher than ours. This large difference is due to the difference in the final year's FCF and because Damodaran considers a residual growth of 6% while we use 5%.

Table 16.11

Difference between Damodaran's Projections and this Valuation (million Dollars)

	2000	2001	2002	2003	2004	2005	2006	2007	2008	2,009
Sales	143	286	236	−601	−3,071	−5,239	−6,787	−7,005	−6,610	−6,469
FCF	−964	−1,089	−1,106	−945	−679	−520	−259	132	642	1,230
Ke	0.9%	0.9%	0.9%	0.9%	0.9%	0.4%	−0.1%	−0.5%	−1.0%	−1.5%
Kd	0.0%	0.0%	0.0%	0.0%	0.0%	−0.2%	−0.3%	−0.3%	−0.5%	−1.0%

16.4. AMERICA ONLINE

America Online's capitalization at the beginning of December 1999 was $181.1 billion. The share price at the beginning of December 1999 was $81/share.[14] However, it had fallen to $34.80 by the end of 2000. The company had more than 12,000 employees.

Figure 16.6 shows the evolution of America Online's share price.

Although this figure shows the significant drop in the company's share price between March and September 1999 (the share price fell from $82/share to $40/share in October), it fell even more in 1996, from $4.50/share in May to $1.50/share in October, as a consequence of the investors questioning the company's business model.

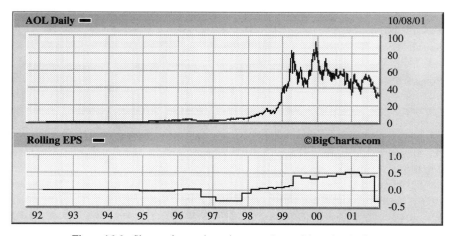

Figure 16.6   Share price, and earnings per share of America Online.

[14]After 7 2 × 1 splits in Nov. 94, April 95, Nov. 95, March 98, Nov. 98, Feb. 99, and Nov. 99.

The most important data from American Online's income statement and balance sheet were:

($ million)	6/1990	6/1991	6/1992	6/1993	6/1994	6/1995	6/1996	6/1997	6/1998	6/1999	6/2000
Net sales	17.3	19.5	26.6	40.0	115.7	394	1,094	1,685	3,091	4,777	6,886
EBITDA	0.7	1.3	4.6	6.0	7.6	−9.18	98.61	41.48	257	851	1,788
Net income	**0.2**	**1.5**	**3.5**	**4.2**	**2.6**	**−38**	**30**	**−499**	**−74**	**762**	**1,232**
Total assets	7.9	7.9	23.6	32.4	154.6	406	959	847	2,874	5,348	10,673
Shareholders' equity	2.0	3.5	18.9	23.8	98.3	218	513	131	996	3,033	6,161
Debt	0.4	0.7	0.0	0.0	9.3	22	22	51	372	348	1,646

AOL was incorporated in 1985. In 2000, it was the leading company in interactive services, Web brands, Internet technologies, and electronic commerce. The company operated two on-line services: America Online with 18 million members and CompuServe with approximately 2 million members. It was also the owner of many Internet brands such as ICQ, AOL Instant Messenger, and Digital City. It also had Internet portals such as Netscape and AOL.com, communication software such as Netscape Navigator, and the largest company in the U.S. in show ticket sales (AOL Movie Phone). Through its strategic alliance with Sun Microsystems, the company develops and sells electronic commerce applications for companies that do business through Internet.

In 1999, AOL's sales had the following breakdown: subscriptions 70%; advertising, commerce, and others 21%, and business services 9%. Customers who had subscribed to the AOL service and CompuServe generated the subscriptions. The companies that advertised to AOL subscribers and users mainly generated the sales from advertising, commerce, and others. They consisted mainly of the rates charged by the company for electronic services and product sales. The sales of business services mainly consisted of fees for using AOL products and technical service, consulting, and training fees.

16.4.1. THE ANALYSTS' RECOMMENDATIONS

In spite of the company's high capitalization and its PER of 250 at the beginning of December 1999, most of the analysts recommended buying: 25 analysts recommended buying, 15 recommended moderate buying, and only 3 recommended holding the stock. None of them recommended selling or selling moderately. In December 2000, the capitalization was $114.3 billion and the PER was 92.6. Most of the analysts continued to recommend buying:

24 analysts recommended buying, 12 recommended moderate buying, 3 recommended holding the stock, and none recommended selling.

16.5. ON-LINE BROKERS: CONSORS, AMERITRADE, E*TRADE, CHARLES SCHWAB, AND MERRILL LYNCH

The course followed by the on-line brokers makes very interesting reading.

Incorporated in 1994, by the year 2000 ConSors was the largest German discount broker in terms of number of customer transactions and the second largest in terms of number of accounts. The largest discount broker (in terms of number of accounts) was Comdirekt. Table 16.12 shows the forecasts made by J.P. Morgan for ConSors at the end of 1999.

ConSors went public in April 1999 (ConSors' largest shareholder, the Schmidt Bank, sold 25% of its shares). During the public offering, the price of its shares tripled on the Neuer Market, achieving a 25% return in the first session. ConSors became the country's fifth largest bank in terms of market capitalization. In August 1999, ConSors' share capital amounted to 44 million shares and its capitalization was 3.3 billion euros. The Schmidt Bank held 70.2% of the company's shares, ConSors customers held 9.1%, and the free float amounted to 18.6% of the total equity.

Figure 16.7 shows the evolution of ConSors' share price and the evolution of the profit and loss statements.

The company's greatest assets were its brand recognition and its customer base. In the opinion of J.P. Morgan, ConSors' success was based on the image of a modern, innovative, competitive company that it conveyed to the

Table 16.12

ConSors, Historic Data and Forecasts (Million euros)

	1996	1997	1998	1999E	2000E	2001E
Total sales, net	4.6	17.2	60.2	128.3	205.0	287.3
Earnings before tax (without marketing costs)	1.4	6.6	18.9	42.3	75.1	106.1
Net income	0.0	2.5	7.0	14.9	25.1	31.4
Number of accounts (thousand)	12	37	86	180	330	555
Number of orders (thousand)	157	631	2,830	6,141	9,874	14,186
Costs/revenues (without marketing costs)	69.5%	61.1%	67.6%	66.3%	62.7%	62.5%
Operations per account	14	19	35	34	29	25
Acquisition cost per customer (euro)	188	86	130	177	205	217

Source: Company records and J.P. Morgan estimates.

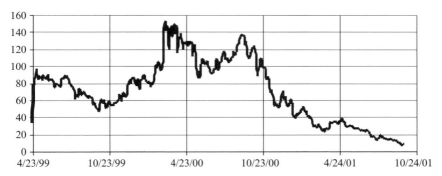

Figure 16.7   ConSors' share price (euros/share) and financial statements.

Figure plus:

(million euros)	dec. 1999	dec. 2000	mar. 2001
Net interest income	22.1	52.7	10.6
Provision for credit losses	−1.8	−6.3	−2.3
Net comission income	102.9	229.0	42.1
Other income	0.7	18.0	−3.1
Trading income	0.0	34.8	6.8
Personnel expenses	−20.4	−65.9	−23.4
Marketing expenses	−23.5	−69.2	−11.1
External services	−24.2	−76.0	−19.3
Depreciation on tangible/intangible assets	−11.9	−32.9	−12.1
Other administrative expenses	−9.1	−26.4	−8.9
Net income	**14.8**	**17.0**	**−15.6**
Total Assets	**1,590.5**	**2,236.9**	**2,299.2**
Amounts payable to banks	69.5	22.8	83.5
Amounts payable to customers	1,214.7	1,554.9	1,576.7
Tax liabilities	5.6	22.9	19.7
Other short term liabilities	16.1	59.8	57.7
Shareholders'equity	**273.7**	**474.8**	**452.6**

market's most active segment. The large number of operations per customer is striking (35 per year in 1998).

The company's goal was to gain a core position as a leader in financial services in Germany and take this leadership to other European markets. ConSors' strategy to achieve this leadership goal consisted of extending its product range beyond mere on-line brokerage services, offering its customers a comprehensive, personalized service. Through Internet, its customers could not only buy shares but also take out insurance, mortgages, etc. By this means, ConSors would increase the number of financial assets managed in its portfolio.

Another reasons for ConSors' success was the composition of its management team: relatively small (six people), young (five of them were in their 30s), and strongly motivated with shares and options. The six managers (including the founders) had options on more than 132,000 shares, with an approximate value of 9.9 million euros.

ConSors, like other European brokers, wished to follow the example of the French Company Cortal and extend its offerings to other European and international markets. Regarding its penetration of other European countries, ConSors would have a competitive advantage compared with its possible competitors if it succeeded in being the first to enter neighboring markets. With this goal in mind, in mid-1999, ConSors bought a small on-line broker in France, Axfin; and, on 14 December 1999 it bought Siaga, a Spanish stockbroker company.

The American brokers had also initiated their expansion in Europe, in spite of having encountered difficulties such as their ignorance of the European market, currencies, and language and cultural differences. To overcome these obstacles, they resorted to agreements and alliances.

E*Trade, the second largest broker in terms of turnover, was present in France, Italy, and the Scandinavian countries. For its part, Ameritrade had an agreement with the French company Cortal, by virtue of which Ameritrade's customers had access to the Paris stock market through Cortal, and Cortal's customers had access to the American stock market through Ameritrade.

At the same time as the Internet was opening up new markets for the banks, it also brought new perils for their business with the entry of new competitors. Indeed, Internet offered many advantages for the banking industry; costs could be reduced enormously while, at the same time, providing the possibility of expanding the services offered and personalizing customer relationships.

The European banks were aware of the Internet's enormous potential. Success would be dependent upon two factors: technology and marketing. The new technologies enabled banks to significantly reduce their costs per operation: the initial outlay required opening a bank web site, and its associated running expenses were much lower than opening and maintaining a bank branch.

Banks in Great Britain, France, Germany, Scandinavia, and Spain were offering their customers all sorts of services over the Internet. However, the European banks' volume of operations was much lower than the U.S. banks, although the number of investors using the Web was growing continuously.

The analysts considered that the German on-line banks and brokers were leading the field in Europe. In Germany, out of a total of 65 million accounts opened, it was possible to access about 10 million on-line.

16.5.1. CONSORS VERSUS AMERITRADE, E*TRADE

Taking into account that Germany has always been considered a very conservative country, it may come as a surprise that the German on-line brokerage industry has a lot in common with the U.S. model:

1. Relatively low fees based on the size of the order. They have not yet adopted the flat rate structure used in America but the fees are similar to those charged by the American brokers Schwab and Fidelity.
2. Marketing costs are growing rapidly, particularly those items related with brand recognition.
3. There is continuous creation of new products.
4. Technological innovation; Strategies are adapted rapidly to new trends in the industry.

Table 16.13 shows the leading on-line brokers' key indicators in 1998: ConSors' return per customer was 45–75% higher than that of its American counterparts and 161% higher than that of Comdirekt. However, if we analyze earnings before tax per operation or the cost/revenues ratio (both parameters exclude marketing costs), we will see that there are no significant differences between the results obtained by ConSors, E*Trade, and Ameritrade. All of this leads us to think that the reason why ConSors' return is

Table 16.13
Key Indicators of the Main on-line Brokers in 1998 (euros)

	ConSors	Comdirekt	Ameritrade	E*Trade
Revenues per customer	979	564	668	638
Costs per customer (without marketing costs)	661	443	449	457
Earnings before tax per customer	**318**	**121**	**219**	**181**
Revenues per operation	28.4	28.4	29.2	35.1
Costs per operation (without marketing costs)	19.2	22.3	22.3	25.1
Earnings before tax per operation	9.2	6.1	6.9	10.0
Operations per customer	35	20	23	18
Costs/revenues (without marketing costs)	67.5%	78.5%	67.2%	71.6%

Source: Company records and J.P. Morgan estimates.

better than the rest is to be found in the number of operations performed by its customers: the number of operations per customer and year was 35 for ConSors, 23 for Ameritrade, and 18 for E*Trade.

In 1999, J.P. Morgan valued the ConSors share at 104 euros. ConSors' market capitalization in December 2000 amounted to 2.697 billion euros. Table 16.14 shows a number of parameters for the leading North American brokers.

Figures 16.8 and 16.9 show the evolution of the share prices of E*Trade, Ameritrade, Charles Schwab, and Merrill Lynch.

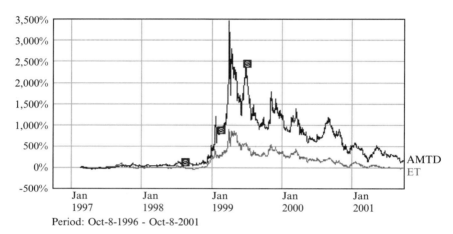

Figure 16.8   Evolution of the share prices of E*Trade (EGRP) and Ameritrade (AMTD).

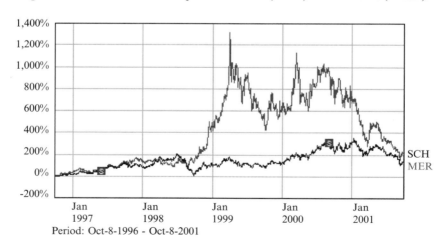

Figure 16.9   Evolution of the share prices of Charles Schwab (SCH) and Merrill Lynch (MER).

Table 16.14

North American Brokers, Main Parameters

December 31, 2000	Million dollars				Sales growth			P/BV	PER	Dividend yield	5 years	
	Capitalization	Net income	Sales	Sales / employee	1 year	3 years					ROE	ROA
Merrill Lynch	52,950	2,618	34,879	0.626	23.4%	7.9%		3.1	17	1.0%	20.9%	0.7%
Charles Schwab	36,062	589	4,713	0.365	53.0%	29.2%		8.6	53	0.2%	25.7%	1.7%
Ameritrade	1,271	–14	654	0.275	107.4%	90.1%		6.0	na	0.0%	12.5%	1.0%
E*Trade	2,261	19	2,201	0.583	232.4%	140.0%		1.2	123	0.0%	–0.3%	0.0%

Between 16 April 1999 and December 2000, Merrill Lynch's return to equity was 48%, while Charles Schwab's return to equity was −40%. In December 2000, Merrill Lynch's capitalization was $52.95 billion and its PER was 17, while the same parameters for Charles Schwab were $36.062 billion and 53.

16.6. MICROSOFT

In February 2000, Microsoft was the company with the world's largest market capitalization. On February 2, 2000, Microsoft's capitalization stood at $521.7 billion, almost twice the capitalization of the 35 companies comprising the Spanish stock market index IBEX 35. On 2 February 2000, its shares sold for $100.80/share,[15] but by the end of 2000, their price had dropped to $43.38.

Bill Gates, the company's founder and largest shareholder, was born on October 28, 1955 in Seattle (Washington). He founded Microsoft in 1975 after dropping out of Harvard. Gates' founder partner was an old school friend, Paul Allen. In 2000, Gates held 15% of Microsoft's equity and Allen held 5%.

Microsoft started business in Alburquerque, NM, developing applications for the BASIC language. The company moved to Seattle in 1979. In 1980, IBM commissioned Microsoft to develop the operating system for its personal computers (PC). Gates bought the QDOS (quick and dirty operating system) operating system from a Seattle programmer for $50,000 and renamed it MS-DOS (Microsoft disk operating system). Many other companies manufactured computers that were compatible with IBM's computer and MS-DOS became the standard operating system for PCs. Microsoft started to develop other programs for personal computers.

In 1985, Microsoft launched Windows, a more user-friendly version of MS-DOS that was inspired by Apple's operating system, Macintosh. In 1993, it launched Windows NT (new technology) to compete with the UNIX operating system in large mainframes and networks. Microsoft bought many software companies and invested unwaveringly in applications development. In 1995, Microsoft entered the Internet with Microsoft Net-

---

[15]After 8 splits: 2 × 1 in Sept. 1987, April 1990, May 1994, Dec. 1996, Feb. 1998, and March 1999; and 3 × 2 in June 1991, and June 1992.

work (MSN), licensed Sun's Java language, and launched the Internet Explorer.

In 1999, the company organized itself by customer groups, instead of by product lines, as it had until then. It also invested $5 billion in AT&T and bought Visio (a company specializing in drawing programs) for $1.3 billion.

Figure 16.10 shows the evolution of Microsoft's share price, earnings per share and PER (the company closes its fiscal year on 30 June).

Table 16.15 shows Microsoft's spectacular growth in sales, employees, and earnings. The growth of Microsoft's sales and earnings over the years is immediately striking. However, even more striking is the fact that, in spite of being the company with world's largest market capitalization, the earnings-sales ratio has also grown over time. It is difficult to account for the company's spectacular growth (growing return with a very large size) without considering some sort of monopoly or quasi-monopoly position.

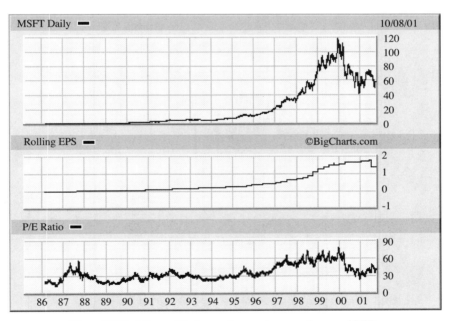

Figure 16.10   Microsoft's share price, earnings per share, and PER.

Table 16.15
Microsoft, Evolution Since 1975

($ million)	1988	1989	1990	1991	1992	1993	1994	1995	1996	1997	1998	1999	2000	2001
Sales	591	804	1,183	1,843	2,759	3,753	4,649	6,075	9,050	11,936	15,262	19,747	22,956	25,296
Net income	124	171	279	463	708	953	1,146	1,453	2,195	3,439	4,462	7,757	9,421	7,346
Earnings/sales	21%	21%	24%	25%	26%	25%	25%	24%	24%	29%	29%	39%	41%	29%
Cash and investments	183	301	449	686	1,345	2,290	3,614	4,750	6,940	8,966	13,927	17,236	23,798	31,600
Total assets	493	721	1,105	1,644	2,640	3,805	5,363	7,210	10,093	14,387	22,357	38,625	52,150	59,257
Shareholders' equity	376	562	919	1,351	2,193	3,242	4,450	5,333	6,908	10,777	16,627	28,438	41,368	47,289
Employees	2,793	4,037	5,635	8,226	11,542	14,430	15,017	17,801	20,561	22,232	27,055	31,575	39,170	47,600

	1975	1976	1977	1978	1979	1980	1981	1982	1983	1984	1985	1986	1987
Sales ($ million)	0.016	0.022	0.38	1.36	2.39	7.52	16.0	24.5	50.1	97.5	140	198	346
Employees	3	7	9	13	28	40	128	220	476	608	910	1,153	1,816

Some Key Dates for Microsoft

April 4, 1975	Incorporation of Microsoft
August 12, 1981	IBM introduces the personal computer with Microsoft's MS-DOS 1.0 operating system
March 13, 1986	Public offering. 2.5 million shares at $21/share
May 22, 1990	Windows 3.0 launched
August 24, 1995	Windows 95 launched
December 7, 1995	Bill Gates announces Microsoft's commitment to support and improve Internet
June 25, 1998	Windows 98 launched
January 2000	Serious legal problems: would the company be split?
February 24, 2000	Windows 2000 launched

Gates' business acumen and his superb perception of information technology innovations have been fundamental factors in Microsoft's success. Gates makes the strategic decisions, also playing a key role in the technical development of new products. For Bill Gates, it is important to know the opinion of his customers and employees and, consequently, he spends a large part of his time meeting with customers and contacting Microsoft employees via e-mail.

Under Gates' leadership, Microsoft's goal has been to continuously improve software technology and make it increasingly easier, cheaper, and more fun for users to use the computer. In 1999, Microsoft invested more than $3 billion in research and development.

16.7. A FINAL COMMENT ON THE VALUATION OF INTERNET COMPANIES

The Internet is a very powerful tool that offers an enormous range of possibilities for companies and users. At present, it is the tool that must be used by virtually all companies if they wish to prosper and grow.[16] Its possibilities are enormous both for commerce with individuals and for commerce between companies.

Although this is true, one is justified in wondering whether the valuations currently made of Internet companies and projects match foreseeable reality or are merely a bubble.

---

[16]On this point, it was amusing to attend corporate presentations to analysts in 1999 and 2000, and observe the frequency with which some executives mentioned (whether or not it was relevant to the occasion) the word Internet. Of course, it did not happen in 2001.

It is very interesting to compare and try to differentiate what the Internet may signify in the first years of the 21st century with the revolutionary effect on society that the railways, freeways, airlines, radio, television, and the telephone had when they first appeared. We also urge the reader to analyze the history of companies such as Levitz, Home Shopping Network, OM Scott, MCI, LTCM, and Boston Chicken.

The Internet is no King Midas. Business ideas related with it must be analyzed with the same rigor as any other business initiative. There are two anecdotes that are very much to the point here. The promoters of a new company for selling gifts by the Internet showed us their business plan together with a series of forecasts that covered several years. When they were asked about the rationale for their forecasts, the reply was: "These forecasts are very conservative because, for example, we are assuming that we will only sell 0.05% of the hams that are sold in Spain." Of course, the next question was how they justify the sale of a single ham. The promoters of another Internet-related company also showed us an extensive business plan accompanied by balance sheet, income statement, and cash flow forecasts, and a valuation. According to them, the company's shares (and it was only a project then) were worth 60 million euros. They were asking my clients for 40 million euros and, in exchange for this investment, offered them 40% of the shares. It is clear that there was a conceptual error in this approach because the company was worth 60 million if the outlay was actually made and zero if it was not. If there were a multitude of investors willing to invest in the company (which was not the case), the 40 million would entitle the investors to 67% of the equity. However, as this was not the case, the 40 million entitled the investors to more than 70% of the equity.

Morals:
A web site is not necessarily a business.
Selling below cost gets you lots of customers, but not much money.

REFERENCES

Copeland, T. E., T. Koller, and J. Murrin (2000), *Valuation: Measuring and Managing the Value of Companies*, third edition, New York: Wiley.

Cooper, M., O. Dimitrov, and R. Rau (2000), "A Rose.com by Any Other Name," Working Paper, Purdue University.

Damodaran, A. (2000), "The Dark Side of Valuation: Firms with No Earnings, No History and No Comparables," Working Paper, Stern School of Business.

Estrada, J. (2001), "The Cost of Equity of Internet Stocks: A Downside Risk Approach," Social Science Research Network, Working Paper No 271044.

Schill, M., and C. Zhou (1999), "Pricing an Emerging Industry: Evidence from Internet Subsidiary Carve-Outs," Working Paper, University of California.

Schwartz, E., and M. Moon (2000), "Rational Pricing of Internet Companies," Working Paper, Anderson School at UCLA.

PART III

Rigorous Approaches to Discounted Cash Flow Valuation

Chapter 17

Discounted Cash Flow Valuation Methods: Perpetuities, Constant Growth, and General Case

17.1. INTRODUCTION

This chapter explores the discounted cash flow valuation methods. We will start the chapter with the simplest case: no-growth, perpetual-life companies. Then we will study the continuous growth case and, finally, the general case.

The different concepts of cash flow used in company valuation are defined: equity cash flow (ECF), free cash flow (FCF), and capital cash flow (CCF). Then the appropriate discount rate is determined for each cash flow depending on the valuation method used.

Our starting point will be the principle by which the value of a company's equity is the same, whichever of the four traditional discounted cash flow formulae is used. This is logical: given the same expected cash flows, it would not be reasonable for the equity's value to depend on the valuation method.

Initially, it is assumed that the debt's market value (D) is equal to its book value (N).[1] Section 17.5 discusses the case in which the debt's book value (N) is not equal to its market value (D), as is often the case, and Section 17.6 analyzes the impact of the use of simplified formulae to calculate the levered beta.

Section 17.7 addresses the valuation of companies with constant growth, and Section 17.11 discusses the general case in company valuation.

---

[1]This means that the required return to debt (Kd) is equal to the interest rate paid by the debt (r).

17.2. COMPANY VALUATION FORMULAE, PERPETUITIES

The cash flows generated by the company are perpetual and constant (there is no growth). The company must invest in order to maintain its assets at a level that enables it to ensure constant cash flows: this implies that the book depreciation is equal to the replacement investment.

We will start with a numerical example, to help the reader become familiar with the concepts.

Income Statements and Cash Flows	
Margin	800
Interest paid (I)	225
Profit before tax (PBT)	575
Taxes (T = 40%)	230
Profit after tax (PAT)	345
+ Depreciation	200
− Investment in fixed assets	−200
ECF	345

$$FCF = ECF + I\,(1 - T) = 345 + 225\,(1 - 0.40) = 480$$

$$CCF = ECF + I = 345 + 225 = 570$$

$R_F = 12\%$. P_M (Market risk premium) = 8%.
Assets' beta (βu) = 1. Equity's beta (β_L) = 1.375.
Cost of debt = 15%.
Debt's beta = 0.375.
Equity market value (E) = 1,500.
Equity book value = 800.
Debt (D) = 1,500.

17.2.1. CALCULATING THE COMPANY'S VALUE FROM THE ECF

The following pages explain the four discounted cash flow methods most commonly used for company valuation in the case of perpetuities. Formula

(17.1) indicates that the equity's value (E) is the present value of the expected ECF discounted at the required return to equity (Ke). The required return to equity (Ke) is often called "cost of equity."

Formula (17.1) is equivalent to the equation we would use to calculate the value of a perpetual bond. This type of bond gives their holders constant cash flows that remain perpetually the same. In order to calculate the value of this bond, we would discount the payment of the regular coupon at the market interest rate for this type of debt. Likewise, the value of a company's equity (E) is the present value of the cash flows that would be paid to its owners (ECF), discounted at that company's required return to equity (Ke).[2]

$$E = ECF/Ke \qquad (17.1)$$

In the example: $E = 345/23\% = 1,500$ because $Ke = R_F + \beta_L\, P_M = 12\%$ $+1.375 \times 8\% = 23\%$.

Consequently, the company's value[3] will be equal to the value of the equity (E) plus the value of the debt (D):

$$E + D = ECF/Ke + I/Kd \qquad (17.2)$$

where $D = I/Kd$,

In the example $E + D = 345/0.23 + 225/0.15 = 1,500 + 1,500 = 3,000$.

The market value of the debt (D) is equal to its book value.[4] The interest paid (I) is equal to the book value of the debt (D) times at the cost of debt (Kd). The beta of the debt is calculated following the CAPM:

$$Kd = R_F + \beta_d P_M; \; 15\% = 12\% + 0.375 \times 8\%$$

17.2.2. Calculating the Company's Value From the FCF

Formula (17.3) proposes that the value of the debt today (D) plus that of the equity (E) is the present value of the expected FCFs that the company will generate, discounted at the weighted cost of debt and equity after tax (WACC).

$$E + D = FCF/WACC \qquad (17.3)$$

---

[2]It is important to remember that the required return (or cost of capital) depends on the funds' use and not on their source.

[3]The value of the equity (E) plus the value of the debt (D) is usually called company's value or value of the company.

[4]For the moment, we will assume that the cost of debt (the interest rate paid by the company) is identical to the required return to debt.

The expression that relates the FCF with the ECF is

$$ECF = FCF - D\ Kd(1 - T) \tag{17.4}$$

In the example $ECF = FCF - D\ Kd(1 - T) = 480 - 1{,}500 \times 0.15 \times (1 - 0.4) = 345$.

As (17.2) and (17.3) must be the same, substituting (17.4) gives:

$$(E + D)WACC = E\ Ke + D\ Kd(1 - T)$$

Consequently, the definition of WACC or "weighted average cost of capital" is

$$WACC = \frac{E\ Ke + D\ Kd(1 - T)}{E + D} \tag{17.5}$$

Note that the WACC is the discount rate that ensures that the value of the company $(E + D)$ obtained using (17.3) is the same as that obtained using (17.2).

In the example: $E + D = 480/0.16 = 3{,}000$; $WACC = [1{,}500 \times 0.23 + 1{,}500 \times 0.15 \times (1 - 0.4)]/(1{,}500 + 1500) = 16\%$

17.2.3. Calculating the Company's Value from the CCFs

Formula (17.6) uses the CCFs as their starting point and proposes that the value of the debt today (D) plus that of the equity (E) is equal to the CCF discounted at the weighted cost of debt and equity before tax $(WACC_{BT})$.[5] The CCF is the cash flow available for all holders of the company's instruments, whether these are debt or capital, and is equal to the ECF plus the debt cash flow (CFd), which, in the case of perpetuities, is the interest paid on the debt (I).

$$E + D = CCF/WACC_{BT} \tag{17.6}$$

The expression that relates the CCF with the ECF and the FCF is

$$CCF = ECF + CFd = ECF + D\ Kd = FCF + D\ Kd\ T \tag{17.7}$$

In the example $CCF = ECF + CFd = 345 + 225 = 570$; $CCF = FCF + IT = 480 + 225 \times 0.4 = 570$.

As (17.2) must be equal to (17.6), using (17.7) gives: $(E + D) WACC_{BT} = E\ Ke + D\ Kd$

And, consequently, the definition of $WACC_{BT}$ is

$$WACC_{BT} = \frac{E\ Ke + D\ Kd}{E + D} \tag{17.8}$$

[5]BT means "before tax."

Note that the expression of WACC$_{BT}$ is obtained by making (17.2) equal to (17.6). WACC$_{BT}$ is the discount rate that ensures that the value of the company obtained using the two expressions is the same.

In the example $E + D = 570/0.19 = 3,000$. Because $CCF = 345 + 225 = 570$ and WACC$_{BT} = (1,500 \times 0.23 + 1,500 \times 0.15)/(1,500 + 1,500) = 19\%$.

17.2.4. ADJUSTED PRESENT VALUE (APV)

The formula for the APV (17.9) indicates that the value of the debt today (D) plus that of the equity (E) of the levered company is equal to the value of the equity of the unlevered company Vu (FCF/Ku) plus the discounted value of the tax shield due to interest payments:

$$E + D = Vu + \text{discounted value of the tax shield}$$
$$= FCF/Ku + \text{discounted value of the tax shield} \qquad (17.9)$$

In the case of perpetuities:

$$DVTS = \text{Discounted value of the tax shield} = DT \qquad (17.10)$$

In the example $E + D = 480/0.2 + 1,500 \times 0.4 = 3,000$.

Expression (17.10) is demonstrated in Section 17.3. This entails not considering leverage costs and shall be discussed further on in this chapter and in Chapter 19.

By equaling formulae (17.2) and (17.9) and taking into account (17.10) and (17.3), it is possible to obtain the relationship between Ku and WACC:

$$WACC = Ku\,[E + D(1 - T)]/(E + D) \qquad (17.11)$$

In the example WACC $= 0.2 \times [1,500 + 1,500 \times (1 - 0.4)]/(1,500 + 1,500) = 16\%$

Formula (17.11) indicates that with tax, in a company with debt, WACC is always less than Ku, and the higher the leverage, the smaller it is. Note also that WACC is independent of Kd and Ke (it depends on Ku). This may seem unintuitive, but it is logical. Note that when $D = 0$, WACC $= Ku$. When $E = 0$, WACC $= Ku(1 - T)$.

By substituting (17.5) in (17.11), we can obtain the relationship between Ku, Ke, and Kd:

$$Ku = \frac{E\,Ke + D\,Kd\,(1 - T)}{E + D\,(1 - T)} = \frac{E\,Ke + D\,Kd\,(1 - T)}{Vu} \qquad (17.12)$$

In the example $Ku = 20\% = [1,500 \times 0.23 + 1,500 \times 0.15 \times (1 - 0.4)]/[1,500 + 1,500 \times (1 - 0.4)]$.

17.2.5. USE OF THE CAPM AND EXPRESSION OF THE LEVERED BETA

Formulae (17.13)–(17.15) are simply the relationship, according to the capital asset pricing model (CAPM), between the required return to equity of the unlevered company (Ku), the required return to equity of the levered company (Ke), and the required return to debt (Kd), with their corresponding betas (β):

$$Ku = R_F + \beta_U \, P_M \qquad\qquad (17.13)$$

$$Ke = R_F + \beta_L \, P_M \qquad\qquad (17.14)$$

$$Kd = R_F + \beta_d \, P_M \qquad\qquad (17.15)$$

R_F = Risk-free interest rate.
β_d = Beta of the debt.
β_U = Beta of the equity of the unlevered company.
β_L = Beta of the equity of the levered company.
P_M = Market risk premium.

In the example $Ku = 12 + 1 \times 8 = 20\%$; $Ke = 12 + 1.375 \times 8 = 23\%$; $Kd = 12 + 0.375 \times 8 = 15\%$.
Another way of expressing (17.12) is,[6] isolating Ke:

$$Ke = Ku + [(Ku - Kd) \, D \, (1 - T)]/E \qquad\qquad (17.16)$$

Substituting Ke, Ku, and Kd in this equation with expressions (17.13)–(17.15), we obtain:

$$\beta_L = \frac{\beta_U[E + D \, (1 - T)] - \beta_d \, D \, (1 - T)}{E} \qquad\qquad (17.17)$$

In the example

$$\beta_L = 1.375 = (1 \times [1{,}500 + 1{,}500 \times 0.6] - 0.375 \times 1{,}500 \times 0.6)/1{,}500.$$

17.3. DVTS IN PERPETUITIES, TAX RISK IN PERPETUITIES

As we stated in the introduction, the value of the levered company ($V_L = E + D$) obtained with all four methods is identical, as shown in

---

[6]This formula "seems" to indicate that if taxes are increased, Ke decreases. However, this is not true. Ke does not depend on T. In the formula, Ku, Kd, and D do not depend on T, and neither does Ke. However, E does depend on T. Performing simple algebraic operations, it is possible to verify that if taxes increase by an amount ΔT, the decrease in the shares' value (ΔE), is $\Delta E = E\Delta T/(1 - T)$.

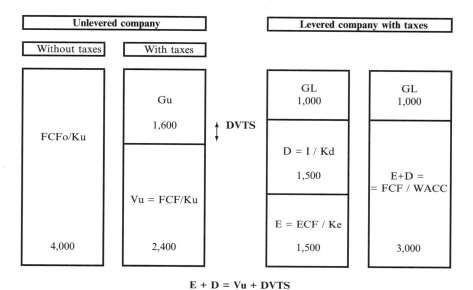

$$\mathbf{E + D = Vu + DVTS}$$

Figure 17.1 Distribution of the company's total value between shareholders, bondholders, and the government. Without leverage costs.

diagram form in Figure 17.1.[7] However, it is important to remember that by forcing fulfillment of the adjusted present value formula (17.9) and (17.10), we are accepting that the company's total value (debt, equity, and tax) is independent of leverage, that is, there are no leverage- generated costs (there is no reduction in the expected FCF nor any increase in the company's risk).

In a world without leverage cost, the following relationship holds:

$$V_u + G_u = E + D + G_L \qquad (17.18)$$

G_U is the present value of the taxes paid by the unlevered company. G_L is the present value of the taxes paid by the levered company.

The DVTS (discounted value of the tax shield) is

$$DVTS = G_u - G_L \qquad (17.19)$$

In a perpetuity, the profit after tax (PAT) is equal to equity cash flow: $PAT = ECF$. This is because in perpetuity, depreciation must be equal to reinvestment in order to keep the cash flow generation capacity constant.

---

[7]Note that we include a third beneficiary element in the company: the state, whose revenues consist of taxes.

We will call FCF_0 the company's free cash flow if there were no taxes, i.e., $PBTu = FCF_0$, then: $FCF = FCF_0(1 - T)$.

For the unlevered company ($D = 0$):

$$Taxes_U = T\ PBTu = T\ FCF_0 = T\ FCF/(1 - T) \qquad (17.20)$$

Consequently, the taxes of the unlevered company have the same risk as FCF_0 (and FCF), and must be discounted at the rate Ku. The required return to tax in the unlevered company (K_{TU}) is equal to the required return to equity in the unlevered company (Ku).[8]

$$K_{TU} = Ku \qquad (17.21)$$

The present value of the taxes of the unlevered company is

$$G_U = T\ FCF/[(1 - T)\ Ku] = T\ Vu/(1 - T) \qquad (17.22)$$

For the levered company:

$$Taxes_L = T\ PBT_L = T\ PAT_L/(1 - T) = T\ ECF/(1 - T) \qquad (17.23)$$

Consequently, the taxes of the levered company have the same risk as the ECF and must be discounted at the rate Ke. Thus, in the case of perpetuities, the tax risk is identical to the equity cash flow risk and, consequently, the required return to tax in the levered company (K_{TL}) is equal to the required return to equity (Ke).[9]

$$K_{TL} = Ke \qquad (17.24)$$

The present value of the taxes of the levered company, that is, the value of the state's interest in the company is[10]

$$G_L = T\ ECF/[(1 - T)\ Ke] = T\ E/(1 - T) \qquad (17.25)$$

The increase in the company's value due to the use of debt is *not* the present value of the tax shield due to interest payments, but the difference between G_U and G_L, which are the present values of two cash flows with different risks:

$$G_U - G_L = [T/(1 - T)]\ (Vu - E) \qquad (17.26)$$

As $Vu - E = D - DVTS$, this gives:

$$DVTS = \text{Discounted value of the tax shield} = DT \qquad (17.10)$$

---

[8]This is only true for perpetuities.

[9]This is only true for perpetuities.

[10]The relationship between profit after tax (PAT) and profit before tax (PBT) is $PAT = PBT(1 - T)$.

In the example $FCF_0 = 800$; $FCF = 480$; $PBTu = 800$; $Taxes_U = 320$; $ECF = 345$; $Taxes_L = 230$. $G_U = 1,600$, $G_L = 1,000$. $D\,T = 600 = 1,600 - 1,000$.

Figure 17.1 shows how $Vu + DT = D + E$.

It is important to note that the discounted value of the tax shield (DVTS) is not (and this is the main error of many books and papers on this topic) the PV of the tax shield, but the difference between two PVs of two flows with different risk: the PV of the taxes paid in the unlevered company (G_U) and the PV of the taxes paid in the levered company (G_L). Formula (17.10) is the difference between the two PVs. Obviously, the flow of taxes paid in the levered company is smaller and riskier than the flow of taxes paid in the unlevered company.

17.4. EXAMPLES OF COMPANIES WITHOUT GROWTH

Table 17.1 shows the valuation of six different companies without growth. The companies differ in the tax rate, the cost of debt, and the size of debt. Column [A] corresponds to the company without debt and without taxes. Column [B] corresponds to the same company paying a tax rate of 35%. Column [C] corresponds to a company with debt equal to 1 billion and without taxes. Columns [D] and [E] correspond to the company with debt equal to 1 billion, a tax rate of 35% and different costs of debt. Column [F] corresponds to a company with a higher level of debt (2 billion) and a tax rate of 35%.

Lines 1 to 5. The companies' income statements.

Lines 8, 9, and 10. Equity cash flow, free cash flow, and capital cash flow.

Line 11. An unlevered beta βu (or assets' beta) equal to 1.0 is assumed.

Line 12. The risk-free rate is assumed to be equal to 12%.

Line 13. The market risk premium is taken to be 8%.

Line 14. With the above data, the required return to unlevered equity (Ku) is 20% in all cases.

Line 15. The value of the unlevered company ($Vu = FCF/Ku$) is 5 billion for the companies without taxes and 3.25 billion for the companies with a 35% tax rate. The difference (1.75 billion) is, logically, the present value of the taxes.

Lines 16 and 17. Company's debt and cost of debt.

Line 18. Beta corresponding to the cost of debt according to formula (17.15).

Line 19. Discounted value of the tax shield due to interest payments, which, in this case (as it is a perpetuity), is DT.

Table 17.1

Example of the Valuation of Six Companies without Growth

	[A] D=0 T=0%	[B] D=0 T=35%	[C] D=1,000 T=0% Kd=13%	[D] D=1,000 T=35% Kd=13%	[E] D=1,000 T=135% Kd=14%	[F] D=2,000 T=35% Kd=14%
1 Margin	1,000	1,000	1,000	1,000	1,000	1,000
2 Interest	0	0	130	130	140	280
3 PBT	1,000	1,000	870	870	860	720
4 Taxes	0	350	0	304,5	301	252
5 PAT	1,000	650	870	565,5	559	468
6 +Depreciation	200	200	200	200	200	200
7 − Investment in fixed assets	−200	−200	−200	−200	−200	−200
8 **ECF**	**1,000**	**650**	**870**	**565,5**	**559**	**468**
9 **FCF**	**1,000**	**650**	**1,000**	**650**	**650**	**650**
10 **CCF**	**1,000**	**650**	**1,000**	**695,5**	**699**	**748**
11 Unlevered beta (βu)	1	1	1	1	1	1
12 R_F	12%	12%	12%	12%	12%	12%
13 $(Rm - R_F) =$ market risk premium	8%	8%	8%	8%	8%	8%
14 Ku	20%	20%	20%	20%	20%	20%
15 **Vu**	**5,000**	**3,250**	**5,000**	**3,250**	**3,250**	**3,250**
16 D	0	0	1,000	1,000	1,000	2,000
17 Kd			13%	13%	14%	14%
18 Beta of debt (βd)			0.125	0.125	0.25	0.25
19 DVTS = DT	0	0	0	350	350	700
20 DVTS + Vu	5,000	3,250	5,000	3,600	3,600	3,950
21 −D = **E1**	**5,000**	**3,250**	**4,000**	**2,600**	**2,600**	**1,950**
22 Levered beta (βL)	1	1	1.21875	1.21875	1.1875	1.5
23 Ke	20%	20%	21.75%	21.75%	21.50%	24%
24 **E2** = ECF / Ke	**5,000**	**3,250**	**4,000**	**2,600**	**2,600**	**1,950**
25 WACC	20%	20%	20%	18.06%	18.06%	16.46%
26 FCF / WACC	5,000	3,250	5,000	3,600	3,600	3,950
27 **E3** = (FCF / WACC) − D	**5,000**	**3,250**	**4,000**	**2,600**	**2,600**	**1,950**
28 WACC$_{BT}$	20%	20%	20%	19.32%	19.42%	18.94%
29 CCF/WACC$_{BT}$	5,000	3,250	5,000	3,600	3,600	3,950
30 **E4** = (CCF/WACC$_{BT}$) − D	**5,000**	**3,250**	**4,000**	**2,600**	**2,600**	**1,950**

Lines 20 and 21. They are the result of applying formula (17.9).

Line 22. Shows the beta of the equity according to formula (17.16).

Line 23. Shows the required return to equity according to formula (17.14).

Line 24. Calculation of the value of the equity is using formula (17.1).

Line 25. Weighted cost of equity and debt, calculated using the formula for WACC (17.5).

Lines 26 and 27. Calculation of the value of the equity is using formula (17.3).

Line 28. Weighted cost of equity and debt, calculated using the formula for $WACC_{BT}$ (17.8).

Lines 29 and 30. Calculation of the value of the equity is using formula (17.6).

Columns [B] and [D] show two very interesting points:

1. As they are perpetuities, according to formula (17.23), the risk of the equity cash flow is identical to the risk of the cash flow for the state (taxes).

2. Formula (17.9) proposes that the value of the levered company $(D + E)$ is equal to value of the unlevered company (Vu) plus the discounted value of the tax shield. Some authors argue that the discounted value of the tax shield must be calculated by discounting the tax shield (interest $\times T = 130 \times 0.35 = 45.5$) at the required return to unlevered equity (Ku).[11] This is not correct. In our example, this PV is 350 million, that is, $1,000 + 2,600 - 3,250 = 1,750 - 1,400$. One can immediately see that 350 is not 45.5/0.2. In this case, $350 = 45.5/0.13$, which explains why it seems that the correct discount rate is Kd.[12] Although *in this case* (perpetuities) the result is the same, we shall see further on that this is incorrect (except for perpetuities).

Table 17.2 highlights the most significant results of Table 17.1.

Other significant findings obtained from Table 17.1 include the following:

1. The required return to equity (Ke) decreases as the cost of debt increases, since the debt becomes an increasingly greater part of the business risk (Ku is constant and is not affected by leverage[13]), line 23, columns D and E.

---

[11]See, for example, Harris and Pringle (1985), Kaplan and Ruback (1995), Ruback (1995), and Tham and Vélez-Pareja (2001). All these papers will be analyzed in Chapter 19.

[12]See, for example, Myers (1974) and Luehrman (1997). These papers will be analyzed in Chapter 19.

[13]This is so because we are assuming that the debt's market value is the same as its nominal value. The required return to debt is equal to the cost of debt.

Table 17.2

**Annual Cash Flows (Million euros), Discount Rates and Value
of the Company without Growth**

	Without taxes		With taxes (35%)	
	No debt $D=0$	With debt $D=1,000$	No debt $D=0$	With debt $D=1,000$
ECF	1,000	870	650	565.5
Taxes	0	0	350	304.5
Debt flow (interest)	0	130	0	130
Total cash flow	1,000	1,000	1,000	1,000
Ke	20%	21.75%	20%	21.75%
Kd	—	13%	—	13%
K_{TL}	—	—	20%	21.75%
E = ECF/Ke	5,000	4,000	3,250	2,600
D = Debt flow/Kd	—	1,000	—	1,000
G = Taxes/K_{TL}	—	—	1,750	1,400
E + D + G	5,000	5,000	5,000	5,000
	[A]	[C]	[B]	[D]
	(Columns of Table 17.1 to which these values correspond.)			

2. The weighted cost of capital (WACC) does not depend on the cost of debt, but on the debt ratio and βu (not how βu is distributed between βd and βL), line 25, columns D and E.

3. For the levered company with taxes, WACC is always less than Ku.

4. As the required return to debt is equal to the cost of debt, the equity value is independent of Kd: it depends on the debt value, but not on Kd. This does not mean that the debt's interest is irrelevant in real life. Obviously, if we think that the appropriate cost for the debt is 13% (thus, the debt has a value of 1,000 million) and the bank wants 14%, the shares' value will decrease because the debt's value is no longer 1,000 but 1,076.9 (140/0.13). However, the fact is that there is no formula that gives us the debt's risk from the business risk and the debt ratio. We only know that the business risk must be distributed between debt and equity in accordance with (17.16). Consequently, the required return to debt has a certain degree of arbitrariness: it must be greater than R_F and less than Ku. Appendix 17.2 provides a formula for the required return to debt in the absence of leverage cost.

17.5. FORMULAE FOR WHEN THE DEBT'S BOOK VALUE (N) IS NOT THE SAME AS ITS MARKET VALUE (D), (R ≠ KD)

N is the debt's book value (the money that the company has borrowed), r is the interest rate, and Nr is the interest paid every year.

Kd is the required return to debt: a "reasonable" return that the bank or the bondholders must (or should) demand, in accordance with the company's risk and the size of the debt.

So far, we have assumed that the cost of debt (r) is equal to the return required by the market on that debt (Kd). However, if this is not so, the value of the debt (D) will no longer be the same as its nominal value (N). All the relationships calculated previously (assuming r = Kd) are valid for perpetuities irrespective of whether r and Kd are equal or not. It is sufficient to consider that in a perpetuity: $D = Nr/Kd$.

If r is equal to Kd, then D and N are equal.

(17.1)–(17.3) and all the formulae seen in this chapter continue to be valid

$$ECF = FCF - Nr (1 - T) = FCF - D Kd (1 - T)$$

17.6. FORMULA FOR ADJUSTED PRESENT VALUE TAKING INTO ACCOUNT THE COST OF LEVERAGE

We will assume now that the company loses value when it is levered. This loss of value is due to the "cost of leverage." Under this hypothesis, formula (17.9) becomes:

$$E + D = FCF/Ku + DVTS_{NCL} - \text{cost of leverage}$$

This formula indicates that the value of the levered company's debt today (D) plus that of its equity (E) is equal to the value of the equity (FCF/Ku) of the unlevered company plus the discounted value of the tax shield with no-cost-of-leverage ($DVTS_{NCL}$) less the cost of leverage.

The cost of leverage includes a series of factors: the greater likelihood of bankruptcy or voluntary reorganization, information problems, reputation, difficulty in gaining access to growth opportunities, differential costs in security issues, and other associated considerations. These costs increase with higher debt levels.

17.6.1. IMPACT ON THE VALUATION OF USING THE SIMPLIFIED FORMULAE FOR THE LEVERED BETA

Two ways of quantifying the cost of leverage is to use the simplified formulae for calculating the levered beta[14] [(17.27) and (17.28)] instead of (17.17):

$$\beta^*_L = \beta_U[D + E^*]/E^* \qquad (17.27)$$

$$\beta'_L = \beta_U[D(1 - T) + E']/E' \qquad (17.28)$$

$$\beta_L = \frac{\beta_U[E + D(1 - T)] - \beta_d D(1 - T)}{E} \qquad (17.17)$$

If these simplified formulae are used, the levered betas obtained (β^*_L and β'_L) will be greater than those obtained using the full formula (17.17).

In addition, the value of the equity (E^* or E') will be less than that obtained earlier (E) because the required return to equity now (Ke^* or Ke') is greater than that used previously (Ke). Logically, the weighted cost of debt and equity now ($WACC^*$ or $WACC'$) is greater than that used earlier ($WACC$).

In the example: $\beta_L = 1.375$; $\beta'_L = 1.659$; $\beta^*_L = 2.333$.

$$E = 1.500; \ E' = 1.365; \ E^* = 1.125.$$

$$Ke = 23\%; \ Ke' = 25.275\%; \ Ke^* = 30.667\%$$

Observe that: $E^* < E' < E$ \qquad and \qquad $Ke^* > Ke' > Ke$

With these simplifications, we introduce cost of leverage in the valuation: in formula (17.9), we must add a term CL that represents the cost of leverage.

$$E^* = FCF/Ku - D(1 - T) - CL^*; \ CL^* = E - E^* \qquad (17.9^*)$$

$$E' = FCF/Ku - D(1 - T) - CL'; \ CL' = E - E' \qquad (17.9')$$

(17.4) continues to be valid: $ECF = FCF - D \ Kd(1 - T)$

In the example $WACC = 16\%$; $WACC' = 16.754\%$; $WACC^* = 18.286\%$. $CL^* = 375$; $CL' = 135$.

---

[14]In Chapters 19 and 21, we will see that the theory we call β' here corresponds to Damodaran (1994) and the theory that we call β^* here corresponds to the practitioners method.

Using these formulae, we obtain the following relationships:

$$CL' = E - E' = D(Kd - R_F)(1 - T)/Ku \qquad (17.29)$$

$$CL^* = E - E^* = [D(Kd - R_F)(1 - T) + DT(Ku - R_F)]/Ku \qquad (17.30)$$

17.6.2. THE SIMPLIFIED FORMULAE AS A LEVERAGE-INDUCED REDUCTION OF THE FCF

The simplified formulae can be viewed as a reduction of the expected FCF (due to the constraints and restrictions caused by the debt) instead of an increase in the required return to equity. In formula (17.9), the FCF is independent of leverage (having the size of D).

If we use formula (17.28): $\beta'_L = \beta u[D(1 - T) + E']/E'$, we can consider that the value E' is obtained from discounting another smaller cash flow (FCF') at the rate of the full formula:

$$E' = \frac{FCF}{Ku} - D + \frac{D[Ku\,T - (1 - T)\,(Kd - R_F)]}{Ku} = \frac{FCF'}{Ku} - D(1 - T) = \frac{ECF'}{Ke},$$

$$(FCF - FCF') = D[(1 - T)\,(Kd - R_F)] = ECF - ECF' \qquad (17.31)$$

This means that when we use the simplified formula (17.28), we are considering that the free cash flow and the equity cash flow are reduced by the quantity $D(1 - T)(Kd - R_F)$.

Likewise, if we use formula (17.27): $\beta^*_L = \beta u[D + E^*]/E^*$, we can consider that the value E* is obtained from discounting another smaller cash flow (FCF*) at rate of the full formula:

$$E^* = \frac{FCF}{Ku} - D + \frac{D[R_F - Kd(1 - T)]}{Ku}$$
$$= \frac{FCF^*}{Ku} - D(1 - T) = \frac{ECF^*}{Ke}$$

$$\begin{aligned}(FCF - FCF^*) &= D[T(Ku - R_F) \\ &+ (1 - T)(Kd - R_F)] = ECF - ECF^*\end{aligned} \qquad (17.32)$$

This means that when we use the simplified formula (17.27), we are considering that the free cash flow (and the equity cash flow) are reduced by $D[T(Ku - R_F) + (1 - T)(Kd - R_F)]$.

17.6.3 THE SIMPLIFIED FORMULAE AS A LEVERAGE-INDUCED INCREASE IN THE BUSINESS RISK (Ku)

Another way of viewing the impact of using the abbreviated formula (17.28) is to assume that what the formula proposes is that the business risk increases with leverage. In order to measure this increase, we call βu the business's beta for each level of leverage. Using formula (17.28) with $\beta u'$ instead of βu, upon performing the algebraic operations, it is seen that:

$$\beta u' = \beta u + \beta_d \, D(1 - T)/[D(1 - T) + E'] \qquad (17.33)$$

Likewise, the impact of using the simplified formula (17.27) $\beta^*_L = \beta u[D + E^*]/E^*$ can be measured by assuming that the formula proposes that the business risk (which we will quantify as βu^*) increases with leverage. Using formula (17.1) with βu^* instead of βu, upon performing the algebraic operations, it is seen that:

$$\beta u^* = \beta u + [\beta_d \, D \, (1 - T) + \beta u \, TD]/[D \, (1 - T) + E^*] \qquad (17.34)$$

It can also be seen that:

$$Ku' = Ku + (Kd - R_F)\frac{D(1 - T)}{E' + D(1 - T)} \qquad (17.35)$$

$$
\begin{aligned}
Ku^* = Ku + (Kd - R_F)&\frac{D(1 - T)}{E^* + D(1 - T)} \\
+ (Ku - R_F)&\frac{DT}{E^* + D(1 - T)}
\end{aligned}
\qquad (17.36)
$$

17.6.4. THE SIMPLIFIED FORMULAE AS A PROBABILITY OF BANKRUPTCY

This model includes the possibility that the company goes bankrupt and ceases to generate cash flows:

$$ECF_{t+1} = ECF_t \qquad \text{with a probability } p_c = 1 - p_q$$
$$0 = E_{t+1} \quad \text{with a probability } p_q$$

In this case, the equity value at $t = 0$ is

$$E^* = ECF(1 - p_q^*)/(Ke + p_q^*) \qquad (17.37)$$

It can be seen immediately that, if $E = ECF/Ke$:

$$p_q* = Ke(E - E*)/(E* + E\ Ke) = (ECF - E*\ Ke)/(E* + ECF)$$

17.6.5. Impact of the Simplified Formulae on the Required Return to Equity

Using the simplified formulae changes the relationship between Ke and Ku. Without costs of leverage, that is, using formula (17.17), the relationship is (17.16):

$$Ke = Ku + [D(1 - T)/E]\ (Ku - Kd) \tag{17.16}$$

Using formula (17.27), the relationship is

$$Ke* = Ku + (D/E*)\ (Ku - R_F) \tag{17.38}$$

Using formula (17.28), the relationship is

$$Ke' = Ku + [D(1 - T)/E']\ (Ku - R_F) \tag{17.39}$$

17.7. VALUING COMPANIES USING DISCOUNTED CASH FLOW, CONSTANT GROWTH

In the previous sections, we defined the concepts and parameters used to value companies without growth and infinite life (perpetuities). In this section, we will discuss the valuation of companies with constant growth.

Initially, we assume that the debt's market value is the same as its book value. Section 17.8.2 addresses the case of mismatch between the debt's book value (N) and its market value (D), which is very common in practical reality. Section 17.8.3 analyzes the impact on the valuation of using simplified betas.

Now, we will assume that the cash flows generated by the company grow indefinitely at a constant annual rate $g > 0$. This implies that the debt to equity (D/E) and working capital requirements to net fixed assets (WCR/NFA) ratios remain constant, or, to put it another way, debt, equity, WCR, and NFA grow at the same rate g as the cash flows generated by the company.

In the case of perpetuities, as FCF, ECF, and CCF were constant, it was not important to determine the period during which the various cash flows used in the valuation formula were generated. On the contrary, in the case of companies with constant growth, it is necessary to consider the period: a period's expected cash flow is equal to the sum of the previous period's cash flow plus the growth g. For example, $FCF_1 = FCF_0(1 + g)$.

17.8. COMPANY VALUATION FORMULAE, CONSTANT GROWTH

With constant growth (g), the discounted cash flow valuation formulae are

$$E = ECF_1/(Ke - g) \qquad (17.1g)$$

$$E + D = \frac{ECF_1}{Ke - g} + \frac{CFd_1}{Kd - g} = \frac{ECF_1}{Ke - g} + \frac{D\ Kd - gD}{Kd - g} \qquad (17.2g)$$

$$E + D = FCF_1/(WACC - g) \qquad (17.3g)$$

$$E + D = CCF_1/(WACC_{BT} - g) \qquad (17.6g)$$

$$E + D = FCF_1/(Ku - g) + DVTS_{NCL} - \text{Cost of leverage} \qquad (17.9g)$$

The formula that relates FCF and ECF is

$$ECF_1 = FCF_1 - D_0[Kd(1 - T) - g] \qquad (17.4g)$$

because $ECF_1 = FCF_1 - I_1(1 - T) + \Delta D_1$; $I_1 = D_0\ Kd$; and $\Delta D_1 = g\ D_0$. The formula that relates CCF with ECF and FCF is

$$CCF_1 = ECF_1 + D_0(Kd - g) = FCF_1 - D_0\ Kd\ T \qquad (17.7g)$$

Although it is obvious, it is useful to point out that the debt's value at $t = 0$ (D_0) is[15]

$$D_0 = \frac{(I - \Delta D)_1}{Kd - g} = \frac{KdD_0 - gD_0}{Kd - g} = D_0$$

17.8.1 RELATIONSHIPS OBTAINED FROM THE FORMULAE

As seen in sections 17.2.2 and 17.2.3, it is possible to infer the same relationships by pairing formulae (17.1g) to (17.9g) and basing this on the fact that the results given must be equal. For the moment, we will assume that the cost of leverage is zero.

As (17.2g) must be equal to (17.3g), using (17.4g), we obtain the definition of WACC (17.5).

As (17.2g) must be equal to (17.6g), using (17.7g), we obtain the definition of $WACC_{BT}$ (17.8).

---

[15]Note that we are assuming that the debt's market value is equal to its nominal or book value.

As (17.3g) must be equal to (17.9g), without cost of leverage, it follows:

$$(E + D) (WACC - g) = (E + D - DVTS) (Ku - g),$$

so:[16]

$$DVTS = (E + D) (Ku - WACC)/(Ku - g)$$

Substituting in this equation the expression for WACC (17.5) and taking into account (17.12), we obtain:

$$DVTS = \frac{D\,T\,Ku}{Ku - g} \qquad (17.10g)$$

We would point out again that this expression is not a cash flow's PV, but the difference between two present values of two cash flows with a different risk: the taxes of the company without debt and the taxes of the company with debt.

One conclusion that is drawn from the above expressions is that the debt cash flow and the equity cash flow (and, therefore, the tax cash flow) depend on Kd, but the value of the debt D (which has been preset and is assumed to be equal to its nominal value), the value of the equity E and, therefore, the value of the taxes *do not depend* on Kd.[17]

If we were to discount the tax shield due to interest payments at the rate Kd, this would give:

$$DVTS = D\ Kd\ T/(Kd - g)$$

which does depend on Kd.

Consequently, *the DVTS is not the present value of the tax shield due to interest payments (D Kd T) at the rate Kd.* The reason is that the discounted value of the tax shield is not the PV of a cash flow (D Kd T, which grows at a rate g), but the difference between the present values of two cash flows with a different risk: the PV of the taxes of the company without debt at the rate K_{TU} and the PV of the taxes of the company with debt at the rate K_{TL}.

17.8.2. FORMULAE WHEN THE DEBT'S BOOK VALUE (N) IS NOT EQUAL TO ITS MARKET VALUE (D)

N is the book value of debt (the money that the company has borrowed), r is the interest rate, and Nr is the annual interest payment.

---

[16]The same result could be obtained by making (17.2) and (17.5) equal [using (17.6)].

[17]This is because we are assuming that the debt's market value (D) is equal to its book value (N).

Kd is the required return to debt: a "reasonable" return that the bond-holders or the bank must (or should) demand, in accordance with the company's risk and the size of the debt, so Kd D is the interest which, from the "reasonable" viewpoint, the company should pay.

Until now, we have assumed that r = Kd, but if this is not so, the debt's market value (D) will not be equal to its nominal value (N).

If the debt grows annually $\Delta N_1 = g\ N_0$, then:

$$D = N(r - g)/(Kd - g) \qquad (17.40)$$

So

$$D\ Kd - Nr = g\ (D - N).$$

The relationship between ECF and FCF is

$$ECF = FCF - Nr\ (1 - T) + gN = FCF - D\ (Kd - g) + N\ r\ T \quad (17.41)$$

As can be seen, when r ≠ Kd the relationship between ECF and FCF is not equal to the relationship when r = Kd.

Substituting (17.41) and (17.1g) in (17.3g):

$$E + D = \frac{ECF + D(Kd - g) - NrT}{WACC - g} = \frac{E\ (Ke - g) + D\ (Kd - g) - NrT}{WACC - g}$$

Upon performing algebraic operations, we obtain:

$$WACC = \frac{E\ Ke + D\ Kd - Nr\ T}{E + D} \qquad (17.42)$$

It can also be shown that the expression for calculating the DVTS is

$$DVTS = \frac{D\ T\ Ku + T[Nr - D\ Kd]}{Ku - g} \qquad (17.43)$$

As we have already seen:

D Kd − D g = N r − N g, it is clear that: N r − D Kd = g(N − D)

Substituting, this gives:

$$DVTS = DT + \frac{T\ g\ N}{Ku - g} = \frac{D\ T\ (Ku - g) + T\ g\ N}{Ku - g}$$

17.8.3. Impact of the Use of the Simplified Formulae

$$\beta*_L = \beta_U[D + E*]/E* \quad \text{and} \quad \beta'_L = \beta_U[D(1 - T) + E']/E'$$

If these simplified formulae are used, the levered beta (β^*_L) will be greater than that obtained using the full formula (19.17):

$$\beta_L = \beta_U + D(1 - T)[\beta_U - \beta_d]/E$$

In addition, the value of the equity (E^* or E') will be less than that obtained previously (E) because the required return to equity now (Ke^* or Ke') is greater than that used previously (Ke). Logically, the weighted cost of debt and equity now ($WACC'$) is greater than that used previously ($WACC$).

With these simplifications, we introduce cost of leverage in the valuation: in formula (17.5), we must add the term CL that represents the cost of leverage: increase of risk and/or a decrease in the FCF when the debt ratio increases.

Using the same methodology followed in the section on perpetuities, we can obtain the different expressions for equity value that are obtained using the full formula (E) or the abbreviated formulae (E', E^*). For a company whose FCF grows uniformly at the annual rate g, they are[18]

$$CL' = E - E' = \frac{D(1 - T)(Kd - R_F)}{Ku - g} \qquad (17.29g)$$

$$CL^* = E - E^* = \frac{D(1 - T)(Kd - R_F)}{Ku - g} + \frac{DT(Ku - R_F)}{Ku - g} \qquad (17.30g)$$

17.9. EXAMPLES OF COMPANIES WITH CONSTANT GROWTH

Table 17.3 shows the balance sheet, income statement, and cash flows of a company with a growth of 5% in all the parameters except net fixed assets, that remain constant.

Lines 1–11 show the forecasts for the company's balance sheet for the next 5 years. Lines 12–20 show the forecast income statements. Lines 21–25 show the calculation of the equity cash flow in each year. Line 26 shows each year's free cash flow. Line 27 shows each year's capital cash flow. Line 28 shows each year's debt cash flow.

The growth of the equity cash flow, free cash flow, capital cash flow, and debt cash flow is 5% per annum.

Table 17.4 shows the valuation of the company with a growth of 5% in all the parameters except net fixed assets, which remain constant. Line 1 shows the beta for the unlevered company (which is equal to the net assets' beta

[18]Note that in all cases we are considering the same debt (D) and the same cost (Kd).

Table 17.3

Balance Sheet, Income Statement and Cash Flows of a Company that Grows at 5%, the Net Fixed Assets Remain Constant, T = 35%

	0	1	2	3	4
1 Cash and banks	100	105	110.25	115.76	121.55
2 Accounts receivable	900	945	992.25	1,041.86	1,093.96
3 Stocks	240	252	264.60	277.83	291.72
4 Gross fixed assets	1,200	1,410	1,630.50	1,862.03	2,105.13
5 − Cum. depreciation	200	410	630.50	862.03	1,105.13
6 Net fixed assets	1,000	1,000	1,000	1,000	1,000
7 Total assets	**2,240**	**2,302**	**2,367.10**	**2,435.46**	**2,507.23**
8 Accounts payable	240	252	264.60	277.83	291.72
9 Debt	500	525	551.25	578.81	607.75
10 Equity (book value)	1,500	1,525	1,551.25	1,578.81	1,607.75
11 Total liabilities	**2,240**	**2,302**	**2,367.10**	**2,435.46**	**2,507.23**
Income statement					
12 Sales	3,000	3,150	3,307.50	3,472.88	3,646.52
13 Cost of sales	1,200	1,260	1,323.00	1,389.15	1,458.61
14 General expenses	600	630	661.50	694.58	729.30
15 Depreciation	200	210	220.50	231.53	243.10
16 Margin	1,000	1,050	1,102.50	1,157.63	1,215.51
17 Interest	75	75	78.75	82.69	86.82
18 PBT	925	975	1,023.75	1,074.94	1,128.68
19 Taxes	323.75	341.25	358.31	376.23	395.04
20 PAT	601.25	633.75	665.44	698.71	733.64
21 + Depreciation		210	220.50	231.53	243.10
22 +Δ Debt		25	26.25	27.56	28.94
23 −Δ WCR		−50	−52.50	−55.13	−57.88
24 − Investments		−210	−220.50	−231.53	−243.10
25 ECF = Dividends		608.75	639.19	671.15	704.70
26 FCF		632.50	664.13	697.33	732.20
27 CCF		658.75	691.69	726.27	762.59
28 Debt cash flow		50.00	52.50	55.13	57.88

Table 17.4

Valuation of a Company that Grows at 5%, the Net Fixed Assets are Constant, T = 35%

	0	1	2	3	4
1 Beta U	1	1	1	1	1
2 R$_F$	12%	12%	12%	12%	12%
3 R$_M$ – R$_F$	8%	8%	8%	8%	8%
4 Ku	20%	20%	20%	20%	20%
5 Vu = FCF/(Ku – g)	4,216.67	4,427.50	4,648.88	4,881.32	5,125.38
Without taxes					
6 FCF WITHOUT TAXES		1,000.00	1,050.00	1,102.50	1,157.63
7 Vu without taxes	6,666.67	7,000.00	7,350.00	7,717.50	8,103.38
With taxes					
8 Kd	15%	15%	15%	15%	15%
9 Beta d	0.375	0.375	0.375	0.375	0.375
10 DTKu/(Ku – g) = DVTS	233.33	245.00	257.25	270.11	283.62
11 DVTS + Vu	4,450.00	4,672.50	4,906.13	5,151.43	5,409.00
12 –D = E 1	3,950	4,148	4,355	4,573	4,801
13 Beta E = β$_L$	1.05142	1.05142	1.05142	1.05142	1.05142
14 Ke	20.41%	20.41%	20.41%	20.41%	20.41%
15 E2 = ECF/(Ke – g)	3,950	4,148	4,355	4,573	4,801
16 WACC	19.213%	19.213%	19.213%	19.213%	19.213%
17 D + E = FCF/(WACC – g)	4,450.00	4,672.50	4,906.13	5,151.43	5,409.00
18 –D = E 3	3,950	4,148	4,355	4,573	4,801
19 WACC$_{BT}$	19.803%	19.803%	19.803%	19.803%	19.803%
20 D + E = CCF/(WACC$_{BT}$ – g)	4,450.00	4,672.50	4,906.13	5,151.43	5,409.00
21 –D = E 4	3,950	4,148	4,355	4,573	4,801

= βu) which has been assumed to be equal to 1. Line 2 shows the risk-free rate, which has been assumed to be 12%. Line 3 shows the market risk premium, which has been assumed to be 8%. These results are used to calculate line 4, which gives Ku = 20%.

Line 5 shows the value of the unlevered company Vu by discounting the future free cash flows at the rate Ku. Lines 6 and 7 show what would be the company's free cash flow if there were no taxes and what would be Vu if there were no taxes. Line 8 shows the cost of debt, which has been assumed to be 15%. Line 9 is the debt's beta (β$_d$) corresponding to its cost (15%), which gives 0.375.

Line 10 shows the discounted value of the tax shield due to interest payments. Line 11 is the application of formula (17.9). Line 12 is obtained by subtracting the value of the debt from line 11, obtaining the value of the equity.

Line 13 shows the equity's beta (β_L). Line 14 shows the required return to equity corresponding to the beta in the previous line. Line 15 is the result of using formula (17.1). It is equal to line 12. Line 16 shows the weighted average cost of capital (WACC). Line 17 shows the present value of the free cash flow discounted at the WACC. Line 18 shows the value of the equity according to formula (17.3), which is also equal to lines 12 and 15.

Line 19 shows the weighted cost of equity and debt before tax ($WACC_{BT}$). Line 20 shows the present value of the capital cash flow discounted at the $WACC_{BT}$. Line 21 shows the value of the equity according to formula (17.4), which is also equal to lines 12, 15 and 18.

It is important to realize that although the cash flows in Tables 17.3 and 17.4 grow at 5%, the economic profit and the EVA do not grow at 5%. The reason is that in these tables, the net fixed assets remain constant (investments = depreciation).

Table 17.5 highlights the most important results obtained from Tables 17.3 and 17.4.

It is important to point out that the tax risk is different from the equity cash flow risk. The risk of both flows will be identical only if the sum of tax and equity cash flow is equal to PBT. This only happens if the ECF is equal to PAT, as tax amounts to 35% of the PBT.

Table 17.5

Cash Flows in Year 1, Discount Rates and
Value of the Company with an Annual Growth $= 5\%$

	Without taxes		With taxes	
	Without debt $D = 0$	With debt $D = 500$	Without debt $D = 0$	With debt $D = 500$
ECF	1,000	950	632.5	608.75
Taxes	—	—	367.5	341.25
Debt cash flow	—	50	—	50
Ke	20%	20.40%	20%	20.41%
Kd	—	15%	—	15%
K_{TL}	—	—	20%	20.39%[a]
$E = ECF/(Ke - g)$	6,667	6,167	4,217	3,950
$G = Taxes/(K_{TL} - g)$	—	—	2,450	2,217
$D = Debt\ cash\ flow/(Kd - g)$	—	500	—	500
Sum	6,667	6,667	6,667	6,667

[a]This is obtained from: $341.25/(K_{TL} - 0.05) = 2.217$.

In Table 17.3 (year 1, D = 500, T = 35%), the equity cash flow (608.75) is less than the PAT (633.75). Consequently, tax has less risk than the equity cash flow.

17.10. TAX RISK AND DVTS WITH CONSTANT GROWTH

Formula (17.18) continues to be valid when a similar development (without leverage costs) to that of Section 17.3 for perpetuities is performed:

$$Vu_t + Gu_t = E_t + D_t + G_{L_t} \qquad (17.18)$$

The discounted value of the tax shields (DVTS) is

$$DVTS_t = Gu_t - G_{L_t} \qquad (17.19)$$

In a company with constant growth and without debt, the relationship between taxes and profit before tax is $Taxes_U = T\ PBTu$.

The relationship between taxes and free cash flow is different from that obtained for perpetuities:

$$\begin{aligned} Taxes_U &= T[FCF + g(WCR + NFA)]/(1 - T) \\ &= T[FCF + g(Ebv + D)]/(1 - T) \end{aligned} \qquad (17.20g)$$

WCR is the net working capital requirements. NFA is the net fixed assets. Ebv is the equity book value.

The present value of taxes in the unlevered company is

$$G_U = Taxes_U/(K_{TU} - g) \qquad (17.22g)$$

In a levered company with constant growth, the relationship between taxes and equity cash flow is different from that obtained for perpetuities:

$$Taxes_L = T(ECF + g\ Ebv)/(1 - T). \qquad (17.23g)$$

The present value of taxes in the levered company is

$$G_L = Taxes_L/(K_{TL} - g) \qquad (17.25g)$$

The increase in the value of the company due to the use of debt *is not* the present value of the tax shield due to the payment of interest but the difference between G_U and G_L, which are the present values of two cash flows with a different risk:

$$DVTS_t = Gu_t - G_{L_t} = [Taxes_U/(K_{TU} - g)] - [Taxes_L/(K_{TL} - g)] \qquad (17.26g)$$

Assuming that there are no costs of leverage, the following is obtained:

$$DVTS_t = D\ T\ Ku/(Ku - g) \qquad (17.10g)$$

17.11. VALUATION OF COMPANIES BY DISCOUNTED CASH FLOW, GENERAL CASE

In the previous sections, valuation parameters and concepts have been defined and applied to two specific cases: perpetuities and constant growth. Now, the subject will be discussed on a general level, i.e., without any pre-defined evolution of the cash flows over the years. In addition, the study period may be finite.

In the course of the following sections, it is shown:

1. The tax shield due to interest payments (DVTS) must *not* be discounted (as many authors propose) neither at the rate Ke (required return to equity) nor at the rate Kd (required return to debt).
2. The discounted value of the tax shield due to interest payments (without costs of leverage) is equal to the PV of the tax shield that would exist if the debt had a cost equal to Ku. This is because this PV is not exactly the present value of a cash flow, but the difference between two present values: that of the flow of taxes paid by the unlevered company and that of the flow of taxes paid by the levered company (flows with different risk).

$$DVTS = PV[D\ Ku\ T;\ Ku]$$

3. Expression of the WACC when the debt's book value is not equal to its "market" value.
4. Expression of the DVTS when the debt's book value is not equal to its "market" value.
5. The impact on the valuation of using the simplified formulae for the levered beta.

17.12. COMPANY VALUATION FORMULAE, GENERAL CASE

There follows four formulae for company valuation using discounted cash flows for a general case. By this we mean that the cash flows generated by the company may grow (or contract) at a different rate each year, and thus, all of the company's parameters can vary from year to year, such as, for example, the level of leverage, the WCR or the net fixed assets.

$$E_0 = \sum_{t=1}^{\infty} \frac{ECF_t}{\prod_1^t (1 + Ke_t)} = PV(Ke; ECF) \tag{17.44}$$

Let us now see the other expressions. The formula which relates the FCF with the company's value is

$$E_0 + D_0 = PV(WACC; FCF) \tag{17.45}$$

The formula that relates the CCF with the company's value is

$$E_0 + D_0 = PV(WACC_{BT}; CCF) \tag{17.46}$$

Other relevant expressions are

$$E_1 = E_0(1 + Ke_1) - ECF_1 \tag{17.47}$$

$$D_1 + E_1 = (D_0 + E_0)(1 + WACC_1) - FCF_1 \tag{17.48}$$

$$D_1 + E_1 = (D_0 + E_0)(1 + WACC_{BT1}) - CCF_1 \tag{17.49}$$

We can also calculate the value of $D_0 + E_0$ from the value of the unlevered company:

$$E_0 + D_0 = PV(Ku; FCF) + DVTS_{NCL} - \text{cost of leverage} \tag{17.50}$$

17.13. RELATIONSHIPS OBTAINED FROM THE FORMULAE, GENERAL CASE

There follows a number of important relationships that can be inferred by pairing formulae (17.44)–(17.46), and (17.50), and taking into consideration that the results they give must be equal.

If $r = Kd$ and Cost of leverage $= 0$.

$$ECF_t = FCF_t + \Delta D_t - I_t(1 - T) \tag{17.51}$$

$$CCF_t = ECF_t - \Delta D_t + I_t \qquad \Delta D_t = D_t - D_{t-1} \qquad I_t = D_{t-1} Kd_t \tag{17.52}$$

$$D_0 = \sum_{t=1}^{\infty} \frac{D_{t-1} Kd_t - (D_t - D_{t-1})}{\prod_1^t (1 + Kd_t)} \tag{17.53}$$

$$WACC_t = \frac{E_{t-1} Ke_t + D_{t-1} Kd_t(1 - T)}{(E_{t-1} + D_{t-1})} \tag{17.54}$$

$$\text{WACC}_{\text{BTt}} = \frac{E_{t-1} \, Ke_t + D_{t-1} \, Kd_t}{(E_{t-1} + D_{t-1})} \tag{17.55}$$

As:

$$Ku_t = \frac{E_{t-1} \, Ke_t + D_{t-1} \, Kd_t(1-T)}{E_{t-1} + D_{t-1}(1-T)} \tag{17.56}$$

which is equivalent to (17.12), gives

$$\text{WACC}_t = \frac{E_{t-1} + D_{t-1}(1-T)}{(E_{t-1} + D_{t-1})} Ku_t \tag{17.57}$$

$$\text{DVTS}_0 = \sum_{t=1}^{\infty} \frac{D_{t-1} \, Ku_t \, T}{\prod_1^t (1 + Ku_t)} \tag{17.58}$$

The following identities must be remembered:

$$Vu_t + G_{U_t} = E_t + D_t + G_{L_t} \tag{17.18}$$

$$Vu_t \, Ku_{t+1} + G_{U_t} \, K_{TU_{t+1}} = E_t \, Ke_{t+1} + D_t \, Kd_{t+1} + G_{L_t} \, K_{TL_{t+1}}$$

$$\text{DVTS}_t = G_{U_t} - G_{L_t} = E_t + D_t - Vu_t \tag{17.19}$$

17.14. AN EXAMPLE OF COMPANY VALUATION

Table 17.6 shows the previous balance sheets of the company Font, Inc. Table 17.7 shows the income statements and the cash flows.

Table 17.8 assumes that the cost of leverage is zero. It shows the valuation by all four methods for a company that is growing (but not at a constant rate) up to year 9. After year 9, a constant growth of 5% has been forecasted. The cash flows grow at 5% from year 11 onward. The cash flows of year 10 are not 5% greater than those of year 9.

For this general case too, it is seen that all our valuation formulae, (17.44)–(17.46) and (17.50), give the same value for the company's equity: at $t = 0$, it is 506 million euros (see lines 43, 46, 50, and 53).

It can also be seen that:

1. The discounted value of the tax shield due to interest payments is 626.72 million (line 41).
2. It would be mistaken to calculate the discounted value of the tax shield by discounting DTKd at the debt interest rate (15%) as that would give 622 million.

Table 17.6
Forecast Balance Sheets for Font, Inc.

	0	1	2	3	4	5	6	7	8	9	10
1 Cash	100	120	140	160	180	200	210	220	230.0	240.0	252.0
2 Accounts receivable	900	960	1,020	1,080	1,140	1,200	1,260	1,320	1,380.0	1,449.0	1,521.5
3 Stocks	300	320	340	360	380	400	420	440	460.0	483.0	507.2
4 Gross fixed assets	1,500	1,800	2,700	3,100	3,300	3,500	3,900	4,204	4,523.2	4,858.4	5,210.3
5 – Cum. depreciation	200	550	900	1,300	1,800	2,100	2,380	2,684	3,003.2	3,338.4	3,690.3
6 Net fixed assets	1300	1,250	1,800	1,800	1,500	1,400	1,520	1,520	1,520.0	1,520.0	1,520.0
7 Total assets	2,600	2,650	3,300	3,400	3,200	3,200	3,410	3,500	3,590.0	3,692.0	3,800.6
8 Accounts payable	300	320	340	360	380	400	420	440	460.0	483.0	507.2
9 Debt	1,800	1,800	2,300	2,300	2,050	1,800	1,700	1,450	1,200.0	1,000.0	1,050.0
10 Equity	500	530	660	740	770	1,000	1,290	1,610	1,930.0	2,209.0	2,243.5
11 Total	2,600	2,650	3,300	3,400	3,200	3,200	3,410	3,500	3,590.0	3,692.0	3,800.6

Table 17.7
Forecast Income Statements and Cash Flows for Font, Inc.

	1	2	3	4	5	6	7	8	9	10	11
14 Sales	3,200	3,400	3,600	3,800	4,000	4,200	4,400	4,600	4,830	5,071.50	5,325.08
15 Cost of sales	1,600	1,700	1,800	1,900	2,000	2,100	2,200	2,300	2,415	2,535.75	2,662.54
16 General expenses	800	850	900	950	1,000	1,050	1,100	1,150	1,207.50	1,267.88	1,331.27
17 Depreciation	350	350	400	500	300	280	304	319.20	335.16	351.92	369.51
18 Margin	450	500	500	450	700	770	796	830.80	872.34	915.96	961.75
19 Interest	270	270	345	345	307.50	270	255	217.50	180	150	158
20 PBT	180	230	155	105	392.50	500	541	613.30	692.34	765.96	804.25
21 Tax	63	80.5	54.25	36.75	137.38	175	189.35	214.66	242.32	268.08	281.49
22 PAT	117	149.5	100.75	68.25	255.13	325	351.65	398.65	450.02	497.87	522.77
23 + Depreciation	350	350	400	500	300	280	304	319.20	335.16	351.92	369.51
24 + Δ Debt	0	500	0	-250	-250	-100	-250	-250	-200	50	52.50
25 - Δ WCR	-80	-80	-80	-80	-80	-70	-70	-70	-79	-84.45	-88.67
26 - Investments	-300	-900	-400	-200	-200	-400	-304	-319.20	-335.16	-351.92	-369.51
27 ECF = Dividends	87	19.5	20.75	38.25	25.13	35	31.65	78.65	171.02	463.42	486.59
28 FCF	262.5	-305	245	512.5	475	310.5	447.40	470.02	488.02	510.92	536.47

Table 17.8
Valuation of Font, Inc.

	0	1	2	3	4	5	6	7	8	9	10
35 Ku	**20%**	**20%**	**20%**	**20%**	**20%**	**20%**	**20%**	**20%**	**20%**	**20%**	**20%**
36 Vu	1,679.6	1,753.1	2,408.7	2,645.4	2,662.0	2,719.4	2,952.8	3,096.0	3,245.1	3,406.1	3,576.5
39 Kd	15%	15%	15%	15%	15%	15%	15%	15%	15%	15%	15%
40 Beta d	0.3750	0.3750	0.3750	0.3750	0.3750	0.3750	0.3750	0.3750	0.3750	0.3750	0.3750
41 DVTS	626.72	626.06	625.28	589.33	546.20	511.94	488.33	466.99	458.89	466.67	490.00
42 DVTS + Vu	2,306.37	2,379.14	3,033.97	3,234.76	3,208.22	3,231.36	3,441.13	3,562.96	3,704.03	3,872.81	4,066.45
43 –D = E1	**506**	**579**	**734**	**935**	**1,158**	**1,431**	**1,741**	**2,113**	**2,504**	**2,873**	**3,016**
44 Beta E	2.4441	2.2626	2.2730	1.9996	1.7190	1.5109	1.3967	1.2788	1.1947	1.1414	1.1414
45 Ke	31.55%	30.10%	30.18%	28.00%	25.75%	24.09%	23.17%	22.23%	21.56%	21.13%	21.13%
46 E 2 = PV(Ke; ECF)	**506**	**579**	**734**	**935**	**1,158**	**1,431**	**1,741**	**2,113**	**2,504**	**2,873**	**3,016**
47 $E_t = E_{t-1}(1 + Ke)$ – ECF	506	579	734	935	1,158	1,431	1,741	2,113	2,504	2,873	3,016
48 WACC	**14.54%**	**14.70%**	**14.69%**	**15.02%**	**15.53%**	**16.10%**	**16.54%**	**17.15%**	**17.73%**	**18.19%**	**18.19%**
49 PV(WACC; FCF)	2,306.37	2,379.14	3,033.97	3,234.76	3,208.22	3,231.36	3,441.13	3,562.96	3,704.03	3,872.81	4,066.45
50 –D = E 3	**506**	**579**	**734**	**935**	**1,158**	**1,431**	**1,741**	**2,113**	**2,504**	**2,873**	**3,016**
51 WACC$_{BT}$	**18.63%**	**18.68%**	**18.67%**	**18.76%**	**18.88%**	**19.03%**	**19.14%**	**19.29%**	**19.43%**	**19.55%**	**19.55%**
52 PV(WACC$_{BT}$; CCF)	2,306.37	2,379.14	3,033.97	3,234.76	3,208.22	3,231.36	3,441.13	3,562.96	3,704.03	3,872.81	4,066.45
53 –D = E 4	**506**	**579**	**734**	**935**	**1,158**	**1,431**	**1,741**	**2,113**	**2,504**	**2,873**	**3,016**

The lines of Tables 17.6–17.8 have the following meanings.

Lines 1 to 11 show the forecast balance sheets for the company over the next 10 years.

Lines 14 to 22 show the forecast income statements.

Lines 23 to 27 show the calculation of each year's equity cash flow.

Line 28 shows each year's free cash flow.

Line 35 shows $Ku = 20\%$. This result comes from a risk-free rate of 12%, a market risk premium of 8%, and a beta for the unlevered company equal to 1.

Line 36 shows the value of the unlevered company (Vu) discounting the future free cash flows at the rate Ku at t = 0 (now), giving Vu = 1,679.65.

Lines 37 and 38 show what would be the company's free cash flow if there were no taxes and what would be Vu with no taxes. If there were no taxes, at t = 0 Vu = 2,917.13.

Line 39 shows the cost of the debt, which has been assumed to be 15%.

Line 40 shows the debt's beta corresponding to its cost, which gives 0.375.

Line 41 shows the discounted value of the tax shield due to interest payments, which at t = 0 is 626.72.

Line 42 is the application of formula (17.50). At t = 0, it gives $D + E = 1,679.65 + 626.72 = 2,306.37$.

Line 43 is the result of subtracting the value of the debt from line 42. At t = 0, the value of the equity is 506 million.

Line 44 shows the equity's beta, using formula (17.17).

Line 45 shows the required return to equity corresponding to the beta in the previous line.

Line 46 is the result of using formula (17.44). This formula too finds that the value of the equity at t = 0 is 506 million. Line 47 shows the evolution of the equity's value according to the formula (17.47). Note that line 47 is the same as line 46.

Line 48 shows the weighted cost of equity and debt after tax, WACC, according to formula (17.54).

Line 49 shows the present value of the free cash flow discounted at the WACC.

Line 50 shows the value of the equity according to formula (17.45), which is also found to be 506 million.

Line 51 shows the weighted cost of equity and debt before tax $WACC_{BT}$, according to formula (17.55).

Line 52 shows the present value of the capital cash flow discounted at the $WACC_{BT}$.

Line 53 shows the value of the equity according to formula (17.46), which is also found to be 506 million.

Table 17.9

Sensitivity Analysis of the Value of the Equity at t = 0 (in Million)

Value of Font, Inc.'s equity in Table 17.3	**506**
Tax rate = 30% (instead of 35%)	594
Risk-free rate (R_F) = 11% (instead of 12%)	653
Market (P_M) = 7% (instead of 8%)	653
βu = 0.9 (instead of 1.0)	622
Residual growth (after year 9) = 6% (instead of 5%)	546

Table 17.9 shows a sensitivity analysis of the equity after making changes in certain parameters.

17.15. VALUATION FORMULAE WHEN THE DEBT'S BOOK VALUE (N) AND ITS MARKET VALUE (D) ARE NOT EQUAL

Our starting point is

$$D_0 = \sum_{t=1}^{\infty} \frac{N_{t-1}\, r_t - (N_t - N_{t-1})}{\prod_1^t (1 + Kd_t)} \qquad (17.59)$$

It is easy to show that:

$$D_1 - D_0 = N_1 - N_0 + D_0\, Kd_1 - N_0\, r_1 \qquad (17.60)$$

Consequently

$$\Delta D = \Delta N + D_0\, Kd_1 - N_0 r_1$$

Taking into account this expression and equations (17.51) and (17.52), we obtain:

$$CCF_t = FCF_t + N_{t-1} r_t\, T \qquad (17.61)$$

The expression for WACC and $WACC_{BT}$ in this case is

$$WACC = \frac{E\, Ke + D\, Kd - N\, r\, T}{E + D} \qquad WACC_{BT} = \frac{E\, Ke + D\, Kd}{E + D} \qquad (17.62)$$

The expression for DVTS in this case is

$$\text{DVTS}_0 = \sum_{t=1}^{\infty} \frac{D_{t-1} \, Ku_t \, T - (N_{t-1} \, r_t - D_{t-1} \, Kd_t)T}{\prod_1^t (1 + Ku_t)} \tag{17.63}$$

17.16. IMPACT ON THE VALUATION WHEN D ≠ N, WITHOUT COST OF LEVERAGE

Table 17.10 shows the impact on the valuation of Font, Inc. if it is assumed that D is not equal to N. In order to calculate the debt's market value (D), the following expressions are used in Table 17.10:

$$\text{Debt} = \sum_{i=1}^{10} \frac{\text{Cash flow to debt}_i}{\prod_{j=1}^{j=i} (1 + Kd_j)} + \frac{\text{Cash flow to debt}_{11}}{(Kd - g)} \times \frac{1}{\prod_{j=1}^{10} (1 + Kd_j)}$$

$$\beta d_i = \frac{Kd_i - Rf_i}{Rm_i - Rf_i}$$

The most significant differences between Tables 17.8 and 17.10 are

(Million euros)	Table 17.8	Table 17.10
Value of debt D	1,800	1,705
Value of equity E	506	568
Value of state's interest	611	644
Total	2,917	2,917

17.17. IMPACT ON THE VALUATION WHEN D ≠ N, WITH COST OF LEVERAGE, IN A REAL-LIFE CASE

The simplified formulae for the levered beta are (17.27) and (17.28). If these simplified formulae are used, the levered beta (β_L*) will be greater than that obtained using the full formula (17.17).

In addition, the value of the equity (E* or E′) will be less than that obtained previously (E) because the required return to equity now

Table 17.10

Valuation of Font, Inc. Assuming that $D \neq N$ $Kd = R_F + (Ku - R_F) \times D(1 - T)/[D(1 - T) + E]$

	0	1	2	3	4	5	6	7	8	9	10
35 Ku	**20%**	**20%**	**20%**	**20%**	**20%**	**20%**	**20%**	**20%**	**20%**	**20%**	**20%**
38 Vu without taxes (Ku)	2,917.1	3,080.6	3,826.7	4,172.0	4,336.4	4,483.7	4,800.4	5,034.5	5,280.6	5,543.4	5,820.5
9 N	1,800	1,800	2,300	2,300	2,050	1,800	1,700	1,450	1,200	1,000	1,050
39 r	*15%*	*15%*	*15%*	*15%*	*15%*	*15%*	*15%*	*15%*	*15%*	*15%*	*15%*
A D	**1,704.4**	**1,729.1**	**2,255.4**	**2,299.8**	**2,093.9**	**1,879.2**	**1,805.3**	**1,576.5**	**1,340.5**	**1,149.8**	**1,207.3**
40 Kd	17.29%	17.14%	17.26%	16.92%	16.37%	15.76%	15.30%	14.68%	14.12%	13.70%	13.70%
B Beta d	0.6609	0.6425	0.6577	0.6152	0.5464	0.4696	0.4123	0.3354	0.2653	0.2122	0.2122
C Nr–DKd		−24.6432	−26.3667	−44.3261	−44.1592	−35.3068	−26.0991	−21.1851	−13.9785	−9.3106	−7.4897
D Ke – Kd	8%	8%	8%	8%	8%	8%	%	8%	8%	8%	8%
E D T Ku+ (Nr – DKd)*T	110.68	110.68	111.81	142.37	145.53	134.22	122.41	118.96	105.46	90.58	77.86
41 DVTS	593.27	601.24	609.68	589.25	561.57	539.67	525.19	511.27	508.06	519.09	545.05
42 DVTS + Vu	2,272.91	2,354.31	3,018.37	3,234.68	3,223.59	3,259.09	3,477.99	3,607.23	3,753.20	3,925.24	4,121.50
43 –D = E1	**568**	**625**	**763**	**935**	**1,130**	**1,380**	**1,673**	**2,031**	**2,413**	**2,775**	**2,914**
44 Beta E	1.6609	1.6425	1.6577	1.6152	1.5464	1.4696	1.4123	1.3354	1.2653	1.2122	1.2122
45 Ke	25.29%	25.14%	25.26%	24.92%	24.37%	23.76%	23.30%	22.68%	22.12%	21.70%	21.70%
46 E 2 = PV(Ke; ECF)	**568**	**625**	**763**	**935**	**1,130**	**1,380**	**1,673**	**2,031**	**2,413**	**2,775**	**2,914**

(continues)

Table 17.10 (*continued*)

	0	1	2	3	4	5	6	7	8	9	10
47 $E_t = E_{t-1}(1+Ke) - ECF$	568	625	763	935	1,130	1,380	1,673	2,031	2,413	2,775	2,914
48 **Reformed WACC**	**15.13%**	**15.25%**	**15.28%**	**15.50%**	**15.84%**	**16.24%**	**16.58%**	**17.08%**	**17.59%**	**18.02%**	**18.02%**
49 PV(WACC; FCF)	2,272.91	2,354.31	3,018.37	3,234.68	3,223.59	3,259.09	3,477.99	3,607.23	3,753.20	3,925.24	4,121.50
50 $-D = E\ 3$	**568**	**625**	**763**	**935**	**1,130**	**1,380**	**1,673**	**2,031**	**2,413**	**2,775**	**2,914**
51 $WACC_{BT}$	**19.29%**	**19.26%**	**19.28%**	**19.23%**	**19.18%**	**19.14%**	**19.15%**	**19.19%**	**19.27%**	**19.35%**	**19.35%**
52 PV($WACC_{BT}$; CCF)	2,272.91	2,354.31	3,018.37	3,234.68	3,223.59	3,259.09	3,477.99	3,607.23	3,753.20	3,925.24	4,121.50
53 $-D = E\ 4$	**568**	**625**	**763**	**935**	**1,130**	**1,380**	**1,673**	**2,031**	**2,413**	**2,775**	**2,914**

(Ke* or Ke′) is greater than that used previously (Ke). Logically, the weighted cost of debt and equity now (WACC′) is greater than that used previously (WACC).

With these simplifications, we introduce cost of leverage in the valuation: in formula (17.50), we must consider the term "cost of leverage," which represents the cost of bankruptcy (increased probability of bankruptcy) and/or a decrease of the expected FCF when the debt ratio is increased.

We assume that the debt's market value is the same as its nominal value. The most important differences in the valuation are shown in Table 17.11 and Figures 17.2 and 17.3.

The value of the equity is 506 million with the full formula, 332 million with the abbreviated formula (17.28) and 81 million with the abbreviated formula (17.27).

Note that, in parallel with formulae (17.29) and (17.30):

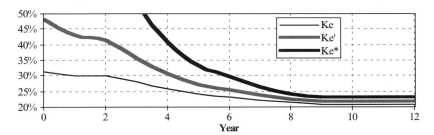

Figure 17.2 Impact of the use of the simplified formulae on the required return to equity of Font, Inc.

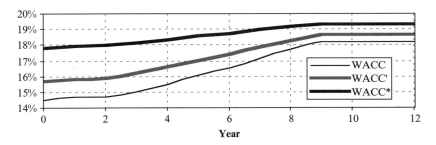

Figure 17.3 Impact of the use of the simplified formulae on the WACC of Font, Inc.

Table 17.11

Impact of the Use of the Simplified Formulae on the Valuation of Font, Inc.

Year	0	1	2	3	4	5	6	7	8	9	10
ECF = Div.		87.00	19.50	20.75	38.25	25.13	35.00	31.65	78.65	171.02	463.42
FCF		262.50	−305.00	245.00	512.50	475.00	310.50	447.40	470.02	488.02	510.92
N	1800	1800	2300	2300	2050	1800	1700	1450	1200	1000	1050
r	15%	15%	15%	15%	15%	15%	15%	15%	15%	15%	15%
E	506	579	734	935	1,158	1,431	1,741	2,113	2,504	2,873	3,016
E'	332	405	560	771	1,006	1,289	1,605	1,983	2,376	2,743	2,880
E*	81	154	310	535	788	1,084	1,410	1,796	2,193	2,556	2,684
Beta E	2.44	2.26	2.27	2.00	1.72	1.51	1.40	1.28	1.19	1.14	1.14
Beta E'	4.53	3.89	3.67	2.94	2.32	1.91	1.69	1.48	1.33	1.24	1.24
BetaE*	23.20	12.66	8.43	5.30	3.60	2.66	2.21	1.81	1.55	1.39	1.39
Ke	31.6%	30.1%	30.2%	28.0%	25.8%	24.1%	23.2%	22.2%	21.6%	21.1%	21.1%
Ke'	48.2%	43.1%	41.4%	35.5%	30.6%	27.3%	25.5%	23.8%	22.6%	21.9%	21.9%
Ke*	197.6%	113.3%	79.4%	54.4%	40.8%	33.3%	29.7%	26.5%	24.4%	23.1%	23.1%
ECF		87.00	19.50	20.80	38.30	25.10	35.00	31.60	78.60	171.00	463.40
ECF'		51.90	−15.60	−24.10	−6.60	−14.90	−0.10	−1.50	50.40	147.60	443.90
ECF*		1.50	−66.00	−88.50	−71.00	−72.30	−50.50	−49.10	9.80	114.00	415.90
Ku	20%	20%	20%	20%	20%	20%	20%	20%	20%	20%	20%
Ku'	22.34%	22.23%	22.18%	21.98%	21.71%	21.43%	21.22%	20.97%	20.74%	20.57%	20.57%
Ku*	26.83%	26.46%	26.05%	25.38%	24.59%	23.79%	23.21%	22.51%	21.92%	21.48%	21.48%

(continues)

Table 17.11 (*continued*)

	0	1	2	3	4	5	6	7	8	9	10
βu	1	1	1	1	1	1	1	1	1	1	1
βu′	1.29	1.28	1.27	1.25	1.21	1.18	1.15	1.12	1.09	1.07	1.07
βu*	1.85	1.81	1.76	1.67	1.57	1.47	1.4	1.31	1.24	1.19	1.19
WACC	14.54%	14.70%	14.69%	15.02%	15.53%	16.10%	16.54%	17.15%	17.73%	18.19%	18.19%
WACC′	15.74%	15.88%	15.94%	16.22%	16.61%	17.06%	17.40%	17.87%	18.31%	18.65%	18.65%
WACC*	17.85%	17.93%	18.02%	18.18%	18.37%	18.60%	18.77%	19.00%	19.20%	19.37%	19.37%

$$506 - 332 = 174 = \sum_{t=1}^{\infty} \frac{D_{t-1}(1 - T)(Kd_t - R_F)}{\prod_{1}^{t}(1 + Ku_t)}$$

$$506 - 81 = 425 = \sum_{t=1}^{\infty} \frac{D_{t-1}[T(Ku - R_F) + (1 - T)(Kd - R_F)]}{\prod_{1}^{t}(1 + Ku_t)}$$

Where:

$$332 = \sum_{t=1}^{\infty} \frac{ECF'_t}{\prod_{1}^{t}(1 + Ke_t)} = \sum_{t=1}^{\infty} \frac{ECF_t}{\prod_{1}^{t}(1 + Ke'_t)}$$

$$81 = \sum_{t=1}^{\infty} \frac{ECF_t{}^*}{\prod_{1}^{t}(1 + Ke_t)} = \sum_{t=1}^{\infty} \frac{ECF_t}{\prod_{1}^{t}(1 + Ke_t{}^*)}$$

APPENDIX 17.1: MAIN VALUATION FORMULAE

Valuation formulae

	Perpetuities (g = 0)	Constant growth	General case
E	$E = \dfrac{ECF}{Ke}$	$E = \dfrac{ECF_1}{Ke - g}$	$E = PV[ECF;\ Ke]$
D	$D = \dfrac{1}{Kd}$	$D_0 = \dfrac{(1-\Delta D)_1}{Kd - g} = \dfrac{KdD_0 - gD_0}{Kd - g}$	$D_0 = \displaystyle\sum_{t=1}^{\infty} \dfrac{D_{t-1}\,Kd_t - (D_t - D_{t-1})}{\prod_1^t (1 + Kd_t)}$
E + D	$E + D = \dfrac{FCF}{WACC}$	$E + D = \dfrac{FCF_1}{WACC - g}$	$E + D = PV[FCF;\ WACC]$
E + D	$E + D = \dfrac{CCF}{WACC_{BT}}$	$E + D = \dfrac{CCF_1}{WACC_{BT} - g}$	$E + D = PV[CCF;\ WACC_{BT}]$
APV	$E + D = \dfrac{FCF}{Ku} + DVTS - CL$	$E + D = \dfrac{FCF_1}{Ku - g} + DVTS - CL$	$E + D = PV[FCF;\ Ku] + DVTS - CL$
if CL = 0	$DVTS = DT$	$DVTS = D\,Ku\,T/(Ku - g)$	$DVTS = PV[D\ Ku\ T;\ Ku]$
DVTS	$DVTS = DT$	$DVTS = \dfrac{D\,T\,Ku + T[Nr - D\,Kd]}{Ku - g}$	$DVTS_0 = \displaystyle\sum_{t=1}^{\infty} \dfrac{D_{t-1}\,Ku_t\,T - (N_{t-1}\,r_t - D_{t-1}\,Kd_t)T}{\prod_1^t (1 + Ku_t)}$
if CL = 0 r ≠ Kd			
if CL = 0	$K_{TU} = Ku \quad K_{TL} = Ke$	$K_{TU} \neq Ku \quad K_{TL} \neq Ke$	$K_{TU} \neq Ku \quad K_{TU} \neq Ke$

Flows relationships

	Perpetuities(g = 0)	Constant growth	General case
r = Kd	$ECF = FCF - D\,Kd(1 - T)$ $CCF = ECF + D\,Kd$ $CCF = FCF - D\,Kd\,T$	$ECF_1 = FCF_1 - Do\,[Kd(1 - T) - g]$ $CCF_1 = ECF_1 + Do\,(Kd - g)$ $CCF_1 = FCF_1 - Do\,Kd\,T$	$ECF_t = FCF_t + \Delta D_t - I_t(1 - T)$ $CCF_t = ECF_t - \Delta D_t + I_t$ $CCF_t = FCF_t + I_t\,T$
r ≠ Kd	$D\,Kd = N\,r$	$D = N(r - g)/(Kd - g)$ $ECF = FCF - Nr(1 - T) + gN$ $ECF = FCF - D(Kd - g) + N\,r\,T$ $CCF_t = FCF_t + N_{t-1}\,r_t\,T$	$D_0 = \displaystyle\sum_{t=1}^{\infty} \dfrac{N_{t-1}\,r_t - (N_t - N_{t-1})}{\prod_1^t (1 + Kd_t)}$

If D = N	$WACC = \dfrac{E\,Ke + D\,Kd(1 - T)}{E + D}$	$WACC_{BT} = \dfrac{E\,Ke + D\,Kd}{E + D}$
If D ≠ N	$WACC = \dfrac{E\,Ke + D\,Kd - N\,r\,T}{E + D}$	$WACC_{BT} = \dfrac{E\,Ke + D\,Kd}{E + D}$
	$CL = 0$	

	CL = 0	CL > 0(β')	CL >> 0(β*)
β_L	$\beta_L = \beta u + \dfrac{D(1 - T)}{E}(\beta u - \beta d)$	$\beta'_L = \beta u + \dfrac{D(1 - T)}{E'}\,\beta u$	$\beta^*_L = \beta u + \dfrac{D}{E^*}\,\beta u$
$DVTS_t = G_{U_t} - G_{L_t} = E_t + D_t - Vu_t$	$Ku = R_F + \beta u\,P_M$	$Kd = R_F + \beta_d\,P_M$	$Ke = R_F + \beta_L\,P_M$

APPENDIX 17.2:   A FORMULA FOR THE REQUIRED RETURN TO DEBT

Formula (17.12) tells us the relationship that must exist between Ku, Ke, and Kd for each level of debt (assuming that the probability of bankruptcy is zero), but we have not found any formula that tells us how to calculate Kd from the company's risk (Ku) and debt ratio. Kd can be interpreted as the "reasonable" return that bondholders or the bank must (or should) demand, considering the company's risk and the size of the debt. For the moment, we are assuming that Kd is also the interest paid by the company on its debt.

The case of maximum debt. When all the cash flow generated by the assets corresponds to debt (ECF = 0), in the absence of leverage costs,[19] the debt's risk at this point must identical to the assets' risk, that is, Kd = Ku.

The case of minimum debt. On the other hand, for a minimum debt, the cost must be R_F.

A description of the debt's cost that meets these two conditions is:

$$Kd = R_F + \frac{D(1-T)(Ku-R_F)}{E+D(1-T)} \qquad (17.64)$$

that implies

$$\beta_d = \beta_U D(1-T)/[D(1-T)+E] \qquad (17.65)$$

Substituting (17.64) in (17.16) gives:

$$Ke = Ku + \frac{D(1-T)(Ku-R_F)}{E+D(1-T)} = Ku + Kd - R_F \qquad (17.66)$$

SUMMARY

- The value of the levered company ($V_L = E + D$) is the same, whichever of the four discounted cash flow methods is applied: discounted ECF, FCF, CCF, or the APV.
- The debt's market value (D) is equal to its book value (N) when the required return to debt (Kd) is equal to the interest rate paid by the debt (r). In perpetuities, the valuation formulae calculated are valid irrespective of whether r and Kd are equal or not. It must only be considered that $D = Nr/Kd$.

---

[19]This can only happen if the owners of the debt and the equity are the same.

- In perpetuities and only in perpetuities, the discount rate that must be applied to discount the taxes of the levered company is the required return to equity (Ke), because, in this case, the risk of the taxes is the same as the risk of the equity cash flow. Likewise, only in perpetuities, the discount rate that must be applied to discount the taxes of the unlevered company is the required return to assets (Ku),
- In companies with constant growth and in the general case, the valuation formulae vary when the debt's cost and the debt's required return are not the equal.
- When the simplified formulae for the levered beta are used, the value obtained for the beta is greater than that obtained using the full formula because the required return to equity is higher when the simplified formulae are used. With these simplifications, a term CL (cost of leverage) must be added to the expression of APV that represents the costs of bankruptcy and/or a decrease in the FCF when the level of debt increases.

REFERENCES

Damodaran, A. (1994), *Damodaran on Valuation*, New York: John Wiley and Sons.

Fernández, P. (2002), "The Value of Tax Shields is NOT Equal to the Present Value of Tax Shields," Working Paper N. 290727, Social Science Research Network.

Harris, R.S., and J.J. Pringle (1985), "Risk-Adjusted Discount Rates Extensions form the Average-Risk Case," *Journal of Financial Research*, (Fall), pp. 237–244.

Kaplan, S., and R. Ruback (1995), "The Valuation of Cash Flow Forecast: An Empirical Analysis," *Journal of Finance*, Vol. 50, No. 4, September.

Luehrman, T. A. (1997), "What's Worth: A General Manager's Guide to Valuation," and "Using APV: A Better Tool for Valuing Operations," *Harvard Business Review*, (May–June), pp. 132–154.

Modigliani, F., and M. Miller, (1958), "The Cost of Capital, Corporation Finance and the Theory of Investment," *American Economic Review*, 48, 261–297.

Modigliani, F., and M. Miller (1963), "Corporate Income Taxes and the Cost of Capital: A Correction," *American Economic Review*, (June), pp. 433–443.

Myers, S.C. (1974), "Interactions of Corporate Financing and Investment Decisions—Implications for Capital Budgeting," *Journal of Finance*, (March), pp. 1–25.

Ruback, R. S. (1995), "A Note on Capital Cash Flow Valuation," Harvard Business School, 9–295–069.

Tham, J., and I. Vélez-Pareja (2001), "The Correct Discount Rate for the Tax Shield: The N-Period Case," SSRN Working Paper.

Chapter 18

Optimal Capital Structure: Problems with the Harvard and Damodaran Approaches

Generally speaking, the optimal capital structure is considered to be that which minimizes the value of the weighted average cost of capital, WACC, and, consequently, maximizes the value of the firm, $D + E$[1]. We will see that if it is assumed that the debt's market value is the same as its book value, then the capital structure that minimizes the WACC also maximizes the share price. However, without this assumption, the minimum value of the WACC may not be the same as the maximum share price.

We will see that for an optimal structure to exist, it is necessary to assume that the firm's total value (debt + equity + present value of taxes) decreases with leverage. This may happen for two reasons: because the expected FCF decreases with the debt level, or because the assets' risk (the FCF's risk and the likelihood of bankruptcy) increases with leverage (or because of a combination of both).[2]

In this chapter we will present an analysis of the optimal structure using two examples: one proposed by the Harvard Business School and the other proposed by Damodaran.

---

[1]It is meaningless to say that the optimal structure is that which maximizes the value of the firm $(D + E)$. This value can be increased simply by asking the bank to increase the cost of debt because $D + E = Vu + DVTS$. Vu is constant and DVTS increases with higher interest payments.

[2]This increase in the assets' risk may be due to their increased volatility or to the increased likelihood of bankruptcy.

18.1. OPTIMAL STRUCTURE ACCORDING TO A HARVARD BUSINESS SCHOOL TECHNICAL NOTE[3]

This note analyzes the relationships between the goal of maximizing each share's price and the objective of achieving an optimal capital structure, understanding this to that which maximizes the firm's value (debt plus equity) and minimizes the weighted average cost of capital (WACC).

The note is based on Table 18.1, which illustrates a very simple example. A company has invested $500,000 in plant, machinery, and working capital. The investment generates annual earnings before tax and interest (EBIT) amounting to $120,000 to perpetuity. Annual depreciation is equal to new investments and the company distributes all its earnings as dividends. As the tax rate on profit is 50%, the free cash flow is $60,000 to perpetuity.

The company wants to select its capital structure from among the debt ratios shown in line 1 of Table 18.1.

Influence of leverage on payments to debt and equity—Lines 1–8 of Table 18.1 show the impact of the leverage on the company's income statement. In this example, the leverage does not influence the company's profit flows (EBIT) or its free cash flow (line 26). As debt is added to the capital structure, interest payments increase and profits (dividends) fall. Total payments to instrument holders (interest plus dividends) increase with the leverage. This increase arises from the discounted value of the tax shield.

Cost of funds—Lines 9 and 10 of Table 18.1 show the required return on debt and the required return on equity, that is, the return demanded by investors in order to purchase the company's debt and equity. As the leverage is increased, both the debt and the equity are exposed to a higher risk. The risk includes both the possibility of bankruptcy and a higher variability in the annual return. As the level of debt increases, investors demand a higher return in return for accepting the increased risk. The required return (lines 9 and 10) is the key assumption in the analysis of the optimal capital structure. The cost of the debt is Kd (line 9), and the company's required return on equity is Ke (line 10). One important point to make is that the cost of the debt may be information provided by banks or financial markets, but the required return on equity is an estimate.

Market value of debt and equity—In a perpetuity, the debt's market value (line 11) is equal to the annual interest payments, divided by the required return on debt (I/Kd). Likewise, the equity's market value (line 12) is equal to the dividends divided by the required return to equity (Div/Ke). The market value of the company as a whole (line 13) is the sum of the market value of its

[3]This section discusses the technical note "Note on the Theory of Optimal Capital Structure," which was included in the book *Case Problems in Finance*, by Fruham et al. (1992), Irwin, 10th edition. This note is analyzed and criticized in the next section.

Table 18.1
Optimal Structure According to a Harvard Business School Technical Note

1 Book value debt ratio (leverage)	0%	10%	20%	30%	40%	50%
2 EBIT, earnings before interest and taxes	120,000	120,000	120,000	120,000	120,000	120,000
3 Interest	0	4,125	8,750	14,625	22,000	31,250
4 Profit before taxes (PBT)	120,000	115,875	111,250	105,375	98,000	88,750
5 Taxes (50%)	60,000	57,938	55,625	52,688	49,000	44,375
6 Profit after taxes (PAT)	60,000	57,938	55,625	52,688	49,000	44,375
7 Dividends = ECF	60,000	57,938	55,625	52,688	49,000	44,375
8 Interest + dividends (3) + (7)	60,000	62,063	64,375	67,313	71,000	75,625
9 Cost of debt: Kd	**8.00%**	**8.25%**	**8.75%**	**9.75%**	**11.00%**	**12.50%**
10 Required return on equity: Ke	**12.00%**	**12.50%**	**13.00%**	**13.50%**	**14.50%**	**16.00%**
11 Market value of debt D (3)/(9)	0	50,000	100,000	150,000	200,000	250,000
12 Market value of equity E (7)/(10)	500,000	463,500	427,885	390,278	337,931	277,344
13 Market value of the firm (11) + (12)	500,000	513,500	527,885	**540,278**	537,931	527,344
14 Book value of debt, N	0	50,000	100,000	150,000	200,000	250,000
15 Book value of equity, Ebv	500,000	450,000	400,000	350,000	300,000	250,000
16 Book value of the firm	500,000	500,000	500,000	500,000	500,000	500,000
17 Return on assets ROA = EBIT (1 − T)/(16)	12.00%	12.00%	12.00%	12.00%	12.00%	12.00%
18 Return on equity = (6)/(15)	12.00%	12.88%	13.91%	15.05%	16.33%	17.75%
19 Number of shares outstanding, NS	5,000	4,513	4,053	3,612	3,141	2,630
20 Price per share, P (12)/(19)	100	102.7	105.5769	**108.06**	107.5862	105.4688
21 Earnings per share, EPS. (6)/(19)	12	12.8375	13.725	14.5875	15.6	16.875

(continues)

Table 18.1 (*continued*)

1 Book value debt ratio (leverage)	0%	10%	20%	30%	40%	50%
22 Price earnings ratio, PER (20)/(21)	8.333333	8	7.692308	7.407407	6.896552	6.25
23 Book value debt ratio (14)/(16)	0%	10%	20%	30%	40%	50%
24 Market value debt ratio (11)/(13)	0.00%	9.74%	18.94%	27.76%	37.18%	47.41%
25 Weighted average cost of capital (WACC)	12.00%	11.68%	11.37%	**11.11%**	11.15%	11.38%
26 Free cash flow, FCF = EBIT (1 – T)	60,000	60,000	60,000	60,000	60,000	60,000
27 Market value of the firm (26)/(25)	500,000	513,500	527,885	**540,278**	537,931	527,344

debt and its equity. In the example, as debt is added to the capital structure, the company's market value (line 13) first increases and then decreases. The highest value of the company, $540,278, is attained with $150,000 of debt.

Company return versus investor return—Lines 14–16 of Table 18.1 give the book value of the debt and the equity. It is assumed that the debt's book value is the same as its market value. Lines 17 and 18 show the company's ROA and ROE. The ROA is not affected by leverage and is always 12%. Without any debt, ROA = ROE, but when debt is added, the ROE moves above the ROA, according to the formula[4]:

$$ROE = ROA + [N/Ebv][ROA - Kd(1 - T)]$$

N and Ebv represent the book value of the debt and the equity, respectively. The ROE represents the return on the equity's book value; however, the shareholders do not obtain this return, because their return depends on the market value. We already saw in Chapters 14 and 15 that the shareholder return has very little bearing with the ROE.

Earnings per share and price earnings ratios—Lines 19 and 20 show the number of shares outstanding and the price per share. These calculations are based on the assumption that, initially, the company has no debt and, in order to attain a certain level of leverage, the company issues debt and buys shares with the proceeds of the debt issue. The following sequence of events is assumed: (1) the company announces its intention to modify its long-term capital structure and issues debt; (2) its shares price changes to reflect the company's new value, and (3) the company repurchases shares at the new price. The share price is obtained from the following equation: $P = (E + D)/5000$.[5]

Lines 21 and 22 of Table 18.1 show the earnings per share (EPS) and the PER. Logically, the higher the debt is (and the smaller the number of shares), the higher the EPS is and, therefore, the higher the debt is, the lower the PER is. Lines 23 and 24 show the debt ratio calculated using book values and market values.

The weighted average cost of capital—Line 25 shows the average cost of capital (WACC) using the market value debt ratio. Line 26 shows the company's free cash flow, which is $60,000. Line 27 shows the company's value, calculated by discounting the free cash flow at the WACC. Logically, it is the same as that calculated in line 13.[6]

---

[4]The reader can deduce this expression from the following formulas, which correspond to the definition of ROA, ROE, and PAT: $ROA = NOPAT/(N + Ebv)$; $ROE = PAT/Ebv$; $PAT = NOPAT - Kd N(1 - T)$

[5]This equation is obtained from $NS \times P = E$ and from $NS = 5,000 - D/P$. NS is the number of shares after repurchase.

[6]The value of the company will increase as the WACC decreases if and only if the free cash flows are unaffected by the higher debt ratio. This is an assumption of the technical note.

Implications—The most important results obtained from Table 18.1 are to be found in lines 13, 20, and 25. The company's optimal capital structure is that which *simultaneously:*

1. Maximizes the company's value (line 13)
2. Maximizes the share price (line 20)
3. Minimizes the company's weighted average cost of capital (WACC)[7] (line 25)

Using the data given in Table 18.1, the optimal capital structure is attained with $150,000 of debt. Figure 18.1 shows how the company's optimal capital structure is determined: the company's value is highest and the WACC is lowest with $150,000 of debt (debt ratio = 30%). Figure 18.2 shows that the share price is also highest with $150,000 of debt (debt ratio = 30%).

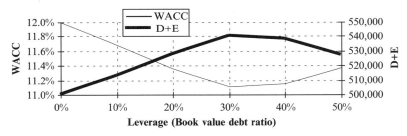

Figure 18.1 Value of the company and WACC at different debt ratios.

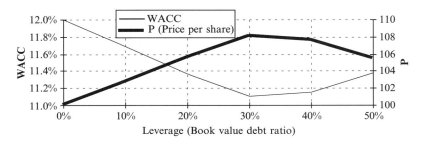

Figure 18.2 Price per share and WACC at different debt ratios.

[7]Because we are maximizing (D + E) in all three cases.

18.2. CRITICAL ANALYSIS OF THE HARVARD BUSINESS SCHOOL TECHNICAL NOTE

The existence of an optimal structure with a debt ratio of 30% depends on the debt and equity costs (lines 9 and 10) assumed by the note's author. The reader can see, for example, that with a graph in which Ke grows linearly with the debt ratio, the company's value increases at higher debt ratios. Likewise, if Ke were to be less than 14.4% (instead of 14.5%) for a debt level of $200,000, the optimal structure would be located at D = $200,000.

In this section, we will highlight certain inconsistencies in the debt and equity costs (lines 9 and 10) assumed by the note's author from a number of view points.

With respect to the cost of the debt, the inconsistency is not the cost of the debt (the bank can charge whatever interest it likes) but in assuming that the debt's cost is the same as its required return (or that the debt's value equals its nominal value).

18.2.1. PRESENT VALUE OF THE CASH FLOWS GENERATED BY THE COMPANY AND REQUIRED RETURN TO ASSETS

The sum of the debt cash flow, equity cash flow, and taxes at different debt levels is shown in line 2 of Table 18.2.

In Chapter 17, we saw that the tax risk in a perpetuity is the same as the equity risk. Consequently, the discount rate that must be used to calculate the taxes' present value is Ke, as shown in line 28.

The company's total value (line 29) decreases with the leverage. There are only two explanations for this:

1. The cash flows generated by the company decrease with the leverage. In this case, this is not so, because it is assumed that the EBIT is $120,000/ year, irrespective of the debt.

2. The company's risk (and that of its assets) increases with the leverage. This causes this company's value to decrease with the leverage, as we shall see in the following section. One explanation for this is that the providers of capital (shareholders, banks, and capital markets) perceive a higher risk (more volatile with a higher likelihood of bankruptcy) in the company as a whole the more debt it includes in its capital structure.

Table 18.2
Value of the Cash Flows Generated by the Company and Required Return to Assets

Book value of debt, D	0	50,000	100,00	150,000	200,000	250,000
5 Taxes	60,000	57,938	55,625	52,688	49,000	44,375
3 Debt cash flow (interest)	0	4,125	8,750	14,625	22,000	31,250
7 Equity cash flow (dividends)	60,000	57,938	55,625	52,688	49,000	44,375
2 **Sum = cash flow generated by the firm = EBIT**	120,000	120,000	120,000	120,000	120,000	120,000
28 Value of taxes, GOV = (5) / Ke	500,000	463,500	427,885	390,278	337,931	277,344
29 **D + E + GOV = (11) + (12) + (28)**	**1,000,000**	**977,000**	**955,769**	**930,556**	**875,862**	**804,688**
30 **Kassets = Ku = (2)/(29)**	**12.00%**	**12.28%**	**12.56%**	**12.90%**	**13.70%**	**14.91%**
31 Δ *Kassets = Ku*		*0.28%*	*0.27%*	*0.34%*	*0.81%*	*1.21%*

The required return to assets (line 30) increases with the leverage,[8] and increases much more when it goes above $150,000 (optimal structure). This sharp increase is the reason why an optimal structure exists.

18.2.2. Leverage Costs

The expression *adjusted present value*, APV, by which the value of the levered company (D + E) is the sum of the value of the unleveraged firm (Vu) plus the discounted value of the tax shield (DT because our firm is a perpetuity) less the cost of leverage, is

$$D + E = Vu + DT - \text{cost of leverage}$$

As we know that Vu = 500,000 (line 16), we can find the value of the cost of leverage (line 32 of Table 18.3). Note that cost of leverage increases sharply when the debt is increased from $150,000–200,000. The optimal structure appears just before the increase in the tax shield (line 34) becomes less than the increase in the cost of leverage (line 33).

18.2.3. Incremental Cost of Debt

In this section, we will analyze the incremental cost of debt. Table 18.4 and Figure 18.3 show this analysis. It will be readily seen that the fact that $100,000 of debt has a cost of 8.75% means that the first $50,000 has a cost of 8.25% and the next $50,000 has a cost of 9.25%. It is a little surprising that the last two $50,000 increments have a cost of 14.75 and 18.5%, particularly considering that the required return to equity in the unlevered company is 12%.

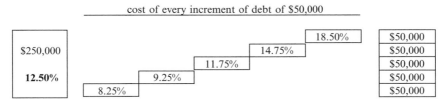

Figure 18.3   Composition of the $250,000 of debt, which has an overall cost of 12.5%.

[8]The required return to equity can also be obtained from the formula Kassets = [EKe + DKd(1 − T)]/[E + D(1 − T)].

Table 18.3

Cost of Leverage

Book value of debt, D	0	50,000	100,000	150,000	200,000	250,000
32 Cost of leverage	0	11,500	22,115	34,722	62,069	97,656
33 Δ Cost of leverage		11,500	10,615	12,607	27,347	35,587
34 Δ(DT)		25,000	25,000	25,000	25,000	25,000

Table 18.4

Incremental Cost of Debt

Book value of debt, D	0	50,000	100,000	150,000	200,000	250,000
35 First 50,000		8.25%	8.25%	8.25%	8.25%	8.25%
36 Next 50,000			9.25%	9.25%	9.25%	9.25%
37 Next 50,000				11.75%	11.75%	11.75%
38 Next 50,000					14.75%	14.75%
39 Next 50,000						18.50%
40 Average		8.25%	8.75%	9.75%	11.00%	12.50%

18.2.4. REQUIRED RETURN TO INCREMENTAL EQUITY CASH FLOW

When the debt level is decreased, dividends increase and the shares' value grows. The required return to incremental equity cash flow is calculated in Table 18.5 and Figure 18.4 by performing an analysis similar to that performed with debt.

The required return to incremental equity cash flow is calculated as follows. E_D is the shares' value when the company has a debt D. With this debt level, the dividends are Div. When the debt level is decreased, dividends increase to $(Div + \Delta Div)$ and the shares' value increases from E_D to $E_{D-} \cdot Ke^{INC}$ is the required return to the additional equity. The following equation must be met:

$$Ke^{INC} = \Delta Div/(E_{D-} - E_D)$$

Note that the required incremental return first falls from 7.63–7.04%, then increases to 7.81% and then falls again. The increase from 7.04–7.81% is an error because the required incremental return should reduce as the leverage decreases.

18.2.5. DIFFERENCE BETWEEN KE AND KD

Table 18.6 shows that the difference between Ke and Kd decreases for debt levels above $100,000.

18.2.6. PRICE PER SHARE FOR DIFFERENT DEBT LEVELS

Table 18.7 shows the price per share if the company's leverage goes from the debt-free situation to the desired level of leverage: it is the same as the

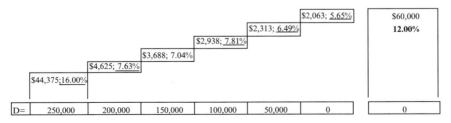

Figure 18.4   Required return to the incremental equity cash flow when the debt level is decreased.

Table 18.5

Required Return to Incremental Equity Cash Flow

Book value of debt, D	0	50,000	100,000	150,000	200,000	250,000
10 Ke	12.00%	12.50%	13.00%	13.50%	14.50%	16.00%
Required return to incremental equity cash flow (from right to left):						
41 Incremental equity cash flow (ΔDiv)		2,063	2,313	2,938	3,688	4,625
42 Required return to incremental equity cash flow		*5.65%*	*6.49%*	*7.81%*	*7.04%*	*7.63%*

Table 18.6

Difference between Ke and Kd

Book value of debt, D	0	50,000	100,000	150,000	200,000	250,000
43 Ke − Kd	4.00%	4.25%	4.25%	3.75%	3.50%	3.50%
44 Ke − Kd (1 − T)	8.000%	8.375%	8.625%	8.625%	9.000%	9.750%

Table 18.7

Price per Share for Each step of the Debt Level

Book value of debt, D	0	50,000	100,000	150,000	200,000	250,000
20 Price per share leveraging the firm from D = 0 until final leverage		102.70	105.58	**108.06**	107.59	105.47
45 Price per share leveraging the firm in steps of $50,000 each		102.70	108.62	**113.38**	106.20	97.77

price per share (line 20) of Table 18.1. Line 45 of Table 18.7 shows the price per share if the company's leverage is increased stepwise: first, $50,000 of debt are added, then another $50,000 and so on.

18.2.7. ADDING THE POSSIBILITY OF BANKRUPTCY TO THE MODEL

This model allocates a probability to the likelihood that the company will go bankrupt and there will be no more dividend or interest payments. In the extreme case that the bondholders recover none of their investment, the value of the interest payments they will receive is

$$I_{t+1} = I_t \quad \text{with a probability } p_c = 1 - p_q$$
$$0 = D_{t+1} \text{ with a probability } p_q$$

In this case, the debt's value at $t = 0$ is

$$D_0 = I(1 - p_q)/(Kd + p_q).$$

Kd is the required return on debt without leverage costs.
Isolating the probability of bankruptcy, we obtain:

$$p_q = (I - D_0 Kd)/(I + D_0)$$

From the shareholders' viewpoint, the value of the dividends they will receive is

$$Div_{t+1} = Div_t \text{ with a probability } p_c = 1 - p_q$$
$$0 = E_{t+1} \text{ with a probability } p_q$$

In this case, the shares' value at $t = 0$ is

$$E_0 = Div(1 - p_q)/(Ke + p_q).$$

Ke is the required return to equity without leverage costs.
Isolating the probability of bankruptcy, we obtain:

$$p_q = (Div - E_0 \ Ke)/(Div + E_0)$$

Table 18.8 shows that the required returns to debt and equity assume that the probability of bankruptcy of the debt exceeds that of the equity at debt levels greater than $150,000, which is absurd.

Upon performing a similar analysis with the entire company (debt, equity, and taxes), the annual expected cash flow for all three is constant, irrespective of the leverage, and is equal to $120,000 (see Table 18.2). Table 18.3 shows these flows' present value. The addition of the probability of bankruptcy (a total bankruptcy in which neither the bondholders nor the shareholders nor

Table 18.8
Probability of Bankruptcy of Debt and Equity

Book value of debt, D	0	50,000	100,000	150,000	200,000	250,000
46 Pq (debt)	0,000%	0.045%	0.307%	0.980%	1.820%	2.810%
47 Pq (shares)	0,000%	0.266%	0.517%	0.727%	1.328%	2.294%
Kd if Pq = 0	*8.00%*	*8.20%*	*8.42%*	*8.67%*	*8.98%*	*9.34%*
Ke if Pq = 0	*12.00%*	*12.20%*	*12.42%*	*12.67%*	*12.98%*	*13.34%*

the State can recover anything) would mean that the expected value of the cash flow for the next period would be

$$120,000 \text{ with a probability } p_c = 1 - p_q$$
$$0 = E_{t+1} + D_{t+1} + GOV_{t+1} \text{ with a probability } p_q$$

For each level of leverage,

$$E_0 + D_0 + GOV_0 = 120,000(1 - p_q)/(Ku + p_q)$$

The probability of total bankruptcy gives:

Debt	0	50,000	100,000	150,000	200,000	250,000
D + E + GOV	1,000,000	976,992	955,770	930,548	875,862	804,688
Equity cash flow, taxes, and debt cash flow	120,000	120,000	120,000	120,000	120,000	120,000
Pq (firm) if Ku = 12%	0.00%	0.25%	0.49%	0.79%	1.50%	2.53%

It can be seen that the probability of bankruptcy almost doubles when the debt level is increased from \$150,000–200,000.

18.2.8. KE AND KD IF THERE ARE NO LEVERAGE COSTS

If we assume that Ku = 12% (the assets' risk does not change with these debt levels and, therefore, there are no leverage costs), line 9′ of Table 18.9 shows the Kd that is obtained after applying formula (17.64):[9]

$$Kd = R_F + \frac{D(1 - T)(Ku - R_F)}{E + D(1 - T)} \tag{17.64}$$

---

[9]The reader can verify the deduction of this and the following equations in Chapter 17.

Table 18.9

Valuation without Leverage Costs

1	Book value debt level (leverage)	0%	10%	20%	30%	40%	50%
9	Cost of debt: r	**8.00%**	**8.25%**	**8.75%**	**9.75%**	**11.00%**	**12.50%**
9'	**Required return on debt: Kd**	**8.00%**	**8.20%**	**8.42%**	**8.67%**	**8.98%**	**9.34%**
10	**Required return on equity: Ke**	**12.00%**	**12.20%**	**12.42%**	**12.67%**	**12.98%**	**13.34%**
11	Market value of debt, D (3)/(9')	0	50,298	103,970	168,600	244,990	334,635
12	Market value of equity, E (7)/(10)	500,000	474,851	448,015	415,700	377,505	332,683
13	Market value of the firm (11) + (12)	500,000	525,149	551,985	584,300	622,495	667,317
19	Number of shares outstanding, NS	5,000	4,524	4,088	3,674	3,268	2,855
20	Price per share, P (12)/(19)	100	104.970	109.603	113.140	115.501	116.537
24	Market value debt level (leverage) (11)/(13)	0.00%	9.58%	18.84%	28.85%	39.36%	50.15%
25	Weighted average cost of capital (WACC)	12.00%	11.43%	10.87%	10.27%	9.64%	8.99%
28	Value of taxes, GOV = (5) / Ke	500,000	474,851	448,015	415,700	377,505	332,683
29	D + E + GOV = (11) + (12) + (28)	1,000,000	1,000,000	1,000,000	1,000,000	1,000,000	1,000,000

In all cases, r > Kd, which is why the debt's value is greater than its nominal value. Similarly, line 10 shows the Ke obtained after applying equation (17.66):

$$Ke = Ku + Kd - R_F \qquad (17.66)$$

Note that in this case:

1. There is no optimal structure. The company's value (line 13) increases with the debt ratio.
2. The debt's value is substantially higher than the nominal value.
3. The difference between Ke and Kd is constant and equal to 4%.

18.2.9. KE AND KD WITH LEVERAGE COSTS

Table 18.10 assumes the existence of leverage costs, shown by the use of the reduced formula for the leveraged beta, which is equivalent to using formula (17.38) for the required return to equity:

$$Ke = Ku + (D/E)(Ku - R_F)$$

This is equivalent to assuming that the required return to assets increases with the leverage (line 30).

Kd is calculated using the formula:

$$Kd = R_F + [D(1 - T)(Kassets - R_F)]/[E + D(1 - T)]$$

In this case, as the leverage is increased, the WACC decreases, and the company's value increases. The maximum price per share occurs at N = $150,000.

Note that lines 31, 33, 34, 42, 43, 46, and 47 no longer have the inconsistencies identified in previous sections.

18.2.10. INFLUENCE OF GROWTH ON THE OPTIMAL STRUCTURE

If a perpetual growth g is applied to the data in Table 18.1 and it is assumed that the first year's investment in net fixed assets and WCR (working capital requirements) is $500,000 × g (all $500,000 of the initial outlay is invested in WCR and fixed assets), for any growth level the optimal structure continues to be a debt level of $150,000.

Table 18.10
Valuation with Leverage Costs

1	Book value debt level (leverage)	0%	10%	20%	30%	40%	50%
9	**Cost of debt: r**	**8.00%**	**8.25%**	**8.75%**	**9.75%**	**11.00%**	**12.50%**
9′	**Required return on debt: Kd**	**8.00%**	**8.22%**	**8.48%**	**8.86%**	**9.41%**	**10.27%**
10	Required return on equity: Ke	**12.00%**	**12.43%**	**12.96%**	**13.72%**	**14.83%**	**16.54%**
11	Market value of debt, D (3)/(9′)	0	50,210	103,174	165,074	233,685	304,337
12	Market value of equity, E (7)/(10)	500,000	466,076	429,150	384,038	330,438	268,346
13	Market value of the firm. (11)+(12)	500,000	516,286	532,324	549,112	564,123	572,683
19	Number of shares outstanding, NS	5,000	4,516	4,055	3,596	3,115	2,588
20	Price per share, P (12)/(19)	100	103.2152	105.8301	**106.8076**	106.0877	103.6692
21	Earnings per share (EPS) (6)/(19)	12	12.8306	13.7173	14.6533	15.7315	17.1432
22	Price-earnings ratio, PER	8.33333	8.04446	7.71506	7.28898	6.74364	6.04724
24	Market value debt level (leverage). (11)/(13)	0.00%	9.73%	19.38%	30.06%	41.42%	53.14%
25	Weighted average cost of capital (WACC)	12.00%	11.62%	11.27%	10.93%	10.64%	10.48%
28	Value of taxes. GOV = (5) / Ke	500,000	466,076	429,150	384,038	330,438	268,346
29	D + E + GOV = (11) + (12) + (28)	**1,000,000**	**982,362**	**961,475**	**933,150**	**894,562**	**841,029**
30	**Kassets = (2) / (29)**	**12.00%**	**12.22%**	**12.48%**	**12.86%**	**13.41%**	**14.27%**
31	Δ *Kassets*		*0.22%*	*0.27%*	*0.38%*	*0.55%*	*0.85%*
32	Δ Cost of leverage	0	8,819	19,263	33,425	52,719	79,486
33	Δ Cost of leverage		8,819	10,444	14,163	19,294	26,766
34	Δ (DT)		25,105	26,482	30,950	34,305	35,326

(continues)

Table 18.10 (*continued*)

1 Book value debt level (leverage)	0%	10%	20%	30%	40%	50%
Required return to incremental equity cash flow (from right to left):						
41 Incremental equity cash flow (ΔDiv)	2,063	2,313	2,938	3,688	4,625	
42 Required return to incremental equity cash flow	*6.08%*	*6.26%*	*6.51%*	*6.88%*	*7.45%*	
43 Ke − Kd	**4.00%**	**4.22%**	**4.48%**	**4.86%**	**5.41%**	**6.27%**
44 Ke − Kd(1 − T)	**8.00%**	**8.32%**	**8.72%**	**9.29%**	**10.12%**	**11.40%**
45 Price per share, Incremental repurchase	0	103.215	108.581	**108.818**	103.985	95.006
46 Pq (debt)	0,000%	0.013%	0.060%	0.170%	0.397%	0.843%
47 Pq (shares)	0,000%	0.204%	0.483%	0.919%	1.610%	2.744%

18.3. BOEING'S OPTIMAL CAPITAL STRUCTURE ACCORDING TO DAMODARAN

Damodaran[10] offers a similar approach to that of the Harvard Business School example analyzed, but applies it to a real company (Boeing in 1990) and assumes a constant cash flow growth of 8.86%.

Damodaran's calculations are summarized in Table 18.11. According to him, Boeing's optimal structure[11] is attained with a debt ratio of 30% (the debt ratio is calculated from the equity's book value). One problem with Table 18.11 is that the value of the firm (D + E) for debt ratios above 70% is less than the value of the debt, which implies a negative value for the equity. Of course, this does not make any sense.

The last column of Table 18.11 shows the cost of the assumed debt increments. It can be seen that increasing the debt by $1.646 billion to take the debt ratio from 30–40% implies contracting that debt at 21.5%, which is an enormous figure. Stranger still is the finding that the next debt increment (which has a higher risk) is cheaper: it costs 19%.

Table 18.12 shows the forecast income statements and cash flows for Boeing with different leverages.

Table 18.11

Optimal Capital Structure for Boeing (Million Dollars), March 1990

Leverage (book value)	Value of the firm	Value of debt	Value of equity	Cost of debt (after tax)	Cost of debt	Incremental debt	Cost of incremental debt
10%	17,683	1,646	16,037	6.40%	9.70%	1,646	**9.70%**
20%	18,968	3,292	15,676	6.93%	10.50%	1,646	**11.30%**
30%	**19,772**	4,938	14,834	7.59%	11.50%	1,646	**13.50%**
40%	18,327	6,584	11,743	9.24%	14.00%	1,646	**21.50%**
50%	17,657	8,230	9,427	9.90%	15.00%	1,646	**19.00%**
60%	14,257	9,876	4,381	11.72%	16.50%	1,646	**24.00%**
70%	10,880	11,522	**−642**	13.90%	18.00%	1,646	**27.00%**
80%	9,769	13,168	**−3,399**	14.42%	**18.00%**	1,646	**18.00%**
90%	8,864	14,814	**−5,950**	14.81%	18.00%	1,646	**18.00%**

Source: Damodaran on valuation, pp. 159.

[10]See Damodaran (1994), *Damodaran on Valuation*. pp. 157–164 and 167–169.
[11]In March 1990, the book value of Boeing's debt stood at $277 million and the market value of its equity was $16.182 billion. Consequently, the company's value, according to Damodaran, was $16.459 billion (0.277 + 16.182).

Table 18.12

Optimal Capital Structure for Boeing, Capital Structure, Income Statements and Cash Flows according to Damodaran (Million Dollars), March 1990

1	D/(D + E) book value	0%	10%	20%	30%	40%	50%	60%	70%	80%	90%
2	(D/E)book value	0%	11%	25%	43%	67%	100%	150%	233%	400%	900%
3	Debt (D)	0	1,646	3,292	4,938	6,584	8,230	9,876	11,522	13,168	14,814
4	Kd	9.7%	9.7%	10.5%	11.5%	14.0%	15.0%	16.5%	18.0%	18.0%	18.0%
5	Taxes	34%	34%	34%	34%	34%	34%	28.96%	22.76%	19.91%	17.70%
6	Beta unleveraged	0.94	0.94	0.94	0.94	0.94	0.94	0.94	0.94	0.94	0.94
	Income statement of year 0										
7	Margin	2,063	2,063	2,063	2,063	2,063	2,063	2,063	2,063	2,063	2,063
8	Depreciation	675	675	675	675	675	675	675	675	675	675
9	Interest	0	160	346	568	922	1,235	1,630	2,074	2,370	2,667
10	Profit before taxes	1,388	1,228	1,042	820	466	154	−242	−686	−982	−1,279
11	Taxes (34%)	472	418	354	279	159	52	−82	−233	−334	−435
12	**Profit after taxes**	**916**	**811**	**688**	**541**	**308**	**101**	**−159**	**−453**	**−648**	**−844**
13	+ Depreciation	675	675	675	675	675	675	675	675	675	675
14	− Investment in fixed assets	800	800	800	800	800	800	800	800	800	800
15	− Investment in working capital	0	0	0	0	0	0	0	0	0	0
16	+ Increase of debt	0	146	292	438	583	729	875	1,021	1,167	1,313
17	**Equity cash flow, ECF**	**791**	**832**	**855**	**854**	**766**	**705**	**591**	**443**	**393**	**344**
18	**Free cash flow, FCF**	**791**	**791**	**791**	**791**	**791**	**791**	**791**	**791**	**791**	**791**
19	g (growth)	8.86%	8.86%	8.86%	8.86%	8.86%	8.86%	8.86%	8.86%	8.86%	8.86%

Source: Damodaran on valuation, pp. 167–169.

Table 18.13 contains the valuation of the cash flows and is the origin of the numbers in Table 18.12. Another error in Table 18.13 is that lines 26 and 27 are only equal[12] for the unlevered company. Why is this so? Basically, for two reasons:

1. Damodaran calculates the WACC using book values in the weighting, instead of market values.
2. Damodaran calculates the interest to be paid in year 0 (line 9 of Table 18.12) by multiplying the debt in year 0 (line 3) by the cost of the debt (line 4). In order to obtain a correct valuation, the interest for year 0 should be calculated by multiplying the debt in the previous year (year −1) by the cost of the debt. This affects the equity cash flow.

Furthermore, the debt is not the percentage of the firm value that Damodaran claims.

We leave the reader to verify that when these two adjustments are made, lines 26 and 27 of Table 18.13 match. The main lines that change are the following:

	D/(D + E) book value	0%	10%	20%	30%	40%	50%	60%	70%	80%	90%
9	Interest**	0.0	146.7	317.5	521.7	846.7	1,134.0	1,496.9	1,905.2	2,177.3	2,449.5
16	+ Increase of debt	0.0	134.0	267.9	401.9	535.9	669.8	803.8	937.8	1,071.7	1,205.7
17	Equity cash flow, ECF	791.1	828.2	849.4	848.7	768.1	712.5	601.4	413.3	314.6	207.1

Santoma (1994) proves that a company with a real production process should not invest in financial assets. The value of the real production process and the financial asset are larger when held separately.

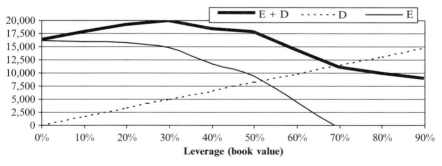

Figure 18.5   Boeing according to Damodaran (1994). Value of the firm (D + E), debt, and equity, for different debt ratios.

---

[12]Line 26 is the equity value (E) calculated by the free cash flow method (also called WACC method). Line 27 is the equity value (E) calculated by the equity cash flow method.

Table 18.13

Optimal Capital Structure for Boeing. Valuation According to Damodaran, Data in Million Dollars, March of 1990

D/(D + E) book value	0%	10%	20%	30%	40%	50%	60%	70%	80%	90%
20 Leveraged beta	0.94	1.0089	1.0951	1.2059	1.3536	1.5604	1.9417	2.6341	3.9514	7.9026
21 Market risk premium	5.5%	5.5%	5.5%	5.5%	5.5%	5.5%	5.5%	5.5%	5.5%	5.5%
22 R_F	9.0%	9.0%	9.0%	9.0%	9.0%	9.0%	9.0%	9.0%	9.0%	9.0%
23 Ke' (calculated with book value)	14.17%	14.55%	15.02%	15.63%	16.44%	17.58%	19.68%	23.49%	30.73%	52.46%
24 WACCbv (calculated with book value)	14.17%	13.73%	13.40%	13.21%	13.56%	13.74%	14.90%	16.77%	17.67%	18.57%
25 (D + E) = PV(FCF; WACC)	16,218	17,683	18,968	19,797	18,323	17,647	14,258	10,887	9,775	8,869
26 −D = E1	16,218	16,037	15,676	14,859	11,739	9,417	4,382	−635	−3,393	−5,945
27 E2 = PV(ECF;Ke)	16,218	15,911	15,095	13,724	10,995	8,805	5,942	3,298	1,958	858

Source: Damodaran on valuation, pp. 167–169.

REFERENCES

Damodaran, A. (1994), *Damodaran on Valuation*, New York: John Wiley and Sons.

Fruhan, W. E., W. C. Kester, S. P. Mason, T. R. Piper, and R. S. Ruback (1992), "Note on the Theory of Optimal Capital Structure," in *Case Problems in Finance*, 10th edition, New York: Irwin.

Santoma, J. (1994), "Investment Allocation Under Limited Liability Rules," IESE Business School Research Paper Db / 266.

Chapter 19

Financial Literature about Discounted Cash Flow Valuation

There is a wealth of literature about discounted cash flow valuation. In this chapter, we will discuss the most important papers,[1] highlighting those that propose different expressions for the present value of the tax shield (DVTS).

The discrepancies between the various theories on the valuation of a company's equity using discounted cash flows originate in the calculation of the DVTS. This chapter illustrates and analyzes seven different theories on the calculation of the DVTS: No-cost-of-leverage, Myers (1974), Miller (1977), Miles and Ezzell (1980), Harris and Pringle (1985), Ruback (1995), Damodaran (1994), and the practitioners' method. We show that Myers' method (1974) gives inconsistent results. This chapter also presents a new interpretation of the theories: it is considered that the difference between the company's value given by no-cost-of-leverage (zero failure costs) and the company's value given by these theories is the leverage cost. When analyzing the results obtained by the different theories, it is advisable to remember that the DVTS is not exactly the present value of the tax shield discounted at a certain rate but the difference between two present values: the present value of the taxes paid by the unlevered company less the present value of the taxes paid by the levered company. The risk of the taxes paid by the unlevered company is less than the risk of the taxes paid by the levered company.

---

[1] It is a good idea to know what the experts on the subject have said in order to not make the mistake that Seneca warned us against: "He who is his own master becomes disciple to an ass."

19.1. A BRIEF REVIEW OF THE MOST SIGNIFICANT PAPERS

Gordon and E. Shapiro (1956) showed that the present value of a flow F growing at the rate g, when discounted at the rate K, is

$$PV_0 = F_1/(K - g)$$

Modigliani and Miller (1958) studied the effect of leverage on the firm's value. Their proposition 1 (1958, formula 3) states that, in the absence of taxes, the firm's value is independent of its debt, i.e., $E + D = Vu$, if $T = 0$. E is the equity value, D is de debt value, Vu is the value of the unlevered company ant T is the tax rate.

In the presence of taxes, their second proposition (1963, formula 12.c) states that the required return on equity flows (Ke) increases at a rate that is directly proportional to the debt to equity ratio (D/E) at market value:

$$Ke = Ku + (D/E) (1 - T) (Ku - Kd) \qquad (19.1)$$

In the presence of taxes and for the case of a perpetuity, their first proposition is transformed into (1963, formula 3):

$$E_0 + D_0 = Vu + DT \qquad (19.2)$$

DT is the DVTS for a perpetuity. But it is important to note that they arrive to the value of DVTS by discounting the present value of the tax savings due to interest payments of a risk free debt $(T\ D\ R_F)$ at the risk free rate (R_F).

As we will prove later on, although the result is correct, to discount the tax savings due to interest payments of a risk free debt at the risk free rate provides inconsistent results for growing companies.

They also state in their paper (1963, formula 33.c) that, in an investment that can be financed totally by debt, the required return on the debt must be equal to the required return on the asset flows: if $D/(D + E) = 100\%$, $Kd = Ku$.

The purpose of Modigliani and Miller was to illustrate the tax impact of debt on value. They never addressed the issue of the riskiness of the taxes and only treated perpetuities. If we relax the no-growth assumption, then new formulas are needed.

In the case of dividends, they said that they were irrelevant if the taxes on dividends and capital gains were the same. Given equal taxes, the shareholder would have no preference between receiving dividends or selling shares.

Modigliani and Miller (1963) give a number of valuation formulas that we shall use in this book:

Their formula (31.c) is

$$WACC = Ku\ [1 - TD/(E + D)]$$

Their formula (11.c) is

$$WACC_{BT} = Ku - DT\ (Ku - Kd)/(E + D)$$

However, in their last equation, Modigliani and Miller (1963) propose calculating the company's target finance structure [D/(D + E)] using book values for D and E, instead of market values. This is obviously incorrect.

Myers (1974) was responsible for introducing the APV (adjusted present value). According to Myers, the value of the levered company is equal to the value of the debt-free company (Vu) plus the present value of the tax shield due to the payment of interest (DVTS). Myers proposes that the DVTS be calculated as follows:

$$DVTS = PV\ [Kd;\ TDKd] \tag{19.3}$$

The argument is that the risk of the tax saving arising from the use of debt is the same as the risk of the debt. Luehrman (1997) recommends to value companies using the APV and he calculates the DVTS as Myers.

And the company's value is

$$APV = E + D = Vu + DVTS = PV\ [Ku;\ FCF] + PV\ [Kd;\ TDKd]$$

We will see later on that this theory provides inconsistent results.

Benninga and Sarig (1997) claim that if there are personal taxes, the tax benefits of the debt should be discounted with after-personal-tax discount rates. According to them,

$$DVTS = PV\ [Kd\ (1 - T_{PD});\ DKd\ [(1 - T_{PD}) - (1 - T)\ (1 - T_{PA})]]$$

The corporate income tax is T, the personal tax rate on shares is T_{PA} and the personal tax rate on debt is T_{PD}. Note that if $T_{PA} = T_{PD}$, then Benninga and Sarig's formula becomes (19.3).

Arditti and Levy (1977) suggest that the company's value be calculated by discounting the capital cash flows, CCF (equity cash flow plus debt cash flow) instead of the free cash flow (FCF). The (CCFS) must be discounted at the $WACC_{BT}$ (WACC before tax). It is readily shown that:

$$D + E = PV\ [WACC;\ FCF] = PV\ [WACC_{BT};\ CCF]$$

where $WACC_{BT}$ is

$$WACC_{BT_t} = Ke\ \frac{E_{t-1}}{E_{t-1} + D_{t-1}} + Kd\ \frac{D_{t-1}}{E_{t-1} + D_{t-1}} \tag{19.4}$$

Arditti and Levy's paper (1977) suffers from one basic problem: they calculate the weights of debt ($D/[E + D]$) and equity ($E/[E + D]$) at book value instead of market value. Hence their statement (page 28) that the company's value obtained by discounting the FCF is different from that obtained by discounting the CCF.

Miller (1977) argues that while there is an optimal debt structure for companies as a whole, such a structure does not exist for each company. Miller argues that due to the clientele effect, debt does not add any value to the company. Consequently, according to Miller, $E + D = Vu$.

He also introduces personal income tax as well as corporate income tax. The tax rate for the company is T, the personal tax rate on shares is T_{PA}, and the personal tax rate on debt is T_{PD}.

According to Miller, for a perpetuity, the value of the debt-free company after personal income tax is

$$Vu = FCF \; (1 - T_{PA})/Ku$$

If the company has debt with a nominal value N, its value is

$$D = NKd \; (1 - T_{PD})/Kd$$

Miller says that the value created by debt, in the case of a perpetuity, is

$$D[1 - (1 - T) \; (1 - T_{PA})/(1 - T_{PD})]$$

But he goes on to say (see page 268) that any attempt by a company to increase its value by increasing its debt would be incompatible with market balance. The increased debt would generate changes in the required returns to debt and equity and in the shares' owners, with the result that the company's value will be independent of debt.

Miller also says that if $T_{PA} = 0$, the aggregate debt supply must be such that it offers an interest $R_0/(1 - T)$, where R_0 is the rate paid by tax-free institutions.

Miller and Scholes (1978) show that, even if the income tax rate is greater than the capital gains tax rate, many investors will not pay more than the capital gains tax rate charged on dividends. They conclude that investors will have no preference between receiving dividends or realizing capital gains if the company buys back shares. According to these authors, the company's value will not depend on its dividend policy, not even in the presence of corporate and personal income tax.

DeAngelo and Masulis (1980) expand on Miller's work. Considering that the marginal tax rate is different for different companies, they predict that companies will use less debt the greater their possibilities for reducing tax by other means: depreciation, deduction of investments, etc.

Miles and Ezzell (1980) maintain that the APV and the WACC give different values: "unless debt and, consequently, Ke are exogenous (they do not depend on the company's value at any given time), the traditional WACC is not appropriate for valuing companies." According to them, a company that wishes to maintain a constant D/E ratio must not be valued in the same way as a company that has a preset amount of debt. Specifically, formula (20) in their paper states that for a company with a fixed target debt ratio [D/(D + E)], the FCF must be discounted at the rate:

$$WACC = Ku - [D/(E + D)] [KdT(1 + Ku)/(1 + Kd)]$$

They arrive at this formula from their formula (11) which, for a growing perpetuity, is

$$E_{t-1} + D_{t-1} = FCF_t/(Ku - g) + KdTD_{t-1}/(Ku - g)$$

They say that the correct rate at which the tax saving due to debt (KdT D_{t-1}) must be discounted is Kd for the first year's tax saving and Ku for the following years' tax savings.

The expression of Ke is their formula (22):

$$Ke = Ku + D (Ku - Kd) [1 + Kd (1 - T)]/[(1 + Kd)E]$$

Miles and Ezzell (1985) show in their formula (27) that the relationship between levered beta and asset beta (assuming that the debt is risk-free and the debt's beta is zero) is

$$\beta_L = \beta u + D\beta u [1 - TR_F/(1 + R_F)]/E$$

Chambers, Harris, and Pringle (1982) compare four discounted cash flow valuation methods: the equity cash flow (ECF) at the rate Ke (required return to equity); the FCF at the WACC; the CCF at the $WACC_{BT}$ (weighted average cost of capital before tax); and Myers' APV. They say that the first three methods give the same value if debt is constant, but different values if it is not constant. They also say that the APV only gives the same result as the other three methods in two cases: in companies with only one period, and in no-growth perpetuities. The reason for their results is an error: they calculate the debt ratio (D/[D + E]) using book values instead of market values. Their Exhibit 3 is proof of this: it is impossible for the WACC and Ke to be constant. If Ke = 11.2%, as they propose, the correct WACC is 6.819% in the first year (instead of their 5.81%) and increases in the following years; and the correct $WACC_{BT}$ is 7.738% in the first year (instead of their 6.94%) and increases in following years. When the debt ratio (D/[D + E]) is calculated using market values, all three procedures give the same value.

Harris and Pringle (1985) propose that the present value of the tax saving due to the payment of interest (DVTS) should be calculated by discounting the tax saving due to the debt (Kd T D) at the rate Ku:

$$DVTS = PV \,[Ku; \; D \; Kd \; T] \tag{19.5}$$

They also propose in their formula (3) that $WACC_{BT} = Ku$ and, therefore, their expression for the WACC is

$$WACC = Ku - D \; Kd \; T/(D + E) \tag{19.6}$$

Harris and Pringle (1985) say

> "the MM position is considered too extreme by some because it implies that interest tax shields are no more risky than the interest payments themselves. The Miller position is too extreme for some because it implies that debt cannot benefit the firm at all. Thus, if the truth about the value of tax shields lies somewhere between the MM and Miller positions, a supporter of either Harris and Pringle or Miles and Ezzell can take comfort in the fact that both produce a result for unlevered returns between those of MM and Miller. A virtue of either Harris and Pringle compared to Miles and Ezzell is its simplicity and straightforward intuitive explanation."

Ruback (1995) assumes in his formula (2.6) that $\beta_L = \beta u(D + E)/ E - \beta dD/E$. With this assumption he arrives at formulas that are identical to those of Harris and Pringle (1985).

Kaplan and Ruback (1995) also calculate the DVTS "discounting interest tax shields at the discount rate for an all-equity firm."

Tham and Vélez-Pareja (2001), following an arbitrage argument, also claim that the appropriate discount rate for the tax shield is Ku, the return to unlevered equity. We will see later on that this theory provides inconsistent results.

Lewellen and Emery (1986) propose three alternative ways to calculate the DVTS. They claim that the most logically consistent is the method proposed by Miles and Ezzell. But one method, that they label Modigliani-Miller, assumes the calculation (see their equation 15) of the DVTS as: PV[Ku; D T Ku]. As will be discussed later in the chapter, this is the only method that provides logically consistent values in a world without cost of leverage.

Taggart (1991) gives a good summary of valuation formulas with and without personal income tax. He proposes that Miles and Ezzell's (1980) formulas should be used when the company adjusts to its target debt ratio once a year and Harris and Pringle's (1985) formulas when the company continuously adjusts to its target debt ratio.

Damodaran (1994) argues[2] that if the business's full risk is borne by the equity, then the formula that relates levered beta (β_L) with asset beta (βu) is:

---

[2]See page 31 of his book *Damodaran on Valuation*. This expression of levered beta appears in many books and is frequently used by consultants and investment banks.

$\beta_L = \beta u + (D/E)\,\beta u\,(1 - T)$. This expression is obtained from the no-cost-of-leverage relationship between levered beta, asset beta, and debt beta,[3] eliminating the debt beta. It is important to realize that it is not the same to eliminate the debt beta as to assume that it is zero, as Damodaran says. If the debt beta were to be zero, the required return to debt should be the risk-free rate. The purpose of eliminating the debt beta is to obtain a higher levered beta (and a higher Ke and a lower equity value) than that given by the no-cost-of-leverage, which is equivalent to introducing leverage costs in the valuation

Another way of relating the levered beta with the asset beta is the following: $\beta_L = \beta u(E + D)/E$. We will call this formula the *practitioners' formula*, as it is a formula commonly used by consultants and investment banks.[4] Obviously, according to this formula, assuming that βu is the same, a higher beta (higher leverage costs) is obtained than according to the no-cost-of- leverage and Damodaran (1994).

Inselbag and Kaufold (1997) argue that if the firm targets the dollar values of debt outstanding, the DVTS is given by Myers' formula. However, if the firm targets a constant debt/value ratio, the DVTS is given by Miles and Ezzell's formula.[5] The authors use the example of a company, Media Inc., with two alternative financing strategies: the first, setting the planned quantity of debt and the second, setting the debt ratio.

According to them, the present value of the tax shield due to the payment of interest (DVTS) is greater if the company sets the planned quantity of debt than if it sets the debt ratio. We do not agree with this for two reasons. The first is that we do not see any companies firing their COO or CFO because they propose a target debt ratio (instead of fixing the quantity of debt). The second is that, as we have already said, the DVTS is the difference between two present values: that of taxes in the unlevered company and that of taxes in the levered company. Inselbag and Kaufold argue that having a target debt ratio is riskier than setting the quantity of debt. If this were to be so, the present value of the taxes to be paid in the levered company should be greater in the company that sets the quantity of debt and, consequently, the DVTS would be less, which is exactly the opposite of what they propose.

Copeland, Koller, and Murrin (2000)[6] treat the APV in their Appendix A. They only mention perpetuities and propose only two ways of calculating the DVTS: Harris and Pringle (1985) and Myers (1974). They conclude *"we leave*

---

[3]The relationship between levered beta, asset beta, and debt beta, according to the no-cost-of-leverage theory is $\beta_L = \beta_U + (D/E)(\beta_U - \beta_d)(1 - T)$. This relationship may also be obtained from Modigliani-Miller (1963) for perpetuities.

[4]One of the many places where it can be found is Ruback (1995), p. 5.

[5]Copeland (2000) suggests only this paper as additional reading on APV (pp. 483).

[6]See page 477.

it to the reader's judgment to decide which approach best fits his or her situation." They also claim that "the finance literature does not provide a clear answer about which discount rate for the tax benefit of interest is theoretically correct."

Fernandez (2001) shows that the discounted value of tax shields is the difference between the present values of two different cash flows with their own risk: the present value of taxes for the unlevered company and the present value of taxes for the levered company. This implies as a first guideline that, for the particular case of a perpetuity and a world without costs of leverage, the discounted value of tax shields is equal to the tax rate times the value of debt (i.e., the no-cost-of-leverage, Myers, and Modigliani-Miller). The discounted value of tax shields can be lower, when costs of leverage exist. In that case, it is shown that, since the existence of leverage costs is independent of taxes, a second guideline for the appropriateness of the valuation method should be that the discounted value of tax shields when there are no taxes is negative.

Twenty-three valuation theories proposed in the literature to estimate the present discounted value of tax shields are analyzed according to their performance relative to the proposed guidelines. By analyzing perpetuities, the author is able to eliminate eight theories that do not provide us with a value of the tax shield of DT (as the candidates for a world without cost-of-leverage should), nor do they provide us with a negative DVTS when there are no taxes (as the candidates for a world with leverage cost should). The eight candidates eliminated due to a lack of consistent results include Harris and Pringle (1985) or Ruback (1995), Miles and Ezzell (1980), and Miller (1977).

By analyzing constant growth companies, the author is able to see there is but one theory that provides consistent results in a world without leverage cost. In accordance with this theory, the DVTS is the present value of DTKu discounted at the unlevered cost of equity (Ku). It is *not* the interest tax shield that is discounted.

The author finds three theories that provide consistent results in a world with leverage cost: Fernandez (2001),[7] Damodaran (1994), and Practitioners. Only Fernandez (2001) is fully applicable, while the other two are applicable up to a certain point. The differences among the theories can be attributed to the implied leverage cost in each of them.

Following an empirical approach, Graham (2000) estimates value creation due to debt at 9.7% of the company's value. If personal income tax is included, value creation is reduced to 4.3% of the company's value. The author concludes saying "I suspect that many debt-conservative firms, if they objectively consider the issue, will reach the conclusion that they should use more debt."

---

[7]According to Fernandez (2001), $DVTS = PV[Ku; D(Ku\ T + R_F - Kd)]$

19.2. MAIN FORMULAE IN THE MOST SIGNIFICANT PAPERS

19.2.1. DIFFERENT EXPRESSIONS OF THE DISCOUNTED VALUE OF THE TAX SHIELD AND OF THE REQUIRED RETURN TO EQUITY

Table 19.1 contains the eight most important theories. For each theory, the table contains the formula for calculating the DVTS and the equation that relates the required return to equity, Ke, with the required return to assets (or required return to unlevered equity), Ku.

According to the no-cost-of-leverage theory, the DVTS is the present value of DTKu (*not* the interest tax shield) discounted at the unlevered cost of equity (Ku). This theory implies that the relationship between the leveraged beta and the unlevered beta is

$$\beta_L = \beta u + \frac{D(1 - T)}{E}(\beta u - \beta d) \qquad (19.7)$$

The second theory is that of Damodaran (1994). Although Damodaran does not mention what should be the discounted value of the tax shield, his formula relating the levered beta with the asset beta

$$\beta_L = \beta u + \frac{D(1 - T)}{E}\beta u \qquad (19.8)$$

implies that

$$DVTS = PV[Ku; DTKu - D (Kd - R_F) (1 - T)]$$

It is important to notice that formula (19.8) is exactly formula (19.7) assuming that $\beta d = 0$. Although one interpretation of this assumption is that "all of the firm's risk is borne by the stockholders (i.e., the beta of the debt is zero),"[8] we think that it is difficult to justify that the return on the debt is uncorrelated with the return on assets of the firm. We rather interpret formula (19.8) as an attempt to introduce leverage cost in the valuation: for a given risk of the assets (βu), by using formula (19.8) we obtain a higher β_L (and consequently a higher Ke and a lower equity value) than with formula (19.7).

We label the third theory as being that of practitioners. The formula that relates the levered beta with the asset beta

$$\beta_L = \beta u + \frac{D}{E}\beta u \qquad (19.9)$$

implies that

[8]See page 31 of Damodaran (1994).

Table 19.1
Competing Theories for Calculating the Value of the Tax Shields

Theories	DVTS	Ke
1 No-cost-of-leverage	$PV[Ku; DTKu]$	$Ke = Ku + \dfrac{D(1-T)}{E}(Ku - Kd)$
2 Damodaran (1994)	$PV[Ku; DTKu - D(Kd - R_F)(1 - T)]$	$Ke = Ku + \dfrac{D(1-T)}{E}(Ku - R_F)$
3 Practitioners	$PV[Ku; T\,D\,Kd - D(Kd - R_F)]$	$Ke = Ku + \dfrac{D}{E}(Ku - R_F)$
4 Harris-Pringle (1985), Ruback (1995)	$PV[Ku; T\,D\,Kd]$	$Ke = Ku + \dfrac{D}{E}(Ku - Kd)$
5 Myers (1974)	$PV[Kd; T\,D\,Kd]$	$Ke = Ku + \dfrac{D - DVTS}{E}(Ku - Kd)$
6 Miles-Ezzell (1980)	$PV[Ku; T\,DKd](1 + Ku)/(1 + Kd_0)$	$Ke = Ku + \dfrac{D}{E}(Ku - Kd)\left[1 - \dfrac{T\,Kd}{1 + Kd}\right]$
7 Miller (1977)	0	$Ke = Ku + \dfrac{D}{E}[Ku - Kd(1 - T)]$
8 Fernandez (2001)	$PV[Ku; D\,(KuT + R_F - Kd)]$	$Ke = Ku + \dfrac{D}{E}[Ku(1 - T) + KdT - R_F]$

PV = present value; T = corporate tax rate; Ku = cost of unlevered equity (required return of unlevered equity); Ke = cost of levered equity (required return of levered equity); Kd = required return of debt = cost of debt; D = value of debt; E = value of equity; R_F = risk free rate; WACC = weighted average cost of capital.

$$DVTS = PV[Ku; \, T \, D \, Ku - D(Kd - R_F)]$$

It is important to notice that formula (19.9) is exactly formula (19.8) eliminating the $(1 - T)$ term. We interpret formula (19.9) as an attempt to introduce still higher leverage cost in the valuation: for a given risk of the assets (βu), by using formula (19.9) we obtain a higher β_L (and consequently a higher Ke and a lower equity value) than with formula (19.8).

Harris and Pringle (1985) and Ruback (1995) propose that the value creation of the tax shield is the present value of the interest tax shield discounted at the unlevered cost of equity (Ku). One straight interpretation of this assumption is that "the interest tax shields have the same systematic risk as the firm's underlying cash flows."[9] But another interpretation comes from analyzing the formula that relates the levered beta with the asset beta:

$$\beta_L = \beta u + \frac{D}{E}(\beta u - \beta d) \qquad (19.10)$$

It is important to notice that formula (19.10) is exactly formula (19.7) eliminating the $(1 - T)$ term. We interpret formula (19.10) as an attempt to introduce still higher leverage cost in the valuation: for a given risk of the assets (βu), by using formula (19.10) we obtain a higher β_L (and consequently a higher Ke and a lower equity value) than with formula (19.7).

According to Myers (1974), the value creation of the tax shield is the present value of the interest tax shield discounted at the cost of debt (Kd). The argument is that the risk of the tax saving arising from the use of debt is the same as the risk of the debt.

The sixth theory is that of Miles and Ezzell (1980). Although Miles and Ezzell do not mention what should be the discounted value of the tax shield, his formula relating the required return to equity with the required return for the unlevered company $[Ke = Ku + (D/E)(Ku - Kd)[1 + Kd(1 - T)]/(1 + Kd)]$ implies that $PV[Ku; \, T \, D \, Kd] \, (1 + Ku)/(1 + Kd_0)$. For a firm with a fixed debt target $[D/(D + E)]$ they claim that the correct rate for discounting the tax saving due to debt ($Kd \, T \, D_{t-1}$) is Kd for the tax saving during the first year, and Ku for the tax saving during the following years.

The seventh theory is Miller (1977). The value of the firm is independent of its capital structure, that is, $DVTS = 0$.

The eighth theory is Fernandez (2001). It quantifies the leverage cost (assuming that no-cost-of-leverage provides the DVTS without leverage costs) as $PV[Ku; \, D \, (Kd - R_F)]$. One way of interpreting this assumption is that the reduction in the value of the firm due to leverage is proportional to

[9]Kaplan and Ruback (1995).

the amount of debt and to the difference of the required return on debt minus the risk free rate. The cost of leverage does not depend on tax rate.[10]

19.2.2. Different Expressions of $WACC$ and $WACC_{BT}$

The corresponding expressions of WACC with their values of Ku are

No-cost-of-leverage:	$WACC = Ku[1 - TD/(E + D)]$
Damodaran (1994):	$WACC = Ku - D[TKu - (1 - T)(Kd - R_F)]/(E + D)$
The practitioners' method:	$WACC = Ku - D[R_F - Kd(1 - T)]/(E + D)$
Harris and Pringle (1985), Ruback (1995):	$WACC = Ku - DKdT/(E + D)$
Myers (1974):	$WACC = Ku - [DVTS(Ku - Kd) + DKdT]/(E + D)$
Miles and Ezzell (1980):	$WACC = Ku - [DKdT(1 + Ku)/(1 + Kd)]/(E + D)$
Miller (1977):	$WACC = Ku$
Fernandez (2001):	$WACC = Ku - D[KuT + R_F - Kd(1 - T)]/(E + D)$

The corresponding expressions of $WACC_{BT}$ with the values of Ku from the previous section are

No-cost-of-leverage:	$WACC_{BT} = Ku - DT(Ku - Kd)/(E + D)$
Damodaran (1994):	$WACC_{BT} = Ku + D[(Kd - R_F) - T(Ku - R_F)]/(E + D)$
The practitioners' method:	$WACC_{BT} = Ku + D(Kd - R_F)/(E + D)$
Harris and Pringle (1985), Ruback (1995):	$WACC_{BT} = Ku$
Myers (1974):	$WACC_{BT} = Ku - DVTS(Ku - Kd)/(E + D)$
Miles and Ezzell (1980):	$WACC_{BT} = Ku - DTKd(Ku - Kd)/[(E + D)(1 + Kd)]$
Miller (1977):	$WACC_{BT} = Ku + DTKd/(E + D)$
Fernandez (2001):	$WACC_{BT} = Ku - D[KuT + R_F - Kd]/(E + D)$

---

[10]This formula can be completed with another parameter φ that takes into account that the cost of leverage is not strictly proportional to debt. φ should be lower for small leverage and higher for high leverage. Introducing the parameter, the cost of leverage is $PV[Ku; \varphi D(Kd - R_F)]$.

19.2.3. DIFFERENT EXPRESSIONS OF THE LEVERED BETA

The different expressions of β_L (levered beta) according to the various papers are

No-cost-of-leverage:[11]	$\beta_L = \beta u + D(1 - T)(\beta u - \beta d)/E$
Damodaran (1994):	$\beta_L = \beta u + D(1 - T)\beta u/E$
The practitioners' method:	$\beta_L = \beta u + D\beta u/E$
Harris and Pringle (1985),[12] Ruback (1995):	$\beta_L = \beta u + D(\beta u - \beta d)/E$
Myers (1974):[13]	$\beta_L = \beta u + (D - DVTS)(\beta u - \beta d)/E$
In the case of a perpetuity growing at a rate g:	$\beta_L = \beta u + D[Kd(1 - T) - g]$ $(\beta u - \beta d)/[E(Kd - g)]$
Miles and Ezzell (1980):[14]	$\beta_L = \beta u + D(\beta u - \beta d)[1 - TKd/(1 + Kd)]/E$
Miller (1977):	$\beta_L = \beta u (D + E)/E - D[\beta d(1 - T) - TR_F/P_M]$
Fernandez (2001):	$\beta_L = \beta u + D[\beta u(1 - T) - \beta d]/E$

19.3. THE BASIC PROBLEM: THE VALUE OF THE TAX SHIELD DUE TO THE PAYMENT OF INTEREST (DVTS)

First, we show that in a world without leverage cost, the discounted value of the tax shields for a perpetuity is DT.

It is assumed that the debt's market value (D) is equal to its book value (N).[15]

19.3.1. ADJUSTED PRESENT VALUE (APV) IN A WORLD WITHOUT COST-OF-LEVERAGE

The formula for the adjusted present value (19.11) indicates that the value of the debt today (D) plus that of the equity (E) of the levered company is

---

[11]This formula is the same as Taggart's (2A.6) (1991), because and he assumes that $\beta d = 0$.

[12]This formula is the same as Taggart's (2C.6) (1991), because and he assumes that $\beta d = 0$.

[13]Note that $D - DVTS = V_U - E$. Copeland, Koller, and Murrin (2000) say in Exhibit A.3 of their book *Valuation: Measuring and Managing the Value of Companies*, that it is not possible to find a formula that relates the levered beta with the unlevered beta. This is not true: the relationship is that given.

[14]This formula is the same as Taggart's (2B.6) (1991), because he assumes that $\beta d = 0$.

[15]This means that the required return to debt (Kd) is the same as the interest rate paid by the debt (r).

equal to the value of the equity of the unlevered company (Vu) plus the discounted value of the tax shield due to interest payments (DVTS).[16]

$$E + D = Vu + DVTS \qquad (19.11)$$

DVTS is the term used to define the increase in the company's value as a result of the tax saving due to the payment of interest (discounted value of the tax shield). $Vu = FCF/Ku$.

It is important to note that the DVTS is not (and this is the main error of many papers on this topic) the PV of the tax shield, but the difference between two PVs of two flows with different risk: the PV of the taxes paid in the unlevered company (Gu) and the PV of the taxes paid in the levered company (G$_L$).

19.3.2. APPROPRIATE DISCOUNT RATE FOR TAXES IN PERPETUITIES

In a world without leverage cost, the following relationship holds:

$$Vu + Gu = E + D + G_L \qquad (19.12)$$

Vu is the value of the unlevered company. Gu is the present value of the taxes paid by the unlevered company. E is the equity value and D is the debt value. G$_L$ is the present value of the taxes paid by the levered company. Equation (19.12) means that the total value of the unlevered company (left-hand side of the equation) is equal to the total value of the levered company (right-hand side of the equation). Total value is the enterprise value (often called value of the firm) plus the present value of taxes.

We designate by K_{TU} the required return to tax in the unlevered company, and by K_{TL} the required return to tax in the levered company.

The DVTS is

$$DVTS = Gu - G_L \qquad (19.13)$$

In a perpetuity, the profit after tax (PAT) is equal to equity cash flow (ECF):

$$PAT = ECF \qquad (19.14)$$

---

[16]As shown in Chapters 17 and 21, the APV always gives the same value as the other most commonly used methods for valuing companies by cash flow discounting: free cash flow discounted at the WACC; equity cash flows discounted at the required return to equity; capital cash flows discounted at the WACC before tax; the business risk-adjusted free cash flows discounted at the required return to assets; the business risk- adjusted equity cash flows discounted at the required return to assets; economic profit discounted at the required return to equity; and EVA discounted at the WACC.

This is because in a perpetuity, depreciation must be equal to reinvestment in order to keep the cash flow generation capacity constant.

In a perpetuity, the free cash flow (FCF) is equal to the profit before tax of the unlevered company (PBTu) multiplied by $(1 - T)$, being T the tax rate.

$$FCF = PBTu \ (1 - T) \tag{19.15}$$

We will call FCF_0 the company's free cash flow if there were no taxes. The FCF_0 is equal to the profit before taxes of the unlevered company (PBTu).

$$FCF_0 = PBTu. \tag{19.16}$$

From (19.15) and (19.16) it is clear that:

$$FCF = FCF_0 \ (1 - T) \tag{19.17}$$

For the unlevered company $(D = 0)$:

$$Taxes_U = T \ PBTu = T \ FCF_0 = T \ FCF/(1 - T) \tag{19.18}$$

The taxes of the unlevered company are proportional to FCF_0 and FCF. Consequently, the taxes of the unlevered company have the same risk as FCF_0 (and FCF), and must be discounted at the rate Ku. The required return to tax in the unlevered company (K_{TU}) is equal to the required return to equity in the unlevered company (Ku).[17]

$$K_{TU} = Ku \tag{19.19}$$

The present value of the taxes of the unlevered company is

$$G_U = T \ FCF/[(1 - T)Ku] = T \ Vu/(1 - T) \tag{19.20}$$

For the levered company:

$$Taxes_L = T \ PBT_L = T \ PAT_L/(1 - T) = T \ ECF/(1 - T) \tag{19.21}$$

Consequently, the taxes of the levered company have the same risk as the ECF and must be discounted at the rate Ke. Thus, in the case of perpetuities, the tax risk is identical to the equity cash flow risk and, consequently, the required return to tax in the levered company (K_{TL}) is equal to the required return to equity (Ke).[18]

$$K_{TL} = Ke \tag{19.22}$$

The present value of the taxes of the levered company, that is, the value of the taxes paid to the government is[19]

---

[17]This is only true for perpetuities.

[18]This is only true for perpetuities.

[19]The relationship between profit after tax (PAT) and profit before tax (PBT), is $PAT = PBT(1 - T)$.

$$G_L = T\ ECF/[(1 - T)Ke] = T\ E/(1 - T) \tag{19.23}$$

The increase in the company's value due to the use of debt is *not* the present value of the tax shield due to interest payments, but the difference between G_U and G_L, which are the present values of two cash flows with different risks:

$$DVTS = G_U - G_L = [T/(1 - T)](Vu - E) \tag{19.24}$$

As $Vu - E = D - DVTS$, this gives:

$$DVTS = \text{discounted value of the tax shield} = DT \tag{19.25}$$

19.3.3. APPROPRIATE DISCOUNT RATE FOR TAXES AND DVTS IN A WORLD WITHOUT COST-OF-LEVERAGE WITH CONSTANT GROWTH

For a growing perpetuity, we cannot give a clear answer about the required return to taxes as we have done for perpetuities.

Equation (19.26) means that the total value of the unlevered company (left-hand side of the equation) is equal to the total value of the levered company (right-hand side of the equation). Total value is the enterprise value (often called value of the firm) plus the present value of taxes. Vu is the value of the unlevered company. Gu is the present value of the taxes paid by the unlevered company. E is the equity value and D is the debt value. G_L is the present value of the taxes paid by the levered company.

$$Vu_t + Gu_t = E_t + D_t + GL_t \tag{19.26}$$

The discounted value of the tax shields (DVTS) is

$$DVTS_t = Gu_t - GL_t \tag{19.27}$$

In a company with constant growth and without debt, the relationship between taxes and profit before tax is

$$\text{Taxes}_U = T\ PBTu. \tag{19.28}$$

The relationship between taxes and free cash flow is different from that obtained for perpetuities:

$$\begin{aligned} \text{Taxes}_U &= T\ [FCF + g(WCR + NFA)]/(1 - T) \\ &= T\ [FCF + g(Ebv + D)]/(1 - T) \end{aligned} \tag{19.29}$$

WCR is the net working capital requirements. NFA is the net fixed assets. Ebv is the equity book value, and g is the constant growth rate.

From equation (19.29) we cannot establish a clear relationship between the required return to taxes and the required return to assets (Ku) as we did for perpetuities in equation (19.18).

The present value of taxes in the unlevered company is

$$Gu = Taxes_U/(K_{TU} - g) \qquad (19.30)$$

In a levered company with constant growth, the relationship between taxes and equity cash flow is different from that obtained for perpetuities:[20]

$$Taxes_L = T(ECF + g\ Ebv)/(1 - T) \qquad (19.31)$$

From equation (19.31) we cannot establish a clear relationship between the required return to taxes and the required return to equity as we did for perpetuities in equation (19.21).

The present value of taxes in the levered company is

$$G_L = Taxes_L/(K_{TL} - g) \qquad (19.32)$$

The increase in the value of the company due to the use of debt *is not* the present value of the tax shield due to the payment of interest but the difference between Gu and G_L, which are the present values of two cash flows with a different risk:

$$DVTS_t = Gu_t - G_{Lt} = [Taxes_U/(K_{TU} - g)] - [Taxes_L/(K_{TL} - g)] \quad (19.33)$$

The relationship between Taxes_U and Taxes_L is

$$Taxes_{Ut+1} - Taxes_{Lt+1} = D_t\ Kd\ T \qquad (19.34)$$

Logically, the taxes of the unlevered company have less risk than the taxes of the levered company, and consequently:

$$K_{TU} < K_{TL} \qquad (19.35)$$

19.3.4. ANALYSIS OF THE THEORIES FOR PERPETUITIES

Table 19.2 reports the implications that each of the 8 theories has for the case of perpetuities. Column [1] contains the general formula for calculating the DVTS according to the 8 theories. Column [2] contains the formula for calculating the DVTS for perpetuities according to the 8 theories when the tax rate is positive. Column [3] contains the formula for calculating the DVTS for perpetuities according to the 8 theories when there are no taxes.

---

[20]For a growing perpetuity, the relationship between ECF and FCF is ECF = FCF − D [Kd(1 − T) − g].

Table 19.2

Perpetuity, Discounted Value of the Tax Shield (DVTS) According to the 8 Theories

Theories	DVTS (general formula) [1]	DVTS in perpetuities ($T > 0$) [2]	DVTS in perpetuities ($T = 0$) [3]
1 No-cost-of-leverage	$PV[Ku; DTKu]$	**DT**	**0**
2 Damodaran	$PV[Ku; DTKu - D(Kd - R_F)(1 - T)]$	$DT - [D(Kd - R_F)(1 - T)]/Ku < $ **DT**	$-D(Kd - R_F)/Ku < $ **0**
3 Practitioners	$PV[Ku; T\,D\,Kd - D(Kd - R_F)]$	$D[R_F - Kd(1 - T)]/Ku < $ **DT**	$-D(Kd - R_F)/Ku < $ **0**
4 Harris-Pringle	$PV[Ku; T\,D\,Kd]$	$T\,D\,Kd/Ku < DT$	0
5 Myers	$PV[Kd; T\,D\,Kd]$	**DT**	**0**
6 Miles-Ezzell	$PV[Ku; T\,D\,Kd](1 + Ku)/(1 + Kd_0)$	$TDKd(1 + Ku)/[(1 + Kd_0)Ku] < DT$	0
7 Miller	0	0	0
8 Fernandez	$PV[Ku; D(KuT + R_F - Kd)]$	$D(KuT + R_F - Kd)/Ku < DT$	$-D(Kd - R_F)/Ku < $ **0**

Necessary conditions	with leverage cost	without leverage cost	
T > 0	$< DT$	DT	
T = 0	< 0	0	
Number of theories:	3	2	
	Damodaran, Practitioners, and Fernandez (2001)	No-cost-of-leverage and Myers	

Three theories do not accomplish the necessary conditions to be considered: Harris and Pringle (1985) or Ruback (1995), Miles and Ezzell (1980), and Miller (1977).

It may be seen that only 2 theories accomplish formula (19.15), which implies DVTS = DT. The two theories are no-cost-of-leverage and Myers.

The other six theories provide a DVTS lower than DT. The difference could be attributed to the leverage cost. These six theories could be applicable in a "real world," where the leverage cost does exist. But if this is the case, leverage cost exists also when there are no taxes. In this situation (column [3] of Table 19.2) these theories should provide a negative DVTS. It only happens in three theories of the six: Damodaran, Practitioners, and Fernandez (2001).

With these two conditions, we are able to eliminate three theories that do not provide us with a value of the tax shield of DT (as the candidates for without cost-of-leverage world should), nor do they provide us with a negative DVTS when there are no taxes (as the candidates for a world with leverage cost should). The three candidates eliminated due to a lack of consistent results are: Harris and Pringle (1985) or Ruback (1995), Miles and Ezzell (1980), and Miller (1977).

The eight candidate theories provide a value of DVTS = 0 if D = 0.

19.3.5. ANALYSIS OF COMPETING THEORIES IN A WORLD WITHOUT COST-OF-LEVERAGE AND WITH CONSTANT GROWTH

It is clear that the required return to levered equity (Ke) should be higher than the required return to assets (Ku). Table 19.3 shows that only no-cost-of-leverage provides us always with Ke > Ku.

Another problem of Myers is that Ke < Ku for high g and/or high T. DVTS is independent of unlevered beta. On top of that, according to Myers, Ke decreases when T (tax rate) increases. According to no-cost-of-leverage Ke increases when T increases.

The only formula that does not present problems is no-cost-of-leverage.

Table 19.3

Problems of the Candidate Formulas to Calculate the DVTS in a World without Cost-of-Leverage and with Constant Growth

	Ke < Ku
No-cost-of-leverage	−Never
Myers	If g > Kd(1 − T)[a]

[a]Ke < Ku if DVTS > D. DTKd/(Kd − g) > D implies g > Kd(1 − T).
It can also be expressed as Vu < E.

When the cost of debt (r) is not equal to the required return to debt (Kd), the discounted value of the tax shield according to no-cost-of-leverage should be calculated as follows:[21]

$$DVTS = PV[Ku; DTKu + T(Nr - DKd)]$$

We would point out again that this expression is not a cash flow's PV, but the difference between two present values of two cash flows with a different risk: the taxes of the company without debt and the taxes of the company with debt.

19.4. DIFFERENCES IN THE VALUATION ACCORDING TO THE MOST SIGNIFICANT PAPERS

19.4.1. GROWING PERPETUITY WITH A PRESET DEBT RATIO OF 30%

Upon applying the above formulas to a company with $FCF_1 = 100$, $Ku = 10\%$, $Kd = 7\%$, $[D/(D + E)] = 30\%$, $T = 35\%$, $R_F = 5\%$, and $g = 5\%$, we obtain the values given in Table 19.4. The value of the unlevered company (Vu) is 2,000 in all cases. Note that, according to Myers, $Ke < Ku = 10\%$, which makes no sense. Neither does it make any sense that $DVTS > D$, which is what happens when $g > Kd(1 - T)$; in the example, when $g > 4.55\%$.

If we make changes to the growth rate, Tables 19.5–19.7 show the valuation's basic parameters at different values of the growth rate g.

Table 19.5 shows that the company's WACC is independent of growth, according to all the theories except Myers'. According to Myers, the WACC falls when growth increases and is equal to growth when $g = Kd$ $[D(1 - T) + E]/(E + D)$; in the example, when $g = 6,265\%$.

Table 19.6 show that the DVTS according to the no-cost-of-leverage and according to Myers are equal for a perpetuity (when there is no growth). When there is growth, the value of the DVTS according to Myers is higher than the DVTS according to the no-cost-of-leverage. All the other theories give values lower than the no-cost-of-leverage theory. According to Myers, the company's value is infinite for growth rates equal or greater than $g = Kd$ $[D(1 - T) + E]/(E + D)$; in the example, when $g \geq 6.265\%$.

Table 19.7 shows that the required return to equity is independent of growth according to all the theories except Myers'. According to Myers, Ke

---

[21]See Fernandez (2001).

Table 19.4

Example of a Company Valuation

	No-cost-of-leverage	Myers	Miller	Miles- Ezzell	Harris-Pringle	Damodaran	Practitioners
WACC	8.950%	8.163%	10.000%	9.244%	9.265%	9.340%	9.865%
Ke	10.836%	9.711%	12.336%	11.256%	11.286%	11.393%	12.143%
$WACC_{BT}$	9.685%	8.898%	10.735%	9.979%	10.000%	10.075%	10.600%
E + D	2,531.65	3,162.06	2,000.00	2,356.05	2,344.67	2,304.15	2,055.50
Vu	2,000.00	2,000.00	2,000.00	2,000.00	2,000.00	2,000.00	2,000.00
E	1,772.15	2,213.44	1,400.00	1,649.23	1,641.27	1,612.90	1,438.85
D	759.49	948.62	600.00	706.81	703.40	691.24	616.65
DVTS	531.65	1,162.06	0.00	356.05	344.67	304.15	55.50
ECF	103.42	104.27	102.70	103.18	103.17	103.11	102.77

$FCF_1 = 100, Ku = 10\%, Kd = 7\%, [D/(D + E)] = 30\%, T = 35\%, R_F = 5\%,$ and $g = 5\%$

Table 19.5

WACC at Different Growth Rates g, [D/(D + E)] = 30%

g	No-cost-of-leverage	Myers	Miller	Miles- Ezzell	Harris-Pringle	Damodaran	Practitioners
0%	8.95%	8.95%	10.00%	9.24%	9.27%	9.34%	9.87%
2%	8.95%	8.82%	10.00%	9.24%	9.27%	9.34%	9.87%
4%	8.95%	8.53%	10.00%	9.24%	9.27%	9.34%	9.87%
6%	8.95%	7.06%	10.00%	9.24%	9.27%	9.34%	9.87%

Table 19.6
DVTS at Different Growth Rates g, [D/(D + E)] = 30%

g	No-cost-of-leverage	Myers	Miller	Miles- Ezzell	Harris-Pringle	Damodaran	Practitioners
0%	117.3	117.3	0.0	81.7	79.3	70.7	13.7
2%	188.8	215.4	0.0	130.4	126.5	112.4	21.5
4%	353.5	540.8	0.0	240.1	232.7	206.0	38.4
6%	889.8	6,934.0	0.0	582.2	562.8	494.0	87.3
7%	1,794.9	∞	0.0	1,122.2	1,081.7	940.2	157.1

Table 19.7
Ke at Different Growth Rates g, [D/(D + E)] = 30%

g	No-cost-of-leverage	Myers	Miller	Miles- Ezzell	Harris-Pringle	Damodaran	Practitioners
0%	10.8%	10.8%	12.3%	11.3%	11.3%	11.4%	12.1%
2%	10.8%	10.7%	12.3%	11.3%	11.3%	11.4%	12.1%
4%	10.8%	10.2%	12.3%	11.3%	11.3%	11.4%	12.1%
5%	10.8%	9.7%	12.3%	11.3%	11.3%	11.4%	12.1%
6%	10.8%	8.1%	12.3%	11.3%	11.3%	11.4%	12.1%

Table 19.8
Present Value of the Tax Shield (DVTS) at Different Debt Ratios (g = 5%), [D/(D + E)] = 30%

D/(D + E)	No-cost-of-leverage	Myers	Miller	Miles-Ezzell	Harris-Pringle	Damodaran	Practitioners
0%	0.0	0.0	0.0	0.0	0.0	0.0	0.0
20%	325.6	649.0	0.0	224.1	217.3	193.0	36.7
40%	777.8	1,921.6	0.0	504.7	487.6	427.2	74.7
60%	1,448.3	5,547.2	0.0	866.3	832.9	717.4	114.2
70%	1,921.6	12,035.1	0.0	1,089.4	1,044.1	890.2	134.5
80%	2,545.5	98,000.0	0.0	1,350.0	1,289.5	1,086.4	155.2
90%	3,405.4	∞	0.0	1,658.7	1,577.8	1,311.3	176.3
100%	4,666.7	∞	0.0	2,030.1	1,921.6	1,571.4	197.8

Table 19.9
Required Return to Equity (Ke) at Different Debt Ratios (g = 5%)

D/(D + E)	No-cost-of-leverage	Myers	Miller	Miles-Ezzell	Harris-Pringle	Damodaran	Practitioners
0%	10.00%	10.00%	10.00%	10.00%	10.00%	10.00%	10.00%
20%	10.49%	9.83%	11.36%	10.73%	10.75%	10.81%	11.25%
40%	11.30%	9.55%	13.63%	11.95%	12.00%	12.17%	13.33%
60%	12.93%	8.99%	18.18%	14.40%	14.50%	14.88%	17.50%
80%	17.80%	7.30%	31.80%	21.73%	22.00%	23.00%	30.00%
90%	27.55%	*3.93%*	59.05%	36.38%	37.00%	39.25%	55.00%
95%	47.05%	*-2.82%*	113.55%	65.69%	67.00%	71.75%	105.00%

Table 19.10

Example of a Company Valuation

	No-cost-of-leverage	Myers	Miller	Miles- Ezzell	Harris-Pringle	Damodaran	Practitioners
WACC	8.950%	8.413%	10.000%	9.197%	9.216%	9.284%	9.835%
Ke	10.836%	9.764%	13.337%	11.372%	11.413%	11.568%	12.901%
WACC$_{BT}$	9.685%	9.048%	10.930%	9.978%	10.000%	10.081%	10.734%
E + D	2,531.65	2,930.38	2,000.00	2,382.59	2,372.15	2,334.18	2,068.35
Vu	2,000.00	2,000.00	2,000.00	2,000.00	2,000.00	2,000.00	2,000.00
E	1,772.15	2,170.89	1,240.51	1,623.09	1,612.66	1,574.68	1,308.86
D	759.49	759.49	759.49	759.49	759.49	759.49	759.49
DVTS	531.65	930.38	0.00	382.59	372.15	334.18	68.35
ECF	103.42	103.42	103.42	103.42	103.42	103.42	103.42
D/(D + E)	30.00%	25.92%	37.97%	31.88%	32.02%	32.54%	36.72%

$FCF_1 = 100$, $Ku = 10\%$, $Kd = 7\%$, $D = 759.49$, $T = 35\%$, $R_F = 5\%$, and $g = 5\%$

falls when growth increases and is equal to Ku when $g = Kd(1 - T)$. In the example, when $g = 4.55\%$. Obviously, this makes no sense.

If the debt ratio is changed, Tables 19.8 and 19.9 show the valuation's basic parameters at different debt ratios.

Table 19.8 shows the DVTS at different debt ratios according to the various theories. The value of the DVTS according to Myers is higher than the DVTS according to the no-cost-of-leverage. All the other theories give values lower than the no-cost-of-leverage theory. It can be seen that the DVTS according to Myers becomes infinite for a debt ratio $D/(D + E)] = (Kd - g)/(TKd)$, in our example, 81.63%.

19.4.2. GROWING PERPETUITY WITH PRESET DEBT

The hypotheses of Table 19.10 are identical to those of Table 19.4, with the sole difference that the initial debt level is set at 759.49 (instead of the debt ratio of 30%). The value of the unlevered company (Vu) is 2,000 in all cases. Note that, according to Myers, $Ke < Ku = 10\%$, which does not make much sense.

APPENDIX 19.1:   IN A WORLD WITH NO LEVERAGE COST THE VALUE OF TAX SHIELDS IS PV[Ku; D T Ku]

Fernandez (2002) proves that the value of tax shields in a world with no leverage cost is the present value of the debt (D) times the tax rate (T) times the required return to the unlevered equity (Ku), discounted at the unlevered cost of equity (Ku): $DTKu/(Ku - g)$.

The proof is as follows. The formula for the adjusted present value (19.36) indicates that the value of the debt today (D) plus that of the equity (E) of the levered company is equal to the value of the equity of the unlevered company (Vu) plus the value of tax shields due to interest payments (DVTS).

$$E + D = Vu + DVTS \qquad (19.36)$$

The relationship between the value of the equity of the unlevered firm and the free cash flow is

$$Vu = FCF/(Ku - g). \qquad (19.37)$$

By substituting (19.37) in (19.36), we get:

$$E + D = FCF/(Ku - g) + DVTS \qquad (19.38)$$

The formula that relates the free cash flow and the equity cash flow in a growing perpetuity is (17.4 g):

$$FCF = ECF + D\ Kd(1 - T) - g\ D \qquad (17.49)$$

By substituting (17.4 g) in (19.38), we get:

$$E + D = [ECF + D\ Kd(1 - T) - g\ D]/(Ku - g) + DVTS \qquad (19.39)$$

By substituting (17.1 g) in (19.39), we get:

$$E + D = [E(Ke - g) + D\ Kd(1 - T) - g\ D]/(Ku - g) + DVTS \qquad (19.40)$$

Multiplying both sides of Eq (19.40) by $(Ku - g)$ we get:

$$(E + D)(Ku - g) = [E(Ke - g) + D\ Kd(1 - T) - g\ D] + VTS(Ku - g) \qquad (19.41)$$

Eliminating $-g(E + D)$ on both sides of Eq (19.41):

$$(E + D)Ku = [E\ Ke + D\ Kd(1 - T)] + DVTS(Ku - g) \qquad (19.42)$$

Eq. (19.42) may be rewritten as:

$$D[Ku - Kd(1 - T)] - E(Ke - Ku) = DVTS(Ku - g) \qquad (19.43)$$

Dividing both sides of Eq. (19.43) by D (debt value), we get:

$$[\ Ku - Kd(1 - T)] - (E/D)(Ke - Ku) = (DVTS/D)(Ku - g) \qquad (19.44)$$

If (E / D) is constant, the left-hand side of equation [19.44] does not depend on growth (g) because for any growth rate (E / D), Ku, Kd, and Ke are constant. We know that for $g = 0$, DVTS = DT (equation [19.25]). Then, Eq. (19.44) applied to perpetuities $(g = 0)$ is:

$$[Ku - Kd(1 - T)] - (E/D)(Ke - Ku) = T\ Ku \qquad (19.45)$$

Substracting (19.45) from (19.44) we get
$0 = (DVTS/D)(Ku - g) - T\ Ku$, which is Eq. (**17.10 g**):

$$\mathbf{DVTS = D\ T\ Ku/(Ku - g)} \qquad (17.10g)$$

One must remember that the DVTS is not the PV of tax shields, but the difference between two present values of two cash flows with a different risk: the PV of the taxes of the unlevered company and the PV of the taxes of the levered company.

One problem of Eq. (19.25) is that DT can be understood as $= D\alpha T/\alpha$. At first glance, α can be anything, related or unrelated to the company that we are valuing. Modigliani and Miller (1963) assume that α is risk-free rate (R_F). Myers (1974) assumes that α is the cost of debt (Kd) and says that the value of tax shields is the present value of the tax savings (D T Kd) discounted at the cost of debt (Kd). But it has been shown that the value of tax shields is the difference between Gu and G_L, which are the present values of two cash flows with different risks: the taxes paid by the unlevered company and the taxes paid by the levered company. In this appendix we have shown that the correct α is the required return to unlevered equity (Ku). It has been shown that for growing companies both Modigliani and Miller (1963) and Myers (1974) provide inconsistent results.

One could say "in practice I do not see why the approach of working out the present value of tax shields themselves would necessarily be wrong, provided the appropriate discount rate was used (reflecting the riskiness of the tax shields)". The problem here is that it is hard to evaluate the riskiness of tax shields because it is the difference of two present flows (the taxes paid by the unlevered company and those paid by the levered company) with different risk. On the other hand, if we were to follow this approach, and calculate the discount rate K^* that accomplish with:

$$VTS = D \; T \; Ku/(Ku - g) = D \; T \; Kd/(K^* - g)$$

The solution is $K^* = Kd + g - Kd \; g/Ku$. Obviously this expression has not any intuition behind. And it is impossible to find a closed form solution for K^* in a general case (instead of a growing perpetuity). Kd is the cost of debt.

To evaluate the riskiness of tax shields is as hard as to evaluate the riskiness of the difference between the Microsoft expected equity cash flow and the GE expected equity cash flow. We may evaluate the riskiness of the expected equity cash flows of each company, but it is difficult (and we think that it does not make any sense) to try to evaluate the riskiness of the difference of the two expected equity cash flows.

REFERENCES

Arditti, F. D., and H. Levy (1977), "The Weighted Average Cost of Capital as a Cutoff Rate: A Critical Examination of the Classical Textbook Weighted Average," *Financial Management*, (Fall), pp. 24–34.

Benninga, S., and O. H. Sarig (1997), *Corporate Finance: A Valuation Approach*, New York: McGraw-Hill.

Chambers, D. R., R. S. Harris, and J. J. Pringle (1982), "Treatment of Financing Mix Analyzing Investment Opportunities," *Financial Management*, (Summer), pp. 24–41.

Copeland, T. E., T. Koller, and J. Murrin (2000). *Valuation: Measuring and Managing the Value of Companies*, third edition, New York: Wiley.

Damodaran, A. (1994), *Damodaran on Valuation*, New York: John Wiley and Sons.

DeAngelo, L., and R. Masulis, (1980), "Optimal Capital Structure under Corporate and Personal Taxation," *Journal of Financial Economics*, 8, March, pp. 3–29.

Fernández, P. (2001), "The Correct Value of Tax Shields. An Analysis of 23 Theories," Working Paper No. 276051, Social Science Research Network.

Fernández, P. (2002), "The Value of Tax Shields is NOT Equal to the Present Value of Tax Shields," Working Paper No. 290727, Social Science Research Network.

Gordon, M., and E. Shapiro (1956), "Capital Equipment Analysis: The Required Rate of Profit," *Management Science*, 3 (Oct.), pp. 102–110.

Graham (2000), "How Big Are the Tax Benefits of Debt?," *Journal of Finance*, Vol. LV, pp. 1901–1941.

Graham (2001), "Taxes and Corporate Finance: A Review," Working Paper, Duke University.

Harris, R. S., and J. J. Pringle (1985), "Risk-Adjusted Discount Rates Extensions Form the Average-Risk Case," *Journal of Financial Research*, (Fall), pp. 237–244.

Inselbag, I., and H. Kaufold (1997), "Two DCF Approaches for Valuing Companies under Alternative Financing Strategies (and How to Choose Between Them)," *Journal of Applied Corporate Finance*, (Spring), pp. 114–122.

Kaplan, S., and R. Ruback (1995), "The Valuation of Cash Flow Forecast: An Empirical Analysis," *Journal of Finance*, Vol. 50, No. 4, September.

Lewellen, W. G., and D. R. Emery (1986), "Corporate Debt Management and the Value of the Firm," *Journal of Financial Quantitative Analysis*, (December), pp. 415–426.

Luehrman, T. A. (1997), "What's Worth: A General Manager's Guide to Valuation," and "Using APV: A Better Tool for Valuing Operations," *Harvard Business Review*, (May-June), pp. 132–154.

Miles, J. A., and J. R. Ezzell, (1980), "The Weighted Average Cost of Capital, Perfect Capital Markets and Project Life: A Clarification," *Journal of Financial and Quantitative Analysis*, (September), pp. 719–730.

Miles, J. A., and J. R. Ezzell, (1985), "Reformulating Tax Shield Valuation: A Note," *Journal of Finance*, Vol. XL, 5 (December), pp. 1485–1492.

Miller, M. H. (1977), "Debt and Taxes," *Journal of Finance*, (May), pp. 261–276.

Miller, M., and F. Modigliani (1961), "Dividend Policy, Growth and the Valuation of Shares", *Journal of Business*, 34, 411–433.

Miller, M., and M. Scholes (1978), "Dividend and Taxes," *Journal of Financial Economics*, (Dec.), pp. 333–364.

Modigliani, F., and M. Miller, (1958), "The Cost of Capital, Corporation Finance and the Theory of Investment," *American Economic Review*, 48, 261–297.

Modigliani, F., and M. Miller (1963), "Corporate Income Taxes and the Cost of Capital: A Correction," *American Economic Review*, (June), pp. 433–443.

Myers, S. C. (1974), "Interactions of Corporate Financing and Investment Decisions—Implications for Capital Budgeting," *Journal of Finance*, (March), pp. 1–25.

Ruback, R. S. (1995), "A Note on Capital Cash Flow Valuation," Harvard Business School, 9-295-069.

Taggart, R. A. Jr. (1991), "Consistent Valuation and Cost of Capital. Expressions with Corporate and Personal Taxes," *Financial Management*, (Autumn), pp. 8–20.

Tham, J., and I. Vélez-Pareja (2001), "The Correct Discount Rate for the Tax Shield: The N-Period Case," SSRN Working Paper.

Chapter 20

Application of the Different Theories to RJR Nabisco

In this chapter, we shall analyze in greater depth the valuation of RJR Nabisco discussed in Chapter 15. The valuations made in Chapter 15 were carried out using the practitioners method.[1] In this chapter, RJR Nabisco is valued using another four theories taken from those introduced in Chapters 17 and 19: No-cost-of-leverage, Damodaran (1994), Ruback (1995), and Myers (1974).

20.1. VALUATION ACCORDING TO NO-COST-OF-LEVERAGE THEORY

Table 20.1 shows the valuation of the pre-bid strategy according to Modigliani-Miller, that is, assuming there are no leverage costs.[2] The valuation has been carried out using the same hypotheses as in Chapter 15 regarding risk-free interest rate (8.5%), market risk premium (8%), assets' beta ($\beta_U = 0.65$), and cash flow growth rate after 1998 (2%).

Line 5 of Table 20.1 shows the β_L, which is obtained from the equation

$$\beta_L = \frac{\beta_U[E + D(1 - T)] - \beta_d D(1 - T)}{E}$$

instead of $\beta_L = \beta_U(D + E)/E$ that we used in Chapter 15.

Line 7 shows the value of the equity (E), which is \$20,286 million. Line 8 shows the value forecast for the debt in each year, and line 9 contains the sum of the debt value and the equity value. Line 10 shows the cost of the debt (Kd) and line 11 the weighted average cost of capital (WACC).

---

[1]The valuation formulas used in this method have been discussed in Chapter 19.

[2]The cost of the debt is equal to the interest paid divided by the debt's nominal amount at the beginning of the year. In this chapter, it is assumed that the debt's value is identical to its nominal amount.

Table 20.1
Pre-Bid Strategy, Valuation According to the No-Cost-of-Leverage Theory

($ Million)	1988	1989	1990	1991	1992	1993	1994	1995	1996	1997	1998
1 Rf		8.5%	8.5%	8.5%	8.5%	8.5%	8.5%	8.5%	8.5%	8.5%	8.5%
2 Pm		8%	8%	8%	8%	8%	8%	8%	8%	8%	8%
3 Beta u		0.65	0.65	0.65	0.65	0.65	0.65	0.65	0.65	0.65	0.65
4 Beta d		0.335	0.313	0.313	0.313	0.313	0.313	0.313	0.313	0.313	
5 Beta L		0.703	0.711	0.709	0.704	0.698	0.691	0.679	0.675	0.665	0.650
6 Ke		14.1%	14.2%	14.2%	14.1%	14.1%	14.0%	13.9%	13.9%	13.8%	13.7%
7 E = PV(ECF; Ke)	20,286	21,820	23,687	25,673	27,520	29,427	31,923	33,554	35,972	39,222	40,007
8 D	5,204	6,018	6,300	6,273	5,982	5,400	4,164	3,727	2,355	0	0
9 D + E	25,490	27,839	29,987	31,946	33,502	34,827	36,086	37,281	38,327	39,222	40,007
10 Kd		11.2%	11.0%	11.0%	11.0%	11.0%	11.0%	11.0%	11.0%	11.0%	0.0%
11 WACC		12.7%	12.7%	12.7%	12.8%	12.9%	13.0%	13.2%	13.2%	13.4%	13.7%
12 PV(FCF; WACC)	25,490	27,839	29,987	31,946	33,502	34,827	36,086	37,281	38,327	39,222	40,007
13 Ku		13.7%	13.7%	13.7%	13.7%	13.7%	13.7%	13.7%	13.7%	13.7%	13.7%
14 FCF		901	1,385	1,856	2,528	2,985	3,261	3,555	3,888	4,246	4,589
15 Vu = PV(FCF; Ku)	24,247	26,667	28,936	31,044	32,768	34,272	35,707	37,043	38,231	39,222	40,007
16 DTKu		242	280	293	292	279	252	194	174	110	0
17 DVTS = PV(DTKu; Ku)	1,243	1,171	1,051	902	733	555	379	238	96	0	0
18 D + E = DVTS + Vu	25,490	27,839	29,987	31,946	33,502	34,827	36,086	37,281	38,327	39,222	40,007
19 CCF		1,099	1,610	2,092	2,763	3,209	3,463	3,711	4,027	4,334	4,589
20 WACC_BT		13.5%	13.5%	13.5%	13.5%	13.5%	13.6%	13.6%	13.6%	13.6%	13.7%
21 D + E = PV(CCF; WACC_BT)	25,490	27,839	29,987	31,946	33,502	34,827	36,086	37,281	38,327	39,222	40,007

Difference between Tables 15.4 and 20.1; Pre-Bid Strategy, Cost of Leverage

($ Million)	1988	1989	1990	1991	1992	1993	1994	1995	1996	1997
Equity value										
No-cost-of-leverage (Table 20.1)	20,286	21,820	23,687	25,673	27,520	29,427	31,923	33,554	35,972	39,222
Table 15.4	19,368	20,961	22,916	25,011	26,982	29,020	31,644	33,379	35,902	39,222
Difference	**918**	**859**	**771**	**662**	**538**	**407**	**278**	**174**	**71**	**0**
DVTS No-cost-of-leverage (Table 20.1)	1,243	1,171	1,051	902	733	555	379	238	96	0
Difference/DVTS	74%	73%	73%	73%	73%	73%	73%	73%	73%	73%

Line 12 is the present value of the forecast *free cash* flow (FCF) discounted at the WACC, that is, the debt value plus the equity value (D + E). As could not be otherwise, this line is the same as line 9.

Line 18 is the debt value plus the equity value (D + E) calculated according to the adjusted present value (APV). As could not be otherwise, this line is the same as lines 9 and 12.

Line 21 is the present value of the forecast capital cash flow (CCF) discounted at the $WACC_{BT}$, that is, the debt value plus the equity value (D + E). As could not be otherwise, this line is the same as lines 9, 12, and 18.

Table 20.2 shows the valuation of the management group's strategy. The valuation has been carried out using the same hypotheses as in Table 20.1. However, in this case, the valuation is performed by grouping the financial instruments comprising the liabilities into *two groups*: equity (shares, preferred stock, and convertible preferred stock) and debt.

Line 6 of Table 20.2 shows the levered beta, which is obtained from the equation

$$\beta_L = \frac{\beta_U[E + Pr + PrCo + D(1 - T)] - \beta_d D(1 - T)}{E + Pr + PrCo}$$

Line 8 shows the value of the shares plus the preferred stock plus the convertible preferred stock. Line 9 shows the forecast value for the debt in each year and line 10 contains the sum of the debt value and the enterprise value (debt plus shares plus preferred stock plus convertible preferred stock). Line 11 shows the weighted average cost of capital (WACC), calculated in accordance with the expression:

$$WACC = \frac{(E + Pr + PrCo)Ke + DKd(1 - T)}{E + Pr + PrCo + D}$$

Line 12 is the present value of the forecast FCF discounted at the WACC. As could not be otherwise, this line is the same as line 10.

Table 20.3 shows the valuation of KKR's strategy. The valuation has been carried out using the same hypotheses as in Table 20.1. However, in this case, the valuation is performed by grouping the financial instruments comprising the liabilities into *two groups*: equity (shares, preferred stock, and convertible preferred stock) and debt.

Line 6 of Table 20.3 shows the required return to equity plus the preferred stock plus the convertible stock. β_L is obtained from the equation

$$\beta_L = \frac{\beta_U[E + Co + Pr + D(1 - T)] - \beta_d D(1 - T)}{E + Co + Pr}$$

Line 7 shows the value of the equity plus the preferred stock plus the convertibles. Line 8 shows the forecast value for the debt in each year and

Table 20.2

Valuation of the Management Group's Strategy According to the No-Cost-of-Leverage Theory

($ million)	1988	1989	1990	1991	1992	1993	1994	1995	1996	1997	1998	1999	2000	2001
1 ECF + CFpref + CFcon = ECF +		0	0	0	0	0	0	0	281	3,331	3,665	3,860	4,146	4,456
2 Rf		8.5%	8.5%	8.5%	8.5%	8.5%	8.5%	8.5%	8.5%	8.5%	8.5%	8.5%	8.5%	8.5%
3 Pm		8%	8%	8%	8%	8%	8%	8%	8%	8%	8%	8%	8%	8%
4 Beta u		0.65	0.65	0.65	0.65	0.65	0.65	0.65	0.65	0.65	0.65	0.65	0.65	0.65
5 Beta d		0.442	0.449	0.455	0.466	0.482	0.499	0.543	0.682	0.682				
6 Beta L		0.924	0.760	0.738	0.717	0.696	0.679	0.663	0.648	0.650	0.650	0.650	0.650	0.650
7 Ke		15.9%	14.6%	14.4%	14.2%	14.1%	13.9%	13.8%	13.7%	13.7%	13.7%	13.7%	13.7%	13.7%
8 E + = PV(ECF +; Ke)	11,632	13,481	15,446	17,671	20,186	23,026	26,235	29,857	33,661	34,942	36,064	37,145	38,088	38,850
9 D	23,204	11,186	10,594	9,676	8,395	6,803	4,857	2,515	0	0	0	0	0	0
10 D + E +	34,836	24,667	26,040	27,347	28,581	29,829	31,092	32,372	33,661	34,942	36,064	37,145	38,088	38,850
Kd		12.0%	12.1%	12.1%	12.2%	12.4%	12.5%	12.8%	14.0%	14.0%	0.0%	0.0%	0.0%	0.0%
11 WACC		10.6%	11.6%	11.8%	12.1%	12.3%	12.6%	13.0%	13.3%	13.7%	13.7%	13.7%	13.7%	13.7%
12 D + E + = PV(FCF; WACC)	34,836	24,667	26,040	27,347	28,581	29,829	31,092	32,372	33,661	34,942	36,064	37,145	38,088	38,850
13 Ku		13.7%	13.7%	13.7%	13.7%	13.7%	13.7%	13.7%	13.7%	13.7%	13.7%	13.7%	13.7%	13.7%
14 FCF	32,390	13,861	1,485	1,767	2,062	2,277	2,507	2,753	3,028	3,331	3,665	3,860	4,146	4,456
15 Vu = PV(FCF; Ku)	32,390	22,967	24,628	26,235	27,768	29,295	30,802	32,269	33,661	34,942	36,064	37,145	38,088	38,850
16 DTKu	2,446	1,081	521	493	451	391	317	226	117	0	0	0	0	0
17 DVTS = PV(DTKu; Ku)	2,446	1,700	1,412	1,111	813	533	290	103	0	0	0	0	0	0
18 D + E + = DVTS + Vu	34,836	24,667	26,040	27,347	28,581	29,829	31,092	32,372	33,661	34,942	36,064	37,145	38,088	38,850
19 CCF		14,810	1,945	2,204	2,464	2,629	2,796	2,966	3,147	3,331	3,665	3,860	4,146	4,456
20 WACC$_{BT}$		13.3%	13.5%	13.5%	13.5%	13.6%	13.6%	13.7%	13.7%	13.7%	13.7%	13.7%	13.7%	13.7%
21 D + E + = PV(CCF; WACC$_{BT}$)	34,836	24,667	26,040	27,347	28,581	29,829	31,092	32,372	33,661	34,942	36,064	37,145	38,088	38,850
E + = E + Pr + PrCo														

Difference between Tables 15.7, 15.18, and 20.2; Management Group's Strategy, Cost of Leverage

($ million)	1988	1989	1990	1991	1992	1993	1994	1995	1996	1997	1998	1999	2000
Enterprise value													
Vu	32,390	22,967	24,628	26,235	27,768	29,295	30,802	32,269	33,661	34,942	36,064	37,145	38,088
No-cost-of-leverage (Table 20.2)	34,836	24,667	26,040	27,347	28,581	29,829	31,092	32,372	33,661	34,942	36,064	37,145	38,088
Table 15.7	30,038	20,764	22,460	24,134	25,773	27,454	29,169	30,910	32,656	34,331	35,779	37,071	38,088
Table 15.18	32,626	23,106	24,729	26,297	27,797	29,299	30,789	32,253	33,661	34,942	36,064	37,145	38,088
Table 20.2 – Table 15.7	**4,797**	**3,902**	**3,579**	**3,213**	**2,808**	**2,375**	**1,923**	**1,462**	**1,005**	**611**	**285**	**74**	**0**
Table 20.2 – Table 15.18	**2,209**	**1,561**	**1,311**	**1,049**	**784**	**530**	**303**	**119**	**0**	**0**	**0**	**0**	**0**
Table 15.18 – Table 15.7	2,588	2,342	2,268	2,163	2,024	1,845	1,620	1,343	1,005	611	285	74	0
DVTS No-cost-of-leverage	2,446	1,700	1,412	1,111	813	533	290	103	0	0	0	0	0

Table 20.3
Valuation of KKR's Strategy According to the No-Cost-of-Leverage Theory

($ Million)	1988	1989	1990	1991	1992	1993	1994	1995	1996	1997	1998	1999	2000
ECF + CFcon + CFpref = ECF +		0	0	0	0	0	0	0	0	3,801	4,319	4,651	5,012
1 Rf		8.50%	8.50%	8.50%	8.50%	8.50%	8.50%	8.50%	8.50%	8.50%	8.50%	8.50%	8.50%
2 Pm		8.00%	8.00%	8.00%	8.00%	8.00%	8.00%	8.00%	8.00%	8.00%	8.00%	8.00%	8.00%
3 Beta u		0.65	0.65	0.65	0.65	0.65	0.65	0.65	0.65	0.65	0.65	0.65	0.65
4 Beta d		0.45	0.45	0.46	0.47	0.48	0.50	0.53	0.69	0.70	-1.06	-1.06	-1.06
5 Beta L		0.85	0.79	0.74	0.72	0.70	0.68	0.67	0.65	0.65	0.65	0.65	0.65
6 Ke		15.3%	14.8%	14.5%	14.3%	14.1%	13.9%	13.8%	13.7%	13.7%	13.7%	13.7%	13.7%
7 E + = PV(ECF +; Ke)	13,902	16,031	18,408	21,068	24,072	27,463	31,294	35,619	40,492	42,238	43,705	45,042	46,200
8 D	21,084	17,353	13,832	12,417	10,677	8,694	6,311	3,479	149	0	0	0	0
9 D + E +	34,986	33,384	32,240	33,485	34,749	36,157	37,605	39,098	40,641	42,238	43,705	45,042	46,200
10 Kd		12.1%	12.1%	12.2%	12.3%	12.4%	12.5%	12.8%	14.0%	14.1%	0.0%	0.0%	0.0%
11 WACC		10.7%	11.0%	11.4%	11.6%	12.3%	12.6%	12.9%	13.3%	13.7%	13.7%	13.7%	13.7%
12 D + E + = PV(FCF; WACC)	34,986	33,384	32,240	33,485	34,749	36,157	37,605	39,098	40,641	42,238	43,705	45,042	46,200
13 Ku		13.7%	13.7%	13.7%	13.7%	13.7%	13.7%	13.7%	13.7%	13.7%	13.7%	13.7%	13.7%
14 FCF		5,343	4,829	2,421	2,620	2,855	3,101	3,364	3,652	3,964	4,319	4,651	5,012
15 Vu = PV(FCF; Ku)	31,813	30,829	30,223	31,942	33,698	35,459	37,216	38,951	40,635	42,238	43,705	45,042	46,200
16 DTKu		982	808	644	578	497	405	294	162	7	0	0	0
17 DVTS = PV(DTKu; Ku)	2,902	2,318	1,827	1,433	1,051	698	389	148	6	0	0	0	0
18 Not-paid interest × T		70	81	106	124	0	0						
19 PV(Not-paid interest T; Ku)	271	238	190	109									
20 D + E + = DVTS + Vu + PV	34,986	33,384	32,240	33,485	34,749	36,157	37,605	39,098	40,641	42,238	43,705	45,042	46,200
21 CCF		6,279	5,625	3,100	3,262	3,304	3,471	3,638	3,817	3,971	4,319	4,651	5,012
22 WACC$_{BT}$		13.4%	13.4%	13.5%	13.5%	13.6%	13.6%	13.6%	13.7%	13.7%	13.7%	13.7%	13.7%
23 D + E + = PV(CCF; WACC$_{BT}$) E + Pr + PrCo = E +	34,986	33,384	32,240	33,485	34,749	36,157	37,605	39,098	40,641	42,238	43,705	45,042	46,200

Difference between Tables 15.11, 15.19, and 20.3; KKR's Strategy, Cost of Leverage

($ Million)	1988	1989	1990	1991	1992	1993	1994	1995	1996	1997	1998	1999	2000
Enterprise value													
Vu	31,813	30,829	30,223	31,942	33,698	35,459	37,216	38,951	40,635	42,238	43,705	45,042	46,200
No-cost-of-leverage theory (Table 20.3)	34,986	33,384	32,240	33,485	34,749	36,157	37,605	39,098	40,641	42,238	43,705	45,042	46,200
Table 15.11	29,832	28,877	28,284	29,993	31,745	33,658	35,621	37,626	39,668	41,674	43,472	45,015	46,200
Table 15.19	32,342	31,250	30,534	32,127	33,732	35,463	37,199	38,927	40,634	42,238	43,705	45,042	46,200
Table 20.3 − Table 15.11	**5,154**	**4,507**	**3,955**	**3,492**	**3,004**	**2,499**	**1,983**	**1,472**	**973**	**564**	**233**	**26**	**0**
Table 20.3 − Table 15.19	**2,644**	**2,135**	**1,705**	**1,358**	**1,017**	**694**	**405**	**171**	**7**	**0**	**0**	**0**	**0**
Table 15.19 − Table 15.11	2,510	2,372	2,250	2,134	1,987	1,805	1,578	1,301	966	564	233	26	0
DVTS No-cost-of-leverage	2,902	2,318	1,827	1,433	1,051	698	389	148	6	0	0	0	0

line 9 contains the sum of the debt value and the enterprise value (debt plus shares plus preferred stock plus convertible preferred stock). Line 11 shows the weighted average cost of capital (WACC), calculated in accordance with the expression:

$$\text{WACC} = (\frac{(E + Co + Pr)Ke + DKd(1 - T) - InpT}{E + Co + Pr + D})$$

Line 12 is the present value of the forecast FCF discounted at the WACC. Logically, this line is the same as line 9.

20.2. VALUATION ACCORDING TO DAMODARAN (1994)

Table 20.4 shows a valuation of the pre-bid strategy. The valuation has been carried out using the same hypotheses as in Table 20.1.

Line 6 of table 20.4 shows the required return to equity. This parameter is calculated from the CAPM: $Ke = 8.5\% + \beta_L \times 8\%$. β_L is obtained from the equity value (E) using the equation $\beta_L = \beta_U[D(1 - T) + E]/E$ instead of $\beta_L = \beta_U(D + E)/E$.

Table 20.5 shows a valuation of the management group's strategy. The valuation has been carried out using the same hypotheses as in Table 20.1. However, note that the valuation has been carried out grouping the financial instruments comprising the liabilities into two groups: equity (shares, preferred stock, and convertible preferred stock) and debt.

Line 7 of Table 20.5 shows the required return to equity plus the preferred stock plus the convertible preferred stock. This parameter is calculated from the CAPM: $Ke = 8.5\% + \beta_L \times 8\%$. β_L is obtained from the equation

$$\beta_L = \frac{\beta_U[E + Pr + PrCo + D(1 - T)]}{E + Pr + PrCo}$$

Line 8 shows the value of the shares plus the preferred stock plus the convertible preferred stock. Line 9 shows the forecast value for the debt in each year, and line 10 contains the sum of debt value and the enterprise value (debt plus shares plus preferred stock plus convertible preferred stock). Line 11 shows the weighted average cost of capital (WACC), calculated according to the expression:

$$\text{WACC} = \frac{(E + Pr + PrCo)Ke + DKd(1 - T)}{E + Pr + PrCo + D}$$

Line 12 is the present value of the forecast FCF discounted at the WACC. This line is the same as line 10.

Table 20.4
Valuation of the Pre-Bid Strategy According to Damodaran (1994)

($ Million)	1988	1989	1990	1991	1992	1993	1994	1995	1996	1997	1998
1 Rf		8.50%	8.50%	8.50%	8.50%	8.50%	8.50%	8.50%	8.50%	8.50%	8.50%
2 Pm		8.00%	8.00%	8.00%	8.00%	8.00%	8.00%	8.00%	8.00%	8.00%	8.00%
3 Beta u		0.65	0.65	0.65	0.65	0.65	0.65	0.65	0.65	0.65	0.65
4 Beta d		0.34	0.31	0.31	0.31	0.31	0.31	0.31	0.31	0.31	
5 Beta L		0.76	0.77	0.77	0.76	0.74	0.73	0.71	0.70	0.68	0.65
6 Ke		14.6%	14.7%	14.6%	14.5%	14.5%	14.3%	14.1%	14.1%	13.9%	13.7%
7 E = PV(ECF; Ke)	19,840	1,406	23,315	25,353	27,260	29,231	31,788	33,469	35,938	39,222	40,007
8 D	5,204	6,018	6,300	6,273	5,982	5,400	4,164	3,727	2,355	0	0
9 D + E	25,044	27,424	29,615	31,626	33,242	34,631	35,952	37,197	38,293	39,222	40,007
10 Kd		11.2%	11.0%	11.0%	11.0%	11.0%	11.0%	11.0%	11.0%	11.0%	0.0%
11 WACC		13.1%	13.0%	13.1%	13.1%	13.2%	13.2%	13.4%	13.4%	13.5%	13.7%
12 PV (FCF; WACC)	25,044	27,424	29,615	31,626	33,242	34,631	35,952	37,197	38,293	39,222	40,007
13 Ku		13.7%	13.7%	13.7%	13.7%	13.7%	13.7%	13.7%	13.7%	13.7%	13.7%
14 FCF		901	1,385	1,856	2,528	2,985	3,261	3,555	3,888	4,246	4,589
15 Vu = PV(FCF; Ku)	24,247	26,667	28,936	31,044	32,768	34,272	35,707	37,043	38,231	39,222	40,007
19 CCF		1,099	1,610	2,092	2,763	3,209	3,463	3,711	4,027	4,334	4,589
20 WACC$_{BT}$		13.9%	13.9%	13.9%	13.8%	13.8%	13.8%	13.8%	13.8%	13.7%	13.7%
21 D + E = PV(CCF; WACC$_{BT}$)	25,044	27,424	29,615	31,626	33,242	34,631	35,952	37,197	38,293	39,222	40,007

Table 20.5
Valuation of the Management Group's Strategy According to Damodaran (1994)

($ Million)	1988	1989	1990	1991	1992	1993	1994	1995	1996	1997	1998	1999	2000
1 ECF + CFpref + CFconv = ECF +		0	0	0	0	0	0	0	281	3,331	3,665	3,860	4,146
2 Rf		8.50%	8.50%	8.50%	8.50%	8.50%	8.50%	8.50%	8.50%	8.50%	8.50%	8.50%	8.50%
3 Pm		8.00%	8.00%	8.00%	8.00%	8.00%	8.00%	8.00%	8.00%	8.00%	8.00%	8.00%	8.00%
4 Beta u		0.65	0.65	0.65	0.65	0.65	0.65	0.65	0.65	0.65	0.65	0.65	0.65
5 Beta d		0.44	0.45	0.45	0.47	0.48	0.50	0.54	0.68	0.68	0.65	0.65	0.65
6 beta L		1.61	1.03	0.96	0.89	0.83	0.78	0.73	0.69	0.65	0.65	0.65	0.65
7 Ke		21.4%	16.8%	16.2%	15.6%	15.2%	14.7%	14.3%	14.0%	13.7%	13.7%	13.7%	13.7%
8 E += PV(ECF +; Ke)	10,351	12,565	14,670	17,043	19,710	22,699	26,042	29,777	33,661	34,942	36,064	37,145	38,088
9 D	23,204	11,186	10,594	9,676	8,395	6,803	4,857	2,515	0	0	0	0	0
10 D + E +=	33,555	23,751	25,264	26,719	28,105	29,502	30,899	32,292	33,661	34,942	36,064	37,145	38,088
Kd		12.0%	12.1%	12.1%	12.2%	12.4%	12.5%	12.8%	14.0%	14.0%	0.0%	0.0%	0.0%
11 WACC		12.1%	12.6%	12.8%	12.9%	13.1%	13.2%	13.4%	13.6%	13.7%	13.7%	13.7%	13.7%
12 D + E += PV (FCF; WACC)	33,555	23,751	25,264	26,719	28,105	29,502	30,899	32,292	33,661	34,942	36,064	37,145	38,088
13 Ku		13.7%	13.7%	13.7%	13.7%	13.7%	13.7%	13.7%	13.7%	13.7%	13.7%	13.7%	13.7%
14 FCF		13,861	1,485	1,767	2,062	2,277	2,507	2,753	3,028	3,331	3,665	3,860	4,146
15 Vu = PV (FCF; Ku)	32,390	22,967	24,628	26,235	27,768	29,295	30,802	32,269	33,661	34,942	36,064	37,145	38,088
19 CCF		14,810	1,945	2,204	2,464	2,629	2,796	2,966	3,147	3,331	3,665	3,860	4,146
20 WACC$_{BT}$		14.9%	14.6%	14.5%	14.4%	14.3%	14.2%	14.1%	14.0%	13.7%	13.7%	13.7%	13.7%
21 D + E += PV(CCF; WACC$_{BT}$)	33,555	23,751	25,264	26,719	28,105	29,502	30,899	32,292	33,661	34,942	36,064	37,145	38,088

Table 20.6 shows a valuation of KKR's strategy. Note that the valuation has been carried out grouping the financial instruments comprising the liabilities into two groups: equity (shares, preferred stock, and convertible stock) and debt.

Line 6 of Table 20.6 shows the required return to equity plus the preferred stock plus the convertible stock. This parameter is calculated from the CAPM: $Ke = 8.5\% + \beta_L \times 8\%$. β_L is obtained from the equation

$$\beta_L = \frac{\beta_U[E + Co + Pr + D(1 - T)]}{E + Co + Pr}$$

Line 7 shows the value of the shares plus the preferred stock plus the convertible stock. Line 8 shows the forecast value for the debt in each year and line 9 contains the sum of the debt value and the enterprise value (debt plus shares plus preferred stock plus convertible stock). Line 11 shows the (WACC), calculated according to the expression:

$$\frac{WACC^* = (E + Co + Pr)Ke + DKd(1 - T) - InpT}{E + Co + Pr + D)}$$

Line 12 is the present value of the forecast FCF discounted at the WACC. This line is the same as line 9.

20.3. VALUATION FROM THE CCF ACCORDING TO RUBACK

Tables 20.7–20.9 show the valuations of the company according to Ruback. According to this method, the enterprise value is the present value of the capital cash flows (CCF) discounted at the required return to assets.

20.4. VALUATION FROM THE APV ACCORDING TO MYERS

Tables 20.10–20.12 show the valuations of the company according to Myers. According to this method, the enterprise value is the value of the unlevered company's equity (Vu) plus the discounted value of the tax shield (DVTS). The value of the unlevered company's equity (Vu) is the present value of the FCFs discounted at the required return to assets. The DVTS is the present value of the annual tax saving (DTKd) discounted at the required return to debt (Kd).

Table 20.6
Valuation of KKR's Strategy According to Damodaran (1994)

($ Million)	1988	1989	1990	1991	1992	1993	1994	1995	1996	1997	1998	1999	2000
ECF + CFconv + CFpre = ECF +		0	0	0	0	0	0	0	0	3,801	4,319	4,651	5,012
1 Rf		8.50%	8.50%	8.50%	8.50%	8.50%	8.50%	8.50%	8.50%	8.50%	8.50%	8.50%	8.50%
2 Pm		8.00%	8.00%	8.00%	8.00%	8.00%	8.00%	8.00%	8.00%	8.00%	8.00%	8.00%	8.00%
3 Beta u		0.65	0.65	0.65	0.65	0.65	0.65	0.65	0.65	0.65	0.65	0.65	0.65
4 Beta d		0.45	0.45	0.46	0.47	0.48	0.50	0.53	0.69	0.70	−1.06	−1.06	−1.06
5 Beta L		1.38	1.15	0.99	0.91	0.85	0.79	0.74	0.69	0.65	0.65	0.65	0.65
6 Ke		19.6%	17.7%	16.4%	15.8%	15.3%	14.8%	14.4%	14.0%	13.7%	13.7%	13.7%	13.7%
7 E + = PV(ECF + ; Ke)	12,360	14,777	17,396	20,254	23,454	27,034	31,036	35,504	40,487	42,238	43,705	45,042	46,200
8 D	21,084	17,353	13,832	12,417	10,677	8,694	6,311	3,479	149	0	0	0	0
9 D + E +	33,444	32,130	31,228	32,671	34,131	35,728	37,347	38,983	40,636	42,238	43,705	45,042	46,200
10 Kd		12.1%	12.1%	12.2%	12.3%	12.4%	12.5%	12.8%	14.0%	14.1%	0.0%	0.0%	0.0%
11 WACC		12.0%	12.2%	12.4%	12.5%	13.0%	13.2%	13.4%	13.6%	13.7%	13.7%	13.7%	13.7%
12 D + E + = PV(FCF; WACC)	33,444	32,130	31,228	32,671	34,131	35,728	37,347	38,983	40,636	42,238	43,705	45,042	46,200
13 Ku		13.7%	13.7%	13.7%	13.7%	13.7%	13.7%	13.7%	13.7%	13.7%	13.7%	13.7%	13.7%
14 FCF		5,343	4,829	2,421	2,620	2,855	3,101	3,364	3,652	3,964	4,319	4,651	5,012
15 Vu = PV (FCF; Ku)	31,813	30,829	30,223	31,942	33,698	35,459	37,216	38,951	40,635	42,238	43,705	45,042	46,200
21 CCF		6,279	5,625	3,100	3,262	3,304	3,471	3,638	3,817	3,971	4,319	4,651	5,012
22 WACC_{BT}		14.8%	14.7%	14.5%	14.5%	14.4%	14.2%	14.1%	14.0%	13.7%	13.7%	13.7%	13.7%
23 D + E + = PV(CCF; WACC_{BT})	33,444	32,130	31,228	32,671	34,131	35,728	37,347	38,983	40,636	42,238	43,705	45,042	46,200
E + Pr + PrCo = E +													

Table 20.7
Valuation of the Pre-Bid Strategy According to Ruback

($ Million)	1988	1989	1990	1991	1992	1993	1994	1995	1996	1997	1998
CCF		1,099	1,610	2,092	2,763	3,209	3,463	3,711	4,027	4,334	4,589
Ku		13.7%	13.7%	13.7%	13.7%	13.7%	13.7%	13.7%	13.7%	13.7%	13.7%
D + E = PV (CCF; Ku)	25,248	27,608	29,780	31,768	33,357	34,718	36,011	37,234	38,308	39,222	40,007

Table 20.8
Valuation of the Management Group's Strategy According to Ruback

($ Million)	1988	1989	1990	1991	1992	1993	1994	1995	1996	1997	1998
CCF		14,810	1,945	2,204	2,464	2,629	2,796	2,966	3,147	3,331	3,665
Ku		13.7%	13.7%	13.7%	13.7%	13.7%	13.7%	13.7%	13.7%	13.7%	13.7%
D + E + = PV (CCF; Ku)	34,568	24,493	25,904	27,248	28,517	29,795	31,081	32,374	33,661	34,942	36,064

Table 20.9
Valuation of KKR's Strategy According to Ruback

($ Million)	1988	1989	1990	1991	1992	1993	1994	1995	1996	1997	1998
CCF		6,279	5,625	3,100	3,262	3,304	3,471	3,638	3,817	3,971	4,319
Ku		13.7%	13.7%	13.7%	13.7%	13.7%	13.7%	13.7%	13.7%	13.7%	13.7%
D + E + = PV (CCF; Ku)	34,679	33,151	32,067	33,360	34,668	36,113	37,590	39,102	40,641	42,238	43,705

Table 20.10

Valuation of the Pre-Bid Strategy According to Myers

($ Million)	1988	1989	1990	1991	1992	1993	1994	1995	1996	1997	1998
Ku		13.7%	13.7%	13.7%	13.7%	13.7%	13.7%	13.7%	13.7%	13.7%	13.7%
FCF		901	1,385	1,856	2,528	2,985	3,261	3,555	3,888	4,246	4,589
Vu = PV (FCF; Ku)	24,247	26,667	28,936	31,044	32,768	34,272	35,707	37,043	38,231	39,222	40,007
DTKd		198	225	236	235	224	202	156	139	88	0
Kd		11.2%	11.0%	11.0%	11.0%	11.0%	11.0%	11.0%	11.0%	11.0%	0.0%
DVTS = PV (DTKd; Kd)	1,097	1,021	909	773	623	468	318	197	79	0	0
D + E = DVTS + Vu	25,343	27,689	29,845	31,817	33,392	34,741	36,025	37,240	38,310	39,222	40,007

Table 20.11

Valuation of the Management Group's Strategy According to Myers

($ Million)	1988	1989	1990	1991	1992	1993	1994	1995	1996	1997	1998
Ku		13.7%	13.7%	13.7%	13.7%	13.7%	13.7%	13.7%	13.7%	13.7%	13.7%
FCF		13,861	1,485	1,767	2,062	2,277	2,507	2,753	3,028	3,331	3,665
Vu = PV (FCF; Ku)	32,390	22,967	24,628	26,235	27,768	29,295	30,802	32,269	33,661	34,942	36,064
DTKd		949	460	437	402	353	289	212	119	0	0
Kd		12.0%	12.1%	12.1%	12.2%	12.4%	12.5%	12.8%	14.0%	14.0%	0.0%
DVTS = PV (DTKd; Kd)	2,262	1,585	1,317	1,040	765	507	281	105	0	0	0
D + E = DVTS + Vu	34,653	24,552	25,945	27,275	28,533	29,802	31,083	32,373	33,661	34,942	36,064

Table 20.12

Valuation of KKR's Strategy According to Myers

($ Million)	1988	1989	1990	1991	1992	1993	1994	1995	1996	1997	1998
Ku		13.7%	13.7%	13.7%	13.7%	13.7%	13.7%	13.7%	13.7%	13.7%	13.7%
FCF		5,343	4,829	2,421	2,620	2,855	3,101	3,364	3,652	3,964	4,319
Vu = PV (FCF; Ku)	31,813	30,829	30,223	31,942	33,698	35,459	37,216	38,951	40,635	42,238	43,705
DTKd		936	796	679	642	449	370	274	166	7	0
Kd		12.1%	12.1%	12.2%	12.3%	12.4%	12.5%	12.8%	14.0%	14.1%	0.0%
DVTS = PV (DTKd; Kd)	2,982	2,406	1,901	1,454	990	664	377	151	6	0	0
D + E = DVTS + Vu	34,795	33,234	32,124	33,396	34,688	36,123	37,593	39,101	40,641	42,238	43,705

Table 20.13

Valuations of the Pre-Bid Strategy

($ Million)	1988	1989	1990	1991	1992	1993	1994	1995	1996	1997
Enterprise value										
No-cost-of-leverage	25,490	27,839	29,987	31,946	33,502	34,827	36,086	37,281	38,327	39,222
Damodaran	25,044	27,424	29,615	31,626	33,242	34,631	35,952	37,197	38,293	39,222
Practitioners	24,572	26,979	29,216	31,284	32,964	34,420	35,808	37,106	38,256	39,222
Myers	25,343	27,689	29,845	31,817	33,392	34,741	36,025	37,240	38,310	39,222
Ruback	25,248	27,608	29,780	31,768	33,357	34,718	36,011	37,234	38,308	39,222
Vu	24,247	26,667	28,936	31,044	32,768	34,272	35,707	37,043	38,231	39,222
Equity value										
No-cost-of-leverage	20,286	21,820	23,687	25,673	27,520	29,427	31,923	33,554	35,972	39,222
Damodaran	19,840	21,406	23,315	25,353	27,260	29,231	31,788	33,469	35,938	39,222
Practitioners	19,368	20,961	22,916	25,011	26,982	29,020	31,644	33,379	35,902	9,222
Myers	20,139	21,671	23,545	25,544	27,410	29,341	31,861	33,513	35,955	39,222
Ruback	20,044	21,590	23,480	25,495	27,375	29,318	31,848	33,507	35,953	39,222
Cost of leverage										
No-cost-of-leverage	0	0	0	0	0	0	0	0	0	0
Damodaran	446	415	372	319	260	197	134	84	34	0
Practitioners	918	859	771	662	538	407	278	174	71	0
Myers	147	150	143	129	110	87	62	40	17	0
Ruback	242	231	207	178	144	109	75	47	19	0

Table 20.14
Valuations of the Management Group's Strategy

($ Million)	1988	1989	1990	1991	1992	1993	1994	1995	1996	1997	1998	1999
Enterprise value												
No-cost-of-leverage	34,836	24,667	26,040	27,347	28,581	29,829	31,092	32,372	33,661	34,942	36,064	37,145
Damodaran	33,555	23,751	25,264	26,719	28,105	29,502	30,899	32,292	33,661	34,942	36,064	37,145
Practitioners	32,626	23,106	24,729	26,297	27,797	29,299	30,789	32,253	33,661	34,942	36,064	37,145
Myers	34,653	24,552	25,945	27,275	28,533	29,802	31,083	32,373	33,661	34,942	36,064	37,145
Ruback	34,568	24,493	25,904	27,248	28,517	29,795	31,081	32,374	33,661	34,942	36,064	37,145
Practitioners Chap. 15	30,038	20,764	22,460	24,134	25,773	27,454	29,169	30,910	32,656	34,331	35,779	37,071
Vu	32,390	22,967	24,628	26,235	27,768	29,295	30,802	32,269	33,661	34,942	36,064	37,145
Cost of leverage												
No-cost-of-leverage	0	0	0	0	0	0	0	0	0	0	0	0
Damodaran	1,281	916	776	627	475	327	193	80	0	0	0	0
Practitioners	2,209	1,561	1,311	1,049	784	530	303	119	0	0	0	0
Myers	183	114	94	72	48	27	9	−2	0	0	0	0
Ruback	268	173	136	99	64	34	11	−2	0	0	0	0
Practitioners Chap. 15	4,797	3,902	3,579	3,213	2,808	2,375	1,923	1,462	1,005	611	285	74

Table 20.15

Valuations of KKR's Strategy

($ Million)	1988	1989	1990	1991	1992	1993	1994	1995	1996	1997	1998	1999
Enterprise value												
No-cost-of-leverage	34,986	33,384	32,240	33,485	34,749	36,157	37,605	39,098	40,641	42,238	43,705	45,042
Damodaran	33,444	32,130	31,228	32,671	34,131	35,728	37,347	38,983	40,636	42,238	43,705	45,042
Practitioners	32,342	31,250	30,534	32,127	33,732	35,463	37,199	38,927	40,634	42,238	43,705	45,042
Myers	34,795	33,234	32,124	33,396	34,688	36,123	37,593	39,101	40,641	42,238	43,705	45,042
Ruback	34,679	33,151	32,067	33,360	34,668	36,113	37,590	39,102	40,641	42,238	43,705	45,042
Practitioners Chap. 15	29,832	28,877	28,284	29,993	31,745	33,658	35,621	37,626	39,668	41,674	43,472	45,015
Vu	31,813	30,829	30,223	31,942	33,698	35,459	37,216	38,951	40,635	42,238	43,705	45,042
Cost of leverage												
No-cost-of-leverage	0	0	0	0	0	0	0	0	0	0	0	0
Damodaran	1,542	1,255	1,012	814	618	429	258	115	5	0	0	0
Practitioners	2,644	2,135	1,705	1,358	1,017	694	405	171	7	0	0	0
Myers	191	150	116	89	61	34	12	−3	0	0	0	0
Ruback	307	233	172	125	81	44	15	−3	0	0	0	0
Practitioners Chap. 15	5,154	4,507	3,955	3,492	3,004	2,499	1,983	1,472	973	564	233	26

20.5. DIFFERENCES IN THE VALUATIONS, SUMMARY

This section summarizes the valuations discussed. It is worth pointing out that in all three valuations, the highest cost of leverage is obtained using the practitioners' theory.

The valuations performed by the management group and KKR also include the valuations obtained in Chapter 15 using the practitioners' method. Note that in this chapter we have grouped the financial instruments into two groups, while in Chapter 15 we valued them separately. It can be seen that when the financial instruments are valued separately, the value obtained is noticeably less than when they are valued as a group.

REFERENCES

Damodaran, A. (1994), *Damodaran on Valuation*, New York: John Wiley and Sons.

Modigliani, F., and M. H. Miller (1963), "Corporate Income Taxes and the Cost of Capital: A Correction," *American Economic Review*, (June), ppg. 433–443.

Fernández, P. (2002), "The Value of Tax Shields is NOT Equal to the Present Value of Tax Shields," Working Paper N. 290727, Social Science Research Network.

Myers, S. C. (1974), "Interactions of Corporate Financing and Investment Decisions—Implications for Capital Budgeting," *Journal of Finance*, (March), ppg. 1–25.

Ruback, R. S. (1995), "A Note on Capital Cash Flow Valuation," Harvard Business School, 9–295–069.

Chapter 21

Eight Methods and Seven Theories for Valuing Companies by Cash Flow Discounting

This chapter is a summarized compendium of all the methods and theories on company valuation using cash flow discounting that we have studied in the previous chapters.

Section 21.1 shows the eight most commonly used methods for valuing companies by cash flow discounting:

1. Free cash flow discounted at the WACC
2. Equity cash flows discounted at the required return to equity
3. Capital cash flows discounted at the WACC before tax
4. Adjusted present value (APV)
5. The business's risk-adjusted free cash flows discounted at the required return to assets
6. The business's risk-adjusted equity cash flows discounted at the required return to assets
7. Economic profit discounted at the required return to equity
8. EVA discounted at the WACC

All eight methods always give the same value. This result is logical, since all the methods analyze the same reality under the same hypotheses; they only differ in the cash flows taken as starting point for the valuation.

Section 21.2 is the application of the eight methods and seven theories studied in Chapter 19 to an example. We will remember that the seven theories are

1. *No-costs-of-leverage*. The relationship between the levered and unlevered beta is $\beta_L = \beta u + D(1 - T)(\beta u - \beta d)/E$

2. *Damodaran (1994)*. To introduce leverage costs, he assumes that the relationship between the levered and unlevered beta is[1] $\beta_L = \beta u + D$ $(1 - T)\beta u/E$,

3. *Practitioners method*. To introduce higher leverage costs, this method assumes that the relationship between the levered and unlevered beta is $\beta_L = \beta u + D\beta u/E$,

4. *Harris and Pringle (1985) and Ruback (1995)*. All of their formulae arise from the assumption that the leverage-driven value creation is DVTS = PV[D Kd T ; Ku].

5. *Myers (1974)*. All of his formulae arise from the assumption that the leverage-driven value creation is DVTS = PV[D Kd T; Kd].

6. *Miles and Ezzell (1980)*. They state that the correct rate for discounting the tax shield (Kd T D) is Kd for the first year, and Ku for the following years.

7. *Modigliani and Miller (1963)*. They calculate the value of tax shields (VTS) by discounting the present value of the tax savings due to interest payments of a risk-free debt (TDR$_F$) at the risk-free rate (R$_F$). Modigliani and Miller (1963, page 436, formula 3): VTS = PV[R$_F$; DTR$_F$].

Appendix 21.1 contains the valuation formulae according to these theories. Appendix 21.2 shows the changes that take place in the valuation formulae when the debt's value does not match its nominal value.

21.1. EIGHT METHODS FOR VALUING COMPANIES BY CASH FLOW DISCOUNTING

There are four basic methods for valuing companies by cash flow discounting[2]:

Method 1. Using the Free Cash Flow and the WACC (Weighted Average Cost of Capital)

Formula (21.1) indicates that the value of the debt (D) plus that of the shareholders' equity (E) is the present value of the expected free cash flows (FCF) that the company will generate, discounted at the weighted average cost of debt and shareholders' equity after tax (WACC):

---

[1]Instead of the relationship obtained from Modigliani and Miller: $\beta_L = \beta u + D (1 - T)$ $(\beta u - \beta d)/E$.

[2]The formulae used in this section are valid if the debt's interest rate matches the required return to debt (Kd), or, to put it another way, if the debt's market value is identical to its book value. The formulae for the case in which this does not happen are given in Appendix 21.2.

$$E_0 + D_0 = PV_0[WACC_t; FCF_t] \tag{21.1}$$

The definition of WACC or "weighted average cost of capital," is given by (21.2):

$$WACC_t = [E_{t-1}Ke_t + D_{t-1}Kd_t(1 - T)]/[E_{t-1} + D_{t-1}] \tag{21.2}$$

Ke is the required return to equity, Kd is the cost of the debt and T is the effective tax rate applied to earnings. $E_{t-1} + D_{t-1}$ are market values.[3]

Method 2. Using the Expected Equity Cash Flow (ECF) and the Required Return to Equity (Ke)

Formula (21.3) indicates that the value of the equity (E) is the net present value of the expected equity cash flows (ECF) discounted at the required return to equity (Ke).

$$E_0 = PV_0[Ke_t; ECF_t] \tag{21.3}$$

Formula (21.4) indicates that the value of the debt (D) is the net present value of the expected debt cash flows (CFd) discounted at the required return to debt (Kd).

$$D_0 = PV_0[Kd_t; CFd_t] \tag{21.4}$$

The expression that relates the FCF with the ECF is[4]

$$ECF_t = FCF_t + \Delta D_t - I_t(1 - T) \tag{21.5}$$

ΔD_t is the increase in debt. I_t is the interest paid by the company. It is obvious that $CFd = I_t - \Delta D_t$

The sum of the values given by formulae (21.3) and (21.4) is identical to the value provided by (21.1):[5]

$$E_0 + D_0 = PV_0[WACC_t; FCF_t] = PV_0[Ke_t; ECF_t] + PV_0[Kd_t; CFd_t]$$

---

[3]In actual fact, "market values" are the values obtained when the valuation is performed using formula (21.1). Consequently, the valuation is an iterative process: the free cash flows are discounted at the WACC to calculate the company's value (D + E) but, in order to obtain the WACC, we need to know the company's value (D + E).

[4]Obviously, the free cash flow is the hypothetical equity cash flow when the company has no debt.

[5]The right way of defining the WACC is as follows. The WACC is the rate at which the FCF must be discounted so that equation (21.2) gives the same result as that given by the sum of (21.3) and (21.4).

Method 3. Using the Capital Cash Flow (CCF) and the $WACC_{BT}$ (Weighted Average Cost of Capital, Before Tax)

The capital cash flows are the cash flows available for all holders of the company's securities, whether these are debt or shares, and are equivalent to the ECF plus the cash flow corresponding to the debt holders (CFd).

Formula (21.6) indicates that the value of the debt today (D) plus that of the shareholders' equity (E), is equal to the capital cash flow (CCF) discounted at the weighted average cost of debt and shareholders' equity before tax ($WACC_{BT}$).

$$E_0 + D_0 = PV[WACC_{BTt}; CCF_t] \qquad (21.6)$$

The definition of $WACC_{BT}$ is (21.7):

$$WACC_{BTt} = [E_{t-1}Ke_t + D_{t-1}Kd_t]/[E_{t-1} + D_{t-1}] \qquad (21.7)$$

The expression (21.7) is obtained by making (21.1) equal to (21.6). $WACC_{BT}$ represents the discount rate that ensures that the value of the company obtained using the two expressions is the same:[6]

$$E_0 + D_0 = PV[WACC_{BTt}; CCF_t] = PV[WACC_t; FCF_t]$$

The expression that relates the CCF with the ECF and the FCF is (21.8):

$$CCF_t = ECF_t + CFd_t = ECF_t - \Delta D_t + I_t = FCF_t + I_t T \Delta D_t$$
$$= D_t - D_{t-1}; I_t = D_{t-1}Kd_t \qquad (21.8)$$

Method 4. Adjusted present value (APV)

The APV formula (21.9) indicates that the value of the debt (D) plus that of the shareholders' equity (E) is equal to the value of the unlevered company's shareholders' equity Vu plus the net present value of the discounted value of the tax shield (DVTS):

$$E_0 + D_0 = Vu_0 + DVTS_0 \qquad (21.9)$$

We already saw in Chapters 17 and 19 that there are several theories for calculating the DVTS.

If Ku is the required return to equity in the debt-free company (also called the required return to assets), Vu is given by (21.10):

---

[6]The right way of defining the $WACC_{BT}$ is as follows. The $WACC_{BT}$ is the rate at which the CCF must be discounted so that equation (21.6) gives the same result as that given by the sum of (21.3) and (21.4).

$$Vu_0 = PV_0[Ku_t; FCF_t] \tag{21.10}$$

Consequently,

$$DVTS_0 = E_0 + D_0 - Vu_0 = PV_0[WACC_t; FCF_t] - PV_0[Ku_t; FCF_t]$$

We can talk of a fifth method (using the business risk-adjusted free cash flow), although this is not actually a new method but is derived from the previous methods.

Method 5. Using the Business Risk-Adjusted Free Cash Flow and Ku (Required Return to Assets)

Formula (21.11) indicates that the value of the debt (D) plus that of the shareholders' equity (E) is the present value of the expected business risk-adjusted free cash flows[7] (FCF\\Ku) that will be generated by the company, discounted at the required return to assets (Ku):

$$E_0 + D_0 = PV_0[Ku_t; FCF_t\backslash\backslash Ku] \tag{21.11}$$

It will be readily seen that the definition of the business risk-adjusted free cash flows[8] (FCF\\Ku) is (21.12):

$$FCF_t\backslash\backslash Ku = FCF_t - (E_{t-1} + D_{t-1})[WACC_t - Ku_t] \tag{21.12}$$

Likewise, we can talk of a sixth method (using the business risk-adjusted equity cash flow), although this is not actually a new method but is derived from the previous methods.

Method 6. Using the Business Risk-Adjusted Equity Cash Flow and Ku (Required Return to Assets)

Formula (21.13) indicates that the value of the equity (E) is the net present value of the expected business risk-adjusted equity cash flows[9] (ECF\\Ku) discounted at the required return to assets (Ku):

$$E_0 = PV_0[Ku_t; ECF_t\backslash\backslash Ku] \tag{21.13}$$

It will be readily seen that the definition of the business risk-adjusted equity cash flows[10] (ECF\\Ku) is (21.14):

$$ECF_t\backslash\backslash Ku = ECF_t - E_{t-1}[Ke_t - Ku_t] \tag{21.14}$$

---

[7]The asset risk-adjusted free cash flow was discussed in Section 17.6.2.
[8]The expression (21.12) is obtained by making (21.11) equal to (21.1).
[9]The asset risk-adjusted equity cash flow was discussed in Section 17.6.2.
[10]The expression (21.14) is obtained by making (21.13) equal to (21.3).

Also, we have the methods analyzed in Chapter 13, using the economic profit and the EVA for valuation purposes.

Method 7 Using the Economic Profit and Ke (Required Return to Equity)

Formula (21.15) indicates that the value of the equity (E) is the equity's book value plus the net present value of the expected economic profit (EP) discounted at the required return to equity (Ke).

$$E_0 = Ebv_0 + PV_0[Ke_t; EP_t] \qquad (21.15)$$

The term economic profit (EP) is used to define the accounting net income or profit after tax (PAT) less the equity's book value (Ebv_{t-1}) multiplied by the required return to equity.

$$EP_t = PAT_t - Ke\ Ebv_{t-1} \qquad (21.16)$$

Method 8. Using the EVA (Economic Value Added) and the WACC

Formula (21.17) indicates that the value of the debt (D) plus that of the shareholders' equity (E) is the book value of the shareholders' equity and the debt ($Ebv_0 + N_0$) plus the present value of the expected EVA, discounted at the weighted average cost of capital (WACC):

$$E_0 + D_0 = (Ebv_0 + N_0) + PV_0[WACC_t; EVA_t] \qquad (21.17)$$

The EVA is the net operating profit after taxes (NOPAT) less the company's book value ($D_{t-1} + Ebv_{t-1}$) multiplied by the WACC. The NOPAT is the profit of the unlevered company (debt-free).

$$EVA_t = NOPAT_t - (D_{t-1} + Ebv_{t-1})WACC_t \qquad (21.18)$$

We could also talk of a ninth method; using the business risk-adjusted capital cash flow and Ku (required return to assets), but the business risk-adjusted capital cash flow is identical to the business risk-adjusted free cash flow (CCF\\Ku = FCF\\Ku). Therefore, this method would be identical to Method 5.

21.2. AN EXAMPLE: VALUATION OF THE COMPANY DELTA INC.

The company Delta Inc. has forecast the balance sheets and income statements for the next few years, as shown in Table 21.1. After year 3, it is

Table 21.1

Balance Sheet and Income Statement Forecasts for Delta Inc.

	0	1	2	3	4
WCR (net current assets)	400	430	515	550	572.00
Gross fixed assets	1,600	1,800	2,300	2,600	2,956.00
– Cum. depreciation		200	450	720	1,000.80
Net fixed assets	1,600	1,600	1,850	1,880	1,955.20
Total assets	**2,000**	**2,030**	**2,365**	**2,430**	**2,527.20**
Debt (N)	1,000	1,000	1,100	1,100	1,144.00
Capital (book value)	1,000	1,030	1,265	1,330	1,383.20
Total Liabilities	**2,000**	**2,030**	**2,365**	**2,430**	**2,527.20**
Income statement					
Margin		300	500	572	603.20
Interest payments		120	120	132	132.00
PBT		180	380	440	471.20
Taxes		63	133	154	164.92
PAT (net income)		**117**	**247**	**286**	**306.28**

expected that the balance sheet and the income statement will grow at an annual rate of 4%.

Using the forecast balance sheets and income statements in Table 21.1, we can readily obtain the cash flows given in Table 21.2. Obviously, the cash flows grow at a rate of 4% after year 4, not after year 3.

The equity's beta (equity of the debt-free company) is 1. The risk-free rate is 10%. The debt's cost is 12%. The tax rate is 35%. The market risk premium is 8%. Consequently, using the CAPM, the required return to assets is 18%.[11] With these parameters, the valuation of this company's equity, using the above formulae, is given in Table 21.3.

The required return to equity (Ke) appears in the second line of the table.[12] Formula (21.3) enables the equity's value to be obtained by discounting the equity cash flows at the required return to equity (Ke).[13] Likewise, formula (21.4) enables the debt's value to be obtained by discounting the debt cash

---

[11] In this example, we use the CAPM: $Ku = R_F + \beta u P_M = 10 + 8 = 18\%$.

[12] The required return to equity (Ke) has been calculated according to the No-cost-of-leverage theory.

[13] The relationship between the value of the equity in two consecutive years is $E_t = E_{t-1}(1 + Ke_t) - ECF_t$.

Table 21.2

Cash Flow Forecasts for Delta Inc.

	0	1	2	3	4	5
Equity cash flow = dividends		87.00	12.00	221.00	253.08	263.20
FCF		165.00	−10.00	306.80	294.88	306.68
CFd		120.00	20.00	132.00	88.00	91.52
CCF		207.00	32.00	353.00	341.08	354.72

flows at the required return to debt (Kd).[14] Another way to calculate the equity's value is using formula (21.1). The present value of the free cash flows discounted at the WACC, formula (21.2), gives us the value of the company, which is the value of the debt plus that of the equity.[15] By subtracting the value of the debt from this quantity, we obtain the value of the equity. Another way of calculating the equity's value is using formula (21.6). The present value of the capital cash flows discounted at the $WACC_{BT}$, formula (21.7), gives us the value of the company, which is the value of the debt plus that of the equity. By subtracting the value of the debt from this quantity, we obtain the value of the equity. The fourth method for calculating the value of the equity is using the APV formula (21.9). The company's value is the sum of the value of the unlevered company, formula (21.10), plus the present value of the discounted value of the tax shield (DVTS).[16]

The business risk-adjusted equity cash flow and free cash flow (ECF\\Ku and FCF\\Ku) are also calculated using formulae (21.14) and (21.12). Formula (21.13) enables the equity's value to be obtained by discounting the business risk-adjusted equity cash flows at the required return to assets (Ku). Another way to calculate the equity's value is using formula (21.11). The present value of the business risk-adjusted free cash flows discounted at the required return to assets (Ku) gives us the value of the company, which is the value of the debt plus that of the equity. By subtracting the value of the debt from this quantity, we obtain the value of the equity.

The example of Table 21.3 shows that the result obtained with all eight valuations is the same. The equity's value today is 1,043.41. As we have

---

[14]The value of the debt matches the nominal value (book value) given in Table 21.1 because we have considered that the required return to debt matches its cost (12%).

[15]The relationship between the company's value in two consecutive years is $(D + E)_t = (D + E)_{t-1}(1 + WACC_t) - FCF_t$.

[16]As the required return to equity (Ke) has been calculated according to the No-costs-of-leverage theory, we must also calculate the DVTS according to the No-costs-of- leverage theory, namely: DVTS = PV(Ku; D T Ku).

Table 21.3

Valuation of Delta Inc.

Formula	0	1	2	3	4
Ku	18.00%	18.00%	18.00%	18.00%	18.00%
Ke	21.74%	21.30%	21.01%	20.86%	20.86%
[1] E + D = PV(WACC; FCF)	2,043.41	2,183.23	2,523.21	2,601.29	2,705.34
[2] WACC	14.92%	15.11%	15.25%	15.34%	15.34%
E = [1] – D	**1,043.41**	**1,183.23**	**1,423.21**	**1,501.29**	**1,561.34**
[3] E = PV(Ke; ECF)	**1,043.41**	**1,183.23**	**1,423.21**	**1,501.29**	**1,561.34**
[4] D = PV(CFd; Kd)	1,000.00	1,000.00	1,100.00	1,100.00	1,144.00
[6] D + E = PV(WACC$_{BT}$; CCF)	2,043.41	2,183.23	2,523.21	2,601.29	2,705.34
[7] WACC$_{BT}$	16.97%	17.04%	17.08%	17.11%	17.11%
E = [6] – D	**1,043.41**	**1,183.23**	**1,423.21**	**1,501.29**	**1,561.34**
DVTS = PV(Ku; D T Ku)	442.09	458.66	478.22	495.00	514.80
[10] Vu = PV(Ku; FCF)	1,601.33	1,724.57	2,044.99	2,106.29	2,190.54
[9] DVTS + Vu	2,043.41	2,183.23	2,523.21	2,601.29	2,705.34
E = [9] – D	**1,043.41**	**1,183.23**	**1,423.21**	**1,501.29**	**1,561.34**
[11] D + E = PV(Ku; FCF\\Ku)	2,043.41	2,183.23	2,523.21	2,601.29	2,705.34
[12] FCF\\Ku		228.00	53.00	376.10	364.18
E = [11] – D	**1,043.41**	**1,183.23**	**1,423.21**	**1,501.29**	**1,561.34**
[13] E = PV(Ku; ECF\\Ku)	**1,043.41**	**1,183.23**	**1,423.21**	**1,501.29**	**1,561.34**
[14] ECF\\Ku		48.00	–27.00	178.10	210.18

(continues)

Table 21.3 (*continued*)

Formula	0	1	2	3	4
[16] EP		−100.38	27.65	20.17	28.87
PV(Ke; EP)	43.41	153.23	158.21	171.29	178.14
[15] **E = PV(Ke; EP) + Ebv**	**1,043.41**	**1,183.23**	**1,423.21**	**1,501.29**	**1,561.34**
[18] EVA		−103.34	18.18	11.05	19.42
PV(WACC; EVA)	43.41	153.23	158.21	171.29	178.14
[17] **E = PV(WACC; EVA) + Ebv + N − D**	**1,043.41**	**1,183.23**	**1,423.21**	**1,501.29**	**1,561.34**

already mentioned, these valuations have been performed according to No-costs-of-leverage theory. The valuations performed using other theories are discussed further on.

The Tables 21.4–21.10 contain the most salient results of the valuation performed on the company Delta Inc., according to Myers (1974), Harris and Pringle (1985), Ruback (1995), Damodaran (1994), Miles and Ezzell (1980), Modigliani and Miller (1963), and the practitioners method.

21.3. HOW IS THE COMPANY VALUED WHEN IT REPORTS LOSSES IN ONE OR MORE YEARS?

In such cases, we must calculate the tax rate that the company will pay and this is the rate that must be used to perform all the calculations. It is as if the tax rate were the rate obtained after subtracting the taxes that the company must pay.

Example. Campa Inc., reports a loss in year 1. The tax rate is 35%. In year 1, it will not pay any tax as it has suffered losses amounting to $220 million. In year 2, it will pay corporate tax amounting to 35% of that year's profit less the previous year's losses (350 − 220). The resulting tax is 45.5, that is, 13% of the PBT for year 2. Consequently, the effective tax rate is zero in year 1, 13% in year 2, and 35% in the other years.

Table 21.4
Valuation of Delta Inc. According to Myers (1974)

	0	1	2	3	4
DVTS = PV(Kd; D Kd T)	514.92	534.71	556.88	577.50	600.60
Ke	20.61%	20.22%	20.17%	19.98%	19.98%
E	**1,116.25**	**1,259.28**	**1,501.86**	**1,583.79**	**1,647.14**
WACC	14.555%	14.721%	14.940%	14.987%	14.987%
E + D	2,116.25	2,259.28	2,601.86	2,683.79	2,791.14
WACC$_{BT}$	16.540%	16.580%	16.716%	16.709%	16.709%
ECF\\Ku		57.90	−15.92	188.41	221.73
FCF\\Ku		237.90	64.08	386.41	375.73

Table 21.5
Valuation of Delta Inc. According to Harris and Pringle (1985) and Ruback (1995)

	0	1	2	3	4
DVTS	294.72	305.77	318.81	330.00	343.20
Ke	24.70%	23.82%	23.22%	22.94%	22.94%
E	**896.05**	**1,030.34**	**1,263.80**	**1,336.29**	**1,389.74**
WACC	15.785%	15.931%	16.046%	16.104%	16.104%
E + D	1,896.05	2,030.34	2,363.80	2,436.29	2,533.74
WACC$_{BT}$	18.000%	18.000%	18.000%	18.000%	18.000%
ECF\\Ku		27.00	−48.00	155.00	187.08
FCF\\Ku		207.00	32.00	353.00	341.08

Table 21.6

Valuation of Delta Inc. According to Damodaran (1994)

	0	1	2	3	4
DVTS	350.86	364.02	379.54	392.86	408.57
Ke	23.46%	22.78%	22.32%	22.09%	22.09%
E	**952.19**	**1,088.58**	**1,324.53**	**1,399.14**	**1,455.11**
WACC	15.439%	15.606%	15.732%	15.799%	15.799%
D + E	1,952.19	2,088.58	2,424.53	2,499.14	2,599.11
WACC$_{BT}$	17.590%	17.617%	17.637%	17.648%	17.648%
ECF\\Ku		35.00	−40.00	163.80	195.88
FCF\\Ku		215.00	40.00	361.80	349.88

Table 21.7

Valuation of Delta Inc. According to the Practitioners Method

	0	1	2	3	4
DVTS	154.38	160.17	167.00	172.86	179.77
Ke	28.59%	27.04%	25.91%	25.46%	25.46%
E	**755.71**	**884.73**	**1,111.99**	**1,179.14**	**1,226.31**
WACC	16.747%	16.833%	16.906%	16.938%	16.938%
D + E	1,755.71	1,884.73	2,211.99	2,279.14	2,370.31
WACC$_{BT}$	19.139%	19.061%	18.995%	18.965%	18.965%
ECF\\Ku		7.00	−68.00	133.00	165.08
FCF\\Ku		187.00	12.00	331.00	319.08

Table 21.8
Valuation of Delta Inc. According to Miles and Ezzell (1980)

	0	1	2	3	4
VTS = PV[Ku; T D Kd]$(1 + Ku)/(1 + Kd_0)$	310.51	322.15	335.89	347.68	361.59
Ke	24.33%	23.52%	22.96%	22.69%	22.69%
E	**911.84**	**1,046.72**	**1,280.88**	**1,353.96**	**1,408.12**
WACC	15.685%	15.838%	15.956%	16.016%	16.016%
D + E	1,911.84	2,046.72	2,380.88	2,453.96	2,552.12
WACC$_{BT}$	17.882%	17.890%	17.896%	17.899%	17.899%
ECF\\Ku		29.25	−45.75	157.48	189.56
FCF\\Ku		209.25	34.25	355.48	343.56

Table 21.9
Valuation of Delta Inc. According to Modigliani and Miller (1963)

	0	1	2	3	4
VTS = PV[R_F; DTR_F]	571.76	593.94	618.33	641.67	667.33
Ke	19.81%	19.48%	19.55%	19.36%	19.36%
E	**1,173.09**	**1,318.51**	**1,563.32**	**1,647.95**	**1,713.87**
WACC	14.285%	14.441%	14.697%	14.731%	14.731%
D + E	2,173.09	2,318.51	2,663.32	2,747.95	2,857.87
WACC$_{BT}$	16.217%	16.253%	16.432%	16.412%	16.412%
ECF\\Ku		65.74	−7.48	196.77	230.71
FCF\\Ku		245.74	72.52	394.77	384.71

Table 21.10
Valuation of Delta Inc. According to the Seven Theories

	E	VTS	Vu	Ke	β_L	WACC	$WACC_{BT}$	ECF\\Ku	FCF\\Ku
Modigliani-Miller	1,173.09	571.76	1,601.33	19.812%	1.226527	14.285%	16.217%	65.741	245.741
Myers	1,116.25	514.92	1,601.33	20.607%	1.325923	14.555%	16.540%	57.895	237.895
No-cost-of-leverage	1,043.41	442.09	1,601.33	21.738%	1.467217	14.917%	16.972%	48.000	228.000
Damodaran	952.19	350.86	1,601.33	23.461%	1.682638	15.439%	17.590%	35.000	215.000
Miles-Ezzell	911.84	310.51	1,601.33	24.333%	1.791669	15.685%	17.882%	29.250	209.250
Harris-Pringle	896.05	294.72	1,601.33	24.696%	1.837006	15.785%	18.000%	27.000	207.000
Practitioners	755.71	154.38	1,601.33	28.586%	2.323265	16.747%	19.139%	7.000	187.000

APPENDIX 21.1: VALUATION FORMULAE ACCORDING TO THE MAIN THEORIES (MARKET VALUE OF THE DEBT = NOMINAL VALUE)

	No-costs-of-leverage	Damodaran (1994)	Practitioners
Ke	$Ke = Ku + \dfrac{D(1-T)}{E}(Ku - Kd)$	$Ke = Ku + \dfrac{D(1-T)}{E}(Ku - R_F)$	$Ke = Ku + \dfrac{D}{E}(Ku - R_F)$
β_L	$\beta_L = \beta u + \dfrac{D(1-T)}{E}(\beta u - \beta d)$	$\beta_L = \beta u + \dfrac{D(1-T)}{E}\beta u$	$\beta_L = \beta u + \dfrac{D}{E}\beta u$
WACC	$Ku\left(1 - \dfrac{DT}{E+D}\right)$	$Ku\left(1 - \dfrac{DT}{E+D}\right) + \left(D\dfrac{(Kd - R_F)(1-T)}{(E+D)}\right)$	$Ku - D\dfrac{R_F - Kd(1-T)}{(E+D)}$
WACC$_{BT}$	$Ku - \dfrac{DT(Ku - Kd)}{(E+D)}$	$Ku - D\dfrac{T(Ku - R_F) - (Kd - R_F)}{(E+D)}$	$Ku + \dfrac{D(Kd - R_F)}{(E+D)}$
DVTS	$PV[Ku; DTKu]$	$PV[Ku; DTKu - D(Kd - R_F)(1-T)]$	$PV[Ku; T\,D\,Kd - D(Kd - R_F)]$
ECF$_t$\\Ku	$ECF_t - D_{t-1}(Ku_t - Kd_t)(1-T)$	$ECF_t - D_{t-1}(Ku - R_F)(1-T)$	$ECF_t - D_{t-1}(Ku_t - R_{Ft})$
FCF$_t$\\Ku	$FCF_t + D_{t-1}Ku_t T$	$FCF_t + D_{t-1}Ku\,T - D_{t-1}(Kd - R_F)(1-T)$	$FCF_t + D_{t-1}[R_{Ft} - Kd_t(1-T)]$

	Harris-Pringle (1985) Ruback (1995)	Myers (1974)	Miles-Ezzell (1980)
Ke	$Ke = Ku + \dfrac{D}{E}(Ku - Kd)$	$Ke = Ku + \dfrac{Vu - E}{E}(Ku - Kd)$	$Ke = Ku + \dfrac{D}{E}(Ku - Kd)\left[1 - \dfrac{T\,Kd}{1+Kd}\right]$
β_L	$\beta_L = \beta u + \dfrac{D}{E}(\beta u - \beta d)$	$\beta_L = \beta u + \dfrac{Vu - E}{E}(\beta u - \beta d)$	$\beta_L = \beta u + \dfrac{D}{E}(\beta u - \beta d)\left[1 - \dfrac{T\,Kd}{1+Kd}\right]$
WACC	$Ku - D\dfrac{KdT}{(E+D)}$	$Ku - \dfrac{DVTS(Ku - Kd) + D\,Kd\,T}{(E+D)}$	$Ku - D\dfrac{Kd\,T}{(E+D)}\dfrac{1+Ku}{1+Kd}$
WACC$_{BT}$	Ku	$Ku - \dfrac{DVTS(Ku - Kd)}{(E+D)}$	$Ku - \dfrac{D\,T\,Kd}{(E+D)}\dfrac{(Ku - Kd)}{(1+Kd)}$
DVTS	$PV[Ku;\ T\,D\,Kd]$	$PV[Kd;\ T\,D\,Kd]$	$PV[Ku;\ T\,D\,Kd]\,(1+Ku)/(1+Kd_0)$
ECF$_t$\\Ku	$ECF_t - D_{t-1}(Ku_t - Kd_t)$	$ECF_t - (Vu - E)(Ku_t - Kd_t)$	$ECF - D\,(Ku - Kd)\dfrac{1+Kd(1-T)}{(1+Kd)}$
FCF$_t$\\Ku	$FCF_t + T\,D_{t-1}\,Kd_t$	$FCF_t + T\,D\,Kd + DVTS\,(Ku - Kd)$	$FCF + T\,D\,Kd\,(1+Ku)/(1+Kd)$

EQUATIONS COMMON TO ALL METHODS

WACC AND WACC$_{BT}$

$$WACC_t = \frac{E_{t-1}Ke_t + D_{t-1}Kd_t(1-T)}{(E_{t-1} + D_{t-1})}$$

$$WACC_{BTt} = \frac{E_{t-1}Ke_t + D_{t-1}Kd_t}{(E_{t-1} + D_{t-1})}$$

$$WACC_{BTt} - WACC_t = \frac{D_{t-1}Kd_tT}{(E_{t-1} + D_{t-1})}$$

RELATIONSHIPS BETWEEN CASH FLOWS

$$ECF_t = FCF_t + (D_t - D_{t-1}) - D_{t-1}Kd_t(1-T)$$

$$CCF_t = FCF_t + D_{t-1}Kd_tT$$

$$CCF_t = ECF_t - (D_t - D_{t-1}) + D_{t-1}Kd_t$$

CASH FLOWS\\KU

$$ECF\backslash\backslash Ku = ECF_t - E_{t-1}(Ke_t - Ku_t)$$

$$FCF\backslash\backslash Ku = FCF_t - (E_{t-1} + D_{t-1})(WACC_t - Ku_t) =$$
$$CCF\backslash\backslash Ku = CCF_t - (E_{t-1} + D_{t-1})(WACC_{BTt} - Ku_t)$$

APPENDIX 21.2:   VALUATION FORMULAE ACCORDING TO THE MAIN THEORIES WHEN THE DEBT'S MARKET VALUE (D) DOES NOT MATCH ITS NOMINAL OR BOOK VALUE (N)

This appendix contains the expressions of the basic methods for valuing companies by cash flow discounting, when the debt's market value (D) does not match its nominal value (N). If the debt's market value (D) does not match its nominal value (N), it is because the required return to debt (Kd) is different from the debt's cost (r).

The interest paid in a period t is

$$I_t = N_{t-1} r_t.$$

The increase in debt in a period t is

$$\Delta N_t = N_t - N_{t-1}.$$

Consequently, the debt cash flow in a period t is

$$CFd = I_t - \Delta N_t = N_{t-1} r_t - (N_t - N_{t-1}).$$

Consequently, the debt's value at $t = 0$ is

$$D_0 = \sum_{t=1}^{\infty} \frac{N_{t-1} r_t - (N_t - N_{t-1})}{\prod_1^t (1 + Kd_t)}$$

It is easy to show that the relationship between the debt's market value (D) and its nominal value (N) is

$$D_t - D_{t-1} = N_t - N_{t-1} + D_{t-1} Kd_t - N_{t-1} r_t$$

Consequently,

$$\Delta D_t = \Delta N_t + D_{t-1} Kd_t - N_{t-1} r_t$$

The fact that the debt's market value (D) does not match its nominal value (N) affects several formulae given in Section 21.1. Formulae (21.1), (21.3), (21.4), (21.6), (21.7), (21.9), and (21.10) continue to be valid, but the other formulae change.

The expression of the WACC in this case is

$$WACC = \frac{E\ Ke + D\ Kd - N\ r\ T}{E + D} \tag{21.2*}$$

The expression relating the ECF with the FCF is

$$ECF_t = FCF_t + (N_t - N_{t-1}) - N_{t-1} r_t (1 - T) \tag{21.5*}$$

The expression relating the CCF with the ECF and the FCF is

$$CCF_t = ECF_t + CFd_t = ECF_t - (N_t - N_{t-1}) + N_{t-1} r_t$$
$$= FCF_t + N_{t-1} r_t T \tag{21.8*}$$

	No-costs-of-leverage	Damodaran (1994)	Practitioners
WACC	$Ku - \dfrac{N\,rT + DT(Ku - Kd)}{(E+D)}$	$Ku - \dfrac{N\,rT + D[T(Ku - R_F) - (Kd - R_F)]}{(E+D)}$	$Ku - \dfrac{N\,rT - D(Kd - R_F)}{(E+D)}$
DVTS	$PV[Ku;\ DTKu + T(Nr - DKd)]$	$PV[Ku;\ T\,N\,r + DT(Ku - R_F) - D(Kd - R_F)]$	$PV[Ku;\ T\,N\,r - D(Kd - R_F)]$
FCF$_t$\\Ku	$FCF_t + D_{t-1}Ku_t\,T + T(N_{t-1}\,r_t - D_{t-1}Kd_t)$	$FCF_t + D_{t-1}Ku_tT + T(N_{t-1}r_t - D_{t-1}Kd_t) - D_{t-1}(Kd_t - R_{Ft})(1-T)$	$FCF_t + T(N_{t-1}\,r_t - D_{t-1}\,Kd_t) + D_{t-1}[R_{Ft} - Kd_t(1-T)]$

	Harris-Pringle (1985) Ruback (1995)	Myers (1974)	Miles-Ezzell (1980)
WACC	$Ku - \dfrac{N\,rT}{(E+D)}$	$Ku - \dfrac{DVTS(Ku - Kd) + N\,rT}{(E+D)}$	$Ku - N\,\dfrac{rT}{(E+D)}\ \dfrac{1 + Ku}{1 + Kd}$
DVTS	$PV[Ku;\ T\,N\,r]$	$PV\,[Kd;\ T\,N\,r]$	$PV[Ku_t;\ N_{t-1}\,r_t T](1 + Ku)/(1 + Kd)$
FCF$_t$\\Ku	$FCF_t + T\,N_{t-1}r_t$	$FCF_t + T\,N\,r + DVTS(Ku - Kd)$	$FCF_t + T\,N\,r(1 + Ku)/(1 + Kd)$

EQUATIONS COMMON TO ALL THE METHODS

WACC AND WACC$_{BT}$

$$WACC_t = \frac{E_{t-1}Ke_t + D_{t-1}Kd_t - N_{t-1}\, r_t T}{(E_{t-1} + D_{t-1})}$$

$$WACC_{BTt} = \frac{E_{t-1}Ke_t + D_{t-1}Kd_t}{(E_{t-1} + D_{t-1})}$$

$$WACC_{BTt} - WACC_t = \frac{N_{t-1}\, r_t\, T}{(E_{t-1} + D_{t-1})}$$

RELATIONSHIPS BETWEEN THE CASH FLOWS

$$ECF_t = FCF_t + (N_t - N_{t-1}) - N_{t-1}r_t(1 - T)$$

$$CCF_t = FCF_t + N_{t-1}r_t T$$

$$CCF_t = ECF_t - (N_t - N_{t-1}) + N_{t-1}r_t$$

REFERENCES

Damodaran, A. (1994), *Damodaran on Valuation*, New York: John Wiley and Sons.

Fernández, P. (2002), "The Value of Tax Shields is NOT Equal to the Present Value of Tax Shields," Working Paper N. 290727, Social Science Research Network.

Harris, R. S., and J. J. Pringle (1985), "Risk-Adjusted Discount Rates Extensions form the Average-Risk Case," *Journal of Financial Research*, (Fall), pp. 237–244.

Miles, J. A., and J. R. Ezzell, (1980), "The Weighted Average Cost of Capital. Perfect Capital Markets and Project Life: A Clarification," *Journal of Financial and Quantitative Analysis* (September), pp. 719–730.

Miles, J. A., and J. R. Ezzell, (1985), "Reformulating Tax Shield Valuation: A Note," *Journal of Finance*, Vol. XL, 5 (December), pp. 1485–1492.

Modigliani, F., and M. Miller, (1958), "The Cost of Capital, Corporation Finance and the Theory of Investment," *American Economic Review* 48, 261–297.

Modigliani, F., and M. Miller (1963), "Corporate Income Taxes and the Cost of Capital: A Correction," *American Economic Review*, (June), pp. 433–443.

Myers, S. C. (1974), "Interactions of Corporate Financing and Investment Decisions — Implications for Capital Budgeting," *Journal of Finance*, (March), pp. 1–25.

Ruback, R. S. (1995), "A Note on Capital Cash Flow Valuation," Harvard Business School, 9–295–069.

PART IV

Real Options and Brands

Chapter 22

Real Options. Valuing Flexibility: Beyond Discounted Cash Flow Valuation

The formulas used to value financial options are based on riskless arbitrage (the possibility of forming a portfolio that provides exactly the same return as the financial option) and are very accurate. However, we will see that very rarely does it make sense to use these formulas directly to value real options because real options are hardly ever replicable. However, we can modify the formulas to take non-replicability into account (see Section 22.7).

The problems we encounter when valuing real options are:

- Difficulty in communicating the valuation due to its higher technical complexity than the present value
- Difficulty in defining the necessary parameters for valuing real options
- Difficulty in defining and quantifying the volatility of the sources of uncertainty
- Difficulty in calibrating the option's exclusiveness
- Difficulty in valuing the options adequately; in any case, their valuation is much less accurate than the valuation of financial options

Although real options are intuitively appealing, we will see that arriving at a value is complicated. Calculating the exact value of a real option is not critical; instead, understanding the value drivers of the option is more important.

22.1. REAL OPTIONS

It is not possible to value correctly a firm or a project that provides some type of future flexibility—*real options*—using the traditional techniques for discounting future flows (NPV or IRR). There are many types of real options: options to exploit mining or oil concessions, options to defer investments, options to expand businesses, options to abandon businesses, options to change the use of certain assets, etc.

A real option exists in an investment project when there are future possibilities for action when the solution of a current uncertainty is known. Oil concessions are a typical example. The oil well will be operated or not depending on the future price of oil. Designing a new product is also a real option: a firm has the option of expanding its production facilities or canceling distribution, depending on the market's future growth. Investments in research and development can also be analyzed using options theory.[1]

Corporate policy strategists and professors have repeatedly reproached finance—and financial analysts—for their lack of tools for valuing investment projects' *strategic implications*. Before using options theory, most new investments were made on the basis solely of qualitative corporate policy criteria. The numbers, if any, were crunched afterward so that they could give the result that the strategist wanted to back his decision. Options theory seems to enable projects' strategic opportunities to be valued: by combining quantitative analysis of the options with qualitative and strategic analysis of the corporate policy, it is possible to make more correct and more rational decisions about the firm's future.

In this chapter, we will study a few simple examples that will enable us to readily see that not considering the options contained in a project may lead us to undervalue it and, in general, turn down projects that we should undertake.[2] We will also analyze a number of real options that are present in many investment projects: the option to expand the project, the option to defer the investment, and the option to use the investment for alternative purposes.

---

[1]See, for example, Grenadier and Weiss (1997).

[2]Similarly, if the projects we are considering contain options that may be exercised by third parties (the future flexibility plays against us), non-consideration of the options contained by the projects will lead us to invest in products we should turn down.

One classification of real options is the following:

Real Options

Contractual options	Growth or learning options	Flexibility options
Oil concessions	Expand	Defer the investment
Mining concessions	Research and development	Downsize the project
Franchises	Acquisitions	Alternative uses
	New businesses	Renegotiations of contracts
	New customers	Outsourcing
	Internet venture	Abandon
	Greater efficiency in increasing entry barriers	Modification of products

People also talk about compound options, which are those that provide new options when they are exercised. Rainbow options is the term used to describe those that have more than one source of uncertainty, for example, an oil concession in which the uncertainty arises from the price of oil, an uncertain quantity of barrels, and uncertain extraction costs.[3]

For example, some of Amazon's real options when it was only a company that sold books were[4]:

- *New business options.* zShops (a marketplace), AmazonAuctions (an auction market) and its new businesses: Drugstore.com (beauty and health products), Ashford.com (jewelry and gift items), Della.com (weddings and gifts), Pets.com (pets) and Greenlight.com (automobiles). Several of these options were exercised by acquisition. Between April 1998 and April 1999, Amazon made 28 acquisitions.
- *Expansion options.* Amazon entered the European market in 1999.
- *Growth options through new customers.* Amazon started to sell music, videos, and DVDs in 1998; software, toys, electronic products and home products in 1999; kitchenware and gardening products in 2000.
- *Efficiency improvement options to increase the entry barriers.* In 1999, Amazon invested more than $300 million to improve its technological infrastructure. It patented the procedure called "1-Click." Free greeting service. Verification of e-mail order.

[3]For a compilation of the different types of real options, see the books published by Trigeorgis (1996), and Amram and Kulatilaka (1999), both with the same title, *Real Options.*

[4]See Collura and Applegate's case study (2000) entitled "Amazon.com: Exploiting the Value of Digital Business Infrastructure."

22.2. EXPLOITATION OF OIL RESERVES

Let us suppose that we are offered the rights for exploiting an oil well for a one-year period. This oil well has already been developed and its reserves are calculated to amount to 10,000,000 barrels. The extraction costs are strictly variable (all the investment in fixed costs has already been made) and will be 20 euros per barrel extracted. These costs will remain constant throughout the next year. The current oil price is 18 euros per barrel.[5] The one-year risk-free interest rate is 5%. We are offered two types of contract:

1. With an obligation to extract oil at some time during the year.
2. With the option of extracting or not.

How much would we be prepared to pay for these two alternative contracts?

22.2.1. WITH AN OBLIGATION TO EXTRACT

If we acquire the obligation to extract the 10,000,000 barrels of oil during the next year, the appropriate technique for valuing the contract is the net present value (NPV).

Table 22.1 shows the calculations that are required to value the contract. All that we have to determine is if we must extract the oil today or wait. The comparison between extracting the oil within one year (NPV = −10.5 million euros) or extracting it now (NPV = −20 million euros) seems to advise in favor of waiting. The intuition behind this result is very simple: as the extraction cost is constant, it will be better to do it as late as possible.

We do not think that the reader will have any problems in calculating the NPV of the cost of extracting one barrel. But he may have problems in calculating the NPV of the revenues (the future price[6] of oil). The NPV of any asset is its expected value in the future discounted at the appropriate rate (that which includes the asset's risk). Likewise, the price of an asset traded on a market is the asset's expected value in the future discounted at the rate considered appropriate by investors. Consequently—and unless we have

---

[5]Note that we are assuming that there is no uncertainty regarding the extraction costs or the oil's quantity or quality: the only uncertainty lies in the oil's future price.

[6]Do not confuse with the price of a futures contract. Although at first sight it may not be intuitive, the price of a futures contract is obtained using an arbitrage formula and has *nothing* to do with the market's expectations about the price on the future date on which the contract will be exercised. The market's expectations about the price's future course are included in the current price.

Table 22.1

Concession for the Exploitation of an Oil Well for One Year

10,000,000 barrels. Extraction cost (variable) = 20 euros/barrel.

Current price of oil = 18 euros/barrel. Annual risk-free interest rate = 5.00%

A/ OBLIGATION TO EXTRACT

A.1/ Extract in one year's time
NPV (cost) = −20/1.05 = −19.0476 euros/barrel. NPV (revenues) = 18 euros/barrel
NPV contract = (− 19.0476 + 18) × 10,000,000 = −10,476,190 euros

A.2/ Extract now
NPV (cost) = −20 euros/barrel. NPV (revenues) = 18 euros/barrel
NPV contract = (− 20 + 18) × 10,000,000 = −20,000,000 euros

B/ OPTION TO EXTRACT

Call (S = 18, K = 20, t = 1 year, r = 1.05)[1]

Volatility	Value (euros)
2%	2,559
5%	596,703
10%	3,298,856
20%	10,101,360
30%	17,237,282

[1]The valuation of the option to extract has been calculated using Black and Scholes' formula. For a demonstration, see Appendix 22.1. The calculations for a volatility of 30% are explained in Section 22.3.

insider information or we think that the market is mistaken in its estimates of the expected value or risk—we must conclude that the NPV of the oil's price in the future is its market price today.

As a result, not only would we refuse to pay anything for this contract, but also we would demand to be paid 10.5 million euros or more for accepting it.

22.2.2. WITH THE OPTION OF EXTRACTING

If the contract gives us the option of extracting the 10,000,000 barrels of oil during next year, the net present value is of no use to us because it assumes that we are obliged to extract the oil. In this case, we must use options theory.

It is obvious that in this case, we *are* willing, at least, to take on the contract free. The reason is that next year we may earn something (we will extract the oil if its price is more than 20 euros/barrel) and we will not lose anything (we will not extract the oil if its price is less than 20 euros/barrel).

The simplicity of this example enables us to value the contract using the simplest formula that exists for valuing options: Black and Scholes's formula[7] for a call on a share that does not pay dividends.

Table 22.1 shows the contract's value with respect to the expected volatility of oil prices. A number of values are given so that the reader can see that the crucial variable in calculating an option's value is volatility. Fortunately, provided that the future period being considered is not very long, we can estimate volatility with a certain amount of precision.

A volatility equal to zero means that we think that the price of the barrel of oil will increase without oscillations and at a constant rate of 5%, which means that its value in one year's time will be $18 \times 1.05 = 18.90$ euros. Obviously, in this case, the contract's value is zero; we will never extract oil because the extraction cost is higher than the selling price. Note that the higher the expected volatility, the greater is the contract's value, as can be seen in Table 22.1.

The most important conclusion to be drawn from Table 22.1 is that if we do not consider the option included in the contract, the result we would obtain would be erroneous and the decision we would be led to make would be wrong.

The NPV can only be used for those projects in which the future cash flows are certain (as in the first contract, with obligation to extract). If a project has any type of future flexibility (as in the second contract, in which we will extract or not depending on the oil price in the future), we must necessarily use options theory: the traditional use of the NPV, without taking into account the possibility of not exercising the option, would lead us to erroneous results and incorrect decisions.

This simple example shows the valuation of a very simple real option.[8] The valuation of other types of real options (option to increase capacity, option to use different raw materials, option to produce different products, option to employ different production processes, etc.) will normally require the use of somewhat more complex valuation techniques.

---

[7]For more complex contracts, we must use the binomial formula.

[8]Note that we have used a large number of simplifying hypotheses, for example, we assume that we know exactly the extraction costs and the quantity of barrels.

22.3. BLACK AND SCHOLES' FORMULA[9] FOR VALUING FINANCIAL OPTIONS

The value of a call on a share, with an exercise price K and which can be exercised at the time t, is the present value of its price at the time t, i.e., MAX $(S_t - K, 0)$, where S_t is the share's price at the time t. Consequently:

$$\text{Call} = \text{NPV} [\text{MAX} (S_t - K, 0)] = \text{NPV} [S_t/S_t > K] \, P[S_t > K] -$$
$$\text{NPV} [K/S_t > K] \, P[S_t > K]$$

The first term of the subtraction is the present value of the share's price (provided that it is greater than K) multiplied by the probability that the share's price will be greater than K. The second term of the subtraction is the present value of the exercise price (Kr^{-t}) multiplied by the probability that the share's price will be greater than K.

It can be shown (see Appendix 22.1) that if the price of the asset with a risk S follows a course

$$S_t = S_0 e^{(\mu t + \sigma \varepsilon \sqrt{t})}$$

and we assume that[10]

$$\mu = \ln(r) - \sigma^2/2, \text{ then:}$$

$$\text{NPV} [S_t/S_t > K] \, P[S_t > K] = S \, N(x)$$

$$\text{NPV} [K/S_t > K] = r^{-t} \, E [K/S_t > K] = Kr^{-t}$$

$$P[S_t > K] = N (x - \sigma\sqrt{t}), \text{ where}^{[11]} x = [\ln (S/Kr^t)/(\sigma\sqrt{t})] + \sigma\sqrt{t}/2$$

Consequently, Black and Scholes' formula is:

Call $= S \, N (x) - K \, r^{-t} \, N (x - \sigma\sqrt{t})$, where $x = [\ln (S/Kr^t)/(\sigma\sqrt{t})] + \sigma\sqrt{t}/2$

$N(x - \sigma\sqrt{t})$ is the probability that the option will be exercised, i.e., $P[S_t > K]$.

---

[9]Readers interested in learning how the formula is obtained can see Appendix 22.1.

[10]This can only be assumed if the option is replicable. This requirement is based on the fact that when a financial instrument can be valued by arbitrage (it can be replicated from other existing instruments), the price ratios move within a risk-free probability range. In this probability range, the expected value of a share's price (and whose price today is S euros) is equal to the expected value of investing those euros at the risk-free rate:

$$E(S_t) = S \, e^{(\mu + \sigma^2/2)t} = S \, r^t \tag{22.4}$$

[11]It is important to realize that $P[S_t > K] = N(x - \sigma\sqrt{t})$ only if $\mu = \ln (r) - \sigma^2/2$. This condition is imposed by the fact that the option can be replicated with shares and bonds.

It is important to remember that this formula assumes that the option can be replicated and, therefore:

1. Considers that $\mu = \ln{(r)} - \sigma^2/2$
2. Calculates the present value using the risk-free rate

Applying Black and Scholes' formula to the call on 10,000,000 shares, where the price of each share is 18 euros, the exercise price is 20 euros per share, the volatility is 30%, the time is 1 year, and the interest rate is 5% (like the oil option), we obtain:

$$x = -0.038568. \ N(x) = 0.4846.$$

$$N(x - \sigma\sqrt{t}) = 0.3675. \ S \ N \ (x) = 87.23 \ \text{million euros}$$

$$Kr^{-t}N \ (x - \sigma\sqrt{t}) = 69.99 \ \text{million euros}$$

And consequently, the call's value is:

Call = 17.24 million euros $= 87.23 - 69.99.$

Table 22.2 shows a sensitivity analysis of this call's value.

Table 22.2

Value of the Call and Analysis of how the Call's Value is Affected by Changes in its Parameters (Million Euros)

Share price	Exercise price	Risk-free rate	Volatility	Time to exercise	Dividends	CALL
180	200	5%	30%	1 year	0	**17.24**
200						28.35
	180					25.51
		6%				17.91
			33%			19.39
				1.1 year		18.63
					20	9.05

22.4. FACTORS THAT DETERMINE A FINANCIAL OPTION'S VALUE

Let us briefly recall the definitions of *call* and *put*. A call is a contract that gives its holder (the buyer) the right (not the obligation) to buy a certain number of shares, at a predetermined price, at any time before a certain date (American option) or only on that date (European option). The buyer has the alternative of exercising or not exercising his right, while the seller must sell at the buyer's order.

A put is a contract that gives its holder (the seller) the right (not the obligation) to sell a certain number of shares, at a predetermined price, at any time before a certain date (American option) or only on that date (European option).

The six basic variables that affect the option's price are

1. **The share price to which the option is referenced (S)**—A call's value increases with the share price, while the put's value decreases. In the case of a European option, this is obvious. At the time of exercising the option, the call's holder may opt for paying the exercise price (K) and receiving a share with a value S: his gain is (S − K), so it is to his interest that S be high. At the time of exercising the option, the holder of a put realizes a gain (K − S) as he receives K in exchange for a share: the lower the share's price, the higher his gain will be.

2. **The option's exercise price (K)**—An increase in the exercise price (K) decreases the value of a call and increases the value of a put. When exercising a call, its holder gains (S − K). Thus, it is to his interest that the payment to be made be small. The situation is the opposite for the holder of a put. If he exercises the option, he will gain (K − S). The exercise price is the amount that he will receive, so it is to his interest that it be high.

3. **The share's volatility**—Both if the option is a call or a put, its value will greater the higher the volatility forecast for the future of the share to which it is referenced. This is because the holder of an option benefits from the oscillations in the share's price in a certain direction (upward if the option is a call and downward if it is a put), while he is protected against movements in the opposite direction.

4. **The risk-free interest rate**—The interest rate affects an option's value because the net present value of the option's exercise price depends on the interest rates. Thus, a call's value increases with higher interest rates, because the exercise price's NPV decreases as the discount rate, that is, the interest rate increases. In the case of a put, the situation is the opposite: its value decreases when the interest rate increases.

5. **The dividends that the share will receive before the exercise date**—Dividends affect the option because when a share pays a dividend, the share's market price is adjusted to reflect the dividend paid (it decreases). Thus, the holder of a call will prefer that the share not pay dividends or that it pays the lowest dividend possible. The holder of a put will prefer that the share pay the highest dividend possible because this will mean that the share's price on the exercise date will be lower.

6. **The time remaining until the last exercise date**—The time to exercise affects the option's value through three variables mentioned previously:
   1. **Volatility**: The longer the time to the exercise date, the greater is the possibility that the share's price will increase or decrease.
   2. **Exercise price**: The longer the time to the exercise date, the lower is the exercise price's NPV.
   3. **Dividends**: The longer the time to the exercise date, the higher are the dividends that the firm will pay.

However, not all these variables affect the option's value in the same way. The total effect will depend on the sum of each of these three variables' partial effects. Generally speaking, in the case of American options, the value of both calls and puts increases the longer the time to the exercise date. In the case of European options, each case must be studied individually.

22.5. REPLICATION OF THE CALL

Let us assume that the price of the shares in the previous example can follow two different courses, as shown in Figure 22.1. A (bullish) course reaches a price in one year's time of 254.66 million euros and the (bearish) course reaches 139 million euros. An intuitive approach to the valuation would conclude that the investor with bullish expectations would be prepared to pay more for the option than the investor with bearish expectations. However, this reasoning is incorrect. Both will agree (if the volatility expected by both is 30%) in valuing the option at 17.24 million euros. The reason for this is that buying today 87.23 million euros of shares and borrowing 69.99 million euros (net outlay: 17.24 million euros) in one year's time will have the same position as buying the option, whatever the future course followed by the share's price.

Figure 22.2 shows the option's replicate if the share price follows the bearish course. Initially, (day 0) 87.231 billion euros in shares (4,846,100 shares) must be bought and 69.994 billion euros must be borrowed.

During the following year, this portfolio must be altered as indicated by Black and Scholes' formula, which is calculated every day. On day 1, the

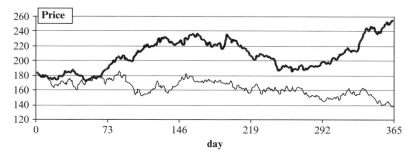

Figure 22.1   Two possible courses for the price of 10,000,000 shares during the next year. The price today is 180 million euros. The price in one year's time according to the bullish course will be 254.6 million euros and 139 million euros according to the bearish course.

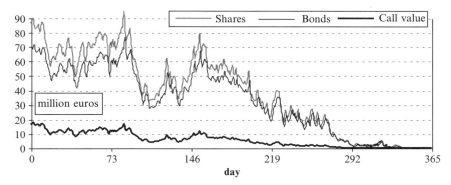

Figure 22.2   Replicate of the call if the share follows the bearish course. In one year's time, both the option and the replicate portfolio will be worth zero (there will be neither shares nor debt).

share's price was 18.05 euros. Calculating the value of the call on day 1 gives 17.44 million euros (88.07 − 70.63). This means that the portfolio on day 1 must have 88.07 million euros invested in shares (if the share's price is 18.05 euros, it must have 4,879,200 shares). As 4,846,100 shares were held on day 0, 33,100 shares must be bought on day 1, which means an outlay of 0.6 million euros. However, this share purchase is financed entirely with debt. On day 1, the total loan will be the loan of day 0 plus one day's interest plus the new loan to buy the 331 shares:

$$69.994 \times 1.05^{1/365} + 0.6 = 70.6 \text{ million euros}$$

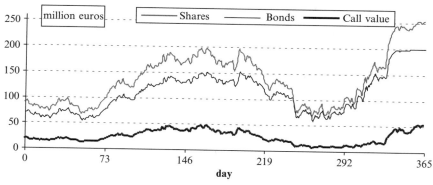

Figure 22.3   Replicate of the share following the bullish course. In one year's time, the call will be worth 54.66 million euros. The replicate portfolio will consist of 254.66 million euros in shares and 200 million euros in debt.

By varying the replicate portfolio in this manner throughout the year (if the share price rises, shares are bought with borrowed money; if the share price falls, shares are sold and part of the loan is repaid), Figure 22.2 shows how the composition of the option's replicate portfolio will vary. On any given day of the year, the call's value is identical to that of the replicate portfolio. At the end (day 364), the option is not worth anything because the share's final price is 13.50 euros. The replicate portfolio on day 365 is not worth anything either because it has neither shares nor debt.

In a similar manner, Figure 22.3 shows the option's replicate portfolio if the share follows a bullish course. On day 365 the option is worth 54.66 million euros, as is also the replicate portfolio, which will have 254.66 million euros in shares and 200 million euros in debt.

22.6. THE EXPECTATIONS REGARDING AN INCREASE IN THE SHARE'S PRICE DO NOT AFFECT THE VALUE OF A REPLICABLE CALL

In the previous section, we have seen that expectations of an increase in the share price do not influence the call's value. A bullish investor and a bearish investor will agree on the call's value because if today they form a portfolio with 87.23 million euros in shares and borrowing 69.99 million euros, in one year's time they will have the same position as with the call, whatever may be the evolution of the share's future price.

The expectations with respect to an increase in the share price can be included in the formula (22.1) given in the Appendix in the parameter μ. Figure 22.4 shows the distribution of the return expected for the share's price by three investors who have identical volatility expectations (30%) but different expectations regarding the return μ: one has μ = −5%, another has μ = 0.379%, and the other has μ = 10%.

Figure 22.5 shows the three investors' distribution of the share price in one year's time. Using equation (22.4), the expected value of the share price is 17.91 for the investor with μ = −5%, 18.90 for the investor with μ = 0.379%, and 20.8087 for the investor with μ = 10%. Note that 18.90 = 18 × 1.05. Thus, the investor with μ = 0.379% expects a return on the share price equal to 5%, which is the risk-free interest rate. This is because μ = 0.379% meets equation (22.5). In spite of their differing expectations about the share's appreciation, all three investors will agree that the option's value is 17.24 million euros.

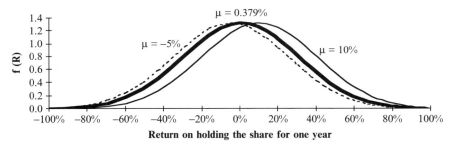

Figure 22.4   Distribution of the share's return in one year's time according to three different expectations.

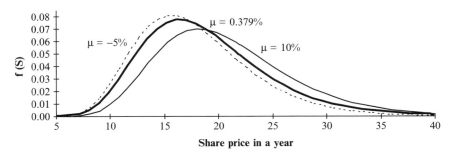

Figure 22.5   Distribution of the share price in one year's time according to three different expectations.

It is vital to realize that Black and Scholes' formula interpreted as net present value considers $\mu = 0.379\% = \ln(r) - \sigma^2/2$ and discounts the option's expected value $E[Max(S - K,0)]$ with the risk-free rate r. This is because the option is replicable: the financial outcome of holding the option is identical to buying today 87.23 million euros in shares and borrowing 69.99 million euros.

It is important to stress again that this formula assumes that the option can be replicated, and therefore:

1. Considers that $\mu = \ln(r) - \sigma^2/2$
2. Calculates the present value using the risk-free rate

22.7. VALUE OF A CALL IF IT CANNOT BE REPLICATED

If the option cannot be replicated, the call's value is not based on riskless arbitrage but on the valuer's expectations: expectations regarding the appreciation of the underlying asset and expectations regarding the investment's risk. In this situation:

$$P\,[S_t > K] = N\,[y - \sigma\sqrt{t}].$$

$$NPV\,[K/S_t > K]\,P\,[S_t > K] = Kr_K^{-t}N\,(y - \sigma\sqrt{t})$$

$$NPV\,[S_t/S_t > K]\,P\,[S_t > K] = Se^{(\mu+\sigma^2/2)t}\,r_K^{-t}\,N(y)$$

$$y = [\ln(S/K) + t\mu + t\sigma^2]/[\sigma\sqrt{t}]$$

$$\textbf{Non-replicable call} = S\,e^{(\mu+\sigma^2/2)t}\,r_K^{-t}\,N(y) - K\,r_K^{-t}\,N(y - \sigma\sqrt{t}) \quad (22.1)$$

The first term can be interpreted as the present value of the cash flows that are expected if the option is exercised. The second term is the present value of the investment required to exercise the option. $N\,(y - \sigma\sqrt{t})$ is the probability of exercising the option.

Table 22.3 shows the value of the option to extract oil in one year's time for different values of μ and r_K. Note that for $\mu = 0.379$ and $r_K = 1.05$, the same value as with Black and Scholes is obtained. This value only makes sense if the option is replicable. If it is not, the option's value also depends on the expected return μ and the discount rate r_K that is appropriate for the project.

Table 22.3

Value of the Option to Extract with Differing Expectations for μ and r_K (Million euros), Volatility = 30%

					μ					
r_K	−5,0%	−2,0%	0,0%	0,379%	1,0%	2,0%	3,0%	4,0%	5,0%	10,0%
1,05	13,00	15,25	16,91	**17,24**	17,79	18,69	19,64	20,61	21,63	27,22
1,06	12,88	15,11	16,75	17,07	17,62	18,52	19,45	20,42	21,42	26,97
1,07	12,76	14,97	16,59	16,92	17,45	18,35	19,27	20,23	21,22	26,71
1,08	12,64	14,83	16,44	16,76	17,29	18,18	19,09	20,04	21,03	26,47
1,09	12,52	14,69	16,29	16,60	17,13	18,01	18,92	19,86	20,83	26,22
1,10	12,41	14,56	16,14	16,45	16,98	17,84	18,74	19,68	20,64	25,98
1,11	12,30	14,43	16,00	16,31	16,82	17,68	18,58	19,50	20,46	25,75

22.8 DIFFERENCES BETWEEN A FINANCIAL OPTION AND A REAL OPTION

The factors that determine the value of a financial option are different from those that affect a real option. These differences in the parameters are shown in Table 22.4.

Equation (22.1) can be rewritten as:

$$\text{Non-replicable call} = \text{NPV(expected cash flows if the option is exercised)} - \text{NPV(investment required to exercise the option)} \quad (22.2)$$

Table 22.4

Parameters that Influence the Value of a Financial Option and of a Real Option

Financial call option	Real call option
Share price	Expected value of cash flows
Exercise price	Cost of investment
Risk-free interest rate	Discount rate with risk
Share's volatility	Volatility of expected cash flows
Time to exercise	Time to exercise
Dividends	Cost of holding the option
Its value does *not* depend on the expected appreciation of the underlying asset	Its value *does* depend on the expected appreciation of the underlying asset
The exercise is instantaneous	Exercise does not happen in an instant

If the project is composed solely of a call, we will undertake the project if "non-replicable call" > 0. If some initial investment must be made to undertake the project, we will undertake it if "non-replicable call" > initial investment:

Undertake the project if:

Non-replicable call – initial investment > NPV (expected cash flows if the option is exercised) – NPV (investment required to exercise the option)

Following the procedure described by Luehrman (1995), we can define:

$$\text{NPV}_{call} = \text{NPV (expected cash flows if the option is exercised)} / \\ [\text{NPV (investment required)} + \text{initial investment)} \qquad (22.3)$$

Obviously, it is interesting to undertake the project if $\text{NPV}_{call} > 1$.

This breakdown enables the following diagram to be drawn, which helps visualize the value of the options and divide them into six types:

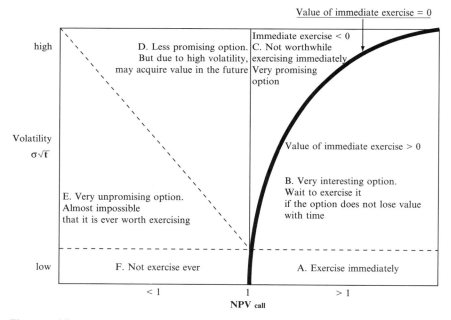

The curved line corresponds to the options in which the present value of immediate exercise is zero. This corresponds to the options with a zero value for $t = 0$. Based on (22.1), if $t = 0: y = \infty, S - K = 0$.

Type A: Very little volatility, NPV_{call} greater than 1 and positive value for immediate exercise. They are options that are worth exercising immediately. Waiting does not add any value due to their low volatility.

Type B: NPV_{call} greater than 1, greater volatility and positive value for immediate exercise. They are options that are worth exercising immediately, but waiting adds value due to the greater volatility.

Type C: NPV_{call} greater than 1, negative value for immediate exercise and high volatility. They are options that are not worth exercising immediately, but waiting adds value due to the volatility. They are very promising options as the volatility expectations make $NPV_{call} > 1$.

Type D: NPV_{call} less than 1, negative value for immediate exercise and high volatility. They are options that are not worth exercising immediately, but waiting adds value due to the volatility. With the present volatility expectations, it will never be worth exercising them as $NPV_{call} < 1$, but it is possible that the option may have value in the future if the volatility increases or the option is improved.

Type E: NPV_{call} less than 1, negative value for immediate exercise and high volatility. They are options that are not worth exercising immediately and, with the present volatility expectations, it will never be worth exercising them as $NPV_{call} < 1$. It is virtually impossible that the option will have value in the future.

Type F: NPV_{call} less than 1, negative value for immediate exercise and very little volatility. They are options that will never be worth exercising.

Figure 22.6 shows the NPV_{call}–volatility diagram for the option in Table 22.1 (assuming that it cannot be replicated) for three initial oil price levels: 18, 20, and 22 euros/barrel. It is assumed that the initial investment to buy the option is 16 million euros.

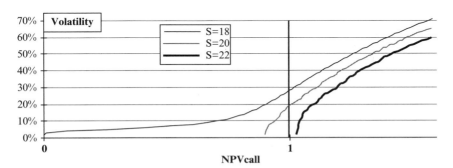

Figure 22.6 NPV_{call}–volatility diagram for the option in Table 22.1 assuming that it is not possible to replicate, for three initial oil price levels. Initial investment = 16 million. $\mu = 1\%$. t = 1 year.

22.9. APPLYING OPTIONS THEORY IN A FIRM

If the real options cannot be replicated, using financial option formulas is completely inappropriate for valuing real options, as all the formulas are based on the existence of a replicate portfolio.[12]

In the following paragraphs, we have included a number of considerations on the practical application of options theory to the analysis of investment projects.

1. High interest rates mean high discount rates, which reduces the present value of future flows. Obviously, this should decrease the value of the option to undertake a project. However, high discount rates also reduce the present value of the option's exercise price. This compensatory effect helps sustain the option's value when interest rates increase, which may give certain types of project—particularly growth options—an enormous value that should be taken into account when analyzing investments.

2. Kester (1984) suggests one feature of options that should be considered: to what extent the holder of an option has an exclusive right to exercise it. Unlike stock options, there are two types of growth options: exclusive and shared. The former are the most valuable because they give their holder the exclusive right to exercise them. These options derive from patents, unique knowledge of the market held by the firm, or technology that its competitors cannot imitate.

    Shared growth options are less valuable. They represent "collective" opportunities held by the industry, for example, the possibility of entering a market that is not protected by high entry barriers or of building a new factory to supply a particular geographical segment of the market. Cost reduction projects are normally shared options, because, as a general rule, they can also be undertaken by competitors.

3. Kester also suggests that when analyzing investment projects, firms should classify the projects in accordance with the options they include. The classification using the traditional criteria of replacement, cost reduction, capacity increase, and new product introduction is not very useful. A more appropriate classification would be to distinguish between projects whose future benefits are mainly generated through cash flows (simple options) and those whose future benefits include subsequent investment options (compound options). Simple growth options,

---

[12]The logic of options theory is based on arbitrage: as it is possible to form a replicate portfolio that will have exactly the same return as the option we are trying to value, (in order to avoid arbitrage) the option must have the same value as the replicate portfolio. If it is not possible to form the replicate portfolio, this reasoning loses its entire basis.

such as routine cost reductions and maintenance and replacement projects, only create value through the cash flows generated by the underlying assets.

Compound growth options like research and development projects, a major expansion in an existing market, entry in a new market, and acquisitions (of new businesses or firms) lead to new investment opportunities and affect the value of the existing growth options. The compound options' complexity, their role in giving shape to the firm's strategy and, even, their impact on the organization's survival require a deeper analysis. The firm must view these projects as part of a larger group of projects or as a series of investment decisions that follow a time continuum. In the light of the firm's strategy, its executives must ask themselves whether a particular option will provide suitable investment opportunities in the appropriate markets, within a suitable time frame, that are matched to their firm's needs.

4. The firm must separate the projects that require an immediate decision on the entire project from those in which there is decision flexibility in the future. Finally, the firm must ask itself if it can realize all the option's benefits or whether they will also be available for other competitors.

5. When examining investment opportunities from the option valuation viewpoint, managers will find it easier to recognize that: (1) the conventional NPV may undervalue certain projects by eliminating the value of the options already existing in the project; (2) projects with a negative NPV can be accepted if the value of the option associated with future flexibility exceeds the NPV of the project's expected cash flows; and (3) the extent of the undervaluation and the degree to which managers can justifiably invest more than what the conventional rules regarding the NPV would indicate can be quantified using options theory.[13]

6. The options' framework indicates that the value of the management's future flexibility is greater in more uncertain environments. This value is greatest in periods with high interest rates and availability of the investment opportunities during extended periods. Consequently, contradicting generally held opinion, greater uncertainty, high interest rates, and more distant investment horizons (when part of the investment can be deferred) are not necessarily harmful for an investment opportunity's value. Although these variables reduce a project's static NPV, they can also increase the value of the project's options (value of management flexibility) to a level that may counteract the previous negative effect.

---

[13]For a good study on the application of real options to mining companies, see Moel and Tufano (2000).

7. A real option will only be valuable if it provides a sustainable competitive advantage. This competitive advantage basically depends on the nature of the competitors (normally, if competition is fierce and the competitors are strong, the advantage's sustainability will be less) and on the nature of the competitive advantage (if it is a scarce resource, for example, scarce buildable land, the advantage's sustainability will be greater).

22.10. USE OF THE BINOMIAL METHOD FOR VALUING REAL OPTIONS

22.10.1. VALUATION OF A PROJECT

A firm has the opportunity of undertaking an investment project that requires an initial investment of 60 million euros. The project consists of developing a new product. There is a considerable degree of uncertainty about the product's acceptance by the market. However, in one year's time, this uncertainty will have disappeared and it will be known whether the product is accepted by the market or not. For simplification purposes, it is assumed that there are only two possible future scenarios:

1. The new product is accepted. In this case, the project value's in one year's time is estimated at 200 million (value of the discounted future cash flows).
2. The new product is not accepted. In this case, the project's value in one year's time is estimated at 50 million (value of the discounted future cash flows).

The annual risk-free interest rate is 10%. The listed firm CCC specializes solely in the development of a product that is identical to ours. The market expects that in one year's time the value of the firm's shares will be 40,000 euros/share if the product is a success, and 10,000 euros/share if it fails. The required return on these shares is 30%. The firm's shares currently trade at 10,000 euros per share because the market is not very optimistic about the new product's success. Note that the share price indicates that the probability of success is estimated at 10% and that of failure at 90%. Therefore, the value of the share today (So) is:

$$So = E (S_1)/(1 + \text{required return})$$
$$= [40,000 \times 0.1 + 10,000 \times 0.9]/1.3 = 10,000 \text{ euros}$$

The question is: Should we accept the investment project?

Today	Year I	
	200 million	probability 10%
V		
	50 million	probability 90%

If we use the net present value for making the decision, we will carry out the following operation:

$$\text{NPV} = \text{E }(V_1)/(1 + \text{required return}) - \text{cost}$$
$$= ([200 \times 0.1 + 50 \times 0.9]/1.3) - 60 = -10 \text{ million euros}$$

Consequently, if we base our decision on the NPV, we should not undertake this project because the cost of doing so (60 million) is greater than what we expect to gain from it (50 million).

If we use options theory, in this case we obtain the same result because *this project is not an option*. The movement that is forecast for the firm CCC's equity is

Today	Year I	
	40,000 euros	probability 10%
10,000 euros		
	10,000 euros	probability 90%

Consequently,[14] $u = 4$; $d = 1$; $r = 1.1.p = 0.0333$. The project's value (V), according to options theory, is

$$V = [pV_u + (1 - p)V_d]/r - \text{cost}$$
$$= ([200 \times 0.03333 + 50 \times 0.9666]/1.1) - 60 = -10 \text{ million euros}$$

The project's value is therefore -10 million euros because we can replicate whatever may happen in one year's time by buying 5,000 shares of the firm CCC:

$$\Delta = (V_u - V_d)/[(u - d)S] = (200 - 50)/[(4 - 1) \times 10,000] = 5,000 \text{ shares}$$

$$B = (uV_d - dV_u)/[(u - d)r] = (4 \times 50 - 1 \times 200)/[(4 - 1) \times 1.1] = 0 \text{ euros}$$

Thus, if the product were a success, the 5,000 shares would be worth 200 million; if the product were a failure, they would be worth 50 million. Consequently, this project's value is

[14]$p = (r - d)/(u - d)$. This parameter arises from the existence of arbitrage, i.e., from the fact that the option can be replicated with shares in the firm CCC and bonds. Any readers interested in exploring the binomial method in greater depth should see Chapter 5 of the book *Options Markets* by Cox and Rubinstein (1985).

5,000 shares × 10,000 euros/share − 60 million = −10 million euros

To put it another way, we would not undertake the project because, in order to obtain 200 million if the product is successful or 50 million if it is not, it is cheaper to buy shares in the firm CCC (50 million) than to make the investment (60 million).

22.10.2. VALUATION OF THE OPTION TO EXPAND THE PROJECT

Let us use the same project from the previous section, but with an additional feature: in one year's time, the firm will be able to expand the project 100% by investing a further 60 million euros. It is obvious that in one year's time the firm will only expand its facilities if the product is successful.

The project can now be represented as:

Today	*Year I*	
V	200 + (200 − 60) million	probability 10%
	50 million	probability 90%

If we use the net present value for making the decision, we will carry out the following operation:

$$\text{NPV} = \text{E } (V_1)/(1 + \text{required return}) - \text{cost}$$
$$= ([340 \times 0.1 + 50 \times 0.9]/1.3) - 60 = 0.769 \text{ million euros}$$

Consequently, if we base our decision on the NPV, we should undertake this project because the cost of doing so today (60 million) is less than what we expect to gain from it (60.769 million).

If we use options theory, we get the opposite result. In this case, the project is an option: in year 1, after knowing whether the product is a success or a failure, the firm has the possibility of expanding the project 100% by investing another 60 million euros. The project's value (V), according to options theory is:

$$V = [pV_u + (1 - p)V_d]/r - \text{cost}$$
$$= ([340 \times 0.03333 + 50 \times 0.9666]/1.1) - 60 = -5.7575 \text{ million euros}$$

The project's value is -5.7575 million euros because we can replicate what may happen in one year's time by buying 9,667 shares in the firm CCC and borrowing 42.4242 million euros at 10%, as can be verified below:

$$\Delta = (V_u - V_d)/[(u - d)S]$$
$$= (340 - 50)/[(4 - 1) \times 10,000] = 9.666,66 \text{ shares}$$

$$B = (uV_d - dV_u)/[(u - d)r]$$
$$= (4 \times 50 - 1 \times 340)/[(4 - 1) \times 1.1] = -42.4242 \text{ million euros}$$

Thus, if the product is a success, the 9,667 shares will be worth 386.67 million and we must return 46.67 million (42.4242 × 1.1) corresponding to the loan. If the product is a failure, the shares will be worth 96.67 million and we will have to repay 46.67 million corresponding to the loan. Consequently, the value of this project is:

$$9,667 \text{ shares} \times 10,000 \text{ euros/share} -$$
$$42.4242 \text{ million} - 60 \text{ million} = -5.7575 \text{ million euros}$$

To put it another way, we would not undertake the project because it is cheaper to obtain 340 million if the product succeeds or 50 million if it fails by forming the replicate portfolio (buying 9,667 shares of the firm CCC and borrowing 42.4242 million euros, which costs us today 54.25 million), than making the investment (60 million).

We can easily calculate the value of the option to expand:

Value of the option to expand =

value of the project with the option to expand—

value of the project without the option to expand

Value of the option to expand $= -5.7575 - (-10) = 4.2424$ million euros
Another way of calculating the value of the option to expand is

Value of the option to expand $= (140 \times 0.03333 + 0 \times 0.96666)/1.1$
$$= 4.2424 \text{ million euros}$$

22.10.3. VALUATION OF THE OPTION TO DEFER THE INVESTMENT

Let us assume the same project of Section 22.10.1, but with an additional feature: the firm can defer commencement of the project until one year later. The investment required in one year's time will be 80 million euros. Obviously, in one year's time the firm will only undertake the project if the product is a success for the firm CCC.

The project can now be represented as:

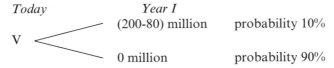

Today	*Year I*	
	(200-80) million	probability 10%
V		
	0 million	probability 90%

If we use the net present value for making the decision, we will carry out the following operation:

$$NPV = E(V_1)/(1 + \text{required return})$$
$$= ([120 \times 0.1 + 0 \times 0.9]/1.3) = 9.2308 \text{ million euros}$$

Consequently, if we base our decision on the NPV, we should keep this project and wait one year before deciding whether to invest or not.

If we use options theory, we get a different result. The project's value (V), according to options theory is:

$$V = [pV_u + (1-p)V_d]/r = ([120 \times 0.03333 + 0 \times 0.9666]/1.1)$$
$$= 3.6363 \text{ million euros}$$

The project's value is 3.6363 million euros because we can replicate whatever may happen in one year's time by buying 4,000 shares of the firm CCC and borrowing 36.3636 million euros at 10%, as can be seen below:

$$\Delta = (V_u - V_d)/[(u-d)S] = (120-0)/[(4-1) \times 10,000] = 4,000 \text{ shares}$$

$$B = (uV_d - dV_u)/[(u-d)r] = (4 \times 0 - 1 \times 120)/[(4-1) \times 1.1]$$
$$= -36.3636 \text{ million euros}$$

Thus, if the product is a success, the 4,000 shares will be worth 160 million euros and we must repay 40 million euros (36.3636 × 1.1) corresponding to the loan. If the product is a failure, the shares will be worth 40 million euros and we must repay 40 million euros corresponding to the loan. Consequently, this project's value is

$$4,000 \text{ shares} \times 10,000 \text{ euros/share} - 36.3636 \text{ million}$$
$$= 3.6363 \text{ million euros}$$

The value of the option to defer the investment is therefore: 3.6363 − (−10) = 13.6363 million euros.

Another way to calculate the value of the option to defer the investment is[15]:

Value of the option to defer the investment =
$$(-80 \times 0.03333 - 50 \times 0.96666)/1.1 + 60 = 13.6363 \text{ million euros}$$

[15]For a more detailed discussion of these options, see the article by McDonald and Siegal (1986).

22.10.4. VALUATION OF THE OPTION TO USE THE INVESTMENT FOR ALTERNATIVE PURPOSES

Let us assume the same project as in Section 22.10.1, but with an additional feature: in one year's time, the firm may sell its facilities for 62 million euros. Obviously, in one year's time the firm will sell its facilities if the product is a failure.

The project can now be represented as:

Today   *Year I*
                           200 million   probability 10%
V
                           62 million   probability 90%

If we use the net present value for making the decision, we will carry out the following operation:

$$NPV = E\ (V_1)/(1 + \text{required return}) - \text{cost}$$
$$= [200 \times 0.1 + 62 \times 0.9]/1.3 - 60 = -1.692 \text{ million euros}$$

Consequently, if we base our decision on the NPV, we should not accept this project.

If we use options theory, we get a different result. The project's value (V), according to options theory is

$$V = [pV_u + (1 - p)V_d]/r - \text{cost}$$
$$= ([200 \times 0.03333 + 62 \times 0.9666]/1.1) - 60 = 0.5454 \text{ million euros}$$

The project's value is 545.454 euros because we can replicate whatever may happen in one year's time by buying 4,600 shares of the firm CCC and investing 14.5454 million euros at 10%, as can be seen below:

$$\Delta = (V_u - V_d)/[(u - d)S] = (200 - 62)/[(4 - 1) \times 10,000] = 4,600 \text{ shares}$$

$$B = (uV_d - dV_u)/[(u - d)r]$$
$$= (4 \times 62 - 1 \times 200)/[(4 - 1) \times 1.1] = 14.5454 \text{ million euros}$$

Thus, if the product is a success, the 4,600 shares will be worth 184 million euros and our fixed income investment will be worth 16 million euros (14.5454×1.1). If the product is a failure, the shares will be worth 46 million euros and our fixed income investment will be worth 16 million euros. Consequently, this project's value is

4,600 shares × 10,000 euros/share + 14.5454 million−

60 million = 0.5454 million euros

The value of the option to use the investment for alternative purposes is, therefore:

0.545454 − (− 10) = 10.545454 million euros

Another way of calculating the value of the option to use the investment for alternative purposes is

Option of using the investment for alternative purposes =
(0 × 0.03333 + 12 × 0.96666)/1.1 = 10.5454 million euros

Another example of a real option arises when an electrical firm considers building a thermal power plant that can use both oil and coal to generate electricity.[16] Obviously, it must only build such a plant instead of a plant that only uses oil (even though the cost of the former is higher) when the excess cost is less than the value of the option to use coal when the price of oil is sufficiently higher than that of coal.

22.11. FREQUENTLY MADE ERRORS WHEN VALUING REAL OPTIONS

The best way to analyze frequently made errors when valuing real options is through an example.

Damodaran (2000, page 38) proposes valuing the option to expand the business of Home Depot. Home Depot is considering the possibility of opening a store in France. The store's cost will be 24 million euros and the present value of the expected cash flows is 20 million euros. Consequently, the project's value will be −4 million euros and it would not be a good idea. However, Home Depot believes that by opening this store, it will have the option to open another larger store in the next 5 years. The cost of the hypothetical second store would be 40 million euros and the present value of the expected cash flows is 30 million euros, although there is a lot of uncertainty regarding this parameter. Home Depot estimates the volatility of the present value of the expected cash flows of the second store at 28.3%. Damodaran uses Black and Scholes' formula to value the option of opening the second store. According to him, the option of opening the second store is a call with the following parameters:

[16]The article of Margrabe (1978) illustrates this aspect.

Option of opening the second store = Call (S = 30; K = 40;
r = 1.06; t = 5 years; σ = 28.3%) = 7.5 million euros

Consequently, according to Damodaran, Home Depot should open the store in France because the project's present value plus the value of the option to expand is −4 + 7.5 = 3.5 million euros.

Some of the errors and problems of this approach are

- *Assuming that the option is replicable.* This is why Black and Scholes' formula is used in the valuation. It is fairly obvious that the option to open a second store is not replicable.[17]
- *The estimation of the option's volatility is arbitrary and has a decisive effect on the option's value.* Damodaran's hypotheses regarding volatility (28.3%), present value of the expected cash flows (30 million), the option's life (5 years), and the option's replicability ($\mu = \ln(r) - \sigma^2/2 = 1.82\%$) are synthesized in the distribution of the expected cash flows in 5 years' time shown in Figure 22.7.[18]

It is obvious that a volatility of 28.3% per year means assuming an enormous scatter of cash flows, which is tantamount to having no idea what these cash flows may be. One thing is that a greater uncertainty increases real options' value and another altogether that real options may have a high value (i.e., must undertake projects), because we don't have the slightest idea of what may happen in the future. Figure 22.7 also shows the shape of two distributions with annual volatilities of 15%.

- As there is no riskless arbitrage, *the value of the option to expand basically depends on Home Depot's expectations about future cash* flows. However, Damodaran assumes that this parameter does not influence the option's value (he does not use it) because he assumes that the option is replicable.
- *It is not appropriate to discount the expected value of the cash* flows *at the risk-free rate* (as is done implicitly when Black and Scholes' formula is used). Although a real option will be exercised when a future uncertainty is settled (in this case, if the first store is a success), this does not mean that it is a risk-free project. The present value of the cash flows (30 million euro in the above example) is calculated using a rate that reflects

---

[17]To get around the non-replicability issue, Amram and Kulatilaka (2000, page 10) define real options as "the subset of strategic options in which the decision to exercise the option is basically determined by financial instruments or assets traded on markets." The problem is that, according to this definition, only a few oil and mining concessions would be real options.

[18]Another way of expressing the scatter is that Damodaran assumes that the value of the expected cash flows in 5 years' time will lie between 22 and 79 with a probability of 66%; and between 12 and 149 with a probability of 95%.

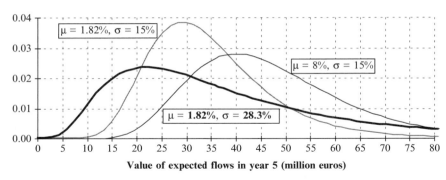

Figure 22.7 Distribution of the expected cash flows in 5 years' time according to Damodaran.

the estimated risk today. Once the outcome of the first store is known, if it is a failure, the second store will not be opened; if it is a success, the second store will be opened, but the project of opening the second store will still have risks: the uncertainty of costs and sales in 5 years' time may be greater or less than that estimated today. Therefore, the cash flows must be discounted at a rate (r_K) that is greater than the risk-free rate.

Table 22.5 shows the value of the option to open the second store using formula 22.6 for a non-replicable option. The table shows that the value of the option to open the second store offsets the 4 million euros of negative value generated by opening the first store if:

1. With low volatilities, the firm has very good prospects regarding the second store's cash flows (large μ).
2. The volatility is very high. In this case, even with extremely unfavorable expectations regarding future cash flows (negative μ), the option's value is high. However, as we have already remarked, it is best to not take too much notice of these values. If we did, firms would have to establish themselves in those countries where they have most uncertainty (countries they do not know or countries whose future is completely unknown to them) because the option of expanding in the future would have a very high value.
    - Damodaran's valuation assumes that we know exactly the cost of opening the second store and that it will be 40 million euros. Obviously, there is uncertainty as to how much it will cost to open a store in 5 years' time. The formula (22.1) used in Table 22.5 assumes that the risk of the opening cost is equal to the risk of the cash flows generated by opening the store, which is not entirely correct. Normally, the cash flows generated by opening the store will have a

Table 22.5

Value of Home Depot's Option to Expand with Different Expectations for μ and volatility, r_K = 1.09; S = 30; K = 40; t = 5years (Million euros)

							μ						
		−20.0%	−10.0%	−5.0%	0.0%	1.82%	4.0%	5.0%	6.0%	7.0%	8.0%	9.0%	10.0%
σ	1.0%	0.0	0.0	0.0	0.0	0.0	0.0	0.0	0.4	1.7	3.1	4.6	6.2
		0.0%	*0.0%*	*0.0%*	*0.0%*	*0.0%*	*0.0%*	*4.6%*	*70.9%*	*99.7%*	*100%*	*100%*	*100%*
	5.0%	0.0	0.0	0.0	0.0	0.0	0.4	0.8	1.4	2.3	3.5	4.9	6.4
		0.0%	*0.0%*	*0.0%*	*0.5%*	*3.9%*	*21.6%*	*36.8%*	*54.4%*	*71.1%*	*84.2%*	*92.7%*	*97.1%*
	10.0%	0.0	0.0	0.0	0.3	0.7	1.5	2.1	2.9	3.8	4.8	6.1	7.4
		0.0%	*0.0%*	*0.8%*	*9.9%*	*19.0%*	*34.7%*	*43.3%*	*52.2%*	*61.0%*	*69.2%*	*76.6%*	*82.9%*
	15.0%	0.0	0.0	0.2	1.1	1.8	3.0	3.7	4.6	5.5	6.6	7.8	9.2
		0.0%	*0.9%*	*5.4%*	*19.6%*	*27.9%*	*39.7%*	*45.5%*	*51.5%*	*57.4%*	*63.1%*	*68.6%*	*73.7%*
	20.0%	0.0	0.2	0.8	2.3	3.3	4.8	5.6	6.6	7.6	8.8	10.1	11.5
		0.2%	*3.9%*	*11.5%*	*26.0%*	*33.0%*	*42.2%*	*46.6%*	*51.1%*	*55.5%*	*59.9%*	*64.2%*	*68.3%*
	25.0%	0.1	0.7	1.7	3.9	5.1	6.9	7.9	8.9	10.1	11.3	12.7	14.2
		1.1%	*7.9%*	*16.8%*	*30.3%*	*36.2%*	*43.8%*	*47.3%*	*50.9%*	*54.4%*	*58.0%*	*61.4%*	*64.8%*
	28.3%	0.2	1.1	2.5	5.2	6.5	8.5	9.5	10.7	11.9	13.3	14.7	16.3
		2.1%	*10.7%*	*19.8%*	*32.5%*	*37.8%*	*44.5%*	*47.6%*	*50.8%*	*53.9%*	*57.0%*	*60.1%*	*63.1%*
	30.0%	0.2	1.4	3.0	5.9	7.3	9.4	10.5	11.7	13.0	14.4	15.9	17.5
		2.7%	*12.0%*	*21.1%*	*33.4%*	*38.5%*	*44.8%*	*47.8%*	*50.7%*	*53.7%*	*56.6%*	*59.6%*	*62.4%*
	35.0%	0.6	2.5	4.7	8.2	10.0	12.4	13.6	15.0	16.5	18.0	19.7	21.5

(continues)

Table 22.5 (continued)

						μ						
	5.0%	15.7%	24.6%	35.7%	40.1%	45.5%	48.1%	50.6%	53.2%	55.7%	58.2%	60.7%
40.0%	**1.2**	**4.0**	**6.8**	**11.1**	**13.2**	**16.0**	**17.4**	**19.0**	**20.6**	**22.4**	**24.3**	**26.3**
	7.5%	*18.9%*	*27.4%*	*37.4%*	*41.3%*	*46.1%*	*48.3%*	*50.5%*	*52.8%*	*55.0%*	*57.2%*	*59.4%*
55.0%	**4.9**	**11.4**	**16.8**	**24.3**	**27.7**	**32.2**	**34.5**	**36.9**	**39.5**	**42.2**	**45.1**	**48.2**
	14.8%	*26.1%*	*33.1%*	*40.8%*	*43.6%*	*47.2%*	*48.8%*	*50.4%*	*52.0%*	*53.6%*	*55.3%*	*56.9%*

The probability of exercising the option is given in Italics.

greater risk than the opening cost and should be discounted at a higher rate.

Other errors.

- *Believe that options' value increases when interest rates increase.* For example, Leslie and Michaels (1997) say, "an increase in interest rates increases the option's value, in spite of its negative effect on the net present value, because it reduces the present value of the exercise price." This is wrong because the negative effect of increased interest rates on the present value of the expected cash flows (as on the value of shares) is always greater than the positive effect of the reduction of the present value of the exercise price.
- *"Play" with volatility.* The best way to explain what we mean when we say "play" is with an example. To value an oil concession where we have uncertainty regarding the number of barrels, Damodaran (1999) proposes calculating the volatility (σ) in the following manner:
- $\sigma^2 = \sigma_p^2 + \sigma_q^2 + \sigma_{pq}$, where σ_p is the volatility of the oil price, σ_q is the volatility of the quantity of barrels of oil, and σ_{pq} is the covariance between price and quantity. Apart from the difficulties in estimating the parameters σ_q and σ_{pq}, it is obvious that, with this method, we will assign a higher value to the option by assigning it a high volatility. The more sources of uncertainty there are, the greater will be the volatility.
- *Valuing contracts as real options when they are not.* For example, the contract held by Áurea, a firm that manages freeway concessions, by virtue of which Dragados will offer Áurea the concession management contracts for all the freeways it is contracted to construct for the next 15 years (this initial term can be extended by mutual agreement between the two parties). The price at which Dragados will offer each concession to Áurea will be 95% of the value determined (at the time of the offer, at the end of the concession) by an independent valuer who is acceptable to both Dragados and Áurea. Áurea has the option of buying (at that time) each concession's equity for 95% of the value determined (at the time of the offer) by the independent valuer.[19] If Áurea exercises the option, it will buy the equity from Dragados and take on the freeway's debt. It is obvious that this contract is composed of a series of real options, one call per concession. However, each of the calls comprising the contract is an *in-the-money* call.[20]

---

[19]The valuations made by independent valuers (that are acceptable to both Dragados and Áurea) of each concession are very accurate, according to the opinion of Valora managers.

[20]An *in-the-money* call is an option whose exercise price is less than the underlying asset's price.

- In this case, the price of the underlying asset is the value determined by the valuer (V), and the exercise price is 95% of this value (0.95 V). Consequently, there is no uncertainty (from a purely economic viewpoint) regarding the future exercise of the options: all of the options will be exercised because they enable a concession having a value V to be bought for 0.95 V.

- This option is similar to a call on a GM share whose exercise price will be 95% of GM's share price at the time of exercise. What is the value of this call? It is 5% of GM's share price today, irrespective of the exercise date and the volatility.

- The value of the contract held by Áurea is, therefore, the present value of 5% of the value of the equity of the concessions that Dragados will offer Áurea during the next 15 years.[21]

22.12. METHODS FOR VALUING REAL OPTIONS

Real options can be valued using the following methods:

- If they are replicable, using Black and Scholes' formula, the formulas developed for valuing exotic options,[22] by simulation, the binomial formula, or by solving the differential equations characterizing the options.

- If they are not replicable, by any of the above methods but taking into account the non-replicability. For example, it is not possible to apply Black and Scholes' formula but rather the modified formula, explained in Section 22.7.

As an exercise, I propose that the reader think how he should value my Argentinean friend's livestock company:

> Dear Pablo: The reason for this message is to briefly consult you about the use of real options. It so happens that I am valuing a livestock company that owns a number of farms in the province of Salta. One of the farms (whose value without options I have already calculated) is located between two towns. The towns have grown and a residential estate has been built very close. There is a distinct possibility of an urban development project in the future and, if this should occur, the land could be worth 8 times more than what it is worth as a livestock farm. The point is that as time goes by, the likelihood that this will happen will increase. Could you give me your opinion?

One last exercise. I propose that the reader identify the errors made in the valuation of Yahoo given in Table 22.6. A renowned international consulting

---

[21]One could consider more years by assigning a probability to the renewal of the contract when the 15-year period has expired.

[22]The reader interested in exotic options can see Nelken (1996) and Zang (1997).

Table 22.6
Valuation of Yahoo Performed by a Renowned International Consulting Firm

1. Value of future flows

(million dollars)	1999	2000	2001	2002	2003	2004	Terminal value
Sales	589	1,078	1,890	3,034	4,165	5,640	
EBIT	188	399	756	1,365	1,999	2,876	
Free cash flow	103	216	445	842	1,255	1,832	104,777
Net present value of free cash flows	52,346						
+ Net cash	600						
Equity value	52,946						

Risk-free rate: 6.3%. Market Risk Premium: 4%. Beta of Yahoo: 1.74. WACC = 13.3%

Long-term growth (free cash flow): 8.25%

2. Value of options (million dollars)

	Electronic commerce		Advertising revenues
Present value of sales	37,684		79,531
Time to exercise (years)	5		5
Exercise price	37,684		79,531
Volatility	88.4%		85.9%
1 + annual interest rate	1.133		1.133
Value of option (sales)	**29,017**		**60,445**

(*continues*)

Table 22.6 (*continued*)

Net margin	45.17%		Net margin	45.17%
Value of option (flows)	**13,107**		**Value of option (flows)**	**27,303**

3. Value of Yahoo shares (million dollars)

Present value of flows	52,946
Value of option on electronic commerce	13,107
Value of option on advertising revenues	27,303
Value of Yahoo shares	**93,355**

firm using what it called "an innovative valuation model" performed the valuation.[23]

The value of the shares (93.355 billion) is the sum of the present value of the cash flows (52.946 billion) and the value of the real options (40.409 billion). The present value of the cash flows is obtained by discounting the free cash flow forecast at a rate of 13.3%. The options' value is calculated using Black and Scholes' formula with the parameters given in Table 22.6.

Some questions to help the reader identify errors:

1. According to the cash flow forecasts, how big will Yahoo be in 2010, in 2020, and in 2050?
2. Is it correct to say that the company's value is the present value of the expected cash flows plus the options on those same flows?
3. Does it make sense to use the WACC to calculate the options' value?
4. What is the sense of the 5–year term used to calculate the options' value?
5. What do you think about the hypothesis that the options' underlying asset is the present value of sales?
6. Is it correct to use Black and Scholes' formula to value the options?
7. What do you think about the volatilities used to value the options?

Finally, one piece of information. Yahoo's equity market value on 23 April 2001 was $10.16 billion.

APPENDIX 22.1: A DERIVATION OF BLACK AND SCHOLES' FORMULA

VALUATION OF A CALL

In this Appendix, we will demonstrate Black and Scholes' formula for valuing a call on a share (therefore, a replicable option) using the simplest procedure. The formula was published for the first time in Black and Scholes (1973).

We assume that the share's return follows a normal process and that its price follows a course such that:

$$S_t = Se^{(\mu t + \sigma \varepsilon \sqrt{t})} \tag{22.4}$$

The share's expected value is given by the equation:

---

[23]The consulting firm also stated that "the advantage of this methodology lies in the fact that it enables absolute valuations to be obtained for Internet companies, avoiding the invariably dangerous valuations of firms operating in this sector."

$$E(S_t) = Se^{(\mu+\sigma^2/2)t} \tag{22.5}$$

Where: μ = return expected by the investor per unit of time.

$\mu t = E[\ln(S_t/S)]$

σ = annual volatility of the share in percent ε = normal random variable of zero mean and variance equal to unity

By definition, the call's value now ($t = 0$) must be the net present value of the future cash flows generated by it. We know the cash flow that the option's holder will receive on the exercise date, i.e., the maximum of the values $(S_t - K)$ and 0: Max $(S_t - K, 0)$. Consequently:

$$\begin{aligned}
C &= NPV \,[\text{Max } (S_t - K, 0)] = NPV \,[(S_t - K)/S_t > K] \, P[S_t > K] \\
&+ NPV \,[0] \, P[S_t > K] = NPV \,[S_t/S_t > K] \, P[S_t > K] \\
&- NPV \,[K/S_t > K] \, P[S_t > K]
\end{aligned} \tag{22.6}$$

Before calculating equation (22.6), we should make clear one important point. If two investors were to calculate the option's NPV using different expectations about the share's future value (with different μ), they would obtain different results. However, if the two investors agree on their volatility expectations, they must also agree on the option's price because the option can be replicated with shares and bonds. Consequently, and this is a general rule for valuing financial instruments that can be constructed from other (replicable instruments), it is not possible to calculate the NPV using the investor's return expectations. Instead, a fixed return expectation must be used, so that all investors use the same expectation even though individually they may have different expectations. When a financial instrument can be valued by riskless arbitrage—it can be replicated from other existing instruments—the price ratios move between a risk-free probability range. In this range, the expected value of a share's price (and whose price today is S euros) is equal to the value expected from investing those euros at the risk-free rate:

$$E(S_t) = Se^{(\mu+\sigma^2/2)t} = Sr^t \tag{22.7}$$

because, where $r = 1+$ risk-free rate:

$$\mu = \ln(r) - \sigma^2/2 \tag{22.8}$$

CALCULATION OF NPV[$K/S_t > K$]P[$S_t > K$]

The present value of K, if $S_t > K$, will be equal to its expected value discounted at the rate r. This value is K, which is a data we know. Thus:

$$\text{NPV } [K/S_t > K] = r^{-t}E \ [K/S_t > K] = K \ r^{-t} \tag{22.9}$$

To calculate the *probability* that the option will be exercised, i.e., the probability that the share's value will be greater than the exercise price on the exercise date, we will take into account equation (22.4). Thus:

$$P[S_t > K] = P[S \ e^{(\mu t + \sigma \varepsilon \sqrt{t})} > K] = P[\mu t + \sigma \varepsilon \sqrt{t} > \ln (K/S)]$$

$$= P[\varepsilon > -\frac{\ln (S/K) + \mu t}{\sigma \sqrt{t}}]$$

ε is a normal random variable of zero mean and variance equal to unity. In a normal distribution, the following equation is met: $P[\varepsilon > -H] = P[\varepsilon < H]$

Consequently, $P[S_t > K] = P[\varepsilon < \dfrac{\ln(S/K) + \mu t}{\sigma \sqrt{t}}]$

Considering (22.8) and substituting in the above equation, we obtain:

$$P[S_t > K] = P[\varepsilon < \frac{\ln(S/K) + \ln(r^t) - t\sigma^2/2}{\sigma \sqrt{t}}]$$

As ε is a normal distribution $(0,1)$, the following equation is met:

$$P[S_t > K] = N[\frac{\ln(Sr^t/K) - t\sigma^2/2}{\sigma \sqrt{t}}].$$

Defining x as:

$$x = \frac{\ln(Sr^t/K) - t\sigma^2/2}{\sigma \sqrt{t}}$$

we obtain the expression:[24]

$$P[S_t > K] = N(x - \sigma \sqrt{t})$$

Taking into account equation (22.9):

$$\text{NPV } [K/S_t > K] \ P[S_t > K] = K \ r^{-t} \ N(x - \sigma \sqrt{t}) \tag{22.10}$$

CALCULATION OF NPV[$S_t/S_t > K$]P[$S_t > K$]

The present value of S_t is equal to its expected value discounted at the rate r:

---

[24]It is important to realize that $P[S_t > K] = N(x - \sigma \sqrt{t})$ only if $\mu = \ln r - \sigma^2/2$. This condition is imposed by the fact that the option can be replicated with shares and bonds.

$$\text{NPV} [S_t/S_t > K] \, P[S_t > K] = r^{-t} E[S_t/S_t > K] \, P[S_t > K] =$$

$$E[S_t/S_t > K] \, P[S_t > K] =$$

$$\int\limits_{-x+\sigma\sqrt{t}}^{\infty} Se^{\left(\mu t + \sigma\varepsilon\sqrt{t}\right)} \frac{e^{-\varepsilon^2/2}}{\sqrt{2\pi}} d\varepsilon = S\, e^{\mu t}$$

$$\int\limits_{-x+\sigma\sqrt{t}}^{\infty} \frac{e^{\left(\sigma\varepsilon\sqrt{t} - \varepsilon^2/2\right)}}{\sqrt{2\pi}} d\varepsilon = S\, e^{\left(\mu + \sigma^2/2\right)t}$$

$$\int\limits_{-x+\sigma\sqrt{t}}^{\infty} \frac{e^{-\left(\frac{\sigma\sqrt{t} - \varepsilon}{2}\right)^2}}{\sqrt{2\pi}} d\varepsilon =$$

To solve this integral, we change variables: $v = \sigma\sqrt{t} - \varepsilon; dv = -d\varepsilon$
Then:

for $S_t = K$; $\varepsilon = -x + \sigma\sqrt{t}$; $v = x$. For $S_t = \infty$; $\varepsilon = \infty$; $v = -\infty$

With these results:

$$E[S_t/S_t > K]P[S_t > K] = Se^{(\mu+\sigma^2/2)t}N(x)$$

On the other hand, taking into account (22.7), the following is met:
$e^{(\mu+\sigma^2/2)t} = r^t$

Therefore:

$$E[S_t/S_t > K]P[S_t > K] = Sr^t N(x)$$

Consequently,

$$\text{NPV}[S_t/S_t > K]P[S_t > K] = r^{-t}E[S_t/S_t > K]P[S_t > K] = SN(x) \quad (22.11)$$

Substituting (22.10) and (22.11) in (22.6), we obtain Black and Scholes' formula for a call:

$$\text{Call} = S\, N(x) - Kr^{-t}N(x - \sigma\sqrt{t})$$

$$\text{where } x = \frac{\ln(Sr^t/K) - t\sigma^2/2}{\sigma\sqrt{t}}$$

$N(x)$ is an integral that has no explicit solution. However, most statistics books contain tables with the cumulative probability function of a normal distribution and many spreadsheets already contain the function $N(x)$.

SUMMARY

A firm or a project that provides some type of future flexibility, real options, cannot be valued correctly using the traditional discounted cash flow techniques. Using the present value, without taking into account the possibility of not exercising the option, would lead to erroneous results and wrong decisions.

The equations to value financial options are valid inly if the options can be replicated. These equations are based on the existence of a replicating port-folio.

The crucial variable in calculating an option's value is expected volatility. The greater the expected volatility, the greater the option's value.

REFERENCES

Amram M., and Nalin Kulatilaka (2000), "Strategy and Shareholder Value Creation: The Real Options Frontier," *Journal of Applied Corporate Finance*, Vol. 13, No. 2, pp. 8–21.

Amram, M. and Nalin Kulatilaka (1999), *Real Options*, Cambridge, MA: Harvard Business School Press.

Black, F., and M. Scholes (1973), "The Pricing of Options and Corporate Liabilities," *The Journal of Political Economy*, May–June, pp. 637–654.

Collura, M. and L. Applegate (2000), "Amazon.com: Exploiting the Value of Digital Business Infrastructure," Harvard Business School Case number 9-800-330.

Cox, J. C., and M. Rubinstein (1985), *Options Markets*, New York: Prentice-Hall.

Damodaran, A., (2000), "The Promise of Real Options," *Journal of Applied Corporate Finance*, Vol. 13, No. 2.

Damodaran, A., (1999), "The Promise and Peril of Real Options," Working Paper, Stern School of Business.

Grenadier, S., and A. Weiss (1997), "Investment in Technological Innovations: An Option Pricing Approach," *Journal of Financial Economics*, 44, pp. 397–416.

Kester, W. C., (1984), "Today's Options for Tomorrow's Growth," *Harvard Business Review*, March–April, pp. 153–160.

Leslie, K. J., and M. P. Michaels (1997), "The Real Power of Real Options," *The McKinsey Quarterly*, No. 3, pp. 5–22.

Luehrman, T. A. (1995), "Capital Projects as Real Options: An Introduction," Harvard Business School, 9-295-074.

McDonald R., and D. Siegal (1986), "The Value of Waiting to Invest," *Quantitative Journal of Economics*, 101, pp. 707–727.

Moel, A., and P. Tufano (2000), "When are Real Options Exercised? An Empirical Study of Mine Closings," Working Paper, Harvard Business School.

Margrabe, W., (1978), "The Value of an Option to Exchange One Asset For Another," *Journal of Finance*, March, pp. 177–198.

Nelken, I., (1996), *The Handbook of Exotic Options*, New York: Irwin.

Trigeorgis, L. (1996), *Real Options*, Cambridge, MA: The MIT Press.

Zang, P. G. (1997), *Exotic Options*, Singapore: World Scientific.

Chapter 23

Valuation of Brands and Intangibles

The consulting firm Interbrand valued the Coca-Cola brand at $72.5 billion and the Microsoft brand at $70.2 billion. The ratio between brand value and market capitalization ranged between 1% for Pampers, 2% for Shell, and 77% for Apple and Nike. For Coca-Cola it was 59%, 14% for Pepsico, and 52% for Kellog (Table 23.1). On February 16, 2001, the newspaper Expansión published a list with the value of the brands of the main soccer and Formula 1 teams. The consulting firm FutureBrand performed the valuation (Table 23.2). According to them, the Real Madrid brand was worth $155 million and the Barcelona brand was worth $85 million. Two questions come to mind: Are these valuations reliable?; and, Does valuing brands achieve anything useful?

In recent years, particularly since the publication of David Aaker's book (1991) *Managing Brand Equity: Capitalizing on the Value of a Brand Name*, the number of consulting firms and research documents proposing methods for determining a brand's value has increased enormously.

The effort is worthwhile because, in the current competitive environment, many consider that the brand constitutes many business sectors' most important commercial and institutional assets. Many people are interested in learning how to create strong, enduring brands. One essential part of this process is to identify each brand's value drivers, that is, the basic parameters for creating, managing, and measuring a brand's value.

However, we feel that we are still a long way from defining exactly the brand concept and, therefore, its value.

In this chapter, our goal is to show the limitations of a number of the methods proposed for valuing brands and intellectual capital and, within

555

Table 23.1

The 80 Most valuable Brands in 2000 (in Billion Dollars),
According to Interbrand

Company	Country	Brand value 2000	1999
1 Coca-Cola	USA	72.5	83.8
2 Microsoft	USA	70.2	56.7
3 IBM	USA	53.2	43.8
4 P&G	USA	48.4	
5 Nestlé	Swizerland	40.3	
6 Intel	USA	39.0	30.0
7 Nokia	Finland	38.5	20.7
8 General Electric	USA	38.1	33.5
9 Unilever	UK	37.1	
10 Ford	USA	36.4	33.2
11 Disney	USA	33.6	32.3
12 McDonald's	USA	27.9	26.2
13 AT&T	USA	25.5	24.2
14 Marlboro	USA	22.1	21.0
15 Mercedes	Germany	21.1	17.8
16 Hewlett-Packard	USA	20.6	17.1
17 Cisco Systems	USA	20	
18 Toyota	Japan	18.9	12.3
19 Citibank	USA	18.9	9.1
20 Gillette	USA	17.4	15.9
21 Sony	Japan	16.4	14.2
22 Amex	USA	16.1	12.6
23 Honda	Japón	15.2	11.1
24 Diageo	UK	14.6	
25 Compaq	USA	14.6	
26 Nescafé	Suiza	13.7	17.6
27 Colgate	USA	13.6	
28 BMW	Germany	13.0	11.3
29 Kodak	USA	11.9	14.8
30 Heinz	USA	11.8	11.8

(*continues*)

Table 23.1 (*continued*)

Company	Country	Brand value 2000	1999
31 Budweiser	USA	10.7	8.5
32 Xerox	USA	9.7	11.2
33 Dell	USA	9.5	9.0
34 Gap	USA	9.3	7.9
35 Nike	USA	8.0	8.2
36 Volkswagen	Germany	7.8	6.6
37 Ericsson	Suecia	7.8	14.8
38 Kelloggs	USA	7.4	7.1
39 Louis Vuitton	Francia	6.9	4.1
40 Pepsi-Cola	USA	6.6	5.9
41 Apple	USA	6.6	4.3
42 MTV	USA	6.4	
43 Yahoo!	USA	6.3	1.8
44 SAP	Germany	6.1	
45 IKEA	Sweden	6.0	3.5
46 Duracell	USA	5.9	
47 Phillips	Holand	5.5	
48 Samsung	Korea	5.2	
49 Gucci	Italy	5.2	
50 Kleenex	USA	5.1	4.6
51 Reuters	UK	4.9	
52 AOL	USA	4.5	4.3
53 amazon.com	USA	4.5	1.4
54 Motorola	USA	4.4	3.6
55 Colgate	USA	4.4	3.6
56 Wrigley's	USA	4.3	4.4
57 Chanel	France	4.1	3.1
58 adidas	Germany	3.8	3.6
59 Panasonic	Japan	3.7	
60 Rolex	Swizerland	3.6	2.4
61 Hertz	USA	3.4	3.5
62 Bacardi	Cuba	3.2	2.9

(*continues*)

Table 23.1 (*continued*)

Company	Country	Brand value 2000	1999
63 BP	UK	3.1	3.0
64 Moet & Chandon	France	2.8	2.8
65 Shell	UK	2.8	2.7
66 Burger King	USA	2.7	2.8
67 Smirnoff	Rusia	2.4	2.3
68 Barbie	USA	2.3	3.8
69 Heineken	Holand	2.2	2.2
70 Wall Street Journal	USA	2.2	
71 Ralph Lauren	USA	1.8	1.6
72 Johnnie Walker	UK	1.5	1.6
73 Hilton	USA	1.5	1.3
74 Jack Daniels	USA	1.5	
75 Armani	Italy	1.5	
76 Pampers	USA	1.4	1.4
77 Starbucks	USA	1.3	
78 Guinness	Ireland	1.2	1.3
79 Financial Times	UK	1.1	
80 Benetton	Italy	1	

Table 23.2

Value of the Brands of Soccer and Formula 1 teams (in Million Dollars), According to Future Brand

Manchester United	259	Juventus	102	Arsenal	82	Ferrari	110
Real Madrid	155	Liverpool	85	Inter Milan	76	McLaren Mercedes	106
Bayern Munich	150	F.C. Barcelona	85	Rangers	53	Williams BMW	79

the limits imposed by the brand's intrinsic reality, establish guidelines for value creation through the study of brands and intellectual capital.

As we will see, the first difficulty encountered is finding a precise definition of what a brand is. This requires determining what part of the cash flows generated by the company are to be attributed to the brand or, to put it another way, what flows would the company generate if it did not have the brand we wish to value.[1]

There is a lot of confusion about brand value. In 2000, a national newspaper published that, according to a renowned marketing professor, "a brand's value can be up to three times more than the market capitalization." Obviously, this is a conceptual error.

Another line of research has been to value the so-called "intellectual capital," which we shall discuss in Section 23.12.

23.1. METHODS USED FOR VALUING BRANDS

A number of authors and consulting firms have proposed different methods for brand valuation. The different methods consider that a brand's value is

1. The market value of the company's shares.
2. The difference between the market value and book value of the company's shares (market value added). Other firms quantify the brand's value as the difference between the shares' market value and its adjusted book value or adjusted net worth (this difference is called goodwill). An example of a company that uses this method is given in Section 23.2.
3. The difference between the market value and the book value of the company's shares minus the management team's managerial expertise (intellectual capital).
4. The brand's replacement value
   • Present value of the historic investment in marketing and promotions[2]

---

[1]There are many definitions for the brand concept but they are not feasible for brand valuation. For example, Aaker defines the brand as "a set of assets and liabilities linked to a brand's name and symbol that adds to or subtracts from the value provided by a product or service to a firm and/or that firm's customers." According to Lance Leuthesser (1995), the brand is "a product's additional value (for its customers) compared with what would be the value of another identical product without the brand." According to the Marketing Science Institute (1998), the brand is the "strong, sustainable, and differentiated advantage with respect to competitors that leads to a higher volume or a higher margin for the company compared with the situation it would have without the brand. This differential volume or margin is the consequence of the behavior of the consumers, the distribution channel and the companies themselves."

[2]This method is inconsistent because there are brands, like Rolls Royce, where marketing costs are negligible and the brand's value is substantial. It is used frequently by Cadbury-Schweppes.

- Estimation of the advertising investment required to achieve the present level of brand recognition
5. The difference between the value of the branded company and that of another similar company that sold unbranded products (generic products or private labels). To quantify this difference, several authors and consulting firms propose different methods:
   - Present value of the price premium (with respect to a private label) paid by customers for that brand
   - Present value of the extra volume (with respect to a private label) due to the brand
   - The sum of the above two values
   - The above sum less all-differential, brand-specific expenses and investments. This is the most correct method, from a conceptual viewpoint. However, it is very difficult to reliably define the differential parameters between the branded and unbranded product, that is, the differential price, volume, product costs, overhead expenses, investments, sales and advertising activities, etc.
   - The difference between the [price/sales] ratios of the branded company and the unbranded company multiplied by the company's sales. This method is discussed in Section 23.3 and is used by Damodaran to value the Kellogg and Coca-Cola brands, as we shall see in Section 23.4. In Section 23.5, we discuss a series of problems or errors that these valuations contain.
   - Differential earnings (between the branded company and the unbranded company) multiplied by a multiple. As we shall see further on, this is the method used by the consulting firm Interbrand.
6. The present value of the company's free cash flow minus the assets employed multiplied by the required return. This is the method used by the firm Houlihan Valuation Advisors and is discussed in Section 23.9.
7. The options of selling at a higher price and/or higher volume and the options of growing through new distribution channels, new countries, new products, new formats . . . due to the brand's existence.

23.2. VALUATION OF THE BRAND "FOR WHOM" AND "FOR WHAT PURPOSE"

When valuing a brand, it is particularly important "for whom" that value is being determined for, since the brand's value is not the same for the company that owns the brand as for a company with a competing brand or for another company operating in the industry with a brand that does not compete directly with it, etc.

Likewise, it is vitally important to define "for what purpose" it is wished to determine a brand's value, whether it is to sell it or to collect a series of royalties, or to facilitate the brand's management, or to capitalize its value in the balance sheet and then depreciate it.

An example will help us understand the importance of this difference. Figure 23.1 shows two valuations of the equity of a consumer products company: that made by the seller (present situation) and that made by the buyer (buyer's expectations). The seller's management team calculated the value of the company's shares (assuming that it will continue to lead the company) as being 838 million euros. The buying company's management team (taking into account its expectations) valued the company's shares at 1.341 billion euros. The difference $(1,341 - 838 = 503)$ is due to a better positioning of the present brand (117 million); savings in sales, distribution, overhead and production costs (146 million); and value of the distribution of the buyer's other brands through the company's channels (240 million).

The seller's management team maintained that the brand's value (including the intellectual capital) under its management was 337 million. However, it is obvious that the brand's value (and the company's value) depended on "for whom." It is also obvious that "for whom" is related with "for what purpose": the buyer's management team would use the company's assets and

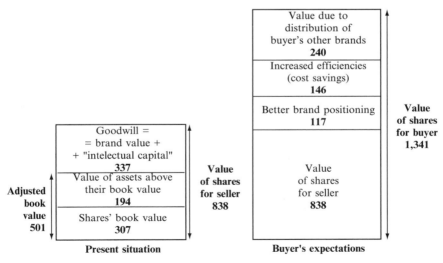

Figure 23.1   Two valuations of the shares of a consumer products company.

the brand in a different way from the seller's management team. It is also obvious that the value of the shares and the brand would be different for another prospective buyer.

This example also highlights the difficulty in separating what is brand value and what is intellectual capital. Can the reader think of a sensible procedure for dividing the 337 million between brand value and intellectual capital?

Finally, the shares were sold for 1.05 billion euros.

23.3. VALUATION OF THE BRAND USING THE DIFFERENCE IN THE PRICE TO SALES RATIOS

It is assumed[2a] that the FCF grows at a rate g until year n and, after year $n + 1$, it grows at a rate g_n. Therefore, the FCF for year n is

$$FCF_n = FCF_1 (1 + g)^{n-1},$$

and the FCF for year $n + 1$ is

$$FCF_{n+1} = FCF_1(1 + g)^{n-1}(1 + g_n)$$

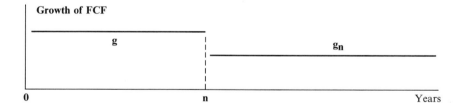

The value of the company $(E + D)$ today is

$$(E + D)_0 = \frac{FCF_1}{WACC - g}\left[1 - \left(\frac{1 + g}{1 + WACC}\right)^n\right]$$
$$+ \frac{FCF_1(1 + g)^{n-1}(1 + g_n)}{(WACC - g_n)(1 + WACC)^n}$$

(23.1)

[2a]This formulation is similar to that of Section 6.9. However, that section only referred to dividends.

This expression reduces to:

$$(E + D)_0 = \frac{FCF_0(1 + g)}{WACC - g}\left[1 - \left(\frac{1 + g}{1 + WACC}\right)^{n-1}\left(\frac{g - g_n}{WACC - g_n}\right)\right] \quad (23.2)$$

The FCF (free cash flow) is the NOPAT less the increase in net fixed assets less the increase in working capital requirements:

$$FCF = NOPAT - \Delta NFA - \Delta WCR \quad (23.3)$$

Dividing (23.3) by the sales (S), we obtain:

$$\frac{FCF}{S} = \frac{NOPAT}{S} - \frac{\Delta NFA}{S} - \frac{\Delta WCR}{S}$$

As[3] $\dfrac{\Delta NFA}{S} + \dfrac{\Delta WCR}{S} = \dfrac{\Delta NFA + \Delta WCR}{\Delta S} \dfrac{\Delta S}{S} = \dfrac{NFA + WCR}{S}$ g gives:

$$\frac{FCF}{S} = \frac{NOPAT}{S} - \frac{NFA + WCR}{S}g \quad (23.4)$$

Dividing the expression (23.2) by the sales (S) and taking into account (23.4), we obtain:

$$\frac{E + D}{S} = \left(\frac{NOPAT}{S} - \frac{NFA + WCR}{S}g\right)\frac{(1 + g)}{WACC - g}$$
$$\left[1 - \left(\frac{1 + g}{1 + WACC}\right)^{n-1}\left(\frac{g - g_n}{WACC - g_n}\right)\right] \quad (23.5)$$

We can consider a price to sales ratio for a branded company and another price to sales ratio for an unbranded company, that is, with private labels or generic products. In this case, the value of the brand is:

$$\text{Value of the brand} = \left[\left(\frac{E + D}{S}\right)_{brand} - \left(\frac{E + D}{S}\right)_{generic}\right]\text{Sales} \quad (23.6)$$

If instead of valuing the company, we only value the shares, the formula (23.1) becomes formula (23.7)

$$E_0 = \frac{ECF_1}{Ke - g}\left[1 - \left(\frac{1 + g}{1 + Ke}\right)^n\right] + \frac{ECF_1(1 + g)^{n-1}(1 + g_n)}{(Ke - g_n)(1 + Ke)^n} \quad (23.7)$$

---

[3]Assuming that the ratio (WCR+NFA)/S remains constant.

The equity cash flow (ECF) is equal to the profit after tax (PAT) multiplied by the payout ratio (p in the first years and p_n in the following years). Dividing the expression (23.7) by the sales gives:

$$\frac{E}{S} = \frac{PAT}{S} \frac{(1+g)p}{Ke-g} \left[1 - \left(\frac{1+g}{1+Ke} \right)^n \right] + \frac{PAT}{S} \frac{p_n(1+g)^n(1+g_n)}{(Ke-g_n)(1+Ke)^n} \quad (23.8)$$

In the same way, we can consider an equity (E) to sales ratio for a branded company and another equity (E) to sales ratio for an unbranded company, that is, with private labels or generic products. The brand's value will then be

$$\text{Value of the brand} = \left[\left(\frac{E}{S} \right)_{brand} - \left(\frac{E}{S} \right)_{generic} \right] \text{Sales} \quad (23.9)$$

23.4. VALUATIONS OF THE KELLOGG AND COCA-COLA BRANDS BY DAMODARAN

Damodaran presents two applications of the method described in the previous section to value the Kellogg and Coca-Cola brands.[4] He uses formulas (23.5) and (23.6) to value Kellogg and formulas (23.8) and (23.9) to value Coca-Cola. Table 23.3 contains both valuations. In the valuation of Kellogg, Damodaran calculates the growth g by multiplying the ROA by the earnings withholding ratio, which is (1 – *payout*). In the valuation of Coca-Cola, he calculates the growth g by multiplying the ROE by the earnings withholding ratio, which is (1 – *payout*), and the ROE is the earnings to sales ratio multiplied to the sales to equity ratio (S/Ebv). Observe that in the case of Kellogg, it is assumed that the growth of fixed assets and working capital requirements (WCR) is zero. In another subsequent valuation, performed in 1998, he priced the value of the Coca-Cola brand[5] at more than $100 billion.

23.5. ANALYSIS OF DAMODARAN'S VALUATIONS

1. *In the valuation of Kellogg, he considers that* (*WCR + NFA*)/*S is zero.* However, in recent years, Kellog's (WCR + NFA)/S ratio has been

---

[4]The valuation of Kellog appears on pages 346–348 of Damodaran (1996). The valuation of Coca-Cola appears on pages 256–257 of Damodaran (1994).

[5]Ver www.stern.nyu.edu/ ~ adamodar/pdfiles/eqnotes/brand.pdf.

Table 23.3
Valuations of the Kellogg and Coca-Cola Brands According to Damodaran

(Kellogg)	Value of the Kellog brand 1995			(Coca-Cola)	Value of the Coca-Cola brand 1993			Coca-Cola 1998		
	Kellogg	Generic	Difference		Coca-Cola	Generic	Difference	Coca-Cola	Generic	Difference
NOPAT / S	14.08%	6.72%	7.36%	PAT / S	14.40%	12.00%	2.40%	18.56%	7.50%	11.06%
(NFA+WCR)/S	0.00%	0.00%	0.00%	S/Ebv	3.364	1.366	2.00	1.67	1.67	0.00
ROA	32.60%	15.00%	17.60%	ROE	48.44%	16.39%	32.05%	31.00%	12.53%	18.47%
p (payout)	44.00%	44.00%	0.00%	p (payout)	39.00%	39.00%	0.00%	35.00%	35.00%	0.00%
g	18.26%	8.40%	9.86%	g	29.55%	10.00%	19.55%	20.15%	8.14%	12.01%
n (years)	5	5	0	n (years)	5	5	0	10	10	0
K_e	13.00%	13.00%	0.00%	K_e	13.325%	13.325%	0.00%	12.13%	12.13%	0.00%
E/(D+E)	92.16%	92.16%	0.00%	p_n	65%	65%	0%	80.65%	52.10%	28.55%
WACC	12.41%	12.41%	0.00%							
g_n	5.00%	5.00%	0.00%	g_n	6.00%	6.00%	0.00%	6.00%	6.00%	0.00%
(E+D) / S	**3.39**	**1.10**	**2.29**	**E / S**	**3.07**	**1.19**	**1.88**	**6.13**	**0.69**	**5.44**

Summary figures:

	Value of the Kellog brand 1995	Value of the Coca-Cola brand 1993	Coca-Cola 1998
Sales ($ million)	6,562 (Sales 1994)	13,074 (Sales 1992)	18,868 (Sales 1997)
Brand value ($ million)	**15,027**	**24,579**	**102,642**
Enterprise / Equity value ($ million)	22,270 (Enterprise value)	40,156 (Equity value)	115,697 (Equity value (E))
Brand value / value	67.5% (Brand value / enterprise value)	61.2% (Brand value / equity value)	88.7% (Brand value / E)

about 50%. Using this ratio, the brand's value is $5.118 million. Figure 23.2 shows the sensitivity of the brand's value (according to Damodaran's methodology) to the (WCR + NFA)/S ratio.

2. *Difficulty in estimating the parameters characterizing a generic brand or private label.* Table 23.4 shows the sensitivity of the brand's value (according to Damodaran's methodology) to two of the generic product's specifications: the NOPAT/S ratio and growth. Observe that when the generic product's growth and the NOPAT/S ratio increase, the brand value decreases considerably.

3. *It assumes that the current sales of the company with a generic brand are identical to those of the branded company.* Figure 23.3 illustrates two situations in diagram form. The diagram on the left shows a branded company with higher cash flow and volume than the company with a generic product (examples of this situation would be Kellogg, Coca-Cola, Pepsi-Cola, and Marlboro). The diagram on the right shows a

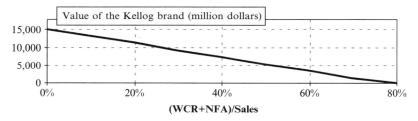

Figure 23.2   Sensitivity of the value of the Kellogg brand to the (WCR + NFA)/sales ratio.

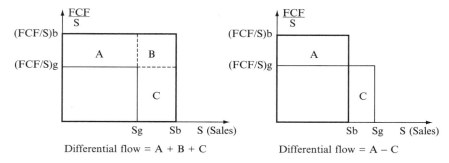

Figure 23.3   Differential cash flows of the branded company (b) compared with the company with a generic product (g).

Table 23.4

Sensitivity of the Value of the Kellogg Brand to the NOPAT/Sales Ratio and Growth of the Generic Product

NOPAT/S	Growth of the generic							
	6%	8%	8.40%	10%	12%	14%	16%	18%
5%	17,389	16,996	16,864	16,536	16,077	15,552	14,961	14,436
6.72%	15,749	15,158	15,027	14,568	13,911	13,255	12,468	11,680
8%	14,502	13,846	13,649	13,124	12,337	11,484	10,630	9,712
10%	12,533	11,680	11,549	10,827	9,843	8,859	7,743	6,562
14%	8,662	7,481	7,284	6,234	4,922	3,478	1,969	328
16%	6,693	5,381	5,118	3,937	2,428	787	−919	−2,756
18%	4,790	3,281	2,953	1,706	0	−1,837	−3,806	−5,906
20%	2,822	1,181	853	−525	−2,428	−4,528	−6,693	−8,990

branded company with a higher cash flow but less volume than the company with the generic product (examples of this situation would be Mercedes, Rolex, and Moet & Chandon). There is also a third situation: a branded company with less cash flow but higher volume than the company with the generic product (examples of this situation would be Amazon, Ikea, Bic, and Wal-Mart). However, Damodaran assumes in his valuations that initial sales of Coca-Cola and the companies with a generic product are identical.

In order to take into account the different volumes, formula (23.9) should be replaced with formula (23.10)

$$\text{Value of the brand} = \left(\frac{E}{S}\right)_{\text{brand}} \text{Sales}_{\text{brand}} - \left(\frac{E}{S}\right)_{\text{generic}} \text{Sales}_{\text{generic}} \quad (23.10)$$

4. *The hypotheses about the future growth of the branded company and that of the company with a generic product are few and very rigid.* Figure 23.4 shows forecast sales and cash flows in Damodaran's model for the Kellogg and Coca-Cola brands. Figure 23.5 shows the difference between the forecasts and subsequent reality. It is obvious that the hypotheses about the brands' growth were very optimistic. During the period 1992–2000, average growth of Coca-Cola's sales was 5.71% and that of its earnings was 3.45%, while the forecast growth for both items was 20.16%. In the case of Kellogg, during the period 1994–2000, average growth of sales was 0.97% and that of its earnings was −3%, while the forecast growth for both items was 15.94%. Observe that in both cases, growth of sales and earnings was below the forecast for the generic products in Table 23.3. This development explains what happened to Kellogg's and Coca-Cola's share prices, which are shown in Figure 23.6. Figure 23.7 shows that, from 1998 onward, Pepsico progressed substantially better than Coca-Cola. Table 23.5 shows the market capitalization and shareholder return for Coca-Cola, Kellogg, and Pepsico between 1989 and 2000.

23.6. INTERBRAND'S VALUATION METHOD[6]

Table 23.2 showed the ranking published by Interbrand in 2000 of the 80 most valuable brands. Interbrand values the brand by multiplying the brand's differential earnings by a multiple. This multiple is obtained by quantifying

---

[6]Interbrand is a multinational specialized in brand creation, strategy, research, design, law, and valuation, www.interbrand.com.

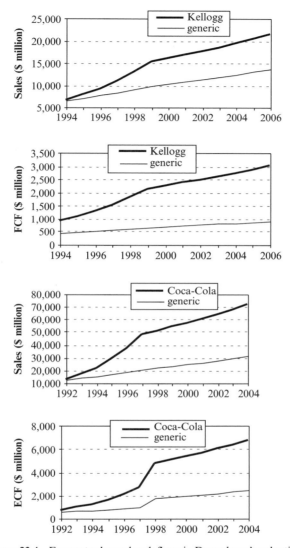

Figure 23.4 Forecast sales and cash flows in Damodaran's valuation.

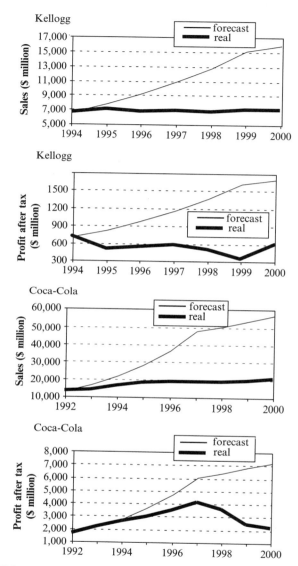

Figure 23.5 Actual and forecast sales and earnings in Damodaran's valuations.

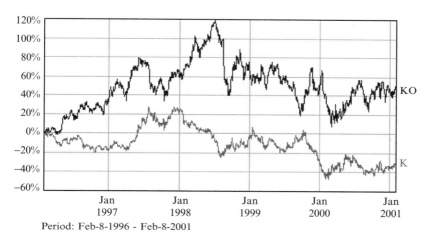

Figure 23.6   Course of Kellogg's (K) and Coca-Cola's (KO) share prices from January 1996.

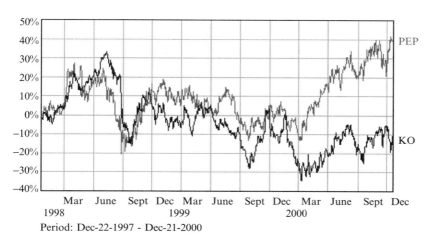

Figure 23.7   Course of Pepsico's (PEP) and Coca-Cola's (KO) share prices from January 1998.

the factors that, according to Interbrand, determine the brand's strength.
Table 23.6 includes an example detailing the steps followed by Interbrand's
method to calculate the brand's differential earnings.

Table 23.5
Growth of Coca-Cola, Kellogg, and PepsiCo

	1989	1990	1991	1992	1993	1994	1995	1996	1997	1998	1999	2000
	Equity market value ($ billion)											
Coca-Cola	26	31	53	55	58	66	93	131	165	165	144	150
Kellogg	8	9	16	16	13	13	17	14	20	14	12	11
PepsiCo	17	20	27	33	33	29	44	45	55	60	51	70
Coca/Pepsi	1.57	1.52	2.00	1.66	1.78	2.31	2.12	2.88	3.00	2.75	2.80	2.14
	Shareholder return											
Coca-Cola	77%	23%	75%	6%	8%	17%	46%	43%	27%	1%	-12%	5%
Kellogg	8%	16%	76%	4%	-13%	5%	36%	-13%	48%	-31%	-6%	-13%
PepsiCo	65%	24%	32%	24%	0%	-10%	57%	6%	22%	10%	-12%	37%

Table 23.6
An Example of the Calculation of the Brand's Differential Earnings According to Interbrand

(Million dollars)	year −2	year −1	year 0	forecast year +1
Earnings before interest and taxes (EBIT)	820	920	824	900
− private label EBIT	300	320	340	360
Brand's differential EBIT	520	600	484	540
Inflation adjustment factor	1.10	1.05	1.00	
Present value of the brand's differential EBIT	572	630	484	
Weighting factor	1	2	3	
Brand's weighted differential EBIT	547			
Allowance for future reduction of EBIT	−			
Capital remuneration	−162			
Brand's differential earnings before tax	385			
Tax	135			
Brand's differential earnings	**250**			

It usually starts with a weighted mean[7] of the historic differential earnings before interest and tax (EBIT) for the last three years (obtained by subtracting the EBIT corresponding to an unbranded or private label generic product[8]) and eliminating the EBIT corresponding to activities not related with the brand's identity. When the weighted mean of the historic EBITs is greater than the brand's forecast EBIT for future years, an allowance is made to take this decrease into account. Capital remuneration and tax are then deducted to give the brand's differential earnings.

In order to calculate the multiple to be applied to the brand's differential earnings, Interbrand calculates the "brand strength," which is a weight composed of seven factors:

1. *Leadership.* A leading brand is more stable and has more value than another brand with a lower market share, because leadership gives market influence, the power to set prices, control of distribution channels, greater resistance to competitors, etc.

2. *Stability.* Brands that have become consolidated over long periods of time or which enjoy a high degree of consumer loyalty obtain high scores in this factor.

3. *Market.* A brand in a stable, growing market with high entry barriers will score very high.

4. *Internationality.* Brands operating in international markets have more value than national or regional brands. However, not all brands are able to cross cultural and national barriers.

5. *Trend.* A brand's tendency to keep up-to-date and relevant for the consumer increases its value.

6. *Support.* Brands that have received investment and support must be considered to be more valuable than those that have not. The quantity and quality of this support is also considered.

7. *Protection.* The robustness and breadth of the brand's protection ("legal monopoly") is a critical factor in its valuation.

---

[7]In many cases, a weighting factor of three times for the present year, twice for the previous year, and once for the year before that is applied. The historic EBITs are also adjusted for inflation.

[8]To quantity the EBIT attributable to the unbranded product, Interbrand recommends considering:

(1) an unbranded product normally does not have the volume or demand stability of a branded product; (2) the brand provides economies of scale from the increased output and demand stability; and (3) a branded product can be sold at a higher price than its unbranded counterpart.

Table 23.7

Examples of Brand Strength Calculations According to Interbrand

Strength factors	Maximum score	Brand A	Brand B	Brand C	Brand D
Leadership	25	19	19	10	7
Stability	15	12	9	7	11
Market	10	7	6	8	6
Internationality	25	18	5	2	0
Trend	10	7	5	7	6
Support	10	8	7	8	5
Protection	5	5	3	4	3
Brand strength	**100**	**76**	**54**	**46**	**38**

Brand A. An international brand that has been established in the toiletries market for many years. The brand was and is number one or number two, depending on the country.

Brand B. Leading national brand in the food industry. It operates in a mature, stable market but in which tastes are changing from traditional products to precooked or easy-to-prepare products. The brand's export sales are limited, and the legal protection is based more on common law than on strong registration rights.

Brand C. National secondary drinks brand with good growth possibilities which was launched five years ago. The market is very dynamic and growing. The brand has received strong support but it is still too soon for this support to give tangible results. The brand has no registration problems in its home country. The brand is being developed for international positioning.

Brand D. A minority but stable regional brand operating in a fragmented but also stable market.

Table 23.7 shows an example of how four brands belonging to different markets are rated.[9]

As Figure 23.8 shows, the brand strength is expressed as a multiple on an 'S'-shaped curve. The multiple's maximum value is mainly determined by the market PER.[10] The maximum multiple varies in different industries and also over time. In the example shown in Figure 23.8, the maximum multiple is 20. In all four cases, we assume that the brand's differential earnings are $250 million.

23.7. COMMENT ON INTERBRAND'S METHOD

Quantifying the brand's differential earnings (basically by estimating the private label's EBIT), brand strength and multiple is a highly subjective

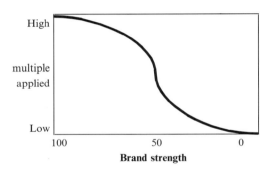

	Brand A	Brand B	Brand C	Brand D
Brand strength	76	54	46	38
Multiple	17.1	11.3	8.8	6.3
Brand's differential earnings	250	250	250	250
Brand value ($ million)	4,275	2,825	2,200	1,575

Figure 23.8   Valuation of the four brands according to Interbrand.

[9]In order to rate each strength factor, it is necessary to carefully study the brand, its positioning in the markets it operates in, activities performed in the past, future plans, brand risks, etc. In addition to making inspection visits to wholesalers and retailers, the packaging, and TV and press advertisements are also examined.

[10]Interbrand makes a more than debatable statement: "the highest multiple on the brand strength scale should be clearly above the average PER of the industry which the company operates in."

matter. Furthermore, brands such as Coca-Cola or Pepsi-Cola are not equally strong on all markets nor in all products (do you know the name of Coca-Cola's tonic water?). Pepsi, for example, has market shares ranging from 1–100%, depending on the country. Even in Spain, the market share in the Canary Islands is close to 50%, while it does not even reach 15% on mainland Spain.

Valuing any brand using this method seems highly subjective to me, not only because of the parameters used but also because of the methodology itself.

However, analyzing the strength factors for each brand/geographical area/format enables comparisons to be made and may provide guidelines for identifying the brand's and company's main value drivers, increasing the brand's strength and, therefore, its value.

23.8. FINANCIAL WORLD'S VALUATION METHOD

One the best-known brand rankings is that created by Financial World (FW). In order to value and rank brands, FW uses a simplified version of Interbrand's method, consisting of obtaining the difference between one brand's earnings and the earnings that should be obtained by a basic, un-branded version of that product. This difference is called "brand-specific net earnings." Finally, FW also applies a multiple calculated with respect to the brand's strength. The result is the brand's value. This model determines the brand's strength by analyzing five components: leadership, stability (consumer loyalty), internationality, continued importance of the brand within its industry, and security of the brand's proprietorship. The model's limitations are identical to those of Interbrand's model. See Table 23.8.

23.9. HOULIHAN VALUATION ADVISORS' METHOD

According to this method, the brand's value is the present value of the company's free cash flow less the assets employed multiplied by the required return. An example provided by Houlihan Valuation Advisors[11] (and corrected) is shown in Table 23.9.

---

[11]See www.houlihan.com/services/brand_article/brand_article.htm. The brand's value according to this is $49.13 billion, instead of $50.34 billion, which is the correct net present value. Houlihan's error lies in the calculation of the terminal value: the consulting firm gives a terminal value of $73.581 million when it is $76.524 million.

Table 23.8
The Most Valuable Brands in 1996 According to Financial World (Million Dollars)

Brand	Brand value	Brand	Brand value
1 Marlboro	44,614	6 Kodak	13,267
2 Coca-Cola	43,427	7 Kellogg's	11,409
3 McDonald's	18,920	8 Budweiser	11,026
4 IBM	18,491	9 Nestlé	10,527
5 Disney	15,358	10 Intel	10,499

Table 23.9
Brand Valuation According to Houlihan Valuation Advisors ($ Million)

Assets employed	Required return	2000	2001	2002	2003	2004	2005
Working capital requirements (WCR)	6%	90.0	91.8	93.6	95.5	97.4	99.4
Net fixed assets	9%	225.0	229.5	234.1	238.8	243.5	248.4
Intangible assets	14%	75.0	76.5	78.0	79.6	81.2	82.8
Patents	15%	10.0	10.2	10.4	10.6	10.8	11.0
Proprietary technology	20%	15.0	15.3	15.6	15.9	16.2	16.6
Company's free cash flow		44.080	44.887	46.956	49.112	51.361	53.705
− Assets employed x required return		−40.645	−41.458	−42.291	−43.133	−43.995	−44.875
Free cash flow attributable to brand		3.435	3.429	4.665	5.979	7.366	8.830
Value of brand	**50.34**	= Present value (brand's free cash flow, 16%). Growth after 2005 = 4%					

Observe that the free cash flow attributable to the brand is somewhat similar to the EVA. This method does not make much sense. It replaces the cash flow attributable to a generic product company with the assets employed by the branded company multiplied by the assets' required return. Can the reader find any justification for this?

23.10. OTHER METHODS PROPOSED BY DIFFERENT CONSULTING FIRMS

The Chicago firm Market Facts has developed a curious method which it calls "conversion model" and which seeks to measure the strength of the psychological commitment between a brand and its consumers. According to this consulting firm, this model's rationale is based on religious conversion studies. The model divides a brand's users into four groups on the basis of the strength of their commitment: unshakable, average, superficial, and convertible. It also classifies non-users on the basis of their willingness to try the brand: approachable, ambivalent, slightly unapproachable, and strongly unapproachable. Market Facts states that the difference between the size of the convertible and approachable segments is a significant indicator of the brand's future health.

Young & Rubicam use the brand asset valuator (BAV), which breaks down the link between brand and consumer into two areas: vitality and stature. In turn, the brand's vitality can be subdivided into relevance and differentiation; and the brand's stature can be subdivided into esteem and familiarity. According to Young & Rubicam, the fact that a brand is differentiated does not mean that consumers wish to buy it; it must also be relevant. A brand has esteem when the consumer appreciates its quality. Familiarity is when the consumer knows the brand. Both factors must be present for the brand's stature to be high. This method only allows a qualitative valuation of the brand.

CDB Research & Consulting conducted a telephone survey of 1191 analysts and pension fund managers to value 1000 companies on 8 factors: potential for cost reductions, innovation, absence of regulatory problems, brand ownership, customer loyalty, capacity for increasing sales, employee relations, and potential for improving productivity. They were asked to rate the companies from 1–10 for each of the eight factors mentioned. Using these scores, an index was calculated (hidden value index) for each company and the 389 companies for which sufficient answers were obtained were ranked.

23.11. BRAND VALUE DRIVERS, PARAMETERS INFLUENCING THE BRAND'S VALUE

Table 23.10 is an adaptation of Table 1.11 for brand value. Obviously, it assumes that brand value is included in enterprise value. Table 23.10 assumes that the enterprise value is the sum of the value of a generic product company plus the value of the brand. The (generic) product contributes part of the enterprise value and the brand contributes another part. The brand value drivers are an adaptation of the value drivers in Table 1.11.

What makes brand valuation different is understanding how they create value for the company and measuring this value creation correctly, so that the level of subjectivity in valuing the company is minimal. The main difficulty lies in measuring "differentials" (return, cash flow growth, operating risk, etc.). In the case of a company whose main business is managing a name (a brand) which it licenses to other companies (franchises) in return for payment of certain royalties, this difficulty disappears because the company's sole activity is managing its brand. However, if the company also manufactures and sells the products, the difficulty lies in determining what part of the cash flows corresponds to the brand, and what part to the generic product.

The main factors affecting the differential return expectations are

- Period of competitive advantage
- Differential assets employed
- Differential margin on sales, that is, the difference between differential prices and costs
- Regulation, brand protection
- Consumer loyalty
- Emotional benefits

The main factors affecting the differential growth expectations are

- Brand-customer relations
- Entry barriers[12]
- Acquisitions / divestitures
- Leadership
- Industry's competitive structure
- New businesses / products
- Technological progress
- Real growth options

---

[12]As Aaker points out, "it is much easier to copy a product than an organization, which has distinctive values, individuals, and programs."

Table 23.10

Brand Value and Main Factors Affecting It (Brand Value Drivers)

Brand value					
Differential flows		Required return			Communication
Differential return *Expectations*	Differential growth *Expectations*	Risk-free interest	Market risk premium	Differential operating risk	Differential financial risk	Quality perceived and offered

The main factors affecting the differential operating risk are

- Legislation
- The brand's internationality
- Buying / buyable brand
- Risk perceived by the market
- Company financing

The main factors affecting the differential financial risk are

- Brand/company liquidity
- Brand size
- Risk control

23.12. WHAT IS THE PURPOSE OF VALUING BRANDS?

To say that the Real Madrid brand is worth $155 million or that the Coca-Cola brand is worth $72.5 billion is useless. As we have already discussed in previous sections, this is due to shortcomings in the valuation methods used and the difficulty in defining which cash flows are attributable to the brand and which are not. However, the brand valuation *process* is very useful, since it helps identify and assess brand value drivers. This assessment consists of comparing a brand's value drivers with those of other brands/companies, with the brand's previous drivers and with the proposed goals.

The brand valuation *process* increases the amount of information held by the company about its brand and it should be developed so that it can be used as a management tool for value creation. A good brand valuation process is a tool that helps maintain a coherent strategy over time and assign marketing resources consistently.

23.13. BRAND VALUE AS A SERIES OF REAL OPTIONS

A brand can be considered as an asset that currently provides certain margins per unit that are higher than those of an unbranded product and a differential volume, and which also provides the brand's owner certain real options for future growth. These real options may be geographical growth, growth through the use of new distribution channels, growth through additional differentiation, growth through the use of new formats, growth through the possibility of gaining access to new market segments, withdrawal facilitated by the use of franchises, etc.

One of the prerequisites of adequate brand management is to take into account the real options provided by the brand for making decisions that increase (and do not decrease) these options' value. This is only possible with a correct long-term analysis because the decisions affecting the real options' value must be made before (sometimes several years before) exercising the options.

23.14. BRAND ACCOUNTING

Should brands be included as a company asset? The advocates of "brand capitalization" point out that a company's brands are often its most important assets, more important even than the bricks, mortar, and machines, whose value *is* included in the accounts. "One cannot ignore brands or intangible assets," insists Chris Pearce, Rentokil's CFO and President of Group 100, a technical committee of CFOs. "They are things that have a real value and are sold between companies on a relatively regularly basis. Companies may pay large sums of money for them and, therefore, they should be included as an asset in the balance sheet."

Its opponents argue that it is impossible (or at least very difficult) to allocate values to brands separately from the companies that create them. It is possible to assign a value to a brand that has recently changed hands, but the inclusion of "home-grown" brands is particularly risky, because there is no generally accepted valuation method.

Capitalizing brands would improve corporate earnings at the cost of worsening cash flow, which, from a financial viewpoint, is nonsense.

Accounting treatment of brands and intangible assets in the United States

Recognition of goodwill: only when buying businesses and as the difference between the price paid and the purchased company's book value. Depreciation of goodwill: over its useful life and not more than 40 years. It may be written off if its value should deteriorate or disappear. Definition of intangible assets: separately identifiable rights that have usefulness and value. Depreciation of intangible assets: over their useful life. They may be depreciated immediately in the event of deterioration.

23.15. VALUATION OF INTELLECTUAL CAPITAL

In recent years, a lot has been spoken about the value of companies' intellectual capital. However, almost all of the studies on the subject are highly descriptive and a long way from obtaining a valuation in euros.[13]

In April 1997, Johan Ross and Göram Ross published the article "A Second Generation of IC-Practices."[14] In the first part of the article, they describe and analyze the "first-generation" intellectual capital practices, the systematic visualization, and measurement of the different forms of intellectual capital. The "second-generation" intellectual capital practices expand on the 'first generation' by consolidating the measurements in an aggregate intellectual capital index. According to these authors, "intellectual capital" (IC) can be described as the difference between a company's market value and its book value.

According to Skandia, a large Swedish insurance and financial services company, the IC consists of human capital and structural capital. The *human capital* represents employees' knowledge, skill and ability to provide satisfactory solutions for clients. The *structural capital* is that which remains when the employees go home: databases, client files, software, manuals, brands, organization structures, etc. It is further subdivided into three IC focuses: renewal and development focus, client focus, and process focus. Table 23.11 shows the application of the Navigator model to one of the divisions: American Skandia[15]. According to Skandia, this type of report provides a more systematic description of the company's ability and potential to transform intellectual capital into financial capital. However, the way we see it, it is simply a series of data on turnover dressed with a few efficiency ratios. Can the reader "visualize" or value intellectual capital by looking at Table 23.11?

The formula given by Roos and Roos for valuing intellectual capital is the following:

$$\text{Equity value} = \text{level of usage} \times (\text{replacement value} + \text{intellectual capital}) + \varepsilon$$

---

[13]They normally do not include employees' salaries in intellectual capital. However, we feel that this is a major component of this capital.

[14]Based on the book by Roos, Roos, Edvinsson, and Dragonnetti (1997).

[15]American Skandia guarantees variable annuities (unit-linked insurance) on the American market. The unit-linked insurance is a life insurance scheme consisting of a combination of national and international mutual funds and in which the client decides in which fund he will invest his contributions, thereby assuming the investment's risk, by choosing the risk/return mix best matched to his investment profile.

Table 23.11

American Skandia, Report on the Company's Potential for Converting Intellectual Capital into Financial Capital

FINANCIAL FOCUS	1997 (6)	1995	HUMAN FOCUS	1997 (6)	1995
Return on invested funds	12.8%	28.7%	Number of full-time employees	509	300
Operating margin (MSEK)	516	355	Number of managers	87	81
Value added/employee (SEK 000s)	1,477	1,904	Female managers	42	28
			Training expenses/employee (SEK 000s)	8.3	2.5
CLIENT FOCUS			PROCESS FOCUS		
Number of contracts	160,087	87,836	Number of contracts/employee	315	293
Savings/contract (SEK 000s)	480	360	Administrative expenses/gross premiums (%)	3.1%	3.3%
Redemption ratio	4.3%	4.1%	IT expenses/administrativeexpenses (%)	5.7%	13.1%
Points of sale	40,063	18,012	Time spent processing new contracts (days)	7	8
RENEWAL AND DEVELOPMENT FOCUS					
Increase in net premiums	35.0%	29.9%			
Development expenses/admin. Expenses	8.7%	10.1%			
Staff under 40	71%	81%			

Source: Skandia.

According to the authors, ε is the value of the company that has no rational explanation and the level of usage is the ratio between the equity's value and its "potential" value. This formula is a step forward compared with assuming that the intellectual capital is the difference between the shares' market value and book value, but we would like to ask the authors how they calculate the level of usage and ε. We imagine they do not know how to calculate ε because, as far as we know, the authors are not the richest men in the world.

We have included this section to point out that valuing intellectual capital is an area in which little work has yet been done. Indeed, it is by no means clear what the company's intellectual capital is, and even less so if we intend to value the company's brand and intellectual capital separately.

REFERENCES

Aaker, D. (1991), *Managing Brand Equity: Capitalizing on the Value of a Brand Name*, New York: Free Press.

Damodaran, A. (1994), *Damodaran on Valuation*, New York: John Wiley and Sons.

Damodaran, A. (1996), *Investment Valuation*, New York: John Wiley and Sons.

Damodaran, A. (1998), www.stern.nyu.edu/~adamodar/pdfiles/eqnotes/brand.pdf.

Houlihan Valuation Advisors, www.houlihan.com/services/brand_article/brand_article.htm.

Interbrand, www.interbrand.com.

Roos, J., G., Roos, L., Edvinsson, and L. Dragonnetti (1997), *Intellectual Capital; Navigating in the New Business Landscape*, New York: Macmillan.

Appendix A
Capital Asset Pricing Model (CAPM)

In 1990, William Sharpe was awarded the Nobel Prize for Economics for his work on the capital asset pricing model (CAPM) published in 1964. Other authors who developed the CAPM simultaneously and independently were John Lintner (1965) and Jan Mossin (1966). Subsequently, the Economics Nobel Prize winner in 1997, Merton (1973), developed the model for continuous time.

In this appendix, we show as simply as possible the model's development, its implications, and the assumptions on which it is based.[1]

The CAPM came about when answering the following question: What equity and bond portfolio should an investor who has risk aversion form? By risk aversion we mean, given equal expected return, an investor will always prefer a lower risk portfolio.

A.1. AN INVESTOR FORMS AN OPTIMAL PORTFOLIO

An investor wishes to form an optimal portfolio.[2] By optimal portfolio we mean that which has the lowest risk for a given expected return (the measure of the risk is the variance[3] of the portfolio return).

The investor forms a portfolio with N securities. The expected return of each security in the following period is R_i and the weight of each security in the portfolio is W_i. The sum of each security's weights in the portfolio is unity:

$$\sum_{i=1}^{N} W_i = 1 \qquad (A.1)$$

---

[1] Readers interested in an alternative derivation of the CAPM can see, for example, page 93 of Ingersoll (1987). Ingersoll derives the CAPM using vectors.

[2] Also called the efficient portfolio.

[3] The volatility is the square root of the variance.

The portfolio's expected return, R_c, is

$$R_c = \sum_{i=1}^{N} W_i R_i \tag{A.2}$$

The expected variance of the portfolio return is

$$\text{Var}(R_c) = \sigma_c^2 = \sum_{i=1}^{N} \sum_{j=1}^{N} \text{Cov}(R_i, R_j) W_i \, W_j \tag{A.3}$$

σ_c is the portfolio's expected volatility. $\text{Cov}(R_i, R_j)$ is the covariance of the expected return of company i with the expected return of company j.

We want to find the weight of each share (W_i) which minimizes the expected variance of the portfolio return, for a given expected return R. Consequently, we have to solve:

$$\text{Min } \sigma_c^2 \text{ with the conditions } R_c = R; \text{ and } \sum_{i=1}^{N} W_i = 1 \tag{A.4}$$

For each expected return, there will be a different portfolio with a minimum variance. This portfolio is usually called the efficient portfolio. These efficient portfolios, taken together, form the efficient frontier (EF).[4]

This problem is solved by minimizing the following Lagrange equation:

$$\text{Lagrange} = \sigma_c^2 + \lambda(R_c - R) + \emptyset\left(\sum_{i=1}^{N} W_i - 1\right) \tag{A.5}$$

To minimize, the Lagrange equation is derived with respect to W_1, W_2, $\ldots W_N$ and is made equal to zero for each of the N derivatives

$$\frac{\partial \sigma_c^2}{\partial W_i} + \lambda \frac{\partial R_c}{\partial W_i} + \phi = 0. \ i = 1, \ldots, N$$

We can simplify these expressions because:

$$\frac{\partial R_c}{\partial W_i} = R_i \tag{A.6}$$

$$\frac{\partial \sigma_c^2}{\partial W_i} = \sum_{j=1}^{N} W_j \text{Cov}(R_i, R_j) = W_1 \text{Cov}(R_i, R_1) + W_2 \text{Cov}(R_i, R_2) + \ldots$$

$$\tag{A.7}$$

$$= \text{Cov}(R_i, \sum_{j=1}^{N} W_j R_j) = \text{Cov}(R_i, R_c)$$

[4]Different efficient portfolios differ in their composition (W_i).

Consequently, the derivatives become:

$$\text{Cov}(R_i, \ R_c) + \lambda R_i + \varnothing = 0; \qquad I = 1, \ 2, \ \ldots, \ N \tag{A.8}$$

If one of the securities is un risk-free bond, with a yield $R_i = R_F$, its covariance with the portfolio is zero: $\text{Cov}(R_F, \ R_c) = 0$. The equation (A.8) for the risk-free bond becomes:

$$\lambda R_F + \varnothing = 0 \tag{A.9}$$

The partial derivative also must be applicable to the portfolio c as a whole. In this case, $R_i = R_c$; $\text{Cov}(R_c, \ R_c) = \text{Var}(R_c)$. Consequently,

$$\text{Var}(R_c) + \lambda R_c + \varnothing = 0; \quad \text{as } \varnothing = -\lambda R_F: \ \text{Var}(R_C) = -\lambda(R_C - R_F);$$

The parameters λ and $\varnothing$ are

$$\lambda = -\text{Var}(R_C)/(R_C - R_F); \quad \varnothing = R_F \text{Var}(R_C)/(R_C - R_F) \tag{A.10}$$

Substituting the values of λ and $\varnothing$ gives:

$$\text{Cov}(R_i, \ R_c) - \frac{\text{Var}(R_c)}{(R_c - R_F)} R_i + \frac{\text{Var}(R_c)}{(R_c - R_F)} \ R_F = 0. \quad i = 1, \ 2, \ \ldots, \ N$$

Isolating the expected return for the share i gives:

$$R_i = R_F + \frac{\text{Cov}(R_i, \ R_c)}{\text{Var}(R_c)} (R_c - R_F). \quad i = 1, \ 2, \ \ldots, \ N$$

If we call $\beta_i = \dfrac{\text{Cov}(R_i, \ R_c)}{\text{Var}(R_c)}. \quad i = 1, \ 2, \ \ldots, \ N$

This gives:

$$\mathbf{R_i = R_F + \beta_i(R_c - R_F)}. \quad i = 1, \ 2, \ \ldots, \ N \tag{A.11}$$

It is important to stress that R_i, $\text{Cov}(R_i, \ R_j)$ and $\text{Var}(R_i)$ are our investor's *expectations* for the next period (which may be one year, one month, etc).

A.2. OPTIMAL PORTFOLIO IF ALL INVESTORS HAVE HOMOGENEOUS EXPECTATIONS

If all investors have the same time horizon and also identical return and risk expectations (volatility of each share and correlation with the other shares) for all shares, then the investors will have the same portfolio and this is the market portfolio M (composed of all the shares on the market). If $E(R_M)$ is the market return expected by all investors (because they all have the same expectations):

$$E(R_i) = R_F + \beta_i(E(R_M) - R_F) \quad i = 1, 2, \ldots \qquad (A.12)$$

This is the expression of the capital asset pricing model (CAPM).

In equilibrium, the investors will have shares in all companies and the portfolio c will be the stock market. All investors will have a portfolio composed of risk-free assets and the diversified portfolio, which is the market.

Figure A.1 shows the line called capital market line (CML), whose equation is:

$$E(R_i) = R_F + [(E(R_M) - R_F)/\sigma_M]\sigma_i$$

The expression $[(E(R_M) - R_F)/\sigma_M]$ is called the required return to risk.

It can be shown that $(E(R_M) - R_F)$ depends on the investors' degree of risk aversion. If we call this parameter A, $E(R_M) - R_F = A\sigma_M^2$. For example, if $\sigma_M = 20\%$ and the degree of risk aversion is 2, $E(R_M) - R_F = 8\%$.

Thus, according to the CAPM, the required return to an asset will be equal to its expected return and will be equal to the risk-free rate plus the asset's beta multiplied by the required market return above the risk-free rate. Figure A.2 is the representation of the CAPM.

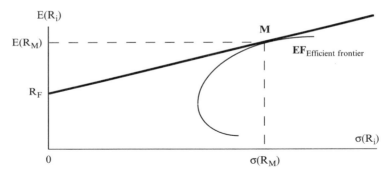

Figure A.1 Capital asset pricing model. In equilibrium, if all investors have identical expectations, all of them will have the market portfolio M, which is on the efficient frontier (EF). The straight line $R_F - M$ is called capital market line (CML): $E(R_i) = R_F + [E(R_M) - R_F] \times [\sigma_i/\sigma_M]$.

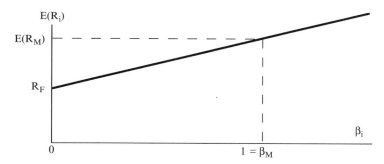

Figure A.2   Capital asset pricing model. In equilibrium, if all investors have identical expectations, each asset's expected return is a linear function of its beta. The straight line is called the security market line (SML).

$$\mathbf{Ke_i = E(R_i) = R_F + \beta_i[E(R_M) - R_F]} \qquad (A.13)$$

A.3. BASIC ASSUMPTIONS OF THE CAPM

The basic assumptions on which the model is based are

1. All investors have homogeneous expectations. This means that all investors have the same expectations about all assets' future return, about the correlations between all asset returns, and about all the assets' volatility.
2. Investors can invest and borrow at the risk-free rate R_F.
3. There are no transaction costs.
4. Investors have risk aversion.
5. All investors have the same time horizon.

A.4. BASIC CONSEQUENCES OF THE CAPM

1. Any combination of risk-free bonds and the market portfolio prevails over any other combination of shares and bonds.
2. All investors will have a portfolio composed in part of risk-free bonds and in part of the market portfolio. The proportions will vary depending on their utility function.
3. The market portfolio is composed of all the assets that exist and each one's quantity is proportional to their market value.

A.5. WHEN THE ASSUMPTIONS OF THE CAPM ARE NOT MET

A.5.1. INVESTORS HAVE DIFFERENT EXPECTATIONS

One of the model's crucial assumptions is that all investors have homogeneous expectations. When this assumption is not met, the market will no longer be the efficient portfolio for all investors. Investors with different expectations will have different portfolios (each one having the portfolio he considers most efficient), instead of the market portfolio. There will also be investors (those who expect that the price of all shares will fall or have a return below the market return) who have no shares but only fixed-income securities in their portfolio.[5]

A.5.2. CAPM IN CONTINUOUS TIME

Merton (1973), the Nobel Economics Prize winner in 1997, derived the CAPM in continuous time, which has the following expression:

$$Ke_i = E(r_i) = r_F + \beta_i[E(r_M) - r_F]$$

where r_F is the instant risk-free rate, $E(r_M)$ is the instant expected market return, and $E(r_i)$ is the instant required return to assets. In Merton's model, the returns follow a lognormal distribution.

A.5.3. IF THE RISK-FREE RATE IS RANDOM

Merton (1990) shows the expression of the CAPM when the risk-free rate is random:

$$E(R_i) = R_F + \beta_{1i}[E(R_M) - R_F] + \beta_{2i}[E(R_N) - R_F]$$

$E(R_N)$ is the expected return of a portfolio N, whose return has a correlation of -1 with the risk-free asset.

A.5.4. THERE IS NO RISK-FREE RATE

Black (1972) provided that in this case, the CAPM is as follows:

$$E(R_i) = E(R_Z) + \beta_i[E(R_M) - E(R_Z)]$$

---

[5] Or short-sell stocks, or sell futures on a stock index.

where $E(R_Z)$ is the expected return of a portfolio Z which has zero beta, which means that its covariance with the market portfolio is zero.

Black, Jensen, and Scholes (1972) showed that the portfolios with zero covariance had a return markedly above the risk-free rate.

A.6. EMPIRICAL TESTS OF THE CAPM

There are many papers that seek to assess whether the predictions of the CAPM are met in reality. One of the most famous was written by Roll[6] in 1977 and it says that that it is not possible to perform tests of the CAPM because two things are being analyzed at the same time: (1) that the market is an efficient portfolio *a priori*,[7] and (2) the expression of the CAPM.

The expression normally used to perform tests of the CAPM is the following:

$$ER_{it} = a_0 + a_1\beta_i + \varepsilon_{it}$$

where $ER_{it} = R_{it} - R_{Ft}$ is the share or portfolio excess return over the risk-free rate.

What should be obtained when the regressions are performed (if the CAPM were to be met exactly) is the following:

1. $a_0 = 0$
2. $a_1 = R_{Mt} - R_{Ft}$ the market return above the risk-free rate.

The most commonly mentioned tests of the CAPM are Friend and Blume (1970), Black, Jensen, and Scholes (1972), Miller and Scholes (1972), Fama and Macbeth (1973), Litzemberger and Ramaswamy (1979), Gibbons (1982), and Shanken (1985). In general, these studies and many others agree that $a_0 \neq 0$ and that $a_1 < R_{Mt} - R_{ft}$. This means that, on average, companies with a small beta have earned more than what the model predicted, and the companies with a large beta have earned less than what the model predicted. In addition, other factors appear that account for the shares' return: the company's size (small companies, on average, are more profitable), the PER (companies with a small PER were more profitable than what the model predicted), dividend yield, market-to-book value, etc.

---

[6]Roll, R. (1977). "A Critique of the Asset Pricing Theory's Tests: Part I: On Past and Potential Testability of Theory." *Journal of Financial Economics*, 4: 129–176.

[7]*A posteriori*, the market portfolio is almost never efficient: there has almost always been another portfolio with higher return and lower volatility.

A.7. FORMULAE FOR CALCULATING THE BETA

A share's historical beta can be calculated by means of any of the following formulae:

$$\beta = \text{Covariance } (R_i, R_M)/\text{Variance } (R_M) \qquad (A.14)$$

$$\beta = \text{Correlation coefficient } (R_i, R_M) \times \text{Volatility } (R_i)/\text{Volatility } (R_M) \qquad (A.15)$$

where: R_i = security return and R_M = market return. To calculate a share's beta, a regression is normally performed between the share's return (R_i) and the market return (R_M). The share's beta (β_i) is the slope of the regression:

$$R_i = a + \beta_i R_M + \varepsilon$$

ε is the error of the regression.

When estimation of beta is based on the CAPM the standard recommendation is to use 5 years of monthly data and a value-weighted index. But Bartholdy and Peare (2001) found that 5 years of monthly data and an equal-weighted index, as opposed to the commonly recommended value-weighted index, provides a more efficient estimate.

A.8. RELATIONSHIP BETWEEN BETA AND VOLATILITY

The relationship between the beta and the volatility (σ) is given by:

$$\sigma_i^2 = \beta_i^2 \sigma_M^2 + \sigma_\varepsilon^2 \qquad (A.16)$$

where σ_i is the volatility of the return R_i, which can be inferred from the graph below, which represents the relationship between the market risk or non-diversifiable risk (β_i, σ_M), and the non-systematic or diversifiable risk (σ_ε):

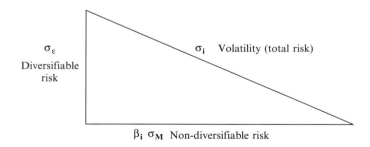

A.9. IMPORTANT RELATIONSHIPS DERIVED FROM THE CAPM

$$\beta_i = \text{Covariance } (R_i, \ R_M)/\sigma_M^2 = \text{Correlation } (R_i, \ R_M)\sigma_i/\sigma_M \quad \text{(A.17)}$$

$$R = \text{Correlation } (R_i, \ R_M) = \text{Covariance } (R_i, \ R_M)/(\sigma_M/\sigma_i) \quad \text{(A.18)}$$

$$R = \text{Correlation } (R_i, \ R_M) = \beta_i \ \sigma_M/\sigma_i \quad \text{(A.19)}$$

$$R^2 = 1 - \sigma_\varepsilon^2/\sigma_i^2 \quad \text{(A.20)}$$

$$\sigma_\varepsilon^2 = \sigma_i^2 - \beta_i^2\sigma_M^2 = \sigma_i^2 - R^2 \ \sigma_i^2 = \sigma_i^2(1 - R^2) \quad \text{(A.21)}$$

Viceira (2001) provides support for the popular recommendation by investment advisors that employed investors should invest in stocks a larger proportion of their savings than retired investors.

Econometric help to deal with beta calculations can be found in Arino and Franses (2000).

SUMMARY

The CAPM is an asset valuation model that relates the risk and the expected return.

The CAPM enables us to determine which is the equity and bond portfolio that gives the highest expected return, assuming a given risk, or has the lowest risk for a given expected return.

In the CAPM, as in any other model, certain assumptions are used to simplify reality and study it better. Almost all the assumptions are reasonable (they are based above all on the fact that investors demand a higher return for accepting a higher risk) except for all investors having homogeneous expectations.

REFERENCES

Arino, M. A., and P. H. Franses (2000), "Forecasting the Levels of Vector Autoregressive Log-Transformed Time Series," *International Journal of Forecasting*, 16, pages 111–116.

Bartholdy, J., and P. Peare (2001), "The Relative Efficiency of Beta Estimates," Social Science Research Network, Working Paper No. 263745.

Black, F. (1972), "Capital Market Equilibrium with Restricted Borrowing," *Journal of Business*, July 1972, pp. 444–455.

Black, F., M. Jensen, and M. Scholes (1972), "The Capital Asset Pricing Model: Some Empirical Findings," in *Studies in the Theory of Capital Markets*, (M. Jensen, ed.), New York: Praeger.

Fama, E. F., and J. D. MacBeth (1973), "Risk, Return and Equilibrium: Empirical Tests," *Journal of Political Economy*, Vol. 81, pp. 607–636.

Friend, I., and M. Blume (1970), "Measurement of Portfolio Performance under Uncertainty," *American Economic Review*, September, pp. 561–575.

Gibbons, M. R. (1982), "Multivariate Tests of Financial Models: A New Approach," *Journal of Financial Economics,* (March), pp. 3–28.

Ingersoll, J. (1987), *Theory of Financial Decision Making*, Totowa, NJ: Rowman & Littlefield.

Lintner, J. (1965), "The Valuation of Risk Assets and the Selection of Risky Investments in Stock Portfolios and Capital Budgets," *Review of Economics and Statistics*, Vol. 47, pp. 13–37.

Litzenberger, R., and K. Ramaswamy (1979), "The Effects of Personal Taxes and Dividends on Capital Asset Prices: Theory and Empirical Evidence," *Journal of Financial Economics*, Vol. 7 (June), pp. 163–195.

Merton, R. C. (1973), "An Intertemporal Capital Asset Pricing Model," *Econometrica*, Vol. 41, No. 5, pp. 867–887.

Merton, R. C. (1990), *Continuous-Time Finance*, Cambridge, MA: Blackwell.

Miller, M., and M. Scholes (1972), "Rates of Return in Relation to Risk: A Re-examination of Some Recent Findings," in *Studies in the Theory of Capital Markets*, (M. Jensen, ed.), New York: Praeger.

Mossin, J. (1966), "Equilibrium in a Capital Asset Market," *Econometrica*, Vol. 34, pp. 768–783.

Roll, R. (1977), "A Critique of the Asset Pricing Theory's Tests: Part I: On Past and Potential Testability of Theory," *Journal of Financial Economics*, 4:129–176.

Shanken, J. (1985), "Multivariate Tests of the Zero-Beta CAPM," *Journal of Financial Economics*, Vol. 14 , pp. 327–348.

Sharpe, W. (1964), "Capital Asset Prices: A Theory of Capital Market Equilibrium under Conditions of Risk," *Journal of Finance*, Vol. 19, pp. 425–442.

Viceira, L. (2001), "Optimal Portfolio Choice for Long-Horizon Investors with Nontradable Labor Income," *Journal of Finance*, 56, No. 2, pp. 433–470.

Glossary

Accounting cash flow Net Income plus depreciation.

Adjusted book value Difference between market value of assets and market value of liabilities. Also called net substantial value or adjusted net worth.

Adjusted present value (APV) The APV formula indicates that the firm value (E + D) is equal to the value of the equity of the unlevered company (Vu) plus the value of the tax shield due to interest payments.

Arbitrage pricing theory (APT) An asset pricing theory that describes the relationship between expected returns on securities, given that there are no opportunities to create wealth through risk-free arbitrage investments.

Arbitrage The purchase and sale of equivalent assets in order to gain a risk-free profit if there is a difference in their prices.

Arbitration Alternative to suing in court to settle disputes between brokers and their clients and between brokerage firms.

Benchmark Objective measure used to compare a firm or a portfolio performance.

Beta A measure of a security's market-related risk, or the systematic risk of a security.

Binomial option pricing model A model used for pricing options that assumes that in each period the underlying security can take only one of two possible values.

Black-Scholes formula An equation to value European call and put options that uses the stock price, the exercise price, the risk-free interest rate, the time to maturity, and the volatility of the stock return. Named for its developers, Fischer Black and Myron Scholes

Book value (BV) The value of an asset according to a firm's balance sheet.

Break-up value Valuation of a company as the sum of its different business units.

Call Option Contract that gives its holder (the buyer) the right (not the obligation) to buy an asset, at a specified price, at any time before a certain date (American option) or only on that date (European option).

Capital asset pricing model (CAPM) Equilibrium theory that relates the expected return and the beta of the assets. It is based on the mean-variance theory of portfolio selection.

Capital cash flow (CCF) Sum of the debt cash flow plus the equity cash flow.

Capital market line In the capital asset pricing model, the line that relates expected standard deviation and expected return of any asset.

Capital structure Mix of different securities issued by a firm.

Capitalization Equity market value.

Cash budget Forecast of sources and uses of cash.

Cash dividend Cash distribution to the shareholders of a company.

Cash earnings (CE) Net income before depreciation and amortization. Also called accounting cash flow and cash flow generated by operations.

Cash flow return on investment (CFROI) The internal rate of return on the investment adjusted for inflation.

Cash value added (CVA) NOPAT plus amortization less economic depreciation less the cost of capital employed.

Collection period The ratio of accounts receivable to daily sales.

Company's value (V_L) Market value of equity plus market value of debt.

Constant growth model A form of the dividend discount model that assumes that dividends will grow at a constant rate.

Consumer price index Measures the price of a fixed basket of goods bought by a representative consumer.

Convertible debentures Bonds that are exchangeable for a number of another securities, usually common shares.

Correlation coefficient The covariance of two random variables divided by the product of the standard deviations. It is a measure of the degree to which two variables tend to move together.

Cost of capital The rate used to discount cash flows in computing its net present value. Sometimes it refers to the WACC and other times to the required return to equity (K_e).

Cost of leverage The cost due to high debt levels. It includes the greater likelihood of bankruptcy or voluntary reorganization, difficulty in getting additional funds to access to growth opportunities, information problems, and reputation.

Covariance It is a measure of the degree to which two asset returns tend to move together.

Credit rating Appraisal of the credit risk of debt issued by firms and governments. The ratings are done by private agencies as Moody's and Standard and Poor's.

Credit risk The risk that the counterpart to a contract will default.

Cumulative preferred stock Stock that takes priority over common stock in regard to dividend payments. Dividends may not be paid on the common stock until all past dividends on the preferred stock have been paid.

Current asset Asset that will normally be turned into cash within a year.

Current liability Liability that will normally be repaid within a year.

Debt cash flow (CFd) Sum of the interest to be paid on the debt plus principal repayments.

Debt's market value (D) Debt cash flow discounted at the required rate of return to debt (may be different than the Debt's book value).

Debt's book value (N) Debt value according to the balance sheet.

Default risk The possibility that the interest of the principal of a debt issue will not be paid.

Default spread Difference between the interest rate on a corporate bond and the interest on a Treasury bond of the same maturity.

Depreciation (book) Reduction in the book value of fixed assets such as plant and equipment. It is the portion of an investment that can be deducted from taxable income.

Depreciation (economic) ED (economic depreciation) is the annuity that, when capitalized at the cost of capital (WACC), the assets' value will accrue at the end of their service life.

Derivative Financial instrument with payoffs that are defined in terms of the prices of other assets.

Discounted dividend model (DDM) Any formula to value the equity of a firm by computing the present value of all expected future dividends.

Discounted value of the tax shields (DVTS) Value of the tax shields due to interest payments.

Dispersion Broad variation of numbers.

Diversifiable risk The part of a security's risk that can be eliminated by combining it with other risky assets.

Diversification principle The theory that by diversifying across risky assets investors can sometimes achieve a reduction in their overall risk exposure with no reduction in their expected return.

Dividend payout ratio (p) Percentage of net income paid out as dividends.

Dividend yield Annual dividend divided by the share price.

Duration A measure of the sensitivity of the value of an asset to changes in the interest rates.

Earnings per share (EPS) Net Income divided by the total number of shares.

Economic balance sheet Balance sheet that has in the asset side working capital requirements.

Economic profit (EP) Profit after tax (net income) less the equity's book value multiplied by the required return to equity.

Economic value added (EVA) NOPAT less the firm's book value multiplied by the average cost of capital (WACC) and other adjustments implemented by the consulting firm Stern Stewart.

Efficient portfolio Portfolio that offers the highest expected rate of return at a specified level of risk. The risk may be measured as beta or volatility.

Enterprise value (EV) Market value of debt plus equity

Equity Book Value (Ebv) Value of the shareholders' equity stated in the balance sheet (capital and reserves). Also called net worth.

Equity cash flow (ECF) The cash flow remaining available in the company after covering fixed asset investments and working capital requirements and after paying the financial charges and repaying the corresponding part of the debt's principal (in the event that there exists debt).

Equity market value (E) Value of all of the company's shares. That is each share's price multiplied by the number of shares. Also called capitalization.

Equity value generation over time Present value of the expected cash flows until a given year.

Exercise price Amount that must be paid for the underlying asset in an option contract. Also called strike price.

Fixed-income security A security such as a bond that pays a specified cash flow over a specific period.

Franchise factor (FF) Measures what we could call the growth's "quality," understanding this to be the return above the cost of the capital employed.

Free cash flow (FCF) The operating cash flow, that is, the cash flow generated by operations, without taking into account borrowing (financial debt), after tax. It is the equity cash flow if the firm had no debt.

Goodwill Value that a company has above its book value or above the adjusted book value.

Gross domestic product (GDP) Market value of the goods and services produced by labor and property in one country including the income of foreign corporations and foreign residents working in the country, but excluding the income of national residents and corporations abroad.

Growth (g) Percentage growth of dividends or profit after tax.

Growth value The present value of the growth opportunities.

Homogenous expectations Situation (or assumption) in which all investors have the same expectations about the returns, volatilities, and covariances of all securities.

IBEX 35 Spanish stock exchange index.

Interest factor The PER the company would have if it did not grow and had no risk. It is, approximately, the PER of a long-term Treasury bond.

Internal rate of return (IRR) Discount rate at which an investment has zero net present value.

Leverage ratio Ratio of debt to debt plus equity.

Leveraged buyout (LBO) Acquisition in which a large part of the purchase price is financed with debt.

Levered beta (β_L) Beta of the equity when the company has debt.

Levered free cash flow (LFCF) Equity cash flow.

Liquidation value Company's value if it is liquidated, that is, its assets are sold and its debts are paid off.

Market portfolio The portfolio that replicates the whole market. Each security is held in proportion to its market value.

Market risk (systematic risk) Risk that cannot be diversified away.

Market value added (MVA) The difference between the market value of the firm's equity and the equity's book value.

Market value of debt (D) Market value of the debt.

Market-to-book ratio (E/Ebv) It is calculated by dividing the equity market value by the equity book value.

Net operating profit after tax (NOPAT) Profit after tax of the unlevered firm.

Non-systematic risk Risk that can be eliminated by diversification. Also called unique risk or diversifiable risk.

Par value The face value of the bond.

Pay in kind (PIK) Financial instruments that pay interest or dividends using new financial instruments of the same type, instead of paying in cash.

Payout ratio (p) Dividend as a proportion of earnings per share.

Perpetuity A stream of cash flows that lasts forever.

Put option Contract that gives its holder the right to sell an asset, at a predetermined price, at any time before a certain date (American option) or only on that date (European option).

Real prices Prices corrected for inflation.

Recurrent cash flows Cash flows related only to the businesses in which the company was already present at the beginning of the year.

Relative PER The company's PER divided by the country's PER or the industry's PER.

Required return to assets (Ku) Required return to equity in the unlevered company.

Required return to equity (Ke) The return that shareholders expect to obtain in order to feel sufficiently remunerated for the risk (also called cost of equity).

Residual income After-tax profit less the opportunity cost of capital employed by the business (see also economic value added and economic profit).

Residual value Value of the company in the last year forecasted.

Retained earnings Earnings not paid out as dividends.

Return on assets (ROA) Accounting ratio: NOPAT divided by total assets.

Also called ROI, ROCE, ROC, and RONA. ROA = ROI = ROCE = ROC = RONA.

Return on capital (ROC) See return on assets.

Return on capital employed (ROCE) See return on assets

Return on equity (ROE) Accounting ratio: PAT divided by equity book value.

Return on investment (ROI) See return on assets.

Reverse valuation Consists of calculating the hypotheses that are necessary to attain the share's price in order to then assess these hypotheses.

Risk free rate (R_F) Rate of return for risk-free investments (Treasury bonds). The interest rate that can be earned with certainty.

Risk premium An expected return in excess of that on risk-free securities. The premium provides compensation for the risk of an investment.

Security market line Graphical representation of the expected return-beta relationship of the CAPM.

Share buybacks Corporation's purchase of its own outstanding stock.

Share repurchase A method of cash distribution by a corporation to its shareholders in which the corporation buy shares of its stock in the stock market.

Share's beta It measures the systematic or market risk of a share. It indicates the sensitivity of the return on a share to market movements.

Shareholder return The shareholder value added in one year divided by the equity market value at the beginning of the year.

Shareholder value added The difference between the wealth held by the shareholders at the end of a given year and the wealth they held the previous year.

Shareholder value creation Excess return over the required return to equity multiplied by the capitalization at the beginning of the period. A company creates value for the shareholders when the shareholder return exceeds the required return to equity.

Shareholder value destroyer A company in which the required return to equity exceeds the shareholders return.

Specific risk Unique risk.

Stock dividend Dividend in the form of stock rather than cash.

Stock split Issue by a corporation of a given number of shares in exchange for the current number of shares held by stockholders. A reverse split decreases the number of shares outstanding.

Substantial value Amount of investment that must be made to form a company having identical conditions as those of the company being valued.

Systematic risk Risk factors common to the whole economy and that cannot be eliminated by diversification.

Tax shield The lower tax paid by the company as a consequence of the interest paid on the debt in each period.

Treasury bill Short-term, highly liquid government securities issued at a discount from the face value and returning the face amount at maturity.

Treasury bond or note Debt obligations of the federal government that make semiannual coupon payments and are issued at or near par value.

Treasury stock Common stock that has been repurchased by the company and held in the company's treasury.

Unique risk See unsystematic risk.

Unlevered company's value (Vu) Value of the equity if a company had no debt.

Unsystematic risk Risk that can be eliminated by diversification.

Variance A measure of the dispersion of a random variable. Equals the expected value of the squared deviation from the mean.

Volatility The annualized standard deviation of the shareholder returns. It measures the share's total risk, that is, the market risk and the diversifiable risk.

Weighted average cost of capital before taxes ($WACC_{BT}$) Appropriate discount rate for the capital cash flow.

Weighted average cost of capital (WACC) Appropriate discount rate for the free cash flow.

Working capital requirements (WCR) The difference between current operational assets and current operational liabilities.

Yield curve A graph of yield to maturity as function of time to maturity.

Yield to maturity Internal rate of return on a bond.

Notation

Abbreviator	Concept
APV	Adjusted present value
BV	Book value
β	Share's beta
βd	Debt's beta
βL	Levered Beta
βU	Unlevered Beta or beta of the assets
CAPM	Capital asset pricing model
CCF	Capital cash flow
CE	Cash earnings
CF	Cash flow
CFd	Debt cash flow
CFROI	Cash flow return on investment
CL	Cost of leverage
CPI	Consumer price index
CVA	Cash value added
D	Market value of the debt
DCF	Discounted cash flow
Dep	Depreciation
Div	Dividends
DPS	Dividend per share distributed by the company
DVTS	Discounted value of the tax shield
E	Market value of the equity
EBIT	Earnings before interest and taxes

(*continues*)

(continued)

Abbreviator	Concept
EBITDA	Earnings before interest, taxes, depreciation, and amortization
EBT	Earnings before tax
Ebv	Equity book value
ECF	Equity cash flow
ED	Economic depreciation
EG	Earnings growth
EMU	European Monetary Union
EP	Economic profit
EPS	Earnings per share
EV	Enterprise value
EVA	Economic value added
EVA spread	Difference between the ROA and the WACC
FAD	Funds available for distribution
FCF	Free cash flow
FF	Franchise factor: $(ROE - Ke)/(ROE \times Ke)$
g	Growth rate
G	Growth factor
G_L	Present value of the taxes paid by the levered company
GNP	Gross National Product
GOV	Present value of taxes paid to the government
G_U	Present value of the taxes paid by the unlevered company
I	Interest payments
IBEX 35	Spanish stock exchange index
Inp	Interest not paid
IRR	Internal rate of return
Kd	Required return to debt, before taxes
Ke	Required return to equity
K_{TL}	Required return to tax in the levered company
K_{TU}	Required return to tax in the unlevered company
Ku	Required return to equity in the unlevered firm or required return to assets
LFCF	Levered free cash flow
MVA	Market value added
N	Debt's book value or nominal value of debt
NFA	Net fixed assets

(continues)

(*continued*)

Abbreviator	Concept
NI	Net income = profit after tax
NOPAT	Net operating profit after tax, also called Earning Before Interest and After Tax (EBIAT), it's also called Net Operating Profit Less Adjusted Taxes (NOPLAT).
NPV	Net present value
NS	Number of shares
P	Share's price.
p	Pay – out ratio
PAT	Profit after tax or net income
PBT	Profit before tax
PER	Price – earnings ratio
P_M	Expected market risk premium
PV	Present value
r	Cost of debt, interest rate of the debt's book value
R_F	Risk-free interest rate
R_M	Market return
ROA	Return on assets—it is calculated by dividing the NOPAT by the equity and debt, both at book value, also called ROI, ROCE, ROC, and RONA, ROA = ROI = ROCE = ROC = RONA
ROC	Return on capital
ROCE	Return on capital employed
ROE	Return on equity, it is calculated by dividing the net income by the shares' book value
ROGI	Return on gross investment
ROI	Return on investment
RONA	Return on net assets
S	Sales
S&P 500	S&P 500 Index
T	Corporate tax rate
T_{PA}	Personal income tax rate on revenues from shares
T_{PD}	Personal income tax rate on revenues from debt
TBR	Total business return
TSR	Total shareholder return
UEC	Union of European Accounting Experts
V_L	Value of the levered company

(*continues*)

(continued)

Abbreviator	Concept
V_U	Value of the unlevered company
WACC	Weighted average cost of capital
$WACC_{BT}$	Weighted average cost of capital before tax
$WACC_{bv}$	Weighted average cost of capital calculated with weights of debt and equity at book value
WCR	Working capital requirements
σ	Volatility

Company Index (Chapters where they are Mentioned)

Name Index (Chapters where they are Mentioned)

Subject Index